THE FOUNDATIONS OF EUROPEAN UNION LAW

AN INTRODUCTION TO THE CONSTITUTIONAL AND ADMINISTRATIVE LAW OF THE EUROPEAN UNION

BY

T C HARTLEY

Professor of Law Emeritus
London School of Economics and Political Science

Eighth Edition

OXFORD
UNIVERSITY PRESS

Great Clarendon Street, Oxford, OX2 6DP,
United Kingdom

Oxford University Press is a department of the University of Oxford.
It furthers the University's objective of excellence in research, scholarship,
and education by publishing worldwide. Oxford is a registered trade mark of
Oxford University Press in the UK and in certain other countries

Fifth edition 2003
Sixth edition 2007
Seventh edition 2010

Impression: 1

Published in the United States of America by Oxford University Press
198 Madison Avenue, New York, NY 10016, United States of America

British Library Cataloguing in Publication Data
Data available

Library of Congress Control Number: 2013956377

ISBN 978–0–19–968145–7

Printed in Great Britain by
Ashford Colour Press Ltd, Gosport, Hampshire

NEW TO THIS EDITION

Key new materials and cases covered in the eighth edition include:

- The financial crisis and the measures to deal with it
- The *Pringle* case
- Preparations for the EU to join the European Convention on Human Rights and what it will mean
- The accession of Croatia to the Union
- Developments regarding the right of citizens to challenge EU measures
- The *Inuit* case and the *Microban* case

PREFACE

The purpose of this book is to explain the principles that constitute the foundations of European Union law. The book is intended as an introduction to the EU legal system for those with no previous knowledge of the subject, and I believe that, for such persons, what is needed first and foremost is an appreciation of the conceptual structure of EU law. This requires an understanding of basic principles and the relationship between them, as well as an understanding of the relationship between the EU system and other legal systems – in particular, national constitutional law and international law. Once this framework has been fully grasped, more detailed rules can be slotted into it, and their relationship with other rules appreciated.

I start with the institutions: the first Part deals with these and is more descriptive than analytical. The second and third Parts cover the EU legal system and the major constitutional issues: they are analytical, though not excessively technical. The final Part takes us into the realm of administrative law and remedies: it is more legal in character and explains some of the things that lawyers will need to know if they are contemplating litigation in the European Court or the General Court. My hope is that each Part will prepare the ground for the next so that a balanced understanding of the whole subject will be possible.

Certain passages in Chapter 3 have been reproduced from my article, 'International Law and the Law of the European Union – A Reassessment' [2002] BYIL 1. I am grateful to Professor James Crawford, the editor of the Yearbook, for granting his permission. Most of the Introduction to Part III is derived from pp. 237–44 of my article, 'The Constitutional Foundations of the European Union' (2001) 117 LQR 225. I would like to thank Professor Francis Reynolds, the editor of the Quarterly, for his permission to re-use it. The section on Denmark in Chapter 8 is taken from pp. 157–9 of my book, *Constitutional Problems of the European Union* (Oxford and Portland, Oregon: Hart Publishing, 1999). I would like to thank Richard Hart for his permission to do so.

I have received a great deal of help from my wife. To her, as always, I owe my greatest debt.

This edition attempts to state the law as it existed on 1 July 2013.

TCH
1 October 2013

USER INFORMATION FOR THIS BOOK

CHANGES IN NOMENCLATURE

One of the characteristic features of the European enterprise is the constant tendency to change the names of things.[1] What is now called the 'European Union' (EU) was originally called the 'European Economic Community' (EEC). This was renamed the 'European Community' (EC) by the Treaty on European Union 1992 (in force in 1993), a treaty which created another entity, the European Union.[2] The Treaty of Lisbon later abolished the European Community and merged its activities into the European Union. So 'European Union' is the correct term today.[3] For ease of understanding, I have adopted the current terminology throughout the book (even when discussing past events) except where it would be clearly inappropriate.[4]

RENUMBERING OF TREATY ARTICLES

The Articles in the main EU Treaties have been renumbered twice, first by the Treaty of Amsterdam 1997 (in force in 1999) and then by the Treaty of Lisbon (in force from 1 December 2009). The Treaty establishing the European Community is now renamed the Treaty on the Functioning of the European Union (TFEU). The new numbering has been used throughout the book (except where it would be misleading); nevertheless, where it was thought useful, the older numbers are shown in square brackets after the current number. For example, a reference to 'Article 267 TFEU [234/177 EC]' is a reference to the provision originally known as 'Article 177 EEC', changed to 'Article 177 EC' as a result of the Treaty on European Union, renumbered 'Article 234 EC' by the Treaty of Amsterdam and now called 'Article 267 TFEU'.[5]

CITATION AND REPORTING OF EUROPEAN COURT CASES

At the beginning of the proceedings, every case is given a number by the Registrar of the European Court or the Registrar of the General Court. Since the establishment of the General Court (formerly the Court of First Instance), cases in the European Court have had the prefix 'C', e.g., 'Case C-9/94'. Cases in the General Court have the prefix 'T' (from the French, *Tribunal*), e.g., 'Case T-9/94'. The figures after the oblique stroke indicate the

[1] Perhaps this gives the appearance of greater progress than has in fact occurred.

[2] The European Union included the European Community, but covered other things as well.

[3] There have been further changes, also adopted throughout the book: 'common market' is replaced by 'internal market'; 'Court of Justice of the European Communities' becomes 'Court of Justice of the European Union', and the Court of First Instance is now to be known as the 'General Court'.

[4] Quotations have not of course been changed.

[5] In some cases, there may have been changes in the text of the provision.

year when the proceedings began. When a case goes on appeal from the General Court to the European Court, it is given a new case number by the Registrar of the European Court; thus Case T-120/89 might become Case C-220/91 P, the different figures after the oblique stroke indicating the difference between the date when the proceedings commenced in the General Court and when the appeal was lodged. 'Opinions' and 'Rulings' of the Court (as distinct from 'Cases') are numbered separately, e.g., Opinion 9/94; Opinions of an Advocate General have the number of the case in which they were given.

CITATIONS IN FOOTNOTES IN THIS BOOK

In footnotes, decisions of the European Court are cited to the European Court Reports (ECR). Where a case is not yet reported in the ECR, the date alone is normally given. Since cases are published in chronological order, this will enable the reader to find them without difficulty when the relevant volume is published.

CITATIONS IN THE TABLE OF CASES

Judgments of the European Court are listed in the Table of Cases for this book in both numerical and alphabetical order. Though the latter may be more convenient to use, the former is more accurate. Cases are cited under their abbreviated name rather than their full name. The abbreviations used are normally those found in the ECR, but since cases are sometimes known under different names, the only sure way of finding a case is to search for it by number.

In the Table of Cases (numerical order), cases are listed first by year (the number after the oblique stroke) and then by the number before it; for each year, 'Opinions' and 'Rulings' are listed before 'Cases', and cases with a C-prefix come before those with a T-prefix.

INTERNET

Judgments of the European Court (and Opinions of Advocates General) may be obtained on the Court's website, http://curia.europa.eu/en/.

BIBLIOGRAPHY AND FURTHER READING

There is a general bibliography provided at the end of the book. Bibliographic material that relates specifically to the subject matter of a chapter is given in the 'Further Reading' after that chapter. The items are listed in date order: readers who wish to find the latest books and articles should look towards the end of the list.

WEBSITE FOR THIS BOOK

The website for this book is www.oxfordtextbooks.co.uk/orc/hartley8e. Updates covering new developments will be posted periodically.

CONTENTS

PART I EUROPEAN UNION INSTITUTIONS

1 THE INSTITUTIONS 13

2 THE EUROPEAN COURT 49

PART II THE UNION LEGAL SYSTEM

3 ACTS OF THE MEMBER STATES 87

4 UNION ACTS 108

5 HUMAN RIGHTS AND GENERAL PRINCIPLES OF LAW 144

6 AGREEMENTS WITH THIRD COUNTRIES 174

PART III UNION LAW AND THE MEMBER STATES

7 DIRECT EFFECT AND NATIONAL REMEDIES 209

8 THE NATIONAL RESPONSE 258

9 PRELIMINARY REFERENCES 281

10 ENFORCEMENT ACTIONS 315

PART IV ADMINISTRATIVE LAW

11 REVIEWABLE ACTS 349

12 *LOCUS STANDI* 367

13 FAILURE TO ACT 392

14 INDIRECT CHALLENGE 410

15 REVIEW AND ANNULMENT 419

16 UNION OBLIGATIONS 443

DETAILED CONTENTS

Alphabetical Table of Cases xxii
Numerical Table of Cases xxxix
Table of English, Scottish, and Irish Cases lv
Table of Legislation lviii
Abbreviations lxiv
Guide to the Online Resource Centre lxvii

PART I EUROPEAN UNION INSTITUTIONS

INTRODUCTION 3
Further Reading 12

1 THE INSTITUTIONS 13
§1 The European Parliament 13
§1.1 Composition 13
§1.2 Privileges and Immunities 16
§1.3 Political Parties 17
§1.4 Committees 17
§1.5 Parliamentary Questions 17
§1.6 Proposals, Inquiries, and Petitions 17
§1.7 The Ombudsman 18
§1.8 Consultation 18
§1.9 Veto Rights 20
§1.10 Approval of the Commission 20
§1.11 Censure of the Commission 20
§1.12 Conclusions 21
§2 The European Council 21
§3 The Council 23
§3.1 Introduction 23
§3.2 Coreper 24
§3.3 Voting 24
§4 The Commission 27
§4.1 Composition 27
§4.2 Rule-making Powers 30
§4.3 Decision-making Procedure 30
§4.4 Assessment 31
§5 The European Central Bank 31
§6 The Court of Auditors 32

§7 The Common Foreign and Security Policy 33
§7.1 Development and Special Features 33
§7.2 The Common Security and Defence Policy 34
§7.3 The High Representative of the Union for Foreign Affairs and Security Policy 34
§8 Bodies, Offices, Agencies, and Other Entities 34
§8.1 The Economic and Social Committee 35
§8.2 The Committee of the Regions 36
§8.3 European Agencies 36
§8.4 The European Stability Mechanism 37
§9 The Ordinary Legislative Procedure 38
§10 The Budgetary Procedure 42
§11 Enhanced Co-operation 43
§12 National Parliaments 44
§13 Assessment 45
Further Reading 47

2 THE EUROPEAN COURT 49
§1 The European Court 49
§1.1 Judges 49
§1.2 Advocates General 51
§1.3 The Registrar 53
§1.4 Legal Secretaries 53
§1.5 Specialized Services 54
§2 The General Court 54
§3 The Civil Service Tribunal 55
§4 Jurisdiction 55
§4.1 Jurisdiction of the General Court 58
§4.2 Appeals from the General Court 59
§4.3 Jurisdiction of the Civil Service Tribunal and Appeals from It 60
§5 Procedure 60
§5.1 The Written Proceedings 60
§5.2 Admissibility 60
§5.3 Preparatory Inquiry 61
§5.4 Oral Procedure 61
§5.5 Judgment 62
§5.6 Execution 62
§5.7 Special Procedures after Judgment 62
§5.8 Preliminary Rulings 63
§5.9 Lawyers 64
§6 Multilingualism 65
§6.1 Introduction 65

§6.2 Court Procedure 67
§6.3 Drafting the Judgment 68
§7 The Form of Judgment 70
§8 Precedent 71
§9 Interpretation 72
§10 Policy 73
§11 The Future 77
Further Reading 79

PART II THE UNION LEGAL SYSTEM

INTRODUCTION 83
Further Reading 85

3 ACTS OF THE MEMBER STATES 87
§1 The Constitutive Treaties 87
§1.1 Introduction 87
§1.2 Amending the Treaties 89
§1.3 New Members 93
§1.4 Suspending Membership Rights 93
§2 Subsidiary Conventions 94
§3 Other Decisions and Agreements 94
§3.1 Acts of the Representatives of the Member States 94
§3.2 Treaties among a Sub-Group of Member States 95
§4 Conflicting Treaties 98
§4.1 Conflicts between EU Treaties 99
§4.2 Conflicts with Non-Union Treaties 100
§4.3 The European Convention on Human Rights 101
§4.4 United Nations Law 104
§4.5 Conclusions 106
Further Reading 107

4 UNION ACTS 108
§1 Classification 108
§1.1 Nominal Classification 108
§1.2 Procedural Classification 111
§1.3 Functional Classification 111
§1.4 Conclusions 112
§2 The Principle of Conferral 112
§2.1 Meaning 112

§2.2 The Theory of Implied Powers 113
§2.3 Open-ended Powers: Article 352 TFEU 114

§3 Union Competence 119

§4 Legal Basis 120

§5 Subsidiarity and Proportionality 122
§5.1 Introduction 122
§5.2 Subsidiarity 123
§5.3 Proportionality 124
§5.4 Procedure 124
§5.5 Judicial Review for Infringement of Subsidiarity 126
§5.6 Conclusions 128

§6 Delegation of Powers 128
§6.1 What is Delegation? 128
§6.2 Delegation to the Commission 129
§6.3 Delegation to other Union Institutions 131
§6.4 Delegation to Outside Bodies 131
§6.5 Delegation to Member States 133
§6.6 Implementing Powers 134
§6.7 Conclusions 135

§7 Form 136
§7.1 Preliminary Acts 136
§7.2 Reasons 136
§7.3 Signature 141

§8 Publication, Notification, and Entry into Force 141

Further Reading 142

5 HUMAN RIGHTS AND GENERAL PRINCIPLES OF LAW 144

§1 Introduction 144

§2 Fundamental Human Rights 146
§2.1 Development of the EU Concept 146
§2.2 The European Convention on Human Rights 153
§2.3 The Charter of Fundamental Rights 156
§2.4 Do EU Human Rights Bind the Member States? 157
§2.5 Human Rights as a Justification for Infringing EU Law 158
§2.6 Human Rights Law Meets International Law 159

§3 Legal Certainty 162
§3.1 Retroactivity and Vested Rights 162
§3.2 Legitimate Expectations 165
§3.3 Revocation of Decisions 167

§4 Proportionality 167

§5 Equality 168

§6 The Right to a Hearing 170
§7 Legal Professional Privilege 172
Further Reading 173

6 AGREEMENTS WITH THIRD COUNTRIES 174
§1 Introduction 174
§1.1 International Agreements as a Source of Union Law 174
§1.2 Legal Personality 174
§1.3 Exclusive and Shared Competence 174
§1.4 Kinds of Agreements 175
§2 The Treaty-Making Powers of the Union 175
§2.1 The Principle of Conferral 175
§2.2 Primary Powers 176
§2.3 Secondary Powers: The Court's Initiative 176
§2.4 The Treaty of Lisbon 185
§2.5 Conclusions 186
§3 Treaty-making Procedure 187
§4 Legal Proceedings 189
§5 Acts of Institutions Established by Agreements with Third Countries 191
§6 International Agreements and the Union Legal System 191
§7 Binding the Union 192
§7.1 Agreements Concluded by the Union 192
§7.2 Agreements Concluded by the Member States 193
§7.3 Mixed Agreements 194
§8 Binding the Member States 196
§9 Effect 196
§9.1 General Principles 196
§9.2 Proceedings in National Courts 197
§9.3 Proceedings in the European Court 198
Further Reading 198

PART III UNION LAW AND THE MEMBER STATES

INTRODUCTION 203
Further Reading 208

7 DIRECT EFFECT AND NATIONAL REMEDIES 209
§1 The Principle of Direct Effect 209
§1.1 Basic Ideas 209
§1.2 Clear and Unambiguous 210

§1.3 Unconditional 211
§1.4 Not Dependent on Further Action 213
§1.5 Conclusions 214

§2 Treaty Provisions 214

§3 Regulations 215

§4 Directives 218
§4.1 The Treaties 218
§4.2 The First Step 218
§4.3 The New Principle 219
§4.4 The Importance of the Deadline 221
§4.5 Differences between Directives and Regulations 222
§4.6 Vertical and Horizontal Direct Effect 224
§4.7 The 'State' 231
§4.8 Indirect Effect 235
§4.9 Governmental Liability for Non-Implementation 239

§5 Decisions 239

§6 General Principles of Law 240

§7 Agreements with Third Countries 240

§8 Acts of Institutions Established by Agreements with Third Countries 243

§9 The Supremacy of Union Law and the Restriction of National Powers 243

§10 Remedies and Procedure in National Courts 245

§11 Governmental Liability in Tort 248
§11.1 The First Step: *Francovich* 248
§11.2 Further Development: *Factortame* 250
§11.3 Maltreatment of Animals: *Hedley Lomas* 252
§11.4 The Transposition of Directives 254
§11.5 Incorrect Decisions by Judges 254
§11.6 Conclusions 255

Further Reading 256

8 THE NATIONAL RESPONSE 258

§1 Introduction 258

§2 Belgium 259

§3 Germany 261

§4 Denmark 266

§5 France 267

§6 Poland 271

§7 The United Kingdom 272
§7.1 The European Communities Act 272

§7.2 The Union Treaties 273
§7.3 Direct Effect 274
§7.4 Implementation 274
§7.5 Enforcement of Judgments 275
§7.6 Supremacy of Union Law 276
§8 Conclusions 278
Further Reading 279

9 PRELIMINARY REFERENCES 281
§1 Introduction 281
§1.1 Meaning of 'Court' 282
§1.2 Entities Covered 282
§1.3 Issues Covered 283
§2 Which Provisions May Be Referred? 283
§2.1 The Treaties 283
§2.2 Subsidiary Conventions 284
§2.3 Acts of the Representatives of the Member States 284
§2.4 Union Acts 284
§2.5 General Principles of Law 284
§2.6 Agreements with non-member States 285
§2.7 Acts of Institutions Established by Agreements with non-member States 287
§2.8 National Provisions Based on Union Law 288
§3 Which Courts Are Covered? 290
§3.1 Power to Refer 290
§3.2 Obligation to Refer 295
§3.3 Preliminary Rulings on Validity 299
§4 Hypothetical Questions and Contrived Proceedings 300
§5 When Should a Reference Be Made? 302
§5.1 The Law 303
§5.2 Discretion 307
§6 Procedure 308
§6.1 English Courts 308
§6.2 The Reference 309
§6.3 Appeals against an Order for Reference 309
§6.4 The European Court 310
§7 Interpretation and Application 311
§8 Effects of Preliminary Rulings 313
Further Reading 313

10 ENFORCEMENT ACTIONS 315
§1 Introduction 315

§2 What Constitutes a Violation? 316
§2.1 Provisions Covered 316
§2.2 Violations by the Legislature or Judiciary of a Member State 317
§2.3 Violation by Popular Action 319
§3 The Administrative Stage 319
§3.1 Introduction 319
§3.2 Commission Discretion 321
§3.3 Recording the Violation 323
§3.4 Time Limit for Commission Action 323
§3.5 Consequences of Procedural Defects 324
§4 The Judicial Stage 325
§5 Remedies Where the Commission Fails to Act 327
§6 Actions by Member States 329
§7 Interim Measures 330
§8 Restitution and Damages 332
§9 The North–South Gradient 335
§10 Compliance 335
§10.1 Defying the Court 335
§10.2 Fines 336
§10.3 Fixing the Penalty in Advance 338
§10.4 General and Persistent Infringements 339
§10.5 Conclusions 339
Further Reading 340

PART IV ADMINISTRATIVE LAW

INTRODUCTION 345
Further Reading 347

11 REVIEWABLE ACTS 349
§1 Introduction 349
§2 The *Noordwijks Cement Accoord* Case 351
§3 Problem Cases 353
§4 Void and Voidable Acts 360
§5 The Author of the Act 364
Further Reading 366

12 *LOCUS STANDI* 367
§1 Privileged Applicants 367
§2 Non-Privileged Applicants: Basic Requirements 368

§3 Individual Concern 369
§3.1 Small Groups 371
§3.2 Closed Categories: Decisions 372
§3.3 Closed Categories: Regulations 374
§4 Quasi-Judicial Determinations 379
§4.1 Competition Proceedings 379
§4.2 Anti-Dumping Proceedings 380
§4.3 State Aid 382
§4.4 Conclusions 383
§5 The Treaty of Lisbon 383
§5.1 Individual Concern after Lisbon 384
§5.2 Regulatory Acts That Do Not Entail Implementing Measures 384
§6 Direct Concern 386
Further Reading 390

13 FAILURE TO ACT 392
§1 Introduction 392
§2 Negative Decisions 393
§3 Definition of Position 395
§4 Parties to the Proceedings 396
§5 Reviewable Omissions 396
§5.1 Preliminary Acts 398
§5.2 Failure to Repeal an Act 399
§6 The Request for Action 402
§6.1 General 402
§6.2 Time Limit for Making Request 404
§7 *Locus Standi* 405
§8 Form of Judgment 408
Further Reading 409

14 INDIRECT CHALLENGE 410
§1 Introduction 410
§2 Treaty Provisions 411
§3 What Acts May Be Challenged? 412
§4 Who May Make the Challenge? 415
§5 In What Proceedings May the Challenge Be Made? 416
§6 On What Grounds May the Challenge Be Made? 416
§7 The Effect of a Successful Challenge 417
§8 Non-Existent Acts 418
Further Reading 418

15 REVIEW AND ANNULMENT 419
§1 Grounds of Review 419
§1.1 Lack of Competence 419
§1.2 Infringement of an Essential Procedural Requirement 420
§1.3 Infringement of the Treaty or of any Rule of Law Relating to its Application 423
§1.4 Misuse of Powers 424
§2 The Time Factor 427
§3 Interest 429
§4 Mistake of Fact 430
§5 Failure to Act 434
§5.1 Requirement to Act 435
§5.2 Power to Act 435
§6 Annulment 436
§6.1 Retroactivity 436
§6.2 Compliance with the Judgment 438
§6.3 Partial Annulment 440
§6.4 Rejection of Application 440
§7 Indirect Challenge 441
Further Reading 441

16 UNION OBLIGATIONS 443
§1 Contract 443
§1.1 Jurisdiction of the European Court 443
§1.2 Choice of Law 445
§2 Restitution 447
§2.1 Substantive Law 448
§2.2 Jurisdiction 449
§3 Tort 450
§3.1 Acts Imputable to the Union 453
§3.2 Damage and Causation 457
§3.3 Fault 460
§4 Liability for Acts Intended to Have Legal Effects 463
§4.1 The '*Plaumann* Doctrine' 465
§4.2 The '*Schöppenstedt* Formula' 467
§4.3 First Requisite 469
§4.4 Second Requisite 471
§4.5 Third Requisite 476
§4.6 Conclusions 478

§5 Concurrent Liability: The Union and the Member States 478
§5.1 Restitution 483
§5.2 Statutory Obligation 483
§5.3 No National Remedy 484
§5.4 Tort 485
§5.5 Conclusions 486
Further Reading 486

Bibliography 487
Index 489

ALPHABETICAL TABLE OF CASES

For 'Parliament', see 'European Parliament'

Abertal v. Commission, Case C-213/91, [1993] ECR 3177 . . . 375
Adam, Case C-267/99, [2001] ECR I-7467 . . . 289
Adams v. Commission, Case 145/83, [1985] ECR 3539; [1986] 1 CMLR 506; [1986] 2 WLR 367 . . . 451, 458, 463
Adeneler, Case C-212/04, [2006] ECR I-6057 . . . 222, 238, 239
Adoui and Cornuaille, Cases 115–116/81, [1982] ECR 1665; [1982] 3 CMLR 631 . . . 151
Agricola Commerciale Olio v. Commission, Case 232/81, [1984] ECR 3881; [1987] 1 CMLR 363 . . . 375, 384
Air France v. Commission, Case T-3/93, [1994] ECR II-121 . . . 362
Airola v. Commission, Case 21/74, [1975] ECR 221 . . . 169
AIUFFASS v. Commission, Case T-380/94, [1996] ECR II-2169 . . . 390
AKZO v. Commission, Case 53/85, [1986] ECR 1965; [1987] 1 CMLR 231 . . . 358
AKZO Chemie v. Commission, Case 5/85, [1986] ECR 2585; [1987] 3 CMLR 716 . . . 131, 358, 362, 365
Akzo Nobel Chemicals Ltd, Case C-550/07 P, [2010] ECR I-8301 . . . 172
Alcan Aluminium v. Commission, Case 69/69, [1970] ECR 385; [1970] CMLR 337 . . . 387–90
Alfieri v. European Parliament, Case 35/64, [1965] ECR 261 . . . 430
Algera v. Assembly, Cases 7/56, 3–7/57, [1957] ECR 39 . . . 167, 355, 361, 458
Al-Jubail Fertilizer v. Council, Case C-49/88, [1991] ECR I-3187 . . . 171
Allied Corporation v. Commission, Cases 239, 275/82, [1984] ECR 1005; [1985] 3 CMLR 572 . . . 377, 380, 381
Almelo and Others, Case C-393/92, [1994] ECR I-1477 . . . 291
Alusuisse v. Council and Commission, Case 307/81, [1982] ECR 3463; [1983] 3 CMLR 388 . . . 370, 377, 380, 381
AM & S v. Commission, Case 155/79, [1982] ECR 1575; [1982] 2 CMLR 264; [1983] 1 All ER 705; [1983] 3 WLR 17 . . . 172
Amylum v. Council, Case 108/81, [1982] ECR 3107 . . . 164, 439
Amylum and Tunnel Refineries v. Council and Commission Cases, 116, 124/77 (one of second Isoglucose Cases), [1979] ECR 3497 . . . 473, 474
Andersson v. Sweden, Case C-321/97, [1999] ECR I-3551; [2000] 2 CMLR 191 . . . 255
Ansaldo Energia, Cases C-279–281/96, [1998] ECR I-5025 . . . 246
Antillean Rice Mills v. Commission, Case C-390/95 P, [1999] ECR I-769 (affirming Cases T-480, 483/93, [1995] ECR II-2305) . . . 373, 377
Antillean Rice Mills v. Council, Case C-451/98, [2001] ECR I-8949 . . . 372, 373, 376, 377
Apesco v. Commission, Case 207/86, [1988] ECR 2151 . . . 370
Arcaro, Case C-168/95, [1996] ECR I-4705 . . . 220, 239
Arposol v. Council, Case 55/86, [1988] ECR 13 . . . 387
Asia Motor France v. Commission, Case C-72/90, [1990] ECR I-2181 . . . 327, 328, 459
Asia Motor France v. Commission, Case C-29/92, [1992] ECR I-3935 . . . 327
ASPEC v. Commission, Case T-435/93, [1995] ECR II-1281 . . . 383, 390
Assicurazioni Generali v. Commission, Case T-87/96, [1999] ECR II-203; [2000] 4 CMLR 312 . . . 359
Assider v. High Authority, Case 3/54, [1955] ECR 63 . . . 436, 440
AssiDomän Kraft Products v. Commission, Case C-310/97 P, [1999] ECR I-5363 (appeal from Case T-227/95, [1997] ECR II-1185) . . . 438, 467
Assurances du Crédit v. Council and Commission, Case C-63/89, [1991] ECR I-1799 . . . 485
Asteris v. Commission, Cases 97, 99, 193, 215/86, [1988] ECR 2181 . . . 375, 402, 438, 439
Asteris v. Greece, Case 106–120/87, [1988] ECR 5515 . . . 484
Atlanta Fruchthandelsgesellschaft (Bananas Case), Case C-465/93, [1995] ECR I-3761 . . . 248

Attorney General v. Burgoa, Case 812/79, [1980] ECR 2787; [1981] 2 CMLR 193 . . . 193, 194
Automec v. Commission (No. 1), Case T-64/89, [1990] ECR II-367 . . . 399
Automec v. Commission (No. 2), Case T-24/90, [1992] ECR II-2223 . . . 399

Balkan-Import-Export, Case 5/73, [1973] ECR 1091 . . . 168
Banks, Case C-128/92, [1994] ECR I-1209 . . . 214
Barber v. Guardian Royal Exchange Assurance Group, Case C-262/88, [1990] ECR I-1889; [1990] 2 All ER 660; [1990] 2 CMLR 513; [1991] 1 QB 344; [1991] 2 WLR 72 . . . 76, 220
Barge v. High Authority, Case 18/62, [1963] ECR 259; [1965] CMLR 330 . . . 138, 431
Barr and Montrose Holdings, Case C-355/89, [1991] ECR I-3479 . . . 293
Barra v. Belgium, Case 309/85, [1988] ECR 355 . . . 76
Bartsch v. Bosch und Siemens Hausgeräte (BSH) Altersfürsorge GmbH, Case C-427/06, [2008] ECR I-7245 . . . 222
BASF v. Commission, Cases T-79, 84/89, [1992] ECR II-315; [1992] 4 CMLR 357 . . . 360, 361, 363
BAT and Reynolds v. Commission, Cases 142, 156/84, [1987] ECR 4487 . . . 380, 399
Beauport v. Council and Commission, Cases 103–9/78, [1979] ECR 17; [1979] 3 CMLR 1 . . . 375
Becher v. Commission, Case 30/66, [1967] ECR 285; [1968] CMLR 169 . . . 479, 480
Becker, Case 8/81, [1982] ELR 53; [1982] CMLR 499 . . . 224
Bela-Mühle, Case 114/76 (one of first Skimmed-Milk Powder Cases), [1977] ECR 1211; [1979] 2 CMLR 83 . . . 168, 169, 471
Belgium v. Commission, Case C-142/87, [1990] ECR I-959 . . . 171
Bergaderm v. Commission, Case C-352/98 P, [2000] ECR I-5291 (appeal from Case T-199/96, [1998] ECR II-2805) . . . 468, 469, 471, 472, 476
Berlusconi, Cases C-387/02, 391/02 and 403/02, [2005] ECR I-3565 . . . 228
Berti v. Commission, Case 131/81, [1985] ECR 645 . . . 459
Bertrand v. Commission, Case 40/75, [1976] ECR 1; [1976] 1 CMLR 220 . . . 457, 459
Beus, Case 5/67, [1968] ECR 83; [1968] CMLR 131 . . . 138
Binderer v. Commission, Case 147/83, [1985] ECR 257 372 . . . 384
Biovilac v. EEC, Case 59/83, [1984] ECR 4057 . . . 460
Biret International v. Council, Case C-93/02 P, [2003] ECR I-10497 . . . 198, 243
Birke v. Commission and Council, Case 543/79, [1981] ECR 2669 . . . 467
Birra Dreher v. Italian Finance Administration, Case 162/73, [1974] ECR 201290 . . . 291
Birra Wührer v. Council and Commission, Cases 256, 257, 265, 267/80, 5/81, [1982] ECR 85 . . . 451, 458
Blaizot v. University of Liège, Case 24/86, [1988] ECR 379; [1989] 1 CMLR 57 . . . 75
Bock v. Commission, Case 62/70, [1971] ECR 897; [1972] CMLR 160 . . . 76, 373, 388–90
Bolton Alimentari, Case C-494/09, [2011] ECR I-647 . . . 415
Bonifaci v. INPS, Cases C-94–5/95, [1997] ECR I-3969 . . . 250, 252
Bonsignore, Case 67/74, [1975] ECR 297; [1975] 1 CMLR 472 . . . 69, 270
Bonu v. Council, Case 89/79, [1980] ECR 553 . . . 140
Borker, Case 138/80, [1980] ECR 1975; [1980] 3 CMLR 638 . . . 300
Bosch, Case 135/77, [1978] ECR 855 . . . 311
Bossi v. Commission, Case 346/87, [1989] ECR 303 . . . 357
Bostock, Case C-2/92, [1994] ECR I-955 . . . 158
Bourgaux v. Common Assembly, Case 1/56, [1956] ECR 361 . . . 432
BP Supergas, Case C-62/93, [1995] ECR I-1883 . . . 245
Brasserie du Pêcheur v. Bundesrepublik Deutschland and The Queen v. Secretary of State for Transport, *ex parte*: Factortame Ltd, Cases C-46/93, 48/93, [1996] ECR I-1029; [1996] 2 WLR 506 . . . 250–2
Bresciani, Case 87/75, [1976] ECR 129; [1976] 2 CMLR 62 . . . 240, 241, 244, 285, 417, 424
Brinkmann Tabakfabriken v. Skatteministeriet, Case C-319/96, [1998] ECR I-5255; [1998] 3 CMLR 673 . . . 255
British Shoe Corporation Footwear Supplies v. Council, Case T-598/97, [2002] ECR II-1155 . . . 382
Broekmeulen, Case 246/80, [1981] ECR 2311; [1982] 1 CMLR 91 . . . 292
Bruckner v. Commission and Council, Case 799/79, [1981] ECR 2697 . . . 467
Buckl, Cases C-15, 108/91, [1992] ECR I-6061 . . . 394, 396, 403
Bundesverband der Bilanzbuchhalter v. Commission, Case C-107/95 P, [1997] ECR I-947 . . . 327
Buralux v. Council, Case C-209/94 P, [1996] ECR I-615 (affirming Case T-475/93, 17 May 1994, not published in ECR) . . . 371, 373, 377
Busseni, Case C-221/88, [1990] ECR I-495 . . . 74

Bussone, Case 31/78, [1978] ECR 2429 . . . 217
Buyl v. Commission, Case 817/79, [1982] ECR 245 . . . 20

Calpak v. Commission, Cases 789, 790/79, [1980] ECR 1949; [1981] 1 CMLR 26 . . . 370, 375
CAM v. Council and Commission, Case 100/74, [1975] ECR 1393 . . . 374
Campo Ebro v. Council, Case T-472/93, [1995] ECR II-421 . . . 371
Canon v. Council, Case 300/85, [1988] ECR 5731 . . . 381
Ca'Pasta v. Commission, Case C-359/98, [2000] ECR I-3977 . . . 360
Capolongo, Case 77/72, [1973] ECR 611; [1974] 1 CMLR 230 . . . 211
Cartesio Oktató és Szolgáltató bt, Case C-210/06, [2008] ECR I-9641 . . . 310
Casagrande v. Munich, Case 9/74, [1974] ECR 773; [1974] 2 CMLR 423 . . . 318
Centro-Com, Case C-124/95, [1997] ECR I-81 . . . 100, 101
Chambre Syndicale de la Sidérurgie Française, Cases 3, 4/64, [1965] ECR 441 . . . 425
Chemial v. DAF, Case 140/79, [1981] ECR 1; [1981] 3 CMLR 350 . . . 301
Chemiefarma v. Commission, Case 41/69, [1970] ECR 661 . . . 20, 130
Chevalley v. Commission, Case 15/70, [1970] ECR 975 . . . 392, 406
CIA Security v. Signalson and Securitel, Case C-194/94, [1996] ECR I-2201; [1996] 2 CMLR 781 . . . 225–9
CIDA v. Commission, Case 297/86, [1988] ECR 3531 . . . 370
CILFIT, Case 283/81, [1982] ECR 3415; [1983] 1 CMLR 472 . . . 305, 306
CIRFS v. Commission, Case C-313/90, [1993] ECR I-1125 . . . 383
CNPAAP v. Council, Case C-87/95 P, [1996] ECR I-2003 (affirming Case T-116/94, [1995] ECR II-1) . . . 377
CNTA v. Commission, Case 74/74, (decision of 14 May 1975), [1975] ECR 533; [1977] 1 CMLR 171; (decision of 15 June 1976), [1976] ECR 797 . . . 166, 457, 469, 470, 483, 485
Cobrecaf v. Commission, Case T-514/93, [1995] ECR II-621 . . . 467
Coca-Cola v. Commission, Cases T-125, 127/97, [2000] ECR II-1733; [2000] 5 CMLR 467 . . . 359
Codorniu v. Council, Case C-309/89, [1994] ECR I-1853 . . . 376–80
COFAZ v. Commission, Case 169/84, [1986] ECR 391; [1986] 3 CMLR 385 . . . 383, 386
Comet v. Produktschap voor Siergewassen, Case 45/76, [1976] ECR 2043; [1977] 1 CMLR 533 . . . 245
Commission v. Austria, Case C-320/03 R, [2003] ECR I-7929, [2003] ECR I-11665, [2004] ECR I-3593 . . . 332
Commission v. Austria, Case C-205/06, [2009] ECR I-01301 . . . 100
Commission v. BASF, Case C-137/92 P, [1994] ECR I-2555 (appeal from Cases T-79/89 (etc.), [1992] ECR II-315) . . . 360, 361, 363
Commission v. Belgium, Case 77/69, [1970] ECR 237 . . . 318
Commission v. Belgium, Case 156/77, [1978] ECR 1881 . . . 413, 415
Commission v. Belgium, Case 102/79, [1980] ECR 1473; [1981] 1 CMLR 282 . . . 223
Commission v. Belgium, Case 149/79, [1980] ECR 3881 and [1982] ECR 1845 . . . 234
Commission v. Belgium, Case 52/84, [1986] ECR 89; [1987] 1 CMLR 710 . . . 334
Commission v. Belgium, Case 293/85 R, [1985] ECR 3521 . . . 331
Commission v. Belgium, Case 293/85, [1988] ECR 305 . . . 320, 323, 325
Commission v. Belgium, Case 298/86, [1988] ECR 4343 . . . 323
Commission v. CO.DE.MI., Case 318/81, [1985] ECR 3693; [1987] 2 CMLR 516 . . . 446
Commission v. Council, Case 22/70 (ERTA Case), [1971] ECR 263; [1971] CMLR 335 . . . 109, 137, 177–9, 186, 187, 190, 194–7, 284, 350, 353
Commission v. Council, Case 81/72 (Staff Salaries Case), [1973] ECR 575; [1973] CMLR 639 . . . 166, 424, 437
Commission v. Council, Case 45/86, [1987] ECR 1493 . . . 120, 138, 367, 422
Commission v. Council, Case 165/87, [1988] ECR 5545 . . . 113, 121, 122
Commission v. Council, Case 383/87, [1988] ECR 4051 . . . 42, 397
Commission v. Council, Case 16/88, [1989] ECR 3457 . . . 131
Commission v. Council, Case C-300/89, [1991] ECR I-2869 . . . 121
Commission v. Council (FAO Case), Case C-25/94, [1996] ECR I-1469 . . . 24, 175, 353
Commission v. Council, Case C-370/07, [2009] ECR I-8917 . . . 120
Commission v. Denmark, Case 211/81, [1982] ECR 4547 . . . 320
Commission v. Denmark, Case C-52/90, [1992] ECR I-2187 . . . 320, 325
Commission v. Edith Cresson, Case C-432/04, [2006] ECR I-6387 . . . 29

Commission v. Feilhauer, Case C-209/90, [1992] ECR I-2613 . . . 444
Commission v. France, Cases 6, 11/69 (Rediscount Rate Case), [1969] ECR 523; [1970] CMLR 43 . . . 327, 361
Commission v. France, Case 26/69, [1970] ECR 565; [1970] CMLR 444 . . . 326
Commission v. France, Case 7/71, [1971] ECR 1003; [1972] CMLR 453 . . . 321–4, 404
Commission v. France, Case 167/73 (French Merchant Seamen Case), [1974] ECR 359; [1974] 2 CMLR 216 . . . 245
Commission v. France, Case 232/78 (Sheep Meat Case), [1979] ECR 2729; [1980] 1 CMLR 418 . . . 335
Commission v. France, Cases 24, 97/80 R (second Sheep Meat Case), [1980] ECR 1319; [1981] 3 CMLR 25 . . . 335, 336
Commission v. France, Case C-265/95, [1997] ECR I-6959 . . . 319
Commission v. France, Case C-304/02, [2005] ECR I-6263 . . . 337, 338
Commission v. France, Case C-239/03, [2004] ECR I-9325 . . . 195
Commission v. France, Case C-177/04, [2006] ECR I-2461 . . . 338
Commission v. France, Case C-121/07, [2008] ECR I-9159 . . . 337, 338
Commission v. Germany (Kohlegesetz), Case 70/72, [1973] ECR 813; [1973] CMLR 741 . . . 164, 333
Commission v. Germany, Case 116/82, [1986] ECR 2519 . . . 416
Commission v. Germany, Case 325/82, [1984] ECR 777; [1985] 2 CMLR 719 . . . 325
Commission v. Germany, Case 195/90 R, [1990] ECR I-3351 . . . 331
Commission v. Germany, Case C-61/94, [1996] ECR I-3989 . . . 316
Commission v. Government of the Italian Republic, Case 16/69, [1969] ECR 377; [1970] CMLR 161 . . . 317, 318
Commission v. Greece, Case 240/86, [1988] ECR 1835 . . . 320
Commission v. Greece, Case 226/87, [1988] ECR 3611 . . . 413, 418
Commission v. Greece, Case C-45/91, [1992] ECR I-2509 . . . 338
Commission v. Greece, Case C-183/91, [1993] ECR I-3131 . . . 413
Commission v. Greece, Case C-387/97, [2000] ECR I-5047 . . . 338
Commission v. Greece (Macedonia Case), Case 120/94 R, [1994] ECR I-3037 . . . 331
Commission v. Greece, Case C-369/07, [2009] ECR I-5703 . . . 338
Commission v. Ireland, Case 61/77 R, [1977] ECR 937 . . . 331
Commission v. Ireland, Case C-13/00, [2002] ECR I-2943 . . . 195, 316
Commission v. Ireland, Case C-494/01, [2005] ECR I-3331 . . . 325, 339
Commission v. Ireland, Case C-418/04, [2007] ECR I-10947 . . . 230
Commission v. Italy, Case 7/61 (Pork Imports Case), [1961] ECR 317; [1962] CMLR 39 . . . 325, 326
Commission v. Ireland, Case C-13/00, [2002] ECR I-2943 . . . 195, 316
Commission v. Italy, Case 10/61, [1962] ECR 1 . . . 98, 100
Commission v. Italy, Case 31/69, [1970] ECR 25; [1970] CMLR 175 . . . 325, 326
Commission v. Italy, Case 8/70, [1970] ECR 961 . . . 318
Commission v. Italy, Case 48/71 (second Art Treasures Case), [1972] ECR 527; [1972] CMLR 69 . . . 326
Commission v. Italy, Case 39/72, [1973] ECR 101; [1973] CMLR 439 . . . 217
Commission v. Italy, Case 79/72, [1973] ECR 667 . . . 335
Commission v. Italy, Case 100/77, [1978] ECR 879; [1979] 2 CMLR 655 . . . 318
Commission v. Italy, Case 28/81, [1981] ECR 2577 . . . 325
Commission v. Italy, Case 166/82, [1984] ECR 459; [1985] 2 CMLR 615 . . . 325
Commission v. Italy, Case 309/84, [1986] ECR 599; [1987] 2 CMLR 657 . . . 320, 326
Commission v. Italy, Case 154/85 R, [1985] ECR 1753 . . . 331
Commission v. Italy, Case 363/85, [1987] ECR 1733 . . . 223
Commission v. Italy, Case 22/87, [1989] ECR 143 . . . 249
Commission v. Italy, Case 119/04, [2006] ECR I-6885 . . . 338
Commission v. Kadi ('Kadi II'), Case C-584/10 P, 18 July 2013 (Grand Chamber) (appeal from Case T-85/09) . . . 106, 162
Commission v. Kronoply and Kronotex, Case C-83/09 P, [2011] ECR I-4441 (Grand Chamber) . . . 383
Commission v. Luxembourg and Belgium, Cases 90, 91/63, [1964] ECR 625; [1965] CMLR 58 . . . 259, 326, 332
Commission v. Malta, Case C-76/08 R, [2008] ECR I-64 . . . 332
Commission v. Netherlands, Case C-341/97, [2000] ECR I-6611 . . . 320, 325

Commission v. Portugal, Case C-70/06, [2008] ECR I-00001 . . . 338
Commission v. Schneider Electric, Case C-440/07 P, [2009] ECR I-6413 (Grand Chamber) . . . 457
Commission v. Spain, Case 278/01, [2003] ECR I-14141 . . . 338
Commission v. Sweden, Case C-249/06, [2009] ECR I-1335 . . . 100
Commission v. Tordeur, Case 232/84, [1985] ECR 3223 . . . 446
Commission v. United Kingdom, Cases 31, 53/77 R (Pig Producers Case), [1977] ECR 921; [1977] 2 CMLR 359 . . . 331
Commission v. United Kingdom, Case 128/78 (Tachograph Case), [1979] ECR 419; [1979] 2 CMLR 45 . . . 217
Commission v. United Kingdom, Case C-466/98 (Open Skies Case), [2002] ECR I-9427 . . . 185
Commission v. Zoubek, Case 426/85, [1986] ECR 4057 . . . 444
Compagnie Continentale France v. Council, Case 169/73, [1975] ECR 117; [1975] 1 CMLR 131 . . . 462
Compagnie d'Approvisionnement v. Commission, Cases 9–11/71, [1972] ECR 391; [1973] CMLR 529 . . . 393, 428, 437, 460, 467, 482
Compagnie des Hauts Fourneaux de Chasse v. High Authority, Case 15/57, [1958] ECR 211 . . . 412, 425, 427
Compagnie Française Commerciale et Financière v. Commission, Case 64/69, [1970] ECR 221; [1970] CMLR 369 . . . 71, 374, 375
Confédération Nationale des Producteurs de Fruits et Légumes v. Council, Cases 16, 17/62, [1962] ECR 471; [1963] CMLR 160 . . . 370
Consorzio Cooperative d'Abruzzo v. Commission, Case 15/85, [1987] ECR 1005 . . . 131, 167, 361
Control Data Belgium v. Commission, Case 294/81, [1983] ECR 911; [1983] 2 CMLR 357 . . . 372, 413
Cook v. Commission, Case C-198/91, [1993] ECR I-2487 . . . 383
Corbiau v. Administration des Contributions, Case C-24/92, [1993] ECR I-1277 . . . 290, 291
Corsica Ferries, Case C-18/93, [1994] ECR I-1783 . . . 290, 291
Costa v. ENEL, Case 6/64, [1964] ECR 585; [1964] CMLR 42583, . . . 206, 259, 296
Council v. European Parliament, Case 34/86, [1986] ECR 2155; [1986] 3 CMLR 94 . . . 42
Council v. European Parliament, Case C-284/90, [1992] ECR I-2277 . . . 42
Council v. European Parliament, Case C-41/95, [1995] ECR I-4411 . . . 42
Cremonini, Case 815/79, [1980] ECR 3583; [1981] 3 CMLR 49 . . . 317
Criminal proceedings against X, Cases C-74 & 129/95, [1996] ECR I-6609 . . . 291
Cristini v. SNCF, Case 32/75, [1975] ECR 1085; [1976] 1 CMLR 573 . . . 312

Da Costa, Cases 28–30/62, [1963] ECR 31; [1963] CMLR 224 . . . 305
Dalmas v. High Authority, Case 1/63, [1963] ECR 303; [1964] CMLR 223 . . . 139
Dalmas v. High Authority, Case 21/64, [1965] ECR 175; [1966] CMLR 46 . . . 413
Danvin v. Commission, Case 26/67, [1968] ECR 315 . . . 448
De Bloos v. Bouyer, Case 59/77, [1977] ECR 2359; [1978] 1 CMLR 511 . . . 415
De Boer Buizen v. Council and Commission, Case 81/86, [1987] ECR 3677 . . . 484
De Coster v. Collège des bourgmestre et échevins de Watermael-Boitsfort, Case C-17/00, [2001] ECR I-9445 . . . 291
De Dapper v. European Parliament, Case 29/74, [1975] ECR 35 . . . 430
De Gezamenlijke Steenkolenmijnen in Limburg v. High Authority, Case 17/57, [1959] ECR 1 . . . 327, 404
De Gezamenlijke Steenkolenmijnen in Limburg v. High Authority, Case 30/59, [1961] ECR 1 . . . 394
De Roubaix v. Commission, Case 25/77, [1978] ECR 1081 . . . 354
De Vleeschauwer v. Commission, Case 144/73, [1974] ECR 957 . . . 430
De Wendel v. Commission, Case 29/67, [1968] ECR 263; [1969] CMLR 354 . . . 140
Deboeck v. Commission, Case 90/74, [1975] ECR 1123 . . . 429, 430
DEFI v. Commission, Case 282/85, [1986] ECR 2469 . . . 382
Defrenne v. Sabena, Case 43/75, [1976] ECR 455; [1976] 2 CMLR 98 . . . 75, 91, 209, 214, 224
Defrenne v. Sabena, Case 149/77, [1978] ECR 1365; [1978] 3 CMLR 312 . . . 152, 157
Degreef v. Commission, Case 80/63, [1964] ECR 391 . . . 448
Dekker, Case C-177/88, [1990] ECR I-3941 . . . 235
Demirel, Case 12/86, [1987] ECR 3719 . . . 158, 195, 241
Demouche and others v. Fonds de garantie automobile and Bureau central français, Case 152/83, [1987] ECR 3833 . . . 283

Demo-Studio Schmidt v. Commission, Case 210/81, [1983] ECR 3045; [1984] 1 CMLR 69 . . . 380, 399
Denkavit v. Commission, Case 14/78, [1978] ECR 2497; [1979] 2 CMLR 135 . . . 328, 459
Denkavit Internationaal v. Bundesamt für Finanzen, Cases C-283, 291 and 292/94, [1996] ECR I-5063 . . . 254
Deshormes v. Commission, Case 17/78, [1979] ECR 189 . . . 352
Dethlefs v. Council and Commission, Case T-112/95, [1998] ECR II-3819 . . . 476
Deuka v. EVGF, Case 78/74, [1975] ECR 421; [1975] 2 CMLR 28 . . . 165, 434
Deutsche Milchkontor v. Germany, Cases 205–215/82, [1983] ECR 2633; [1984] 3 CMLR 586 . . . 245
Deutsche Post and Germany v. Commission, Case C-463/10 P, [2011] ECR I-9639 . . . 350, 357
Deutsche Shell, Case C-188/91, [1993] ECR I-363 . . . 191, 287
Deutz und Geldermann v. Council, Case 26/86, [1987] ECR 941 . . . 375
Devred v. Commission, Case 257/78, [1979] ECR 3767 . . . 169
DGV v. Commission and Council, Cases 241, 242, 245–50/78 (one of second Quellmehl and Gritz Cases), [1979] ECR 3017 . . . 472, 485
Dias, Case C-343/90, [1992] ECR I-4673 . . . 302, 303
Dietz v. Commission, Case 126/76, [1977] ECR 2431; [1978] 2 CMLR 608 . . . 485
Dillenkofer v. Germany, Cases C-178–9, 188–190/94, [1996] ECR I-4845 . . . 251, 254
Dior v. Tuk Consultancy, Cases C-300, 392/98, [2000] ECR I-11307 . . . 195, 241, 287
Dorsch Consult, Case C-54/96, [1997] ECR I-4961 . . . 290, 291
Dorsch Consult v. Council and Commission, Case T-184/95, [1998] ECR II-667; affirmed Case C-237/98 P [2000] ECR I-4549 . . . 460
Dow Benelux v. Commission, Case 85/87, [1989] ECR 3137; [1991] 4 CMLR 410 . . . 152
Dow Chemical Ibérica v. Commission, Cases 97–99/87, [1989] ECR 3165; [1991] 4 CMLR 410 . . . 152
Draehmpaehl v. Urania Immobilienservice OHG, Case C-180/95, [1997] ECR I-2195 . . . 225
Ducros v. Commission, Case T-149/95, [1997] ECR II-2031 . . . 383
Dumortier v. Council, Cases 64, 113/76, 167, 239/78, 27, 28, 45/79 (one of second Quellmehl and Gritz Cases), [1979] ECR 3091 . . . 459, 472, 485
Dzodzi, Cases C-297/88, 197/89, [1990] ECR I-3763 . . . 288

E and F, Case C-550/09, [2010] ECR I-6213 . . . 415
Eco Swiss v. Benetton International, Case C-126/97, [1999] ECR I-3055; [2000] 5 CMLR 816 . . . 293
ECSC v. Ferriere Sant'Anna, Case 168/82, [1983] ECR 1681 . . . 169
Einfuhr- und Vorratsstelle v. Köster, Case 25/70, [1970] ECR 1161; [1972] CMLR 255 . . . 20, 130, 131, 148
Elz v. Commission, Case 56/75, [1976] ECR 1097 . . . 167
Emerald Meats v. Commission, Cases C-106, 317/90, 129/91, [1993] ECR I-209 . . . 376
Emesa Sugar (Free Zone) NV v. Aruba, Case C-17/98, [2000] ECR I-665 . . . 52
EMI, Case 51/75, [1976] ECR 811; [1976] 2 CMLR 235 . . . 311
Emmott, Case C-208/90, [1991] ECR I-4269 . . . 246
Emrich v. Commission, Case C-371/89, [1990] ECR I-1555 . . . 327
Enka, Case 38/77, [1977] ECR 2203; [1978] 2 CMLR 212 . . . 220, 223
ENU v. Commission, Case C-107/91, [1993] ECR I-599 . . . 407
Eridania, Case 230/78, [1979] ECR 2749 . . . 216
Eridania v. Commission, Cases 10, 18/68, [1969] ECR 459 . . . 386, 400, 401, 428
ERT, Case C-260/89, [1991] ECR I-2925 . . . 157
Essevi, Cases 142–3/80, [1981] ECR 1413 . . . 323
European Parliament v. Commission, Case C-156/93, [1995] ECR I-2019 . . . 368, 425
European Parliament v. Council, Case 13/83 (Transport Case), [1985] ECR 1513; [1986] 1 CMLR 138 . . . 395
European Parliament v. Council, Case 302/87 (Comitology Case), [1988] ECR 5615 . . . 75, 367, 395, 398
European Parliament v. Council, Case 377/87 (Draft Budget Case), [1988] ECR 4017 . . . 42, 397–99
European Parliament v. Council, Case C-70/88 (Chernobyl Case), [1990] ECR I-2041 . . . 72, 74, 367, 395, 396
European Parliament v. Council, Case C-65/90, [1992] ECR I-4593 . . . 20
European Parliament v. Council, Case C-295/90, [1992] ECR I-4193 . . . 121, 438
European Parliament v. Council, Cases C-181, 248/91, [1993] ECR I-3685 . . . 42, 365

European Parliament v. Council, Case C-316/91, [1994] ECR I-625 . . . 121, 351, 368
European Parliament v. Council, Case C-388/92, [1994] ECR I-2067 . . . 20
European Parliament v. Council, Case C-65/93, [1995] ECR I-643 . . . 19
European Parliament v. Council, Case C-360/93, [1996] ECR 1195 . . . 437
European Parliament v. Council, Case C-417/93, [1995] ECR I-1185 . . . 19, 20, 131
European Parliament v. Council, Case C-21/94, [1995] ECR I-1827 . . . 20
European Parliament v. Council, Case C-392/95, [1997] ECR I-3213 . . . 20
European Parliament v. Innamorati, Case C-254/95 P, [1996] ECR I-3423 . . . 140
European Parliament v. Council, Case C-166/07, [2009] ECR I-7135 . . . 122
European Parliament v. Council, Case C-355/10, 5 September 2012 (Grand Chamber) . . . 130, 131, 367
Eurotunnel v. SeaFrance, Case C-408/95, [1997] ECR I-6315 . . . 415
Evans Medical and Macfarlan Smith, *see* R v. Secretary of State for the Home Department, *ex parte* Evans Medical and Macfarlan Smith (Generics Case), Case C-324/93
EVGF v. Mackprang, Case 2/75, [1975] ECR 607 . . . 165
Exporteurs in Levende Varkens v. Commission, Cases T-481, 484/93, [1995] ECR II-2941 . . . 377
Extramet Industrie v. Council, Case C-358/89, [1991] ECR I-2501 . . . 370, 381, 382

Fabrique de Fer de Charleroi v. Commission, Cases 351, 360/85, [1987] ECR 3639 . . . 426
Faccini Dori v. Recreb, Case C-91/92, [1994] ECR I-3325 . . . 220, 225, 226, 229, 231, 237
Fédération Charbonnière de Belgique (Fédéchar) v. High Authority, Case 8/55, [1956] ECR 245 and 292 . . . 83, 113, 168, 354, 393, 425, 427
Fédération Européenne de la Santé Animale v. Council, Case 160/88 R, [1988] ECR 4121 . . . 375
Fédération nationale du commerce extérieur v. France, Case C-354/90, [1991] ECR I-5505 . . . 359
Federconsorzi, Case C-88/91, [1992] ECR I-4035 . . . 289
FEDIOL v. Commission, Case 191/82, [1983] ECR 2913; [1984] 3 CMLR 244 . . . 382
FEDIOL v. Commission, Case 70/87, [1989] ECR 1781 . . . 198, 461
FIAMM v. Council and Commission, Cases C-120–121/06, [2008] ECR I-6513 . . . 198, 243, 460, 469
Finsider v. Commission, Cases C-363, 364/88, [1992] ECR I-359 . . . 464
Fiskano v. Commission, Case C-135/92, [1994] ECR I-2885 . . . 171
Flemmer, Cases C-80–82/99, [2001] ECR I-7211 . . . 444, 446, 476
Foglia v. Novello, Case 104/79, [1980] ECR 745; [1981] 1 CMLR 45229, . . . 301, 304
Foglia v. Novello, Case 244/80, [1981] ECR 3045; [1982] 1 CMLR 585 . . . 229, 301, 302
Foster v. British Gas, Case C-188/89, [1990] ECR I-3313; [1990] 2 CMLR 833 . . . 232, 233, 235
Foto-Frost, Case 314/85, [1987] ECR 4199 . . . 299
Fournier, [1992] Case C-73/89, ECR I-5621 . . . 289
France v. Commission, Case C-202/88, [1991] ECR I-1223; [1992] 5 CMLR 552 . . . 30
France v. Commission, Case C-366/88, [1990] ECR I-3571 . . . 353
France v. Commission, Case C-303/90, [1991] ECR I-5315 . . . 353
France v. Commission, Case C-325/91, [1993] ECR I-3283 . . . 353
France v. Commission, Case C-327/91, [1994] ECR I-3641 . . . 30, 114, 184, 285, 365, 420
France v. Commission, Case C-57/95, [1997] ECR I-1627 . . . 353
France v. European Parliament, Cases 358/85, 51/86, [1988] ECR 4821 . . . 4, 353
France v. European Parliament, Case C-345/95, [1997] ECR I-5215 . . . 4
France v. High Authority, Case 1/54, [1954] ECR 1 . . . 427
France v. United Kingdom, Case 141/78, [1979] ECR 2923; [1980] 1 CMLR 6 . . . 330
France, Italy and the United Kingdom v. Commission, Cases 188–90/80, [1982] ECR 2545; [1982] 3 CMLR 144 . . . 30
Francovich v. Italy, Cases C-6, 9/90, [1991] ECR I-5357; [1993] 2 CMLR 66 . . . 212, 248, 250, 251, 254, 255, 334
Fratelli Costanzo v. Comune di Milano, Case 103/88, [1989] ECR 1839; [1990] 3 CMLR 239 . . . 232
Fresh Marine Company v. Commission, Case T-178/98, [2000] ECR II 3331; [2001] 3 CMLR 35; upheld on appeal, Case C-472/00 P, [2003] ECR I-7541; [2003] 2 CMLR 39 . . . 462, 467
Frilli v. Belgium, Case 1/72, [1972] ECR 457; [1973] CMLR 386 . . . 169

Front National v. Parliament, Case C-486/01 P-R and Case C-488/01 P-R, [2002] ECR I-1843; Case C-486/01 P, [2004] ECR I-6289 . . . 17

GAARM v. Commission, Case 289/83, [1984] ECR 4295; [1986] 3 CMLR 15 . . . 328, 459
Gabalfrisa, Cases C-110–147/98, [2000] ECR I-1577 . . . 290, 291
Galli, Case 31/74, [1975] ECR 47; [1975] 1 CMLR 211 . . . 215
Garofalo, Cases C-69–79/96, [1997] ECR I-5603 . . . 290, 292
GB-INN0-BM, Case C-362/88, [1990] ECR I-667 . . . 150
Geitling v. High Authority, Cases 36–38, 40/59, [1960] ECR 423 . . . 147
GEMA v. Commission, Case 125/78, [1979] ECR 3173; [1980] 2 CMLR 177 . . . 380, 399, 407
Geotronics v. Commission, Case C-395/95 P, [1997] ECR I-2271 . . . 359, 360
Germany v. Commission, Case 24/62 (Brennwein Case), [1963] ECR 63; [1963] CMLR 347 . . . 136–8, 140, 141
Germany v. Commission, Cases 52, 55/65, [1966] ECR 159; [1967] CMLR 22 . . . 326
Germany v. Commission, Case 50/69 R, [1969] ECR 449; [1971] CMLR 724 . . . 431, 433
Germany v. Commission, Cases 281, 283–5, 287/85, [1987] ECR 3203; [1988] 1 CMLR 11 . . . 30, 113
Germany v. Council Case C-280/93, (Bananas Case), [1994] ECR I-4973 . . . 198, 417, 424, 461
Germany v. European Parliament and Council (Tobacco Advertising Case), Case C-376/98, [2000] ECR I-8419; [2000] 3 CMLR 1175 . . . 127, 420
Germany v. High Authority, Case 3/59 (Railway Tariffs Case), [1960] ECR 53 . . . 413
Gesellschaft für Getreidehandel v. EVGF, Case 55/72, [1973] ECR 15; [1973] CMLR 465 . . . 413
Gestetner Holdings v. Commission and Council, Case C-156/87, [1990] ECR I-781 . . . 358
Gestevisión Telecinco v. Commission, Case T-95/96, [1998] ECR II-3407; [1998] 3 CMLR 1112 . . . 383, 407
Gibraltar v. Council, Case C-298/89, [1993] ECR I-3605 . . . 375
Giloy, Case C-130/95, [1997] ECR I-4291 . . . 248, 289
Giordano v. Commission, Case 11/72, [1973] ECR 417 . . . 451
Giuffrida v. Council, Case 105/75, [1976] ECR 1395 . . . 426
Gmurzynska-Bscher, Case C-231/89, [1990] ECR I-4003 . . . 288
Grad, Case 9/70, [1970] ECR 825; [1971] CMLR 1 . . . 218, 240
Granaria, Case 116/76 (one of first Skimmed-Milk Powder Cases), [1977] ECR 1247; [1979] 2 CMLR 83 . . . 168, 471
Grands Moulins de Paris v. Council and Commission, Case 50/86, [1987] ECR 4833 . . . 476
Grands Moulins des Antilles v. Commission, Case 99/74, [1975] ECR 1531 . . . 483
Greece v. Commission, Case 192/83, [1985] ECR 2791 . . . 402
Greece v. Commission, Case 30/88, [1989] ECR 3711 . . . 191, 316
Greek Canners v. Commission, Case 250/81, [1982] ECR 3535; [1983] 2 CMLR 32 . . . 370
Greenpeace v. Council, Case T-585/93, [1985] ECR II-2205 . . . 377
Greenpeace v. Council, Case C-321/95 P, [1998] ECR I-1651 (affirming Case T-585/93), [1985] ECR II-2205 . . . 377
Greis Unterweger, Case 318/85, [1986] ECR 955 . . . 300
Grifoni v. Commission, Case C-308/87, [1990] ECR I-1203 . . . 458
Grimaldi, Case C-322/88, [1989] ECR 4407 . . . 109, 235, 284
Group of the European Right v. European Parliament, Case 78/85, [1988] ECR 1753 . . . 353
Groupement des Industries Sidérurgiques Luxembourgeoises, Cases 7, 9/54, [1956] ECR 175 . . . 327
Guérin Automobiles v. Commission, Case C-282/95, [1997] ECR I-1503 (appeal from Case T-186/94, [1995] ECR II-1753) . . . 358, 396, 399, 407
Gutmann v. Commission, Cases 18, 35/65, [1966] ECR 103 . . . 425, 426

Haaga, Case 32/74, [1974] ECR 1201; [1975] 1 CMLR 32 . . . 284
Haegeman v. Belgium, Case 181/73, [1974] ECR 449; [1975] 1 CMLR 515 . . . 174, 285–7
Haegeman v. Commission, Case 96/71, [1972] ECR 1005; [1973] CMLR 365 . . . 481–3
HAG GF, Case C-10/89, [1990] ECR I-3711 . . . 71, 72
Haim v. Kassenzahnärztliche Vereinigung Nordrhein, Case C-424/97, [2000] ECR I-5123 . . . 255
Handelsvereniging Rotterdam, Cases 73, 74/63, [1964] ECR 1; [1964] CMLR 198 . . . 413, 416

Hauer v. Land Rheinland-Pfalz, Case 44/79, [1979] ECR 3727; [1980] 3 CMLR 42 . . . 152
Hauptzollamt Bielefeld v. König, Case 185/73, [1974] ECR 607 . . . 142
Hauptzollamt Bremerhaven v. Massey-Ferguson, Case 8/73, [1973] ECR 897 . . . 116
Hauts Fourneaux de Chasse v. High Authority, Case 2/57, [1958] ECR 199 . . . 427
Hauts Fourneaux et Aciéries Belges v. High Authority, Case 8/57, [1958] ECR 245 . . . 169, 425
Heinrich, Case C-345/06, [2009] ECR I-1659 . . . 141, 363
Hermès v. FHT, Case C-53/96, [1998] ECR I-3603 . . . 195, 287
Herpels v. Commission, Case 54/77, [1978] ECR 585 . . . 167
HNL v. Council and Commission, Cases 83, 94/76, 4, 15, 40/77, [1978] ECR 1209; [1978] 3 CMLR 566 . . . 468, 471, 472
Hoechst v. Commission, Cases 46/87, 227/88, [1989] ECR 2859; [1991] 4 CMLR 410 . . . 152, 171
Hoffmann-La Roche v. Centrafarm, Case 107/76, [1977] ECR 957; [1977] 2 CMLR 334 . . . 290, 297, 298
Hoffmann-La Roche v. Commission, Case 85/76, [1979] ECR 461; [1979] 3 CMLR 211 . . . 171
Holtz & Willemsen v. Council, Case 134/73, [1974] ECR 1; [1975] 1 CMLR 91 . . . 393
Holtz & Willemsen v. Council and Commission, Case 153/73, [1974] ECR 675; [1975] CMLR 91 . . . 483
Hoogovens v. High Authority, Case 14/61, [1962] ECR 253; [1963] CMLR 73 . . . 145, 167
HSB-Wohnbau GmbH, Case C-86/00, [2001] ECR I-5353 . . . 291
Huber v. Commission, Case 78/63, [1964] ECR 367; [1964] CMLR 576 . . . 357
Humblet v. Belgium, Case 6/60, [1960] ECR 559 . . . 30
Hurd v. Jones (Inspector of Taxes), Case 44/84, [1986] ECR 29; [1986] 2 CMLR 1; [1986] QB 892; [1986] 3 WLR 189 . . . 211, 284

IBC v. Commission, Case 46/75, [1976] ECR 65 . . . 483, 485
IBM v. Commission, Case 60/81, [1981] ECR 2639; [1981] 3 CMLR 635 . . . 357, 360
ICI v. Commission, Case 48/69, [1972] ECR 619; [1972] CMLR 557 . . . 142
Inter-Environnement Wallonie v. Région Wallonne, Case C-129/96, [1997] ECR I-7411 . . . 222, 230, 238, 239
International Chemical Corporation, Case 66/80, [1981] ECR 1191; [1983] 2 CMLR 593 . . . 417
International Fruit Company v. Commission, Cases 41–4/70, [1971] ECR 411; [1975] 2 CMLR 515 . . . 71, 374, 387, 417
International Fruit Company, Cases 21–4/72, [1972] ECR 1219; [1975] 2 CMLR 1 . . . 105, 192–4, 197, 241, 242, 417, 424
Internationale Handelsgesellschaft, Case 11/70, [1970] ECR 1125; [1972] CMLR 255 . . . 148, 168, 261
Interquell v. Commission and Council, Cases 261, 262/78 (one of second Quellmehl and Gritz Cases), [1979] ECR 3045 . . . 472, 485
Intertanko, Case C-308/06, [2008] ECR I-4057 . . . 193, 198
Inuit Tapiriit Kanatami v. Parliament and Council, Case T-18/10, [2011] ECR II-5599 (for appeal *see* Case C-583/11 P) 385
Inuit Tapiriit Kanatami v. Parliament and Council, Case C-583/11 P (appeal from Case T-18/10), 3 October 2013 (Grand Chamber) . . . 385
Inuit Tapiriit Kanatami, Case T-526/10, 25 April 2013 . . . 385
IRCA, Case 7/76, [1976] ECR 1213 . . . 149, 164
Ireks-Arkady v. Commission and Council, Case 238/78 (one of second Quellmehl and Gritz Cases), [1979] ECR 2955 . . . 472, 485
Irish Cement v. Commission, Cases 166, 220/86, [1988] ECR 6473; [1989] 2 CMLR 57 . . . 396
Irish Creamery Milk Suppliers Association v. Ireland, Cases 36, 71/80, [1981] ECR 735; [1981] 2 CMLR 455 . . . 307
ISA v. High Authority, Case 4/54, [1955] ECR 91 . . . 136, 436
ISO v. Council, Case C 118/77, [1979] ECR 1277 . . . 381
Italy v. Commission, Case 13/63, [1963] ECR 165; [1963] CMLR 289 . . . 432
Italy v. Commission, Case 32/65, [1966] ECR 389; [1969] CMLR 39 . . . 410, 415
Italy v. Commission, Case 151/88, [1989] ECR 1255 . . . 350
Italy v. Commission, Case C-47/91, [1992] ECR I-4145 . . . 359
Italy v. High Authority, Case 2/54, [1954] ECR 37 . . . 422, 436
Italy v. High Authority, Case 20/59, [1960] ECR 325 . . . 436

Jégo-Quéré v. Commission, Case T-177/01, [2002] ECR II-2365; on appeal, Case C-263/02 P, [2004] ECR I-3425 . . . 378

Job Centre, Case C-111/94, [1995] ECR I-3361 . . . 290, 291, 300
Johnson v. Chief Adjudication Officer, Case C-410/92, [1994] ECR I-5483 . . . 246
Johnston v. Chief Constable of the RUC, Case 222/84, [1986] ECR 1651; [1986] 3 CMLR 240 . . . 232, 233

Kadi v. Council and Commission ('Kadi I'), Case T-315/01, [2005] ECR II-3649 (reversed on appeal: Cases C-402/05 P and 415/05 P) . . . 98, 101, 104, 105, 161
Kadi v. Council and Commission ('Kadi I'), Cases C-402/05 P and 415/05 P, [2008] ECR I-6351 . . . 91, 98, 101, 104, 105, 161, 197
Kadi v. Commission ('Kadi II'), Case T-85/09, [2010] ECR II-5177 (affirmed on appeal: Case C-584/10 P) . . . 106, 162
Kaefer and Procacci, Cases C-100, 101/89, [1990] ECR I-4647 . . . 294
Kalsbeek v. Sociale Verzekeringsbank, Case 100/63, [1964] ECR 565; [1964] CMLR 548 . . . 164
Kampffmeyer v. Commission, Cases 5, 7, 13–24/66, [1967] ECR 245 . . . 451, 452, 457, 462, 477, 479
Kampffmeyer v. Council and Commission, Cases 56–60/74, [1976] ECR 711 . . . 458
Kergall v. Common Assembly, Case 1/55, [1955] ECR 151 . . . 432, 446, 458
Kleinwort Benson v. City of Glasgow District Council, Case C-346/93, [1995] ECR I-615 . . . 289
Klöckner-Werke v. Commission, Case 119/81, [1982] ECR 2627; [1983] 3 CMLR 341 . . . 422
Kloppenburg, Case 70/83, [1984] ECR 1075; [1985] 1 CMLR 205 . . . 222, 235, 263, 265
Köbler v. Austria, Case C-224/01, [2003] ECR I-10239 . . . 254
Kofisca Italia, Case C-1/99, [2001] ECR I-207 . . . 289
Kohler v. Court of Auditors, Cases 316/82, 40/83, [1984] ECR 641 . . . 362
Köllensperger and Atzwanger, Case C-103/97, [1999] ECR I-551 . . . 291
Kolpinghuis Nijmegen, Case 80/86, [1987] ECR 3969 . . . 224, 235, 236, 239
Konle v. Austria, Case C-302/97, [1999] ECR I-3099 . . . 255
Konstantinidis, Case C-168/91, [1993] ECR I-1191 . . . 158
Koschniske (Wördsdorfer), Case 9/79, [1979] ECR 2717; [1980] 1 CMLR 87 . . . 306
Koyo Seiko v. Council and Commission, Case 120/77 (Japanese Ball-Bearing Cases), [1979] ECR 1337; [1979] 2 CMLR 257 . . . 381
Kramer, Cases 3, 4, 6/76, [1976] ECR 1279; [1976] 2 CMLR 440 . . . 180, 183, 184, 186, 187
Kremzow, Case C-299/95, [1997] ECR I-2629 . . . 158
Krohn v. Commission, Case 175/84, [1986] ECR 753; [1987] 1 CMLR 745 . . . 467, 484
Krupp v. Commission, Cases 275/80, 24/81, [1981] ECR 2489 . . . 361
KSH v. Council and Commission, Case 101/76, [1977] ECR 797; [1980] 2 CMLR 669 . . . 371
KSH v. Council and Commission, Case 143/77 (one of second Isoglucose Cases), [1979] ECR 3583 . . . 473, 474
Kücükdeveci v. Swedex, Case C-555/07, [2010] ECR I-365 . . . 230, 240
Kupferberg, Case 104/81, [1982] ECR 3641; [1983] 1 CMLR 1 . . . 83, 240, 241
Küster v. European Parliament, Case 79/74, [1975] ECR 725 . . . 354
Kziber, Case C-18/90, [1991] ECR I-199 . . . 241

Laguillaumie, Case C-116/00, [2000] ECR I-4979 . . . 302
Lassalle v. European Parliament, Case 15/63, [1964] ECR 31; [1964] CMLR 259 . . . 354
Legros v. Réunion, Case C-163/90, [1992] ECR I-4625 . . . 302
Lehtonen and Castors Braine, Case C-176/96, [2000] ECR I-2681 . . . 302
Lemmens, Case C-226/97, [1998] ECR I-3711 . . . 226
Lemmerz-Werke v. High Authority, Cases 53, 54/63, [1963] ECR 239; [1964] CMLR 384 . . . 361
Lemmerz-Werke v. High Authority, Case 111/63, [1965] ECR 677; [1968] CMLR 280 . . . 167
Leroy v. High Authority, Case 35/62, 16/63, [1963] ECR 197; [1964] CMLR 562 . . . 432
L'Etoile Commerciale v. Commission, Cases 89, 91/86, [1987] ECR 3005 . . . 387
Leur-Bloem, Case C-28/95, [1997] ECR I-4161 . . . 289
Levy, Case C-158/91, [1993] ECR I-4287 . . . 98, 100, 101, 243, 287
Lord Bethell v. Commission, Case 246/81, [1982] ECR 2277; [1982] 3 CMLR 300 . . . 380, 406, 407
Lührs, Case 78/77, [1978] ECR 169; [1979] 1 CMLR 657 . . . 165
Lütticke v. Commission, Case 48/65, [1966] ECR 19; [1966] CMLR 378 . . . 327, 394, 396, 407

Lütticke v. Commission, Case 4/69, [1971] ECR 325 . . . 328, 459, 466, 467
Lutz GmbH, Case C-182/00, [2002] ECR I-547 . . . 291
Lux v. Court of Auditors, Case 69/83, [1984] ECR 2447 . . . 425
Luxembourg v. European Parliament, Case 230/81, [1983] ECR 255; [1983] 2 CMLR 726 . . . 4
Luxembourg v. European Parliament, Case 108/83, [1984] ECR 1945; [1986] 2 CMLR 507 . . . 4
Luxembourg v. European Parliament, Cases C-213/88, C-39/89 [1991] ECR I-5643 . . . 4
Lyckeskog, Case C-99/00, [2002] ECR I-4839 . . . 297

Mackprang v. Commission, Case 15/71, [1971] ECR 797; [1972] CMLR 52 . . . 393, 406
Maïseries de Beauce v. ONIC, Case 109/79, [1980] ECR 2883 . . . 418, 441
Maizena v. Council, Case 139/79, [1980] ECR 3393 . . . 19, 422
Mangold, Case C-144/04, [2005] ECR I-9981 . . . 77, 222, 229–31, 239, 240, 301
Mannesmann v. High Authority, Cases 4–13/59, [1960] ECR 113 . . . 448, 449
Mannesmann Röhrenwerke v. Council, Case 333/85, [1987] ECR 1381 . . . 387
Marcato v. Commission, Case 37/72, [1973] ECR 361 . . . 429
Marcopoulos v. European Court of Justice, Cases T-32, 39/89, [1990] ECR II-281; [1990] 3 CMLR 309 . . . 357
Marleasing, Case C-106/89, [1990] ECR I-4135; [1992] 1 CMLR 305 . . . 236–8
Marshall v. Southampton & South West Hampshire Area Health Authority (Teaching), Case 152/84, [1986] ECR 723; [1986] 1 CMLR 688; [1986] 2 WLR 780; [1986] 2 All ER 584 . . . 224, 229, 231, 232, 236, 237, 239, 244
Marshall v. Southampton & South West Hampshire Area Health Authority (No. 2), Case C-271/91, [1993] ECR I-4367, [1993] WLR 1054 (ECJ) . . . 225, 248
Martinez v. European Parliament, Cases T-222, 327 and 329/99, [2001] ECR II-2823: *see* Front National v. Parliament, Case C-486/01 P, [2002] ECR I-1843
Masdar (UK) Ltd v. Commission, Case 47/07 P, [2008] ECR I-9761 . . . 448, 449
Maso v. INPS and Italy, Case C-373/95, [1997] ECR I-4051 . . . 250, 252
Matra v. Commission, Case C-225/91, [1993] ECR I-3203 . . . 383
Mattheus v. Doego, Case 93/78, [1978] ECR 2203; [1979] 1 CMLR 551 . . . 301
Maurissen v. Commission, Cases 193–4/87, [1989] ECR 1045 . . . 364
Mazzalai, Case 111/75, [1976] ECR 657; [1977] 1 CMLR 105 . . . 220, 284
Meilicke, Case C-83/91, [1992] ECR I-4871 . . . 302, 303
Merkur v. Commission, Case 43/72, [1973] ECR 1055 . . . 467, 482
Meroni v. High Authority, Case 9/56, [1958] ECR 133 . . . 131, 137, 145, 412
Meroni v. High Authority, Case 10/56, [1958] ECR 157 . . . 412
Meroni v. High Authority (No. 5), Cases 21–26/61, [1962] ECR 73 . . . 401
Metro v. Commission, Case 26/76, [1977] ECR 1875; [1978] 2 CMLR 1 . . . 380
Metro v. Commission (No. 2), Case 75/84, [1986] ECR 3021; [1987] 1 CMLR 118 . . . 380
Meyer-Burckhardt v. Commission, Case 9/75, [1975] ECR 1171 . . . 318, 328
Michailidis v. Commission, Case T-100/94, [1998] ECR II-3115 . . . 377
Michel v. European Parliament, Case 195/80, [1981] ECR 2861 . . . 140
Michelin v. Commission, Case 322/81, [1983] ECR 3461; [1985] 1 CMLR 282 . . . 171
Microban v. Commission, Case T-262/10, [2011] ECR II-7697 . . . 385, 386
Mij PPW International, Case 61/72, [1973] ECR 301 . . . 66
Milac, Case 131/77, [1978] ECR 1041 . . . 311, 431
Milch- Fett- und Eierkontor, Case 29/68, [1969] ECR 165; [1969] CMLR 390 . . . 313
Miles v. European Schools, Case C-196/09, [2011] ECR I-5105 (Grand Chamber) . . . 290, 294
Mirossevich v. High Authority, Case 10/55, [1956] ECR 333 . . . 426, 432
Moksel v. BALM, Case 55/87, [1988] ECR 3845 . . . 66
Moksel v. Commission, Case 45/81, [1982] ECR 1129 . . . 375
Mollet v. Commission, Case 75/77, [1978] ECR 897 . . . 171
Moulijn v. Commission, Case 6/74, [1974] ECR 301 . . . 66
Moulins de Pont-à-Mousson, Cases 124/76, 20/77 (one of first Quellmehl and Gritz Cases), [1977] ECR 1795; [1979] 2 CMLR 445 . . . 441, 472, 485
Mulder, Case 120/86 (first Mulder Case), [1988] ECR 2321 . . . 475

Mulder v. Council and Commission, Cases C-104/89, 37/90 (second Mulder Case), [1992] ECR I-3061 . . . 446, 458, 459, 474, 475
Municipality of Differdange v. Commission, Case 222/83, [1984] ECR 2889; [1985] 3 CMLR 638 . . . 369
Musique Diffusion Française v. Commission, Cases 100–3/80, [1983] ECR 1825; [1983] 3 CMLR 221 . . . 152, 171

Nachi Europe, Case C-239/99, [2001] ECR I-1197 . . . 381, 415
Nachi Fujikoshi v. Council, Case 121/77 (Japanese Ball-Bearing Cases), [1979] ECR 1363; [1979] 2 CMLR 257 . . . 381
Nakajima v. Council, Case C-69/89, [1991] ECR I-2069 . . . 198, 461
Nashua Corporation v. Commission and Council, Cases C-133, 150/87, [1990] ECR I-719 . . . 358, 382
National Carbonising v. Commission, Cases 109, 114/75, [1977] ECR 381 . . . 361
National Panasonic v. Commission, Case 136/79, [1980] ECR 2033; [1980] 3 CMLR 169; [1981] 2 All ER 1 . . . 152
NBV and NVB v. Commission, Case T-138/89, [1992] ECR II-2181 . . . 359
Nederlandse Spoorwegen, Case 36/73, [1973] ECR 1299; [1974] 2 CMLR 148 . . . 291
Nederlandse Spoorwegen, Case 38/75, [1975] ECR 1439; [1976] 1 CMLR 167 . . . 105, 193
Netherlands v. Commission, Case 59/70, [1971] ECR 639 . . . 324, 404
Netherlands v. Commission, Case 13/72, [1973] ECR 27; [1974] 1 CMLR 161 . . . 140
Netherlands v. High Authority, Case 6/54, [1955] ECR 103 . . . 422, 425
Netherlands v. High Authority, Case 25/59, [1960] ECR 355 . . . 323, 436
Nippon Seiko v. Council and Commission, Case 119/77 (Japanese Ball-Bearing Cases), [1979] ECR 1303; [1979] 2 CMLR 257 . . . 381
Nold v. Commission, Case 4/73, [1974] ECR 491; [1974] 2 CMLR 338 . . . 148
Nold v. High Authority, Case 18/57, [1957] ECR 121 . . . 361
Noordwijks Cement Accoord, Cases 8–11/66, [1967] ECR 75; [1967] CMLR 77 . . . 110, 351, 352, 357, 361, 362
Norbrook Laboratories v. Ministry of Agriculture, Case C-127/95, [1998] ECR I-1531; [1998] 3 CMLR 809 . . . 255
Nordgetreide v. Commission, Case 42/71, [1972] ECR 105; [1973] CMLR 177 . . . 393, 396, 407, 408, 465
Nordsee v. Reederei Mond, Case 102/81, [1982] ECR 1095 . . . 293
NTN v. Council, Case 113/77 (Japanese Ball-Bearing Cases), [1979] ECR 1185; [1979] 2 CMLR 257 . . . 370, 381
Nuova Ceam v. Commission, Case 205/87, [1987] ECR 4427 . . . 381
Nuovo Campsider v. Commission, Case 25/85, [1986] ECR 1531 . . . 403

Oceano Grupo Editorial v. Rocio Murciano Quintero, Cases C-240–44/98, [2000] ECR 1-4941 . . . 227
Ölmühle Hamburg, Cases 119, 120/76 (one of first Skimmed-Milk Powder Cases), [1977] ECR 1269; [1979] 2 CMLR 83 . . . 168, 471
Omega, Case C-36/02, [2004] ECR I-9609 . . . 104, 159
Open Skies Case, *see* Commission v. United Kingdom, Case C-466/98
Opinion 1/75, Local Cost Standard, [1975] ECR 1355 . . . 180, 365
Opinion 1/76, Laying-up Fund for Inland Waterway Vessels, [1977] ECR 741 . . . 73, 180, 181, 184, 187, 189
Opinion 1/78, International Agreement on Natural Rubber, [1979] ECR 2871; [1979] 3 CMLR 639 . . . 175, 189
Opinion 1/91, First EEA Case, [1991] ECR 6079 . . . 5, 73, 83, 289, 316
Opinion 2/91, ILO Convention 170 Case, [1993] ECR I-1061, [1993] 3 CMLR 800 . . . 190
Opinion 1/92, Second EEA Case [1992] ECR I-2821 . . . 6
Opinion 2/92, OECD Case, [1995] ECR I-521 . . . 183, 184
Opinion 1/94, WTO Case, [1994] ECR I-5267 . . . 99, 178, 183, 184
Opinion 2/94, ECHR Case, [1996] ECR I-1759 . . . 73, 118, 152, 154, 185, 189, 267
Opinion 3/94, Bananas Case, [1995] ECR I-4577 . . . 189
Opinion 1/03, Lugano Convention Case, [2006] ECR I-1145 . . . 185
Opinion 1/08, GATS, [2009] ECR I-11129 . . . 183
Opinion 1/09, Patents Court, [2011] ECR I-1137 (Full Court) . . . 73
Organisation des Modjahedines du peuple d'Iran (OMPI) v. Council, Case T-228/02, [2006] ECR II-4665 . . . 105
Orkem v. Commission, Case 374/87, [1989] ECR 3283; [1991] 4 CMLR 502 . . . 171
Oslizlok v. Commission, Case 34/77, [1978] ECR 1099 . . . 171

Palmisani v. INPS, Case C-261/95, [1997] ECR I-4025 . . . 250, 252
Papiers Peints de Belgique v. Commission, Case 73/74, [1975] ECR 1491; [1976] 1 CMLR 589 . . . 139
Parfums Christian Dior v. Evora, Case C-337/95, [1997] ECR I-6013 . . . 294, 296, 299
Parliament, *see* 'European Parliament'
Parti Ecologiste 'Les Verts' v. European Parliament, Case 294/83, [1986] ECR 1339; [1987] 2 CMLR 343 . . . 15, 74, 83, 364, 375, 384
Parti Ecologiste 'Les Verts' v. European Parliament, Case 190/84, [1988] ECR 1017 . . . 353
Pastätter, Case C-217/89, [1990] ECR I-4585 . . . 475
Patents Court Case, Opinion 1/09, [2011] ECR I-1137 (Full Court) Pecastaing v. Belgium, Case 98/79, [1980] ECR 691; [1980] 3 CMLR 685 . . . 152
Pedersen (Frimodt) v. Commission, Case 301/86, [1987] ECR 3123 . . . 381
Pellegrini v. Commission, Case 23/76, [1976] ECR 1807; [1977] 2 CMLR 77 . . . 446
Peterbroeck v. Belgium, Case C-312/93, [1995] ECR I-4599 . . . 246
Pfeiffer, Cases C-397–403/01, [2004] ECR I-8835 . . . 228–31, 238
Pigs Marketing Board v. Redmond, Case 83/78, [1978] ECR 2347; [1979] 1 CMLR 177 . . . 245
Pinna, Case 41/84, [1986] ECR 1 . . . 76
Piraiki-Patraiki v. Commission, Case 11/82, [1985] ECR 207; [1985] 2 CMLR 46 . . . 373, 390
Plaumann v. Commission, Case 25/62, [1963] ECR 95; [1964] CMLR 29 . . . 369, 370, 376, 378–80, 385, 452, 465–7
Politi v. Italy, Case 43/71, [1971] ECR 1039; [1973] CMLR 60 . . . 290, 291
Polydor v. Harlequin Record Shops, Case 270/80, [1982] ECR 329; [1982] 1 CMLR 677; [1982] FSR 358 . . . 83, 240, 241
Port, Case C-68/95, [1996] ECR I-6065 . . . 248, 407, 484
Porta v. Commission, Case 109/81, [1982] ECR 2469 . . . 447
Portugal v. Commission, Case C-89/96, [1999] ECR I-8377 . . . 438
Portugal v. Council, Case C-149/96, [1999] ECR I-8395 . . . 198, 242, 461
Prais v. Council, Case 130/75, [1976] ECR 1589; [1976] 2 CMLR 708 . . . 169
Pretore di Cento v. A Person or Persons Unknown, Case 110/76, [1977] ECR 851; [1977] 2 CMLR 515 . . . 300
Pretore di Genova v. Banchero, Case C-157/92, [1993] ECR I-1085 . . . 302, 309
Pretore di Salò v. X (sub nom. Criminal proceedings against a Person or Persons Unknown), Case 14/86, [1987] ECR 2545 . . . 224, 239, 300
PreussenElektra, Case C-379/98, [2001] ECR I-2099 . . . 301
Pringle v. Government of Ireland, Case C-370/12, 27 November 2012 (Full Court) . . . 38, 90, 97, 414, 415
Procureur Général v. Arbelaiz-Emazabel, Case 181/80, [1981] ECR 2961 . . . 193
Providence Agricole v. ONIC, Case 4/79, [1980] ECR 2823 . . . 418, 441

Quiller v. Council and Commission, Cases T-195 and 202/94, [1997] ECR II-2247 . . . 476

R v. Bouchereau, Case 30/77, [1977] ECR 1999; [1977] 1 CMLR 269 . . . 69, 317
R v. HM Treasury, *ex parte* British Telecommunications, Case C-392/93, [1996] ECR I–1631; [1996] 3 WLR 203 . . . 251, 254
R v. Intervention Board for Agricultural Produce, *ex parte* Accrington Beef, Case C-241/95, [1996] ECR I-6699 . . . 415
R v. Kirk, Case 63/83, [1984] ECR 2689; [1984] 3 CMLR 522 . . . 152
R v. Ministry of Agriculture, *ex parte* Hedley Lomas, Case C-5/94, [1996] ECR I-2553 . . . 235, 251–3
R v. National Insurance Commissioner, *ex parte* Warry, Case 41/77, [1977] ECR 2085; [1977] 2 CMLR 783 . . . 298
R v. Royal Pharmaceutical Society, Cases 266–7/87, [1989] ECR 1295 . . . 232
R v. Secretary of State for Home Affairs, *ex parte* Santillo, Case 131/79, [1980] ECR 1585; [1980] 2 CMLR 308; [1981] 2 All ER 897; [1981] 2 WLR 362 . . . 216
R v. Secretary of State for the Home Department, *ex parte* Evans Medical and Macfarlan Smith (Generics Case), Case C-324/93, [1995] ECR I-563 . . . 100, 286, 287
R v. Secretary of State for Social Security, *ex parte* Sutton, Case C-66/95, [1997] ECR I-2163 . . . 251
R v. Secretary of State for Transport, *ex parte* Factortame (No. 2), Case C-213/89, [1990] ECR I-2433; [1990] 3 WLR 818; [1990] 3 CMLR 1 . . . 247, 308
R v. Secretary of State for Transport, *ex parte* Factortame (No. 3), Case C-221/89, [1991] ECR I-3905; [1991] 3 CMLR 589 . . . 247, 250
Racke, Case 136/77, [1978] ECR 1245 . . . 434

Racke, Case 98/78, [1979] ECR 69; [1979] 1 CMLR 552 . . . 164
Racke, Case C-162/96, [1998] ECR I-3655; [1998] 3 CMLR 219 . . . 417, 424
Ratti, Case 148/78, [1979] ECR 1629; [1980] 1 CMLR 96 . . . 215, 220–4, 230, 239, 244
Rau v. BALM, Cases 133–6/85, [1987] ECR 2289 . . . 414
Razzouk and Beydoun v. Commission, Cases 75, 117/82, [1984] ECR 1509 . . . 169
Rechberger v. Austria, Case C-140/97, [1999] ECR I-3499 . . . 255
Région Wallonne v. Commission, Case C-95/97, [1997] ECR I-1787 . . . 368
Regione Autonoma Friuli-Venezia v. Commission, Case T-288/97, [1999] ECR II-1871 . . . 368
Regione Toscana v. Commission, Case C-180/97, [1997] ECR I-5245 . . . 368
Rewe-Handelsgesellschaft Nord v. Hauptzollamt Kiel, Case 158/80, [1981] ECR 1805; [1982] CMLR 440 . . . 136, 246
Rewe-Zentrale, Case 37/70, [1971] ECR 23; [1971] CMLR 238 . . . 164, 433
Rewe-Zentralfinanz, [1976] Case 33/76, ECR 1989 . . . 245
Reynolds Tobacco v. Commission, Case C-131/03 P, [2006] ECR I-7795 . . . 360
Rey Soda v. Cassa Conguaglio Zucchero, Case 23/75, [1975] ECR 1279; [1976] 1 CMLR 185 . . . 131, 134
Rheinmühlen, Case 146/73, [1974] ECR 139; [1974] 1 CMLR 523 . . . 294, 309
Rheinmühlen, Case 166/73, [1974] ECR 33; [1974] 1 CMLR 523 . . . 294
Richez-Parise v. Commission, Cases 19, 20, 25, 30/69, [1970] ECR 325 . . . 462
Rienks, Case 5/83, [1983] ECR 4233; [1985] 1 CMLR 144 . . . 232
Rijksdienst voor Werknemerspensioenen v. Vlaeminck, Case 132/81, [1982] ECR 2953; [1983] 3 CMLR 557 . . . 303
Roquette, Case C-228/92, [1994] ECR I-1445 . . . 418
Roquette v. Commission, Case 26/74, [1976] ECR 677 . . . 457, 484
Roquette v. Commission, Case 20/88, [1989] ECR 1553 . . . 451, 484
Roquette v. Council, Case 138/79, [1980] ECR 3333 . . . 19, 375, 422
Roquette v. Council, Case 110/81, [1982] ECR 3159 . . . 439
Roquette v. Council, Case T-298/94, [1996] ECR II-1531 . . . 377
Roquette v. France, Case 34/74, [1974] ECR 1217 . . . 484
Roquette v. French Customs, Case 145/79, [1980] ECR 2917 . . . 418, 441, 484
Royal Scholten-Honig, Cases 103, 145/77 (one of first Isoglucose Cases), [1978] ECR 2037; [1979] 1 CMLR 675 . . . 473, 474
Royer, Case 48/75, [1976] ECR 497; [1976] 2 CMLR 619 . . . 69, 270
Ruckdeschel, Cases 117/76, 16/77 (one of first Quellmehl and Gritz Cases), [1977] ECR 1753; [1979] 2 CMLR 445 . . . 441, 472, 485
Rutili, Case 36/75, [1975] ECR 1219; [1976] 1 CMLR 140 . . . 152, 157, 270

Sabbatini v. European Parliament, Case 20/71, [1972] ECR 345; [1972] CMLR 945 . . . 169, 416
SACE, Case 33/70, [1970] ECR 1213; [1971] CMLR 123 . . . 218
Salerno v. Commission and Council, Cases 87, 130/77, 22/83, 9–10/84, [1985] ECR 2523 . . . 375
Salonia, Case 126/80, [1981] ECR 1563; [1982] CMLR 64 . . . 303
Salumi, Cases 212–17/80, [1981] ECR 2735 . . . 164
Salzmann, Case C-178/99, [2001] ECR I-4421 . . . 291
Sayag v. Leduc, Case 5/68, [1968] ECR 395; [1969] CMLR 12 . . . 30, 455
Sayag v. Leduc, Case 9/69, [1969] ECR 329 . . . 452, 454
Schlüter, Case 9/73, [1973] ECR 1135 . . . 105, 193, 211, 241, 242, 417, 424
Schmid, Case C-516/99, [2002] ECR I-4573 . . . 291
Schmidberger, Case C-112/00, [2003] ECR I-5659 . . . 104, 158, 159
Schöning-Kougebetopoulou, Case C-15/96, [1998] ECR I-47 . . . 255
Schroeder v. Germany, Case 40/72, [1973] ECR 125; [1973] CMLR 824 . . . 428
Schwarze, Case 16/65, [1965] ECR 877; [1966] CMLR 172 . . . 137, 139
Serio v. Commission, Case 115/73, [1974] ECR 341 . . . 430
Sermes v. Commission, Case 279/86, [1987] ECR 3109 . . . 381
Sevince, Case C-192/89, [1990] ECR I-3461 . . . 74, 191, 241, 243, 287, 316
SFEI v. Commission, Case C-39/93 P, [1994] ECR I-2681 (appeal from Case T-36/92, [1992] ECR II-2479) . . . 358, 380, 399
SGEEM v. European Investment Bank, Case C-370/89, [1992] ECR I-6211 . . . 454, 455
Sideradria v. Commission, Case 41/85, [1986] ECR 3917 . . . 413

Simmenthal, Case 70/77, [1978] ECR 1453; [1978] 3 CMLR 670 . . . 290
Simmenthal, Case 106/77, [1978] ECR 629; [1978] 3 CMLR 263 . . . 243, 309
Simmenthal v. Commission, Case 92/78, [1979] ECR 777; [1980] 1 CMLR 25 . . . 412, 414
Simon v. Court of Justice, Case 15/60, [1961] ECR 115 . . . 167
Singer and Geigy, Cases 290, 291/81, [1983] ECR 847 . . . 286
SIOT, Case 266/81, [1983] ECR 790 . . . 242
Skoma-Lux, Case C-161/06, [2007] ECR I-10841 . . . 141, 364
SNUPAT v. High Authority, Cases 32–33/58, [1959] ECR 127 . . . 132, 365, 416
SNUPAT v. High Authority, Cases 42, 49/59, [1961] ECR 53; [1963] CMLR 60 . . . 167, 353, 438, 439
Société des Usines à Tubes de la Sarre v. High Authority, Cases 1, 14/57, [1957] ECR 105 . . . 361
Société d'Initiatives et de Coopération Agricoles v. Commission, Case 114/83, [1984] ECR 2589; [1985] 2 CMLR 767 . . . 328, 459
Société pour l'Exportation des Sucres v. Commission, Case 88/76, [1977] ECR 709 . . . 164, 165, 374
Sofrimport v. Commission, Case C-152/88, [1990] ECR I-2477 . . . 375, 474
Sonito v. Commission, Case C-87/89, [1990] ECR I-1981 . . . 327
Sotgiu v. Deutsche Bundespost, Case 152/73, [1974] ECR 153 . . . 169
Spagl, Case C-189/89, [1990] ECR I-4539 . . . 475
Spain v. Commission, [1992] Cases C-271, 281, 289/90, ECR I-5833 . . . 30
Spain v. Lenzing, Case C-525/04 P, [2007] ECR I-9947 . . . 383, 434
Spain v. United Kingdom, Case C-145/04, [2006] ECR I-7917 . . . 16, 103, 104
SPI, Cases 267–9/81, [1983] ECR 801; [1984] 1 CMLR 354 . . . 74, 155, 193, 241, 242, 285, 286, 316
Spijker v. Commission, Case 231/82, [1983] ECR 2559; [1984] 2 CMLR 284 . . . 372, 377, 384
SPUC v. Grogan, Case C-159/90, [1991] ECR I-4685; [1991] 3 CMLR 849 . . . 150, 152, 158
Stahlwerke Peine-Salzgitter v. Commission, Case T-120/89, [1991] ECR II-279 (CFI) affirmed Case C-220/91 P, [1993] ECR I-2393 . . . 458, 464, 474
Star Fruit v. Commission, Case 247/87, [1989] ECR 291 . . . 327, 407
Stauder v. City of Ulm, Case 29/69, [1969] ECR 419; [1970] CMLR 112 . . . 66, 147, 148
Steenhorst-Neerings, Case C-338/91, [1993] ECR I-5475 . . . 246
Steinike und Weinlig v. Germany, Case 78/76, [1977] ECR 595; [1977] 2 CMLR 688 . . . 215, 262, 326
Stichting Zuid-Hollandse Mileufederatie, Case C-138/05, [2006] ECR I-8339 . . . 222
Stoeckel, Case C-345/89, [1991] ECR I-4047 . . . 101
Stork v. High Authority, Case 1/58, [1959] ECR 17 . . . 147
Sürül, Case C-262/96, [1999] ECR I-2685; [2001] 1 CMLR 4 . . . 76

Telemarsicabruzzo v. Circostel, Cases C-320–322/90, [1993] ECR I-393 . . . 302, 309
Terres Rouges v. Commission, Case T-47/95, [1997] ECR II-481 . . . 377
Timex v. Council and Commission, Case 264/82, [1985] ECR 849; [1985] 3 CMLR 550 . . . 382
Tobacco Advertising Case, *see* Germany v. European Parliament and Council, Case C-376/98
Toepfer v. Commission, Cases 106–7/63, [1965] ECR 405; [1966] CMLR 111 . . . 372, 388, 432, 479
Tomatis, Case C-384/89, [1991] ECR I-127 . . . 289
Töpfer v. Commission, Case 112/77, [1978] ECR 1019 . . . 165
Toyo v. Council, Case 240/84, [1987] ECR 1809 . . . 381
Traghetti del Mediterraneo SpA v. Italy, Case C-173/03, [2006] ECR I-5177 . . . 254
Transocean Marine Paint v. Commission, Case 17/74, [1974] ECR 1063; [1974] 2 CMLR 459 . . . 53, 160, 170, 171, 421, 422, 440
Tunnel Refineries v. Council, Case 114/81, [1982] ECR 3189 . . . 439
TWD, Case C-188/92, [1994] ECR I-833 . . . 71, 414

UCDV v. Commission, Case C-244/88, [1989] ECR 3811 . . . 375
UNECTEF v. Heylens, Case 222/86, [1987] ECR 4097 . . . 247
Unibet (London) Ltd and Unibet (International) Ltd v. Justitiekanslern, Case C-432/05, [2007] ECR I-2271 . . . 245
UNICME v. Council, Case 123/77, [1978] ECR 845 . . . 374
Unifrex v. Commission and Council, Case 281/82, [1984] ECR 1969 . . . 484, 485
Unifruit Hellas v. Commission, Case T-489/93, [1994] ECR II-1201 . . . 375

Unilever Italia v. Central Food, Case C-443/98, [2000] ECR I-7535; [2001] 1 CMLR 21 . . . 226, 228, 229
Unil-it, Case 30/75, [1975] ECR 1419; [1976] 1 CMLR 115 . . . 240
Unión de Pequeños Agricultores v. Council, Case C-50/00 P, [2002] ECR I-6677 . . . 77, 377
Union des Minotiers de la Champagne v. France, Case 11/74, [1974] ECR 877; [1975] 1 CMLR 75 . . . 169
Union Deutsche Lebensmittelwerke v. Commission, Case 97/85, [1987] ECR 2265 . . . 377
Union Malt, Cases 44–51/77, [1978] ECR 57; [1978] 3 CMLR 703 . . . 165
Union Nationale des Coopératives Agricoles de Céréales, Cases 95–8/74, 15, 100/75, [1975] ECR 1615 . . . 165
Union Royale Belge v. Bosman, Case C-415/93, [1995] ECR I-4921 . . . 76
United Kingdom v. Commission, Case 114/86, [1988] ECR 5289 . . . 356
United Kingdom v. Council, Case 68/86, [1988] ECR 855 . . . 422
United Kingdom v. Council, Case 131/86, [1988] ECR 905 . . . 141, 367
United Kingdom v. Council, Case C-84/94, [1996] ECR I-5755 . . . 127
Universität Hamburg, Case 216/82, [1983] ECR 2771 . . . 413
UPA, *see* Unión de Pequeños Agricultores v. Council
Usinor v. Commission, Cases 81, 119/85, [1986] ECR 1777 . . . 464

Vaassen, Case 61/65, [1966] ECR 261; [1966] CMLR 508 . . . 290, 292
Valsabbia v. Commission, Case 154/78, [1980] ECR 907; [1981] 1 CMLR 613 . . . 152
Van den Broeck v. Commission, Case 37/74, [1975] ECR 235 . . . 169
Van der Kooy v. Commission, Cases 67, 68, 70/85, [1988] ECR 219; [1989] 2 CMLR 804 . . . 382
Van Duyn v. Home Office, Case 41/74, [1974] ECR 1337; [1975] 1 CMLR 1 . . . 213, 218–21, 223, 224, 240, 270
Van Gend en Loos, Case 26/62, [1963] ECR 1; [1963] CMLR 105 . . . 83, 209, 210, 214, 315
Van Parys, Case C-377/02, [2005] ECR I-1465 . . . 197, 243
Van Schijndel, Cases C-430–1/93, [1995] ECR I-4705 . . . 246
Van Zuylen v. HAG, Case 192/73, [1974] ECR 731 . . . 71, 72
Vaneetveld v. Le Foyer, Case C-316/93, [1994] ECR I-763 . . . 225
Variola, Case 34/73, [1973] ECR 981 . . . 216
VBVB v. Commission, Cases 43, 63/82, [1984] ECR 19 . . . 362
Verbond van Nederlandse Ondernemingen, Case 51/76, [1977] ECR 113; [1977] 1 CMLR 413 . . . 220
Victoria Film, Case C-134/97, [1998] ECR I-7023 . . . 291, 300
Vinal v. Orbat, Case 46/80, [1981] ECR 77; [1981] 3 CMLR 524 . . . 301
Vloeberghs v. High Authority, Cases 9, 12/60, [1961] ECR 197; [1963] CMLR 44 . . . 327, 459, 464, 466, 476
Von Colson and Kamann v. Land Nordrhein-Westfalen, Case 14/83, [1984] ECR 1891; [1986] 2 CMLR 430 . . . 212, 213, 236, 237, 246
Von Deetzen, Case 170/86, [1988] ECR 2355 . . . 475
Von Deetzen, Case C-44/89, [1991] ECR I-5119 . . . 475
Von Lachmüller v. Commission, Cases 43, 45, 48/59, [1960] ECR 463 . . . 447
Vreugdenhil v. Commission, Case C-282/90, [1992] ECR I-1937 . . . 477, 483, 485
Vreugdenhil v. Minister van Landbouw en Visserij, Case 22/88, [1989] ECR 2049 . . . 477

Wachauf, Case 5/88, [1989] ECR 2609; [1991] 1 CMLR 328 . . . 157
Wagner v. Commission, Case 162/78, [1979] ECR 3467 . . . 375
Walrave and Koch v. Union Cycliste Internationale, Case 36/74, [1974] ECR 1405; [1975] 1 CMLR 320 . . . 312
Watson and Belmann, Case 118/75, [1976] ECR 1185; [1976] 2 CMLR 552 . . . 224, 270
Webb v. EMO Air Cargo, Case C-32/93, [1994] ECR 3567 . . . 237
Weddel v. Commission, Case C-354/87, [1990] ECR I-3487 . . . 376
Weddel & Co. BV v. Commission, Case C-54/90, [1992] ECR I-871 . . . 30
Weighardt v. Euratom Commission, Case 11/64, [1965] ECR 285; [1966] CMLR 1 . . . 357
Wells, Case C-201/02, [2004] ECR I-723 . . . 227, 229
Werhahn v. Council and Commission, Cases 63–9/72, [1973] ECR 1229 . . . 452
Westzucker, Case 57/72, [1973] ECR 321 . . . 431, 433

Westzucker, Case 1/73, [1973] ECR 723 . . . 163, 164
Wiljo v. Belgium, Case C-178/95, [1997] ECR I-585 . . . 415
Willame v. Commission, Case 110/63, [1965] ECR 649; [1966] CMLR 231 . . . 448, 458
Wöhrmann v. Commission, Cases 31, 33/62, [1962] ECR 501; [1963] CMLR 152 . . . 412
Wollast v. EEC, Case 18/63, [1964] ECR 85 . . . 448
Worms v. High Authority, Case 18/60, [1962] ECR 195; [1963] CMLR 1 . . . 454, 456, 457
Wybot v. Faure, Case 149/85, [1986] ECR 2391 . . . 16

X v. Commission, Case C-404/92 P, [1994] ECR I-4737 . . . 152

Zuckerfabrik Bedburg v. EEC, Case 281/84, [1987] ECR 49 . . . 485
Zuckerfabrik Schöppenstedt v. Council, Case 5/71, [1971] ECR 975 . . . 452, 466, 467
Zuckerfabrik Süderdithmarschen, Cases C-143/88, 92/89, [1991] ECR I-415 . . . 248, 308
Zunis Holding, Case T-83/92, [1993] ECR II-1169 . . . 394
Zwartveld, Case C-2/88, [1990] ECR I-4405; [1990] 3 CMLR 457 54ZZ, Case C-300/11, 4 June 2013 (Grand Chamber) . . . 56

NUMERICAL TABLE OF CASES

*Cases brought before the Court of First Instance (prefix 'T') are listed after those brought (in the same year) before the European Court (prefix 'C'). Judgments designated 'Opinion' or 'Ruling' are listed (for convenience) before those (in the same year) designated 'Case'.

Case 1/54, France v. High Authority, [1954] ECR 1 . . . 427
Case 2/54, Italy v. High Authority, [1954] ECR 37 . . . 422, 436
Case 3/54, Assider v. High Authority, [1955] ECR 63 . . . 436, 440
Case 4/54, ISA v. High Authority, [1955] ECR 91 . . . 136, 436
Case 6/54, Netherlands v. High Authority, [1955] ECR 103 . . . 422, 425
Cases 7, 9/54, Groupement des Industries Sidérurgiques Luxembourgeoises v. High Authority, [1956] ECR 175 . . . 327
Case 1/55, Kergall v. Common Assembly, [1955] ECR 151 . . . 432, 446
Case 8/55, Fédération Charbonnière de Belgique (Fédéchar) v. High Authority, [1956] ECR 245 and 292 . . . 83, 113, 168, 354, 393, 425, 427
Case 10/55, Mirossevich v. High Authority, [1956] ECR 333 . . . 426, 432
Case 1/56, Bourgaux v. Common Assembly, [1956] ECR 361 . . . 432
Cases 7/56, 3–7/57, Algera v. Assembly, [1957] ECR 39 . . . 167, 355, 361, 458
Case 9/56, Meroni v. High Authority, [1958] ECR 133 . . . 131, 137, 145, 412
Case 10/56, Meroni v. High Authority, [1958] ECR 157 . . . 412
Cases 1, 14/57, Société des Usines à Tubes de la Sarre v. High Authority, [1957] ECR 105 . . . 361
Case 2/57, Hauts Fourneaux de Chasse v. High Authority, [1958] ECR 199 . . . 427
Case 8/57, Hauts Fourneaux et Aciéries Belges v. High Authority, [1958] ECR 245 . . . 169, 425
Case 15/57, Compagnie des Hauts Fourneaux de Chasse v. High Authority, [1958] ECR 211 . . . 412, 425, 427
Case 17/57, De Gezamenlijke Steenkolenmijnen in Limburg v. High Authority, [1959] ECR 1 . . . 327, 404
Case 18/57, Nold v. High Authority, [1957] ECR 121 . . . 361
Case 1/58, Stork v. High Authority, [1959] ECR 17 . . . 147
Cases 32–3/58, SNUPAT v. High Authority, [1959] ECR 127 . . . 132, 365, 416, 456
Case 3/59, Germany v. High Authority (Railway Tariffs Case), [1960] ECR 53 . . . 413
Cases 4–13/59, Mannesmann v. High Authority, [1960] ECR 113 . . . 448, 449
Case 20/59, Italy v. High Authority, [1960] ECR 325 . . . 436
Case 25/59, Netherlands v. High Authority, [1960] ECR 355 . . . 323, 436
Case 30/59, De Gezamenlijke Steenkolenmijnen in Limburg v. High Authority, [1961] ECR 1 . . . 394
Cases 36–38, 40/59, Geitling v. High Authority, [1960] ECR 423 . . . 147
Cases 42, 49/59, SNUPAT v. High Authority, [1961] ECR 53; [1963] CMLR 60 . . . 167, 353, 438, 439
Cases 43, 45, 48/59, Von Lachmüller v. Commission, [1960] ECR 463 . . . 447
Case 6/60, Humblet v. Belgium, [1960] ECR 559 . . . 30
Cases 9, 12/60, Vloeberghs v. High Authority, [1961] ECR 197; [1963] CMLR 44 . . . 327, 459, 464, 466, 476
Case 15/60, Simon v. Court of Justice, [1961] ECR 115 . . . 167
Case 18/60, Worms v. High Authority, [1962] ECR 195; [1963] CMLR 1 . . . 454, 456, 457
Case 7/61, Commission v. Italy (Pork Imports Case), [1961] ECR 317; [1962] CMLR 39 . . . 325, 326
Case 10/61, Commission v. Italy, [1962] ECR 1 . . . 98, 100
Case 14/61, Hoogovens v. High Authority, [1962] ECR 253; [1963] CMLR 73 . . . 145, 167
Cases 21–6/61, Meroni v. High Authority (No. 5), [1962] ECR 73 . . . 401
Cases 16–17/62, Confédération Nationale des Producteurs de Fruits et Légumes v. Council, [1962] ECR 471; [1963] CMLR 160 . . . 370
Case 18/62, Barge v. High Authority, [1963] ECR 259; [1965] CMLR 330 . . . 138, 431
Case 24/62, Germany v. Commission (Brennwein Case), [1963] ECR 63; [1963] CMLR 347 . . . 136–8, 140, 141
Case 25/62, Plaumann v. Commission, [1963] ECR 95; [1964] CMLR 29 . . . 369, 370, 376, 378–80, 385, 452, 465–7

Case 26/62, Van Gend en Loos, [1963] ECR 1; [1963] CMLR 105 . . . 83, 209, 210, 214, 315
Cases 28–30/62, Da Costa, [1963] ECR 31; [1963] CMLR 224 . . . 305
Cases 31, 33/62, Wöhrmann v. Commission, [1962] ECR 501; [1963] CMLR 152 . . . 412
Case 35/62, 16/63, Leroy v. High Authority, [1963] ECR 197; [1964] CMLR 562 . . . 432
Case 1/63, Dalmas v. High Authority, [1963] ECR 303; [1964] CMLR 223 . . . 139
Case 13/63, Italy v. Commission, [1963] ECR 165; [1963] CMLR 289 . . . 432
Case 15/63, Lassalle v. European Parliament, [1964] ECR 31; [1964] CMLR 259 . . . 354
Case 18/63, Wollast v. EEC, [1964] ECR 85 . . . 448
Cases 53–4/63, Lemmerz-Werke v. High Authority, [1963] ECR 239; [1964] CMLR 384 . . . 361
Cases 73–4/63, Handelsvereniging Rotterdam, [1964] ECR 1; [1964] CMLR 198 . . . 413, 416
Case 78/63, Huber v. Commission, [1964] ECR 367; [1964] CMLR 576 . . . 357
Case 80/63, Degreef v. Commission, [1964] ECR 391 . . . 448
Cases 90, 91/63, Commission v. Luxembourg and Belgium, [1964] ECR 625; [1965] CMLR 58 . . . 259, 326, 332
Case 100/63, Kalsbeek v. SocialeVerzekeringsbank, [1964] ECR 565; [1964] CMLR 548 . . . 164
Cases 106–7/63, Toepfer v. Commission, [1965] ECR 405; [1966] CMLR 111 . . . 372, 388, 432, 479
Case 110/63, Willame v. Commission, [1965] ECR 649; [1966] CMLR 231 . . . 448, 458
Case 111/63, Lemmerz-Werke v. High Authority, [1965] ECR 677; [1968] CMLR 280 . . . 167
Cases 3–4/64, Chambre Syndicale de la Sidérurgie Française, [1965] ECR 441 . . . 425
Case 6/64, Costa v. ENEL, [1964] ECR 585; [1964] CMLR 425 . . . 83, 206, 259, 296
Case 11/64, Weighardt v. Euratom Commission, [1965] ECR 285; [1966] CMLR 1 . . . 357
Case 21/64, Dalmas v. High Authority, [1965] ECR 175; [1966] CMLR 46 . . . 413
Case 35/64, Alfieri v. European Parliament, [1965] ECR 261 . . . 430
Case 16/65, Schwarze, [1965] ECR 877; [1966] CMLR 172 . . . 137, 139
Cases 18, 35/65, Gutmann v. Commission, [1966] ECR 103 . . . 425, 426
Case 32/65, Italy v. Commission, [1966] ECR 389; [1969] CMLR 39 . . . 410, 415
Case 48/65, Lütticke v. Commission, [1966] ECR 19; [1966] CMLR 378 . . . 327, 394, 396, 407
Cases 52, 55/65, Germany v. Commission, [1966] ECR 159; [1967] CMLR 22 . . . 326
Case 61/65, Vaassen, [1966] ECR 261; [1966] CMLR 508 . . . 290, 292
Cases 5, 7, 13–24/66, Kampffmeyer v. Commission, [1967] ECR 245 . . . 451, 452, 457, 462, 477, 479
Cases 8–11/66, Noordwijks Cement Accoord, [1967] ECR 75; [1967] CMLR 77 . . . 110, 351, 352, 357, 361, 362
Case 30/66, Becher v. Commission, [1967] ECR 285; [1968] CMLR 169 . . . 479, 480
Case 5/67, Beus, [1968] ECR 83; [1968] CMLR 131 . . . 138
Case 26/67, Danvin v. Commission, [1968] ECR 315 . . . 448
Case 29/67, De Wendel v. Commission, [1968] ECR 263; [1969] CMLR 354 . . . 140
Case 5/68, Sayag v. Leduc (No. 1), [1968] ECR 395; [1969] CMLR 12 . . . 30, 455
Cases 10, 18/68, Eridania v. Commission, [1969] ECR 459 . . . 386, 400, 401, 428
Case 29/68, Milch-, Fett- und Eierkontor, [1969] ECR 165; [1969] CMLR 390 . . . 313
Case 4/69, Lütticke v. Commission, [1971] ECR 325 . . . 328, 459, 466, 467
Cases 6, 11/69, Commission v. France (Rediscount Rate Case), [1969] ECR 523; [1970] CMLR 43 . . . 327, 361
Case 9/69, Sayag v. Leduc, [1969] ECR 329 . . . 452, 454
Case 16/69, Commission v. Government of the Italian Republic, [1969] ECR 377; [1970] CMLR 161 . . . 317, 318
Cases 19–20, 25, 30/69, Richez-Parise v. Commission, [1970] ECR 325 . . . 462
Case 26/69, Commission v. France, [1970] ECR 565; [1970] CMLR 444 . . . 326
Case 29/69, Stauder v. City of Ulm, [1969] ECR 419; [1970] CMLR 112 . . . 66, 147, 148
Case 31/69, Commission v. Italy, [1970] ECR 25; [1970] CMLR 175 . . . 325, 326
Case 41/69, Chemiefarma v. Commission, [1970] ECR 661 . . . 20, 130
Case 48/69, ICI v. Commission, [1972] ECR 619; [1972] CMLR 557 . . . 142
Case 50/69 R, Germany v. Commission, [1969] ECR 449; [1971] CMLR 724 . . . 431, 433
Case 64/69, Compagnie Française Commerciale et Financière v. Commission, [1970] ECR 221; [1970] CMLR 369 . . . 71, 374, 375
Case 69/69, Alcan Aluminium v. Commission, [1970] ECR 385; [1970] CMLR 337 . . . 387–90
Case 77/69, Commission v. Belgium, [1970] ECR 237 . . . 318

Case 8/70, Commission v. Italy, [1970] ECR 961 . . . 318
Case 9/70, Grad, [1970] ECR 825; [1971] CMLR 1 . . . 218, 240
Case 11/70, Internationale Handelsgesellschaft, [1970] ECR 1125; [1972] CMLR 255; [1974] 2 CMLR 540 . . . 148, 168, 261
Case 15/70, Chevalley v. Commission, [1970] ECR 975 . . . 392, 406
Case 22/70, Commission v. Council (ERTA Case), [1971] ECR 263; [1971] CMLR 335 . . . 109, 137, 177–9, 186, 187, 190, 194–7, 284, 350, 353
Case 25/70, Einfuhr- und Vorratsstelle v. Köster, [1970] ECR 1161; [1972] CMLR 255 . . . 20, 130, 131, 148
Case 33/70, SACE, [1970] ECR 1213; [1971] CMLR 123 . . . 218
Case 37/70, Rewe-Zentrale, [1971] ECR 23; [1971] CMLR 238 . . . 164, 433
Cases 41–4/70, International Fruit Company v. Commission, [1971] ECR 411; [1975] 2 CMLR 515 . . . 71, 374, 387, 417
Case 59/70, Netherlands v. Commission, [1971] ECR 639 . . . 324, 404
Case 62/70, Bock v. Commission, [1971] ECR 897; [1972] CMLR 160 . . . 76, 373, 388–90
Case 5/71, Zuckerfabrik Schöppenstedt v. Council, [1971] ECR 975 . . . 452, 466, 467
Case 7/71, Commission v. France (Euratom Case), [1971] ECR 1003; [1972] CMLR 453 . . . 321–24, 404
Cases 9–11/71, Compagnie d'Approvisionnement v. Commission (No. 2), [1972] ECR 391; [1973] CMLR 529 . . . 393, 428, 437, 460, 467, 482
Case 15/71, Mackprang v. Commission, [1971] ECR 797; [1972] CMLR 52 . . . 393, 406
Case 20/71, Sabbatini v. European Parliament, [1972] ECR 345; [1972] CMLR 945 . . . 169, 416
Case 42/71, Nordgetreide v. Commission, [1972] ECR 105; [1973] CMLR 177 . . . 393, 396, 407, 408, 465
Case 43/71, Politi v. Italy, [1971] ECR 1039; [1973] CMLR 60 . . . 290, 291
Case 48/71, Commission v. Italy (second Art Treasures Case), [1972] ECR 527; [1972] CMLR 699 . . . 326
Case 96/71, Haegeman v. Commission, [1972] ECR 1005; [1973] CMLR 365 . . . 481–3
Case 1/72, Frilli v. Belgium, [1972] ECR 457; [1973] CMLR 386 . . . 169
Case 11/72, Giordano v. Commission, [1973] ECR 417 . . . 451
Case 13/72, Netherlands v. Commission, [1973] ECR 27; [1974] 1 CMLR 161 . . . 140
Cases 21–4/72, International Fruit Company (third), [1972] ECR 1219; [1975] 2 CMLR 1 . . . 105, 192–4, 197, 241, 242, 417, 424
Case 37/72, Marcato v. Commission, [1973] ECR 361 . . . 429
Case 39/72, Commission v. Italy, [1973] ECR 101; [1973] CMLR 439 . . . 217
Case 40/72, Schroeder v. Germany, [1973] ECR 125; [1973] CMLR 824 . . . 428
Case 43/72, Merkur v. Commission, [1973] ECR 1055 . . . 467, 482
Case 55/72, Gesellschaft für Getreidehandel v. EVGF, [1973] ECR 15; [1973] CMLR 465 . . . 413
Case 57/72, Westzucker, [1973] ECR 321 . . . 431, 433
Case 61/72, Mij PPW International, [1973] ECR 301 . . . 66
Cases 63–9/72, Werhahn v. Council and Commission, [1973] ECR 1229 . . . 452
Case 70/72, Commission v. Germany (Kohlegesetz), [1973] ECR 813; [1973] CMLR 741 . . . 164, 333
Case 77/72, Capolongo, [1973] ECR 611; [1974] 1 CMLR 230 . . . 211
Case 79/72, Commission v. Italy, [1973] ECR 667 . . . 335
Case 81/72, Commission v. Council (first Staff Salaries Case), [1973] ECR 575; [1973] CMLR 639 . . . 166, 424, 437
Case 1/73, Westzucker, [1973] ECR 723 . . . 163, 164
Case 4/73, Nold v. Commission, [1974] ECR 491; [1974] 2 CMLR 338 . . . 148
Case 5/73, Balkan-Import-Export, [1973] ECR 1091 . . . 168
Case 8/73, Hauptzollamt Bremerhaven v. Massey-Ferguson, [1973] ECR 897 . . . 116
Case 9/73, Schlüter, [1973] ECR 1135 . . . 105, 193, 211, 241, 242, 417, 424
Case 34/73, Variola, [1973] ECR 981 . . . 216
Case 36/73, Nederlandse Spoorwegen, [1973] ECR 1299; [1974] 2 CMLR 148 . . . 291
Case 115/73, Serio v. Commission, [1974] ECR 341 . . . 430
Case 134/73, Holtz & Willemsen v. Council, [1974] ECR 1; [1975] 1 CMLR 91 . . . 393
Case 144/73, De Vleeschauwer v. Commission, [1974] ECR 957 . . . 430
Case 146/73, Rheinmühlen, [1974] ECR 139; [1974] 1 CMLR 523 . . . 294, 309
Case 152/73, Sotgiu v. Deutsche Bundespost, [1974] ECR 153 . . . 169
Case 153/73, Holtz & Willemsen v. Council and Commission, [1974] ECR 675; [1975] CMLR 91 . . . 483

Case 162/73, Birra Dreher v. Italian Finance Administration, [1974] ECR 201 . . . 290, 291
Case 166/73, Rheinmühlen, [1974] ECR 33; [1974] 1 CMLR 523 . . . 294
Case 167/73, Commission v. France (French Merchant Seamen Case), [1974] ECR 359; [1974] 2 CMLR 216 . . . 245
Case 169/73, Compagnie Continentale France v. Council, [1975] ECR 117; [1975] 1 CMLR 131 . . . 462
Case 181/73, Haegeman v. Belgium, [1974] ECR 449; [1975] 1 CMLR 515 . . . 174, 285–7
Case 185/73, Hauptzollamt Bielefeld v. König, [1974] ECR 607 . . . 142
Case 192/73, Van Zuylen v. HAG, [1974] ECR 731 . . . 71, 72
Case 6/74, Moulijn v. Commission, [1974] ECR 301 . . . 66
Case 9/74, Casagrande v. Munich, [1974] ECR 773; [1974] 2 CMLR 423 . . . 318
Case 11/74, Union des Minotiers de la Champagne v. France, [1974] ECR 877; [1975] 1 CMLR 75 . . . 169
Case 17/74, Transocean Marine Paint v. Commission, [1974] ECR 1063; [1974] 2 CMLR 459 . . . 53, 160, 170, 171, 421, 422, 440
Case 21/74, Airola v. Commission, [1975] ECR 221 . . . 169
Case 26/74, Roquette v. Commission, [1976] ECR 677 . . . 457, 484
Case 29/74, De Dapper v. European Parliament, [1975] ECR 35 . . . 430
Case 31/74, Galli, [1975] ECR 47; [1975] 1 CMLR 211 . . . 215
Case 32/74, Haaga, [1974] ECR 1201; [1975] 1 CMLR 32 . . . 284
Case 34/74, Roquette v. France, [1974] ECR 1217 . . . 484
Case 36/74, Walrave and Koch v. Union Cycliste Internationale, [1974] ECR 1405; [1975] 1 CMLR 320 . . . 312
Case 37/74, Van den Broeck v. Commission, [1975] ECR 235 . . . 169
Case 41/74, Van Duyn v. Home Office, [1974] ECR 1337; [1975] 1 CMLR 1 . . . 213, 218–21, 223, 224, 240, 270
Cases 56–60/74, Kampffmeyer v. Council and Commission, [1976] ECR 711 . . . 458
Case 67/74, Bonsignore, [1975] ECR 297; [1975] 1 CMLR 472 . . . 69, 270
Case 73/74, Papiers Peints de Belgique v. Commission, [1975] ECR 1491; [1976] 1 CMLR 589 . . . 139
Case 74/74, CNTA v. Commission, (decision of 14 May 1975), [1975] ECR 533; (decision of 15 June 1976), [1976] ECR 797; [1977] 1 CMLR 171 . . . 166, 457, 469, 470, 483, 485
Case 78/74, Deuka v. EVGF, [1975] ECR 421; [1975] 2 CMLR 28 . . . 165, 434
Case 79/74, Küster v. European Parliament, [1975] ECR 725 . . . 354
Case 90/74, Deboeck v. Commission, [1975] ECR 1123 . . . 429, 430
Cases 95–8/74, 15, 100/75, Union Nationale des Coopératives Agricoles de Céréales, [1975] ECR 1615 . . . 165
Case 99/74, Grands Moulins des Antilles v. Commission, [1975] ECR 1531 . . . 483
Case 100/74, CAM v. Commission, [1975] ECR 1393 . . . 374
Opinion 1/75, Local Cost Standard Case, [1975] ECR 1355 . . . 180, 365
Case 2/75, EVGF v. Mackprang, [1975] ECR 607 . . . 165
Case 9/75, Meyer-Burckhardt v. Commission, [1975] ECR 1171 . . . 318, 328
Case 23/75, Rey Soda v. Cassa Conguaglio Zucchero, [1975] ECR 1279; [1976] 1 CMLR 185 . . . 131, 134
Case 30/75, Unil-it, [1975] ECR 1419; [1976] 1 CMLR 115 . . . 240
Case 32/75, Cristini v. SNCF, [1975] ECR 1085; [1976] 1 CMLR 573 . . . 312
Case 36/75, Rutili, [1975] ECR 1219; [1976] 1 CMLR 140 . . . 152, 157, 270
Case 38/75, Nederlandse Spoorwegen, [1975] ECR 1439; [1976] 1 CMLR 167 . . . 105, 193
Case 40/75, Bertrand v. Commission, [1976] ECR 1; [1976] 1 CMLR 220 . . . 457, 459
Case 43/75, Defrenne v. Sabena (second), [1976] ECR 455; [1976] 2 CMLR 98 . . . 75, 91, 209, 214, 224
Case 46/75, IBC v. Commission, [1976] ECR 65 . . . 483, 485
Case 48/75, Royer, [1976] ECR 497; [1976] 2 CMLR 619 . . . 69, 270
Case 51/75, EMI, [1976] ECR 811; [1976] 2 CMLR 235 . . . 311
Case 56/75, Elz v. Commission, [1976] ECR 1097 . . . 167
Case 87/75, Bresciani, [1976] ECR 129; [1976] 2 CMLR 62 . . . 240, 241, 244, 285, 417, 424
Case 105/75, Giuffrida v. Council, [1976] ECR 1395 . . . 426
Cases 109, 114/75, National Carbonising v. Commission, [1977] ECR 381 . . . 361
Case 111/75, Mazzalai, [1976] ECR 657; [1977] 1 CMLR 105 . . . 220, 284
Case 118/75, Watson and Belmann, [1976] ECR 1185; [1976] 2 CMLR 552 . . . 224, 270
Case 130/75, Prais v. Council, [1976] ECR 1589; [1976] 2 CMLR 708 . . . 169

Opinion 1/76, Laying-up Fund for Inland Waterway Vessels, [1977] ECR 741 . . . 73, 180, 181, 184, 187, 189
Cases 3–4, 6/76, Kramer (North-East Atlantic Fisheries Convention Case), [1976] ECR 1279; [1976] 2 CMLR 440 . . . 180, 183, 184, 186, 187
Case 7/76, IRCA, [1976] ECR 1213 . . . 149, 164
Case 23/76, Pellegrini v. Commission, [1976] ECR 1807; [1977] 2 CMLR 77 . . . 446
Case 26/76, Metro v. Commission, [1977] ECR 1875; [1978] 2 CMLR 1 . . . 380
Case 33/76, Rewe-Zentralfinanz, [1976] ECR 1989 . . . 245
Case 45/76, Comet v. Produktschap voor Siergewassen, [1976] ECR 2043; [1977] 1 CMLR 533 . . . 245
Case 51/76, Verbond van Nederlandse Ondernemingen, [1977] ECR 113; [1977] 1 CMLR 413 . . . 220
Cases 64, 113/76, 167, 239/78, 27–28, 45/79, Dumortier v. Council (one of second Quellmehl and Gritz Cases), [1979] ECR 3091; [1982] ECR 1733 . . . 459, 472, 485
Case 78/76, Steinike und Weinlig v. Germany, [1977] ECR 595; [1977] 2 CMLR 688; [1980] 2 CMLR 531 . . . 215, 262, 326
Cases 83, 94/76, 4, 15, 40/77, HNL v. Council and Commission (second Skimmed Milk Powder Case), [1978] ECR 1209; [1978] 3 CMLR 566 . . . 468, 471, 472
Case 85/76, Hoffmann-La Roche v. Commission, [1979] ECR 461; [1979] 3 CMLR 211 . . . 171
Case 88/76, Société pour l'Exportation des Sucres v. Commission, [1977] ECR 709 . . . 164, 165, 374
Case 101/76, KSH v. Council and Commission, [1977] ECR 797; [1980] 2 CMLR 669 . . . 371
Case 107/76, Hoffmann-La Roche v. Centrafarm, [1977] ECR 957; [1977] 2 CMLR 334 . . . 290, 297, 298
Case 110/76, Pretore di Cento v. A Person or Persons Unknown, [1977] ECR 851; [1977] 2 CMLR 515 . . . 300
Case 114/76, Bela-Mühle (one of first Skimmed-Milk Powder Cases), [1977] ECR 1211; [1979] 2 CMLR 83 . . . 168, 169, 471
Case 116/76, Granaria (one of first Skimmed-Milk Powder Cases), [1977] ECR 1247; [1979] 2 CMLR 83 . . . 168, 471
Cases 117/76, 16/77, Ruckdeschel (one of first Quellmehl and Gritz Cases), [1977] ECR 1753; [1979] 2 CMLR 445 . . . 441, 472, 485
Cases 119–20/76, Ölmühle Hamburg (one of first Skimmed-Milk Powder Cases), [1977] ECR 1269; [1979] 2 CMLR 83 . . . 168, 471
Cases 124/76, 20/77, Moulins de Pont-à-Mousson (one of first Quellmehl and Gritz Cases), [1977] ECR 1795; [1979] 2 CMLR 445 . . . 441, 472, 485
Case 126/76, Dietz v. Commission, [1977] ECR 2431; [1978] 2 CMLR 608 . . . 485
Case 25/77, De Roubaix v. Commission, [1978] ECR 1081 . . . 354
Case 30/77, R v. Bouchereau, [1977] ECR 1999; [1977] 1 CMLR 269 . . . 69, 317
Cases 31, 53/77 R, Commission v. United Kingdom (Pig Producers Case), [1977] ECR 921; [1977] 2 CMLR 359 . . . 331
Case 34/77, Oslizlok v. Commission, [1978] ECR 1099 . . . 171
Case 38/77, Enka, [1977] ECR 2203; [1978] 2 CMLR 212 . . . 220, 223
Case 41/77, R v. National Insurance Commissioner, *ex parte* Warry, [1977] ECR 2085; [1977] 2 CMLR 783 . . . 298
Cases 44–51/77, Union Malt, [1978] ECR 57; [1978] 3 CMLR 703 . . . 165
Case 54/77, Herpels v. Commission, [1978] ECR 585 . . . 167
Case 59/77, De Bloos v. Bouyer, [1977] ECR 2359; [1978] 1 CMLR 511 . . . 415
Case 61/77 R, Commission v. Ireland, [1977] ECR 937 . . . 331
Case 70/77, Simmenthal, [1978] ECR 1453; [1978] 3 CMLR 670 . . . 290
Case 75/77, Mollet v. Commission, [1978] ECR 897 . . . 171
Case 78/77, Lührs, [1978] ECR 169; [1979] 1 CMLR 657 . . . 165
Cases 87, 130/77, 22/83, 9–10/84, Salerno v. Commission and Council, [1985] ECR 2523 . . . 375
Case 100/77, Commission v. Italy, [1978] ECR 879; [1979] 2 CMLR 655 . . . 318
Cases 103, 145/77, Royal Scholten-Honig (one of first Isoglucose Cases), [1978] ECR 2037; [1979] 1 CMLR 675 . . . 473, 474
Case 106/77, Simmenthal, [1978] ECR 629; [1978] 3 CMLR 263 . . . 243, 309
Case 112/77, Töpfer v. Commission, [1978] ECR 1019 . . . 165
Case 113/77 etc., NTN v. Council (Japanese Ball-Bearing Cases), [1979] ECR 1185; [1979] 2 CMLR 257 . . . 370, 381
Cases 116, 124/77, Amylum and Tunnel Refineries v. Council and Commission (one of second Isoglucose Cases), [1979] ECR 3497 . . . 473, 474
Case 118/77, ISO v. Council, [1979] ECR 1277 . . . 381

Case 119/77, Nippon Seiko v. Council and Commission (Japanese Ball-Bearing Cases), [1979] ECR 1303; [1979] 2 CMLR 257 . . . 381
Case 120/77, Koyo Seiko v. Council and Commission (Japanese Ball-Bearing Cases), [1979] ECR 1337; [1979] 2 CMLR 257 . . . 381
Case 121/77, Nachi Fujikoshi v. Council (Japanese Ball-Bearing Cases), [1979] ECR 1363; [1979] 2 CMLR 257 . . . 381
Case 123/77, UNICME v. Council, [1978] ECR 845 . . . 374
Case 131/77, Milac, [1978] ECR 1041 . . . 311, 431
Case 135/77, Bosch, [1978] ECR 855 . . . 311
Case 136/77, Racke, [1978] ECR 1245 . . . 434
Case 143/77, KSH v. Council and Commission (one of second Isoglucose Cases), [1979] ECR 3583 . . . 473, 474
Case 149/77, Defrenne v. Sabena, [1978] ECR 1365; [1978] 3 CMLR 312 . . . 152, 157
Case 156/77, Commission v. Belgium, [1978] ECR 1881 . . . 413, 415
Opinion 1/78, International Agreement on Natural Rubber, [1979] ECR 2871; [1979] 3 CMLR 639 . . . 175, 189
Case 14/78, Denkavit v. Commission, [1978] ECR 2497; [1979] 2 CMLR 135 . . . 328, 459
Case 17/78, Deshormes v. Commission, [1979] ECR 189 . . . 352
Case 31/78, Bussone, [1978] ECR 2429 . . . 217
Case 83/78, Pigs Marketing Board v. Redmond, [1978] ECR 2347; [1979] 1 CMLR 177 . . . 245
Case 92/78, Simmenthal v. Commission, [1979] ECR 777; [1980] 1 CMLR 25 . . . 412, 414
Case 93/78, Mattheus v. Doego, [1978] ECR 2203; [1979] 1 CMLR 551 . . . 301
Case 98/78, Racke, [1979] ECR 69; [1979] 1 CMLR 552 . . . 164
Cases 103–9/78, Beauport v. Council and Commission, [1979] ECR 17; [1979] 3 CMLR 1 . . . 375
Case 125/78, GEMA v. Commission, [1979] ECR 3173; [1980] 2 CMLR 177 . . . 380, 399, 407
Case 128/78, Commission v. United Kingdom (Tachograph Case), [1979] ECR 419; [1979] 2 CMLR 45 . . . 217
Case 141/78, France v. United Kingdom, [1979] ECR 2923; [1980] 1 CMLR 6 . . . 330
Case 148/78, Ratti, [1979] ECR 1629; [1980] 1 CMLR 96 . . . 215, 220–24, 230, 239, 244
Case 154/78, Valsabbia v. Commission, [1980] ECR 907; [1981] 1 CMLR 613 . . . 152
Case 162/78, Wagner v. Commission, [1979] ECR 3467 . . . 375
Case 230/78, Eridania, [1979] ECR 2749 . . . 216
Case 232/78, Commission v. France (Sheep Meat Case), [1979] ECR 2729; [1980] 1 CMLR 418 . . . 335
Case 238/78, Ireks-Arkady v. Commission and Council (one of second Quellmehl and Gritz Cases), [1979] ECR 2955 . . . 472, 485
Cases 241–2, 245–50/78, DGV v. Commission and Council (one of second Quellmehl and Gritz Cases), [1979] ECR 3017 . . . 472, 485
Case 257/78, Devred v. Commission, [1979] ECR 3767 . . . 169
Cases 261–2/78, Interquell v. Commission and Council (one of second Quellmehl and Gritz Cases), [1979] ECR 3045 . . . 472, 485
Case 4/79, Providence Agricole v. ONIC, [1980] ECR 2823 . . . 418, 441
Case 9/79, Koschniske (Wördsdorfer), [1979] ECR 2717; [1980] 1 CMLR 87 . . . 306
Case 44/79, Hauer v. Land Rheinland-Pfalz, [1979] ECR 3727; [1980] 3 CMLR 42 . . . 152
Case 89/79, Bonu v. Council, [1980] ECR 553 . . . 140
Case 98/79, Pecastaing v. Belgium, [1980] ECR 691; [1980] 3 CMLR 685 . . . 152
Case 102/79, Commission v. Belgium, [1980] ECR 1473; [1981] 1 CMLR 282 . . . 223
Case 104/79, Foglia v. Novello, [1980] ECR 745; [1981] 1 CMLR 45 . . . 229, 301, 304
Case 109/79, Maïseries de Beauce v. ONIC, [1980] ECR 2883 . . . 418, 441
Case 131/79, R v. Secretary of State for Home Affairs, *ex parte* Santillo, [1980] ECR 1585; [1980] 2 CMLR 308; [1981] 2 All ER 897; [1981] 2 WLR 362 . . . 216
Case 136/79, National Panasonic v. Commission, [1980] ECR 2033; [1980] 3 CMLR 169; [1981] 2 All ER 1 . . . 152
Case 138/79, Roquette v. Council, [1980] ECR 3333 . . . 19, 375, 422
Case 139/79, Maizena v. Council, [1980] ECR 3393 . . . 19, 422
Case 140/79, Chemial v. DAF, [1981] ECR 1; [1981] 3 CMLR 350 . . . 301
Case 145/79, Roquette v. French Customs, [1980] ECR 2917 . . . 418, 441, 484
Case 149/79, Commission v. Belgium, [1980] ECR 3881 and [1982] ECR 1845 . . . 234
Case 155/79, AM & S v. Commission, [1982] ECR 1575; [1982] 2 CMLR 264; [1983] 1 All ER 705; [1983] 3 WLR 17 . . . 172
Case 543/79, Birke v. Commission and Council, [1981] ECR 2669 . . . 467
Cases 789–90/79, Calpak v. Commission, [1980] ECR 1949; [1981] 1 CMLR 26 . . . 370, 375
Case 799/79, Bruckner v. Commission and Council, [1981] ECR 2697 . . . 467

Case 812/79, Attorney General v. Burgoa, [1980] ECR 2787; [1981] 2 CMLR 193 . . . 193, 194
Case 815/79, Cremonini, [1980] ECR 3583; [1981] 3 CMLR 49 . . . 317
Case 817/79, Buyl v. Commission, [1982] ECR 245 . . . 20
Cases 24, 97/80 R, Commission v. France (second Sheep Meat Case), [1980] ECR 1319; [1981] 3 CMLR 25 . . . 335, 336
Cases 36, 71/80, Irish Creamery Milk Suppliers Association v. Ireland, [1981] ECR 735; [1981] 2 CMLR 455 . . . 307
Case 46/80, Vinal v. Orbat, [1981] ECR 77; [1981] 3 CMLR 524 . . . 301
Case 66/80, International Chemical Corporation, [1981] ECR 1191; [1983] 2 CMLR 593 . . . 417
Cases 100–3/80, Musique Diffusion Française v. Commission, [1983] ECR 1825; [1983] 3 CMLR 221 . . . 152, 171
Case 126/80, Salonia, [1981] ECR 1563; [1982] CMLR 64 . . . 303
Case 138/80, Borker, [1980] ECR 1975; [1980] 3 CMLR 638 . . . 300
Cases 142–3/80, Essevi, [1981] ECR 1413 . . . 323
Case 158/80, Rewe-Handelsgesellschaft Nord v. Hauptzollamt Kiel, [1981] ECR 1805; [1982] CMLR 440 . . . 136, 246
Case 181/80, Procureur Général v. Arbelaiz-Emazabel, [1981] ECR 2961 . . . 193
Cases 188–90/80, France, Italy and the United Kingdom v. Commission, [1982] ECR 2545; [1982] 3 CMLR 144 . . . 30
Case 195/80, Michel v. European Parliament, [1981] ECR 2861 . . . 140
Cases 212–17/80, Salumi, [1981] ECR 2735 . . . 164
Case 244/80, Foglia v. Novello (No. 2), [1981] ECR 3045; [1982] 1 CMLR 585 . . . 229, 301, 302
Case 246/80, Broekmeulen, [1981] ECR 2311; [1982] 1 CMLR 91 . . . 292
Cases 256–7, 265, 267/80, 5/81, Birra Wührer v. Council and Commission, [1982] ECR 85 . . . 451, 458
Case 270/80, Polydor v. Harlequin Record Shops, [1982] ECR 329; [1982] 1 CMLR 677; [1982] FSR 358 . . . 83, 240, 241
Cases 275/80, 24/81, Krupp v. Commission, [1981] ECR 2489 . . . 361
Case 8/81, Becker, [1982] ECR 53; [1982] CMLR 499 . . . 224
Case 28/81, Commission v. Italy, [1981] ECR 2577 . . . 325
Case 45/81, Moksel v. Commission, [1982] ECR 1129 . . . 375
Case 60/81, IBM v. Commission, [1981] ECR 2639; [1981] 3 CMLR 635 . . . 357, 360
Case 102/81, Nordsee v. Reederei Mond, [1982] ECR 1095 . . . 293
Case 104/81, Kupferberg, [1982] ECR 3641; [1983] 1 CMLR 1 . . . 83, 240, 241
Case 108/81, Amylum v. Council, [1982] ECR 3107 . . . 164, 439
Case 109/81, Porta v. Commission, [1982] ECR 2469 . . . 447
Case 110/81, Roquette v. Council, [1982] ECR 3159 . . . 439
Case 114/81, Tunnel Refineries v. Council, [1982] ECR 3189 . . . 439
Cases 115–16/81, Adoui and Cornuaille, [1982] ECR 1665; [1982] 3 CMLR 631 . . . 151
Case 119/81, Klöckner-Werke v. Commission, [1982] ECR 2627; [1983] 3 CMLR 341 . . . 422
Case 131/81, Berti v. Commission, [1985] ECR 645 . . . 459
Case 132/81, Rijksdienst voor Werknemerspensioenen v. Vlaeminck, [1982] ECR 2953; [1983] 3 CMLR 557 . . . 303
Case 210/81, Demo-Studio Schmidt v. Commission, [1983] ECR 3045; [1984] 1 CMLR 69 . . . 380, 399
Case 211/81, Commission v. Denmark, [1982] ECR 4547 . . . 320
Case 230/81, Luxembourg v. European Parliament, [1983] ECR 255; [1983] 2 CMLR 726 . . . 4
Case 232/81, Agricola Commerciale Olio v. Commission, [1984] ECR 3881; [1987] 1 CMLR 363 . . . 375, 384
Case 246/81, Lord Bethell v. Commission, [1982] ECR 2277; [1982] 3 CMLR 300 . . . 380, 406, 407
Case 250/81, Greek Canners v. Commission, [1982] ECR 3535; [1983] 2 CMLR 32 . . . 370
Case 266/81, SIOT, [1983] ECR 790 . . . 242
Cases 267–9/81, SPI, [1983] ECR 801; [1984] 1 CMLR 354 . . . 74, 193, 241, 242, 285, 286, 316
Case 283/81, CILFIT, [1982] ECR 3415; [1983] 1 CMLR 472 . . . 305, 306
Cases 290–1/81, Singer and Geigy, [1983] ECR 847 . . . 286
Case 294/81, Control Data Belgium v. Commission, [1983] ECR 911; [1983] 2 CMLR 357 . . . 372, 413
Case 307/81, Alusuisse v. Council and Commission, [1982] ECR 3463; [1983] 3 CMLR 388 . . . 370, 377, 380, 381
Case 318/81, Commission v. CO.DE.MI., [1985] ECR 3693; [1987] 2 CMLR 516 . . . 446
Case 322/81, Michelin v. Commission, [1983] ECR 3461; [1985] 1 CMLR 282 . . . 171

Case 11/82, Piraiki-Patraiki v. Commission, [1985] ECR 207; [1985] 2 CMLR 46 . . . 373, 390
Cases 43, 63/82, VBVB v. Commission, [1984] ECR 19 . . . 362
Cases 75, 117/82, Razzouk and Beydoun v. Commission, [1984] ECR 1509 . . . 169
Case 116/82, Commission v. Germany, [1986] ECR 2519 . . . 416
Case 166/82, Commission v. Italy, [1984] ECR 459; [1985] 2 CMLR 615 . . . 325
Case 168/82, ECSC v. Ferriere Sant'Anna, [1983] ECR 1681 . . . 169
Case 191/82, FEDIOL v. Commission, [1983] ECR 2913; [1984] 3 CMLR 244 . . . 382
Cases 205–15/82, Deutsche Milchkontor v. Germany, [1983] ECR 2633; [1984] 3 CMLR 586 . . . 245
Case 216/82, Universität Hamburg, [1983] ECR 2771 . . . 413
Case 231/82, Spijker v. Commission, [1983] ECR 2559; [1984] 2 CMLR 284 . . . 372, 377, 384
Cases 239, 275/82, Allied Corporation v. Commission, [1984] ECR 1005; [1985] 3 CMLR 572 . . . 377, 380, 381
Case 264/82, Timex v. Council and Commission, [1985] ECR 849; [1985] 3 CMLR 550 . . . 382
Case 281/82, Unifrex v. Commission and Council, [1984] ECR 1969 . . . 484, 485
Cases 316/82, 40/83, Kohler v. Court of Auditors, [1984] ECR 641 . . . 362
Case 325/82, Commission v. Germany, [1984] ECR 777; [1985] 2 CMLR 719 . . . 325
Case 5/83, Rienks, [1983] ECR 4233; [1985] 1 CMLR 144 . . . 232
Case 13/83, European Parliament v. Council (Transport Case), [1985] ECR 1513; [1986] 1 CMLR 138 . . . 395
Case 14/83, Von Colson and Kamann v. Land Nordrhein-Westfalen, [1984] ECR 1891; [1986] 2 CMLR 430 . . . 212, 213, 236, 237, 246
Case 59/83, Biovilac v. EEC, [1984] ECR 4057 . . . 460
Case 63/83, R v. Kirk, [1984] ECR 2689; [1984] 3 CMLR 522 . . . 152
Case 69/83, Lux v. Court of Auditors, [1984] ECR 2447 . . . 425
Case 70/83, Kloppenburg, [1984] ECR 1075; [1985] 1 CMLR 205; [1988] 3 CMLR 1 . . . 222, 235, 263, 265
Case 108/83, Luxembourg v. European Parliament, [1984] ECR 1945; [1986] 2 CMLR 507 . . . 4
Case 114/83, Société d'Initiatives et de Coopération Agricoles v. Commission, [1984] ECR 2589; [1985] 2 CMLR 767 . . . 328, 459
Case 145/83, Adams v. Commission, [1985] ECR 3539; [1986] 1 CMLR 506; [1986] 2 WLR 367 . . . 451, 458, 463
Case 147/83, Binderer v. Commission, [1985] ECR 257 . . . 372, 384
Case 152/83, Demouche and others v. Fonds de garantie automobile and Bureau central français, [1987] ECR 3833 . . . 283
Case 192/83, Greece v. Commission, [1985] ECR 2791 . . . 402
Case 222/83, Municipality of Differdange v. Commission, [1984] ECR 2889; [1985] 3 CMLR 638 . . . 369
Case 289/83, GAARM v. Commission, [1984] ECR 4295; [1986] 3 CMLR 15 . . . 328, 459
Case 294/83, Parti Ecologiste 'Les Verts' v. European Parliament, [1986] ECR 1339; [1987] 2 CMLR 343 . . . 15, 74, 83, 353, 364, 375, 384
Case 41/84, Pinna, [1986] ECR 1 . . . 76
Case 44/84, Hurd v. Jones (Inspector of Taxes), [1986] ECR 29; [1986] 2 CMLR 1; [1986] QB 892; [1986] 3 WLR 189 . . . 211, 284
Case 52/84, Commission v. Belgium, [1986] ECR 89; [1987] 1 CMLR 710 . . . 334
Case 75/84, Metro v. Commission (No. 2), [1986] ECR 3021; [1987] 1 CMLR 118 . . . 380
Cases 142, 156/84, BAT and Reynolds v. Commission, [1987] ECR 4487 . . . 380, 399
Case 152/84, Marshall v. Southampton & South West Hampshire Area Health Authority (Teaching), [1986] ECR 723; [1986] 1 CMLR 688; [1986] 2 WLR 780; [1986] 2 All ER 584 . . . 224, 229, 231, 232, 236, 237, 239, 244
Case 169/84, COFAZ v. Commission, [1986] ECR 391; [1986] 3 CMLR 385 . . . 383, 386
Case 175/84, Krohn v. Commission, [1986] ECR 753; [1987] 1 CMLR 745 . . . 467, 484
Case 190/84, Parti Ecologiste 'Les Verts' v. European Parliament, [1988] ECR 1017 . . . 353
Case 222/84, Johnston v. Chief Constable of the RUC, [1986] ECR 1651; [1986] 3 CMLR 240 . . . 232, 233
Case 232/84, Commission v. Tordeur, [1985] ECR 3223 . . . 446
Case 240/84, Toyo v. Council, [1987] ECR 1809 . . . 381
Case 281/84, Zuckerfabrik Bedburg v. Council and Commission, [1987] ECR 49 . . . 485
Case 309/84, Commission v. Italy, [1986] ECR 599; [1987] 2 CMLR 657 . . . 320, 326
Case 5/85, AKZO Chemie v. Commission, [1986] ECR 2585; [1987] 3 CMLR 716 . . . 131, 358, 362, 365

Case 15/85, Consorzio Cooperative d'Abruzzo v. Commission, [1987] ECR 1005 . . . 131, 167, 361
Case 25/85, Nuovo Campsider v. Commission, [1986] ECR 1531 . . . 403
Case 41/85, Sideradria v. Commission, [1986] ECR 3917 . . . 413
Case 53/85, AKZO Chemie v. Commission, [1986] ECR 1965; [1987] 1 CMLR 231 . . . 358
Cases 67–8, 70/85, Van der Kooy v. Commission, [1988] ECR 219; [1989] 2 CMLR 804 . . . 382
Case 78/85, Group of the European Right v. European Parliament, [1988] ECR 1753 . . . 353
Cases 81, 119/85, Usinor v. Commission, [1986] ECR 1777 . . . 464
Case 97/85, Union Deutsche Lebensmittelwerke v. Commission, [1987] ECR 2265 . . . 377
Cases 133–6/85, Rau v. BALM, [1987] ECR 2289 . . . 414
Case 149/85, Wybot v. Faure, [1986] ECR 2391 . . . 16
Case 154/85 R, Commission v. Italy, [1985] ECR 1753 . . . 331
Cases 281, 283–5, 287/85, Germany v. Commission, [1987] ECR 3203; [1988] 1 CMLR 11 . . . 30, 113
Case 282/85, DEFI v. Commission, [1986] ECR 2469 . . . 382
Case 293/85 R, Commission v. Belgium, [1985] ECR 3521 . . . 331
Case 293/85, Commission v. Belgium, [1988] ECR 305 . . . 320, 323, 325
Case 300/85, Canon v. Council, [1988] ECR 5731 . . . 381
Case 309/85, Barra v. Belgium, [1988] ECR 355 . . . 76
Case 314/85, Foto-Frost, [1987] ECR 4199 . . . 299
Case 318/85, Greis Unterweger, [1986] ECR 955 . . . 300
Case 333/85, Mannesmann Röhrenwerke v. Commission, [1987] ECR 1381 . . . 387
Cases 351, 360/85, Fabrique de Fer de Charleroi v. Commission, [1987] ECR 3639 . . . 426
Cases 358/85, 51/86, France v. European Parliament, [1988] ECR 4821 . . . 4, 353
Case 363/85, Commission v. Italy, [1987] ECR 1733 . . . 223
Case 426/85, Commission v. Zoubek, [1986] ECR 4057 . . . 444
Case 12/86, Demirel, [1987] ECR 3719 . . . 158, 195, 241
Case 14/86, Pretore di Salò v. X, [1987] ECR 2545 (sub nom. Criminal proceedings against a Person or Persons Unknown) . . . 224, 239, 300
Case 24/86, Blaizot v. University of Liège, [1988] ECR 379; [1989] 1 CMLR 57 . . . 76
Case 26/86, Deutz und Geldermann v. Council, [1987] ECR 941 . . . 375
Case 34/86, Council v. European Parliament, [1986] ECR 2155; [1986] 3 CMLR 94 . . . 42
Case 45/86, Commission v. Council (Tariff Preferences Case), [1987] ECR 1493 . . . 120, 138, 367, 422
Case 50/86, Grands Moulins de Paris v. Council and Commission, [1987] ECR 4833 . . . 476
Case 55/86, Arposol v. Council, [1988] ECR 13 . . . 387
Case 68/86, United Kingdom v. Council, [1988] ECR 855 . . . 422
Case 80/86, Kolpinghuis Nijmegen, [1987] ECR 3969 . . . 224, 235, 236, 239
Case 81/86, De Boer Buizen v. Council and Commission, [1987] ECR 3677 . . . 484
Cases 89, 91/86, L'Etoile Commerciale v. Commission, [1987] ECR 3005 . . . 387
Cases 97, 99, 193, 215/86, Asteris v. Commission, [1988] ECR 2181 . . . 375, 402, 438, 439
Case 114/86, United Kingdom v. Commission, [1988] ECR 5289 . . . 359
Case 120/86, Mulder (first Mulder Case), [1988] ECR 2321 . . . 475
Case 131/86, United Kingdom v. Council, [1988] ECR 905 . . . 141, 367
Cases 166, 220/86, Irish Cement v. Commission, [1988] ECR 6473; [1989] 2 CMLR 57 . . . 396
Case 170/86, Von Deetzen, [1988] ECR 2355 . . . 475
Case 207/86, Apesco v. Commission, [1988] ECR 2151 . . . 370
Case 222/86, UNECTEF v. Heylens, [1987] ECR 4097 . . . 247
Case 240/86, Commission v. Greece, [1988] ECR 1835 . . . 320
Case 279/86, Sermes v. Commission, [1987] ECR 3109 . . . 381
Case 297/86, CIDA v. Commission, [1988] ECR 3531 . . . 370
Case 298/86, Commission v. Belgium, [1988] ECR 4343 . . . 323
Case 301/86, Frimodt Pedersen v. Commission, [1987] ECR 3123 . . . 381
Case 22/87, Commission v. Italy, [1989] ECR 143 . . . 249
Cases 46/87, 227/88, Hoechst v. Commission, [1989] ECR 2859; [1991] 4 CMLR 410 . . . 152, 171
Case 55/87, Moksel v. BALM, [1988] ECR 3845 . . . 66
Case 70/87, Fediol v. Commission, [1989] ECR 1781 . . . 198, 461

Case 85/87, Dow Benelux v. Commission, [1989] ECR 3137; [1991] 4 CMLR 410 . . . 152
Cases 97–9/87, Dow Chemical Ibérica v. Commission, [1989] ECR 3165; [1991] 4 CMLR 410 . . . 152
Case 106–20/87, Asteris v. Greece, [1988] ECR 5515 . . . 484
Cases C-133, 150/87, Nashua Corporation v. Commission and Council, [1990] ECR I-719 . . . 358, 382
Case C-142/87, Belgium v. Commission, [1990] ECR I-959 . . . 171
Case C-156/87, Gestetner Holdings v. Commission and Council, [1990] ECR I-781 . . . 358
Case 165/87, Commission v. Council (Commodity Coding Case), [1988] ECR 5545 . . . 113, 121, 122
Cases 193–4/87, Maurissen v. Commission, [1989] ECR 1045 . . . 364
Case 205/87, Nuova Ceam v. Commission, [1987] ECR 4427 . . . 381
Case 226/87, Commission v. Greece, [1988] ECR 3611 . . . 413, 418
Case 247/87, Star Fruit v. Commission, [1989] ECR 291 . . . 327, 407
Cases 266–7/87, R v. Royal Pharmaceutical Society, [1989] ECR 1295 . . . 232
Case 302/87, European Parliament v. Council (Comitology Case), [1988] ECR 5615 . . . 75, 367, 395, 398
Case C-308/87, Grifoni v. Commission, [1990] ECR I-1203 . . . 458
Case 346/87, Bossi v. Commission, [1989] ECR 303 . . . 357
Case C-354/87, Weddel v. Commission, [1990] ECR I-3487 . . . 376
Case 374/87, Orkem v. Commission, [1989] ECR 3283; [1991] 4 CMLR 502 . . . 171
Case 377/87, European Parliament v. Council (Draft Budget Case), [1988] ECR 4017 . . . 42, 397–9
Case 383/87, Commission v. Council, [1988] ECR 4051 . . . 42, 397
Case C-2/88, Zwartveld, [1990] ECR I-4405; [1990] 3 CMLR 457 . . . 56
Case 5/88, Wachauf, [1989] ECR 2609; [1991] 1 CMLR 328 . . . 157
Case 16/88, Commission v. Council, [1989] ECR 3457 . . . 131
Case 20/88, Roquette v. Commission, [1989] ECR 1553 . . . 451, 484
Case 22/88, Vreugdenhil v. Minister van Landbouw en Visserij, [1989] ECR 2049 . . . 477
Case 30/88, Greece v. Commission, [1989] ECR 3711 . . . 191, 316
Case C-49/88, Al-Jubail Fertilizer v. Council, [1991] ECR I-3187 . . . 171
Case C-70/88, European Parliament v. Council (Chernobyl Case), [1990] ECR I-2041 . . . 72, 74, 367, 395, 396
Case 103/88, Fratelli Costanzo v. Comune di Milano, [1989] ECR 1839; [1990] 3 CMLR 239 . . . 232
Cases C-143/88, 92/89, Zuckerfabrik Süderdithmarschen, [1991] ECR I-415 . . . 248, 308
Case 151/88, Italy v. Commission, [1989] ECR 1255 . . . 350
Case C-152/88, Sofrimport v. Commission, [1990] ECR I-2477 . . . 375, 474
Case 160/88 R, Fédération Européenne de la Santé Animale v. Council, [1988] ECR 41351 . . . 375
Case C-177/88, Dekker, [1990] ECR I-3941 . . . 235
Case C-202/88, France v. Commission, [1991] ECR I-1223; [1992] 5 CMLR 552 . . . 30
Cases C-213/88, C-39/89, Luxembourg v. European Parliament, [1991] ECR I-5643 . . . 4
Case C-221/88, Busseni, [1990] ECR I-495 . . . 74
Case C-244/88, UCDV v. Commission, [1989] ECR 3811 . . . 375
Case C-262/88, Barber v. Guardian Royal Exchange Assurance Group, [1990] ECR I-1889; [1990] 2 All ER 660; [1990] 2 CMLR 513; [1991] 1 QB 344; [1991] 2 WLR 72 . . . 76, 220
Cases C-297/88, 197/89, Dzodzi, [1990] ECR I-3763 . . . 288
Case C-322/88, Grimaldi, [1989] ECR 4407 . . . 109, 235, 284
Case C-362/88, GB-INN0-BM, [1990] ECR I-667 . . . 150
Cases C-363–4/88, Finsider v. Commission, [1992] ECR I-359 . . . 464
Case C-366/88, France v. Commission, [1990] ECR I-3571 . . . 353
Case C-10/89, HAG GF, [1990] ECR I-3711 . . . 71, 72
Case C-44/89, Von Deetzen, [1991] ECR I-5119 . . . 475
Case C-63/89, Assurances du Crédit v. Council and Commission, [1991] ECR I-1799 . . . 485
Case C-69/89, Nakajima v. Council, [1991] ECR I-2069 . . . 198, 461
Case C-73/89, Fournier, [1992] ECR I-5621 . . . 289
Case C-87/89, Sonito v. Commission, [1990] ECR I-1981 . . . 327

Cases C-100–1/89, Kaefer and Procacci, [1990] ECR I-4647 . . . 294
Cases C-104/89, 37/90, Mulder v. Council and Commission (second Mulder Case), [1992] ECR I-3061 . . . 446, 458, 459, 474, 475
Case C-106/89, Marleasing, [1990] ECR I-4135; [1992] 1 CMLR 305 . . . 236–8
Case C-188/89, Foster v. British Gas, [1990] ECRI-3313; [1990] 2 CMLR 833 . . . 232, 233, 235
Case C-189/89, Spagl, [1990] ECR I-4539 . . . 475
Case C-192/89, Sevince, [1990] ECR I-3461 . . . 74, 191, 241, 243, 287, 316
Case C-213/89, R v. Secretary of State for Transport, *ex parte* Factortame (No. 2), [1990] ECR I-2433; [1990] 3 WLR 818; [1990] 3 CMLR 1 . . . 247, 308
Case C-217/89, Pastätter, [1990] ECR I-4585 . . . 475
Case C-221/89, R v. Secretary of State for Transport, *ex parte* Factortame (No. 3), [1991] ECR I-3905; [1992] 1 QB 680; [1992] 3 WLR 288; [1991] 3 All ER 769 . . . 247, 250
Case C-231/89, Gmurzynska-Bscher, [1990] ECR I-4003 . . . 288
Case C-260/89, ERT, [1991] ECR I-2925 . . . 157
Case C-298/89, Gibraltar v. Council, [1993] ECR I-3605 . . . 375
Case C-300/89, Commission v. Council (Titanium Dioxide Case), [1991] ECR I-2867 . . . 121
Case C-309/89, Codorniu v. Council, [1994] ECR I-1853 . . . 376–80
Case C-345/89, Stoeckel, [1991] ECR I-4047 . . . 101
Case C-355/89, Barr and Montrose Holdings, [1991] ECR I-3479 . . . 293
Case C-358/89, Extramet Industrie v. Commission, [1991] ECR I-2501 . . . 370, 381, 382
Case C-370/89, SGEEM v. European Investment Bank, [1992] ECR I-6211 . . . 454, 455
Case C-371/89, Emrich v. Commission, [1990] ECR I-1555 . . . 327
Case C-384/89, Tomatis, [1991] ECR I-127 . . . 289
Cases T-32, 39/89, Marcopoulos v. European Court of Justice, [1990] ECR II-281; [1990] 3 CMLR 309 . . . 357
Case T-64/89, Automec v. Commission (No. 1), [1990] ECR II-367 . . . 399
Cases T-79/89 etc., BASF v. Commission: *see* Commission v. BASF, Case C-137/92 P 360, 361, 363
Case T-120/89, Stahlwerke Peine-Salzgitter v. Commission, [1991] ECR II-279 (CFI); affirmed Case C-220/91 P, [1993] ECR I-2393 . . . 458, 464, 474
Case T-138/89, NBV and NVB v. Commission, [1992] ECR II-2181 . . . 359
Cases C-6, 9/90, Francovich v. Italy, [1991] ECR I-5357; [1993] 2 CMLR 66 . . . 212, 248, 250, 251, 254, 255, 334
Case C-18/90, Kziber, [1991] ECR I-199 . . . 241
Case C-52/90, Commission v. Denmark, [1992] ECR I-2187 . . . 320, 325
Case C-54/90, Weddel & Co. BV v. Commission, [1992] ECR I-871 . . . 30
Case C-65/90, European Parliament v. Council, [1992] ECR I-4593 . . . 20
Case C-72/90, Asia Motor France v. Commission, [1990] ECR I-2181 . . . 327, 328, 459
Cases C-106, 317/90, 129/91, Emerald Meats v. Commission, [1993] ECR I-209 . . . 376
Case C-159/90, SPUC v. Grogan, [1991] ECR I-4685; [1991] 3 CMLR 849 . . . 150, 152, 158
Case C-163/90, Legros, [1992] ECR I-4625 . . . 302
Case 195/90R, Commission v. Germany, [1990] ECR I-3351 . . . 331
Case C-208/90, Emmott, [1991] ECR I-4269 . . . 246
Case C-209/90, Commission v. Feilhauer, [1992] ECR I-2613 . . . 444
Cases C-271, 281, 289/90, Spain v. Commission, [1992] ECR I-5833 . . . 30
Case C-282/90, Vreugdenhil v. Commission, [1992] ECR I-1937 . . . 477, 483, 485
Case C-284/90, Council v. European Parliament, [1992] ECR I-2277 . . . 41
Case C-295/90, European Parliament v. Council (Student Right of Residence Case), [1992] ECR I-4193 . . . 121, 438
Case C-303/90, France v. Commission, [1991] ECR I-5315 . . . 353
Case C-313/90, CIRFS v. Commission, [1993] ECR I-1125 . . . 383
Cases C-320–2/90, Telemarsicabruzzo v. Circostel, [1993] ECR I-393 . . . 302, 309
Case C-343/90, Dias, [1992] ECR I-4673 . . . 302, 303
Case C-354/90, Fédération Nationale du Commerce Extérieur v. France, [1991] ECR I-5505 . . . 359
Case T-24/90, Automec v. Commission (No. 2), [1992] ECR II-2223 . . . 399
Opinion 1/91, First EEA Case, [1991] ECR I-6079 . . . 5, 73, 83, 289, 316
Opinion 2/91, ILO Convention 170 Case, [1993] ECR I-1061; [1993] 3 CMLR 800 . . . 190
Cases C-15, 108/91, Buckl, [1992] ECR I-6061 . . . 394, 396, 403

Case C-45/91, Commission v. Greece, [1992] ECRI-2509 . . . 338
Case C-47/91, Italy v. Commission, [1992] ECR I-4145 . . . 359
Case C-83/91, Meilicke, [1992] ECR I-4871 . . . 302, 303
Case C-88/91, Federconsorzi, [1992] ECRI-4035 . . . 289
Case C-107/91, ENU v. Commission, [1993] ECR I-599 . . . 407
Case C-158/91, Levy, [1993] ECR I-4287 . . . 98, 100, 101, 243, 287
Case C-168/91, Konstantinidis, [1993] ECRI-1191 . . . 158
Cases C-181, 248/91, European Parliament v. Council, [1993] ECR I-3685 . . . 42, 365
Case C-183/91, Commission v. Greece, [1993] ECR I-3131 . . . 413
Case C-188/91, Deutsche Shell, [1993] ECR I-363 . . . 191, 287
Case C-198/91, Cook v. Commission, [1993] ECR I-2487 . . . 383
Case C-213/91, Abertal v. Commission, [1993] ECR I-3265 . . . 375
Case C-225/91, Matra v. Commission, [1993] ECR I-3203 . . . 383
Case C-271/91, Marshall v. Southampton and South West Hampshire Area Health Authority (No. 2), [1993] ECR I-4367; [1993] WLR 1054 (ECJ) . . . 225, 248
Case C-316/91, European Parliament v. Council, [1994] ECR I-625 . . . 121, 351, 368
Case C-325/91, France v. Commission, [1993] ECR I-3283 . . . 353
Case C-327/91, France v. Commission, [1994] ECR I-364130, . . . 114, 184, 285, 365, 420
Case C-338/91, Steenhorst-Neerings, [1993] ECRI-5475 . . . 246
Opinion 1/92, Second EEA Case, [1992] ECR I-2821 . . . 6
Opinion 2/92, OECD Case, [1995] ECR I-521 . . . 183, 184
Case C-2/92, Bostock, [1994] ECR I-955 . . . 158
Case C-24/92, Corbiau v. Administration des Contributions, [1993] ECR I-1277 . . . 290, 291
Case C-29/92, Asia Motor France v. Commission, [1992] ECR I-3935 . . . 327
Case C-91/92, Faccini Dori v. Recreb, [1994] ECR I-3325 . . . 220, 225, 226, 229, 231, 237
Case C-128/92, Banks, [1994] ECR I-1209 . . . 214
Case C-135/92, Fiskano v. Commission, [1994] ECR I-2885 . . . 171
Case C-137/92 P, Commission v. BASF, [1994] ECR I-2555 (appeal from Cases T-79/89 (etc.), [1992] ECR II-315) . . . 360, 361, 363
Case C-157/92, Pretore di Genova v. Banchero, [1993] ECR I-1085 . . . 302, 309
Case C-188/92, TWD, [1994] ECR I-833 . . . 71, 414
Case C-228/92, Roquette, [1994] ECR I-1445 . . . 418
Case C-388/92, European Parliament v. Council, [1994] ECR I-2067 . . . 20
Case C-393/92, Almelo and Others, [1994] ECRI-1477 . . . 291
Case C-404/92 P, X v. Commission, [1994] ECR I-4737 . . . 152
Case C-410/92, Johnson v. Chief Adjudication Officer, [1994] ECR I-5483 . . . 246
Case T-36/92, SFEI v. Commission, [1992] ECRII-2479 . . . 358, 358
Case T-83/92, Zunis Holding, [1993] ECR II-1169 . . . 394
Case C-18/93, Corsica Ferries, [1994] ECR I-1783 . . . 290, 291
Case C-32/93, Webb v. EMO Air Cargo, [1994] ECR 3567 . . . 237
Case C-39/93 P, SFEI v. Commission, [1994] ECR I-2681 (appeal from Case T-36/92, [1992] ECR II-2479) . . . 358, 380, 399
Cases C-46/93, 48/93, Brasserie du Pêcheur v. Bundesrepublik Deutschland and The Queen v. Secretary of State for Transport, *ex parte* Factortame Ltd, [1996] ECR I-1029; [1996] 2 WLR 506 . . . 250–2
Case C-62/93, BP Supergas, [1995] ECR I-1883 . . . 245
Case C-65/93, European Parliament v. Council, [1995] ECR I-643 . . . 19
Case C-156/93, European Parliament v. Commission, [1995] ECR I-2019 . . . 368, 425
Case C-280/93, Germany v. Council (Bananas Case), [1994] ECR I-4973 . . . 198, 417, 424, 461
Case C-312/93, Peterbroeck v. Belgium, [1995] ECR I-4599 . . . 246
Case C-316/93, Vaneetveld, [1994] ECR I-763 . . . 225
Case C-324/93, R v. Secretary of State for the Home Department, *ex parte* Evans Medical and Macfarlan Smith (Generics Case), [1995] ECR I-563 . . . 100, 286, 287
Case C-346/93, Kleinwort Benson v. City of Glasgow District Council, [1995] ECR I-615 . . . 289

Case C-360/93, European Parliament v. Council, [1996] ECR 1195 . . . 437

Case C-392/93, R v. HM Treasury, *ex parte* British Telecommunications, [1996] ECR I–1631; [1996] 3 WLR 203 . . . 251, 254

Case C-415/93, Union Royale Belge v. Bosman, [1995] ECR I-4921 . . . 76

Case C-417/93, European Parliament v. Council, [1995] ECR I-1185 . . . 19, 20, 131

Cases C-430–1/93, Van Schijndel, [1995] ECR I-4705 . . . 246

Case C-465/93, Atlanta Fruchthandelsgesellschaft (Bananas Case), [1995] ECR I-3761 . . . 248

Case T-3/93, Air France v. Commission, [1994] ECR II-121 . . . 362

Case T-435/93, ASPEC v. Commission, [1995] ECR II-1281 . . . 383, 390

Case T-472/93, Campo Ebro v. Council, [1995] ECR II-421 . . . 371

Case T-475/93: *see* Case C-209/94 P, Buralux v. Council

Cases T-481, 484/93, Exporteurs in Levende Varkens v. Commission, [1995] ECR II-2941 . . . 377

Case T-489/93, Unifruit Hellas v. Commission, [1994] ECR II-1201 . . . 375

Case T-514/93, Cobrecaf v. Commission, [1995] ECR II-621 . . . 467

Case T-585/93, Greenpeace v. Council, [1985] ECR II-2205 . . . 377

Opinion 1/94, WTO Case, [1994] ECR I-5267 . . . 99, 178, 183, 184

Opinion 2/94, ECHR Case, [1996] ECR I-1759 . . . 73, 118, 152, 154, 185, 189, 267

Opinion 3/94, Bananas Case, [1995] ECR I-4577 . . . 189

Case C-5/94, R v. Ministry of Agriculture, *ex parte* Hedley Lomas, [1996] ECR I-2553 . . . 235, 251–3

Case C-21/94, European Parliament v. Council, [1995] ECR I-1827 . . . 20

Case C-25/94, Commission v. Council (FAO Case), [1996] ECR I-1469 . . . 24, 175, 353

Case C-61/94, Commission v. Germany, [1996] ECR I-3989 . . . 316

Case C-84/94, United Kingdom v. Council, [1996] ECR I-5755 . . . 127

Case C-111/94, Job Centre, [1995] ECR I-3361 . . . 290, 291, 300

Case 120/94 R, Commission v. Greece (Macedonia Case), [1994] ECR I-3037 . . . 331

Cases C-178–9, 188–190/94, Dillenkofer v. Germany, [1996] ECR I-4845 . . . 251, 254

Case C-194/94, CIA Security v. Signalson and Securitel, [1996] ECR I-2201; [1996] 2 CMLR 781 . . . 225–9

Case C-209/94 P, Buralux v. Council, [1996] ECR I-615 (affirming Case T-475/93, 17 May 1994, not published in ECR) . . . 371, 373, 377

Cases C-283, 291 and 292/94, Denkavit Internationaal v. Bundesamt für Finanzen, [1996] ECR I-5063 . . . 254

Case T-100/94, Michailidis v. Commission, [1998] ECR II-3115 . . . 377

Case T-186/94, Guérin Automobiles v. Commission, [1995] ECR II-1753 . . . 358

Cases T-195, 202/94, Quiller v. Council and Commission, [1997] ECR II-2247 . . . 476

Case T-298/94, Roquette v. Council, [1996] ECR II-1531 . . . 377

Case T-380/94, AIUFFASS v. Commission, [1996] ECR II-2169 . . . 390

Case C-28/95, Leur-Bloem, [1997] ECR I-4161 . . . 289

Case C-41/95, Council v. European Parliament, [1995] ECR I-4411 . . . 42

Case C-57/95, France v. Commission, [1997] ECR I-1627 . . . 353

Case C-66/95, R v. Secretary of State for Social Security, *ex parte* Sutton, [1997] ECR I-2163 . . . 251

Case C-68/95, Port, [1996] ECR I-6065 . . . 248, 407, 484

Cases C-74 & 129/95, Criminal proceedings against X, [1996] ECR I-6609 . . . 291

Case C-87/95 P, CNPAAP v. Council, [1996] ECR I-2003 (affirming Case T-116/94, [1995] ECR II-1) . . . 377

Cases C-94–5/95, Bonifaci v. INPS, [1997] ECR I-3969 . . . 250, 252

Case C-107/95 P, Bundesverband der Bilanzbuchhalter v. Commission, [1997] ECR I-947 . . . 327

Case C-124/95, Centro-Com, [1997] ECR I-81 . . . 100, 101

Case C-127/95, Norbrook Laboratories v. Ministry of Agriculture, [1998] ECR I-1531; [1998] 3 CMLR 809 . . . 255

Case C-130/95, Giloy, [1997] ECR I-4291 . . . 248, 289

Case C-168/95, Arcaro, [1996] ECR I-4705 . . . 220, 239

Case C-178/95, Wiljo v. Belgium, [1997] ECR I-585 . . . 415

Case C-180/95, Draehmpaehl v. Urania Immobilienservice OHG, [1997] ECR I-2195 . . . 225

Case C-241/95, R v. Intervention Board for Agricultural Produce, *ex parte* Accrington Beef, [1996] ECR I-6699 . . . 415

Case C-254/95 P, European Parliament v. Innamorati, [1996] ECR I-3423 . . . 140
Case C-261/95, Palmisani v. INPS, [1997] ECR I-4025 . . . 250, 252
Case C-265/95, Commission v. France, [1997] ECR I-6959 . . . 319
Case C-282/95, Guérin Automobiles v. Commission, [1997] ECR I-1503 (appeal from Case T-186/94, [1995] ECR II-1753) . . . 358, 396, 399, 407
Case C-299/95, Kremzow, [1997] ECR I-2629 . . . 158
Case C-321/95 P, Greenpeace v. Council, [1998] ECR I-1651 (affirming Case T-585/93, [1985] ECR II-2205) . . . 377
Case C-337/95, Parfums Christian Dior v. Evora, [1997] ECR I-6013 . . . 294, 296, 299
Case C-345/95, France v. European Parliament, [1997] ECR I-5215 . . . 4
Case C-373/95, Maso v. INPS and Italy, [1997] ECR I-4051 . . . 250, 252
Case C-390/95 P, Antillean Rice Mills v. Commission, [1999] ECR I-769 (affirming Cases T-480, 483/93, [1995] ECR II-2305) . . . 373, 377
Case C-392/95, European Parliament v. Council, [1997] ECR I-3213 . . . 20
Case C-395/95 P, Geotronics v. Commission, [1997] ECR I-2271 . . . 359, 360
Case C-408/95, Eurotunnel v. SeaFrance, [1997] ECR I-6315 . . . 415
Case T-47/95, Terres Rouges v. Commission, [1997] ECR II-481 . . . 377
Case T-112/95, Dethlefs v. Council and Commission, [1998] ECR II-3819 . . . 476
Case T-149/95, Ducros v. Commission, [1997] ECR II-2031 . . . 383
Case T-184/95, Dorsch Consult v. Council and Commission, [1998] ECR II-667; affirmed Case C-237/98 P [2000] ECR I-4549 . . . 460
Case C-15/96, Schöning-Kougebetopoulou, [1998] ECR I-47 . . . 255
Case C-53/96, Hermès v. FHT, [1998] ECR I-3603 . . . 195, 287
Case C-54/96, Dorsch Consult, [1997] ECR I-4961 . . . 290, 291
Cases C-69–79/96, Garofalo, [1997] ECR I-5603 . . . 290, 292
Case C-89/96, Portugal v. Commission, [1999] ECR I-8377 . . . 438
Case C-129/96, Inter-Environnement Wallonie v. Région Wallonne, [1997] ECR I-7411 . . . 222, 230, 238, 239
Case C-149/96, Portugal v. Council, [1999] ECR I-8395 . . . 198, 242, 461
Case C-162/96, Racke, [1998] ECR I-3655; [1998] 3 CMLR 219 . . . 417, 424
Case C-176/96, Lehtonen and Castors Braine, [2000] ECR I-2681 . . . 302
Case C-262/96, Sürül, [1999] ECR I-2685; [2001] 1 CMLR 4 . . . 76
Cases C-279–281/96, Ansaldo Energia, [1998] ECR I-5025 . . . 246
Case C-319/96, Brinkmann Tabakfabriken v. Skatteministeriet, [1998] ECR I-5255; [1998] 3 CMLR 673 . . . 255
Case T-87/96, Assicurazioni Generali v. Commission, [1999] ECR II-203; [2000] 4 CMLR 312 . . . 359
Case T-95/96, Gestevisión Telecinco v. Commission, [1998] ECR II-3407; [1998] 3 CMLR 1112 . . . 383, 407
Case C-95/97, Région Wallonne v. Commission, [1997] ECR I-1787 . . . 368
Case C-103/97, Köllensperger and Atzwanger, [1999] ECR I-551 . . . 291
Case C-126/97, Eco Swiss v. Benetton International, [1999] ECR I-3055; [2000] 5 CMLR 816 . . . 293
Case C-134/97, Victoria Film, [1998] ECR I-7023 . . . 291, 300
Case C-140/97, Rechberger v. Austria, [1999] ECR I-3499 . . . 255
Case C-180/97, Regione Toscana v. Commission, [1997] ECR I-5245 . . . 368
Case C-226/97, Lemmens, [1998] ECR I-3711 . . . 226
Case C-302/97, Konle v. Austria, [1999] ECR I-3099 . . . 255
Case C-310/97 P, AssiDomän Kraft Products v. Commission, [1999] ECR I-5363 (appeal from Case T-227/95, [1997] ECR II-1185) . . . 438, 467
Case C-321/97, Andersson v. Sweden, [1999] ECRI-3551; [2000] 2 CMLR 191 . . . 255
Case C-341/97, Commission v. Netherlands, [2000] ECR I-6611 . . . 320, 325
Case C-387/97, Commission v. Greece, [2000] ECR I-5047 . . . 338
Case C-424/97, Haim v. Kassenzahnärztliche Vereinigung Nordrhein, [2000] ECR I-5123 . . . 255
Cases T-125, 127/97, Coca-Cola v. Commission, [2000] ECR II-1733; [2000] 5 CMLR 467 . . . 359
Case T-288/97, Regione Autonoma Friuli-Venezia v. Commission, [1999] ECR II-1871 . . . 368

Case T-598/97, British Shoe Corporation Footwear Supplies v. Council, [2002] ECR II-1155 . . . 382
Case C-17/98, Emesa Sugar (Free Zone) NV v. Aruba, [2000] ECR I-665 . . . 52
Cases C-110–147/98, Gabalfrisa, [2000] ECR I-1577 . . . 290, 291
Cases C-240–44/98, Oceano Grupo Editorial v. Rocio Murciano Quintero, [2000] ECR 1–4941 . . . 227
Cases C-300, 392/98, Dior v. Tuk Consultancy, [2000] ECR I-11307 . . . 195, 241, 287
Case C-352/98 P, Bergaderm v. Commission, [2000] ECR I-5291 (appeal from Case T-199/96, [1998] ECR II-2805) . . . 468, 469, 471, 472, 476
Case C-359/98, Ca'Pasta v. Commission, [2000] ECR I-3977 . . . 360
Case C-376/98, Germany v. European Parliament and Council (Tobacco Advertising Case), [2000] ECR I-8419; [2000] 3 CMLR 1175 . . . 127, 420
Case C-379/98, PreussenElektra, [2001] ECR I-2099 . . . 301
Case C-443/98, Unilever Italia v. Central Food, [2000] ECR I-7535; [2001] 1 CMLR 21 . . . 226, 228, 229
Case C-451/98, Antillean Rice Mills v. Council, [2001] ECR I-8949 . . . 372, 373, 376, 377
Case C-466/98, Commission v. United Kingdom, [2002] ECR I-9427 . . . 185
Case T-178/98, Fresh Marine Company v. Commission, [2000] ECR II 3331; [2001] 3 CMLR 35; upheld on appeal, Case C-472/00 P, [2003] ECR I-7541; [2003] 2 CMLR 39 . . . 462, 467
Case C-1/99, Kofisca Italia, [2001] ECR I-207 . . . 289
Cases C-80–82/99, Flemmer, [2001] ECR I-7211 . . . 444, 446, 476
Case C-178/99, Salzmann, [2001] ECR I-4421 . . . 291
Case C-239/99, Nachi Europe, [2001] ECR I-1197 . . . 381, 415
Case C-267/99, Adam, [2001] ECR I-7467 . . . 289
Case C-516/99, Schmid, [2002] ECR I-4573 . . . 291
Cases T-222, 327 and 329/99, Martinez v. European Parliament, [2001] ECR II-2823: *see* Case C-486/01 P, [2004] ECR I-6289
C-13/00, Commission v. Ireland, [2002] ECR I-2943 . . . 195
Case C-17/00, De Coster v. Collège des bourgmestre et échevins de Watermael-Boitsfort, [2001] ECR I-9445 . . . 291
Case C-50/00 P, Unión de Pequeños Agricultores v. Council, [2002] ECR I-6677 . . . 77, 377
Case C-86/00, HSB-Wohnbau GmbH, [2001] ECR I-5353 . . . 291
Case C-99/00, Lyckeskog, [2002 ECR I-4839 . . . 297
Case C-116/00, Laguillaumie, [2000] ECR I-4979 . . . 302
Case C-182/00, Lutz GmbH, [2002] ECR I-547 . . . 291
Case C-112/00, Schmidberger, [2003] ECR I-5659 . . . 104, 158, 159
Case C-472/00 P: *see* Case T-178/98
Case C-224/01, Köbler v. Austria, [2003] ECR I-10239 . . . 254
Case 278/01, Commission v. Spain, [2003] ECR I-14141 . . . 338
Cases C-397–403/01, Pfeiffer, [2004] ECR I-8835 . . . 228–31, 238
Case C-494/01, Commission v. Ireland, [2005] ECR I-3331 . . . 325, 339
Case C-486/01 P, Front National v. Parliament, [2004] ECR I-6289 . . . 17
Cases C-486/01 P-R and C-488/01 P-R, Front National v. Parliament [2002] ECR I-1843; Case C-486/01 P, [2004] ECR I-6289 . . . 17
Case T-177/01, Jégo-Quéré v. Commission, [2002] ECR II-2365 (for appeal, see Case C-263/02 P, [2004] ECR I-3425) . . . 378
Case T-315/01, Kadi v. Council and Commission ('Kadi I'), [2005] ECR II-3649 (reversed on appeal: Cases C-402/05 P and 415/05 P) . . . 98, 101, 104, 105, 161
Case C-36/02, Omega, [2004] ECR I-9609 . . . 104, 159
Case C-93/02 P, Biret International v. Council, [2003] ECR I-10497 . . . 198, 243
Case C-201/02, Wells, [2004] ECR I-723 . . . 227, 229
Case C-263/02 P, Jégo-Quéré v. Commission, [2004] ECR I-3425 . . . 378
Case C-304/02, Commission v. France, [2005] ECR I-6263 . . . 337, 338
Case C-377/02, Van Parys, [2005] ECR I-1465 . . . 197, 243
Cases C-387/02, 391/02 and 403/02, Berlusconi, [2005] ECR I-3565 . . . 228
Case T-228/02, Organisation des Modjahedines du peuple d'Iran (OMPI) v. Council, [2006] ECR II-4665 . . . 105
Opinion 1/03, Lugano Convention Case, [2006] ECR I-1145 . . . 185
Case C-131/03 P, Reynolds Tobacco v. Commission [2006] ECR I-7795 . . . 360

Case C-173/03, Traghetti del Mediterraneo SpA v. Italy, [2006] ECR I-5177 ... 254
Case C-239/03, Commission v. France, [2004] ECR I-9325 ... 195, 317
Case C-320/03 R, Commission v. Austria, [2003] ECR I-7929, [2003] ECR I-11665, [2004] ECR I-3593 ... 332
Case 119/04, Commission v. Italy, [2006] ECR I-6885 ... 338
Case C-144/04, Mangold, [2005] ECR I-9981 ... 77, 222, 229–31, 239, 240, 301
Case C-145/04, Spain v. United Kingdom, [2006] ECR I-7917 ... 16, 103, 104, 155
Case C-177/04, Commission v. France, [2006] ECR I-2461 ... 338
Case C-212/04, Adeneler, [2006] ECR I-6057 ... 222, 238, 239
Case C-418/04, Commission v. Ireland, [2007] ECR I-10947 ... 230
Case C-432/04, Commission v. Edith Cresson, [2006] ECR I-6387 ... 29
Case C-525/04 P, Spain v. Lenzing, [2007] ECR I-9947 ... 383, 434
Case C-138/05, Stichting Zuid-Hollandse Mileufederatie, [2006] ECR I-8339 ... 222
Cases C-402/05 P and 415/05 P, Kadi v. Council and Commission ('Kadi I') [2008] ECR I-6351 ... 91, 98, 101, 104, 105, 161, 197
Case C-432/05, Unibet (London) Ltd and Unibet (International) Ltd v. Justitiekanslern, [2007] ECR I-2271 ... 245
Case C-70/06, Commission v. Portugal, [2008] ECR I-00001 ... 338
Case C-120–121/06, FIAMM v. Council and Commission, [2008] ECR I-6513 ... 198, 243, 460, 469
Case C-161/06, Skoma-Lux, [2007] ECR I-10841 ... 141, 364
Case C-205/06 Commission v. Austria, [2009] ECR I-01301 ... 100
Case C-210/06, Cartesio Oktató és Szolgáltató bt, [2008] ECR I-9641 ... 310
Case C-249/06 Commission v. Sweden, [2009] ECR I-1335 ... 100
Case C-308/06, Intertanko, [2008] ECR I-4057 ... 193, 198
Case C-345/06, Heinrich, [2009] ECR I-1659 ... 141, 363
Case C-427/06, Bartsch v. Bosch und Siemens Hausgeräte (BSH) Altersfürsorge GmbH, [2008] ECR I-7245 ... 222
Case 47/07 P, Masdar (UK) Ltd v. Commission, [2008] ECR I-9761 ... 448, 449
Case C-121/07, Commission v. France, [2008] ECR I-9159 ... 337, 338
Case C-166/07, European Parliament v. Council, [2009] ECR I-7135 ... 122
Case C-369/07, Commission v. Greece, [2009] ECR I-5703 ... 338
Case C-370/07, Commission v. Council, [2009] ECR I-8917 ... 120
Case C-440/07 P, Commission v. Schneider Electric, [2009] ECR I-6413 (Grand Chamber) ... 457
Case C-550/07 P, Akzo Nobel Chemicals Ltd, [2010] ECR I-8301 ... 172
Case C-555/07, Kücükdeveci v. Swedex, [2010] ECR I-365 ... 230, 240
Opinion 1/08 GATS, [2009] ECR I-11129 ... 183
Case C-76/08 R, Commission v. Malta, [2008] ECR I-64 ... 332
Opinion 1/09, Patents Court Case, [2011] ECR I-1137 (Full Court) ... 73
Case C-83/09 P, Commission v. Kronoply and Kronotex, [2011] ECR I-4441 (Grand Chamber) ... 383
Case C-494/09, Bolton Alimentari, [2011] ECR I-647 ... 415
Case C-550/09, E and F, [2010] ECR I-6213 ... 415
Case C-196/09, Miles v. European Schools, [2011] ECR I-5105 (Grand Chamber) ... 290, 294
Case T-85/09, Kadi v. Commission ('Kadi II'), [2010] ECR II-5177 (affirmed on appeal: Case C-584/10 P) ... 106, 162
Case C-355/10, European Parliament v. Council, 5 September 2012 (Grand Chamber) ... 130, 131, 367
Case C-463/10 P, Deutsche Post and Germany v. Commission, [2011] ECR I-9639 ... 350, 357
Case C-584/10 P, Commission v. Kadi ('Kadi II'), 18 July 2013 (Grand Chamber) ... 106, 162
Case T-18/10, Inuit Tapiriit Kanatami v. Parliament and Council, [2011] ECR II-5599 (for appeal, see Case C-583/11 P) 385
Case T-262/10, Microban v. Commission, [2011] ECR II-7697 ... 385, 386
Case T-526/10, Inuit Tapiriit Kanatami, 25 April 2013 ... 385
Case C-300/11, ZZ, 4 June 2013 (Grand Chamber) ... 56
Case C-583/11 P, Inuit Tapiriit Kanatami v. Parliament and Council, (appeal from Case T-18/10), 3 October 2013 (Grand Chamber) ... 385
Case C-370/12, Pringle v. Government of Ireland, 27 November 2012 (Full Court) ... 38, 90, 97, 414, 415

TABLE OF ENGLISH, SCOTTISH, AND IRISH CASES

Ahmad v. ILEA [1977] 3 WLR 396; [1978] 1 All ER 574 (CA) . . . 170

Allgemeine Gold und Silberscheideanstalt v. Commissioners of Customs and Excise [1978] 2 CMLR 292; affirmed [1980] QB 390; [1980] 2 WLR 555; [1980] 2 All ER 138 (CA) . . . 157

Biggs v. Somerset County Council [1966] ICR 364 (CA) . . . 246

Bosphorus Hava Yollari Turizm Ve Ticaret Anonim Sirketi v. Ireland [2006] 42 EHRR 1 . . . 155

Bulk Oil v. Sun International [1984] 1 WLR 147 (CA) . . . 293

Bulmer v. Bollinger [1974] Ch 401; [1974] 3 WLR 202; [1974] 2 All ER 1226 (CA) . . . 303–7

Church of Scientology of California v. Customs and Excise Commissioners [1981] 1 All ER 1035 (CA) . . . 307

Customs and Excise Commissioners v. Samex [1983] 1 All ER 1042; [1983] 3 CMLR 194 . . . 307

Doughty v. Rolls-Royce [1992] ICR 538; [1992] IRLR 126; The Times, 14 January 1992 (CA) . . . 233, 234

Duke v. GEC Reliance (formerly Reliance Systems) [1988] AC 618; [1988] 2 WLR 359; [1988] 1 All ER 626 (HL); [1988] 1 CMLR 719 . . . 238, 277

Finnegan v. Clowney Youth Training Programme [1990] 2 AC 407; [1990] 2 WLR 1035; [1990] 2 All ER 546; [1990] 2 CMLR 859 . . . 238

Foster v. British Gas [1991] 2 AC 306 . . . 234

Fothergill v. Monarch Airlines Ltd [1981] AC 251 . . . 204

Gardner & Co. v. Cone [1928] Ch. 995 . . . 163

Garland v. British Rail Engineering Ltd [1983] 2 AC 751; [1982] 2 WLR 918; [1982] 2 All ER 402 (HL) . . . 236, 277

Griffin v. South West Water Services [1995] IRLR 15 . . . 233

Henn and Darby v. DPP, *see* R v. Henn and Darby

Holiday in Italy, Re a [1975] 1 CMLR 184 . . . 298

James Buchanan & Co. Ltd v. Babco Forwarding and Shipping (UK) Ltd [1978] AC 141 . . . 204

Kaur (Surjit) v. Lord Advocate [1980] 3 CMLR 79 (Court of Session) . . . 157

Litster v. Forth Dry Dock & Engineering Co. [1990] 1 AC 546; [1989] 2 WLR 634; [1989] 1 All ER 1134; [1989] 2 CMLR 194 . . . 238

Macarthys Ltd v. Smith [1979] 3 All ER 325; [1981] 1 All ER 111 . . . 277

McWhirter v. Attorney-General [1972] CMLR 882 . . . 272

Matthews v. United Kingdom, (1999) 28 EHRR 361 . . . 102, 103, 155

Magnavision, *see* SA Magnavision NV

National Smokeless Fuels Ltd v. IRC [1986] 3 CMLR 227 . . . 277

NUT v. St Mary's School [1997] 3 CMLR 630; [1997] ICR 334 (CA) . . . 233, 234

Östreicher v. Secretary of State for the Environment [1978] 1 WLR 810; [1978] 3 All ER 82 (CA) . . . 170

Polydor v. Harlequin Record Shops [1980] 2 CMLR 413 (CA) . . . 304

R v. Brixton Prison Governor, *ex parte* Soblen [1963] 2 QB 243 . . . 427

R v. Commissioners of Customs and Excise, *ex parte* Cooke and Stevenson [1970] 1 All ER 1068 . . . 430

R v. Henn and Darby [1978] 1 WLR 1031; [1978] 3 All ER 1190 (CA); [1980] 2 WLR 597; [1980] 2 All ER 166; [1980] 2 CMLR 229 (HL) . . . 306, 307

R v. HM Treasury, *ex parte* British Telecommunications, The Times, 2 December 1993 (CA) . . . 247, 248

R v. HM Treasury, *ex parte* Smedley [1985] 1 QB 657; [1985] 2 WLR 576; [1985] 1 All ER 589 (CA) . . . 273
R v. International Stock Exchange, *ex parte* Else [1993] QB 534; [1993] 2 WLR 70; [1993] 1 All ER 420 (CA) . . . 307, 308
R v. Manchester Crown Court, *ex parte* DPP [1993] 1 WLR 693 (QBD); reversed on other grounds [1993] 1 WLR 1524 (HL) . . . 16
R v. Minister of Agriculture, *ex parte* Fédération Européenne de la Santé Animale [1988] 3 CMLR 661 (Eng. High Ct.) . . . 275
R v. Plymouth Justices, *ex parte* Rogers [1982] 3 WLR 1; [1982] 2 All ER 175; [1982] 3 CMLR 221 (Div. Ct.) . . . 304
R v. Secretary of State for Foreign and Commonwealth Affairs, *ex parte* Lord Rees-Mogg [1993] 3 CMLR 101; [1994] 2 WLR 115 (DC) . . . 7
R v. Secretary of State for Social Services, *ex parte* Bomore Medical Supplies [1986] 1 CMLR 228 (CA) . . . 306
R v. Secretary of State for Transport, *ex parte* Factortame [1990] 2 AC 85; [1989] 2 WLR 997; [1989] 2 All ER 692; [1989] 3 CMLR 1 (judgment of House of Lords before the reference) . . . 247, 248, 276
R v. Secretary of State for Transport, *ex parte* Factortame (No. 2) [1991] 1 AC 603; [1990] 3 WLR 856; [1991] 1 All ER 70; [1990] 3 CMLR 375 (judgment of House of Lords after the reference) . . . 247, 248
R v. Secretary for Transport, *ex parte* Factortame (No. 5) [1999] 3 WLR 1062; [1999] 4 All ER 906; [1999] 3 CMLR 597 (HL) . . . 252

SA Magnavision NV v. General Optical Council (No. 1) [1987] 1 CMLR 887 (Div. Ct.) . . . 306
SA Magnavision NV v. General Optical Council (No. 2) [1987] 2 CMLR 262 (Div. Ct.) . . . 306, 308
Shields v. E. Coomes (Holdings) Ltd [1978] 1 WLR 1408; [1979] 1 All ER 456 (CA) . . . 277
Stirling District Council v. Allan, 1995 SC 420; [1995] IRLR 301 . . . 238

Thoburn v. Sunderland District Council [2002] 3 WLR 247; [2002] 1 CMLR 50 (DC) . . . 205, 275, 277

Webb v. EMO Air Cargo [1993] 1 WLR 49; [1992] 4 All ER 929 (HL) . . . 238
Webb v. EMO Air Cargo (No. 2) [1995] 1 WLR 1454 (HL) . . . 238

Cases from other National and International Courts

Belgium

Minister for Economic Affairs v. Fromagerie Franco-Suisse 'Le Ski', Cour de Cassation, 21 May 1971 [1972] CMLR 230 . . . 259, 260, 272, 332

Denmark

Carlsen v. Rasmussen, Supreme Court, 6 April 1988, Case I 361/1997, [1999] 3 CMLR 854 . . . 205, 206, 266

European Commission of Human Rights

CFDT (Confédération Française Démocratique du Travail) Case [1978] 12 Decisions and Reports 213 . . . 155
M & Co [1990] 64 Decisions and Reports 138 . . . 155
MSS v. Belgium and Greece, 21 January 2011 (Appeal 30696/09) (Grand Chamber) . . . 155

European Court of Human Rights

Vermuelen v. Belgium [1996] I Reports of Judgments and Decisions 224 . . . 52

France

Boisdet Case, Conseil d'Etat, 24 September 1990, [1991] 1 CMLR 3 . . . 269
Bourrée Case, Conseil d'Etat, 26 July 1944, Rec. Lebon, 217 . . . 455
Cohn-Bendit Case, Conseil d'Etat, 22 December 1978, Dalloz, 1979, 155 . . . 269, 270
Conseil Constitutionnel: Decision of 9 April 1992, [1993] 3 CMLR 345 . . . 270
Conseil Constitutionnel: Decision of 2 September 1992, (Case 92–312) [1992] JORF 12095 . . . 270
Conseil Constitutionnel: Decision of 23 September 1992 (Case 92–313) [1992] JORF 13337 . . . 270
Conseil d'Etat, 13 June 1986, [1986] RTDE 533 . . . 271
Cour de Cassation, 10 December 1986, [1986] RTDE 195 . . . 271
Directeur Général des Douanes v. Société Vabre & Société Weigel, Cour de Cassation, 24 May 1975, [1975] 2 CMLR 336 . . . 268
Maïseries de Beauce Case, Conseil d'Etat, 26 July 1985, [1985] Recueil des Décisions du Conseil d'Etat 233; [1985] AJDA 615, [1986] RTDE 158 . . . 271
Nicolo Case, Conseil d'Etat, 20 October 1989, [1990] 1 CMLR 173 . . . 269

Semoules Case, Conseil d'Etat, 1 March 1968, [1970] CMLR 395 . . . 269, 318

Germany

Brunner v. European Union Treaty, Bundesverfassungsgericht, 12 October 1993, [1994] 1 CMLR 57; (1994) 33 ILM 388; BVerfGE 155 . . . 7, 205, 206, 262, 264, 265

Decision of 25 April 1985, Bundesfinanzhof, (VR 123/84) [1989] 1 CMLR 873 . . . 263

Decision of 8 April 1987, Bundesverfassungsgericht, (2 BvR 687/85), [1987] RIW 878; [1988] 3 CMLR 1 . . . 264

Decision of 30 June 2009, Bundesverfassungsgericht (2 Bve 2/08) . . . 265

Export of Oat Flakes, Re [1969] CMLR 85 . . . 168

Internationale Handelsgesellschaft v. EVGF, Bundesverfassungsgericht, 29 May 1974, [1974] 2 CMLR 540 . . . 261, 262

M GmbH v. Bundesregierung (Tobacco Advertising Case), 12 May 1989, Case 2 BvQ 3/89, [1990] 1 CMLR 570 . . . 262

Value Added Tax Directives, Re, Bundesfinanzhof, 16 July 1981, [1982] 1 CMLR 527 . . . 263

Wunsche Handelsgesellschaft case, Bundesverfassungsgericht, 22 October 1996, [1987] 3 CMLR 225 . . . 264

International Court of Justice

Danzig Railways Officials Case (1928) PCIJ Ser. B No. 15 . . . 205

Italy

Frontini Case, Corte Costituzionale, 27 December 1973, [1974] 2 CMLR 372 . . . 258

Poland

Case K 11/03 . . . 271

Case K 33/03 . . . 271

Case K 15/04 . . . 271

Case K 18/04 . . . 271

Case K 24/04 . . . 271

Case P 1/05 . . . 271

Netherlands

Reinvoorde Case, Hoge Raad, 7 April 1970, [1973] CMLR 175 . . . 303

US

Foster and Elam v. Neilson 2 Pet. 253 . . . 204

Roe v. Wade, 410 US 113 (1973) . . . 150

TABLE OF LEGISLATION

TREATIES AND CONVENTIONS

Accession Treaty 1972 (UK, Denmark and Ireland) . . . 4, 5, 88
art.1(3) . . . 283
arts.2–4 . . . 93
art.9 . . . 14
art.3(1), (2) . . . 273
art.155 . . . 65
Accession Treaty 1979 (Greece) . . . 5, 88
Accession Treaty 1985 (Spain and Portugal) . . . 5, 88
Accession Treaty 1994 (Austria, Finland, and Sweden) . . . 6, 88
Accession Treaty 2003 (Czech Republic, Estonia, Cyprus, Latvia, Lithuania, Hungary, Malta, Poland, Slovenia and Slovakia) . . . 88
Accession Treaty 2005 (Bulgaria and Romania) . . . 88
Accession Treaty 2011 (Croatia) . . . 25, 88
art.9(2) . . . 54
art.20 . . . 25
Agreement on the European Economic Area (EEA Agreement) 1974 . . . 5, 6
Agreement on Trade-Related Aspects of Intellectual Property Rights (TRIPs) 1994 . . . 183
art.50 . . . 195, 196

Brussels Convention on Jurisdiction and the Enforcement of Judgments in Civil and Commercial Matters 1968 . . . 94, 289
art.6 (3) . . . 445
Budgetary Treaty 1970 . . . 6, 88
Budgetary Treaty 1975 . . . 6, 88

Charter of Fundamental Rights of the European Union . . . 8, 9, 156, 158, 230, 377
arts.14, 15 . . . 156
art.21(1) . . . 230
art.25 . . . 156
arts.29, 35 . . . 156
art.47 . . . 377, 450
art.51(1) . . . 158
art.52(2) . . . 157, 158
art.52(3) . . . 157
Convention for the Prevention of Marine Pollution from Land-Based Sources 1975 . . . 185
Convention on Certain Institutions Common to the European Communities 1957 . . . 88, 92

EAEC Treaty (Euratom) . . . 3–5, 14, 30, 75, 88, 92, 99, 101, 175, 177, 186, 187, 324, 407
Title II, Chapter VI . . . 324
art.53 . . . 407
art.76(2) . . . 324
art.101 . . . 177
art.102 . . . 175
art.106a . . . 99
art.107(2) . . . 14
art.108(1) . . . 101
art.108(3) . . . 14
art.141 . . . 324
art.146 . . . 75, 367
art.148 . . . 407
art.184 . . . 174
art.188 . . . 455
art.188(1) . . . 446
art.208 . . . 3
EC Treaty (*see* Treaty on the Functioning of the European Union)
ECSC Treaty . . . 3–5, 30, 65, 74, 87, 92, 131, 145, 327, 328, 336, 354, 361, 365, 404, 405, 412, 413, 416, 431, 432, 434, 451, 460, 465
art.4(c) . . . 404
art.8 . . . 476
art.14 . . . 355, 362
art.33 . . . 149, 327, 328, 401, 404, 405, 425, 432, 434, 448, 456, 464
art.34 . . . 464, 465, 474
art.35 . . . 327, 328, 404, 405, 416,
art.36 . . . 145, 416
art.38 . . . 74
art.40 . . . 69, 456, 464, 474
art.41 . . . 299
art.80 . . . 464
art.88 . . . 328, 336, 404, 413, 476
art.92 . . . 132
art.95 . . . 74
art.97 . . . 3
art.98 . . . 4
art.100 . . . 65
European Convention on Human Rights (ECHR) 1950 . . . 11, 21, 73, 101, 102–4, 118, 144, 152–4, 156, 157, 159, 185, 187–9, 206, 255, 377

art.6 . . . 52, 152, 281, 377
arts.7, 8 . . . 152
art.8(1) . . . 152
art.10(1) . . . 152
art.13 . . . 152, 377
art.14 . . . 102
art.36 . . . 155
art.59 . . . 154
art.63 . . . 102
Protocol 1 . . . 152
European Schools Convention 1994 . . . 294
European Social Charter 1961 . . . 152

General Agreement on Tariffs and Trade (GATT) 1994 . . . 193, 241–3, 286, 316
General Agreement on Trade in Services (GATS) 1995 . . . 183

International Labour Organisation, Convention 111, 1958 . . . 152

Lomé Convention II 1979 . . . 356
Luxembourg Convention 1956 . . . 181

Mannheim Convention 1868 . . . 181
Merger Treaty 1965 (Treaty Establishing a Single Council and a Single Commission of the European Communities) . . . 4, 88

North American Free Trade Agreement (NAFTA) 1994 . . . 5
North-East Atlantic Fisheries Convention 1959 . . . 180

Protocols to the EU Treaties—
Protocol No. 1 on the Role of National Parliaments in the European Union . . . 44
arts.3, 4 . . . 102
Protocol No. 2 on the Application of the Principles of Subsidiarity and Proportionality . . . 124
arts.2–5 . . . 124
art.6 . . . 125
art.8 . . . 126, 127
Protocol No. 3 on the Statute of the Court of Justice of the European Union . . . 49, 52, 309
art.3 . . . 451
art.4 . . . 50
art.6 . . . 50
art.9A . . . 50
art.16 . . . 50
art.16(3), (4) . . . 50
art.19 . . . 64
art.23 . . . 309
art.23a . . . 311
art.42 . . . 62
arts.43, 44 . . . 63
art.48 . . . 54
arts.49, 50 . . . 55
art.50(2) . . . 55
art.51 . . . 58
art.54(2) . . . 71
arts.56–61 . . . 59
art.61(2) . . . 71
art.62c . . . 55
Annex I—The European Union Civil Service Tribunal . . . 55
art.1 . . . 60
art.2 . . . 55
arts.9–13 . . . 60
art.11 . . . 55
Protocol No. 7 on the Privileges and Immunities of the European Union . . . 30
arts.7–9 . . . 16
art.11–15 [12–16] . . . 30
art.11(a) . . . 455
art.17 [18] . . . 30, 455
Protocol No. 14 on the Euro Group . . . 154
Protocol No.17 concerning Article 141 of the Treaty establishing the European Community 1992 . . . 76
Protocol No. 19 integrating the Schengen Acquis into the Framework of the European Union . . . 96
Protocol No. 20 on the Application of Certain Aspects of Article 26 of the Treaty on the Functioning of the European Union to the United Kingdom and Ireland . . . 96
Protocol No. 21 on the Position of the United Kingdom and Ireland in Respect of the Area of Freedom, Security and Justice . . . 96
Protocol No. 22 on the Position of Denmark . . . 96
Protocol No. 30 on the Application of the Charter of Fundamental Rights of the European Union to Poland and to the United Kingdom . . . 9
Protocol No. 36 on Transitional Provisions—
art.3(2) . . . 26
art.3(3) . . . 25

Rome Convention on the Law Applicable to Contractual Obligations 1980 . . . 94
art.20 . . . 99
Rules of Procedure of the European Court of Justice 1991 . . . 50, 191, 363
art.4 . . . 50
art.10 . . . 55
art.11(1) . . . 55
art.12 . . . 50, 363
art.14 . . . 51
art.14(1), (2) . . . 55
art.17 . . . 55

art.18 . . . 53, 55
art.19 . . . 55
arts.36–41 . . . 67
art.37(3) . . . 67
art.38(4) . . . 67
art.38(8) . . . 68
art.44(5a) . . . 444
art.102 . . . 64
art.103 . . . 62
arts.105, 106 . . . 64
arts.107, 108 . . . 191
arts.107–114 . . . 64
arts.115–118 . . . 65
arts.133–146 . . . 64
art.155 . . . 62
art.157 . . . 62
arts.158, 159 . . . 63
arts.185–189 . . . 65

Single European Act 1986 . . . 7, 54, 88, 123, 153
Preamble . . . 153
art.2 . . . 22
art.3(1) . . . 13
Statute of the International Court of Justice—
art. 38(1)(c) . . . 144

Treaty Amending Certain Provisions of the Protocol on the Statute of the European Investment Bank 1975 . . . 88
Treaty Creating the Court of Justice of the Cartagena Agreement 1979—
arts.28–31 . . . 281
Treaty Establishing the European Community (EC Treaty) (see Treaty on the Functioning of the European Union)
Treaty Establishing the European Stability Mechanism 2012 (ESM Treaty) . . . 10, 38, 96–98
Recital 6 . . . 38
art.8(1) . . . 38
art.37(2), (3) . . . 97
Treaty of Amsterdam 1997 . . . 8, 88, 96, 153, 368
art.6 . . . 100
art.9 . . . 3, 4
Treaty of Lisbon 2007 . . . 8–10, 15, 23, 49, 54, 64, 88, 89, 99, 106, 111, 112, 115, 118, 130, 137, 156, 174, 185, 187, 272, 338, 364, 368, 370, 379, 385, 386, 412, 438
Protocol No 2 to the Lisbon Treaty Amending the Treaty Establishing the EAEC . . . 99
art.3 . . . 99
Treaty on European Union 1992 (TEU) . . . 7, 8, 27, 88, 99, 156, 175, 266, 270, 364, 367, 368
Preamble . . . 153
Title IV [ex Title VII] . . . 8
Title V [ex Title V] . . . 8
ex Title VI . . . 8
art.1 . . . 8
art.2 . . . 93, 94
art.2(5) . . . 117
art.3 . . . 115
art.3(3) . . . 115
art.4(1) . . . 112
art.4(3) [5 EC] . . . 210, 211, 249, 319, 320
art.5 . . . 118
art.5(1) . . . 112
art.5(2) . . . 56
art.5(3) . . . 123
art.5(4) . . . 124
art.6 . . . 156, 438
art.6(1) . . . 106, 153, 230
art.6(2) [F(2)] . . . 153, 154
art.7 . . . 93, 153, 158, 438
art.7(1) . . . 93
art.7(2) . . . 15
art.8(2) . . . 176
art.10(4) . . . 17
art.12 . . . 438
art.13 . . . 13, 364, 450, 454
art.13(4) . . . 35
art.14 [189/137 EC] . . . 13
art.14(2) . . . 15
art.14(3) . . . 14
art.15 . . . 22
art.15(4) . . . 22
art.15(6)(a) . . . 24
art.16(2) [203/146 EC] . . . 23
art.16(4) . . . 26
art.16(7) . . . 24
art.16(9) . . . 24
art.17(1) . . . 114, 321
art.17(3) . . . 28
art.17(4), (5) . . . 27
art.17(6) . . . 28
art.17(7) [214/158 EC] . . . 20, 27
art.17(8) . . . 28
art.18 . . . 34
art.18(2) . . . 34
art.18(3) . . . 24
art.19 [220/164 EC] . . . 49, 145, 146
art.19(1) . . . 435
art.19(2) . . . 54
art.20 . . . 43
art.20(2) . . . 44
art.20(4) . . . 44
art.24 . . . 134
art.24(1) . . . 33, 316
art.26 . . . 134
art.27(3) . . . 34
art.31(1), (2) . . . 33
art.37 . . . 176
art.40 . . . 33, 117

art.42(1)–(3) . . . 34
art.48 . . . 89–92, 118
art.48(2), (3) . . . 89
art.48(5)–(7) . . . 90
art.49 . . . 93, 153
art.49(2) . . . 93
art.50 . . . 93
art.51 . . . 88
art.55 . . . 65
Protocol Concerning Article 141 [119] of the Treaty Establishing the European Community . . . 76
Protocols common to the EU Treaties *see* Protocols to the EU Treaties
Treaty of Nice 2002 . . . 8, 88, 367
Treaty on Stability, Co-ordination and Governance in the Economic and Monetary Union (Fiscal Compact) 2012 . . . 10, 96–8
art.2(1), (2) . . . 97
art.3(2) . . . 97
art.8 . . . 97
Treaty on the Functioning of the European Union (TFEU) (formerly the Treaty Establishing the European Community (EC Treaty) . . . 3–5, 9, 30, 87, 94–6, 99, 101, 123, 156, 175, 178, 189
ex Part One . . . 179, 197
art.2(1), (2) . . . 119
art.2(5) . . . 119
art.3 . . . 119
art.3(2) . . . 176, 185, 186
art.4(3), (4) . . . 119
ex art.5/3b . . . 420
art.6 . . . 119
ex art.9 . . . 117
art.16(4), (5) . . . 135
art.18 [12/6 EC] . . . 145, 168
art.20(20(a) . . . 322
ex art.27 . . . 116, 117
ex art.28 . . . 117
art.30 [25/12 EC] . . . 209, 210
art.31 [26/28 EC] . . . 121
art.34 [28/30 EC] . . . 319
art.36 [30/36 EC] . . . 252, 253
art.40(2) [34(2/40(3) EC] . . . 168, 169
art.43(2) [37(2)/43(2) EC] . . . 130
art.45 [39/48 EC] . . . 234
art.45(2) [39(2)/48(2) EC] . . . 234
art.45(3) [39(3)/48(3) EC] . . . 212, 213, 219
art.45(4) [39(4)/48(4) EC] . . . 234, 235
art.48(6) . . . 37
art.52 [45/56 EC] . . . 151
art.52(1) [46(1)/56(1) EC] . . . 151
art.62 [55/66 EC] . . . 151
arts 67 [61/73i EC] . . . 96
art.76 . . . 125
art.79(3) [art. 63 pts 3, 4/73k(3), (4) EC] . . . 176
art.101 [81/85 EC] . . . 170, 351, 359
art.101(1) [81(1)/85(1) EC] . . . 351, 352
art.101(3) [81(3)/85(3) EC] . . . 351, 352
art.103 [83/87 EC] . . . 130
art.106 [86/90 EC] . . . 413
art.106(3) [86(3)/90(3) EC] . . . 327
arts.107–109 [87–89/92–94 EC] . . . 211
art.107 [87/92 EC] . . . 211, 359
art.107(1) [87(1)/92(1) EC] . . . 211
art.108 [88/93 EC] . . . 333, 334, 413
art.108(2) [88(2)/93(2) EC] . . . 211, 315, 333, 413
art.109 [89/94 EC] . . . 333
ex art.111 . . . 117
ex art.113 . . . 117, 120, 121
art.114 [95/100a EC] . . . 121, 122
art.114(9) [95(9)/100a(4) EC] . . . 315
art.115 [94/100 EC] . . . 114
art.122(2) . . . 37
art.125(1) . . . 37
art.136 . . . 37
art.153 [137/118 EC] . . . 113, 114
art.157 [141/119 EC] . . . 75, 76, 169, 213
art.165(1) [149(1)/126(1) EC] . . . 118
art.186 [170/130m EC] . . . 176
ex art.189(2) EC . . . 14
ex art.190(1)/138(1) EC . . . 101
art.190(4)/138(3) EC . . . 14
art.191(4) [art.174(4)/130r(4) EC] . . . 123, 176
art.192 [175/130s EC] . . . 121, 122
ex art.203/146 EC . . . 23
art.207 [133/113 EC] . . . 176, 188
art.207(1)/151 (1) EC . . . 24
art.209(2) [179(2)/130w EC] . . . 176
art.216(1) . . . 176, 185, 186
art.216(2) [300(7)/228(7) EC] . . . 192, 196, 242, 316
art.217 [310/238 EC] . . . 176
art.218 [300/228 EC] . . . 154, 187
art.218(6)(a)(iii) [300(3)/228(3)] . . . 191
art.218(6)(b) [300(3)/228(3)] . . . 188
art.218(11) [300(6)/228(6) EC] . . . 118, 183, 184, 189–91, 196
art.219 [111/109 EC] . . . 176, 188
art.223(1) [190(4)/138(3) EC] . . . 15, 102
art.225 [192/138b EC] . . . 17
art.226 [193/138c EC] . . . 17
ex art.226 EEC . . . 432, 433
ex art.226(3) EEC . . . 433
art.227 [194/138d EC] . . . 18
art.228 [195/138e EC] . . . 18
art.228(1) [195(1)/138e(1) EC] . . . 44
art.230 [197/140 EC] . . . 17, 130

art.231 [198/141 EC] . . . 41
art.234 [201/144 EC] . . . 20
art.235 . . . 24
art.235(1) . . . 22
art.238 [205(1), (3)/148(1), (3)EC] . . . 26
art.238(1) [205(1)/148(3) EC] . . . 25
art.238(4) [205(3)/148(3) EC] . . . 25, 33
art.240 [207(1)/151(1) EC] . . . 24
art.240(2) [207(2)/151(2) EC] . . . 24
art.245 [213/157 EC] . . . 28
art.246 [215/159 EC] . . . 28
art.247 [216/160 EC] . . . 28
art.248 [217(2) EC] . . . 29
art.250 [219/163 EC] . . . 30
arts.251–281 [221–245/165–188 EC] . . . 49
art.251 [221/165 EC] . . . 50, 102
art.252 [222/166 EC] . . . 51
art.252(2) . . . 51
art.253 [223/167 EC] . . . 49, 95
art.253(5) . . . 53
art.254 [224/168 EC] . . . 55
art.254(2), (3) . . . 55
art.255 . . . 49, 78
art.256 [225/168a EC] . . . 58
art.256(1) . . . 59
art.257 [225a EC] . . . 55, 60
art.257(4) . . . 55
art.258 [226/169 EC] . . . 92, 103, 242, 245, 249, 259, 302, 316, 318–21, 323, 324, 329–32, 334, 336, 339, 404, 407, 408, 411, 413, 416, 459, 479
arts.258–260 [226–228/169–171 EC] . . . 315, 332–4
art.259 [227/170 EC] . . . 103, 269, 327, 329, 330, 479
art.260 [228/171 EC] . . . 326, 331, 333, 334, 336, 338, 339
art.260(3) . . . 338, 339
art. 261 [229/172 EC] . . . 411
art.263 [230/173 EC] . . . 35, 58, 74, 75, 104, 120, 126, 127, 146, 160, 189, 198, 284, 285, 326, 327, 349–54, 357, 362, 364, 365, 367, 368, 375, 379, 382, 384, 385, 392, 393, 395–403, 405–8, 411, 413–19, 434, 451, 459, 461, 465, 467
art.264 [231/174 EC] . . . 349, 437, 438, 441
art.265 [232/175 EC] . . . 58, 127, 392–408, 411, 416, 435, 451, 466
art.266 [233/176 EC] . . . 400, 408, 438–41, 465
art.267 [234/177 EC] . . . 35, 64, 192, 219, 220, 237, 246, 248, 263, 264, 275, 282–4, 286, 288–99, 303, 305, 306, 308, 311–13, 316–18, 323, 327, 332, 410, 412, 416, 417, 441
art.267(a) . . . 283, 284
art.267(b) . . . 282, 284, 285
art.268 [235/178 EC] . . . 58, 411, 449, 450, 466
art.270 [236/179 EC] . . . 58, 354, 416, 449
art.271 [237/180 EC] . . . 315, 364
art.272 [238/181 EC] . . . 58, 411, 443, 444
art.273 . . . 97
art.274 [240/183 EC] . . . 441, 444
art.275 . . . 33
art.276 . . . 394
art.277 [241/184 EC] . . . 411–13, 415, 416
art.279 [243/186 EC] . . . 331, 336
art.280 [244/187 EC] . . . 62
art.282(1), (3) . . . 31
art.283(2) . . . 31
arts.285–287 [246–248/188a–188c EC] . . . 32
art.288 [249/189 EC] . . . 108, 109, 110, 137, 206, 215–19, 223, 224, 240, 263, 350, 449
art.289 . . . 111, 350
art.289(1)–(3) . . . 111
art.289(4) . . . 111
art.290 . . . 129, 135, 136
art.290(1) . . . 111
art.291 . . . 111, 134–6
art.291(1), (2) . . . 134
art.293 [250/189a EC] . . . 39
art.293(1) [250(1)/189a(1)] . . . 41
art.294 [251/189b EC] . . . 38
art.294(14) [251(7)/189b(7) EC] . . . 40
art.296 [253/190 EC] . . . 110, 138
art.296(2) . . . 136–40, 422
art.297 [254/191 EC] . . . 141, 217, 363
art.297(1), third para [254(1)/191(1) EC] . . . 141
art.297(2), second para [254(1)/191(1) EC] . . . 141
art.297(2), third para [254(3)/191(3) EC] . . . 142
art.299 [256/192 EC] . . . 62
art.300(2)–(4) . . . 35, 36
art.304 [262/198 EC] . . . 36
art.308 [266/198d EC] . . . 35, 185
ex art.309 . . . 153
art.309 [267/198e EC] . . . 35
arts.313–319 [268–280/199–209a EC] . . . 42
art.314 [272/203 EC] . . . 42
art.317 [274/205 EC] . . . 43
art.319 [276/206 EC] . . . 43
arts.326–334 [arts.27a–27e, 40–40b, 43–45 TEU, 11, 11a EC] . . . 43
art.329(2) . . . 44
art.331 [arts.27a–27e, 40–40b, 43–45 TEU, 11, 11a EC] . . . 44
art.335 [282/211 EC] . . . 452
art.340 [288/215 EC] . . . 146, 166, 198, 411, 445, 446, 449, 450, 452–5, 459–61, 464–8, 473, 475, 482, 484, 485

art.342 [290/217 EC] . . . 65
art.348 [298/225 EC] . . . 315, 331
art.351 [307/234 EC] . . . 100, 103, 105, 106, 151, 161, 194, 287
art.352 [308/235 EC] . . . 95, 114, 116–21, 185, 186, 266, 267, 420
art.352(2) . . . 117, 119
art.352(3)–(4) . . . 113, 117
art.354 [309/236 EC] . . . 94, 158
art.355 [299(2)–(6)/227(2)–(5)] . . . 293
art.355(3) [299(4)/227(4) EC] . . . 102
art.356 [312/240 EC] . . . 3
art.357 [313/247 EC] . . . 9
art.358 . . . 65
Protocols see Protocols to the EU Treaties

United Nations Charter 1945 . . . 91, 105, 106, 161
art.25 . . . 104
Chapter VII . . . 104
art.41 . . . 161
art.48(2) . . . 161
art.103 . . . 104, 161
art.108 . . . 91

Vienna Convention on the Law of Treaties 1969 . . . 92, 271
art.4 . . . 92, 98
art.5 . . . 91, 98, 99
art.30 . . . 92, 98, 100, 103
art.30(1) . . . 104
art.30(2) . . . 92, 98, 100
art.30(3) . . . 92, 98
art.30(4) . . . 98
art.30(4)(a) . . . 98
art.30(4)(b) . . . 99
art.53 . . . 83, 105
art.54(b) . . . 92
WTO Agreement 1995 . . . 183, 193, 242, 461

UNITED KINGDOM STATUTES

British Nationality Act 1981 . . . 89
Carriage of Goods by Sea Act 1971—
s.2(1) . . . 204
Civil Jurisdiction and Judgments Act 1982 . . . 289
s.16(3) . . . 289
Sch.4 . . . 289
art.5(1), (3) . . . 289
European Communities Act 1972 . . . 210, 259, 272, 276–8, 308
s.1(1) . . . 87
s.1(2), (3) . . . 273
s.2 . . . 276
s.2(1) . . . 205, 274, 276, 308
s.2(2) . . . 274, 275, 277
s.2(4) . . . 275, 276
s.3(1) . . . 272, 276, 313
Sch.1, Part.I . . . 87
Sch.1, Part.II . . . 274
Sch.2 . . . 275
para.1 . . . 275
para.2(1) . . . 274
para.2(2) . . . 274
European Communities (Amendment) Act 1993 . . . 7
European Parliamentary Elections Act 2002—
s.12 . . . 273
European Parliament (Representations) Act 2003—
Part.2 . . . 103
European Union Act 2011 . . . 206
s.18 . . . 278
European Union (Amendment) Act 2008—
Sch.1(1), para.1 . . . 274
Equal Pay Act 1970 . . . 76
Gas Act 1972—
s.2(1) . . . 234
ss.4, 7, 29 . . . 234
Human Rights Act 1998 . . . 206
s.3 . . . 206
s.4 . . . 206
Merchant Shipping Act 1988—
Pt.II . . . 247
Weights and Measures Act 1985 . . . 277

UNITED KINGDOM STATUTORY INSTRUMENTS

Civil Procedure Rules 1998 (SI No 1998/3132) . . . 308
Part 68 . . . 308, 309
r.68.2(1) . . . 305, 308
r.68.2(1)(a) . . . 303
r.68.3(1) . . . 308
r.68.4 . . . 308
PD.68 . . . 308
PD.68, para 2.1 . . . 308
European Communities (Definition of Treaties) Order (SI No 1976/217) . . . 87
European Communities (Enforcement of Community Judgments) Order 1972 (SI No 1972/1590) . . . 275
European Parliamentary Elections (Combined Region and Campaign Expenditure) (United Kingdom and Gibraltar) Order 2004 (SI No 2004/366) . . . 103
Merchant Shipping (Registration of Fishing Vessels) Regulations 1988 (SI No 1988/1926) . . . 247

ABBREVIATIONS

AJDA	L'Actualité Juridique: Droit Aministratif
Am. Jo. Comp. L.	American Journal of Comparative Law
Am. J. Int. L.	American Journal of International Law
BYIL	British Yearbook of International Law
BVerfGE	Bundesverfassungsgericht
CDE	Cahiers de Droit Européen
CFSP	Common Foreign and Security Policy
CJEL	Columbia Journal of European Law
CLJ	Cambridge Law Journal
CLP	Current Legal Problems
CMLR	Common Market Law Reports
CMLRev.	Common Market Law Review
COREPER	Committee of Permanent Representatives
CPR	Civil Procedure Rules
EAEC	European Atomic Energy Community (also known as Euratom)
EC	European Community
ECB	European Central Bank
EC Bull.	Bulletin of the European Communities
ECHR	European Convention for the Protection of Human Rights and Fundamental Freedoms
ECJ	Court of Justice (European Court)
ECLR	European Competition Law Review
ECOSOC	Economic and Social Committee
ECR	European Court Reports (official reports of the judgments of the European Court, English version)
ECSC	European Coal and Steel Community
EEA	European Economic Area
EEC	European Economic Community
EFSM	European Financial Stability Mechanism
EFSF	European Financial Stability Facility
EFTA	European Free Trade Association
EHRR	European Human Rights Reports
ELJ	European Law Journal
ELRev.	European Law Review

EP	European Parliament
EPC	European Political Co-operation
ERTA	European Road Transport Agreement
ESM	European Stability Mechanism
EU	European Union
Euratom	European Atomic Energy Community
FIDE	International Federation for European Law
GATS	General Agreement on Trade in Services
GATT	General Agreement on Tariffs and Trade
ICJ	International Court of Justice
ICLQ	International and Comparative Law Quarterly
ILM	International Legal Materials
ILO	International Labour Organization
JCMS	Journal of Common Market Studies
JO	Journal Officiel (French version of OJ)
JORF	Journal Officiel de la République Française
LIEI	Legal Issues of European Integration
LQR	Law Quarterly Review
MCA	Monetary Compensatory Amount
MEP	Member of the European Parliament
MLR	Modern Law Review
NAFTA	North American Free Trade Agreement
OJ	Official Journal (of the European Communities)
OJLS	Oxford Journal of Legal Studies
PCIJ	Permanent Court of International Justice
PL	Public Law
RDI	Rivista di Diritto Internazionale
Rec.	Recueil de la jurisprudence de la Cour de Justice des Communautés européennes (French version of ECR)
RIW	Recht der Internationalen Wirtschaft
RMC	Revue du Marché Commun
RTDE	Revue Trimestrielle de Droit Européen
SEA	Single European Act
SEW	Sociaal-Economische Wetgeving
TEU	Treaty on European Union (Maastricht Agreement)
TFEU	Treaty on the Functioning of the European Union
TRIPs	Agreement on Trade-Related Aspects of Intellectual Property Rights
TSCG	Treaty on Stability, Co-ordination and Governance (the 'Fiscal Compact')

UNCTAD	United Nations Conference on Trade and Development
WTO	World Trade Organization
WTO DSB	World Trade Organization Dispute Settlement Body
YEL	Yearbook of European Law

GUIDE TO THE ONLINE RESOURCE CENTRE

The Foundations of European Union Law is accompanied by a free Online Resource Centre which contains a range of resources designed to support you throughout your EU law module.

www.oxfordtextbooks.co.uk/orc/hartley8e /

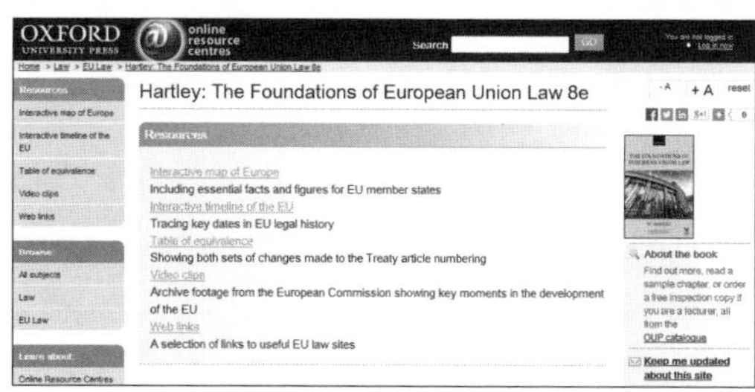

Get started . . .

If you're studying EU law for the first time the Online Resource Centre provides a range of resources to help build your understanding and prepare for your first lectures including:

- Interactive map of the EU with key facts on each Member State
- Interactive timeline of the development of the EU
- Video clips of key moments in the EU's development
- Quick-reference and searchable guide of all EU Article renumbering

Prepare for exams . . .

The Online Resource Centre includes a guide to further web resources to help you pursue areas of interest and help with your revision.

Stay up to date . . .

The Online Resource Centre provides updates from the authors on key developments in EU law as well as links to the latest EU law blogs and the European Commission's YouTube channel.

PART I

EUROPEAN UNION INSTITUTIONS

INTRODUCTION

What is now known as the 'European Union' was previously called the 'European Community'. In the past, there were three Communities. The first to be established was the European Coal and Steel Community (ECSC). The ECSC Treaty was signed on 18 April 1951, and stated that it was concluded for a period of fifty years.[1] It entered into force on 23 July 1952 and terminated in 2002.

The signatories to the ECSC Treaty were the six original Member States: Germany, Belgium, France, Italy, Luxembourg, and the Netherlands. The United Kingdom was invited to take part, but declined to do so. The signing took place in Paris – for this reason it is sometimes called the 'Treaty of Paris' – and the French version was the sole authentic text. Four principal institutions were created: the Council (representing the Member States); the Commission (a supranational executive, which was originally called the 'High Authority'); the Assembly; and the Court. Except for the Assembly, which normally met in Strasbourg, they were all located in Luxembourg.

Next came the European Economic Community (EEC) (subsequently renamed the 'European Community' or 'EC') and the European Atomic Energy Community ('EAEC' or 'Euratom'). The EEC Treaty and the EAEC Treaty[2] were both signed in Rome on 25 March 1957 and entered into force on 1 January 1958. They were concluded for an unlimited period.[3] The United Kingdom was again invited to participate but dropped out of the preliminary discussions. The signatories were therefore the same six States, but this time the texts in each of their official languages – German, French, Italian, and Dutch – were equally authentic. Separate Commissions and Councils were created for each of the new Communities, but all three shared the same Assembly and Court.[4] The new Councils and Commissions met in Brussels.

The three Treaties contained many common features, but there were also important differences. One difference was that the ECSC Treaty was more specific as regards the policy to be pursued; the EEC Treaty, on the other hand, was concerned mainly with creating a framework, and left the creation of policy to the institutions. The consequence of this was that the institutions were required to play a more

[1] Art. 97 ECSC.

[2] The reason a separate Treaty was signed governing the non-military use of atomic energy was the fear that the EEC Treaty might be rejected by the French Parliament. It was hoped that, in such an eventuality, at least the EAEC Treaty could be saved.

[3] Art. 356 TFEU [312/240 EC]; Art. 208 EAEC.

[4] The establishment of a single Assembly and Court for the three Communities was effected by a separate Treaty: the Convention on Certain Institutions Common to the European Communities, which entered into force on the same date as the EEC and EAEC Treaties. It was repealed by Art. 9 of the Treaty of Amsterdam, its operative provisions having been moved to the other Treaties.

creative role in the EEC. This difference was in turn responsible for another distinction between the ECSC and EEC Treaties: under the former, the Commission had much more independent power (and the Council correspondingly less) than under the EEC Treaty. In the EEC, therefore, the balance of power was more in favour of the Council.

On the purely legal level, the EEC and EAEC Treaties are very similar – many provisions concerning legal remedies are identical – while significant differences were to be found in the ECSC Treaty. This can be explained by the fact that the EEC and EAEC Treaties were drafted at the same time and the drafters were obviously influenced by the experience gained from the operation of the ECSC Treaty.

It was, of course, illogical and inconvenient for the two most important institutions to be triplicated, so a Merger Treaty (officially known as the Treaty Establishing a Single Council and a Single Commission of the European Communities) was signed in Brussels on 8 April 1965 and entered into force on 1 July 1967.[5] This Treaty did not merge the Communities themselves but merged the three Commissions to form a single Commission and merged the three Councils to form a single Council. The new Council and Commission were located in Brussels.[6] In order to compensate Luxembourg for this loss, it was agreed that some Council meetings would be held there. In addition, certain other EU activities are run from Luxembourg, and the European Court still sits there. The European Parliament sits in Strasbourg but holds some sessions, as well as its committee meetings, in Brussels;[7] its secretariat is based in Luxembourg.[8] The end result is highly inconvenient and inefficient and shows that, even in the simplest matters, common objectives have to give way before national interests.

The next step was the widening of membership. Britain's original attitude of disdain changed in the early 1960s, and in 1961 the Conservative Government of Mr Harold Macmillan took the decision to seek entry. Initially, Britain's application was blocked by General De Gaulle; but Britain persevered, and on 22 January 1972 the Final Act was signed which embodied the instruments of accession of the United Kingdom, Ireland, Denmark, and Norway.[9] Norway dropped out when a referendum showed

[5] It was repealed by Art. 9 of the Treaty of Amsterdam, its operative provisions having been moved to the other Treaties.

[6] For a long time the institutions were given only temporary seats and it was not until the 1992 Edinburgh Summit that these were made permanent.

[7] For litigation prior to the Edinburgh decision on the seat of the Parliament, see *Luxembourg v. European Parliament*, Case 230/81, [1983] ECR 255 and *France v. European Parliament*, Cases 358/85, 51/86, [1988] ECR 4821. For litigation subsequent to the Edinburgh decision, see *France v. European Parliament*, Case C-345/95, [1997] ECR I-5215.

[8] Attempts by the Parliament itself to rationalize the situation by moving its staff to its places of work were declared illegal by the European Court at the suit of Luxembourg: *Luxembourg v. European Parliament*, Case 108/83, [1984] ECR 1945. See also *Luxembourg v. European Parliament*, Cases C-213/88, C-39/89, [1991] ECR I-5643.

[9] The new Member States actually joined the EEC and EAEC through ratification of the Treaty of Accession, and the ECSC by depositing an instrument of accession on the basis of the Decision of Accession. The latter was a decision of the Council of the European Communities under Art. 98 ECSC. The terms of admission are

that a majority of the Norwegian electorate opposed entry; but the other three new Member States joined on 1 January 1973. English, Danish, and Irish became official languages and the translations into these languages of the EEC and EAEC Treaties were declared to be authentic texts.

Greece was the next country to join. On 28 May 1979 the Treaty of Accession and other relevant instruments were signed in Athens, and Greece became the tenth Member State on 1 January 1981. Spain and Portugal followed. The relevant instruments were signed on 12 June 1985 and membership came into effect on 1 January 1986. There were then twelve Member States, and the official languages included Greek, Portuguese, and Spanish.

In 1991, negotiations were concluded with the members of the European Free Trade Area (EFTA) – Norway, Sweden, Finland, Iceland, Switzerland, Liechtenstein,[10] and Austria – for an agreement to establish the European Economic Area (EEA).[11] This agreement, which some saw originally as a substitute for membership, was intended to integrate the EFTA countries economically into the Union (then the Community) without giving them a role in its institutions. In the relevant areas,[12] Union law from all sources – treaty provisions, legislation, and rules laid down by the European Court – was made applicable to them.[13] This covered not only the law as it existed when the agreement was concluded, but also new legislation which might be adopted in the future, as well as future decisions of the European Court. Under the terms of the agreement, if the EFTA countries refused to accept these new rules, they risked losing their rights in the sector in question. This scheme had great attractions – it created the world's largest trading area[14] – but it also had serious drawbacks. In particular, it meant that the EFTA countries would have to apply rules of law, in the making of which they would have had virtually no say.[15]

In 1991, the European Court declared the EEA Agreement incompatible with the EEC Treaty.[16] The reasons for this were complex, but they centred on the European Court's objection to the creation of a rival court, the proposed EEA Court. Since this would have had jurisdiction to interpret EEA law, it would have had great influence on the development of Union law. The European Court's objections were not assuaged by

laid down in the Act of Accession, which is an integral part of both the Treaty of Accession and the Decision of Accession.

[10] At the time, Liechtenstein was not a member of EFTA but had applied to join.

[11] On the Union side, the parties were the EEC and the ECSC as legal entities and the twelve individual Member States; on the EFTA side, they were the States just listed.

[12] These include free movement of goods (but only regarding products originating in the Contracting States), persons, services, and capital. Agriculture is excluded.

[13] In some cases, modifications were made.

[14] Though smaller in area than the territory covered by the North American Free Trade Agreement (NAFTA), it had more consumers and a greater gross domestic product.

[15] For details, see Reymond, 'Institutions, Decision-Making Procedure and Settlement of Disputes in the European Economic Area' (1993) 30 CMLRev. 449; Cremona, 'The "Dynamic and Homogeneous" EEA: Byzantine Structures and Variable Geometry' (1994) 19 ELRev. 508; Christiansen, 'The EFTA Court' (1997) 22 ELRev. 539.

[16] *First EEA Case*, Opinion 1/91, [1991] ECR I-6079.

the fact that the majority of judges on the EEA Court would have been judges from the European Court; indeed, this was an added grievance.[17]

The agreement was then amended to meet the European Court's objections and the new version was approved by the Court in 1992.[18] A further setback occurred when the agreement was rejected by the Swiss voters in a referendum, which meant that Switzerland had to drop out.[19] However, it eventually came into force on 1 January 1994 between the Union countries and Norway, Sweden, Finland, Iceland, and Austria. Liechtenstein joined later, after a referendum in 1995.

Even before the EEA Agreement had come into force, most of the EFTA countries had applied to join the Union. The Swiss dropped out of these negotiations when their electorate rejected the EEA,[20] but Austria, Finland, Norway, and Sweden persevered. The Accession Treaty for these countries was signed on 24 June 1994. Referendums in Austria, Finland, and Sweden approved membership; but the Norwegian electorate again rejected it. On 1 January 1995, Austria, Finland, and Sweden became Member States of the Union; only Iceland, Liechtenstein, and Norway remained in EFTA. The Union then had fifteen members; Finnish and Swedish became official Union languages.[21]

The next group of new members consisted of eight former Communist countries (Lithuania, Latvia, Estonia, Poland, the Czech Republic, Slovakia, Hungary, and Slovenia) and two Mediterranean islands (Malta and Cyprus). They joined on 1 May 2004. The Union then had twenty-five members. Lithuanian, Latvian, Estonian, Polish, Czech, Slovak, Hungarian, Slovenian, and Maltese became official languages. Bulgaria and Romania joined on 1 January 2007, adding their languages to the total; while Croatia became a Member State on 1 July 2013: its language was also included. There are now twenty-eight Member States and twenty-three official languages. The translation difficulties are immense.

In 1985 Greenland left the Union following a referendum held in 1982 in which there was a narrow majority in favour of withdrawal. Greenland was not a Member State but, being associated with Denmark (though with internal self-government), was part of the Union.[22]

The structure of the Union has already undergone considerable change in the course of its development. In addition to the treaties previously mentioned, amendments have been made by the first and second Budgetary Treaties, 1970 and 1975, and by the

[17] See, further, Hartley, 'The European Court and the EEA' (1992) 41 ICLQ 841.

[18] *Second EEA Case*, Opinion 1/92, [1992] ECR I-2821. The Agreement was finally signed in Oporto, Portugal, on 2 May 1992.

[19] As a result, the Agreement had to be amended by a Protocol signed in Brussels on 17 March 1993.

[20] In 2001, a referendum was held in Switzerland on a proposal that the Government should commence negotiations for membership of the European Union. It was rejected by a majority of approximately 3:1.

[21] For further details, see Goebel, 'The European Union Grows: The Constitutional Impact of the Accession of Austria, Finland and Sweden' (1995) 18 *Fordham International Law Journal* 1092; Lee Miles (ed.), *The European Union and the Nordic Countries* (1996).

[22] It is now associated with the Union. For further details, see Weiss, 'Greenland's Withdrawal from the European Communities' (1985) 10 ELRev. 173.

Single European Act of 1986, which came into force on 1 July 1987. Other changes have resulted from the establishment of political (constitutional) conventions and practices which have developed without any formal legal foundation.

Further changes resulted from the Treaty on European Union (TEU). This was signed in Maastricht, a provincial town in the Netherlands, on 7 February 1992 and came into force on 1 November 1993. Of all the amending treaties (up until then), this had the most difficult birth. It was rejected by a referendum in Denmark (though this was reversed in a later referendum, held after a Union summit in Edinburgh had produced a gloss on the Treaty provisions of most concern to Denmark)[23] and almost rejected by a referendum in France. Opinion polls in both Germany and Britain showed considerable opposition.

In the United Kingdom, the necessary legislation[24] was passed only after great turmoil; indeed, it could have brought the Government down.[25] The anti-Maastricht forces then resorted to the courts: an action was brought by a well-known journalist, Lord Rees-Mogg, for a declaration that the United Kingdom could not lawfully ratify the Treaty.[26] Only when this had failed, was the way open for British ratification.

In the end, Britain was not the last country to ratify. Germany's ratification was delayed even longer by legal proceedings in the Constitutional Court and, though ratification was eventually permitted, the judgment made clear that the German Constitution (*Grundgesetz*) imposes definite limits on Germany's participation in a federal Europe.[27]

The Treaty on European Union brought about important changes of a conceptual nature. The European Economic Community (EEC) was renamed the European Community (EC) and a new entity was created, the European Union (EU). This was 'founded on the European Communities, supplemented by the policies and forms of

[23] The meeting was held on 12 December 1992 and resulted in a Decision and a Declaration by all the Member States, and a Declaration by Denmark alone. For the contents and legal effect of these instruments, see Hartley, 'Constitutional and Institutional Aspects of the Maastricht Agreement' (1993) 42 ICLQ 213 at 234–7; Howarth, 'The Compromise on Denmark and the Treaty on European Union: A Legal and Political Analysis' (1994) 31 CMLRev. 765.

[24] The European Communities (Amendment) Act 1993.

[25] This was not due to any widespread anti-European sentiment among British MPs: officially at least, the Treaty enjoyed overwhelming support. However, the die-hard anti-European faction in the parliamentary Conservative Party, though small, was greater than the Conservative majority. This was exploited by the Labour Party, which voted for motions that, though not ostensibly anti-Maastricht, would have had the practical effect of killing the Bill. In this way, Labour could embarrass the Government without compromising their official support for the Bill. It was finally passed in the Commons only when the Prime Minister stated that he would call a general election if the Government lost the vote. Since the Conservative Party would almost certainly have lost the election and many Conservative rebels would have lost their seats, this threat of self-destruction proved effective. For a full discussion, see Rawlings, 'Legal Politics: The United Kingdom and the Ratification of the Treaty on European Union' [1994] PL 254.

[26] *R. v. Secretary of State for Foreign and Commonwealth Affairs, ex parte Lord Rees-Mogg* [1994] 2 WLR 115; [1993] 3 CMLR 101 (DC).

[27] *Bundesverfassungsgericht*, 12 October 1993, [1993] NJW 3047; [1994] 1 CMLR 57. For constitutional proceedings in France, see *Conseil Constitutionnel*, 9 April 1992, [1993] 3 CMLR 345; see also Oliver, 'The French Constitution and the Treaty of Maastricht' (1994) 43 ICLQ 1.

co-operation' established by the Treaty on European Union.[28] The latter were two in number: a 'common foreign and security policy'[29] and 'co-operation in the fields of justice and home affairs'.[30] The result was that two entities – the European Community and the European Union – existed side by side, the European Community being contained in the European Union.

The most important result of the Treaty on European Union was the establishment of a common currency for the Union – the euro. However, the United Kingdom,[31] Denmark,[32] and Sweden[33] rejected it, and many of the former Communist Member States are not yet ready for it; so it does not apply in all the EU countries.

The Treaty of Amsterdam was signed in 1997, and came into force on 1 May 1999. It saw the insertion into the Treaty on European Union of a new Title[34] on what was then known as 'closer co-operation' (further developed and renamed 'enhanced co-operation' in the Treaty of Nice). Once called 'variable geometry', this means allowing some Member States to go ahead with further integration while others opt out.

The next major development was the Treaty of Nice,[35] which was signed on 26 February 2001 and entered into force on 1 February 2003. Although originally rejected by the voters of Ireland, it was accepted in a second referendum held in October 2002. Its main purpose was to reform the institutions of the Union in preparation for further enlargement.

A Charter of Fundamental Rights was adopted by proclamation of the Commission, Council, and Parliament in December 2000.[36] Until the Treaty of Lisbon came into effect, it had no binding force.

The most ambitious project in recent times has been the attempt to give the Union a Constitution. A body known as the 'European Convention' or the 'Convention on the Future of Europe' was set up for the purpose. It consisted of representatives of:

- the existing Member States and the applicant Member States;
- the national Parliaments of the existing and applicant Member States;
- the European Parliament; and
- the Commission.

28 Art. 1 TEU as it then existed.

29 See what was then (and is now) Title V TEU.

30 See what was then Title VI TEU. These provisions have now been replaced by provisions in various Articles in the TFEU.

31 The United Kingdom is not obliged to adopt the common currency unless the British Government and Parliament so decide: see the Protocol on certain provisions relating to the United Kingdom of Great Britain and Northern Ireland.

32 See the Protocol on certain provisions relating to Denmark; see also the Decision of the Heads of State and Government, section B, adopted at the Edinburgh Summit on 12 December 1992. Denmark held a referendum in September 2000, in which adoption of the euro was rejected.

33 Since the Treaty gives it no opt-out and it meets the criteria for adoption of the euro, Sweden's refusal to join is actually illegal, but no one wants to make an issue of this.

34 Title VII (now Title IV) TEU.

35 Published in OJ 2001, C 80. For a summary of its provisions, see Bradley, 'Institutional Design in the Treaty of Nice' (2001) 38 CMLRev. 1095.

36 OJ 2000, C 364/8.

It was chaired by a former President of France, Mr Valéry Giscard d'Estaing.

In due course, it produced a Constitution, contained in a draft treaty: the Treaty Establishing a Constitution for Europe. After a setback at a meeting of the Heads of State or Government in Brussels on 12 and 13 December 2003, it was finally agreed by the national Governments in October 2004. It then had to be ratified by each Member State according to its constitutional requirements. In many Member States, this required a referendum. Although the approval of the voters was obtained in several States, the process ground to a halt when the Constitution was rejected, first by the people of France and then by the people of the Netherlands.[37] Since France had initiated the process of European integration and the Netherlands was its most enthusiastic supporter, this was a mortal blow. The Constitution was dead.

It was then decided to try something more modest. The result was embodied in the Treaty of Lisbon (also called the 'Reform Treaty'), which was signed in the Portuguese capital on 13 December 2007. This too suffered a set-back when it was rejected in a referendum in Ireland in June 2008. After political concessions were made to meet the concerns of the Irish voters, it was put to a second referendum on 2 October 2009. This time, it was approved (by an overwhelming majority): perhaps the downturn in Ireland's economic fortunes had concentrated people's minds.

A new obstacle then emerged: a group of Czech senators brought a second constitutional challenge – a previous challenge having been unsuccessful – before the Czech Constitutional Court. President Klaus could not sign the Instrument of ratification while this was pending; moreover, some statements indicated that he would not sign at all.

President Klaus's opposition was overcome when the other Member States agreed to give the Czech Republic an opt-out on the Charter of Fundamental Rights similar to that already obtained by Poland and the United Kingdom;[38] so, when the Czech Constitutional Court rejected the new challenge on 3 November, the Instrument of ratification was signed by President Klaus on behalf of the Czech Republic and deposited with the Italian Government in accordance with Article 357 TFEU. Accordingly, the Treaty of Lisbon came into force on 1 December 2009.

Although there was rejoicing in some quarters, the ratification was not to everyone's liking. The *Daily Express*, a newspaper billed (by itself) as 'The World's Greatest Newspaper', announced the event under the banner headline 'BRITAIN: THE END', a sentiment hardly justified by the terms of the Treaty.[39]

David Cameron, the Conservative leader, who had previously given a 'cast-iron' guarantee (to readers of *The Sun*) that if the Conservatives came to power, there would

[37] This must have come as a relief to the British Government, since it was politically committed to a referendum in the United Kingdom, a referendum in which the Constitution would almost certainly have been rejected.

[38] The opt-out for Poland and the United Kingdom is contained in Protocol No. 30. The Czechs wanted a similar opt-out because they believed – probably wrongly – that the Charter could be used by Germans expelled after the Second World War to regain their property.

[39] *Daily Express*, 4 November 2009, p. 1.

be a referendum on the Treaty, announced that this would no longer be possible. *The Sun* forgave him for this,[40] but some of his supporters regarded it as a betrayal.

Despite the fuss, the Treaty of Lisbon will probably have less practical impact than some of the earlier agreements. Many of its provisions merely involve a tidying-up of the law or a streamlining of procedures (those relevant to this book will be considered in subsequent chapters). There are also terminological and legal changes. It abolishes the European Community and merges it with the Union; so the previous distinction between Community and Union no longer exists: the entire operation is now known as the 'European Union', though the European Atomic Energy Community continues to function.

In 2010, Europe was shaken by a financial crisis that threatened to destroy the euro. Investors began to doubt the solvency of some Euro-Area States, mainly in the South. Ireland, Portugal, Greece, Cyprus, Spain, and Italy were the worst affected. Interest rates rose on the sovereign debt of these States, and there was a real risk they would default. The European Union came to their rescue, setting up mechanisms – temporary at first,[41] but then of a permanent nature[42] – to provide financial support.[43]

This, however, came at a price: the recipients were required to make drastic cuts in government spending in order to reduce the need for borrowing. This entailed a massive cut in social-welfare spending, and large reductions in funding for public health and education. As a result, the economy slumped and unemployment soared.

This in turn caused political dissension, both within the countries affected, and between the latter and the more prosperous Euro-Area Members in northern Europe. The Northerners felt that the profligacy and imprudence of politicians in the South threatened to destroy what the Northerners had so painstakingly built up. The Southerners, on the other hand, accused the Northerners of a lack of solidarity. In some countries – Greece, for example – Germany, the biggest Euro-Area country, was openly taunted with its Nazi past.

In many European countries, both in the North and the South, ugly political movements sprang up, seeking scapegoats – usually foreigners or racial minorities – for the country's ills. Prejudice against immigrants, both from within and outside the Union, increased markedly.

[40] *The Sun*, Editorial, 4 November 2009, p. 6. They said that Labour was guilty of an act of treachery by agreeing to it.

[41] Council Regulation 407/ 2010 of 11 May 2010 establishing a European financial stabilisation mechanism, OJ 2010, L 118/1; Decision of the representatives of the Governments of the Euro Area meeting within the Council of the European Union, Council document 9614/10 of 10 May 2010.

[42] Treaty Establishing the European Stability Mechanism (adopted 2 February 2012; in force 27 September 2012). For further details, see Chap. 1, § 8.4.

[43] In addition, an agreement signed by all the Member States except the United Kingdom and the Czech Republic, the Treaty on Stability, Co-ordination and Governance in the Economic and Monetary Union (commonly known as the 'Fiscal Compact'), concluded in Brussels on 2 March 2012, established rules and procedures intended to prevent monetary crises happening again in the future.

In part, the contrast in attitudes between North and South stems from differences in the way people view membership of the Union in general and the Euro Area in particular. In the North, it has been regarded as a challenge as well as an opportunity; in the South, on the other hand, it has been widely seen as conferring an entitlement, an entitlement to the same standard of living as that enjoyed in the North.

Politicians in the South responded to these expectations by making use of the low interest rates that membership of the Euro Area initially produced in order to borrow recklessly on the international markets to finance projects producing short-term benefits but of doubtful long-term utility. When the time came to repay the money, the unwillingness of the Northerners to pick up the bill was seen by many in the South as a betrayal of what the Union stood for.

In Britain, the Eurosceptics gained ground, and there were calls for the United Kingdom to leave the Union, calls which the Prime Minister, David Cameron, answered by promising a referendum once his attempts to reform the Union had been concluded. Where this will lead is impossible to foresee.

Eurosceptics point to the defects of the Union as a justification for leaving, but they do not seem to have considered the alternatives. The Commonwealth is no longer a meaningful economic entity and the United States is far more interested in a trade agreement with the Union than it would be in an agreement with the United Kingdom alone. Some people say the United Kingdom could increase its trade with developing countries like China, but there is no reason to believe that this would be easier outside the Union than within it; indeed, the opposite would be the case.

If the United Kingdom left, it might be able to negotiate a trade agreement with the Union, but the price would include the obligation to respect EU law – including rules laid down by the European Court – over a wide area. Since one of the main objections to membership is the obligation to obey EU law, exit would make no sense, especially since the United Kingdom would no longer have any say in the making of those laws.

What is the Union, as it exists today? It is not easy to compare it with other political entities: it contains some of the features of a traditional international organization and, less prominently, some features of a federation.[44] Perhaps it is best regarded as the forerunner of a new breed of enhanced international organizations which have real power over their Member States. Though less advanced, the WTO and the Council of Europe (European Convention on Human Rights) are other examples. The term 'supranational' is sometimes used to refer to the features which distinguish such organizations.

The hybrid nature of the Union must constantly be borne in mind when considering its structure. The three political organs – the Council, the Commission, and the Parliament – each contain both inter-governmental and supranational elements,

[44] Interestingly, the federal elements are strongest with regard to the judicial and legal system of the Union; they are weakest in the political area, including such vital matters as legislative and executive powers, taxation, and defence.

though the former are more noticeable in the case of the Council and the latter in the case of the Commission.

The most important characteristic of a traditional international organization is that it is really only a form of institutionalized inter-governmental co-operation. It is based on the principle that no Member State may be bound without its consent. If the decisions of the organization are taken by majority vote, they are no more than mere declarations; if, on the other hand, they are to have any real 'bite', they must be approved by each Member State.

In contrast to this, the organs of the Union have a significant measure of autonomy, and unanimity is required only in special cases. Nor can it be doubted that the Union has real teeth: EU law is binding on Member States and (in many cases) on individuals; it is frequently applied by national courts. Moreover, in certain cases fines can be levied on companies, individuals, and even Member States, for breach of EU law. The decisions of the Union derive their binding force from the fact that they are taken by organs endowed with the appropriate power by the Treaties and not because each decision has been individually agreed to by the Member States. These features give the Union its supranational character.

FURTHER READING

Items are listed in date order, the most recent being at the end.

John Gillingham, *European Integration, 1950–2003* (2003).

Walter van Gerven, *The European Union, A Polity of States and Peoples* (2005).

Craig, 'The Treaty of Lisbon: Process, Architecture and Substance' (2008) 33 ELRev. 137.

Robert Schütze, *From Dual to Co-operative Federalism: The Changing Structure of European Law* (2009).

Jean-Claude Piris, *The Lisbon Treaty: A Legal and Political Analysis* (2010).

1

THE INSTITUTIONS

According to the Treaties,[1] the Union has seven institutions:

- the European Parliament;
- the European Council;
- the Council;
- the European Commission (usually called simply 'the Commission');
- the Court of Justice of the European Union;
- the European Central Bank;
- the Court of Auditors.

The Court of Justice will be discussed in the next chapter. The others will be considered here. We will also deal with the three most important political posts:

- the President of the European Council;
- the President of the Commission;
- the High Representative of the Union for Foreign Affairs and Security Policy.

§1 THE EUROPEAN PARLIAMENT

§1.1 COMPOSITION

The European Parliament[2] is intended to provide the democratic element in the EU system: it represents the citizens of the Union.[3]

In the beginning, Members of the European Parliament (MEPs) were not directly elected by the people, but selected by the national Parliaments. The Treaties provided that the Parliament would draw up proposals for direct elections and that the Council, acting unanimously, would 'lay down the appropriate provisions', which it would

[1] Art. 13 TEU.

[2] Referred to in the original Treaties as the 'Assembly', the European Parliament adopted its present name in 1962 (EP Resolution of 30 March 1962, JO 1962, p. 1045). This was recognized by the Member States in the Single European Act: see Art. 3(1) SEA.

[3] Art. 14 TEU [189/137 EC].

recommend to Member States for adoption in accordance with their respective constitutional requirements.[4] The Parliament first drew up proposals in 1960, but it took a further sixteen years for the Council to reach a decision.[5] The necessary measures had then to be adopted at national level, which involved further difficulties and delays, not least in the United Kingdom; so the first elections were not held until 1979. Thereafter, they have been, and will be, held every five years.[6]

The instrument providing for elections took an unusual form, since all its substantive provisions were in an Act annexed to the Council Decision. The legal nature of this Act is controversial. Did it take effect as an international agreement between the Member States based on a draft recommended by the Council? Or did it take effect as a decision of the Council to which the Member States agreed? Perhaps the best view is that Articles 190(4) [138(3)] EEC and 108(3) EAEC laid down a special procedure for amending the Treaties which derogated from the normal procedure. If this view is correct, the Act took effect as an agreement between the Member States but formed part of the Treaties.[7] The importance of this question is that the jurisdiction of the European Court to annul, interpret, or enforce the Act depends on its legal status.[8]

At the present time (2013) there are a total of 765 seats (not counting the President), which are allocated as follows:[9]

Germany	99
France	74
Italy, United Kingdom	73 each
Spain	54
Poland	51
Romania	32
Netherlands	26
Belgium, Czech Republic, Greece, Hungary, Portugal	22 each
Sweden	20
Austria	19
Bulgaria	18
Denmark, Slovakia, Finland	13 each

[4] Arts 190(4) [138(3)] EEC and 108(3) EAEC.

[5] Council Decision 76/787 and the annexed Act concerning the election of the representatives of the Assembly by direct universal suffrage, OJ 1976, L 278/1. See, further, Forman, (1977) 2 ELRev. 35.

[6] Art. 14(3) TEU. Previously, the relevant provision was Art. 3 of the Act annexed to Council Decision 76/787 providing for direct elections (see n. 5).

[7] See Joliet, *Institutions*, at pp. 75–7, where the problem is fully discussed.

[8] If the third view is correct, the European Court cannot annul the Act, even if it infringes the Treaties, but it can interpret or enforce it where the Treaties so provide.

[9] Act of Accession (Bulgaria and Romania) 2005, Art. 9, replacing Art. 189(2) EC and Art. 107(2) EAEC.

Ireland, Croatia, Lithuania	12 each
Latvia	9
Slovenia	8
Estonia, Cyprus, Luxembourg, Malta	6 each

The next elections will be in 2014, after which the total number of MEPs will be reduced to 750 (not counting the President). To achieve this reduction, Germany will lose three MEPs and Romania, Greece, Belgium, Portugal, the Czech Republic, Hungary, Austria, Bulgaria, Ireland, Croatia, Lithuania, and Latvia will lose one each.

This distribution is based on principles laid down in the Treaty of Lisbon.[10] Under them, the total number of MEPs must not exceed 750;[11] representation must be 'degressively proportional', which means that the bigger a Member State is, the fewer seats it will have relative to population. The minimum number of seats for a Member State must be six, the maximum ninety-six.

The idea that small States should be allocated more seats than big ones (relative to population) has been the governing principle all along; nevertheless, it is open to question. For example, the population of the United Kingdom is more than 130 times that of Luxembourg. If it is right for Luxembourg to have six seats (as it does at present), the United Kingdom should have something like 780 seats, instead of the seventy-three it has presently. To put it another way: the vote of one Luxembourger is worth more than those of ten British citizens. This is not consistent with the principle of equality among voters.[12]

For many years, each Member State was free to choose for itself the electoral system under which its MEPs would be elected,[13] though the intention has always been that a uniform system would eventually be adopted. In 2002, agreement was reached on

[10] Art. 14(2) TEU (as amended by the Treaty of Lisbon).

[11] This is not counting the President of the Parliament.

[12] It is sometimes said that this unequal allocation of seats is necessary in order to ensure that all parties in the smaller countries can gain representation. Such an argument cannot, however, justify a departure from the basic principle of equality of voting rights, nor can it explain why Northern Ireland, with its distinctive and diverse political scene, should have only half as many seats as Luxembourg, even though it has more than four times as many voters. The fact that Northern Ireland is not an independent State is irrelevant, since the European Parliament is not intended to provide a forum to represent States, a function fulfilled by the Council. Similar arguments may be made with regard to Scotland and Wales, as well as with regard to culturally distinct regions in other Member States – for example, the Basque Country in Spain.

[13] Art. 7(2) of the Act providing for direct elections, as it stood originally. In *Parti Ecologiste – 'Les Verts' v. European Parliament*, Case 294/83, [1986] ECR 1339, a grant by the European Parliament to the European political parties to cover election expenses was held invalid by the European Court. The Ecologist Party (the Greens) had challenged the grant on the ground that it was distributed in a way that was unfair to the newer parties, but the European Court annulled it on the ground that the conduct of elections was a matter for the Member States. See, further, Joliet and Keeling, 'The Reimbursement of Election Expenses: A Forgotten Dispute' (1994) 19 ELRev. 243.

certain principles, laid down in a Council Decision,[14] which were binding on Member States. These include proportional representation under either the list system or the single transferable vote. National law continues to apply to matters not governed by the Decision.[15]

Article 223(1) TFEU requires the European Parliament to draw up a proposal for a uniform electoral procedure in all Member States. The Council, acting unanimously and after obtaining the consent of the European Parliament,[16] must lay down the necessary provisions. These must be approved by the Member States in accordance with their respective constitutional requirements. Similar provisions for the adoption of a uniform electoral procedure have existed in the past, but full agreement has never been reached. It remains to be seen whether the new provision will be more successful.

In the past, Members of the European Parliament could also be members of their national Parliaments, but this is no longer permitted.[17] There are a number of other offices that MEPs cannot hold – for example, Member of the Commission; Judge, Advocate General, or Registrar of the European Court; or active official of a Union institution.[18] Similar rules apply at national level with regard to members of the national Parliaments – for example, the British House of Commons. Their purpose is to avoid a conflict of interests.

§1.2 PRIVILEGES AND IMMUNITIES

MEPs are entitled to various privileges and immunities[19] of which the most important are, first, freedom of movement to and from the meeting place of the Parliament; secondly, immunity from legal proceedings in respect of opinions expressed, or votes cast, in the performance of their duties; and thirdly, in their own Member State, the same immunities as are enjoyed by members of their national Parliament and, in other Member States, freedom from detention and immunity from legal proceedings. Immunities in the third category apply only during parliamentary sessions but, as these last virtually all the year,[20] this limitation is of little importance.[21] Immunities in this category may be waived by the Parliament itself.

[14] Decision 2002/772, OJ 2002, L 772/1, amending the Act annexed to Decision 76/787 providing for direct elections.

[15] On the citizenship requirement for voting, and the right of persons in Gibraltar to vote, see *Spain v. United Kingdom*, Case C-145/04, [2006] ECR I-7917.

[16] The European Parliament must act by a majority of its component members.

[17] Art. 6 of the Act annexed to Council Decision 76/787, as amended by Decision 2002/772.

[18] *Ibid.*

[19] See Protocol No. 7 on the Privileges and Immunities of the European Union, Arts 7–9.

[20] The length of the sessions is a matter for the Parliament itself to decide. Although it does not actually sit throughout the year, it holds various ancillary activities, such as committee meetings, during most of the year and, for the purpose of Parliamentary immunity, is regarded as in session until the formal closing of the session, which takes place immediately before the opening of the new session. See *Wybot v. Faure*, Case 149/85, [1986] ECR 2391.

[21] As to whether a former MEP may be prosecuted in England for dishonestly obtaining money for expenses from the European Parliament, see *R. v. Manchester Crown Court, ex parte DPP* [1993] 1 WLR 693, QBD, reversed on other grounds [1993] 1 WLR 1524 (HL). According to the House of Lords (*ibid.* at 1530–1), the decision of the Divisional Court in this case, having been made without jurisdiction, will not be binding on any other court.

§1.3 POLITICAL PARTIES

Members of the European Parliament sit according to their political group (party), not their country.[22] EU political groups are not parties in the normal sense, however: they exist simply for the purpose of the internal functioning of the Parliament, not for fighting elections. Elections are fought under the normal national labels – for example, Conservative and Labour in the United Kingdom.[23]

§1.4 COMMITTEES

A characteristic feature of the European Parliament is the role of committees. There are a number of standing committees, and much of the work of the Parliament is done in these committees. When matters come before the Parliament for discussion, they are usually considered first in the appropriate committee and the subsequent debate on the floor of the House is based on the Committee's report.

§1.5 PARLIAMENTARY QUESTIONS

Parliamentary questions have become an important part of the Parliament's proceedings. Article 230, second paragraph, TFEU [197/140 EC] requires the Commission to reply orally or in writing to questions put to it by the Parliament or by its Members. The Council also replies to questions. The answers to Parliamentary questions are published in the Official Journal.

§1.6 PROPOSALS, INQUIRIES, AND PETITIONS

Three special rights may conveniently be mentioned at this point: the right of the Parliament to request proposals, its right to set up inquiries, and the right of citizens (and others) to petition the Parliament.

The second paragraph of Article 225 TFEU [192/138b EC] gives the Parliament the right, acting by a majority of its members, to request the Commission to submit any 'appropriate proposal' on matters on which it considers that a Union act is required for the purpose of implementing the Treaties. There is no obligation on the Commission to comply, but, if it does not do so, it must give the reason.

Article 226 TFEU [193/138c EC] gives the Parliament the right to set up (temporary) committees of inquiry, at the request of a quarter of its members, to investigate alleged contraventions or maladministration in the implementation of Union law (except where the matter is pending before a court).

[22] Art. 10(4) TEU states that political parties at European level contribute to forming 'European political awareness' and to 'expressing the will' of citizens of the Union.

[23] For litigation on the formation of political groups, see *Front national v. Parliament*, Case C-486/01 P, [2004] ECR I-6289.

Article 227 TFEU [194/138d EC] gives any citizen of the European Union, acting individually or in association with others, the right to petition the European Parliament on a matter within the Union's fields of activity which affects him directly.[24] This gives legal recognition to a practice which had existed for some time and can be a valuable means of putting pressure on the Union.[25]

§1.7 THE OMBUDSMAN

Article 228 TFEU [195/138e EC] gives the Parliament the power to appoint an Ombudsman,[26] who can receive complaints from any citizen of the Union[27] concerning maladministration in the activities of any Union institution or body except the Court of Justice of the European Union acting in its judicial role. The appointment is made after each Parliamentary election and the Ombudsman holds office until the next election. He (or she) is eligible for reappointment. The status of the Ombudsman is in some ways similar to that of a member of the Commission: he is completely independent in the performance of his duties and can be dismissed only if the European Court, at the request of the Parliament, finds that he no longer fulfils the conditions required for the performance of his duties or is guilty of serious misconduct.

Where the Ombudsman establishes an instance of maladministration, he must refer the matter to the institution concerned, which has three months to inform him of its views. The Ombudsman then forwards a report to the Parliament and the institution concerned. The person lodging the complaint must be informed of the outcome. The Parliament does not, however, have power to provide redress in the event that the complaint is upheld. Perhaps it is hoped that the institution or body concerned will do this.[28]

§1.8 CONSULTATION

The Parliament plays an important role in the ordinary legislative procedure. This will be discussed later, in § 9. There are, however, certain instances in which the Treaties give the Parliament no more than the right to be consulted. What this entails will be considered here.

[24] The right also extends to non-citizens residing in a Member State (as well as to companies having their registered office there).

[25] For further details, see Marias, 'The Right to Petition the European Parliament after Maastricht' (1994) 19 ELRev. 169; Pliakos, 'Les conditions d'exercise du droit de pétition' [1993] CDE 317.

[26] The office of Ombudsman originated in Scandinavia (the Parliamentary Commissioner for Administration in Britain is based on the Scandinavian model). The first Ombudsman was a Finn (Jacob Soderman), appointed in 1995.

[27] This right, too, extends to non-citizens residing in a Member State, and to companies having their registered office there.

[28] For further details, see Pliakos, 'Le Médiateur de l'Union européenne' [1994] CDE 563; Magliveras, 'Best Intentions but Empty Words: The European Ombudsman' (1995) 20 ELRev. 401.

Where the Parliament has the right to be consulted, it must be given a reasonable opportunity to formulate its views and to make them known. The leading case is *Roquette v. Council*,[29] which was decided at a time when the Parliament's role in the legislative process was only consultative. The Council had sent a proposal for legislation to the Parliament in March 1979. As the measure was to enter into force on 1 July of that year, the Council asked that the opinion be given during the April session. This proved impossible because the draft resolution proposed by the Parliamentary committee to which the proposal had been sent was rejected by the Parliament in plenary session. This meant that the matter had to go back to the committee for reconsideration and the resulting delay made it impossible to complete the procedure during the April session. The Parliament was willing to convene an extraordinary session should the Council or Commission so desire, but the Council made no such request. Instead it adopted the measure on 25 June 1979, referring in the preamble to the fact that the Parliament had been 'consulted', rather than (as was normal) referring to its opinion.

Is it sufficient that the Parliament has been *asked* for its opinion or must it actually *give* its opinion? If the latter were the case, the Parliament could delay matters indefinitely by the simple expedient of not giving an opinion. If such stonewalling were possible, the right to be consulted would turn into a veto power.

In its judgment, the Court said that observance of the requirement of consultation 'implies that the Parliament has expressed its opinion. It is impossible to take the view that the requirement is satisfied by the Council's simply asking for the opinion.'[30] The Council had argued that the Parliament, by its own conduct, had made observance of the requirement impossible. The Court, however, pointed out that the Council had not exhausted all the possibilities of obtaining an opinion; in particular it had not asked for an extraordinary session. The Council had not, therefore, proved its allegations; and the Court declared the measure void. It was, however, careful to leave open the questions of principle raised by the Council.

In 1995, the question again came before the Court. This time, however, the fault lay with the Parliament: it had not done everything possible to give an opinion in sufficient time; so the Court held that it could not complain that the Council had gone ahead and adopted the measure without waiting for its opinion. The measure was, therefore, valid.[31]

What is the position where, after the Parliament has given its opinion, the proposal is amended? If it was always necessary to ask the Parliament for a new opinion on the amended proposal, the procedure would become very cumbersome, since amendments

[29] Case 138/79, [1980] ECR 3333. See also *Maizena v. Council*, Case 139/79, [1980] ECR 3393.

[30] Para. 34 of the judgment.

[31] *European Parliament v. Council*, Case C-65/93, [1995] ECR I-643. See also *European Parliament v. Council*, Case C-417/93, [1995] ECR I-1185, where the Court ruled that the Council is entitled to take a preliminary decision on the measure in question before obtaining the Parliament's opinion, provided that such a decision is not definitive. For a comment on both cases, see Boyron, 'The Consultation Procedure: Has the Court of Justice Turned against the European Parliament?' (1996) 21 ELRev. 145.

often have to be made in order to secure the assent of the Member States in the Council. In view of this, the Court has held that, if the provisions of the final text of the measure are 'substantially identical' to those in the version submitted to the Parliament, or if any amendment is substantially in accordance with the Parliament's own proposal, there is no need for a second consultation.[32] Where, however, the amended text differs in substance from the one on which the Parliament was consulted, the Parliament must be consulted again. If this is not done, the measure will be annulled.[33]

§1.9 VETO RIGHTS

There are a number of circumstances in which the Parliament must give its assent to action taken by the Council, and in such cases the Parliament has a right of veto. These will be considered where appropriate in due course.

§1.10 APPROVAL OF THE COMMISSION

Here, the Parliament has two powers: first, it must elect the President of the Commission;[34] secondly, the President and the other members of the Commission[35] nominated by the Member States are subject 'as a body' to a vote of approval by the Parliament.[36] Before it grants its approval, the Parliament requires the President-elect and the would-be Commissioners to appear before it to answer questions. Some nominees are said to find these sessions gruelling.

The power to approve Commissioners other than the President is weakened by the fact that the Parliament must approve the nominations *en bloc*; so it cannot veto individual nominations. However, if it objects strongly enough to a particular appointment, it can threaten to reject the whole Commission unless the offending nominee is replaced.

§1.11 CENSURE OF THE COMMISSION

The Parliament also has the power to obtain the resignation of the Commission by passing a vote of censure. This is laid down by Article 234 TFEU [201/144 EC], which

[32] *Chemiefarma v. Commission*, Case 41/69, [1970] ECR 661 (paras 68 and 69 of the judgment); *Buyl v. Commission*, Case 817/79, [1982] ECR 245 (paras 23 and 24 of the judgment). The Court has also held that where power to implement a measure is delegated by the Council, either to the Commission or to itself, it is not necessary to consult the Parliament on the implementing measures, provided the Parliament was consulted on the original measure: *Einfuhr- und Vorratsstelle v. Köster*, Case 25/70, [1970] ECR 1161; *European Parliament v. Council*, Case C-417/93, [1995] ECR I-1185. For a discussion of delegation, see Chap. 4, § 6.

[33] *European Parliament v. Council*, Case C-65/90, [1992] ECR I-4593; *European Parliament v. Council*, Case C-388/92, [1994] ECR I-2067; *European Parliament v. Council*, Case C-21/94, [1995] ECR 1827; *European Parliament v. Council*, Case C-392/95, [1997] ECR I-3213.

[34] It must do this by a majority of its component members.

[35] Including the High Representative for Foreign Affairs and Security Policy.

[36] Art. 17(7), last para., TEU [214/158 EC].

provides that the Commission must resign *en bloc* if such a motion is passed by a two-thirds majority of votes cast, representing a majority of all members. However, the Commission remains in office until a new Commission is appointed; so if the Parliament does not approve the new nominees put forward by the Council – who could in fact be the same individuals – the existing Commissioners will continue to act until their term of office expires under the normal rules.

The most important occasion on which resort has been had to this procedure was in January 1999, when there was a motion of censure against the Commission headed by Mr Santer. This failed to achieve a two-thirds majority;[37] but the Commission had to accept the establishment of a committee of independent experts to investigate allegations against it of fraud, mismanagement, and nepotism. When the experts produced a damning report, the whole Commission resigned on 15 March 1999. However, the Member States failed to appoint a new Commission and, in accordance with the rule mentioned previously, the existing Commissioners continued to carry out their duties – and draw their salaries – until their terms of office expired in January of the following year.[38]

§1.12 CONCLUSIONS

It will be clear from what has been said that the powers of the European Parliament fall short of those normally enjoyed by the legislature of a modern State. Nevertheless, they are gradually increasing and the days are long past when it could be dismissed as no more than a 'talking shop'. Moreover, its most important powers, those concerning legislation and the budget, have yet to be considered.

§2 THE EUROPEAN COUNCIL

EU terminology can be confusing. The 'European Council', the 'Council', and the 'Council of Europe' are three quite different things. The first two are European Union institutions. The latter is not even part of the Union, but is an entirely separate European organization, whose most important achievement is the European Convention on Human Rights. It is important not to confuse these three bodies. In this Section, we consider the European Council; the Council will be discussed later, in § 3.

The European Council represents the Member States at the highest level. It is the top decision-making body in the Union. However, it was not part of the original structure of the Union and has only reached its present position through a process of gradual evolution.

[37] There were 292 votes in favour and 232 against.

[38] See Tomkins (1999) 62 MLR 744.

In 1974 it was agreed that the Heads of State or of Government[39] of the Member States, together with their foreign ministers, would hold summit conferences at regular intervals. In time, these meetings became formalized and were known as 'the European Council'. In 1986, the European Council was given legal recognition by Article 2 of the Single European Act,[40] but it was still regarded as being no more than a special version of the Council. It was only with the Treaty of Lisbon that it came to enjoy the status of a separate institution.

Today, the governing provision is Article 15 TEU, which states that the European Council will provide the European Union with the necessary impetus for its development, and will define its general political directions and priorities. It consists of the Heads of State or Government of the Member States, together with its President and the President of the Commission.[41] The High Representative of the Union for Foreign Affairs and Security Policy takes part in its work. It meets twice every six months, convened by its President. Special (additional) meetings may also be convened.

Where specific powers are conferred on the European Council, the Treaties specify how it takes decisions – usually by a qualified majority or by unanimity. Where it acts in a political capacity, it takes decisions by consensus.[42]

The President of the European Council may be destined to become a key figure. He (or she) is elected by the European Council (by a qualified majority) for a term of two-and-a-half years, renewable once.[43] He is not allowed to hold any national office, though former Heads of Government are strong candidates. The first appointment (November 2009) was Mr Herman van Rompuy, who was Prime Minister of Belgium before becoming President. The former British Prime Minster, Mr Tony Blair, was a keen contender, but failed to secure the appointment.

The President's job is to chair the European Council and 'drive forward' its work. It is intended that he will provide cohesion and dynamism. Exactly how his functions will mesh in with those of the High Representative of the Union for Foreign Affairs and Security Policy (discussed later, in § 7.3) is controversial. The Treaty says:

> The President of the European Council shall, at his level and in that capacity, ensure the external representation of the Union on issues concerning its common foreign and security policy, without prejudice to the powers of the High Representative of the Union for Foreign Affairs and Security Policy.

[39] This formula was adopted to allow the French President (Head of State) to represent France, while all other Member States were represented by their Heads of Government – for example, the British Prime Minister or the German Chancellor.

[40] Now repealed.

[41] The President of the European Council and the President of the Commission are not entitled to vote: Art. 235(1) TFEU. On the appointment of the President of the Commission, see § 4.1.

[42] Art. 15(4) TEU states that, except where the Treaties provide otherwise, its decisions are taken by consensus.

[43] He may be removed from office by the same procedure in the event of an impediment or of serious misconduct.

Perhaps it is hoped that the two appointees will work together, with the President dealing with foreign Heads of State or Government, and the High Representative operating at foreign-minister level.

§3 THE COUNCIL

§3.1 INTRODUCTION

The Council takes the final decision on most EU legislation (normally acting jointly with the Parliament) and, together with the Parliament, decides on the Union budget. It consists of the delegates of the Member States, each State being represented by a government minister who is authorized to commit his Government.[44] Which minister attends depends on the 'configuration' in which the Council is meeting, which in turn depends on the matter to be discussed. When general matters are to be discussed, Member States will normally be represented by their foreign ministers; but other ministers will attend for specialist discussions – for example, ministers of agriculture for meetings dealing with agriculture and ministers of finance for financial meetings. Ministers attending Council meetings are usually accompanied by officials. A representative of the Commission also takes part.

Prior to the Treaty of Lisbon, the Presidency of the Council rotated among the Member States at six-monthly intervals.[45] The Member State holding the Presidency would work in partnership with the State that held the Presidency immediately before, and immediately after. While it held the Presidency, a Member State would provide the chairman for all meetings of the Council and other Union bodies on which the Member States were represented.[46] The functions of the President were to call meetings, to preside at them, to call for a vote, and to sign acts adopted at the meeting. The Presidency also involved a general responsibility to ensure the smooth running of the Council.

In the negotiations leading up to the Treaty of Lisbon, some Member States (mainly the bigger ones) wanted to abandon this system. They thought it was inefficient to keep changing the team running the Council; they also thought that some of the smaller Member States were not capable of doing a good job. Their solution was to have a permanent President. Other Member States (mainly the smaller ones) regarded the rotating Presidency as an important way of ensuring that the bigger States would not become too dominant.

In the end, a rather messy compromise was reached. It was agreed that the President of the European Council would be a specially appointed individual, but he would be appointed for only two-and-a-half years (renewable once), not the five

[44] Art. 16(2) TEU [203/146 EC]. [45] Art. 203 [146] EC as it then stood.

[46] These bodies included COREPER, and committees and working groups of the Council.

years originally proposed. The rotating Presidency would continue largely as before,[47] though it would no longer chair the European Council or the Council in its Foreign Affairs Configuration: the former would be chaired by the President of the European Council[48] and the latter by the High Representative of the Union for Foreign Affairs and Security Policy.[49]

The Council has its own General Secretariat staffed by permanent officials.[50] It is similar to, but much smaller than, the Commission staff. It is divided into Directorates General and headed by a Secretary General. It has its own Legal Service.

§3.2 COREPER

The ministers are able to be in Brussels only for short periods. In order to provide continuity, a Committee of the Permanent Representatives of the Member States, usually known by its French acronym, 'COREPER', was set up to prepare the work of the Council.[51] The Permanent Representatives are the ambassadors of the Member States to the Union and the Committee represents the Member States at a lower level than the ministers. COREPER itself meets on two levels: deputy Permanent Representatives for more technical questions; and the Permanent Representatives themselves for the more important political questions. At a lower level still, the Council has many committees and working groups, staffed by national officials based in Brussels or in their home countries.

COREPER plays an important role in the Council machinery. Matters to be decided by the Council come to it first. If unanimous agreement is reached in COREPER, the item will be adopted by the Council without discussion. Negotiations with the Commission take place in COREPER: if a Commission proposal is unacceptable, attempts will be made to induce the Commission to amend it in order to secure agreement. As a result, COREPER operates as an integral part of the Council decision-making process and could be regarded as an extension of the Council itself.[52]

§3.3 VOTING

There are different systems of voting in the Council depending on the matter to be decided. For some matters – mainly of a procedural or administrative nature – the Council acts by a 'simple' majority, which means that there must be a majority of its

[47] See Art. 16(9) TEU; Art. 235 TFEU and Declaration (No. 9) on Article 16(9) of the Treaty on European Union concerning the European Council decision on the exercise of the Presidency of the Council (with a draft decision of the European Council annexed).

[48] Art. 15(6)(a) TEU. [49] Art. 18(3) TEU. [50] Art. 240(2) TFEU [207(2)/151(2) EC].

[51] Arts 16(7) TEU and 240 TFEU [207(1)/151(1) EC].

[52] In *Commission v. Council* (*FAO* case), Case C-25/94, [1996] ECR I-1469, the European Court held that, not being an institution of the Union, COREPER has no power to take decisions in its own name. However, an amendment to Art. 207(1) [151(1)] EC brought about by the Treaty of Amsterdam allowed it to adopt procedural decisions in cases provided for in the Council's Rules of Procedure. See now Art. 240 TFEU.

component Members in favour of the proposal.[53] Under this procedure, abstentions have the same effect as negative votes.

In other matters – usually of special importance – there must be unanimity, which does not, however, mean that every Member of the Council must vote in favour: abstentions by Members present at the meeting do not prevent the adoption of the proposal.[54] Here, as long as the Member in question is present, abstentions have the same effect as positive votes.

Most matters are decided by what is called a 'qualified majority'. This is an attempt to solve one of the most intractable problems facing supranational organizations all over the world. Once you get away from the idea that nothing can be done without unanimity, it is necessary to decide how voting is to be conducted. If each State were given equal voting power, it would mean that Luxembourg would be on the same footing as the United States or China. This would be absurd. However, to base voting power solely on population would be unacceptable to most States. In the UN Security Council, the problem is solved by giving each State one vote, but, in addition, giving a veto to those which were originally regarded as the most important States.

In the European Union, a different solution has been adopted. When qualified-majority voting takes place in the Council, the votes of the Member States are weighted. The votes given to each State are in essence a compromise between the principle of equality and the principle that votes should reflect population.

Certain additional factors also play a role, in particular, the idea of grouping States together. This latter idea produces anomalies. In the past, Germany, France, Italy, and the United Kingdom were all approximately the same size; so it made sense to give them the same voting power. This changed with German reunification. However, France was unwilling to allow Germany to have more votes than it had; so Germany remains grouped with the other members of the 'Big Four'.

The allocation of votes has been subject to frequent changes. At present, it is as follows:[55]

Germany, France, Italy, United Kingdom	29 votes each
Spain, Poland	27 votes each
Romania	14 votes
Netherlands	13 votes
Belgium, Czech Republic, Greece, Hungary, Portugal	12 votes each
Bulgaria, Austria, Sweden	10 votes each
Denmark, Ireland, Croatia, Lithuania, Slovakia, Finland	7 votes each
Estonia, Cyprus, Latvia, Luxembourg, Slovenia	4 votes each
Malta	3 votes

[53] Art. 238(1) TFEU. [54] Art. 238(4) TFEU.

[55] Protocol (No. 36) on Transitional Provisions, Art. 3(3), as amended by Art. 20 of the Accession Treaty for Croatia 2011.

The total number of votes is 352. A qualified majority is 260, which is approximately 74 per cent of the total.

There are, however, two additional rules which must also be satisfied if the proposal is to be adopted. The first concerns the number of Member States voting in favour: if the act is adopted on a proposal from the Commission, there must (in addition to a qualified majority of votes) also be a majority of Member States in favour; if the act is not adopted on a proposal from the Commission, there must (in addition to a qualified majority of votes) also be a two-thirds majority of Member States.[56] This rule benefits the smaller States, since it prevents their being outvoted by the larger ones. However, there is a second additional rule, which benefits the larger States. This is the rule that when a decision is adopted by a qualified majority, any Member State may request verification of the fact that the States making up the qualified majority represent at least 62 per cent of the total population of the Union. If this is not shown to be the case, the proposal will fail. This requirement prevents a coalition of small States from outvoting the larger States.[57]

According to Article 16(4) TEU, a simpler system will apply from 1 November 2014. Under this, a measure will be passed if, but only if, two conditions are fulfilled: first, the States voting in favour must constitute at least 55 per cent of the total number of Member States (comprising at least fifteen Member States); secondly, those States must account for at least 65 per cent of the total population of the Union.[58] However, Article 3(2) of the Protocol (No. 36) on Transitional Provisions provides that, until 31 March 2017, the old system will be applied if any member of the Council so requests.

Although important, the provisions of the Treaties tell only part of the story. International bodies usually work on a system of give and take. States try to achieve what they want by influencing other Member States, either by offering something in return – 'We will vote for you on issue X if you support us on issue Y'– or by threatening to cause trouble. In the latter category, three tactics (in order of increasing stringency) are: threatening to block progress on other, unrelated issues; threatening to boycott future meetings; and threatening to withdraw. Negative tactics of this kind can, if the threats are credible, be very effective, but there is a price to be paid. Bad feeling is created and other States will be less co-operative. Moreover, boycott or withdrawal will hurt the State concerned more than the others. For these reasons manœuvres of this kind are used only if a country feels that its vital interests are at stake (though a relatively powerful country will feel able to take tougher measures than a weaker one).

In view of this, a number of political understandings have grown up – understandings that are important even though they may be subject to constant change. In general, it is accepted that voting must not be used to push through a decision that

[56] *Ibid.* [57] *Ibid.*

[58] Art. 16(4) TEU. However, the measure will be deemed to pass unless at least four Member States are opposed. For further rules, see Art. 238 TFEU.

causes serious harm to the vital national interests of a given State, unless there are imperative reasons why it is needed. In the past, there was a kind of constitutional convention to this effect, usually regarded as based on the 'Luxembourg Accords'.[59] Today, majority voting is used more and more; nevertheless, some sort of understanding still exists.

§4 THE COMMISSION

The Commission is intended to give expression to the Union interest. Its most important activities are: formulating proposals for new Union policies; mediating between the Member States to secure the adoption of these proposals; co-ordinating national policies; and overseeing the execution of existing Union policies. It could be regarded as the EU executive.

§4.1 COMPOSITION

There is one Commissioner[60] from each Member State.[61] The Treaty on European Union provides that this will change for appointments made after 31 October 2014 (when there are supposed to be only two-thirds as many Commissioners as Member States), but, as part of the package offered to Ireland to secure ratification of the Treaty of Lisbon, it was agreed that Ireland would continue to have its Commissioner.[62] In view of this, the European Council adopted a decision on 22 May 2013[63] that the old system will continue in force. This decision will be reviewed in due course,[64] but it remains to be seen whether it will change.[65]

The procedure for appointing members of the Commission is laid down in Article 17(7) TEU.[66] The first step is to elect the President of the Commission. The European Council (acting by a qualified majority) proposes a candidate to the European Parliament. The candidate must be elected by the European Parliament by a majority of its component members. If the first candidate fails to be elected, the European Council must propose a new one within a month, who must be elected by the same majority.

Once the President of the Commission has been elected, the next step is for the Council, acting by common accord with the President-elect, to adopt a list of the other persons it proposes to appoint to the Commission. They are selected on the basis of

[59] On this, see pp. 21–2 of the 6th edn of this book.

[60] This includes the President of the Commission and the High Representative of the Union for Foreign Affairs and Security Policy.

[61] Art. 17(4) TEU.

[62] Presidency Conclusions, Brussels European Council, 11 and 12 December 2008, para. 1(2).

[63] EUCO 119/13.

[64] *Ibid.*

[65] This decision was taken under Art. 17(5) TEU, which allows the European Council (acting unanimously) to alter the number of Commissioners.

[66] See § 1.10.

suggestions made by Member States.[67] The President, the High Representative for Foreign Affairs and Security Policy, and the other members of the Commission are subject as a body to a vote of consent by the European Parliament. After this has been obtained, they are appointed by the European Council, acting by a qualified majority. The appointments are for a (renewable) period of five years.[68]

In 2009, José Manuel Barroso, a former Prime Minister of Portugal, was re-elected as President of the Commission for a second term.

Members of the Commission cannot be dismissed during their term of office by the national Governments or by the Council, but the whole Commission must resign *en bloc* if a vote of no confidence is passed by the European Parliament.[69] Commissioners cannot be dismissed individually in this way; but the European Court can compel a Commissioner to retire on grounds of serious misconduct or because he no longer fulfils the conditions required for the performance of his duties.[70]

In addition, a Commissioner must resign if the President of the Commission so requests.[71] This could be used to get rid of a Commissioner who was incompetent, whose activities were politically objectionable, or who was thought to be corrupt.

According to the Treaties, Commissioners are supposed to be above national loyalties. This is provided for by the third paragraph of Article 17(3) TEU:

> In carrying out its responsibilities, the Commission shall be completely independent...[T]he members of the Commission shall neither seek nor take instructions from any Government or other institution, body, office or entity. They shall refrain from any action incompatible with their duties or the performance of their tasks.

In addition, Article 245 TFEU [213 EC] states:

> The Members of the Commission shall refrain from any action incompatible with their duties. Member States shall respect their independence and shall not seek to influence them in the performance of their tasks.

Any overt breach of these principles could lead to the compulsory retirement of the Commissioner concerned.[72]

[67] It is likely that the practice before the Treaty of Lisbon will continue. Under this, the suggestions of each Member State regarding 'their' Commissioner were adopted unless the person concerned was clearly unacceptable.

[68] Art. 17(3) TEU.

[69] Art. 17(8) TEU, discussed in § 1.11.

[70] Art. 247 TFEU. The procedure is set in motion by an application by the Council (acting by a simple majority) or the Commission.

[71] Art. 17(6), last para., TEU. This means that there are six different ways in which a Commissioner may cease to hold office: (1) death; (2) expiry of his term of office; (3) individual (voluntary) resignation; (4) collective (compulsory) resignation (following a motion of no confidence in the European Parliament); (5) compulsory retirement by the Court; (6) compulsory resignation at the request of the President. Except in the first, third, and fifth of these cases, he remains in office until his successor has been appointed. See Art. 246 TFEU [215/159 EC].

[72] It is further stated that a Commissioner must not engage in any other occupation, whether gainful or not, during his (or her) term of office (though in practice certain academic activities are allowed). After he has ceased to hold office, he must behave with integrity and discretion as regards the acceptance of appointments

These provisions do not, however, prevent governments (or private interests) from lobbying individual Commissioners or the Commission as a whole. The balance of power in the Union is such that, though the Commission is an independent force in its own right, it cannot fulfil its functions without the co-operation of national governments; so Commissioners have to listen carefully when the national governments make representations to them.

The President of the Commission allocates portfolios to Commissioners so that each is responsible for one or more subjects.[73] Since some subjects are more important than others, there is intense lobbying when this is done, with each government trying to ensure that its person gets a plum job. The President of the Commission may also reshuffle portfolios during the Commission's term of office.[74] These developments suggest that the President's role will come to resemble that of a British Prime Minister.

The Commission is divided into departments known as Directorates General. Not all of these are of equal importance or prestige; hence the scramble for portfolios. Each Directorate General is headed by a Director General, who is responsible to the relevant Commissioner. Directorates General are subdivided into Directorates (headed by a Director) and these in turn are made up of Divisions (each under a Head of Division). There are also a number of specialized services. One of these is the Legal Service, which gives legal advice to all Directorates General and represents the Commission in legal proceedings. Appointments to the higher posts are subject to intense national rivalry. The decision is taken by the Commissioners themselves and depends in part on ensuring that each country maintains its share of posts. This means that the best person will not always get the job, a fact which is damaging to morale.

Each Commissioner is assisted by his *Cabinet*, a group of officials personally appointed by him and directly responsible to him, who are not necessarily on the permanent staff of the Commission. The head of the *Cabinet* (*Chef de Cabinet*) plays an important role as his Commissioner's right-hand man. The *Chefs de Cabinet* of all the Commissioners meet regularly to co-ordinate activities and prepare the ground for Commission meetings. If the *Chefs de Cabinet* reach unanimous agreement on a question, their decision is normally adopted by the Commission without debate.[75]

and benefits. Disregard of these obligations could lead to compulsory retirement (if still in office) or loss of pension. Proceedings under this provision were brought for the first time in 1999, when the Council applied to the Court for an order depriving Mr Bangemann of his pension rights because he accepted a position with a Spanish telecommunications company. Mr Bangemann was the outgoing Commissioner responsible for telecommunications in the disgraced Santer Commission. The proceedings were withdrawn when he agreed not to take up the position for a year, and not to engage in negotiations with Union institutions for two years. Deprivation of pension rights can also be used to punish misbehaviour in office that does not come to light until afterwards. This happened to Ms Cresson, who was also a member of the Santer Commission. She had given her dentist a scientific appointment with the Commission, even though he was clearly unqualified. The Court found that she had committed a breach of the obligations arising from her office, but decided not to deprive her of her pension. See *Commission v. Edith Cresson*, Case C-432/04, [2006] ECR I-6387, a case suggesting that the Court has a fairly relaxed attitude towards nepotism.

[73] Art. 248 TFEU. [74] *Ibid.*

[75] Compare the role played by COREPER with regard to the Council (discussed in § 3.2).

Officials of the Commission (and the other Union institutions) enjoy various privileges and immunities under Union law,[76] the most important of which are immunity from legal proceedings in national courts in respect of acts performed by them in their official capacity[77] and immunity from national income tax on their Union salary.[78] They are, however, subject to a special Union income tax, though the rate of taxation is low. All the privileges and immunities enjoyed by Union officials are granted to them solely in the interests of the Union, and the institution concerned is obliged to waive the immunity whenever it considers that such waiver is not contrary to the interests of the Union.[79]

§4.2 RULE-MAKING POWERS

Under the ECSC Treaty, the Commission was the main legislative authority, though sometimes it had to obtain the approval of the Council. Under the EEC and EAEC Treaties, on the other hand, it had legislative powers in only a few cases, though, where granted, they were regarded as legislative in the true sense.[80] Today, although the Commission retains powers to lay down rules that are functionally legislative, they are not regarded as 'legislative' in terms of the new terminology introduced by the Treaty of Lisbon. In a much wider range of cases, the Commission enjoys powers delegated to it by the Council. Here the basic principles must be laid down in the Council measure which delegates the power: the Commission can then adopt measures that fill in the details.[81]

§4.3 DECISION-MAKING PROCEDURE

The Commission takes decisions by a simple majority vote.[82] Frequently, however, use is made of the so-called 'written procedure' under which draft decisions are circulated

[76] See Protocol No. 7 on the Privileges and Immunities of the European Communities, Arts 11–15 [12–16]. These privileges and immunities also apply to members of the Commission.

[77] As to the meaning of this, see *Sayag v. Leduc* (*No. 1*), Case 5/68, [1968] ECR 395.

[78] Member States are also prohibited from taking an official's salary into account for the purpose of determining the tax payable by the official's spouse: *Humblet v. Belgium*, Case 6/60, [1960] ECR 559.

[79] Protocol No. 7 on the Privileges and Immunities of the European Communities, Art. 17 [18]. See *Weddel & Co. BV v. Commission*, Case C-54/90, [1992] ECR I-871.

[80] *France, Italy and United Kingdom v. Commission*, Cases 188–190/80, [1982] ECR 2545 (paras 4–7 of the judgment). See, further, *France v. Commission*, Case C-202/88, [1991] ECR I-1223; *Spain v. Commission*, Cases C-271, 281, 289/90, [1992] ECR I-5833. The European Court also held that whenever the EU Treaties conferred a specific task on the Commission, they impliedly granted the Commission the powers (including legislative powers) that were indispensable in order to carry out that task: *Germany v. Commission*, Cases 281, 283–5, 287/85, [1987] ECR 3203 (para. 28 of the judgment). See Hartley, 'The Commission as Legislator under the EEC Treaty' (1988) 13 ELRev. 122. However, the Commission had no implied power under the EU Treaties to conclude international agreements, even on a subject matter (such as competition) with regard to which it has internal executive power: *France v. Commission*, Case C-327/91, [1994] ECR I-3641.

[81] See Chap. 4, § 6.2.

[82] Art. 250 TFEU [219/163 EC].

among the Commissioners and, if no objections are made within a given period, the proposal is regarded as adopted.

§4.4 ASSESSMENT

In the early days, Commission officials were idealists. Today, it often appears that they are more concerned with furthering their careers. Although few are actually corrupt, there seems to exist a widespread culture of looking after one's own interests and ignoring those of the Union. This came most glaringly to light in the scandal surrounding the Santer Commission (discussed in § 1.11), in which the whole Commission resigned after a report by a committee of independent experts set up by the European Parliament said that it was increasingly difficult to find anyone in the Commission with 'even the slightest sense of responsibility'.[83]

In 2012, the Maltese Commissioner for Health, John Dalli, resigned after being accused of corruption. It was alleged that, in return for a bribe of €60 million, he offered to ensure that a forthcoming directive on tobacco would be amended to suit the interests of Swedish tobacco companies. Mr Dalli protested his innocence, but resigned nevertheless.

Despite these shortcomings, the Commission enjoys a powerful position in the Union, mainly because it is seen as being above national rivalries. This raises the question whether it is right for a bureaucracy that is subject to little political control to have such an important role.

§5 THE EUROPEAN CENTRAL BANK

The European Central Bank (ECB) became an institution only when the Treaty of Lisbon came into force. It has the important task of managing the euro, the common currency of many Member States. It conducts the monetary policy of the Union in conjunction with the central banks of those Member States whose currency is the euro.[84] It is independent in the exercise of its powers.[85] It has legal personality.[86]

Its Governing Council consists of the members of its Executive Board plus the Governors of the national central banks of those Member States that have the euro. The Executive Board of the ECB consists of its President, its Vice-President, and four other members.[87] They are appointed by the European Council, acting by a qualified majority, from among persons of recognized standing and professional experience in monetary or banking matters, on a recommendation from the (EU) Council, after it has consulted the European Parliament and the Governing Council of the ECB.[88] Their

[83] Committee of Independent Experts, *First Report on Allegations of Fraud, Mismanagement and Nepotism in the European Commission* (15 March 1999). See Tomkins (1999) 62 MLR 744.

[84] Art. 282(1) TFEU. [85] Art. 282(3) TFEU. [86] *Ibid.* [87] Art. 283(2) TFEU.

[88] *Ibid.*

term of office is eight years and is not renewable. Only nationals of Member States may be members of the Executive Board. The President of the (EU) Council and a Member of the Commission may participate (without having the right to vote) in meetings of the Governing Council of the ECB; likewise, the President of the ECB participates in (EU) Council meetings when the Council is discussing matters relating to the objectives and tasks of the ECB.

§6 THE COURT OF AUDITORS

Though established some time previously, the Court of Auditors attained institutional status only in 1993. It sits in Luxembourg, and its structure and status are in many ways similar to those of the European Court.[89]

It consists of one national from each Member State. They must be persons who belong, or have belonged, to external audit bodies in their respective countries or who are specially qualified for such an office. They are appointed for a term of six years by the Council, acting by a qualified majority (after consulting the European Parliament), on the basis of proposals made by each Member State. They are eligible for reappointment.

The President of the Court of Auditors is elected by the Court from among its own members for a period of three years. He or she may be re-elected. The members of the Court must be completely independent in the performance of their duties, and they may neither seek nor take instructions from any government or other body. They must refrain from any action incompatible with their duties.

A member of the Court of Auditors may be deprived of his office (or his right to a pension or other benefits) if the European Court, at the request of the Court of Auditors, finds that he no longer fulfils the requisite conditions or meets the obligations arising from his office. The provisions of the Protocol on the Privileges and Immunities of the European Union applicable to the judges of the European Court also apply to the members of the Court of Auditors.

The function of the Court of Auditors is to examine the accounts of revenue and expenditure of the Union. Where able to do so, it must provide the European Parliament and the Council with a statement assuring them of the reliability of the accounts, and of the legality and regularity of the underlying transactions. It examines whether revenue has been received and expenditure incurred in a lawful and regular manner, and decides whether financial management has been sound. It draws up an annual report after the close of each financial year, which is forwarded to the other institutions of the Union and is published (together with their replies to its observations) in the Official Journal. It acts by a majority of its members.

[89] The relevant provisions are Arts 285–287 TFEU [246–248/188a–188c EC]. See also Kok, 'The Court of Auditors of the European Communities: "The Other European Court in Luxembourg"' (1989) 26 CMLRev. 345, an article written before the Court of Auditors became an institution of the Union.

Fraud and financial mismanagement are serious problems in the Union. The importance of these problems was recognized by the Member States when they gave the Court of Auditors the status of a Union institution.

§7 THE COMMON FOREIGN AND SECURITY POLICY

§7.1 DEVELOPMENT AND SPECIAL FEATURES

For many years, the Union has been an active player in the foreign-policy and defence areas, though a striking feature of its activity in the beginning was that this took place entirely outside the institutional framework established by the Treaties. This gradually began to change, but, until the coming into force of the Treaty of Lisbon, the common foreign and security policy (together with police and judicial co-operation in criminal matters) were kept separate from other activities. This was done through the distinction between the European Community (EC) and the European Union: the common foreign and security policy (CFSP) and police and judicial co-operation in criminal matters, while falling within the scope of the Union, were outside that of the EC, the entity under which the other policies were conducted. Now that the EC has been abolished, there is no longer any conceptual difference between the CFSP and other areas of Union activity. Nevertheless, the CFSP still retains distinctive features: legislative powers are lacking;[90] the jurisdiction of the European Court is largely excluded;[91] and decision-making is based on the principle that no Member State should be bound against its will.

This latter principle finds expression in the rule that decisions in the European Council and the Council must be taken by unanimity.[92] However, there is a rule that a Member State may abstain from voting while making a formal declaration referring to Article 31(1), second sub-paragraph. The effect of this is that the measure will be passed – an abstention by a Member State that is present does not prevent its adoption[93] – but, by virtue of Article 31(1), second sub-paragraph, the Member State in question will not itself be bound. This allows individual Member States to opt out of EU policies without preventing the others from going ahead. Nevertheless, the

[90] Art. 24(1), second sub-para., second sentence, TEU; Art. 31(1), first sub-para., second sentence, TEU.

[91] Art. 24(1) (second para.) TEU, together with the second para. of Art. 275 TFEU. Under these provisions, the European Court's jurisdiction with regard to the Common Foreign and Security Policy is limited to two peripheral issues: first, monitoring compliance with Art. 40 TEU (a provision designed to prevent encroachment by the Common Foreign and Security Policy on the general powers of the Union) and, secondly, reviewing the legality of decisions providing for restrictive measures against natural or legal persons (individuals or corporations).

[92] Art. 31(1), first sub-para., TEU. Limited exceptions are laid down by Art. 31(2), first sub-para., but these are largely nullified by the second sub-para.

[93] Art. 238(4) TFEU. 'Unanimity' for this purpose means that no Member State must oppose the measure: see § 3.3.

Member State in question must accept that the Union is bound, and it must not itself actively undermine the policy.

§7.2 THE COMMON SECURITY AND DEFENCE POLICY

The common security and defence policy could be said to contain the seeds of a future European Army, though this will not come into being for a long time, if indeed it comes into being at all. According to the Treaties, the common security and defence policy, which is an integral part of the CFSP, is intended to provide the Union with an operational capacity which can be used in military operations outside the Union.[94] It involves the progressive framing of a Union defence policy.[95] There is also a European Defence Agency charged with the task of improving the military capabilities of the Member States.[96]

§7.3 THE HIGH REPRESENTATIVE OF THE UNION FOR FOREIGN AFFAIRS AND SECURITY POLICY

This office was newly created by the Treaty of Lisbon. Under Article 18 TEU, the High Representative is appointed by the European Council (acting by a qualified majority), with the agreement of the President of the Commission.[97] He or she (the first appointee was a woman, Baroness Cathy Ashton, a British politician who was previously a member of the Commission) has the task of conducting the CFSP: she contributes to its development and carries it out as mandated by the Council.[98] She presides over the Foreign Affairs Council (the Council in its foreign affairs configuration) and is one of the Vice-Presidents of the Commission.[99] She is assisted by a European External Action Service, a kind of embryonic EU diplomatic service, which operates in co-operation with the diplomatic services of the Member States, and consists of officials from the relevant departments of the Council Secretariat and the Commission, as well as staff seconded from the national diplomatic services of the Member States.[100]

§8 BODIES, OFFICES, AGENCIES, AND OTHER ENTITIES

In addition to the seven institutions of the Union (listed at the beginning of this chapter), there are a number of other entities – some of greater importance than

[94] Art. 42(1) TEU. [95] Art. 42(2) TEU. [96] Art. 42(3) TEU.
[97] The High Representative may be removed from office by the same procedure.
[98] The High Representative has similar powers with regard to the Common Security and Defence Policy.
[99] Art. 18(2) TEU. [100] Art. 27(3) TEU.

others – which play a role in the functioning of the Union.[101] These fall into two broad categories. First, there is a diverse group, created by the Treaties or by Union legislation, which are referred to by the general formula 'bodies, offices and agencies', a phrase that appears in the Treaties on a number of occasions.[102] Secondly, there are certain other entities which defy categorization, but which play an important role in the EU system, especially with regard to the euro. The most important of these is the European Stability Mechanism (ESM). They will be considered separately at the end of this section.

We start by considering the first category. There does not seem to be any clear dividing line between bodies, offices, and agencies; indeed, the entities in question go by all these names[103] and several others besides.[104] There is no definition of these terms in the Treaties, though 'agency' has come to have a fairly well established meaning (see § 8.3). Taken together, as they appear in the phrase 'bodies, offices and agencies', they cover any entity created by Union law that plays a role in the executive functioning of the Union.

Because they are so diverse, there is little to be gained by attempting a classification, though there is a distinction between entities directly created by the Treaties and those created by Union legislation. The former include two advisory bodies[105] (the Economic and Social Committee, and the Committee of the Regions, discussed in § 8.1 and § 8.2 respectively); an important financial institution, the European Investment Bank;[106] and the European Ombudsman (discussed in § 1.7).

There are more than twenty entities created by Union acts. They are generally regarded as falling under the rubric 'agency', though this word will not necessarily appear in their official title.

We will look briefly at the two advisory bodies mentioned previously, and then consider European agencies in general.

§8.1 THE ECONOMIC AND SOCIAL COMMITTEE

This Committee is intended to represent sectional interests. According to Article 300(2) TFEU, it consists of representatives of employers' organizations, employees' organizations (trade unions), and other representatives of civil society, including those in professional and cultural areas. Its members are appointed for five-year terms by the Council on the basis of proposals made by each Member State. Though intended to represent particular groups, its members may not be bound by mandatory instructions and must

[101] We are not here concerned with bodies created under Member State law, such as the 'outside bodies' discussed in Chap. 4, § 6.4.

[102] See, for example, Arts 263 and 267 TFEU.

[103] For example, the European Aviation Safety Agency and the European Public Prosecutor's Office.

[104] For example, 'centre' (European Centre for Disease Prevention and Control); 'foundation' (European Foundation for the Improvement of Living and Working Conditions); and 'authority' (European Food Safety Authority).

[105] Art. 13(4) TEU.

[106] Arts 308 and 309 TFEU.

be completely independent in the performance of their duties.[107] Where the Treaties so provide, the Committee has the right to be consulted by the Parliament, the Council, or Commission;[108] in all other cases, it may be consulted if appropriate. It may also issue an opinion of its own initiative. Where consultation takes place, the European Parliament, the Council, or Commission may set it a time limit (of at least one month), and, if no opinion is given within that period, go ahead without it.

§8.2 THE COMMITTEE OF THE REGIONS

The Committee of the Regions represents (elected) regional and local bodies within the Union.[109] It operates in much the same way as the Economic and Social Committee.

§8.3 EUROPEAN AGENCIES

European agencies are usually set up to perform a task for which a certain degree of independence is desirable – for example, to give unbiased opinions based on objective criteria. They are of many different kinds and fulfil many different functions:[110] they may give opinions and recommendations which provide the technical and scientific basis for the Commission's decisions;[111] they may carry out inspections and issue reports setting out their findings;[112] or they may adopt individual decisions which are legally binding on third parties.[113] Although extremely diverse, they have certain characteristics in common: they are created by Union regulations to perform specific tasks; they have legal personality; and they enjoy a certain degree of organizational and financial autonomy.[114]

Two general categories have been identified,[115] though there are some agencies that do not fall into either. The first category consists of what are called 'executive agencies'. Today, they are governed by general provisions contained in a Council Regulation, Regulation 58/2003.[116] They are responsible for purely managerial tasks and assist the Commission in implementing Union programmes.[117] They are not intended to have a significant policy-making role. The second category consists of regulatory agencies. They have wider powers and are actively involved in executive functions. They may be able to adopt legally binding acts.

[107] Art. 300(4) TFEU. [108] Art. 304 TFEU. [109] Art. 300(3) TFEU.

[110] See the Commission communication entitled 'The Operating Framework for the European Regulatory Agencies' COM (2002) 718, pp. 2–5.

[111] For example, the European Food Safety Authority.

[112] For example, the European Maritime Safety Agency.

[113] For example, the European Aviation Safety Agency.

[114] 'The Operating Framework for the European Regulatory Agencies' COM (2002) 718, p. 3.

[115] *Ibid.*, pp. 3–4. [116] OJ 2003, L 11/1.

[117] 'The Operating Framework for the European Regulatory Agencies' (see n. 114), p. 3; Reg. 58/2003, Art. 6.

§8.4 THE EUROPEAN STABILITY MECHANISM

When it became apparent that some Euro-Area Member States might default on their debts, the EU moved swiftly to rescue them. The problem was that, while collective action was essential to provide the necessary resources, non-euro Member States – in particular, the United Kingdom – were unwilling to commit funds for the defence of a currency which they had not adopted. This meant that the response had to be restricted to the Euro-Area Member States, something which could be regarded as compromising the unity of the EU system.

In May 2010, the Council adopted a Regulation creating the European Financial Stability Mechanism (EFSM),[118] which enabled loans to be given to Member States in financial difficulties. In addition, the representatives of the Governments of the Euro-Area Member States, meeting within the Council, took a Decision establishing the European Financial Stability Facility (EFSF), a decision which committed the Euro-Area Member States to provide assistance of up to €440 billion.[119] At the same time, the representatives of the Governments of all the Member States, meeting within the Council, took a Decision agreeing that functions could be conferred on the Commission for this purpose.[120] This two-pronged response – Union assistance based on a Union act (the EFSM Regulation) and Member State assistance based on an inter-governmental act (the EFSF Decision) – was necessary because the Union by itself lacked the resources to carry through the operation.

This rescue package created legal problems. The first difficulty was that Article 125(1) TFEU, generally known as the 'no-bailout clause', expressly forbids both the Union and the Member States from being liable for, or assuming, the financial commitments of a Member State. This could have been regarded as prohibiting the entire operation. Secondly, it was open to doubt whether the Treaties empowered the Union to adopt the EFSM Regulation. It had been adopted under Article 122(2) TFEU, which allows the Union to give financial assistance to a Member State threatened by severe difficulties caused by natural disasters or exceptional circumstances beyond its control. It could be argued that the difficulties of the Member States in question were caused by their own lack of prudence, not by circumstances beyond their control.

To solve these problems, an amendment of the Treaty was necessary. This was done by using (for the first time) the simplified revision procedure laid down in paragraph 6 of Article 48 TFEU (explained in Chapter 3, § 1.2).[121]

[118] Council Regulation 407/ 2010, OJ 2010, L 118/1.

[119] Council document 9614/10 of 10 May 2010. The EFSF was actually a private company set up under Luxembourg law, of which the seventeen Euro-Area Member States were the shareholders.

[120] *Ibid.* For details, see http://www.efsf.europa.eu.

[121] European Council Decision 2011/199/EU of 25 March 2011 amending Article 136 of the Treaty on the Functioning of the European Union with regard to a stability mechanism for Member States whose currency is the euro, OJ 2011 L 91/1.

These measures constituted the initial response to the crisis. However, it soon became apparent that a permanent solution was needed. This took the form of an international financial institution, the European Stability Mechanism (ESM). It was created by the Treaty Establishing the European Stability Mechanism 2012 (ESM Treaty), a treaty adopted by the seventeen Euro-Area Member States[122] on 2 February 2012. It came into force on 27 September 2012. The ESM has now taken over the tasks of the EFSF and the EFSM. Its authorized capital stock is €700 billion[123] and its initial maximum lending volume of €500 billion.[124]

The ESM is an intergovernmental organization under public international law. Its Members are the seventeen Euro-Area Member States. It might seem strange that an intergovernmental organization established under international law by only some of the Member States should play such a vital role in the protection of the euro. It shows how the Union has become increasingly fragmented as core Member States become more and more integrated, while others – especially the United Kingdom – remain on the periphery.

The constitutional legality of this arrangement was upheld by the European Court in *Pringle v. Government of Ireland*,[125] a case which originated with a claim brought before the Irish courts by a member of the *Dáil* (Irish Parliament), Mr Pringle. He argued that the ESM Treaty was contrary to Union law because it allowed a group of Member States to do something which could be done only by the Union itself. The Irish Supreme Court referred the matter to the European Court, which sat as a Full Court (all twenty-seven judges) because the matter was of such importance. After holding that the seventeen Euro-Area Member States were obliged to respect Union law and that it had jurisdiction to ensure that this was done, the European Court ruled that the ESM Treaty did not infringe exclusive Union competence. No doubt, a sigh of relief was heard in Euro-Area ministries of finance when this judgment was announced.

§9 THE ORDINARY LEGISLATIVE PROCEDURE

The decision-making process in the Union depends on the particular treaty Article giving the Union competence with regard to the matter in question. In this section we will discuss what is called the 'ordinary legislative procedure', the procedure most often used to adopt Union legislation. The financial procedure (budget) will be considered in § 10.

The key provision is Article 294 TFEU. The procedure starts with the Commission, which normally has the power of initiative. The first step is for the Commission to

[122] Belgium, Germany, Estonia, Ireland, Greece, Spain, France, Italy, Cyprus, Luxembourg, Malta, the Netherlands, Austria, Portugal, Slovenia, Slovakia, and Finland.

[123] ESM Treaty, Art. 8(1).

[124] ESM Treaty, Recital 6.

[125] Case C-370/12, 27 November 2012 (Full Court).

draw up its proposal. A draft will be submitted to the national Governments. The latter will comment and a series of meetings will be convened to discuss the draft. If these proceed well, the text will gradually be moulded into a shape acceptable to the Member States. It is essential to obtain the general consent of the Member States; otherwise, the proposal will be rejected by the Council, where a qualified majority will be needed for its adoption.

When general agreement has been reached, the Commission will submit its proposal to the European Parliament and the Council. The European Parliament will usually send it to a committee. The committee report will eventually be debated by the European Parliament, which will adopt its position on the proposal. This will normally involve amendments. The proceedings in the European Parliament at this stage are called the 'first reading' and the text as amended by the European Parliament is called its 'position at first reading'. This is communicated to the Council.

The Council will consider the European Parliament's position at first reading. If it approves it, the act will be adopted with the amendments proposed by the European Parliament. If (as is more likely) it does not approve the European Parliament's position, it will adopt its own position and send it to the European Parliament. This will probably involve rejecting some of the European Parliament's amendments and substituting some of its own. The result will constitute the Council's position at first reading.

At this point, an important general rule should be mentioned. This is the rule laid down in Article 293 TFEU that where, pursuant to the Treaties, the Council acts on a proposal from the Commission, it may amend that proposal only by acting unanimously. (As we shall see later, this does not apply under the conciliation procedure; nor does it apply with regard to the budget.) However, the Commission may itself amend the proposal at any time. What normally happens, therefore, is that if the Member States want changes made, the Commission will amend its proposal to fall in with their wishes. So it is only where the Commission refuses to do this that the rule about acting unanimously comes into play. In such a situation, the measure may fail if the Commission refuses to back down.

Assuming that the Council adopts a position, this will be considered by the European Parliament at second reading. A time limit of three months applies. If the European Parliament approves the text as proposed by the Council, or if it takes no action, the act will be deemed to have been adopted. The text proposed by the Council in its position at first reading will prevail.

This means that the European Parliament can reject the measure only by positive action: if it is unable to take a decision or neglects to do so within the time limit, the measure will be adopted by default. Moreover, a rejection of the Council's position can be adopted only if a majority of the European Parliament's component members (absolute majority) vote in favour of rejection: it is not sufficient if there is merely a majority of votes. So if the Council's text is rejected by a majority of votes, but not by an absolute majority, it will be deemed to have been adopted. In this situation, abstentions (or no-shows) by MEPs have the same effect as votes against the motion to reject.

Neither of these outcomes is likely. What will probably happen is that the European Parliament will want to amend the Council's position. Perhaps it will try to obtain a compromise. This is possible, but again there must be an absolute majority (majority of members). If this happens, the amended text will be forwarded to the Council and the Commission. The latter will give its opinion on the amendments.

We now come to the third stage. Again there is a time limit of three months. If, within this period, the Council approves the text as amended by the European Parliament, it will be deemed to have been adopted. A qualified majority is needed for such approval, unless the Commission expressed a negative opinion with regard to any of the amendments. In such a case, the amendment in question may be approved only if the Council acts unanimously.[126]

If the Council fails to approve all the amendments by the three-month deadline (by a qualified majority or unanimously, as the case may be), the President of the Council, acting in agreement with the President of the European Parliament, must convene a meeting of a Conciliation Committee. This must take place within six weeks.

The next stage is conciliation. The Conciliation Committee consists of the members of the Council (or their representatives) and an equal number of MEPs representing the European Parliament. It has the task of reaching agreement on a joint text, which will normally be some kind of compromise. In doing this, each side acts independently of the other. On the Council side, there must be a qualified majority; on the European Parliament's side, there must be a majority of the MEPs (absolute majority). The proposal can be adopted only if both sides agree. Again, there is a deadline: six weeks. If no agreement is reached within this time, the measure is lost. The Commission takes part, but its role is simply that of a conciliator.

If the Conciliation Committee approves a joint text within the six-week time limit, the final stage begins. This is the third reading. The joint text must be approved by both the Council and the European Parliament. The deadline is again six weeks. During this period, the European Parliament must approve the joint text (by a majority of votes cast: an absolute majority is not necessary) and the Council must approve it by a qualified majority. If either fails to do so, the proposed act is deemed not to have been adopted.[127]

It is interesting to analyse the voting majorities needed under this procedure. The Council votes by a qualified majority[128] (except where it wishes to approve an amendment to which the Commission objects). The Parliament normally acts by an absolute

[126] This rule does not apply where, in those special cases provided for in the Treaties, a legislative act is submitted to the ordinary legislative procedure on the initiative of a group of Member States, on a recommendation by the European Central Bank, or at the request of the European Court. In such cases, the Commission is free to give an opinion, but a negative opinion will not have the consequence that the Council must act unanimously.

[127] The periods of three months and six weeks which apply at various points in the procedure may be extended, by a maximum of one month and two weeks respectively, at the initiative of the European Parliament or the Council: Art. 294(14) TFEU.

[128] In a Conciliation Committee this may be a qualified majority of the representatives of the Council.

majority of its members, but this does not apply where it approves the position of the Council at first reading: in such a case no specified majority is mentioned, which means that it acts by a majority of votes cast.[129] Moreover, no more than a majority of votes is required for approving a joint text agreed by the Conciliation Committee. In other words, a majority of members is required where the Parliament wishes to block the Council's proposals, but a majority of votes is sufficient if it approves the Council's proposals. Since the European Parliament is a large and cumbersome body, some of whose members may be unable to attend a particular session, this is an important difference.

How does the Commission fare under this procedure? In general, the foundation of the Commission's power is its right to make proposals. However, the right to make proposals is of little value if those proposals can be easily amended. Consequently, the Commission gains considerable bargaining power from the rule that the Council must be unanimous in order to amend its proposals. It is true that the Council can refuse to adopt a measure unless the Commission agrees to amend it, but if the Commission is determined, it may well be able to force the Council to accept a compromise.

Prior to the convening of the Conciliation Committee, the Commission's prerogatives are fully respected: amendments proposed by the European Parliament which are not accepted by the Commission may be adopted by the Council only if it is unanimous. Once the Conciliation Committee has been convened, however, the position is different: a text accepted by the Conciliation Committee may be adopted by the Council by a qualified majority even if the Commission objects.[130] Moreover, the unanimity rule does not apply to proceedings in the Conciliation Committee. Once the conciliation procedure comes into operation, therefore, the Commission loses its power to require the Council to act unanimously. This is a significant weakening of the Commission's power: the Commission's loss is the Parliament's gain.

The Conciliation Committee is convened whenever the Council does not approve the Parliament's amendments within three months. Consequently, if the Council wishes to approve an amendment proposed by the Parliament which the Commission rejects, but the Council cannot muster a unanimous vote, it merely has to wait for three months and convene the Conciliation Committee, which may adopt the amendment by a qualified majority on the Council side. The amendment may then be approved by the Council, acting by a qualified majority. In other words, the only effect of a Commission veto is to delay adoption of the measure. The result is that, while the Council still cannot itself amend the Commission's proposals unless it is unanimous, it may by this means adopt the Parliament's amendments by a qualified majority even if the Commission objects.

129 Art. 231 TFEU. 130 Art. 293(1) TFEU.

§10 THE BUDGETARY PROCEDURE

The budget is adopted under a special legislative procedure, a variant of the ordinary legislative procedure.[131] The financial year runs from 1 January to 31 December; so the budget must be adopted before the end of the previous year. The first step is for each institution (except for the ECB) to draw up its estimates of expenditure. These are sent to the Commission, which consolidates them into a draft budget. The draft budget, which must also contain estimates of revenue and expenditure, is sent to the European Parliament and the Council. This must take place no later than 1 September of the year preceding that in which the budget will apply.

The next stage is for the Council to adopt its position and forward it to the European Parliament. This must be done by 1 October. In doing this, and in taking all other decisions concerning the budget, the Council acts by a qualified majority. It is not bound by the proposals of the Commission: the normal rules which prevent the Council from making amendments to Commission proposals except by unanimity do not apply here.

The third stage takes place in the European Parliament. The deadline is forty-two days. If the European Parliament approves the position of the Council, the budget is adopted. If it takes no decision during this period, the budget is deemed to have been adopted. Neither of these is likely to occur. What is most likely is that the European Parliament will adopt amendments. This must be done by a majority of its members (absolute majority). If it does this, the amendments are forwarded to the Council and to the Commission.

If the Council approves the amendments within ten days, the budget is adopted. If (as is more likely) it does not do so, a Conciliation Committee will be convened by the President of the Parliament in agreement with the President of the Council.

The Conciliation Committee is composed – and operates – in the same way as under the ordinary legislative procedure: each side must agree independently of the other – the Council representatives by a qualified majority, and the MEPs by an absolute majority (majority of members). The deadline, however, is shorter: it is twenty-one days. If, within this period, no agreement is reached, the budget is regarded as rejected, and the Commission must submit a new draft. If a joint text is accepted, it is forwarded to the European Parliament and to the Council for their agreement. They have fourteen days to give this.

[131] The main provisions on Union finance are Arts 313–319 TFEU [268–280/199–209a EC]. The main provisions on the budgetary procedure are contained in Art. 314 TFEU [272/203 EC]. For litigation between the institutions on the budget prior to the Treaty of Lisbon, see *Council v. European Parliament*, Case 34/86, [1986] ECR 2155; *European Parliament v. Council* (*Draft Budget*), Case 377/87, [1988] ECR 4017; *Commission v. Council*, Case 383/87, [1988] ECR 4051; *Council v. European Parliament*, Case C-284/90, [1992] ECR I-2277; *European Parliament v. Council*, Cases C-181, 248/91, [1993] ECR I-3685; *Council v. European Parliament*, Case C-41/95, [1995] ECR I-4411. The main sources of Union revenue ('own resources') are agricultural levies, customs duties on imports from outside the Union, a slice of the proceeds of the value added tax (VAT) imposed by the Member States on the basis of EC rules, and funds from the Member States.

If, within this period, the European Parliament and the Council both approve the joint text or fail to take a decision, or if one approves the joint text while the other fails to take a decision, the budget is deemed to be definitively adopted on the basis of the joint text. If, on the other hand, the European Parliament, acting by a majority of its component members (absolute majority), and the Council both reject the joint text, or if one rejects it while the other one fails to take a decision before the deadline, the budget is regarded as having been rejected and the Commission must submit a new one. The same applies if the European Parliament (acting by a majority of members) rejects it and the Council approves it.

If, within the fourteen-day period, the European Parliament accepts the budget but the Council rejects it, the position is more complicated. The European Parliament may, within fourteen days, confirm some or all of the amendments it made to the Council's original text (before the Conciliation Committee). This must be done by a majority of members (absolute majority) and a three-fifths majority of votes. If an amendment is not confirmed, the position agreed in the Conciliation Committee on the budget heading which is the subject of the amendment will be retained. The budget will be deemed to be definitively adopted on this basis.

The budget is implemented by the Commission in co-operation with the Member States.[132] At the end of the financial year, the European Parliament, acting on a recommendation from the Council (which itself acts by a qualified majority), gives a discharge to the Commission after considering the accounts and financial statement submitted by the Commission and the annual report of the Court of Auditors.[133]

§11 ENHANCED CO-OPERATION

Sometimes it may happen that some Member States want the Union to go ahead in a given area while others do not. The latter may be able to block the adoption of any EU measure. Can the former then go ahead on their own and obtain the enactment of Union measures that apply only to them? The answer is that, in certain circumstances, they can. The EU term used to describe this is 'enhanced co-operation'. The relevant provisions are Article 20 TEU, which establishes the basic principles, and Articles 326 to 334 TFEU, which fill in the details.

Enhanced co-operation, which can apply only in areas where the European Union has non-exclusive competence,[134] involves the use by the Member States concerned of EU institutions to attain objectives which they could normally attain by acting outside the EU framework. At least nine Member States must want to participate.[135] They must first request the Commission to make a proposal. If it decides not to do so, the Commission must give its reasons. If it makes the proposal, the decision to authorize

[132] Art. 317 TFEU [274/205 EC]. [133] Art. 319 TFEU [276/206 EC].

[134] On this, see Chap. 4, §3.

[135] This means that a minority can go ahead even if the majority are opposed.

enhanced co-operation is taken by the Council, but only those Member States wishing to participate are allowed to vote. The consent of the European Parliament must also be obtained.[136]

The resulting measures are binding only on the participating Member States. Other Member States can join in at any time,[137] but they are not obliged to do so. This applies also to new Member States that join the Union after the adoption of the scheme: they too are not obliged to participate if they do not wish to.[138]

In the past, enhanced co-operation was regarded with suspicion, since it runs counter to the idea of a united (and uniform) Europe. However, the political dynamics of the Union are such that Member States cannot easily be forced to do things they do not want to do. The majority cannot coerce the minority. Nevertheless, it would be wrong for the minority to prevent the majority from going ahead with things they regard as important. In this situation, enhanced co-operation is the only option.

However, the old hostility still lingers: Article 20(2) TEU expressly provides that the decision authorizing enhanced co-operation may be adopted by the Council only as a last resort, when it has established that the objectives of such co-operation cannot be attained within a reasonable period by the Union as a whole. Moreover, the procedural requirements laid down by the Treaties make clear that a group of Member States cannot go ahead with enhanced co-operation just because they want to. The Commission and the European Parliament must agree.[139]

§12 NATIONAL PARLIAMENTS

Since national Parliaments are not EU institutions, they ought not (strictly speaking) to feature in this chapter. However, one of the innovations of the Treaty of Lisbon is to give them a role in the Union system in order to encourage them to involve themselves more in the activities of the European Union. This is perhaps an attempt to do something about the perceived lack of democracy in the Union and the feeling on the part of many European citizens that it is aloof and remote.

The provisions relating to the national Parliaments are set out in a special protocol, Protocol (No. 1) on the Role of National Parliaments in the European Union. Their main right is to be informed in good time of Commission documents and draft legislative acts. The latter must normally be sent to them at least eight weeks before they are

[136] The procedure is different in the case of enhanced co-operation within the framework of the common foreign and security policy: see Art. 329(2) TFEU.

[137] They will have to comply with any conditions of participation laid down by the authorizing decision; they must also comply with acts already adopted within the framework of the scheme: see Art. 228(1) TFEU. The Commission has a role in this procedure: see Art. 331 TFEU.

[138] Art. 20(4) TEU.

[139] This does not apply to enhanced co-operation within the framework of the common foreign and security policy.

put on the Council agenda. With regard to subsidiarity, however, their role is greater. This will be discussed in Chapter 4, § 5.4 and § 5.5.

§13 ASSESSMENT

What has been explained so far sets out the bare bones of the European Union. Enough has already been said, however, to make it possible to assess certain aspects of the institutional structure.

It was suggested previously that the European Union is an uneasy amalgam of two different concepts: an international organization and a federal State. The truth of this will be apparent from what has already been said. The institutional structure of the Union was designed to mediate between different interests to find generally acceptable solutions. By far the most important players are the national Governments. For this reason, the European Union is closer to an international organization than to anything else. However, the collective interest of the Union, as something other than the lowest common denominator of the various national interests, is also recognized. This is the supranational element.

The interests of the national Governments find expression in the European Council and in the Council. The collective interest is promoted by the Commission. Sectional interests within Member States gain a voice through the Economic and Social Committee (though they can also do so by lobbying national Governments); local and regional interests are represented by the Committee of the Regions.

Where does this leave the European Parliament? It is supposed to represent the citizens of Europe. It is often said that it provides the 'democratic element' in the Union structure. This way of putting it, however, is symptomatic of the problem. It implies that democracy is something added to the general mixture, like spice to a stew. It is true that the European Parliament is elected by the citizens of Europe. However, democracy is more than elections. It is more than a procedure: it is an objective.

Democracy means that citizens should have a real say in government policy, a real influence on the most important decisions. If elections do not bring this about, they are without value, at least as far as democracy is concerned. The way elections achieve democracy in Western countries is through the establishment of a chain of responsibility. The party system is an essential element. In the West, the Government is always the Government of a party. In Britain it is usually a single party; on the Continent it may be a coalition of parties. That party (or those parties) are responsible for what the Government does and they have to answer to the electorate.

At the time of writing (2013), there is (unusually for Britain) a coalition between the Conservative Party and the Liberal Democrats. The Prime Minister is a Conservative, Mr David Cameron. If he does things badly, the electorate will hold the Conservatives (and perhaps also the Liberal Democrats) responsible. When the next elections take place, the voters will give their verdict. Electors who disapprove of what the Government has done can vote for another party (or not vote at all). The Conservatives know this.

They know that if the voters think they have done a good job, they will be returned to office – perhaps without even having to form a coalition. If the voters think that they have done a bad job, they will lose power. For this reason they have to pay attention to what the people want.

It cannot be denied that the system has its imperfections. The Government may try to mislead the people by putting up a smokescreen of lies and propaganda. This will deceive some of the people some of the time. A free press is supposed to counteract this, but all too often the press is itself under the control of vested interests. Even if not deceived, the voters may feel that the other parties are even worse; so they may vote for the government party for lack of an alternative. Despite all these failings, however, the democratic system as it operates in Western countries still succeeds in establishing real (though limited) democratic control of the Government.

In the European Union, things do not work like this. There is no chain of responsibility. Political parties exist – see § 1.3 – but party government does not. No party is in power. No party is responsible for what the Union does. When the Union institutions take decisions, there is no way in which the persons concerned will be responsible to the voters for what they have done. In any event, this will not occur through European elections.[140] In practice, nothing European political parties do, or do not do, will have the slightest effect on the outcome of the next elections. Apart from any other reason, this is because the vast majority of citizens are totally unaware of what goes on in the European Parliament.

The outcome of European elections is not determined by what has taken place in the European Parliament (or in the other institutions of the Union). It depends entirely on national considerations. If the national Government in a Member State is doing well, the electorate will reward it by voting *in the European elections* for the party in power in that Member State. If it is doing badly, they will vote against it. One of the striking features of European elections, at least in Britain, is that issues are often raised that have nothing whatsoever to do with the European Union.

These facts are widely recognized. The problem is that they cannot be solved without turning the Union into a federal State in which the Government is responsible to the European Parliament in the same way that a British Government is responsible to the British Parliament. However, this will not happen because it is not wanted by the national Governments or by the citizens of the Member States. Most people in most countries want ultimate power to remain with the national Governments. They do not want a European super-state. So democratic control, if it operates at all, will have to operate through the national Governments and the national Parliaments. The European Parliament will remain a useful forum for debate and a fertile field in which power brokers and lobbyists can ply their trade on behalf of vested interests, especially big business. But it will not bring democracy to the EU.

[140] There might be indirect repercussions through the national political systems.

FURTHER READING

Items are listed in date order, the most recent being at the end.

WEILER, 'The Community System: The Dual Character of Supranationalism' (1981) 1 YEL 267.

RENÉ JOLIET, *Le droit institutionnel des Communautés européennes: Les institutions; Les sources; Les rapports entre ordres juridiques* (1983), pp. 1–109.

LENAERTS, 'Regulating the Regulatory Process: "Delegation of Powers" in the European Community' (1993) 18 ELRev. 23.

TEASDALE, 'The Life and Death of the Luxembourg Compromise' (1993) 31 JCMS 567.

BONO, 'Co-Decision: An Appraisal of the Experience of the European Parliament as Co-legislator' (1994) 14 YEL 21.

DASHWOOD, 'Community Legislative Procedures in the Era of the Treaty on European Union' (1994) 19 ELRev. 343.

FOSTER, 'The New Conciliation Committee under Article 198b EC' (1994) 19 ELRev. 185.

MARIAS, 'The Right to Petition the European Parliament after Maastricht' (1994) 19 ELRev. 169.

FIONA HAYES-RENSHAW AND HELEN WALLACE, *The Council of Ministers* (1996).

JONES, 'The Committee of the Regions, Subsidiarity and a Warning' (1997) 22 ELRev. 312.

HARDEN, 'When Europeans Complain – The Work of the European Ombudsman' (2000) 2 *Cambridge Yearbook of European Studies* 199.

BRADLEY, 'Institutional Design in the Treaty of Nice' (2001) 38 CMLRev. 1095.

DASHWOOD, 'The Constitution of the European Union after Nice: Law-Making Procedures' (2001) 26 ELRev. 215.

JOHN PETERSON AND MICHAEL SHACKLETON (EDS), *The Institutions of the European Union* (2002).

SIMON HIX, *The Political System of the European Union* (2003).

JACQUÉ, 'The Principle of Institutional Balance' (2004) 41 CMLRev. 383.

WALTER VON ARNIM, '"Fraudulent and Unacceptable"? The Uncontrolled Growth in Allowances in the European Parliament' (2004) 29 ELRev. 698.

VAN GERVEN, *The European Union, A Polity of States and Peoples* (2005).

LEFEVRE, 'Rules of Procedure Do Matter: The Legal Status of the Institutions' Power of Self-Organization' (2005) 30 ELRev. 802.

PAUL CRAIG, *EU Administrative Law* (2006).

STEVE PEERS, *EU Justice and Home Affairs Law*, 2nd edn (2006).

RICHARD CORBETT, FRANCIS JACOBS, AND MICHAEL SHACKLETON, *The European Parliament*, 7th edn (2007).

TSADIRAS, 'The Position of the European Ombudsman in the Community system of Judicial Remedies' (2007) 32 ELRev. 607.

SNELL, '"European Constitutional Settlement", an Ever-Closer Union and the Treaty of Lisbon: Democracy or Relevance?' (2008) 33 ELRev. 619.

GRILLER AND ORATOR, 'Everything under Control? The "Way Forward" for European Agencies in the Footsteps of the Meroni Doctrine' (2010) 35 ELRev. 3.

Chamon, 'EU Agencies between Meroni and Romano or the Devil and the Deep Blue Sea' (2011) 48 CMLRev. 1055.

Cygan, 'The Parliamentarisation of EU Decision-Making? The Impact of the Treaty of Lisbon on National Parliaments' (2011) 36 ELRev. 480.

Kiiver, 'The Early-Warning System for the Principle of Subsidiarity: The National Parliament as a *Conseil d'Etat* for Europe' (2011) 36 ELRev. 98.

De Waele and Broeksteeg, 'The Semi-Permanent European Council Presidency: Some Reflections on the Law and Early Practice' (2012) 49 CMLRev. 1039.

Tsadiras, 'The European Ombudsman's Remedial Powers: An Empirical Analysis in Context' (2013) 38 ELRev. 52.

2

THE EUROPEAN COURT

We start with the new terminology introduced by the Treaty of Lisbon. Under this, 'Court of Justice of the European Union' is an umbrella term covering all the judicial bodies set up by the Treaties. These are:

- the Court of Justice (generally known as the 'European Court');
- the General Court (formerly known as the 'Court of First Instance'); and
- specialized courts (at the moment, only the Civil Service Tribunal).

The main functions of these courts are: to ensure that the law is enforced (especially against Member States); to act as referee between the Member States and the Union as well as between the Union institutions *inter se*; and to ensure the uniform interpretation and application of EU law throughout the Union. The powers of the courts and the law which they administer are considered in detail in the following chapters of this book. Here the stage will be set by discussing their institutional structure.[1]

§1 THE EUROPEAN COURT

§1.1 JUDGES

There is one Judge from each Member State: twenty-eight at present. They are appointed by the common accord of the Member States.[2] It is stated in the Treaties[3] that Judges

[1] The relevant provisions are Art. 19 TEU; Arts 251–281 TFEU; Protocol (No. 3) on the Statute of the Court of Justice of the European Union (a protocol to the Treaties) and the Rules of Procedure. There are separate Rules of Procedure for the Court of Justice, the General Court, and the Civil Service Tribunal. Some of these instruments have been amended; references to them in this chapter are to the versions in force in July 2013. Current versions may be found on the court's website: http://curia.europa.eu.

[2] Art. 19 TEU. In practice, each Member State puts forward its candidate, who is normally accepted by the others. The Treaty of Lisbon (Art. 255 TFEU) has, however, made provision for a panel to be set up to give an opinion on candidates' suitability to perform the duties of Judge and Advocate General of the Court of Justice and the General Court. The panel consists of seven persons chosen from among former members of the European Court and the General Court, members of national supreme courts and lawyers of recognized competence, one of whom will be proposed by the European Parliament.

[3] Art. 253 TFEU.

must be 'persons whose independence is beyond doubt and who possess the qualifications required for appointment to the highest judicial offices in their respective countries or who are jurisconsults of recognized competence'. The latter provision permits academic lawyers to be appointed, even if they are not eligible for appointment to the judiciary in their own countries. Many members of the Court do in fact have academic backgrounds.

Judges are appointed for staggered terms of six years, so that every three years fourteen of the posts fall vacant. They are eligible for reappointment and this frequently occurs; there is no retirement age. The Member States cannot remove a Judge during his (or her) term of office, but he may be dismissed if, in the unanimous opinion of the other Judges and Advocates General, 'he no longer fulfils the requisite conditions or meets the obligations arising from his office'.[4] So far this procedure has never been put into operation.

The President and Vice-President of the Court are elected by their brother Judges for a renewable term of three years.[5] The election is by secret ballot.[6] The President's function is to direct the judicial and administrative business of the Court and to preside at sessions of the Full Court. The Court is divided into Chambers and the President of each Chamber is also elected by the Judges.[7]

On taking up his duties, a Judge gives a solemn undertaking that, both during and after his term of office, he will respect the obligations arising from his appointment. He is not permitted to hold any political or administrative (governmental) office; nor may he engage in any occupation, whether gainful or not, unless exemption is granted by the Council.[8] Several Judges have in fact been permitted to undertake academic functions. Even after they have ceased to hold office, Judges must behave with integrity and discretion as regards the acceptance of appointments or benefits.[9]

As the Court reaches decisions by a majority, and the President has no casting vote, there must always be an uneven number of Judges deciding a case. If one Judge has to withdraw – for example, through illness – the most junior remaining Judge will abstain from taking part in the deliberations.[10]

The Court normally sits in Chambers; it sits as a full Court only in exceptional cases.[11] In addition to Chambers of three or five Judges, there is provision for a Grand Chamber, consisting of fifteen Judges. It is presided over by the President of the Court. The Court will sit as a Grand Chamber where a Member State or a Union institution which is a party to the proceedings so requests.[12] The Court will normally sit in plenary formation (full Court) only in the special cases laid down in the Statute – for example, the compulsory retirement of a member of the Commission for misconduct.[13]

[4] See Art. 6 of the Statute of the Court.
[5] Art. 9a of the Statute.
[6] Art. 8(3) of the Rules of Procedure.
[7] Art. 12 of the Rules of Procedure.
[8] Art. 4 of the Statute of the Court.
[9] *Ibid.*
[10] Rules of Procedure, Art. 33. If the most junior Judge is the Judge-Rapporteur, the next most junior Judge stands down.
[11] Art. 251 TFEU and Art. 16 of the Statute.
[12] Art. 16, third para., of the Statute.
[13] Art. 16, fourth para., of the Statute.

However, a Chamber will be able to refer a case of exceptional importance to the full Court.[14]

It might be thought that the comparatively short terms of office, as well as the appointment procedure, would lessen the independence of the Judges. This does not, however, appear to be the case. It is widely accepted that the members of the Court are, in general, completely independent from their national Governments. A Judge does not, just because he is British, consider himself to be representing Britain on the Court. There is in fact a sense of corporate identity and solidarity among the Judges and Advocates General and, though they may be influenced by the different traditions of their respective legal systems, they have rarely been accused of taking national advantage into account; on the contrary, the Court is generally regarded as one of the most 'European-minded' institutions in the Union.

The most important protection the Judges have against national pressure is the fact that there is always just one 'judgment of the Court' without any separate concurring or dissenting judgments. Since, moreover, the Judges swear to uphold the secrecy of their deliberations, it is never known how individual Judges voted. Therefore it is impossible to accuse a Judge of being insufficiently sensitive to national interests or of having 'let his Government down'; no one outside the Court can ever know whether he vigorously defended the position adopted by his own country or was in the forefront of those advocating a 'Union solution'.

The background of the Judges is varied: many previously held academic, diplomatic, administrative, or judicial offices; some were in private practice.[15]

§1.2 ADVOCATES GENERAL

In addition to the Judges, there are also eight Advocates General.[16] Although not required by law, this normally includes one from each of the big countries. They have the same status as Judges: the same provisions regarding appointment, qualifications, tenure, and removal apply to them as to Judges; they receive the same salary, and they rank equally in precedence with the Judges according to seniority in office. One Advocate General is designated First Advocate General.[17] When administrative matters concerning the functioning of the Court are being discussed, the Advocates General sit with the Judges; but they play no part in the Court's deliberations in judicial matters.

Their function has no parallel in the English legal system, though it is similar to that of a *commissaire du gouvernement* in the French *Conseil d'Etat*. In the words of the Treaty:[18] 'It shall be the duty of the Advocate-General, acting with complete impartiality and independence, to make, in open court, reasoned submissions on cases which, in accordance

[14] Art. 16, last para., of the Statute.

[15] Brief biographies of the members of the Court may be found on the Court's website.

[16] Art. 252 TFEU. The Council, acting unanimously, may increase the number at the request of the Court.

[17] Art. 14 of the Rules of Procedure.

[18] Art. 252, second para., TFEU.

with the Statute of the Court of Justice of the European Union, require his involvement.' When each new case comes to the Court, it is assigned by the First Advocate General to one of the Advocates General. The Advocate General to whom the case is assigned, together with his (or her) legal secretary (discussed later, in § 1.4), will study the issues involved and undertake any legal research they think necessary. After the parties have concluded their submissions to the Court, the Advocate General will give his opinion. This opinion is not binding on the Court, but will be considered with great care by the Judges when they make their decision. It is printed, together with the judgment, in the law reports.

Impartiality and independence are important characteristics of the Advocate General's office. He represents neither the Union nor any Member State: he speaks only for the public interest. He works quite separately and independently from the Judges; one could say that he gives a 'second opinion' which is in fact delivered first. This opinion shows the Judges what a trained legal mind, equal in quality to their own, has concluded on the matter before them. It could be regarded as a point of reference, or starting point, from which they can begin their deliberations. In many cases they follow the Advocate General fully; in others they deviate from his opinion either wholly or in part. But always his views will be of great value.

An Advocate General's job must in many ways be more satisfying than that of a Judge. A Judge works as a member of a committee: any proposal he puts forward regarding a judgment must be agreed to by at least a majority of his colleagues. He cannot, therefore, put his personal stamp upon a judgment in the same way that an English judge can; and even if he succeeds in winning over his brother Judges to his way of thinking on a particular issue, the result is always anonymous: no one outside the closed circle of the Court will ever know that it was his work. The Advocate General, on the other hand, is on his own: his opinion is his own work (though he may receive assistance from his legal secretary) and he alone is responsible for it. He will receive praise or blame according to his deserts.

One feature of the European Court which has sometimes given rise to comment is that there is no appeal from its judgments.[19] In most cases it may be regarded as a court of first and last resort. This puts a heavy burden on the Judges, a burden not made any lighter by the uneven quality of the lawyers who appear before it. The Court cannot always draw the same assistance from counsel as an English court would. In these circumstances, the role of the Advocate General is especially important. His opinion could in fact be regarded as a judgment of first instance which is subject to instant and invariable appeal. It is, however, an appeal of a special nature, since the parties normally have no opportunity to comment on the opinion before the Court begins its deliberations.[20]

[19] However, the European Court itself hears appeals from the General Court.

[20] It could be argued that the absence of such an opportunity is an infringement of Art. 6 of the European Convention on Human Rights. The Court has rejected this view: *Emesa Sugar (Free Zone) NV v. Aruba*, Case C-17/98, [2000] ECR I-665 (Order of 4 February 2000). However, the European Court of Human Rights may take a different view: see *Vermeulen v. Belgium* [1996] I *Reports of Judgments and Decisions* 224 (distinguished by the European Court in the *Emesa Sugar* case).

The Advocate General's opinion is usually much easier to read than the Court's judgment. The latter, being the work of a committee, is often lacking in logical rigour; its terse and formal style is unattractive – at least to those brought up in the common law tradition – while the need to achieve consensus may produce obscurities and inconsistencies. The Advocate General's opinion, on the other hand, is closer in style to an English judgment, this similarity being especially marked – as one would expect – in the case of an English Advocate General. In it, one normally finds a discussion of the facts, reference to (and quotation from) the relevant legislative provisions, and a full consideration of previous decisions of the Court. In some cases, the Advocate General will provide a short comparative survey, prepared with the assistance of the Court 'Documentation Service', of the way in which the point at issue would be dealt with in the different legal systems of the Member States. He will also analyse the arguments put forward by the parties, and finally give his own views on the issues before the Court.

In reaching his conclusions, the Advocate General is not restricted to the arguments advanced by the parties. A good example of a case in which the Advocate General put forward an original solution, which had not occurred to the parties, was *Transocean Marine Paint Association v. Commission*.[21] This case will be considered in detail later;[22] here all that need be said of the facts is that it was an attempt to set aside a decision of the Commission which was unfavourable to the interests of the applicants. They advanced various grounds for their contention; but it was Advocate General Warner, drawing on the law of the Member States – and particularly on that of England – who proposed that it should be annulled for failure to comply with natural justice. This was accepted by the Court and the rule *audi alteram partem* was incorporated into the Union legal system as a general principle of law.

§1.3 THE REGISTRAR

The Registrar of the European Court plays a more important role than his equivalent in most national systems. He (or she) is appointed by the Court for a term of six years and is eligible for reappointment.[23] His functions are twofold. The Registry is responsible for all procedural matters; documents filed with the Court are the responsibility of the Registry, which distributes them to the members of the Court and serves them on the parties. Secondly, the Registrar is in charge of the administration of the Court and is present when the Court holds an administrative meeting, though he does not have a vote. In all these activities, he is responsible to the President of the Court.

§1.4 LEGAL SECRETARIES

Each Judge and Advocate General has a number of assistants, officially known as 'legal secretaries' (*référendaires* in French). They usually belong to a younger generation than

[21] Case 17/74, [1974] ECR 1063. [22] See Chap. 5, § 6.

[23] Art. 253, fifth para., TFEU; Rules of Procedure, Art. 18. A secret ballot is held: *ibid*.

the Judges and Advocates General; they may be lecturers or practising lawyers, and they usually spend a few years at the Court before returning to their careers in their own countries. Their main task is to carry out legal research and to assist in the preparation of opinions or other legal writing. They are chosen by the Judge or Advocate General for whom they work.

§1.5 SPECIALIZED SERVICES

The Court has an excellent library, with materials covering the legal systems of the Member States as well as that of the Union. There is at least one lawyer on the staff from each Member State, and the Research and Documentation Division provides the Judges and Advocates General with background papers on Union law and comparative surveys of national law.

There is a Translation Directorate which translates legal documents, including the judgments of the Court and the opinions of the Advocates General, into the various languages of the Court. There is also an Information Office, which provides lawyers (and others) with information on recent cases and other aspects of the Court's work.

§2 THE GENERAL COURT

The General Court was established in 1989, following amendments contained in the Single European Act.[24] It was originally called the 'Court of First Instance', before being renamed by the Treaty of Lisbon. The aim when creating this court was to lessen the workload of the European Court by relieving it of some of the cases with no political or constitutional importance, especially those involving complex facts. The European Court could then concentrate on the task of deciding the more important cases and maintaining the unity of Union law. A right of appeal to the European Court on points of law would ensure that the General Court stayed in line. It was hoped that the establishment of the General Court would reduce the backlog of cases pending before the European Court. The General Court has indeed relieved the European Court of a significant number of cases, but the unremitting build-up of new cases continues to cause serious problems.[25]

The General Court consists of at least one Judge from each Member State.[26] At present, there are twenty-eight Judges.[27] The provisions regarding their appointment and terms of office are the same as those for the European Court, but the provision concerning their qualifications is slightly different: they must possess the 'ability required

[24] For the background, see Kennedy, 'The Essential Minimum: The Establishment of the General Court' (1989) 14 ELRev. 7; see also 'Reflections on the Future Development of the Community Judicial System' (a discussion paper issued by the General Court in 1990) (1991) 16 ELRev. 175.

[25] See 'Editorial Comments' (2011) 48 CMLRev. 987.

[26] Art. 19(2), second para., TEU.

[27] Art. 48 of the Statute (as amended by the Treaty of Accession for Croatia, Art. 9(2)).

for appointment to high judicial office'.[28] They elect one of their number as President for a renewable term of three years.[29] There are no Advocates General as such, but when the General Court sits in Plenary Session, the President of the General Court designates a Judge to act as Advocate General.[30] A Chamber of the General Court may be assisted by an Advocate General if the legal difficulty or factual complexity of the case so requires.[31] The decision to designate an Advocate General in a particular case is taken by the General Court sitting in plenary session at the request of the Chamber concerned.[32]

The General Court usually sits in Chambers of three or five Judges or in a Grand Chamber of thirteen Judges.[33] It may also be constituted by a single Judge.[34] It sits in plenary session in certain special instances – for example, if the difficulty or importance of the case so justify.[35]

§3 THE CIVIL SERVICE TRIBUNAL

Article 257 TFEU makes provision for the establishment of specialized courts, which are intended to lessen the workload of the General Court by relieving it of some of the less important cases. Acting under this provision, the Council has established the European Civil Service Tribunal,[36] which hears disputes involving the European Union Civil Service. At present, it consists of seven Judges, appointed by the Council acting unanimously. They are appointed for a renewable period of six years[37] and are chosen from among persons who 'possess the ability required for appointment to judicial office'.[38] An appeal from their decisions (on points of law only) lies to the General Court.[39]

§4 JURISDICTION

This section is concerned with the jurisdiction of the European Court, the General Court, and the Civil Service Tribunal. Initially, no distinction will be made between them and, for ease of explanation, they will all be referred to as 'the European Court'.

[28] Art. 254, second para., TFEU. [29] Art. 254, third para., TFEU.

[30] See the Rules of Procedure of the General Court, Art. 17; see also Art. 49 of the Statute of the Court.

[31] Rules of Procedure of the General Court, Art. 18.

[32] Rules of Procedure of the General Court, Art. 19.

[33] Rules of Procedure of the General Court, Art. 10.

[34] Art. 50 of the Statute. See also Art. 14(2) of the Rules of Procedure of the General Court.

[35] Art. 50, second para., of the Statute; Art. 11(1) of the Rules of Procedure and the provisions referred to therein, including Art. 14(1). [36] Art. 62c of the Statute and Annex I to the Statute.

[37] Art. 2 of Annex I to the Statute. [38] Art. 257, fourth para., TFEU.

[39] Art. 257, third para., TFEU; Art. 11 of Annex I to the Statute.

The Treaties give the European Court only limited jurisdiction.[40] There are a number of specific heads of jurisdiction and a case must be brought within one of them if the Court is to hear it. The various kinds of actions will be analysed in detail in the chapters that follow; here it is enough to give an overall picture. Diagram 2.1 illustrates the principal heads of jurisdiction under the EU Treaties.

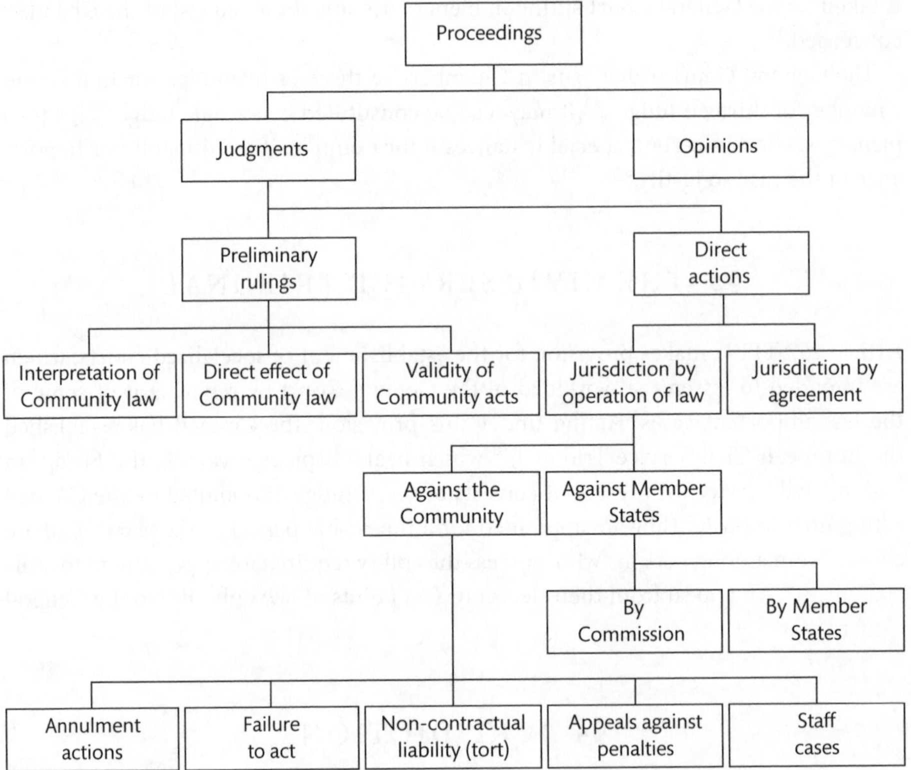

Diagram 2.1 The Principal Heads of Jurisdiction of the European Court under the EU Treaties

There are several criteria according to which the Court's jurisdiction may be classified. The most basic distinction is between judgments, on the one hand, and opinions or rulings, on the other. The latter are very much rarer than the former, but they occur in

[40] As an institution of the Union, the European Court must 'act only within the limits of the competences conferred upon it by the Member States in the Treaties': Art. 5(2) TEU. In spite of this, the Court interprets its jurisdiction generously and in some cases clearly goes beyond the limits set by the Treaties (see, for example, *Zwartveld*, Case C-2/88, [1990] ECR I-4405). It may even consider that it has the power to confer jurisdiction on itself, though it has not said so expressly. For a general discussion of the question, see Arnull, 'Does the Court of Justice Have Inherent Jurisdiction?' (1990) 27 CMLRev. 683; Usher, 'How Limited is the Jurisdiction of the European Court?' in J Dine, S Douglas-Scott, and I Persaud (eds), *Procedure and the European Court* (1991), at pp. 72 *et seq.*

a number of situations, for example, where the Council, the Commission, or a Member State requests an opinion on whether an international agreement which the Union intends to conclude with a non-member State is compatible with the EU Treaties. Though advisory, these opinions have legal consequences: if, in the above example, the opinion is adverse, the agreement may enter into force only if the EU Treaties are amended to accommodate it.

As far as judgments are concerned, the most fundamental distinction is between actions begun in the European Court (direct actions) and actions begun in a national court from which a reference for a preliminary ruling is made to the European Court. This distinction is important because, if an action is begun in the European Court, it will end in the European Court: the Court's judgment will constitute a final determination of the dispute between the parties and will grant any remedies that may be appropriate; it is not subject to appeal.[41]

If, on the other hand, the action is begun in a national court, it will end in a national court: the European Court's ruling will be transmitted to the national court and the latter will then decide the case. Here the European Court's ruling, though binding and not subject to appeal, is merely a determination of an abstract point of law: the European Court does not decide the case as such. The national court decides any relevant questions of fact and then applies the law – including relevant provisions of Union law as interpreted by the European Court – to the facts; it also exercises any discretion it may have as to the remedy to be given.

In spite of the limited role played by the European Court, preliminary rulings are of great importance because they concern the relationship between Union law and national law. It is only to the extent that it penetrates the national legal systems and confers rights and imposes obligations directly on private citizens that Union law can be really effective. It is through its power to give preliminary rulings that the European Court has established the doctrine of direct effect and the doctrine of the supremacy of Union law over national law.[42] The European Court will give a preliminary ruling only when requested to do so by a national court which considers that a question of Union law is relevant to its decision: any court or tribunal *may* make such a request; a court or tribunal from which there is no appeal *must* do so. The issues which may be referred to the European Court are of three kinds: the interpretation of a provision of Union law, the effect of such a provision in the national legal system (which, in theory, is also a question of interpretation), and, in the case of a measure passed by the Union itself, the validity of such a provision.

Direct actions may be divided into two categories: those over which the Court has jurisdiction by virtue of an agreement between the parties and those where the Court's jurisdiction is conferred by direct operation of the law. The former are not very important in practice; the main example is actions arising out of a contract concluded by the Union which contains a clause giving jurisdiction to the European Court.

[41] There are, however, appeals (on points of law) from the General Court to the European Court and from the Civil Service Tribunal to the General Court.

[42] See Chaps 7 and 9.

Direct actions where the Court's jurisdiction does not depend on consent may be classified according to whether the defendant is the Union or a Member State. A number of different kinds of action may be brought against the Union. The two most important are actions for judicial review and actions for damages for non-contractual liability (tort). Actions for judicial review may be brought either to annul a Union measure or to oblige a Union institution to pass a measure which it had previously refused to pass. Such proceedings are brought against the relevant Union institution;[43] they may be brought by a Member State, another Union institution, or – in certain special cases – by a private individual.

Actions for damages for non-contractual liability may be brought against the Union by either a Member State or a private individual. The applicant must prove that he has suffered loss as a result of Union action (or inaction).

Other proceedings in which a Union institution is the defendant include appeals against penalties imposed under Union regulations (if the regulation in question so provides), and employment disputes between the Union and its staff.

Actions against a Member State are called enforcement actions. They may be brought against a Member State alleged to have violated Union law. The applicant may be either the Commission or another Member State; in practice it is almost always the Commission. There is a preliminary procedure in which an opinion is given by the Commission after the Member State has explained its position: if the Member State refuses to abide by this opinion, the Commission (or the other Member State) brings the action before the Court.

§4.1 JURISDICTION OF THE GENERAL COURT

The European Court (Court of Justice) has jurisdiction in all the above instances, except where jurisdiction has been conferred on the General Court or the Civil Service Tribunal.

The rules governing the jurisdiction of the General Court are to be found in Article 256 TFEU, and Article 51 of the Statute. They are rather complex. The Treaty Articles confer jurisdiction on the General Court in a fairly wide range of cases[44] (annulment actions, actions for failure to act, tort actions, staff actions, and contract cases where the contract so provides), with the exception of those assigned to a specialized court (the Civil Service Tribunal); however, they also provide, first, that the Statute may reserve some of these cases for the European Court and, secondly, that it may give the General Court jurisdiction in other cases. Article 51 of the Statute does not give the General Court any additional jurisdiction; however, it reserves a number of cases for the European Court. These cover a wide range of proceedings brought by Member States or Union institutions. The result is that cases before the General Court consist

[43] They may also be brought against bodies, offices, or agencies of the Union.

[44] Arts 263, 265, 268, 270, and 272 TFEU.

mainly, though not entirely, of cases brought by private persons (usually companies) against the Union (usually the Commission). Competition cases, anti-dumping cases, and trade mark cases are the most important. The full list is as follows:[45]

- annulment actions, or actions for failure to act, by private persons against Union institutions or agencies;
- actions by Member States against the Commission;
- actions by Member States against the Council, though only regarding acts adopted in the fields of State aid and dumping, and acts by which the Council exercises implementing powers;
- actions in tort against the Union;
- actions in contract where the contract expressly confers jurisdiction on the General Court;
- actions relating to Union trade marks;
- appeals (on points of law) against decisions of the Civil Service Tribunal; and
- actions brought against decisions of the Plant Variety Office or the European Chemicals Agency.

§4.2 APPEALS FROM THE GENERAL COURT

There is a right of appeal, on points of law only, from the General Court to the European Court.[46] The grounds of appeal are lack of competence (equivalent to *ultra vires*); a breach of procedure (which must adversely affect the interests of the appellant); or any other infringement of Union law.[47]

Appeals may be brought by a party or intervener; however, a Member State or Union institution may appeal even if it is not a party or intervener. Interveners other than Union institutions or Member States may appeal only where the decision of the General Court directly affects them.

If the General Court annuls a Union regulation, the annulment does not take effect until the time for bringing an appeal has expired; if an appeal is brought, the annulment does not take effect unless and until the appeal is dismissed.

If the European Court allows the appeal, it quashes the judgment of the General Court. It may then either give final judgment itself, or it may refer the case back to the General Court for final judgment.[48]

[45] See http://curia.europa.eu/jcms/jcms/Jo2_7033/#compet.

[46] Art. 256(1) TFEU, together with Arts 56–61 of the Statute.

[47] An appeal may not be taken only on the amount of costs or the party ordered to pay them.

[48] For statistics on appeals from the General Court up to the end of 1994, see Brown, 'The First Five Years of the Court of First Instance and Appeals to the Court of Justice: Assessment and Statistics' (1995) 32 CMLRev. 743. On the basis of these statistics, Professor Brown concludes (at 757) that, of the cases decided by the General Court, only about one in ten is appealed and, of these appeals, only one in ten is wholly successful; consequently, only one decision in a hundred is completely overturned on appeal.

§4.3 JURISDICTION OF THE CIVIL SERVICE TRIBUNAL AND APPEALS FROM IT

The jurisdiction of the Civil Service Tribunal is limited to disputes between the Union and its staff.[49] There is a right of appeal on points of law from its decisions to the General Court.[50] Most of what was said previously regarding appeals from the General Court also applies to appeals from the Civil Service Tribunal.

§5 PROCEDURE

This section focuses on the European Court, but most of what is said applies to the other courts as well. The procedure in the European Court is laid down partly in the Statute of the Court and partly in the Rules of Procedure,[51] which were originally modelled on those of the International Court of Justice.

The two most important ways in which the procedure in the European Court differs from that in an English court are the greater importance of written documents (and the consequent downgrading of oral proceedings) and the more active role played by the Court. Both of these features are generally characteristic of Continental courts.

The normal procedure in a direct action may be divided into four stages: the written proceedings, the preparatory inquiry, the oral hearing, and the judgment.

§5.1 THE WRITTEN PROCEEDINGS

Direct actions in the European Court are begun with a document called an application, in which the applicant (claimant) sets out the basis of his claim. This is not served on the defendant but lodged with the Court; the Registrar will serve it on the defendant, who then has one month to lodge his defence. The applicant is entitled to reply to the defence by means of a document called a reply, and the defendant may answer this in a rejoinder. Then the pleadings are closed.

§5.2 ADMISSIBILITY

At this point the defendant may make a preliminary objection regarding admissibility. This concerns the question whether the Court is able to hear the case, in particular whether the subject matter is within the Court's jurisdiction, whether the applicant has *locus standi*, and whether the proceedings were brought within the relevant time limit. A preliminary objection to admissibility is made in a separate document, to which the applicant is entitled to reply. There is a special hearing on the point and the Advocate

[49] Art. 1 of Annex I to the Statute.

[50] Art. 257 TFEU; Arts 9–13 of Annex I to the Statute.

[51] See n. 1.

General gives an opinion. The Court will then give judgment: it may uphold the objection (in which case the action will be at an end), or dismiss it (in which case the proceedings will continue from the point where they were broken off), or it may decide to reserve its decision until the final judgment: in this case the main action will continue, but in the end the Court may decide that it was inadmissible and reject it without going into the merits.

§5.3 PREPARATORY INQUIRY

The second stage is the preparatory inquiry. This is concerned with the determination of questions of fact. Unlike the English procedure, however, it is the Court which decides what evidence is needed. As soon as the application has been lodged, the President of the Court will assign the case to one of the Chambers and designate a Judge from that Chamber as 'Judge-Rapporteur'; the First Advocate General will then decide which Advocate General will take the case. After the close of pleadings, the Judge-Rapporteur will prepare a preliminary report dealing with the issues of fact arising in the case. The Court will then decide, at a so-called general meeting (formerly 'administrative meeting'), what issues of fact (if any) need to be proved and what evidence is necessary for this purpose. In practice, questions of fact are not often in dispute and the Court will usually content itself with requiring the production of documents, and, possibly, putting questions to the parties. Where witnesses are called, the procedure is rather different from that in an English court. The witnesses are always witnesses of the Court, not the parties. (If a party wishes a certain witness to be called, he must make a request to the Court.) A witness is summoned by an order of the Court which will indicate the facts on which he is to be examined. The witness is heard before a Chamber of the Court in the presence of the parties or their representatives; the presiding Judge will examine the witness, but the parties – as well as the other Judges and the Advocate General – may put questions as well. The testimony is put into writing and signed by the witness after being read back to him.

§5.4 ORAL PROCEDURE

This corresponds to the 'day in court' in English procedure. However, since the evidence has already been taken at an earlier stage, it is much less important to the outcome of the case. A few weeks beforehand, the Judge-Rapporteur issues his report for the hearing, which is distributed to the parties so that they can comment on it at the hearing. The report sets out the facts of the case and contains a summary of the arguments put forward by the parties.

At the hearing, counsel will address the Court and expound their contentions. After the main speeches, each side is allowed a brief reply. The Judges and the Advocate General may address questions to counsel. The Court then usually adjourns and the Advocate General prepares his opinion; the hearing resumes at a later date for him to deliver it. The parties have no right to comment on it: the hearing is now over and the Court must consider its judgment.

§5.5 JUDGMENT

The Court always reserves judgment. The Judges meet in a special deliberation room to decide on their judgment; no one other than the Judges themselves may be present, not even secretaries or interpreters. The Judge-Rapporteur has the task of preparing a draft of the judgment which is then put before the other Judges; if necessary a vote is taken. The procedure is that each Judge gives his opinion in turn, starting with the most junior.

When a decision is finally reached, the judgment is signed by all the Judges sitting and is delivered in open court. It is also published: the operative part (formal ruling) in the Official Journal and the whole judgment, together with the Advocate General's opinion, in the official law reports.

§5.6 EXECUTION

In most cases the defendant is either the Union (or an institution thereof) or a Member State; in neither of these cases is it possible to obtain execution of the judgment. The judgment is binding, and it is assumed that it will be obeyed. The question of execution only arises, therefore, in those rare cases where the defendant is a private individual and damages are awarded against him, or where the applicant is a private person and costs are awarded against him. In these cases the judgment creditor must go to the appropriate national court to obtain enforcement according to national procedure; enforcement is, however, automatic and the national court has no right to question the judgment.[52]

§5.7 SPECIAL PROCEDURES AFTER JUDGMENT

There is no appeal from judgments of the European Court; there are, however, three special procedures which, to a very limited extent, might be said to serve a similar function. These are third-party proceedings, revision, and interpretation. The first two allow a request to be made to the European Court to review a judgment previously given by it; under the third, the Court may be asked to clarify the meaning of its judgment.[53] Though of theoretical interest, these proceedings are rare in practice.

Third-party proceedings provide a means whereby a person who was not a party to the original action may contest a judgment which is prejudicial to his rights.[54] The proceedings are begun by an application to which similar rules apply as in the case of an ordinary action, and which is lodged with the Court and served by the Registrar on all the parties to the original proceedings. The third party must show that the judgment

[52] Arts 280 and 299 TFEU. For the procedure in the United Kingdom, see Chap. 8, § 7.5.

[53] Clerical mistakes, errors in calculation, and obvious slips in the judgment may also be corrected by the Court of its own motion, or on application of a party within two weeks after the delivery of the judgment; see Art. 103 of the Rules of Procedure. A party may apply within one month for the Court to make good any omission in its judgment: Art. 155 of the Rules of Procedure.

[54] Art. 42 of the Statute. See also Art. 157 of the Rules of Procedure.

is prejudicial to his rights and give good reasons why he was unable to take part in the original action (normally this would be because it was not brought to his notice). The proceedings must be brought within two months of the publication of the judgment in the Official Journal.

When a new fact comes to light after the judgment which would have had a decisive impact on it, a party to the original proceedings may apply for revision.[55] The fact must not have been before the Court when it gave judgment and must also have been unknown to the party making the application. The proceedings must be brought within three months of the discovery of the new fact and also within ten years of the original judgment. When an application is made, the Court first decides whether the new fact is of sufficient importance to warrant the reopening of the case; if it decides that this is so, it will then reconsider the original judgment in the light of the new fact. The other party is, of course, allowed to contest the application, both at the stage of admissibility and when the judgment is reviewed.

An application for the interpretation of a judgment may be brought by a party to the original case, or by a Union institution even if it was not a party.[56] The request may be directed only to the actual ruling or the reasoning on which it was based; the clarification of *obiter dicta* may not be requested.

§5.8 PRELIMINARY RULINGS

The procedure is different where the European Court is asked by a national court to give a preliminary ruling. Here there are, strictly speaking, no parties; the proceedings are not regarded as contentious: the European Court views its function simply as assisting the national court. The parties to the national proceedings cannot, therefore, take the initiative before the European Court: the national court sets the procedure in motion by making an order for reference, and the judgment of the European Court is sent back to the national court where the case will continue on its course. The events in the European Court are only an episode in the national proceedings.

When an order for reference reaches the European Court, the Registrar will transmit copies to the parties in the national proceedings and also to the Member States, the Commission, and, where a measure of the Council is in issue, to the Council. These persons and bodies may submit written observations to the Court and they may also attend the oral hearing. At the hearing, submissions are made by those attending; then the Advocate General presents his opinion, and judgment is given in the normal way. The parties to the national proceedings may not request revision or interpretation of the judgment; but the national court may, if it wishes, make a second reference in order to deal with a new issue or to clarify the original ruling.

[55] Art. 44 of the Statute. See also Art. 159 of the Rules of Procedure.

[56] Art. 43 of the Statute. See also Art. 158 of the Rules of Procedure.

In certain cases, at the request of the national court or, exceptionally, of the Court's own motion, references may be dealt with under an urgent procedure.[57] Where this applies, the procedure is somewhat different – for example, time limits may be shorter. Where the reference is made with regard to a person in custody, the European Court must 'act with the minimum delay'.[58]

§5.9 LAWYERS

The rules regarding legal representation differ according to whether the party is, on the one hand, a private person or company or, on the other hand, a Member State or Union institution.[59] In the former case, representation by a lawyer is obligatory; the only exception is that in references for preliminary rulings the national rules apply: therefore, if a party is permitted to appear in person in the court from which the reference was made, he will be allowed to do so in the European Court.

Member States and Union institutions are represented by an agent appointed for the particular case; the agent may be assisted by an adviser or lawyer. National Governments often choose a civil servant (normally with legal qualifications) as their agent; alternatively they may brief a barrister. The Council, Commission, and Parliament are normally represented by a member of their legal services; sometimes outside lawyers may be briefed.

The right of a lawyer to appear before the European Court depends on national law. In direct actions, any lawyer entitled to practise before a court of any Member State may appear before the European Court; in preliminary references, anyone (even if not legally qualified) entitled to represent a party before the court or tribunal which made the reference may do so before the European Court. Agents and advisers of Member States and Union institutions may appear even if not entitled to plead in national courts.

In direct actions, the general rule is that costs are awarded to the successful party if he has asked for them.[60] Where costs are granted, the unsuccessful party must not only pay his own costs (for example, lawyers' fees, travelling expenses, etc.) but also those of the successful party. In the event of a dispute, either party may apply for costs to be taxed by the Court. In preliminary rulings, on the other hand, the European Court does not award costs: they are regarded as costs in the case before the national court and any ruling made by it applies to them as well.

[57] Arts 107–114 of the Rules of Procedure. For an assessment, see Barnard, 'The PPU: Is it Worth the Candle? An Early Assessment' (2009) 34 ELRev. 281. There is also provision for an 'expedited procedure', applicable both to preliminary rulings (Arts 105 and 106 of the Rules of Procedure) and to direct actions (Arts 133–136 of the Rules of Procedure).

[58] Art. 267, last para., TFEU. This provision was added by the Treaty of Lisbon.

[59] See Art. 19 of the Statute. See also Arts 43–47 of the Rules of Procedure.

[60] The rules regarding costs in the European Court are to be found in Arts 137–146 (direct actions) and Art. 102 (preliminary rulings) of the Rules of Procedure.

A person who is wholly or partly unable to meet the costs of proceedings in the European Court may apply for legal aid.[61] The application is made to the Court itself and is heard by a Chamber. Legal representation is not necessary for such an application.

§6 MULTILINGUALISM

§6.1 INTRODUCTION

One of the characteristics of the Union is that it is multilingual. Between them, the Member States have twenty-four official languages – Bulgarian, Croatian, Czech, Danish, Dutch, English, Estonian, Finnish, French, German, Greek, Hungarian, Irish, Italian, Latvian, Lithuanian, Maltese, Polish, Portuguese, Romanian, Slovak, Slovene, Spanish, and Swedish.

The principle of linguistic equality was not fully accepted in the beginning. When the ECSC Treaty was signed in 1951, Germany (and, to some extent, Italy) were in a weak political position as a consequence of the war; Britain had chosen to stand aloof from Europe. Therefore it was hardly surprising that France played the leading role and that the French language enjoyed a special position. The result was that the Treaty was drawn up in a single text in French.[62] There was no express statement that only the French text was authentic, but this was generally regarded as following from the fact that it was the original. Official translations were, however, made into Dutch, German, and Italian and, subsequently, into the official languages of the new Member States. The EU Treaties, on the other hand, are authentic in the official languages of all the Member States.[63]

All the official languages except Irish are working languages of the institutions.[64] Union legislation is published in all the working languages, and it is generally accepted that all versions are equally authentic.[65] When Denmark, Ireland, and the United Kingdom joined, pre-accession Union measures still in force were translated into Danish and English, and Article 155 of the Act of Accession stated that they would have the same authenticity as the versions in the other languages. This was also done when other Member States joined later.

[61] For the European Court, see Arts 115–118 and 185–189 of the Rules of Procedure. See also Kennedy, 'Paying the Piper: Legal Aid in Proceedings before the Court of Justice' (1988) 27 CMLRev. 559.

[62] See Art. 100 ECSC.

[63] Art. 55 TEU; Art. 358 TFEU.

[64] See Art. 342 TFEU, together with Regulation 1 (EC), JO 1958, p. 385 and Regulation 1 (EAEC), JO 1958, p. 401, as amended on the accession of new Member States. As far as the ECSC was concerned, see P. Reuter, *La Communauté Européenne du Charbon et de l'Acier* (1953), pp. 81–2, referring to an unpublished decision of the foreign ministers of the original Six, taken at a meeting in Paris on 23 and 24 July 1952, that Dutch, French, German, and Italian would be the working languages.

[65] See H. Kutscher, 'Methods of Interpretation as Seen by a Judge at the Court of Justice', p. 17 (paper delivered at the Judicial and Academic Conference held at the European Court in 1976).

The interpretation of multilingual texts poses particular problems. In public international law, various theories on the interpretation of multilingual treaties have been put forward. They include the following: that the least onerous version should be preferred (theory of minimum obligation); that each Contracting State should be bound only by the version in its own language; and that the text in the original language should prevail.[66] However, theories which might be appropriate for international law are not necessarily appropriate for Union law. In particular, it would be unacceptable for the obligations of Member States to vary because of differences in the texts.[67]

In practice, the European Court does not appear to have been troubled by linguistic differences in the texts. The reason is simple: even when there are no linguistic problems, the Court does not put a great deal of weight on the literal meaning of the words. Policy considerations play a particularly important role and sometimes prevail over the literal meaning even when it is clear.[68] Linguistic discrepancies are, therefore, treated in the same way as other obscurities in the text: the Court adopts the meaning which, in its view, best accords with the purpose of the provision and the policy objectives pursued by the Court.[69] This applies both in those cases where the same term is used in all the versions but its meaning differs in the various national systems and also in those cases where different terms are used.

The chapters that follow contain many examples of the Court's practice of choosing between the various versions on the basis of policy objectives. Here it is sufficient to mention one: *Stauder v. City of Ulm*.[70] This case, which is considered further in Chapter 5, § 2.1, concerned a Union scheme under which persons in receipt of welfare benefits could obtain butter at a reduced price on presentation of a coupon. The scheme had been established by a Commission decision addressed to all the Member States, and the German version stated that the coupon had to contain the beneficiary's name; the Dutch version was similar, but the French and Italian texts stated merely that the coupon had to be 'individualized'.

The German authorities charged with implementing the scheme had looked only to the German version and had issued vouchers which had to contain the name and address of the beneficiary. The plaintiff in the case maintained that it was a humiliation to have to reveal his identity to the shopkeeper when he bought the butter; he even went so far as to argue that this constituted a violation of his human rights. He therefore brought legal proceedings in the German courts and the case came before the European Court on a reference for a preliminary ruling on the interpretation and validity of the Commission decision. The Court held that it should be interpreted so as

[66] See Dickschat, 'Problèmes d'interprétation des traités européens résultant de leur plurilinguisme' [1968] *Revue Belge de Droit International* 40 at 43–4.

[67] See the quotation from *Stauder v. City of Ulm* set out later.

[68] See § 10.

[69] See *Mij PPW Internationaal*, Case 61/72, [1973] ECR 301 (para. 14 of the judgment) and *Moulijn v. Commission*, Case 6/74, [1974] ECR 1287 (paras 10 and 11 of the judgment); see further Kutscher, 'Methods of Interpretation' (n. 65), p. 20.

[70] Case 29/69, [1969] ECR 419. See also *Moksel v. BALM*, Case 55/87, [1988] ECR 3845 (paras 14–19 of the judgment).

not to require the recipient's name to be revealed. The relevant passage of the judgment reads as follows:[71]

> When a single decision is addressed to all the Member States the necessity for uniform application and accordingly for uniform interpretation makes it impossible to consider one version of the text in isolation but requires that it be interpreted on the basis of both the real intention of its author and the aim he seeks to achieve, in the light in particular of the versions in all four languages.
>
> In a case like the present one, the most liberal interpretation must prevail, provided that it is sufficient to achieve the objectives pursued by the decision in question. It cannot, moreover, be accepted that the authors of the decision intended to impose stricter obligations in some Member States than in others.

The consequence of this judgment is that, even when a Union decision is addressed to a Member State, that State must be prepared to consider all the linguistic versions if it wants to be sure of the correct interpretation.[72]

§6.2 COURT PROCEDURE

What languages may be used in Court proceedings? The question depends on what is known as the 'language of the case'.[73] Any one of the official languages of the Member States (including Irish) may be chosen, and the theory behind the rules governing the choice of language is that the Union is regarded as multilingual and consequently able to operate in any official language. Union institutions are therefore required to accommodate themselves to the needs of the other party.

In direct actions, the basic rule is that the applicant has the choice of language. However, where the defendant is a Member State, the language of the case is the official language of that State. (Where the Member State has more than one official language – as, for example, is the case with Belgium – the applicant may choose between them.) Except in the rare cases where a Member State brings enforcement proceedings against another Member State, the Union will always be a party to a direct action; the effect of these rules, therefore, is to benefit the other party. The Court may depart from the rules at the request of the parties; however, where the request is not made jointly by the parties, the Advocate General and the other party must be heard.

In the case of a preliminary ruling, the language of the case is that of the national court or tribunal which made the reference,[74] though other Member States may submit observations in their own languages.[75]

In general, the language of the case is used for all purposes in the proceedings, and documents in other languages must be translated into it. Members of the Court,

[71] [1969] ECR at 424–5 (paras 3 and 4 of the judgment).
[72] See Kutscher, 'Methods of Interpretation' (n. 65), pp. 18–19.
[73] See Arts 36–41 of the Rules of Procedure.
[74] Art. 37(3) of the Rules of Procedure. Again, the use of another language may be permitted.
[75] Art. 38(4) of the Rules of Procedure.

however, may use any official language of their choice. This applies to comments and questions during the hearing, and to the Advocate General's opinion.[76] There is simultaneous translation at the oral hearing. Court publications, including law reports, are published in the working languages of the Union (i.e., in all the official languages except Irish).

It will readily be appreciated that litigants in the European Court face linguistic problems not encountered in domestic courts. The private litigant normally has the choice of language; however, a litigant who chooses, for example, Finnish must be aware of the fact that most Judges cannot understand this language. The precision of the pleadings may suffer on translation, and at the hearing the eloquence of counsel may have little effect when it is heard through the earphones of the simultaneous-translation apparatus. Clearly, a French-speaking lawyer – or an English-speaking one – will find it easier to present his case.

§6.3 DRAFTING THE JUDGMENT

In order to maintain the secrecy of their discussions, the Judges do not allow any interpreters into the deliberation room. In these circumstances multilingualism is impossible and the Court has informally adopted French as its working language. This choice was made when the Court was first set up and is another example of the special position enjoyed by the French in those days. Indeed, the choice of French was almost inevitable in view of the fact that it was an official language of three of the six original Member States (France, Belgium, and Luxembourg). Today, English is more widely spoken in the majority of Union countries, but it is unlikely, for a considerable time at least, to replace French as the working language of the Court: once made, a choice of language is hard to change, since appointments to the Court are made with this in mind.

The choice of French as the working language of the Court means that the Judges are supposed to speak French when they discuss their judgment. All drafting is done in French and the final version approved by the Court is in French, even if this is not the language of the case. The French text of the judgment is then translated into the language of the case and this text is signed by the Judges and delivered in open court. The result is that the text signed by the Judges may be in a language which many of them do not understand. This throws a great deal of responsibility on those Judges who are fluent in the language of the case to ensure that the translation truly reflects what was agreed on.

One drawback of the unilingual mode of operation of the Court is that it puts Judges whose mother tongue is not French at a disadvantage. Most people feel less confident about giving their opinions in a group discussion if they are not fully at home in the language spoken. French-speaking Judges must therefore enjoy a subtle psychological

[76] Art. 38(8) of the Rules of Procedure.

advantage over their colleagues. The use of French in the deliberation room must, moreover, work to some extent in favour of French legal thinking: it is hard to draft a judgment in French without using French legal terminology, while concepts peculiar to other systems might be ignored simply because they cannot easily be expressed in French.

Another difficulty is that, although the official version of the judgment is in the language of the case, the French-language version is the one actually agreed on by the Court and therefore might be said to represent the opinion of the Court more accurately than the former. One can imagine that, if there is a discussion in the deliberation room as to exactly what was decided in a previous case, it is the French text which will be examined. Consequently, a lawyer trying to convince the Court that it ought to follow its previous decision would be well advised to study the French text as well as that in his own language, even if the latter is the authentic version; where this is not the case, it is especially important not to rely exclusively on the one version.

It is almost impossible for even the best translator to find a form of words with exactly the same meaning as the original; translations, therefore, can never be exact. Sometimes there is simply no equivalent word in the other language. For example, Article 40 ECSC used the phrase '*faute de service*' in the French version; this is a French legal term which cannot be translated directly into English: the translators of the Treaty therefore had to make do with the circumlocution 'wrongful act or omission [on the part of the Union] in the performance of its functions', a phrase which entirely lacks the precise connotations of the French. (One can imagine that if the English word 'trust' were translated into French, the translators might well come up with something equivalent to 'legal relationship in which one person has a beneficial interest in property nominally owned by another', a phrase which can have little meaning for someone ignorant of English law.)

In addition to the inaccuracies which inevitably result from translation, actual mistakes sometimes occur. For example, in the English version of the judgment in *Royer*,[77] the word 'save' was omitted from the following passage: 'the procedure of appeal to a competent authority must precede the decision ordering expulsion [save] in cases of emergency'. This was a simple slip; a less obvious, and thus more insidious, error occurred in the *Bonsignore* case.[78] Here the phrase '*Gefährdungen der öffentlichen Ordnung*' in the authentic German version of the judgment – '*des menaces à l'ordre public*' in the French version – was mistranslated into English as 'breaches of the peace', a mistake which caused difficulties in a later case when an English court made a reference for a preliminary ruling on the same issue.[79]

[77] Case 48/75, [1976] ECR 497 at para. 59 of the judgment. The authentic version of this judgment was in French.

[78] Case 67/74, [1975] ECR 297 at 307.

[79] *R v. Bouchereau*, Case 30/77, [1977] ECR 1999; see *per* Advocate General Warner at 2024. 'Threats to public policy' would be a literal translation of the German and French texts.

§7 THE FORM OF JUDGMENT

Judgments of the European Court consist of three main parts. The first[80] is based on the report of the Judge-Rapporteur and contains a statement of the facts, the legal background, and a summary of the arguments of the parties; the second part[81] contains the reasoning of the judgment; the final part is the actual ruling.[82] For easy reference, the judgment is drawn up in numbered paragraphs.

For lawyers, the second part is the important one, since this gives the Court's reasons for its decision. After a certain amount of experimentation in the early days, the Court adopted a style based on that of the French courts. This is formal, terse, and abstract. In the beginning, the French version was written in the form of one long sentence, each paragraph beginning with the words '*Attendu que*...' ('Whereas...') or simply '*que*' ('that') and ending with a semicolon. These subordinate clauses would all lead up to the final ruling that, for example, the application was dismissed. This was broken up into separate sentences in the English version (a style now adopted in French as well) but it still reads as a series of *ex cathedra* statements, completely lacking the close reasoning of an English or American judgment.

This style was probably necessitated by the decision-making procedure adopted by the Court. For the reasons discussed earlier, the Court gives a single judgment: concurring or dissenting judgments are not permitted. However, it is the policy of the Court to involve all the Judges in the drafting of the judgment in an attempt to attain the maximum consensus. Though the Judge-Rapporteur might be expected to play a special role, the judgment is the collective work of the whole Court, and it is apparently not uncommon for each sentence to be subject to lengthy discussion. Committee procedure of this kind does not lend itself to the production of a discursive judgment of the English sort.

This does not, of course, mean that a court which gives a single judgment must inevitably adopt the French style. The judgments of the Privy Council in the days before it allowed dissenting and concurring judgments are evidence of this. However, if it were desired to produce a judgment in the English style, it would be necessary to sacrifice any attempt to gain a consensus: the drafting of the judgment would have to be entrusted to a single Judge – who would no doubt be the member of the Court whose views most clearly represented those of the majority – and the role of the others would be limited to the suggesting of minor alterations.

Two further consequences of the attempt to attain consensus are evident in the Court's judgments. In some cases there appear to be two separate lines of reasoning, both leading to the same conclusion. Since these may be quite different, the result is

[80] It is now headed 'Report for the Hearing', but previously such headings as 'Issues of Fact and Law', 'Facts', or 'Facts and Issues' have been used. Since the beginning of 1994, it has been omitted from the European Court Reports.

[81] It is now headed 'Judgment', but previously headings such as 'Grounds of Judgment', 'Law', or 'Decision' have been used.

[82] This is usually set in bold type in the official reports.

disconcerting for the lawyer trying to extract the *ratio decidendi*. The reason for this appears to be that, though there was a majority in favour of the result, there were two different schools of thought as to the reasons. The inclusion of both sets of reasons may be an attempt to satisfy both groups.

The second expedient adopted in the case of dissension among the Judges is to take the opposite course: instead of putting in something to please both groups, the Court deletes anything which might displease either. The result is that no reasons of substance are given at all. Examples of both these methods of arriving at a consensus may be found in the following sections.[83]

§8 PRECEDENT

Does the doctrine of precedent apply in the European Court?[84] The answer is that there is no legal doctrine of *stare decisis*, but the Court does follow its previous decisions in almost all cases. The case-law of the European Court is just as important for the development of Union law as that of English courts is for modern English law: the following chapters contain ample proof of this. However, though lawyers and Advocates General have always cited copious precedents, the Court itself used to refer to its previous decisions only in rare instances. One almost got the impression that it was trying to disguise the extent to which it followed precedent:[85] sometimes it would reproduce sentences, or even whole paragraphs, from previous judgments, without quotation marks or any acknowledgement of source. Today the position has changed, though the Court usually cites precedents only when they support its reasoning: it does not normally cite them in order to distinguish them.[86]

There are a number of important instances where the Court has not followed precedent.[87] These are the result of changing circumstances or a change of opinion among the Judges, possibly following criticism by Advocates General or academic writers. Where

[83] See *Compagnie Française v. Commission*, Case 64/69, [1970] ECR 221, where two lines of reasoning were given, and *International Fruit Company v. Commission*, Cases 41–4/70, [1971] ECR 411, where virtually no reasons at all were given.

[84] See Arnull, 'Owning Up to Fallibility: Precedent and the Court of Justice' (1993) 30 CMLRev. 247. For the position in the General Court, see Arnull at pp. 262–4, where it is suggested that the General Court is not bound either by its own previous decisions or even by those of the European Court. There is an exception to the latter proposition where the European Court allows an appeal from the General Court and refers the case back to the latter for a final judgment: here the General Court is bound by the decision of the European Court on points of law (Art. 61, second para. of the Statute). A second exception arises where the European Court rules that the General Court, not the European Court, has jurisdiction in a case – the General Court cannot then decide that it lacks jurisdiction: Art. 54, second para., of the Statute.

[85] The Court may have been under the influence of the Continental theory that precedents cannot constitute a formal source of law.

[86] There are some exceptions: see, for example, *TWD*, Case C-188/92, [1994] ECR I-833 (paras 19–24 of the judgment). See also Arnull, 'Owning Up to Fallibility' (see n. 84), pp. 253–60.

[87] For examples, see the Opinion of Advocate General Jacobs in the *HAG GF* case (see n. 90) at I-3747–50.

this happens, the Court does not normally overrule the earlier case as an English court would: it simply ignores it. The most prominent exception to this,[88] and indeed the most famous example of a *volte face* by the European Court, is its decision in *HAG GF*.[89]

The striking feature of this case is that it arose on largely the same facts as a previous case decided some sixteen years earlier, *Van Zuylen v. HAG*.[90] The issue was the right of the holder of a trade mark to block the importation from another Member State of goods bearing that mark. Both the earlier and the later case involved the same mark, 'HAG', a brand of decaffeinated coffee. In the later case, the Court confronted the issue directly and said that it had decided to reconsider its previous judgment. After considering the policy factors involved, it reversed it.[91] The following passage from the Opinion of Advocate General Jacobs is of interest:[92]

> The Court has consistently recognised its power to depart from previous decisions...That the Court should in an appropriate case expressly overrule an earlier decision is I think an inescapable duty, even if the Court has never before expressly done so.

That the Court did so in *HAG GF* was probably due to the close factual links between the two cases, though the persuasiveness of the Advocate General no doubt played its part.

The opinions of Advocates General are frequently cited by lawyers (and Advocates General) in cases before the Court. Do they have any weight as precedents? Obviously a great deal depends on whether the Court itself has pronounced on the issue. The first possibility is that the Court did not consider the point in the previous case. Here, the Advocate General's opinion has a value somewhat similar to that of a judgment at first instance which is upheld (or reversed) on appeal on different grounds without the appellate court expressing any opinion on the ground on which the case was originally decided. The second possibility is that the Advocate General's opinion was rejected by the Court in the previous case. Even here it will be cited by counsel, but they will have to show that the Advocate General was right and the Court wrong. The third possibility is that the Court followed the Advocate General. Here the main value of his opinion will be to explain and clarify the judgment, something which is often necessary in view of the brevity of the Court's reasoning.

§9 INTERPRETATION

The interpretation of the Treaties and Union legislation is one of the principal tasks of the Court. To some extent the Court's approach to this is the same as that of an English court: it looks at the words used and considers their meaning in the context of the instrument as a whole. In doing this, it tries to give the provision an interpretation

[88] *European Parliament v. Council* (*Chernobyl*), Case C-70/88, [1990] ECR I-2041, is another exception.

[89] Case C-10/89, [1990] ECR I-3711.

[90] Case 192/73, [1974] ECR 731.

[91] It seems that the Court felt that the rather drastic solution adopted in the earlier case was, after all, not needed in order to protect the functioning of the internal market.

[92] At I-3749–50.

which fits in with the general scheme of the instrument, though it is much more willing than an English court to depart from the literal meaning of the words to achieve this.

Beyond this, the Court makes little attempt to establish the actual subjective intention of the authors of the text. The preparatory documents (*travaux préparatoires*) for the Treaties have never been published; there are certain national materials, such as official statements by the national Governments to their Parliaments during ratification debates, but these are little used. As far as Union legislation is concerned, Commission proposals (including an explanatory memorandum) and the opinions of the European Parliament and the Economic and Social Committee (where these bodies have been consulted) are available, but not often considered by the Court.

One reason for disregarding the subjective intention of the authors of the text is that, in the case of an agreement reached after hard bargaining, there may be no common intention – only an agreement on a form of words. A more important reason is that the Court prefers to interpret texts on the basis of what it thinks they should be trying to achieve; it moulds the law according to what it regards as the needs of the Union.[93]

This is sometimes called the 'teleological method of interpretation', but it really goes beyond interpretation properly so called: it is decision-making on the basis of judicial policy.

§10 POLICY

One of the distinctive characteristics of the European Court is the extent to which its decision-making is based on policy. By policy is meant the values and attitudes of the Judges – the objectives they wish to promote. The policies of the European Court are basically the following:

1. strengthening the Union (and especially the federal elements in it);
2. increasing the scope and effectiveness of Union law;
3. enlarging the powers of Union institutions.[94]

[93] Thus Judge Kutscher (a former President of the European Court) has said extrajudicially: 'Interpretations based on the original situation would in no way be in keeping with a Community law orientated towards the future' (Kutscher, 'Methods of Interpretation' (see n. 65), p. 22).

[94] This also applies to the Court itself. One of the most prominent features of its case-law is the tenacity with which it fights off threats to its legal hegemony. In 1977, it declared the Agreement for the Laying-Up Fund for Inland Waterways to be incompatible with EU (then EEC) law, mainly because it objected to the creation of a tribunal that could, within an extremely small area, threaten its supremacy: *Laying-up Fund for Inland Waterway Vessels*, Opinion 1/76, [1977] ECR 741 (discussed in Chap. 6, § 2.3). This was followed in 1991 by a case in which it declared the EEA Agreement incompatible with EU (EEC) law: it was opposed to the creation of a rival authority, the proposed EEA Court (see *First EEA* case, Opinion 1/91, [1991] ECR 6079; discussed in the Introduction to Part I of this book). In 1996, it ruled that the Union could not, without an amendment to the Treaties, become a Party to the European Convention on Human Rights: if it had become a Party to the Convention, the European Court would have been subordinated to the European Court of Human Rights (ECtHR) when questions of human rights arose: see *ECHR* case, Opinion 2/94, [1996] ECR I-1759, discussed in Chap. 5, § 2.2. Then, in 2011, it ruled that the creation of the proposed European and Community Patents Court was against EU law: Opinion 1/09, [2011] ECR I-1137 (Full Court).

They may be summed up in one phrase: the promotion of European integration.

All courts are of course influenced by policy, but, in the European Court, policy plays a particularly important role: occasionally the Court will ignore the clear words of the Treaty in order to attain a policy objective. An example of this is *Parti Ecologiste – 'Les Verts' v. European Parliament*,[95] which concerned a decision of the European Parliament authorizing the payment of grants from the Union budget to political parties, ostensibly to cover an information campaign to explain the work of the Parliament to the electors at the time of the 1984 elections, but in reality to contribute towards the parties' election expenses. The formula adopted for the distribution of the money was strongly biased in favour of those parties represented in the Parliament before the elections and discriminated against those parties seeking representation for the first time. One party in the latter category, the French Ecologists, brought proceedings in the European Court to annul the decision.

The proceedings were brought under Article 173 EEC which, as it stood at the time of the case, provided: 'The Court of Justice shall review the legality of acts of the Commission and the Council.' This provision was perfectly clear and did not mention acts of the Parliament; nevertheless, the Court held that acts of the Parliament were covered. It reached this conclusion in four steps. The first step was to state that the Union is based on the rule of law, and acts of both the Member States and the Union institutions are subject to judicial review to ensure that they conform to the Treaty. The second step was to explain that no power had been given in what was then the EEC Treaty to review the acts of the Parliament because, at the time when the Treaty was drawn up, the Parliament did not possess the power to pass measures which could affect the rights of third parties.[96] The third step was to point out that it subsequently obtained such powers, notably in the Budgetary Treaties and the Decision and Act on direct elections. The fourth step was to conclude that it would be contrary to the spirit and system of the Treaty if the acts of the Parliament were not now subject to review. Therefore, the Court decided, Article 173 EEC covered acts of the Parliament.

The logic of this ruling should be fully understood: what the Court did was to say that the acts of the Parliament *ought* to be reviewable; therefore, they *were* reviewable. This logic, which also formed the basis of the decision in the *SPI* case (discussed later),[97] ignores the distinction between what the law ought to be and what it is, a distinction which is fundamental to the Western concept of law.

An equally striking example is provided by the *Chernobyl* case,[98] which also concerned the European Parliament. This case was in some ways the reverse of the *Parti Ecologiste* case: the issue was whether the Parliament could bring proceedings under

[95] Case 294/83, [1986] ECR 1339. Other examples are mentioned elsewhere in this book: they include *Sevince*, Case C-192/89, [1990] ECR I-3461; *Busseni*, Case C-221/88, [1990] ECR I-495; and *SPI*, Cases 267–9/81, [1983] ECR 801.

[96] The Court pointed out that under the ECSC Treaty (now expired), where the Parliament did have such powers (see Art. 95, fourth para.), its acts were reviewable: see Art. 38 ECSC.

[97] See Chap. 9, § 2.6.

[98] *European Parliament v. Council*, Case C-70/88, [1990] ECR I-2041. For the background to the case, see Chap. 12, § 1.

Article 146 EAEC[99] to annul an act of the Council. As it stood at the time, this provision did not cover the Parliament. The Court recognized this,[100] but nevertheless held that the Parliament *could* bring proceedings (though only for a limited purpose). It said:[101]

> The absence in the Treaties of any provision giving the Parliament the right to bring an action for annulment may constitute a procedural gap, but it cannot prevail over the fundamental interest in the maintenance and observance of the institutional balance laid down in the Treaties establishing the European Communities. Consequently, an action for annulment brought by the Parliament against an act of the Council or the Commission is admissible.

It is hard to imagine a clearer example of changing the law while supposedly interpreting it.

The Court's decisions in these cases did not represent a challenge to the interests of the national Governments.[102] Where this is the case, the Court moves more carefully. A common tactic is to introduce a new doctrine gradually: in the first case that comes before it, the Court will establish the doctrine as a general principle, but suggest that it is subject to various qualifications; the Court may even find some reason why it should not be applied to the facts of the case before it. The principle, however, is now established. If there are not too many protests, it will be reaffirmed in later cases; the qualifications can then be whittled away and the full extent of the doctrine revealed.

This process is well illustrated by the lines of cases concerning the treaty-making power of the Union and the direct effect of directives. These are both discussed in later chapters;[103] here a case will be considered which reveals in a particularly stark form the interplay between law and policy, principle and expediency: the second *Defrenne* case.[104] This concerned what was then Article 119 EEC, which, as it stood at the time, provided: 'Each Member State shall during the first stage ensure and subsequently maintain the application of the principle that men and women should receive equal pay for equal work.'

The first stage for bringing the Treaty into operation ended on 31 December 1961, but the Member States felt that they were not in a position to implement Article 119 by this date. They therefore held a conference which laid down a fresh timetable: the new date was 31 December 1964. This deadline was not, however, met by all the Member States, and the Commission then convened various meetings and drew up a series of reports in an attempt to bring the recalcitrant Governments into line. Finally, the Commission announced that it would take enforcement proceedings against those Member States which had not complied by 18 July 1973, but this threat was not carried

[99] At the time, this was identical to Art. 173 EEC.

[100] In a previous case, *European Parliament v. Council* (*Comitology*), Case 302/87, [1988] ECR 5615, it had in fact given an express ruling to this effect.

[101] Paras 26 and 27 of the judgment.

[102] This is shown by the fact that the Treaty on European Union amended the Treaties in question to make them accord with both rulings.

[103] In Chap. 6, § 2.3 and Chap. 7, § 4, respectively.

[104] *Defrenne v. Sabena*, Case 43/75, [1976] ECR 455.

out. Then, on 10 February 1975, the Council issued a directive on equal pay which had to be implemented within one year.

In 1970, however, Gabrielle Defrenne, an air hostess who had worked for the Belgian airline Sabena, brought proceedings against it in the Belgian courts because it had paid her less than male cabin crew doing the same work. She claimed that it had no right to do this and demanded back-payment of the difference. The Belgian courts referred various questions of Union law to the European Court for a preliminary ruling; in particular, they wished to know whether Article 119 conferred rights directly on individuals, even though it had not been implemented, and, if so, from what date it did this.

These questions raised highly delicate issues. In particular, if back-pay could be claimed by all women who had suffered discrimination, the economic consequences would be serious: according to the United Kingdom Government, many British firms would be driven into bankruptcy if the right to equal pay were backdated to Britain's entry into the Union.[105] As far as the law was concerned, the principal issue was whether Article 119 was directly effective. There were quite strong reasons for believing that it was not,[106] but such a ruling would have conflicted with the Court's policy of enhancing the scope and effectiveness of Union law. On this point, policy triumphed: the Court ruled that Article 119 conferred rights directly on individuals in the Member States and that the various resolutions putting off the date for implementation were of no effect. This meant that there had been a right to equal pay in the original Member States since 1 January 1962 and in the United Kingdom, Ireland, and Denmark since 1 January 1973.

However, the Court felt it expedient to sweeten the pill by ruling that only those workers who had instituted legal proceedings (or made equivalent claims) before the date of the judgment could rely on the direct effect of Article 119 in order to claim back-pay for periods prior to that date. Thus Ms Defrenne won her case but the Member States were shielded from an avalanche of similar claims.[107]

This ruling neatly reconciled the Court's policy with the interests of the Member States. But it did so at the expense of legal principle: there was no possible ground in law for limiting the effect of the judgment in this way: if Article 119 was directly effective for Ms Defrenne, it must have been directly effective for all other workers; claims for back-pay might be affected by national statutes of limitation, but

[105] The Equal Pay Act 1970 only came into force on 29 December 1975; consequently, the Court's decision could have made employers liable for claims going back three years.

[106] Art. 119 was far from clear and it envisaged action by the Member States to bring it into force: see Chap. 7, § 1.4.

[107] The principle has also been applied in *Pinna*, Case 41/84, [1986] ECR 1; *Barra v. Belgium*, Case 309/85, [1988] ECR 355; *Blaizot v. University of Liège*, Case 24/86, [1988] ECR 379; *Barber v. Guardian Royal Exchange Assurance Group*, Case C-262/88, [1990] ECR I-1889 (on this see the Protocol Concerning Article 141 [119] EC, a Protocol to the Treaty on European Union); *Union Royale Belge v. Bosman*, Case C-415/93, [1995] ECR I-4921; *Sürül*, Case C-262/96, [1999] ECR I-2685.

there was no legal ground for making the date of the judgment in the *Defrenne* case decisive.[108]

These cases are extreme examples; nevertheless, they prompt the question whether it is right to allow policy to play so dominant a role. In this connection, it is desirable to draw a distinction between those cases where the Court makes a choice on policy grounds between two or more legally tenable solutions, and those cases where it allows policy considerations to dictate a solution that conflicts with generally accepted legal principles. The former is perfectly proper, but the latter may be criticized as going beyond the proper function of a court.[109] It might be argued that this activist approach is necessary to promote European integration; however, if the Union is to fulfil the expectations of its founders, it must be firmly based on the rule of law: this could be jeopardized if policy is allowed to override clear provisions of law.[110]

§11 THE FUTURE

What is the future likely to hold? Criticism of the Court for its failure to pay regard to the terms of the Treaties continues as before.[111] Some of the critics are persons of the highest standing – for example, the Chancellor of the Austrian Republic and a former President of Germany, a man who had also been President of the Federal Constitutional Court of Germany.[112]

However, criticism of an entirely different kind is also beginning to be heard. Following the most recent enlargements of the Union, questions are being asked concerning the technical ability as lawyers of some of the Judges. Thus, for example, an Editorial in the *Common Market Law Review* said, of the inept citation of authority in the Court's much-criticized judgment in *Mangold*,[113] that it would have provoked 'thick red underlining' if it had occurred in a student essay.[114]

[108] The reasons given by the Court in its judgment were: first, the economic difficulties feared by the British and Irish Governments (it said that these could not affect the *future* application of the law, thereby implying that they could affect its application as regards the past); secondly, the fact that the conduct of the Member States and the views adopted by the Commission had led employers to continue their violation of the principle of equal pay; and thirdly, that the general level at which pay would have been fixed could not be known (a rather doubtful proposition). These latter arguments, however, apply just as much to workers who made claims before the *Defrenne* judgment as to those who began proceedings after it. They therefore provide no justification for the Court's ruling.

[109] For evidence that the Court may have changed its attitude in recent years, see *Unión de Pequeños Agricultores v. Council*, Case C-50/00 P, [2002] ECR I-6677 (para. 44 of the judgment).

[110] This theme is explored more fully in Hartley, *Constitutional Problems of the European Union* (1999), Chaps 2 and 3; see also Hartley, 'The European Court, Judicial Objectivity and the Constitution of the European Union' (1996) 112 LQR 95. For a critique of this latter article, see Arnull, 'The European Court and Judicial Objectivity: A Reply to Professor Hartley' (1996) 112 LQR 411. See also Tridimas, 'The Court of Justice and Judicial Activism' (1996) 21 ELRev. 187; Arnull, 'Me and My Shadow: The European Court of Justice and the Disintegration of European Union Law' (2008) 31 *Fordham Law Review* 1174.

[111] See Editorial, 'The Court of Justice in the Limelight – Again' (2008) 45 CMLRev. 1571.

[112] *Ibid.* [113] Case C-144/04, [2005] ECR I-9981, discussed in Chap. 7, § 4.6.

[114] (2006) 43 CMLRev. 1 at 8.

This is linked to another problem. The rule that there is one Judge from each Member State means that the Court has come to be dominated by Judges from the smaller countries. In the Union today, there are three Member States with a population of under one million, and nine with a population of under five million. The combined population of these nine smallest Member States is less than a quarter of that of Germany; yet they have nine Judges to Germany's one – this, despite the fact that Germany has a highly developed legal culture that has produced jurists of the greatest renown. Only one Judge can be selected from this ample pool of talent, while nine come from a group of States that, even together, cannot be regarded as having attained the same level of juristic achievement.

There is a further problem: the enormous disparity between public-service salary levels in many of the new Member States compared with those in the Union institutions means that a judgeship in the European Court is seen as a glittering prize by many potential candidates. This could tempt national Governments to regard an appointment as an opportunity to exercise political patronage, something that would seriously distort the selection process.[115]

This problem could be solved only if the selection process were taken out of the hands of politicians, and candidates were appointed on the basis of merit, rather than nationality or politics. Although fair representation should be given to major geographical regions and groups of legal systems – the Scandinavian legal family, the German legal family, the French legal family, the East European legal family, and the common law – it should no longer be necessary to have a Judge from each Member State.

A small step in the right direction has already been taken. The Treaty of Lisbon made provision for the setting up of a panel to give an opinion on candidates' suitability to perform the duties of Judge and Advocate General of the European Court and the General Court.[116] The panel consists of seven persons chosen from among former members of the European Court and the General Court, members of national supreme courts and lawyers of recognized competence, one of whom is proposed by the European Parliament. They give their opinion on each candidate before appointment is considered.[117]

In a best-case scenario, a negative opinion from the panel would mean that the person concerned was not appointed. However, politics may intrude again: the Member State which proposed the unacceptable candidate might threaten to block all other appointments unless its candidate was accepted. Whether this happens in practice is not known: the details of the appointments process are not made public.

[115] See Barents, 'The Court of Justice after the Treaty of Lisbon' (2010) 47 CMLRev. 709 at 712–14.

[116] Art. 255 TFEU.

[117] See Barents, 'The Court of Justice after the Treaty of Lisbon' (see n. 115), pp. 712–14.

FURTHER READING

Items are listed in date order, the most recent being at the end.

HJALTE RASMUSSEN, *On Law and Policy in the European Court of Justice* (1986).

BORGSMIDT, 'The Advocate General at the European Court of Justice: A Comparative Study' (1988) 13 ELRev. 106.

KENNEDY, 'Paying the Piper: Legal Aid in Proceedings before the Court of Justice' (1988) 27 CMLRev. 559.

RASMUSSEN, 'Between Self-Restraint and Activism: A Judicial Policy for the European Court' (1988) 13 ELRev. 28.

COURT OF FIRST INSTANCE, 'Reflections on the Future Development of the Community Judicial System' (a discussion paper issued in 1990) (1991) 16 ELRev. 175.

VESTERDORF, 'The Court of First Instance of the European Communities After Two Full Years in Operation' (1992) 29 CMLRev. 897.

ARNULL, 'Owning Up to Fallibility: Precedent and the Court of Justice' (1993) 30 CMLRev. 247.

ARNULL, 'The Community Judicature and the 1996 IGC' (1995) 20 ELRev. 599.

BROWN, 'The First Five Years of the Court of First Instance and Appeals to the Court of Justice: Assessment and Statistics' (1995) 32 CMLRev. 743.

EDWARD, 'How the Court of Justice Works' (1995) 20 ELRev. 539.

MANCINI AND KEELING, 'Language, Culture and Politics in the Life of the European Court of Justice' (1995) CJEL 397.

VAN GERVEN, 'The Role and Structure of the European Judiciary Now and in the Future' (1996) 21 ELRev. 211.

SCOREY, 'A New Model for the Communities' Judicial Architecture in the New Union' (1996) 21 ELRev. 224.

TRIDIMAS, 'The Court of Justice and Judicial Activism' (1996) 21 ELRev. 199.

HJALTE RASMUSSEN, *European Court of Justice* (Copenhagen, 1998).

KENNEY, 'The Members of the Court of Justice of the European Communities' (1998/99) 5 CJEL 101.

TREVOR C HARTLEY, *Constitutional Problems of the European Union* (1999), Chaps 2 and 3.

FORWOOD, 'The Evolving Role of the Court of First Instance of the European Communities – Some Comments on the Changes Agreed at Nice as They Affect the Judicial Architecture of the Community Court' (2000) 3 *Cambridge Yearbook of European Studies* 139.

ALEC STONE SWEET, *Governing with Judges: Constitutional Politics in Europe* (2000).

KAREN J ALTER, *Establishing the Supremacy of European Law* (2001).

ALAN DASHWOOD AND ANGUS JOHNSTON (EDS), *The Future of the European Judicial System* (2001).

JOHNSTON, 'Judicial Reform and the Treaty of Nice' (2001) 38 CMLRev. 499.

SCHØNBERG AND FRICK, 'Finishing, Refining, Polishing: The Use of *travaux préparatoires* as an Aid to the Interpretation of Community Legislation' (2003) 28 ELRev. 149.

VESTERDORF, 'The Community Court System Ten Years from Now' (2003) 28 ELRev. 303.

JACOBS, 'Recent and Ongoing Measures to Improve the Efficiency of the European Court of Justice' (2004) 29 ELRev. 823.

R CREECH, *Law and Language in the European Union: The Paradox of a Babel 'United in Diversity'* (2005).

ANTHONY ARNULL, *The European Union and its Court of Justice*, 2nd edn (2006).

BARBIER DE LA SERRE, 'Accelerated and Expedited Procedures before EC Courts: A Review of the Practice' (2006) 43 CMLRev. 783.

NOREEN BURROWS AND ROSA GREAVES, *The Advocate General and EC Law* (2007).

ARNULL, 'Me and My Shadow: The European Court of Justice and the Disintegration of European Union Law' (2008) 31 *Fordham Law Review* 1174.

KAREN J ALTER, *The European Court's Political Power* (2009).

BARNARD, 'The PPU: Is it Worth the Candle? An Early Assessment' (2009) 34 ELRev. 281.

BARENTS, 'The Court of Justice after the Treaty of Lisbon' (2010) 47 CMLRev. 709.

SCHILLING, 'Beyond Multilingualism: On Different Approaches to the Handling of Diverging Language Versions of a Community Law' (2010) 16 ELJ 47.

TRIDIMAS AND GARI, 'Winners and Losers in Luxembourg: A Statistical Analysis of Judicial Review before the European Court of Justice and the Court of First Instance' (2010) 35 ELRev. 13

GUNNAR BECK, *The Legal Reasoning of the Court of Justice of the EU* (2013).

PART II

THE UNION LEGAL SYSTEM

INTRODUCTION

The Union legal system was created by a set of treaties. It depends for its validity on those treaties; and the treaties depend for their validity on international law. Ultimately, therefore, Union law is a sub-system of international law. However, if a group of States conclude a set of treaties to govern their relations with each other in a given area, international law permits them to create a new system of law that is self-contained and separate from international law.[1] The normal rules of international law will not necessarily apply within that system. (Peremptory norms of international law, also known as *jus cogens*,[2] constitute an exception, though these will not often be relevant in Union law.) Consequently, the Union Treaties will not necessarily be interpreted in the same way as ordinary treaties, a point much emphasized by the European Court.[3]

Though the Union Treaties are treaties under international law, they are treaties of a special character. They are treaties that create a new international organization of the supranational kind. They also create a new legal system. For this reason, they may be regarded as a kind of constitution, though that term should not be regarded as calling into question their status as treaties.[4]

Although Union law forms a coherent system, there are various purposes for which it is necessary to make distinctions, on the basis of their origin, between different provisions of Union law. Thus proceedings for judicial review may be brought only with respect to legally binding acts of the Union institutions; in determining the validity of such acts, the Court may have regard to the Treaties and 'any rule of law relating to their application'; enforcement actions may be brought against Member States for a failure to fulfil an obligation 'under' the Treaties. There are also special problems as to which questions of Union law may be referred by a national court to the European Court for interpretation in a preliminary ruling; and the doctrine of direct effect depends in part

[1] *Van Gend en Loos*, Case 26/62, [1963] ECR 1 at 12. See also *Costa v. ENEL*, Case 6/64, [1964] ECR 585 at 593, where the European Court said that, unlike ordinary treaties, the EU Treaties (then the EEC Treaty) created their own legal system; and *per* Advocate General Lagrange in *Fédération Charbonnière de Belgique v. High Authority*, Case 8/55, [1956] ECR 245 at 277, where it is said that the rules of law derived from the Treaties constitute the internal law of the Union.

[2] A peremptory norm of international law is defined in Art. 53 of the 1969 Vienna Convention on the Law of Treaties as 'a norm accepted and recognized by the international Union of States as a whole as a norm from which no derogation is permitted and which can be modified only by a subsequent norm of general international law having the same character'.

[3] This is vividly illustrated by cases such as *Polydor*, Case 270/80, [1982] ECR 329, in which a provision in an agreement between the Union and a non-member State was given a different interpretation by the European Court from a similar provision in the EU Treaties (then the EEC Treaty). See also *Kupferberg*, Case 104/81, [1982] ECR 3641 at paras 28–31 of the judgment; *First EEA Case*, Opinion 1/91, [1991] ECR I-6079 at para. 14 of the judgment.

[4] See *Les Verts – Parti Ecologiste v. European Parliament*, Case 294/83, [1986] ECR 1339, where the European Court said that the Treaties constituted the 'constitutional charter' of the Union (then the Community) (para. 23 of the judgment).

on the nature of the provision in question. For all these reasons, but above all in order to delimit the extent of the system as a whole, it is necessary to analyse the sources of Union law.

In the analysis of Union law according to its sources, the most important distinction is between enacted and non-enacted law. Enacted law is law created by some authority; non-enacted law is not so created. It is, of course, true that the existence of non-enacted law is not certain unless it has been recognized by a court; and it could be argued that it, too, is created – by the courts. There are, however, important differences between judge-made law and enacted law, and it is therefore reasonable to use this distinction as the basis for the classification of Union law.

Enacted Union law may be created either by a Union institution or by the Member States. The second distinction, therefore, is between acts of Union institutions (Union acts) and acts of the Member States. In this context it is important to stress that, though the most important Union institution, the Council, is composed of representatives of the Member States, its acts are Union acts, not acts of the Member States. If, on the other hand, the representatives of the Member States meet when they are *not* acting in their capacity as members of the Council, their decisions will be acts of the Member States. Such meetings may take place in the Council: the important question is not the place where they meet, but the capacity in which they meet.

Non-enacted Union law consists of the so-called 'general principles of law' – the 'common law' of the Union – which have been adopted by the European Court. They are an important source of Union law and have a significant role to play in the Union legal system.

International agreements with non-member States constitute another source of Union law. They may be concluded either by the Union alone, by the Union acting jointly with the Member States, or, in certain special cases, by the Member States alone. These agreements are thus either acts of the Member States or Union acts; because of their special nature, however, it is desirable to consider them separately.

It is possible, therefore, to establish the following four major sources of Union law:

1. acts of the Member States;
2. Union acts;
3. general principles of Union law;
4. international agreements with non-member States.

These will be considered in turn in the chapters in this Part of the book.

Finally, it should be said that it is not always easy to discern exactly where a legal system begins and ends: the Union legal system, like most other legal systems, has fuzzy edges. A legal system is made up of legal rules; a legal rule is a rule that has legal effects; a legal effect involves a change in the legal position of some person: all this is easy to say, but sometimes difficult to apply in practice. In the Union context, there is a range of instruments – Resolutions, Statements in Minutes, Joint Declarations, Interinstitutional Agreements, Codes of Conduct, Recommendations, and many more – that are often on the edge of the Union legal system, sometimes falling on the one side and sometimes on the other. Moreover, legal effect is not an all-or-nothing characteristic: an instrument may have some legal effects but not others – for example, an instrument may not have direct legal consequences in its own right, but may affect the interpretation of another instrument and thus have indirect legal consequences. The term 'soft law' is sometimes used to designate instruments with doubtful, or only partial, legal effects.[5] Some such instruments have already been mentioned; others will be discussed in the appropriate places.

FURTHER READING

Items are listed in date order, the most recent being at the end.

PIERRE PESCATORE, *L'ordre juridique des Communautés européennes* (1975).

WYATT, 'New Legal Order, or Old?' (1982) 7 ELRev. 147.

DOWRICK, 'A Model of the European Communities' Legal System' (1983) 3 YEL 169.

FRANCIS G JACOBS, *European Union Law and Public International Law – Two Different Legal Orders?* (Institut für Internationales Recht an der Universität Kiel, 1983).

SØRENSEN, 'Autonomous Legal Orders' (1983) 32 ICLQ 559.

WELLENS AND BORCHARDT, 'Soft Law in European Union Law' (1989) 14 ELRev. 267.

BIEBER AND SALOMÉ, 'Hierarchy of Norms in European Law' (1996) 33 CMLRev. 907.

PELLET, 'Les fondements juridiques internationaux du droit communautaire' (1997) 5 Collected Courses of the Academy of European Law, Book 2, 193.

HARTLEY, 'International Law and the Law of the European Union – A Reassessment' [2002] BYIL 1.

[5] For a fuller discussion, see Klabbers, 'Informal Instruments before the European Court of Justice' (1994) 31 CMLRev. 997; Wellens and Borchardt, 'Soft Law in European Union Law' (1989) 14 ELRev. 267.

3

ACTS OF THE MEMBER STATES

For purposes of discussion, acts of the Member States may be divided into a number of categories. The constitutive Treaties are the most important.

§1 THE CONSTITUTIVE TREATIES

§1.1 INTRODUCTION

The constitutive Treaties lay the foundations of the European Union. They may be regarded as the constitution of the Union: they set up the various organs of the European Union and grant them their powers.[1] They also contain many provisions of a non-institutional nature which would not normally be found in a constitution. These are mainly concerned with economic and social law, and are evidence of the hybrid nature of the Treaties, and, indeed, of the Union itself.

Which are the constitutive Treaties? They may be defined as the Treaties which created the Union (originally the three Communities), together with the Treaties which amend or supplement them. The principal Treaties falling within this category are as follows:[2]

1. ECSC Treaty (18 April 1951: now expired and no longer in force);
2. Treaty on the Functioning of the European Union, usually abbreviated to 'TFEU' (25 March 1957: previously called the 'Treaty establishing the European Community', a phrase usually abbreviated to 'EC Treaty' or 'TEC', also known as the 'Treaty of Rome');

[1] Certain Council decisions are also of a constitutional nature, for example the decision providing for direct elections to the European Parliament, discussed in Chap. 1, § 1.1.

[2] There is no official list of these Treaties, but see the European Communities Act 1972, s. 1(1) (as amended) and Sch. 1, Part I, and the European Communities (Definition of Treaties) Order 1976 (SI 1976/217). Certain other instruments are also listed in s. 1(1) – for example, certain Decisions of the Council on the Communities' system of 'own resources'.

3. EAEC Treaty (25 March 1957);
4. Convention on Certain Institutions Common to the European Communities (25 March 1957: now repealed);
5. Merger Treaty (Convention Establishing a Single Council and a Single Commission of the European Communities) (8 April 1965: now largely repealed);
6. First Budgetary Treaty (22 April 1970);
7. First Treaty of Accession (22 January 1972: entry of Denmark, Ireland, and the United Kingdom);
8. Treaty amending certain Provisions of the Protocol on the Statute of the European Investment Bank (10 July 1975);
9. Second Budgetary Treaty (22 July 1975);
10. Second Treaty of Accession (28 May 1979: entry of Greece);
11. Third Treaty of Accession (12 June 1985: entry of Spain and Portugal);
12. Single European Act (17 and 28 February 1986);
13. Treaty on European Union, usually abbreviated to 'TEU' (7 February 1992: also known as the 'Maastricht Agreement');
14. Fourth Treaty of Accession (24 June 1994: entry of Austria, Finland, and Sweden);
15. Treaty of Amsterdam (2 October 1997);
16. Treaty of Nice (26 February 2001);
17. Fifth Treaty of Accession (16 April 2003: entry of the Czech Republic, Estonia, Cyprus, Latvia, Lithuania, Hungary, Malta, Poland, Slovenia, and Slovakia);
18. Sixth Treaty of Accession (25 April 2005: entry of Bulgaria and Romania);
19. Treaty of Lisbon (13 December 2007: also known as the 'Reform Treaty');
20. Seventh Treaty of Accession (9 December 2011: entry of Croatia).[3]

The history and objectives of these Treaties were outlined briefly in Chapter 1; here certain legal points of a general nature will be considered.

Appended to many of the Treaties there are certain supplementary instruments. Annexes and Protocols are an integral part of the Treaty to which they relate.[4] The status of the declarations annexed to the Treaties – some of which are joint declarations on the part of all the Contracting States and some of which are unilateral declarations by one Contracting State only – is not entirely clear. Many of them were apparently intended to be only of political significance; others have an indirect legal effect. For example, certain provisions in the EU Treaties grant rights to nationals of the Member States. The Treaties contain no definition of who is a national, and it may be assumed that the intention was that each Member State should decide who its own nationals are (subject to any relevant provisions of EU law). When the United Kingdom acceded to the European

[3] Decisions of the Council and agreements of the representatives of the Governments of the Member States have not been listed, even though they may amend the constitutive Treaties.

[4] See Art. 51 TEU.

Union, the Government of the United Kingdom made a Declaration regarding the definition of a UK national for EU purposes.[5] This Declaration would therefore have effect in EU law to the extent that EU law refers to national law on this matter.

§1.2 AMENDING THE TREATIES

Important changes in the procedure for amending the constitutive Treaties were brought about by the Treaty of Lisbon. Article 48 TEU now provides two methods of amendment: the ordinary revision procedure and the simplified revision procedure. The ordinary procedure may be used for any amendments, even those increasing the powers of the Union; the simplified procedure may be used only in limited cases.

Under the ordinary procedure, proposals may be submitted to the Council by a Member State, the European Parliament, or the Commission. The Council passes them on to the European Council; it will also notify the national Parliaments.[6]

The next step[7] is for the European Council to consider the proposal (after consulting the European Parliament and the Commission). If the European Council adopts (by a simple majority) a decision to examine the proposals, the President of the European Council convenes a Convention composed of:

- representatives of the national Parliaments;
- the Heads of State or Government of the Member States;
- the European Parliament; and
- the Commission.[8]

The task of the Convention is to decide whether to recommend moving on to the next stage, the convening of an inter-governmental conference. In making this decision, the Convention acts by consensus.

The second paragraph of Article 48(2) TEU provides, however, that the European Council may decide to omit the Convention, and move directly to the next step, the convening of an inter-governmental conference.[9] It would do this where the proposed amendments are not of sufficient importance to justify a Convention.

The inter-governmental conference has the task of deciding what amendments (if any) to make. It acts by common accord (unanimity) but smaller countries will be subject to heavy political pressure if they do not go along with what the bigger ones want. Any amendments agreed have to be ratified by each Member State in accordance with its constitutional requirements. In the case of some Member States, this could entail a referendum. This is not constitutionally required in the United Kingdom, but the

[5] This was made necessary by the complicated and confusing state of British nationality law. In 1982 it was replaced by a new Declaration, following the enactment of the British Nationality Act 1981.

[6] Art. 48(2) TEU. [7] Art. 48(3) TEU.

[8] The European Central Bank (ECB) must also be consulted if the proposals involve institutional changes in the monetary area.

[9] The European Council acts by a simple majority after obtaining the consent of the European Parliament.

Government may decide for political reasons to call one. Legal challenges are also possible and have not been uncommon in the past. So far, the courts have never blocked ratification, though (as we will see in Chapter 8) these challenges sometimes result in important legal pronouncements.

What happens if one Member State fails to ratify? There have been a number of occasions in the past (discussed in the Introduction to Part I) in which the voters of a particular Member State have delivered a negative verdict. In the case of the proposed 'Constitution for Europe', in which the voters of two important Member States – France and the Netherlands – rejected it, the project collapsed. Where only one small State rejects it, the solution in the past has been to require that State to hold a second referendum, usually after certain political concessions have been made in order to allay the concerns of voters. So far this has worked.

The Treaty of Lisbon has taken a first, hesitant step in the direction of finding a solution to this problem. Article 48(5) TEU now provides:

> If, two years after the signature of a treaty amending the Treaties, four fifths of the Member States have ratified it and one or more Member States have encountered difficulties in proceeding with ratification, the matter shall be referred to the European Council.

This is all that is said. What the European Council will do about it is left entirely open. One would imagine that the usual mixture of inducements and threats (depending on how powerful the Member State is) will be employed.

The simplified revision procedure is laid down in paragraphs 6 and 7 of Article 48 TEU. It may be used only in limited circumstances. Paragraph 6 is for amendments to Part Three of the TFEU, relating to the internal policies and action of the Union. The procedure cannot be used, however, to increase the competences conferred on the Union.

Where paragraph 6 applies, a proposal may be made by a Member State, the European Parliament, or the Commission. The proposal is made to the European Council, which may adopt a decision to make the desired amendments.[10] The decision must be unanimous and the European Parliament and the Commission must be consulted.[11] The decision must also be approved by all the Member States in accordance with their respective constitutional requirements. It will not come into force until this has happened.

Paragraph 7 provides for a simplified procedure in two special cases. The first is to change a requirement (in certain instances)[12] that the Council must act unanimously in a given area or case, to a requirement that it must act by a qualified majority. The second is to change a requirement in the Treaty on the Functioning of the European Union that the Council must adopt a legislative act by a special procedure,

[10] In *Pringle v. Government of Ireland*, Case C-370/12, 27 November 2012 (Full Court), the European Court held that it has jurisdiction to consider, first, whether the procedural rules laid down in Art. 48 have been followed; secondly, whether the amendments concern only Part Three of the TFEU and, thirdly, whether they increase the competences of the Union (paras 30–37 of the judgment).

[11] The ECB must also be consulted if the proposals involve institutional changes in the monetary area.

[12] It applies only to the Treaty on the Functioning of the European Union and Title V of the Treaty on European Union. It does not apply to decisions having military or defence implications.

to a requirement that it will adopt it by the ordinary procedure. In both these cases, the European Council may make the amendment by taking a decision to that effect. In doing so, it must be unanimous; the European Parliament (acting by a majority of its component members) must give its consent. In addition, the national Parliaments must be notified: if any of them objects within a period of six months, the European Council cannot adopt the decision.

It will be seen from what has been said that there is no way in which the Treaties may be amended without the consent of all Member States. In fact, the EU treaty-amendment procedures, which accord greater respect to national sovereignty than those laid down in some other multilateral treaties,[13] largely follow the rules of international law that would be applicable in the absence of any express provision. There are, however, a few additional requirements – for example, concerning the European Parliament – and the question might arise whether the Treaties could be validly amended if these were not satisfied.

Most EU lawyers who have considered the issue take the view that the Treaties may be amended only by the procedures laid down in them,[14] and there is no doubt that this would be the view of the European Court.[15] This is the answer that one inevitably gets if one considers the matter from within the EU system. However, the position might also be considered from the viewpoint of international law.

What is the position under international law? If the treaty setting up an international organization specifies a given procedure for its amendment, and – let us assume – states that it may be amended in no other way, may the Member States nevertheless amend it[16] by a new treaty to which they all agree? The matter is somewhat controversial; nevertheless, it is suggested that the amending treaty would be valid.[17] Although Article 48

[13] For example, the UN Charter may be amended (for all members) if the amendment is adopted by a two-thirds majority in the General Assembly and ratified by two-thirds of the members, including all the permanent members of the Security Council: see Art. 108 of the Charter. See De Witte, 'Rules of Change in International Law: How Special is the European Community?' (1994) 25 *Netherlands Yearbook of International Law* 299 at 331–2.

[14] See the citations in De Witte, 'Rules of Change in International Law' (see n. 13), p. 315, note 54.

[15] Compare *Kadi and Al Barakaat International Foundation v. Council and Commission*, Cases C-402 and 415/05 P, [2008] ECR I-6351, discussed in § 4.4; see also *Defrenne v. Sabena*, Case 43/75, [1976] ECR 455 at para. 58 of the judgment.

[16] It is assumed that their intention to amend it is clear. A mere conflict of treaties without any express intention to amend the earlier one would be a different matter. On this, see § 4.

[17] Deliège-Sequaris, 'Révision des traités européens en dehors des procédures prévues' [1980] CDE 539 at 542–8 (where the competing arguments and the views of other writers are carefully analysed); Weiler and Haltern, 'Response: The Autonomy of the Community Legal Order – Through the Looking Glass' (1996) 37 *Harvard Journal of International Law* 411 at 418, note 26. For the opposite view, see Pellet 'Les fondements juridiques internationaux du droit communautaire' (1997) 5 *Collected Courses of the Academy of European Law*, Book 2, 193 at 214–17. Pellet bases his view on Art. 5 of the 1969 Vienna Convention on the Law of Treaties, but this cannot give the rules of an international organization any greater force and effect than they would have had apart from the Vienna Convention; it therefore leaves open the position under customary international law. It should be noted that Weiler and Haltern do not consider that international law is applicable; however, they believe that, if it were applicable, it would permit the EU Treaties to be amended without following Art. 48. Pellet, on the other hand, considers that international law *is* applicable, but that it requires the Parties to respect Art. 48; nevertheless, he admits that if they did not do so, the European Court could not (and probably should not) do anything about it.

imposes certain procedural requirements on the Member States, requirements that might well produce consequences within the EU system,[18] it does not divest them of the *capacity* to enter into a new treaty: the conclusion of the new treaty may be a violation of EU law (as laid down in the existing treaties), but this would not make it invalid under international law.

There would then be a conflict of treaties: a conflict between the earlier treaty, which says that it cannot be amended (except under a procedure which, we assume, has not been followed) and the later treaty, which nevertheless amends it. The solution to such a conflict is to be found in Article 30(3) of the 1969 Vienna Convention on the Law of Treaties.[19] This states that where all the Parties to the earlier treaty are also Parties to the later treaty (and the latter does not provide that it is subject to the former),[20] the earlier treaty applies only to the extent that its provisions are compatible with those of the later treaty. It follows from this that, in the situation we are considering, the amendments would be valid under international law. This conclusion makes sense, since the purpose of a treaty must, first and foremost, be to serve the interests of the States that are Parties to it. If they all want to amend it, they should not be barred from doing so by what they previously agreed.[21] Moreover, since the Parties to a treaty are free to terminate it at any time by mutual consent, irrespective of its terms,[22] it would be strange if its terms could restrict their power to amend it.

It will be seen from this that there are two possible views on this matter. Which would prevail in practice would depend on the balance of political forces at the time in question. On two occasions in the past, the ECSC Treaty was amended without complying with the procedures laid down in it: the validity of these amendments has never been questioned.[23]

[18] The Commission might bring proceedings under Art. 258 TFEU [226/169 EC] to prevent the Member States from concluding the new treaty, though the prospect of such an action against *all* the Member States is somewhat bizarre. If the Member States refused to obey any judgment given by the European Court, the Commission could bring further proceedings for the Court to impose a fine on them. If they refused to pay the fine, there would be no way in which it could be enforced.

[19] Strictly speaking, the Vienna Convention does not apply to treaties concluded before it entered into force: see Art. 4 of the Vienna Convention. However, the Vienna Convention is regarded in general as declaratory of customary international law: see Sir Ian Sinclair, *The Vienna Convention on the Law of Treaties*, 2nd edn (1984), pp. 10–21; Anthony Aust, *Modern Treaty Law and Practice* (2000), pp. 10–11. There can be little doubt that Art. 30 represents customary international law: Mus, 'Conflicts between Treaties in International Law' (1998) 45 *Netherlands International Law Journal* 208 at 213.

[20] See Art. 30(2) of the Vienna Convention.

[21] It might be argued that the interests of the peoples of Europe should also be considered, but these can be better protected through the national ratification processes than through consulting the European Parliament.

[22] Art. 54(b) of the 1969 Vienna Convention.

[23] The first was the Treaty of 27 October 1956, which brought about certain amendments consequent on the return of the Saar to Germany, and the second was the Convention on Certain Institutions Common to the European Communities, which was signed at the same time as the EEC and EAEC Treaties: see Pierre Pescatore, *L'ordre juridique des Communautés européennes* (1975), pp. 62–3.

§1.3 NEW MEMBERS

A special form of amendment procedure applies when new Member States join the Union.[24] Any European State may apply for admission, provided it respects the values set out in Article 2 TEU, which states:

> The Union is founded on the values of respect for human dignity, freedom, democracy, equality, the rule of law and respect for human rights, including the rights of persons belonging to minorities. These values are common to the Member States in a society in which pluralism, non-discrimination, tolerance, justice, solidarity and equality between women and men prevail.

The application is addressed to the Council,[25] which must act unanimously, after consulting the Commission and obtaining the assent of the European Parliament (which acts by an absolute majority of its members). The conditions of admission and the resulting adjustments to the EU Treaties are laid down in a treaty between the applicant State and the existing Member States; this treaty must be ratified by the applicant State and the existing Member States in accordance with their respective constitutional requirements.[26] When it joins the European Union, the new Member State must accept all existing EU law, including EU legislation and the case-law of the European Court.[27]

§1.4 SUSPENDING MEMBERSHIP RIGHTS

There is no provision for expelling a Member State, but Article 7 TEU provides that the rights of a Member State under the Treaties may be suspended for a serious and persistent breach of the values referred to in Article 2 (set out in § 1.3).

There are two procedures. The first, which appears to be intended as a warning to the recalcitrant Member State, is laid down in paragraph 1 of Article 7. Under it, the Council takes the decision. It may declare that there is a 'clear risk' of a serious breach of the values in Article 2.[28] In doing so, it acts by a majority of four-fifths of its members[29] after obtaining the consent of the European Parliament.[30] Before doing so, the Council must hear the Member State and may address recommendations to it.[31] The Treaty does not specify any particular consequences of such a decision. No doubt it would have a political effect.

[24] Art. 49 TEU. On withdrawal from the EU, see Art. 50 TEU.

[25] The European Parliament and the national Parliaments are notified of the application.

[26] Art. 49, second para., TEU.

[27] See, for example, Arts 2–4 of the first Act of Accession, which cover acts of the Member States, EU acts, and international agreements.

[28] The procedure is set in motion by a reasoned proposal by one-third of the Member States, by the European Parliament or by the Commission.

[29] Not counting the 'accused' Member State.

[30] The Parliament acts by a two-thirds majority of votes cast, representing a majority of members.

[31] It does this under the same procedure.

The second procedure is laid down by paragraph 2. Here the decision is taken by the European Council: it may determine the existence of a 'serious and persistent breach' by the Member State of the values referred to in Article 2. The procedure is the same, except that the European Council acts by unanimity. Under both paragraphs, however, the vote of the 'accused' Member State is not counted.[32]

When a decision under the second paragraph has been taken, the Council (acting by a qualified majority)[33] may suspend some of the rights of the Member State under the Treaties, including its voting rights in the Council. The Council can subsequently vary or revoke the suspension.

§2 SUBSIDIARY CONVENTIONS

In addition to the constitutive Treaties, there were in the past certain other international agreements between the Member States, which, in some cases at least, were part of EU law. Today, most of them have been brought fully within the EU system.[34]

§3 OTHER DECISIONS AND AGREEMENTS

We finally consider acts of the Member States that do not fall into any of the previously mentioned categories. The most important are, first, what are generally called 'acts of the representatives of the Member States'; and, second, treaties on Union matters concluded by a sub-group of Member States.

§3.1 ACTS OF THE REPRESENTATIVES OF THE MEMBER STATES

This is a somewhat anomalous group of acts adopted by the representatives of the Governments of the Member States, meeting in the Council. The representatives here are the delegates sent to the Council by the Member States, i.e., ministers in their respective Governments; but, since they do not act in their capacity as members of the Council when they adopt these acts, the acts are not acts of the Council but are acts of the Member States.

32 Art. 354 TFEU. As regards the other Member States, the abstention of a member of the Council who is present in person or is represented does not prevent the adoption of the decision.

33 Not counting the vote of the 'guilty' Member State.

34 Examples include the Convention on Jurisdiction and the Enforcement of Judgments in Civil and Commercial Matters of 27 September 1968, OJ 1972, L 299/32 (now replaced by an EU Regulation, the Brussels I Regulation, Reg. 44/2001, OJ 2001, L 12/1; in turn replaced by Reg. 1215/2012, OJ 2012, L 351/1), and the Convention on the Law Applicable to Contractual Obligations, opened for signature in Rome on 19 June 1980, OJ 1980, L 266/1 (now replaced by the Rome I Regulation, Reg. 593/2008, OJ 2008, L 177/6).

These acts are usually designated either 'Decision of the Representatives of the Governments of the Member States, meeting in the Council' or 'Agreement between the Representatives'. They are usually published in the Official Journal and are often signed by the President of the Council. They are an established feature of the European Union – first used as long ago as 1954 – and they deal with a wide variety of subjects. Where they are referred to as 'agreements' they are often subject to ratification; but this is not the case where they carry the designation 'decision'. The subjects they deal with are relevant to the functioning of the European Union, though they do not normally fall within any specific power to adopt an EU act.[35] The Commission often plays a part in their preparation.

What is the status of these acts? They probably all fall into one of three categories. Some of them are international agreements concluded in simplified form. In this case, they have the same status as the subsidiary conventions discussed earlier, and are part of the EU legal system. Others, however, are not intended to be legally binding at all: their consequences are merely political. The 'Luxembourg Accords' are probably an example. Acts falling into this category have no legal effects and are not part of any legal system, including the EU legal system. Finally, some acts of the representatives of the Member States constitute the exercise of a power conferred jointly on the Member States. For example, Article 253 TFEU [223/167 EC] provides that Judges and Advocates General of the European Court are appointed 'by common accord of the Governments of the Member States': such appointments are made by acts of the representatives of the Member States. Acts falling into this category – though they must be adopted by unanimous agreement of all the Member States – take effect, not as international agreements, but by virtue of the Treaty provision in question. They plainly fall within the EU legal system.

§3.2 TREATIES AMONG A SUB-GROUP OF MEMBER STATES

It can happen that some, but not all, of the Member States conclude a treaty among themselves on an EU matter. This usually occurs when certain Member States want to extend the EU system to a new area, but others do not. This is a feature of the measures taken to defend the euro, but it has also occurred previously. The principal 'nay-sayer' (country refusing to participate) has almost always been the United Kingdom.

Two early examples were the so-called 'Social Chapter' and the Schengen Agreement. The Social Chapter was originally intended to be part of the TFEU (then the EC Treaty), but the United Kingdom, which had a Conservative Government at the time, refused to accept it; so it had to be adopted in the form of a separate treaty, the Agreement on Social Policy, to which the United Kingdom was not a party. When the Labour Party won the election in 1997, the new Government decided to opt in. Effect was given to

[35] They may, however, fall within the scope of the general power contained in Art. 352 TFEU [308/235 EC].

this by the Treaty of Amsterdam 1997, which re-inserted the Social Chapter into the body of the TFEU.[36]

The Schengen Agreement made provision for the abolition of entry controls on persons travelling from one Member State to another.[37] The scheme started with two agreements, signed in Schengen, Luxembourg, in 1985 and 1990 between France, Germany, and the Benelux countries, under which it was agreed that controls would be gradually lifted. Subsequently, all the other Member States except Britain and Ireland joined in. Two non-member States, Iceland and Norway, became associated with the scheme. These agreements were subsequently brought into the main body of EU law through a Protocol annexed to the Treaty on European Union and the TFEU (then the EC Treaty) by the Treaty of Amsterdam.[38] Two further Protocols allowed Britain and Ireland a permanent opt-out.[39] A fourth Protocol gave a more limited opt-out to Denmark.[40]

What happened in the case of the Schengen Agreement and the Social Chapter shows that there are two ways of achieving the same objective: one is a treaty among a sub-group of Member States and the other is a provision in one of the constitutive Treaties with an opt-out for those Member States which do not wish to participate.[41] There are, however, two important differences. The first is that the latter solution requires the consent of all the Member States, even those that do not wish to participate: they have to allow the Treaties to be amended, even though the new provision will not apply to them. The second difference is that, in the former case, it could be maintained that the treaty does not constitute Union law properly so called, something which could have a number of consequences.

These problems became more acute when the economic crisis threatened the euro. The survival of the euro required a co-ordinated response, but the non-euro States were unwilling to commit funds for this purpose. The result was a patchwork of measures, some Union acts, some acts of the representatives of the Member States, and some agreements among a sub-group of Member States.[42] The last of these consisted of two important measures, the Treaty Establishing the European Stability Mechanism 2012 (ESM Treaty), which was intended to provide the funds to bail out Member States in financial difficulties, and the Treaty on Stability, Co-ordination and Governance 2012 (TSCG, commonly known as the 'Fiscal Compact'), which was intended to strengthen budgetary discipline in the hope of avoiding further crises in the future.

[36] See now Arts 151 *et seq.* TFEU.

[37] See what were then Arts 61–69 EC, introduced by the Treaty of Amsterdam. See now Arts 67 *et seq.* TFEU.

[38] See now Protocol (No. 19) on the Schengen *Acquis* Integrated into the Framework of the European Union.

[39] See now Protocol (No. 20) on the Application of Certain Aspects of Article 26 of the Treaty on the Functioning of the European Union to the United Kingdom and to Ireland; and Protocol (No. 21) on the Position of the United Kingdom and Ireland in Respect of the Area of Freedom, Security and Justice.

[40] Protocol (No. 22) on the Position of Denmark.

[41] Another way of achieving this result is through the use of the enhanced-co-operation mechanism discussed in Chap. 1, § 11. However, this would lead to a Union act (such as a regulation), not a Member State act.

[42] See Chap. 1, § 8.4 for further details.

The ESM Treaty was concluded by the Euro-Area Member States alone. In the case of the TSCG, it was originally expected that all the Member States would be Parties, but the United Kingdom (subsequently followed by the Czech Republic) refused to sign; so it came into force among all the other Member States.

Since neither the ESM Treaty nor the TSCG constituted an amendment to the constitutive Treaties, their relationship to the constitutive Treaties was problematic. With this in mind, Article 2(1) of the TSCG states: 'This Treaty shall be applied and interpreted by the Contracting Parties in conformity with the Treaties on which the European Union is founded...' Article 2(2) goes on to provide:

> The provisions of this Treaty shall apply insofar as they are compatible with the Treaties on which the Union is founded and with European Union law. They shall not encroach upon the competences of the Union to act in the area of the economic union.

This makes clear that the TSCG is subordinate to the constitutive Treaties: in the event of a conflict, the constitutive Treaties prevail. There is no equivalent provision in the ESM Treaty, but under EU law the same principles would apply.[43]

Another issue was the role of the Union institutions. This was particularly important with regard to the European Court since it was desirable for it to have jurisdiction to resolve legal disputes with regard to the two treaties. Luckily, Article 273 TFEU provides the answer. This confers jurisdiction on the European Court in any dispute between Member States which relates to the subject matter of the Treaties if the dispute is submitted to it under a 'special agreement' between the parties. In *Pringle v. Government of Ireland*,[44] the European Court held that the 'special agreement' required by Article 273 could be given in advance, with reference to a whole class of pre-defined disputes.[45]

In reliance on Article 273, Article 37(2) of the ESM Treaty provides that any dispute regarding the interpretation or application of the ESM Treaty is to be decided, in the first instance, by the ESM Board of Governors; Article 37(3) then states that if an ESM Member (a Member State that is a party to the ESM Treaty) contests the decision of the Board of Directors, the dispute will be submitted to the European Court. The decision of the European Court is 'binding on the parties in the procedure'.[46]

In the TSCG, the European Court is given jurisdiction by Article 8 TSCG to determine whether a Contracting Party has failed to comply with the requirement in Article 3(2) TSCG to transpose the principles of the compact into national law. Failure to comply with a judgment of the European Court in this respect can lead to the imposition of a fine on the defaulting State. This can be as high as 0.1 per cent of its gross domestic product.[47]

[43] This is implicit in the whole of the judgment of the European Court in *Pringle v. Government of Ireland*, Case C-370/12, 27 November 2012 (Full Court) and is expressly stated in paras 69 and 101.

[44] Case C-370/12, 27 November 2012 (Full Court).

[45] Para. 172 of the judgment.

[46] ESM Treaty, Art. 37(3).

[47] On the role of the Commission in this procedure, see Craig, 'The Stability, Co-ordination and Governance Treaty: Principle, Politics and Pragmatism' (2012) 37 ELRev. 231 at 245–7.

In both treaties, the Commission is given certain functions. In the case of the ESM Treaty, this is authorized by a decision of the representatives of the Governments of all the Member States.[48] There is no equivalent authorization in the case of the TSCG, though it is possible that no new powers are conferred on the Commission, and that the Commission's activities under the TSCG simply involve the use of existing powers in a new context.[49]

§4 CONFLICTING TREATIES

The next question to consider is what happens when one of the EU Treaties conflicts with some other treaty. Here, the outcome might depend on whether one was looking at the matter from the viewpoint of international law or EU law. In some cases in the past, the European Court has accepted that international law provides the solution;[50] as we shall see (in § 4.4), however, the European Court has recently taken the view that this is not always the case.[51] We shall consider both points of view.

The rules applicable under international law are complex,[52] but Article 30 of the 1969 Vienna Convention on the Law of Treaties is generally regarded as setting them out.[53] According to Article 30(2) of the Vienna Convention, if one of the conflicting treaties provides that the other one prevails, that other treaty will prevail. If neither treaty contains such a rule, paragraphs 3 and 4(a) of Article 30 apply. They may be summarized as follows:

1. If the Parties to the two treaties are the same, the second one prevails.
2. Even if the Parties are not the same, the second one prevails if all the Parties to the first treaty are also Parties to the second.
3. If only some of the Parties to the first treaty are also Parties to the second, the latter prevails as between those States which are Parties to both treaties.

[48] Decision of 20 June 2011, Council Document 12114/11 of 24 June 2011.

[49] See Craig, 'The Stability, Co-ordination and Governance Treaty' (see n. 47), pp. 242–5.

[50] *Italy v. Commission*, Case 10/61, [1962] ECR 1, at 10. This case concerned a conflict between the EEC Treaty (now the TFEU) and a GATT agreement signed in Geneva. The Commission based its argument on 'the principles of international law' and the Court held that its interpretation was 'well founded'. See also *Levy*, Case C-158/91, [1993] ECR I-4287 at para. 12 of the judgment.

[51] *Kadi and Al Barakaat International Foundation v. Council and Commission*, Cases C-402 and 415/05 P, [2008] ECR I-6351 (ECJ), reversing Case T-306/01 and Case T-315/01, [2005] ECR II-3533 and [2005] ECR II-3649.

[52] Jenks, 'The Conflict of Law-Making Treaties' (1953) 30 BYIL 401; Sir Ian Sinclair, *The Vienna Convention on the Law of Treaties*, 2nd edn (1984), pp. 93–8; Mus, 'Conflicts Between Treaties in International Law' (1998) 45 NILJ 208.

[53] The Constitutive Treaties were originally concluded before the Vienna Convention entered into force (for the original Parties) on 27 January 1980. Since Art. 4 of the Vienna Convention provides that it applies only to treaties concluded after it entered into force, it cannot as such apply to the original EU Treaties; nevertheless, it may be regarded as stating the customary international law previously applicable. It should also be said that Art. 5 of the Vienna Convention states that the Convention applies to a treaty which is the constituent instrument of an international organization, and to any treaty adopted within an international organization, 'without prejudice to any relevant rules of the organization'. This means that a principle laid down in the Convention cannot apply if it conflicts with such a rule, unless that principle would have applied under customary international law if the Convention had not been adopted.

These rules solve only some of the possible problems. If none of them applies, Article 30(4)(b) of the Convention comes into operation. It provides: as between a State Party to both treaties and a State Party to only one of the treaties, the treaty to which both States are Parties governs their mutual rights and obligations.

This means that if State X concludes a treaty with State Y and a second treaty with State Z, the first treaty governs its relations with State Y and the second with State Z. This is clearly correct, but is unhelpful if the two treaties contain inconsistent provisions. If the treaties are of a contractual nature, State X could no doubt carry out its obligations under one of them, and pay compensation to the State with which it concluded the other treaty. However, if the treaties are of a legislative nature, Article 30(4)(b) is of no assistance to a court which needs to know which treaty to apply.

It will be seen from this that international law does not always provide a clear answer, though it does do so in some cases. With this in mind, we will now consider how these rules apply in particular circumstances.

§4.1 CONFLICTS BETWEEN EU TREATIES

Since the Parties to all the EU Treaties are the same, the rule of international law is that the later treaty prevails, unless it contains a provision to the contrary. This means that, in general, the TEU and the TFEU, as amended by the Treaty of Lisbon, prevail over all other international agreements in the EU system.

The Treaty of Lisbon contains a Protocol (Protocol No 2) which deals with the Treaty establishing the European Atomic Energy Community (EAEC Treaty or Euratom Treaty). The Protocol makes various amendments to the EAEC Treaty, and states that certain provisions of the TEU and TFEU apply to it; subject to this, it is provided in Article 3 of the Protocol (which inserts a new Article 106a into the EAEC Treaty) that the provisions of the TEU and the TFEU do not derogate from the EAEC Treaty. In other words, the EAEC Treaty prevails, except as otherwise provided.[54]

Subsidiary Conventions and other acts of the Member States were intended to be subordinate to the constitutive Treaties and often have a provision to this effect.[55] Even in the absence of such a provision, the European Court would normally interpret them as being subject to the constitutive Treaties. This would probably be in accord with international law.[56] So far, therefore, EU law and international law coincide.

[54] This does not mean that provisions from the other Treaties cannot apply in the EAEC sphere if they do not conflict with the provisions of the EAEC Treaty: *WTO* case, Opinion 1/94, [1994] ECR I-5267 at para. 24 of the Opinion.

[55] See, for example, Art. 20 of the Rome Convention on the Law Applicable to Contractual Obligations, 1980 (now terminated).

[56] This would clearly be the case where they were concluded before the TEU and TFEU. Even if they were not, the same result would probably ensue under Art. 5 of the Vienna Convention, which states that the Convention applies to a treaty which is the constituent instrument of an international organization, and to any treaty adopted within an international organization, 'without prejudice to any relevant rules of the organization'.

§4.2 CONFLICTS WITH NON-UNION TREATIES

More difficult questions arise where one of the EU Treaties conflicts with a non-EU treaty to which some or all of the Member States are Parties. Here the first paragraph of Article 351 TFEU [307/234 EC][57] would be relevant. It provides:

> The rights and obligations arising from agreements concluded before 1 January 1958 or, for acceding States, before the date of their accession,[58] between one or more Member States on the one hand, and one or more third countries on the other, shall not be affected by the provisions of this Treaty.[59]

According to the European Court, the purpose of this provision is to make clear, in accordance with the principles of international law, that the application of the EU Treaties does not affect the commitment of the Member State concerned to respect the rights of non-member States under an earlier agreement.[60] As was pointed out by the European Court in *Italy v. Commission*,[61] the word 'rights' in Article 351 [307/234 EC] refers to the rights of the non-member State and the word 'obligations' refers to the obligations of the Member State. Thus the obligations of the EU State towards the non-member State are not affected: the *rights* of the EU State may very well be affected.[62]

Article 351 was probably adopted because some States might have been reluctant to conclude the EU Treaties if this could have given rise to obligations inconsistent with those arising out of earlier treaties with other States. There is no equivalent provision in

[57] In subsequent paragraphs, Art. 351 [307/234 EC] requires the Member State in question to take all appropriate steps to eliminate the incompatibilities. On this, see *Commission v. Sweden*, Case C-249/06, [2009] ECR I-1335; *Commission v. Austria*, Case C-205/06, 3 March 2009 (Grand Chamber).

[58] The original text of the EEC Treaty spoke simply of 'agreements concluded before the entry into force of this Treaty'. This was amended by the Treaty of Amsterdam 1997, Art. 6 (heading I, point 78), by deleting the words 'before the entry into force of this Treaty' and replacing them with 'before 1 January 1958 or, for acceding States, before the date of their accession'. Since the relevant date for the EU Treaties is that of entry into force, not that on which the text was adopted, it might be argued that the relevant date for the other agreement (the date on which it was 'concluded') should also be that on which it entered into force. Under Art. 30 of the 1969 Vienna Convention, however, the relevant date appears to be that on which the text is adopted, not that on which the treaty enters into force: Sir Ian Sinclair, *The Vienna Convention on the Law of Treaties*, 2nd edn (1984), p. 98; Anthony Aust, *Modern Treaty Law and Practice* (2000), p. 183; Mus, 'Conflicts Between Treaties in International Law' (1998) 45 NILJ 208 at 220–2. A different view is advanced in Vierdag, 'The Time of the "Conclusion" of a Multilateral Treaty: Art. 30 of the Vienna Convention on the Law of Treaties and Related Provisions' (1988) 59 BYIL 75, but this seems to be incorrect for the reasons given in Mus (see earlier). According to the European Court, Art. 351 [307/234] was intended to reflect the principles of international law: *Commission v. Italy*, Case 10/61, [1962] ECR 1 at 10. In view of this, it would make sense to interpret it (in this respect) in the same way as Art. 30 of the Vienna Convention. Moreover, if the purpose of Art. 351 [307/234] is to protect Member States from the embarrassment of conflicting obligations, the relevant date should be that on which the text of the other agreement was adopted, rather than that on which it entered into force.

[59] On the effect of Art. 351 [307/234] in international law, see Art. 30(2) of the 1969 Vienna Convention.

[60] *Levy*, Case C-158/91, [1993] ECR I-4287 at para. 12 of the judgment.

[61] Case 10/61, [1962] ECR 1 at 10. See also *Evans Medical and Macfarlan Smith*, Case C-324/93, [1995] ECR I-563 at para. 27 of the judgment; and *Centro-Com*, Case C-124/95, [1997] ECR I-81 at para. 56 of the judgment.

[62] Thus in *Italy v. Commission*, Italy's right under the GATT agreement to charge the higher rate of duty was affected in so far as it conflicted with the rights of other EC countries under the EC Treaty.

the EAEC Treaty, probably because it was thought unlikely that it would conflict with any other treaty.

The *Levy* case[63] is an illustration of the operation of Article 351 TFEU [307/234 EC]. Prior to the conclusion of the EEC Treaty (now the TFEU), France had concluded an ILO agreement which provided that women would not be permitted to work at night. France gave effect to this agreement by passing appropriate legislation. Subsequently, the European Union adopted a directive on sex equality in employment,[64] which gave women the same rights as men to work at night.[65] There was thus a conflict between, on the one hand, the ILO agreement and the French legislation and, on the other hand, the directive. Levy, an employer who had infringed the French legislation, was prosecuted. Normally, the directive would have given him a good defence,[66] but because the French legislation was adopted to give effect to France's obligations under the ILO agreement, the European Court ruled that the directive would not take effect in France to the extent to which it prevented France from complying with its obligations under the ILO agreement. It made clear, however, that this would be the case only if the performance of the agreement could still be required by States that were Parties to it and were not Parties to the EU Treaties.[67]

In a later case, *Kadi and Al Barakaat International Foundation v. Council and Commission*,[68] however, the European Court laid down an important qualification to this rule: it said that, although the agreement with the non-member State prevails over ordinary provisions of the EU Treaties, it cannot prevail over provisions forming part of the constitutional foundations of the EU system. This is discussed further in § 4.4.

§4.3 THE EUROPEAN CONVENTION ON HUMAN RIGHTS

The most noteworthy instance in which these problems have arisen is where the EU Treaties have been in conflict with the European Convention on Human Rights. The leading case concerns the right of persons resident in Gibraltar to vote in elections to the European Parliament. Originally, the EU Treaties provided that the European Parliament (then called the 'Assembly') would consist of delegates designated by Member State Parliaments from among their own number.[69] The Treaties went on to state, however, that the European Parliament would draw up proposals for direct elections. These had to be agreed by the Council and adopted by the Member States 'in

[63] Case C-158/91, [1993] ECR I-4287. See also *Centro-Com*, Case C-124/95, [1997] ECR I-81 at paras 56–61.

[64] The Equal Treatment Directive, 76/207, OJ 1976, L 39/40.

[65] *Stoeckl*, Case C-345/89, [1991] ECR I-4047.

[66] See *Stoeckl* (see n. 65). This would have been a case of 'vertical' direct effect, since the other party was the State, the prosecutor in the criminal proceedings. On the meaning of 'vertical' direct effect, see Chap. 7, § 4.6.

[67] There was some doubt as to whether the ILO agreement had been terminated or suspended under international law by virtue of later agreements, a question which the European Court held was for the French court to decide.

[68] Cases C-402 and 415/05 P, [2008] ECR I-6351 (ECJ), reversing Case T-306/01 and Case T-315/01, [2005] ECR II-3533 and [2005] ECR II-3649.

[69] Arts 138(1) EEC and 108(1) EAEC.

accordance with their respective constitutional requirements'.[70] After a long delay, the Council adopted a decision to which was annexed an 'Act' providing for direct elections.[71] The Act was ratified as a treaty by the Member States, and, though there is some controversy surrounding its legal status, it is best regarded as a treaty amending the relevant EU Treaties.[72] The Act specifies how many representatives will be elected in each Member State; it also states in Annex II that the United Kingdom will apply the provisions of the Act only in respect of the United Kingdom itself. Article 15 of the Act states that the Annexes form an integral part of the Act. Since Gibraltar, though a British dependency, is not constitutionally part of the United Kingdom, this had the effect of excluding Gibraltarians from participating in elections to the European Parliament, even though the EU Treaties apply, in part, to Gibraltar and, to that extent, the European Parliament has jurisdiction over Gibraltar.[73]

In *Matthews v. United Kingdom*,[74] Ms Matthews, a resident of Gibraltar, brought proceedings before the European Court of Human Rights, claiming that the denial of her right to vote in European elections constituted a violation of Article 3 of Protocol No. 1 to the Convention, a provision which guarantees the right to free elections.[75] The United Kingdom argued that the Act constituted a treaty which was binding on it, and that it could not be liable for any infringement of the Convention that resulted from the Act. The Court rejected this argument: even though the Act was a treaty, the United Kingdom had chosen to conclude it, and it was, therefore, liable for any resulting infringement.[76] It ruled that Article 3 of Protocol No. 1 does not apply only to the legislature of a State, but can also apply to that of an international organization. It then held that, as a result of increases in the powers of the European Parliament following amendments brought in by the Treaty on European Union,[77] the Parliament now constitutes a 'legislature' for the purpose of Article 3. It concluded, therefore, that the United Kingdom had violated the Convention.[78]

As a result of this decision, there was a conflict between two treaties binding on the United Kingdom, the European Convention on Human Rights, which required voting rights to be given to Gibraltarians, and what was then the EC Treaty (now the TFEU), which forbade it. This put the United Kingdom in a difficult position. It had

[70] Arts 138(3) EEC and 108(3) EAEC. [71] Decision 76/787, OJ 1976, L 278/1.

[72] See Chap. 1, § 1.01.

[73] The Treaties applied to Gibraltar by virtue of Art. 299(4) [227(4)] EC (see now Art. 355(3) TFEU). However, the Treaty of Accession by which the United Kingdom joined the EU provides that many parts of the EU Treaties, including those dealing with such important matters as the free movement of goods and the Common Agricultural Policy, would not apply to Gibraltar. [74] (1999) 28 EHRR 361.

[75] She also invoked Art. 14 of the Convention, which provides that the enjoyment of the rights laid down in the Convention must be secured without discrimination. The Convention applies to Gibraltar by virtue of a declaration made by the United Kingdom on 23 October 1953 under what was then Art. 63 of the Convention; Protocol No. 1 applies by virtue of a declaration made on 25 February 1988 under Art. 4 of Protocol No. 1.

[76] For the case-law of the European Court of Human Rights on this issue (both before and after the *Matthews* case), see Chap. 5, § 2.2.

[77] The Treaty on European Union provided that, in certain cases, legislation would be enacted jointly by the European Parliament and the Council: see Art. 251 [189b] EC, as it stood at the time.

[78] The judgment was largely declaratory, but the applicant was awarded £45,000 for costs and expenses.

no objection to allowing Gibraltarians to vote in European elections,[79] and the obvious course was to ask the other EU States to amend the Act. However, Spain did not agree, since it was campaigning for the return of Gibraltar to Spanish sovereignty.

The United Kingdom then decided to carry out its obligations under the European Convention on Human Rights by giving Gibraltarians the right to vote in elections to the European Parliament as part of one of the electoral regions in England and Wales.[80] Spain objected, and brought proceedings against the United Kingdom under Article 259 TFEU [227/170 EC].[81]

The position under both Article 30 of the Vienna Convention and under Article 351 TFEU [307/234 EC] is complicated; nevertheless, it is arguable that the European Convention on Human Rights enjoyed priority by virtue of Article 351 TFEU [307/234 EC].[82] The European Court did not, however, decide the case on this basis. In a judgment that carefully avoided the issue of conflicting treaties, it simply held that, since the United Kingdom had done no more than was necessary to comply with the judgment in the *Matthews* case, Spain's application should be dismissed.

The issue of conflicting treaties was clouded because Spain and the United Kingdom had concluded an informal agreement in 2002, under which the United Kingdom could take the steps necessary to comply with the judgment in the *Matthews* case, provided it did so in accordance with EU law. This agreement was reflected in a Declaration made by the United Kingdom on 18 February 2002, which was recorded in the minutes of the Council.[83] In the proceedings before the Court, Spain was, therefore, unable to argue that Gibraltarians could not be allowed to vote at all. It did, however, argue that the United Kingdom had infringed what was then the EC Treaty by allowing them to cast their votes in Gibraltar: they should have been required to travel to the United Kingdom to vote or to vote by post.[84] None of this, however, was relevant to whether the United Kingdom had infringed the EC Treaty. An agreement between two Member States (even if noted by the others) cannot amend the Treaty; nor can it absolve one Member State from its obligation to comply with the Treaty.

[79] The reason Gibraltarians were originally excluded was that there were too few of them to make up a constituency (electoral district) on their own, and they were too remote from the United Kingdom to be joined to any constituency there. The United Kingdom had, however, decided that future elections in the United Kingdom to the European Parliament would be held under a system of proportional representation; so that reason no longer applied.

[80] European Parliament (Representation) Act 2003, Part 2; European Parliamentary Elections (Combined Region and Campaign Expenditure) (United Kingdom and Gibraltar) Order 2004, SI 2004/366.

[81] *Spain v. United Kingdom*, Case C-145/04, [2006] ECR I-7917. The Commission had refused to bring proceedings against the United Kingdom under Art. 226 [169] EC, and even went so far as to appear in the proceedings in support of the United Kingdom.

[82] See Hartley, 'International Law and the Law of the European Union – A Reassessment' (2001) 72 BYIL 1 at 32–5.

[83] This should have settled the matter; however, there was a change of Government in Spain and the new Government was less sympathetic to the British position.

[84] It also objected to the fact that electoral challenges could be brought before the courts of Gibraltar and that certain administrative activities took place there.

As we shall see in Chapter 5, human rights constitute a 'general principle of law' in the EU system and, as such, override EU legislation. However, they cannot on this basis override a Treaty provision. The judgment in *Spain v. United Kingdom* must, therefore, be regarded as laying down a tacit rule that the European Convention on Human Rights (and possibly other human rights conventions) override the constitutive Treaties in the event of a conflict,[85] something that was hinted at by the Court in two earlier cases.[86] This is based on the 'privileged position accorded to the protection of fundamental rights by the Community [EU] legal order'.[87] The position may, therefore, be different where the conflict is with a treaty that is not concerned with human rights.

§4.4 UNITED NATIONS LAW

Recently the European Court has had to deal with a conflict between EU human rights law and a Resolution of the UN Security Council that was contrary to human rights. This was in joined cases *Kadi and Al Barakaat International Foundation v. Council and Commission* (discussed further in Chapter 5, § 2.6).[88]

The Security Council had adopted a series of Resolutions under Chapter VII of the UN Charter freezing the assets of certain named individuals and organizations on the ground that they were associated with the Taliban and Osama Bin Laden. The European Union then adopted regulations to give effect to the Resolutions. The applicants, a person resident in Saudi Arabia with assets in Sweden (*Kadi*), and a Swedish organization giving assistance to Somali refugees (*Al Barakaat*), had been named in a Security Council Resolution and in an EU regulation. Sweden had been obliged to give effect to the regulation. The applicants brought annulment proceedings against the EU regulation under Article 263 TFEU [230/173 EC]. Since the applicants' property had been seized without any judicial proceedings or hearing or other right of redress and without their even being told what they were supposed to have done wrong, their human rights had been violated. Without the Security Council Resolution, the regulation would have been annulled on this ground. However, the General Court (which heard the cases in the first instance) held it valid.

Its reasoning was as follows.[89] Under international law, the Security Council Resolution was binding on all members of the United Nations,[90] and prevailed over all treaties, whether prior or subsequent;[91] therefore, it was binding on the Member States

[85] See *per* Advocate General Tizzano at paras 118–121 of his Opinion in *Spain v. United Kingdom*.

[86] *Schmidberger*, Case C-112/00, [2003] ECR I-5659 at para. 74 of the judgment; *Omega*, Case C-36/02, [2004] ECR I-9609 at para. 35 of the judgment.

[87] Advocate General Tizzano at para. 118 of his Opinion in *Spain v. United Kingdom*.

[88] Cases C-402 and 415/05 P, [2008] ECR I-6351 (ECJ), reversing Case T-306/01 and Case T-315/01, [2005] ECR II-3533 and [2005] ECR II-3649 (General Court).

[89] See paras 233–259 of the judgment.

[90] Art. 25 of the UN Charter.

[91] Art. 103 of the UN Charter. Art. 30(1) of the Vienna Convention on the Law of Treaties 1969 expressly provides that the rules it lays down are subject to Art. 103.

of the Union and had to be carried out even if it conflicted with the EU Treaties. Since the Member States of the European Union became Parties to the UN Charter before they concluded the EU Treaties,[92] the first paragraph of Article 351 TFEU [307/234 EC] (discussed in § 4.2) required the Union not to prevent the Member States from fulfilling their obligations under the Resolution; consequently, under EU law the Resolution prevailed over EU law. Although the Union was not bound by the Resolution under international law, it was bound under EU law: this followed from a principle originally laid down by the European Court in the third *International Fruit Company* case,[93] a principle under which the European Union will, in certain situations, become bound by obligations entered into by the Member States (discussed in Chapter 6, § 7.2). As a consequence, the Union was obliged to adopt the regulation,[94] an obligation that overrode the requirement to respect human rights.[95]

This judgment was reversed by the European Court. Although it had no jurisdiction to review the lawfulness of Resolutions of the Security Council, it did have jurisdiction to review the lawfulness of EU regulations. The fact that the regulation was adopted to give effect to the obligations of the Member States under the Security Council Resolutions did not affect the matter. Under international law, the Resolutions of the Security Council prevail over any other treaty obligations, but the position is different under EU law. EU law has its own hierarchy of norms (ranking of different legal rules), which is not necessarily the same as that under international law. This was a statement of principle by the European Court of great constitutional importance.

Previously, the hierarchy of norms in EU law depended on their source. As we have seen, the constitutive Treaties come first. However, in *Kadi* the European Court created a special 'super category' of legal norms, which derive their status, not from their source, but from their function in the EU system. In *Kadi*, these were variously called 'constitutional principles';[96] 'the very foundations of the Community';[97] 'the principles enshrined...as a foundation of the Union';[98] and 'the principles that form part of the very foundations of the Community legal order'.[99] We shall refer to them as the 'constitutional foundations' of the EU system. Although they are based on provisions of the constitutive

[92] Germany was an exception, but its duty to carry out its obligations under the Charter followed from certain other international agreements that pre-dated the EC Treaty.

[93] Cases 21–4/72, [1972] ECR 1219. See also *Schlüter*, Case 9/73, [1973] ECR 1135 and *Nederlandse Spoorwegen*, Case 38/75, [1975] ECR 1439.

[94] The only exception existed under the international law doctrine of *jus cogens* (on which see Art. 53 of the 1969 Vienna Convention on the Law of Treaties). However, the General Court found that the violation of the applicants' rights was not sufficiently serious to bring this principle into operation.

[95] It is interesting to contrast the judgment of the General Court in *Kadi* with its later judgment in *Organisation des Modjahedines du peuple d'Iran (OMPI) v. Council*, Case T-228/02, [2006] ECR II-4665, which also concerned the freezing of the assets of an organization accused of being associated with terrorism. Although the freezing of OMPI's assets was part of the same programme as that in the earlier cases, there was one important difference: it was the EU Council, not the Security Council, that had designated OMPI as being associated with terrorism. The General Court held, therefore, that the EU had had a choice in the matter: it was not just following instructions from the Security Council. For this reason, it was obliged to observe the EU law requirement of a fair hearing. Since it had not done so, the decision designating OMPI was annulled.

[96] Para. 285 of *Kadi*. [97] Paras 282 and 290. [98] Para. 303. [99] Para. 304.

Treaties – for example, Article 6(1) TEU[100] – they are in reality very much the work of the European Court.

The European Court rejected the view that Article 351 TFEU [307/234 EC] protected the regulation from challenge. We have seen (in § 4.2) that a treaty with a non-member State concluded by a Member State before it joined the Union enjoys primacy over EU measures such as regulations to the extent necessary to avoid forcing it to violate its obligations towards the non-member State. The European Court has even held that such a treaty can enjoy primacy over a provision in one of the constitutive Treaties.[101] However, in *Kadi* it said that it can never enjoy primacy over provisions (such as the protection of fundamental human rights) that form part of the constitutional foundations of the Union.[102]

The European Court appeared not to accept the General Court's view that, under EU law, the European Union is bound by the UN Charter, but it said that even if what was then Article 300(7) EC (which provides that international agreements concluded by the Union are binding on the institutions and the Member States) were applicable to the UN Charter – in other words, even if the UN Charter were binding on the Union – the Charter would still not enjoy primacy over the constitutive Treaties (what the European Court called 'primary law'), much less over legal rules forming part of the constitutional foundations of the EU system.[103]

For these reasons, the European Court allowed the appeal and set aside the judgment of the General Court. The regulation was annulled in so far as it concerned the applicants, though its effects were maintained for a limited period.[104]

This judgment opened up an inconsistency between the EU legal system and international law. This could have exposed the Member States to conflicting obligations, but it has the merit of giving greater protection to human rights.

§4.5 CONCLUSIONS

We can see from what has been said that though the European Court normally applies the rules of international law to treaty conflicts (or at least rules of EU law that coincide with those of international law), there are some instances in which it refuses to follow international law and insists on applying the European Union's own hierarchy of norms.

Under this, legal rules forming part of the constitutional foundations of the Union enjoy primacy over all other legal rules. Other provisions in the constitutive Treaties

[100] As it applied at the time (it has been amended by the Treaty of Lisbon), Art. 6(1) stated that the Union is founded on the principles of liberty, democracy, respect for human rights and fundamental freedoms, and the rule of law.

[101] *Centro-Com*, Case C-124/95, [1997] ECR I-81 at paras 56–61.

[102] Paras 300–304 of the judgment.

[103] Paras 305–309 of the judgment. The European Court accepted that it would enjoy primacy over EU legislation (what it called 'secondary Community law').

[104] For further discussion, see Chap. 5, § 2.6. For further developments, see *Commission v. Kadi*, Case C-584/10 P (18 July 2013) (Grand Chamber) (appeal from *Kadi v. Commission*, Case T-85/09, [2010] ECR II-5177).

come next. They prevail over most other rules, but they may be suspended to a limited extent where they conflict with a treaty with a non-member State concluded by a Member State before it joined the European Union. On the other hand, they prevail over agreements with non-member States concluded by the Union (and *a fortiori* over agreements concluded by Member States after they join the Union).[105]

FURTHER READING

Items are listed in date order, the most recent being at the end.

BEBR, 'Acts of Representatives of the Governments of the Member States' [1966] SEW 529.

PESCATORE, 'Remarques sur la nature juridique des "décisions des représentants des Etats Membres réunis au sein du Conseil"' [1966] SEW 579.

RASMUSSEN, 'A New Generation of Community Law?' (1978) 15 CMLRev. 249.

RENÉ JOLIET, *Le droit institutionnel des Communautés européennes: Les institutions; Les sources; Les rapports entre ordres juridiques* (1983), pp. 127–38.

WEILER AND MODRALL, 'Institutional Reform: Consensus or Majority?' (1985) 10 ELRev. 316.

KLABBERS, 'Informal Instruments before the European Court of Justice' (1994) 31 CMLRev. 997.

HARTLEY, 'International Law and the Law of the European Union – A Reassessment' (2001) 72 BYIL 1.

DOUGLAS-SCOTT, 'A Tale of Two Courts: Luxembourg, Strasbourg and the Growing European Human Rights *Acquis*' (2006) 43 CMLRev. 629.

ALMQVIST, 'A Human Rights Critique of European Judicial Review: Counter Terrorism Sanctions' (2008) 57 ICLQ 303.

HALBERSTAM AND STEIN, 'The United Nations, the European Union, and the King of Sweden: Economic Sanctions and Individual Rights in a Plural World Order' (2009) 46 CMLRev. 13.

KUNOY AND DAWES, 'Plate Tectonics in Luxembourg: The *Ménage à Trois* between EC Law, International Law and the European Convention on Human Rights Following the UN Sanctions Cases' (2009) 46 CMLRev. 73.

TRIDIMAS AND GUTIÉRREZ-FONS, 'EU Law, International Law and Economic Sanctions against Terrorism: The Judiciary in Distress?' (2009) 32 *Fordham Journal of International Law* 901.

CRAIG, 'The Stability, Co-ordination and Governance Treaty: Principle, Politics and Pragmatism' (2012) 37 ELRev. 231.

[105] For further discussion of the relationship between EU law and international law, see *Commission v. Ireland*, Case C-459/03, [2006] ECR I-4635.

4

UNION ACTS

This chapter deals with measures ('legal acts' in EU terminology) adopted by the Union. We discuss the powers of the Union institutions and the procedures followed to exercise those powers. We start with the classification of legal acts.

§1 CLASSIFICATION

Legal acts may be classified in at least three ways: they may be classified according to the label they have been given (what they call themselves); they may be classified according to the procedure used to adopt them; and they may be classified according to their function. All three methods are relevant for different purposes. We shall refer to the first as 'nominal' classification; the second as 'procedural' classification; and the third as 'functional' classification. We start with nominal classification.

§1.1 NOMINAL CLASSIFICATION

Article 288 TFEU [249/189 EC] lists five different kinds of acts that may be adopted if other provisions confer the power to do so. They are:

1. regulations;
2. directives;
3. decisions;
4. recommendations;
5. opinions.

Article 288 also contains a short statement of the characteristics each kind of act is supposed to have. A regulation is essentially normative in character: it lays down general rules which are binding both at the EU level and at the national level. Directives and decisions differ from regulations, in that they are not binding in quite the same way. Directives may be addressed only to Member States and they are binding only as to the result to be achieved: they leave to the national authorities 'the choice of form and methods'. This suggests that they lay down an objective and allow each national Government to achieve it by the means it regards as most suitable. A decision, on the other hand, is binding in its entirety; however, if it specifies those to whom it is addressed (which it usually does), it is binding only on them. Recommendations and opinions are not binding at all.[1]

These provisions appear to form a neat and tidy system in which formal designations correspond to differences in function. The differences suggest a hierarchy. Regulations appear to be at the top, since they are both wide in scope, being binding on everybody, and lay down directly applicable rules. One might think that decisions came next: although they may bind only a limited category of persons (those to whom they are addressed), their obligatory quality is just as intense as that of a regulation. Directives, on the other hand, appear to be the weakest form: they are binding only as to their objective.

Unfortunately, things are not as simple as this. The first complication is that the formal designation of an act – the label given to it by its author – is not always a reliable guide to its contents. An act may be called a regulation but bear all the characteristics of a decision; or it may be called a directive but leave little choice as to form and methods. Faced with this situation, the European Court has sometimes rejected the formal designation and looked instead at the substance of the act. If an act in the form of a regulation does not lay down general rules but is concerned with deciding a particular case, the Court may call it a 'disguised decision' and treat it for certain purposes as if it were a decision. This is what we have called 'functional' classification. It is not clear, however, how far the Court will go in this 'relabelling' process: in the past, it has done so mainly for the purpose of deciding questions of *locus standi* (standing) in judicial review.[2]

A second complication is that in practice the differences between the various kinds of acts are not as great as might appear from the Treaty provisions. In particular, judgments of the European Court have had the effect of upgrading directives so that they are now much closer to regulations: even if they have not been implemented by the Member State to which they are addressed, they can directly confer rights on private citizens which may be invoked against public authorities.[3]

A third complication is that the European Court has ruled that the list in what is now Article 288 is not exhaustive: it is possible to have a legally binding act which does not fall into any of the categories enumerated in the Treaty. Acts falling into this residual category are usually called, for want of a better name, acts *sui generis*. The case in which the European Court gave this ruling was the *ERTA* case,[4] which concerned the negotiations leading to the European Road Transport Agreement (ERTA) and, in particular, a Council 'resolution'– to use a neutral term – in which it was settled what

[1] They cannot, therefore, create rights upon which individuals may rely before a national court: *Grimaldi*, Case C-322/88, [1989] ECR 4407 (para. 16 of the judgment); nevertheless, the European Court has said that a measure in the form of a recommendation may have to be examined to see whether its content is consistent with its form (para. 14).

[2] See § 1.3. [3] For the details, see Chap. 7, § 4.

[4] *Commission v. Council*, Case 22/70, [1971] ECR 263; discussed further in Chap. 6, § 2.3.

negotiating procedure would be adopted at the conference. The Commission disagreed with the content of this 'resolution' and wished to obtain a ruling from the Court on whether the negotiating procedure laid down in it was in accord with EU law. The only means available of bringing this issue before the Court was an action for the annulment of the 'resolution'.

One question which the Court had to decide was whether the 'resolution' could in fact form the subject of annulment proceedings.[5] If the Court had decided this in the negative, it would have been obliged to declare the proceedings inadmissible and would thus have been deprived of the opportunity to rule on the substantive issues involved, principally the capacity of the Union to conclude international agreements. The Court was, however, faced with a problem: if it decided that the 'resolution', which was not in the form of any legal act listed in what is now Article 288, was in fact a regulation, directive, or decision, it would have been obliged to annul it for lack of reasons, since at the time in question there was a rule, laid down in what was then Article 190 EEC, that regulations, directives, and decisions had to state the reasons on which they were based.[6]

The Court was clearly reluctant to annul the 'resolution', since this might have meant that the negotiations for the ERTA, which had been concluded by the time the judgment was given, would have had to begin all over again. Since the Agreement had already been signed by at least some Member States, this would have been most undesirable and might have made non-member States reluctant to enter into similar negotiations in the future. In view of this, one can see the attractiveness, from a policy point of view, of declaring the 'resolution' to be a legal act *sui generis*: by holding it to be a legal act, the Court was able to declare the proceedings admissible and could therefore rule on the substantive issues; and by declaring that it was not a regulation, a decision, or a directive, it could hold that what was then Article 190 EEC did not apply to it, and it did not need to be annulled for lack of reasons. The Court was thus able to give a judgment in which the substantive issues were decided in principle in favour of the Commission – which was all the Commission wanted – and at the same time avoid upsetting the Agreement. There were, therefore, strong policy reasons why the Court classified the 'resolution' as an act *sui generis*; had it not been for these considerations, the Court would probably have declared it to be a decision.[7]

It will be seen from what has been said that nominal classification has severe limitations. It was partly for this reason – though also for other reasons – that the Treaty of Lisbon introduced a new kind of classification: what we have called 'procedural' classification.

[5] For a general discussion of which measures are subject to annulment by the Court, see Chap. 11.

[6] Today, Art. 296(2) TFEU provides that *legal acts* must state the reasons on which they are based. See § 7.2.

[7] This was the solution adopted in another case in which the act carried no formal designation, the *Noordwijks Cement Accoord* case, discussed in Chap. 11, § 2.

§1.2 PROCEDURAL CLASSIFICATION

The Treaty of Lisbon created a new concept of EU law, that of a 'legislative act'. This is defined by Article 289(3) TFEU as a legal act 'adopted by legislative procedure'. Article 289 TFEU recognizes two kinds of legislative procedure: ordinary legislative procedure and special legislative procedure. The ordinary legislative procedure was outlined in Chapter 1, § 9. It consists in the joint adoption by the European Parliament and the Council of a regulation, directive, or decision on a proposal from the Commission.[8] The special legislative procedure, which may be used only in the specific cases provided for by the Treaties, consists in the adoption of a regulation, directive, or decision by the European Parliament with the participation of the Council, or by the latter with the participation of the European Parliament.[9] In either case, the result is a 'legislative act'.[10]

Legal acts that do not fall within the definition of a 'legislative act' constitute 'non-legislative acts'. They may still be legally binding – they may indeed be in the form of a regulation, directive, or decision – and they may operate functionally as legislation – they may lay down general rules – but they will not be entitled to the designation 'legislative act'.

Two other kinds of legal acts referred to in the Treaties are 'delegated' acts and 'implementing' acts. Delegated acts are discussed in § 6. They may be adopted where a legislative act delegates power to the Commission to adopt non-legislative acts of general application (functionally legislative or normative) to supplement or amend non-essential elements of the legislative act.[11]

Implementing acts are measures to implement legally binding acts.[12] They may be adopted either by the Member States (in which case they will not be EU acts at all) or, where uniformity is needed, by the Commission (or, in certain special cases, by the Council).

§1.3 FUNCTIONAL CLASSIFICATION

Functional classification is classification of a legal act according to what it actually does – the way it functions – rather than according to what it calls itself or the procedure used to adopt it. It is a separate method of classification because, as we have seen, the way a measure operates is not necessarily indicated either by its official designation or by the procedure used to adopt it.

From a functional point of view, the difference between a legislative (normative) act and an executive act (decision) is generally said to be that a legislative act is a measure that lays down general rules that bind everyone within its scope, while an executive act deals with a particular case. Thus, a legislative act may lay down the rate of customs duty to be paid when goods are imported; an executive act will determine exactly how

[8] Art. 289(1) TFEU. [9] Art. 289(2) TFEU.

[10] Art. 289(4) TFEU goes on to say that in the specific cases provided for by the Treaties, legislative acts may be adopted on the initiative of a group of Member States or of the European Parliament, on a recommendation from the European Central Bank, or at the request of the Court of Justice, or the European Investment Bank.

[11] Art. 290(1) TFEU. [12] Art. 291 TFEU.

much must be paid by the importer of a particular consignment of goods. In principle, the former should be a regulation in the EU system and the latter a decision. It is because this has not always been the case in practice that the European Court has sometimes classified legal acts on a functional basis.

This has taken place mainly in the context of judicial review and was made necessary by the fact that (in the past) individuals (as distinct from EU institutions and national Governments) could challenge only decisions, not regulations or directives. The European Court thought it was unfair that individuals should be deprived of their rights simply because an act carried the wrong designation. So it began to classify acts on a functional basis to allow it to review measures that, though in the form of a regulation, operated functionally as decisions.

Since the coming into force of the Treaty of Lisbon, functional classification is no longer necessary for this purpose; however, it has been used by the General Court in order to decide whether a measure constitutes a 'regulatory act' for the purpose of judicial review under a different provision.[13]

§1.4 CONCLUSIONS

It is important to realize that these three methods of classification are independent and can cut across each other. A 'legislative act' in the procedural sense will not necessarily be functionally legislative: it will not necessarily lay down general rules binding on all those who fall within its scope. As we have seen, a regulation, though intended to be legislative in the functional sense, may not actually be so. Moreover, a 'legislative act' in the procedural sense may not be in the form of a regulation: the Treaties make clear that it may take the form of either a regulation, a decision, or a directive – this despite the fact that decisions are supposed to function as executive acts. For these reasons, it is necessary for the EU lawyer to think on three planes, so to speak: he must keep in mind the procedural classification of an act, its nominal classification, and its functional classification. Each may be relevant for different purposes.

§2 THE PRINCIPLE OF CONFERRAL

§2.1 MEANING

According to the Treaties, the limits of the Union's powers are governed by the principle of conferral.[14] This means that the Union possesses only such powers as are conferred upon it by the Treaties. Any powers not conferred remain with the Member States.[15] It follows from these provisions that the Union cannot confer powers on itself: it does not have what the Germans call '*Kompetenz-Kompetenz*' (the power to confer power on yourself or – what comes to the same thing – to determine conclusively the limits

[13] See Chap. 12, § 5.2. [14] Art. 5(1) TEU. [15] Art. 4(1) TEU.

of your powers). As a result, if the Union acts beyond its powers, the act in question will be invalid ('*ultra vires*' in traditional English terminology). If it is a legal act (an act which purports to produce legal effects), it will be annulled by the European Court.

Of course, the European Court is itself part of the Union. It is an institution of the Union. So if the Court's decision as to the limits of the powers of the Union was conclusive, it could be said that, in a sense, the Union *did* have *Kompetenz-Kompetenz:* it could determine the limits of its own powers. Since this might seem at odds with the principle of conferral, the highest constitutional courts in several Member States – for example, Germany, Denmark, and Poland – have made it clear that, in their view, the European Court does not have the final say on this point: the Member State courts do. The European Court does not accept this; so the matter remains controversial. We return to it in Chapter 8.

While it is undoubtedly true that the Union has no inherent powers[16] and must keep within the powers conferred on it by the Treaties, the practical significance of this is diminished by two factors: first, the European Court interprets the empowering provisions of the Treaties in a wide manner, partly on the basis of the theory of implied powers; secondly, some Treaty provisions, notably Article 352 TFEU [308/235 EC], confer on the Union what might seem to be an open-ended power.

§2.2 THE THEORY OF IMPLIED POWERS

This theory, which was originally developed in the constitutional and administrative law of such countries as the United States and England, and which has been recognized as a principle of international law,[17] may be expressed in both a narrow and a wide formulation. According to the narrow formulation, the existence of a given power implies also the existence of any other power which is reasonably necessary for the exercise of the former; according to the wide formulation, the existence of a given *objective* or *function* implies the existence of any power reasonably necessary to attain it.

The narrow formulation was adopted by the European Court as long ago as 1956;[18] the wide formulation was applied (with regard to the Commission) in 1987. This was in *Germany v. Commission*,[19] a case arising out of what was then Article 118 EEC (see now Article 153 TFEU). As it existed at the time, Article 118 EEC provided: 'the Commission shall have the task of promoting close co-operation between Member

[16] The European Court has, however, come very close to claiming inherent powers for itself: see Arnull, 'Does the Court of Justice Have Inherent Jurisdiction?' (1990) 27 CMLRev. 683; Usher, 'How Limited is the Jurisdiction of the European Court of Justice?' in J Dine, S Douglas-Scott, and I Persaud (eds), *Procedure and the European Court* (1991), p. 72.

[17] See International Court of Justice, *Advisory Opinion on Reparation for Injuries Suffered in the Service of the United Nations* [1949] ICJ 174 at 182. See, further, Lauwaars, *Lawfulness and Legal Force of Community Decisions* (1973), pp. 94–8.

[18] *Fédération Charbonnière de Belgique v. High Authority*, Case 8/55, [1956] ECR 245 at 280; see also *Commission v. Council*, Case 165/87, [1988] ECR 5545 at para. 8 of the judgment.

[19] Cases 281, 283–5, 287/85, [1987] ECR 3203.

States in the social field, particularly in matters relating to…'. This provision gave the Commission a task, but nowhere did it confer on the Commission any legislative power. The authors of the Treaty probably thought that it was not necessary. However, in 1985 the Commission, acting under Article 118 EEC, adopted a decision which obliged the Member States to consult with the Commission regarding certain matters, and to inform it of draft measures and agreements concerning the topic in question. This decision was challenged by some of the Member States, but it was upheld by the Court (except for certain provisions).

The Court held that, whenever a provision of the Treaties confers a specific task on the Commission, that provision must also be regarded as impliedly conferring on the Commission 'the powers which are indispensable in order to carry out that task.'[20] Since the EU Treaty confers many tasks on the Commission, including such wide-ranging functions as that of ensuring the application of the Treaties and of measures adopted by the institutions pursuant to them,[21] this judgment is potentially significant, though so far it has not been widely applied.[22]

§2.3 OPEN-ENDED POWERS: ARTICLE 352 TFEU

A second, and more important, limitation to the principle of conferral is that not all Treaty provisions lay down clear limits to the powers they confer. For example, Article 115 TFEU [94/100 EC] empowers the Council to issue directives for the 'approximation' (harmonization) of such laws, regulations, or administrative provisions of the Member States as 'directly affect the establishment or functioning of the internal market.'[23] This gives wide scope to the Union to adopt measures.

Article 115 TFEU might still be regarded as granting a specific power; but another provision goes much further. The first paragraph of Article 352 TFEU provides:

> If action by the Union should prove necessary, within the framework of the policies defined in the Treaties, to attain one of the objectives set out in the Treaties, and the Treaties have not provided the necessary powers, the Council, acting unanimously on a proposal from the Commission and after obtaining the consent of the European Parliament, shall adopt the appropriate measures. Where the measures in question are adopted by the Council in accordance with a special legislative procedure, it shall also act unanimously on a proposal from the Commission and after obtaining the consent of the European Parliament.

[20] Para. 28 of the judgment. The Court immediately went on to use the word 'necessary' instead of 'indispensable', and then applied the new doctrine in a way which suggests that it will adopt a generous view of what is 'necessary': see Hartley, 'The Commission as Legislator under the EU Treaty' (1988) 13 ELRev. 122.

[21] Art. 17(1) TEU.

[22] For a case in which the Court might have applied it but did not, see *France v. Commission*, Case C-327/91, [1994] ECR I-3641.

[23] When acting under this procedure, the Council must be unanimous.

This may be regarded as an express adoption (with regard to the Council) of the wide formulation of the doctrine of implied powers; broadly speaking, it grants power to take whatever measures are necessary to attain the objectives of the Treaties.

In order to appreciate the precise extent of this power, the conditions prescribed for its exercise must be analysed. These may be divided into procedural and substantive requirements. The former contain two special features: the Council must be unanimous; and the European Parliament must give its consent.[24]

The substantive requirements are as follows:

1. the power must be used in order to attain one of the objectives set out in the Treaties;
2. action by the Union must be necessary for this purpose;
3. the attainment of the objective must take place within the framework of the policies defined in the Treaties;
4. the Treaties must not have provided the necessary powers;
5. the measure must be appropriate.

Each of these will be considered in turn.

There are various provisions of the Treaties that set out the objectives of the Union. Article 3 TEU is the most important. Even a casual glance at it will show that the objectives are extremely wide. They include, for example, the promotion of peace and the well-being of the peoples of the Union; the sustainable development of Europe based on balanced economic growth and price stability; full employment and social progress; a high level of protection and improvement of the quality of the environment; and equality between women and men. There are many others. It needs little imagination to appreciate that almost anything could be justified as necessary to attain one or other of them.

The second requirement is that action by the Union must be necessary to attain the objective. Although a determination that a Union act is necessary may seem to be a pure decision of fact, it actually involves a large measure of discretion; in the first instance at least, it will be made by the Commission and the Council. It is unlikely, except in extreme cases, that the Court will substitute its own judgment for that of the institutions to which the power to act is given by the Treaty.[25]

The third requirement is that the objective must be attained within the framework of the policies defined by the Treaties. Previously, the requirement was a little different: the objective had to be attained in the 'course of the operation of the common market'. The new version (laid down in the Treaty of Lisbon) appears to have been intended to widen the formulation – the establishment of a common market (now referred to as an 'internal market')[26] is only one of the policies defined by the Treaties – and to bring the English text closer to some of the other linguistic versions: the previous German and Dutch texts meant 'within the framework of the common market' ('*im Rahmen des Gemeinsamen*

[24] This latter requirement is new: before the Treaty of Lisbon, the European Parliament merely had to be consulted.

[25] But see Dashwood, 'The Limits of European Union Powers' (1996) 21 ELRev. 113 at 123.

[26] Art. 3(3) TEU.

Marktes' and '*in het kader van de gemeenschappelijke markt*'). Again, it can be said that this requirement will hardly ever constitute a significant limitation on the powers of the Union.

The fourth requirement is that a specific provision of the Treaty should not have provided the necessary powers. This seems straightforward enough, but in fact more problems have been created by this requirement than by any other. For instance, what is the position where the Treaty expressly covers the matter in issue but grants powers which are regarded as insufficient?

This question arose in *Hauptzollamt Bremerhaven v. Massey-Ferguson*,[27] which concerned a regulation on the valuation of goods for customs purposes. The object of the regulation, which had been enacted under what was then Article 235 EEC (an earlier version of Article 352 TFEU), was to ensure that uniform rules were applied throughout the Union: this was clearly necessary to ensure the proper functioning of the customs union. However, Article 27 EC (now repealed) was concerned with just this question, though it granted only the power to make recommendations. Since recommendations are not legally binding, it could be argued that Article 27 did not grant the necessary powers. On the other hand, it could be maintained that, since the authors of the Treaty had expressly dealt with the matter and had seen fit to give the power only to make recommendations, they must be regarded as having impliedly excluded the use of greater powers. The Advocate General, however, preferred the former argument and this was implicitly accepted by the European Court, which upheld the validity of the regulation. One can conclude, therefore, that the express grant of a power considered insufficient does not preclude resort to Article 352 TFEU.

A second objection to the validity of the regulation in the *Massey-Ferguson* case was that the necessary power *was* in fact granted by certain other provisions in the Treaty, provided these were given a sufficiently broad interpretation in line with the doctrine of implied powers (narrow formulation).[28] Advocate General Trabucchi took the view, however, that the interpretation of these other powers was subject to doubt; therefore, even if they were sufficiently wide, recourse to what was then Article 235 was legitimate. He expressed his opinion as follows:[29]

> Even supposing that this Regulation could have been adopted by a simpler procedure under a different rule or by implication on the basis of a number of specific rules and powers provided by the Treaty, one cannot see what damage to the public interest has been caused by the adoption of such a measure on the basis and under the procedure of Article 235. It would certainly be against the spirit of the system created by the Treaty if the Commission or the Council were to consider it necessary to act on the basis of Article 235 in a case where other provisions of the Treaty already clearly provide suitable powers of action. But we do not have to consider what legal consequences could result on such a hypothesis. In the present case, in the absence of an express and clear provision of the Treaty specifically empowering the enactment of this Regulation, one must dismiss the idea that because this provision was prudently based on the general authorizing rule of Article 235, such fact could possibly constitute an irregularity liable to render it invalid.

[27] Case 8/73, [1973] ECR 897. [28] See *per* Advocate General Trabucchi, [1973] ECR at 913–14.

[29] See *per* Advocate General Trabucchi, [1973] ECR at 914.

This was accepted by the Court; the relevant passage reads as follows:[30]

> If it is true that the proper functioning of the customs union justifies a wide interpretation of Articles 9, 27, 28, 111 and 113 of the Treaty and of the powers which these provisions confer on the institutions to allow them thoroughly to control external trade by measures taken both independently and by agreement, there is no reason why the Council could not legitimately consider that recourse to the procedure of Article 235 was justified in the interest of legal certainty. This is the more so as the Regulation in question was adopted during the transitional period.
>
> By reason of the specific requirements of Article 235 this course of action cannot be criticized since, under the circumstances, the rules of the Treaty on the forming of the Council's decisions or on the division of powers between the institutions are not to be disregarded.

Recourse to Article 352 TFEU [308/235 EC] is, however, impermissible where the power to act is clearly given by another provision of the Treaty.[31]

The fifth requirement for the exercise of the power granted by Article 352 is that the act must be appropriate. This means that it must be reasonably suitable for achieving the objective in question. It probably also means that any hardship caused must not be disproportionate to the benefits accruing from the attainment of the objective: this follows from the doctrine of 'proportionality', a general principle of EU law (see § 5.3 of this chapter and Chapter 5, § 4).

Finally, it should be said that there is a general requirement which applies to all Union legislation but which applies with particular force to measures adopted under Article 352. This is the requirement of subsidiarity. It will be discussed in § 5.

Prior to the Treaty of Lisbon, these were the only requirements expressly set out in Article 352 TFEU [308/235 EC]. However, paragraphs 2 to 4 of Article 352 now lay down three further requirements. The first is that the Commission must draw the attention of the national Parliaments to proposals based on Article 352.[32] This is done through the procedure for monitoring the subsidiarity principle, a procedure that will be considered further in § 5.4. The second requirement is that measures based on Article 352 must not entail harmonization of Member States' laws or regulations in cases where the Treaties exclude such harmonization.[33] The final requirement is that Article 352 cannot serve as a basis for attaining objectives pertaining to the common foreign and security policy.[34]

[30] *Ibid.* at 908 (para. 4). The phrase at the very end of this passage, 'are not to be disregarded', appears in the French text as '*ne se trouvent pas déjouées*'. In the context, a better translation would have been 'have not been prejudiced'.

[31] See the cases discussed in § 4.

[32] Art. 352(2) TFEU.

[33] Art. 352(3) TFEU. This appears to refer to an express exclusion, such as that found in Art. 2(5), second sub-para., TEU.

[34] Art. 352(4) TFEU. This paragraph goes on to provide that acts adopted pursuant to Art. 352 must respect the limits set out in Art. 40, second para., TEU, a provision which states that the implementation of general EU policies must not affect the application of the procedures and the extent of the powers of the institutions laid down by the Treaties for the exercise of the Union competences under the common foreign and security policy. Measures taken under Art. 352 are thus subject to the same limitations.

In addition to the requirements laid down in Article 352 itself, there are certain other limits and requirements that result from general principles or from the case-law of the European Court under the predecessors of Article 352 [308/235 EC]. One obvious limit is that measures taken under Article 352 TFEU [308/235 EC] must not be contrary to an express prohibition contained in the Treaty.[35]

Secondly, Article 352 should not be used to adopt measures which would constitute an amendment of the Treaty: Treaty amendments are expressly dealt with by Article 48 TEU, which, it will be remembered,[36] provides for the calling of a conference of Member States; it also lays down that any amendments must be ratified by each Member State according to its constitutional provisions. It is suggested that this procedure must be used, not only where a provision of the Treaty is expressly amended, but also where the basic constitutional structure set up by the Treaty is modified. These limitations are quite reasonable when one remembers that, even in a fully-fledged federation, the federal organs do not normally have power to make constitutional amendments without going through special procedures, usually involving either a referendum or the agreement of the constituent States.

This limitation on the use of Article 352 TFEU [308/235 EC] was affirmed by the European Court in its Opinion on the accession of the Union to the European Convention on Human Rights, a case decided before express provision for such accession was made by the Treaty of Lisbon.[37] This case is discussed further in Chapter 5, § 2.2 and Chapter 6, § 2.3; here, all we will do is to quote two paragraphs from the judgment (the references to Article 235 should now be read as references to Article 352):[38]

> Article 235 is designed to fill the gap where no specific provisions of the Treaty confer on the Community institutions express or implied powers to act, if such powers appear none the less to be necessary to enable the Community to carry out its functions with a view to attaining one of the objectives laid down by the Treaty.
>
> That provision, being an integral part of an institutional system based on the principle of conferred powers, cannot serve as a basis for widening the scope of Community powers beyond the general framework created by the provisions of the Treaty as a whole and, in particular, by those that define the tasks and the activities of the Community. On any view, Article 235 cannot be used as a basis for the adoption of provisions whose effect would, in substance, be to amend the Treaty without following the procedure which it provides for that purpose.

The Court concluded that the suggested use of Article 352 TFEU [308/235 EC] would involve a modification of the Union system that would be 'of constitutional significance'; consequently, the Court ruled, it would go beyond the scope of Article 352 TFEU [308/235 EC].[39] It could be brought about only by an amendment to the Treaty.

[35] See, for example, Art. 165(1) TFEU, which, while giving the Union a certain role in education, makes it clear that the Member States are responsible for the content of teaching and the organization of education systems; consequently, any attempt to use Art. 352 with regard to these matters would be wrong.

[36] See Chap. 3, § 1.2.

[37] *ECHR* case, Opinion 2/94, [1996] ECR I-1759. This Opinion (in effect, a binding judgment) was given under what was then Art. 228(6) EC, now Art. 218(11) TFEU, a provision discussed in Chap. 6, § 4.

[38] Paras 29 and 30. [39] Para. 35.

The extensive scope of Article 352 might appear of little significance in view of the rule that measures passed under it must be agreed to by all the members of the Council. This means that any Member State has the power to veto a proposal. However, if Article 352 did not exist, the Member States would be obliged to enter into a convention or treaty and this would be subject to ratification, which normally entails the approval of the national parliaments. The importance of Article 352, therefore, is that it allows Governments to bypass this procedure, thus making democratic control at the national level less effective. For the reasons explained in Chapter 1, § 13, requiring the consent of the European Parliament is not an adequate substitute. Perhaps this is why Article 352(2) now requires the Commission to draw the attention of the national Parliaments to proposals based on Article 352.

§3 UNION COMPETENCE

The powers (competence) conferred on the Union may be exclusive or shared. When the Treaties confer exclusive competence on the Union, only the Union may legislate and adopt legally binding acts in the area in question: the Member States may do so only if the Union grants them power (delegation, discussed in § 6.5), or if the Member State act is adopted for the implementation of a Union act.[40] (On the latter, see § 1.2 and § 6.6.)

When the Treaties confer a shared competence on the Union in a specific area, the Union and the Member States may both legislate and adopt legally binding acts in that area.[41] However, the Member States may exercise their competence only to the extent that the Union has not done so; nevertheless, if the Union decides to cease exercising its competence in a given area, the Member States may again exercise their competence.

In addition, the Union has competence in certain areas to carry out actions to support, coordinate, or supplement the actions of the Member States, without thereby superseding their competence.[42] There is no official term in the Treaties for this last kind of competence; we shall call it 'supplementary competence'.

The areas in which the Union enjoys exclusive competence are specified in Article 3 TFEU.[43] Where the Treaties confer competence on the Union that does not relate to one of these areas or to one of those specified in Article 6 TFEU (what we have called supplementary competence), the competence is shared. The main areas in this category are set out in Article 5 TFEU.[44]

These distinctions are important because if no competence is conferred on the Union, it may not act (principle of conferral); however, it the competence is exclusive, the Member States may not act.

[40] Art. 2(1) TFEU. [41] Art. 2(2) TFEU. [42] Art. 2(5) TFEU.

[43] The customs union is an example.

[44] These include important matters such as the internal market, agriculture, and the environment. There are certain other areas where the Union can carry out activities without preventing the Member States from doing so: see Art. 4(3) and (4) TFEU. The areas in question – for example, research and technological development, and humanitarian aid – are all areas in which action by one party will not undermine action by the other.

§4 LEGAL BASIS

It will be seen from what was said previously that the powers of the Union and its institutions vary depending on the Treaty provision under which action is taken. Since some Treaty provisions are rather unclear and open-ended, it is often difficult to decide which one is appropriate in a given case. The question we now consider is whether adopting a measure on the wrong legal basis (proceeding under the wrong Treaty Article) means that the measure will be annulled. We will deal with only a small selection of the European Court's case-law on the subject, from which it will be seen that the Court often displays a rather surprising attitude. Since the relevant cases were decided in the past, the significance of proceeding under one Article rather than another was often different from what it is today; nevertheless, the principles are the same.

In the second paragraph of the passage from the Court's judgment in the *Massey-Ferguson* case quoted in § 2.3, the European Court said that a measure might be annulled for being adopted on the wrong legal basis if this affects 'the rules of the Treaty on the forming of the Council's decisions' (for example, the voting procedure) or 'the division of powers between the institutions' (for example, the powers of the European Parliament).

The former situation is illustrated by the *Tariff Preferences* case,[45] which concerned Council regulations giving tariff preferences to imports from developing countries. As the regulations dealt with tariffs and trade, the Commission considered that they were covered by what was then Article 113 EEC. The Council, on the other hand, took the view that, since their purpose was developmental (aid), they could be adopted only under what was then Article 235 EEC (equivalent to what is now Article 352 TFEU, discussed in § 2.3). The significance of this dispute was that Article 113 EEC allowed for qualified majority voting,[46] while Article 235 EEC required unanimity. The Council tried to avoid the issue by not specifying any particular Treaty Article as the legal basis of the measure: the reference in the Commission proposal to Article 113 was deleted and the preamble simply referred to the EEC Treaty as a whole.

In annulment proceedings brought by the Commission, the Court held that the regulations could have been adopted under Article 113 and declared them void on two separate grounds: first, that the failure to specify the precise legal basis was an infringement of an essential procedural requirement;[47] and, secondly, that, as the regulations could have been adopted under Article 113 EEC, the Council was not justified

[45] *Commission v. Council*, Case 45/86, [1987] ECR 1493.

[46] By this time, the transitional period was over.

[47] This is one of the recognized grounds for the annulment of a measure: see Art. 263 TFEU [230/173 EC]. The Court stated that failure to refer to a precise provision of the Treaty does not necessarily constitute an infringement of an essential procedural requirement when the legal basis of the measure may be determined from other parts of the measure, but it held that explicit reference is indispensable where the parties and the Court would otherwise be left uncertain as to the precise legal basis: see para. 9 of the judgment. For a more recent case on this point, see *Commission v. Council*, Case C-370/07, [2009] ECR I-8917.

in adopting them under Article 235 EEC. The Court expressly mentioned that the two Articles 'entail different rules regarding the manner in which the Council may arrive at its decision'.[48] What is surprising about this is that if the Council was unanimous, there must necessarily have been a qualified majority in favour of the measure; nevertheless, following the wrong procedure was sufficient to annul it.

What is the position where a measure comes partly within the area covered by one Article and partly within that covered by another? According to the *Commodity Coding*[49] case, the procedural requirements of both Articles must be satisfied.[50] This case again concerned a measure which, in the view of the Commission, could have been adopted under what was then Article 113 EEC. The Council, however, amended the Preamble to give what were then Articles 28 and 235 EEC (in addition to Article 113) as its legal basis. In annulment proceedings brought by the Commission, the Court held that Articles 28 and 113 together constituted the appropriate legal basis for the measure. The requirements of both these provisions had to be fulfilled, but recourse to Article 235 was impermissible. However, at the time in question, Article 28 (like Article 235) required unanimity; so the addition of Article 235 as a legal basis did not affect the voting procedure in the Council. Consequently, the Court did not annul the measure.[51]

It is interesting to note that in another respect there *was* a significant difference between Article 235, as it stood at the time, and Article 28: the former, but not the latter, required the European Parliament to be consulted. This had taken place, but the Court held that while wrongful failure to consult the European Parliament leads to nullity, legally unnecessary consultation does not do so, since the Council is always entitled to ask the European Parliament for its opinion.[52]

A further twist was given to the law by the *Titanium Dioxide* case,[53] which concerned a Council measure intended to lay down uniform environmental-protection standards for the titanium dioxide industry. This measure, the Court held, had two purposes: to protect the environment and (because it laid down uniform standards in all Member States) to promote fair competition between producers in different Member States. The former was covered by what was then Article 130s EEC (which required unanimity in the Council and the consultation of the European Parliament) and the latter fell within the scope of what was then Article 100a EEC (which envisaged qualified

[48] Para. 12 of the judgment.

[49] *Commission v. Council*, Case 165/87, [1988] ECR 5545.

[50] Para. 11 of the judgment.

[51] See para. 19 of the judgment, where the Court said that the illegality which resulted from using the wrong legal basis was 'only a purely formal defect which cannot make the measure void'.

[52] Para. 20 of the judgment. In a later case, *European Parliament v. Council*, Case C-316/91, [1994] ECR I-625, the Parliament considered that the measure should have been adopted under a provision that would have given it the right to be consulted. The Council argued that, since the Parliament had in any event been consulted (on a voluntary basis), the application for annulment should be declared inadmissible. This argument was rejected by the Court, which held that the application was admissible (though in the end it was dismissed on the merits).

[53] *Commission v. Council*, Case C-300/89, [1991] ECR I-2867. See also *European Parliament v. Council*, Case C-295/90, [1992] ECR I-4193, where the Treaty provision under which the measure should have been adopted involved the co-operation procedure, as distinct from the Parliament's merely giving its opinion.

majority voting in the Council and what was called the 'co-operation procedure' (a procedure now abolished) with regard to the European Parliament).

On the basis of the Court's judgment in the *Commodity Coding* case,[54] one would have thought that the correct procedure would have been to follow the requirements of both provisions. This would have entailed applying the more onerous requirement with regard to each aspect of the procedure, in other words, applying the unanimity rule as far as voting in the Council was concerned, and following the co-operation procedure as far as the role of the European Parliament was concerned.

This, however, created a problem. As the law stood at the time, the main difference between the co-operation procedure and simple consultation was that, under the former, the Council could override a negative opinion on the part of the European Parliament only if it was unanimous. However, if the Council had to be unanimous in any event, the opinion lost its sting: it made no difference what the European Parliament said. In view of this, the Court held that its ruling in the *Commodity Coding* case could not be applied: one or other of the two Treaty provisions had to be chosen as the sole legal basis. After some discussion, the Court selected Article 100a. The Commission had proposed this provision as the legal basis for the measure, but the Council had substituted Article 130s. As a result, the Court annulled the measure.[55]

This series of cases provides an insight into the policies pursued by the European Court. Where a measure is adopted by a public authority under the wrong enabling provision, most courts would be concerned to ensure only that the substantive and procedural requirements of the correct provision had been satisfied. Where the correct provision provided for majority voting, but the authority acted by unanimity because this was required by the provision under which the measure was adopted, most courts would take the view that since the requirements of both provisions had been met, there was no need to annul the measure. The fact that the European Court has followed a different policy shows that it has not been concerned simply with ensuring respect for the law, but has had a more political objective: that of pushing the Union in the direction of greater integration. It is also noticeable that where the Court has had to decide which of two provisions constituted the correct legal basis for a measure, it has more often than not come down in favour of the one providing for qualified majority voting, rather than unanimity.

§5 SUBSIDIARITY AND PROPORTIONALITY

§5.1 INTRODUCTION

According to Article 5 TEU, the limits of Union competences are governed by the principle of conferral, while the use of Union competences is governed by the principles of

[54] See earlier discussion.

[55] For a different approach in a more recent case, see *European Parliament v. Council*, Case C-166/07, [2009] ECR I-7135.

subsidiarity and proportionality. In other words, the principle of conferral determines what powers the European Union possesses; the principles of subsidiarity and proportionality determine how those powers are to be exercised. Having discussed the principle of conferral, as well as the powers actually conferred, we are now in a position to consider subsidiarity and proportionality.

The principle of subsidiarity was made part of EU law by the Treaties.[56] It had been a principle of German constitutional law[57] and was brought into EU law as a means of preventing an unrestrained growth of EU legislation.[58] Proportionality, on the other hand, though it also derives from German constitutional law, was first developed by the European Court as a general principle of EU law and only subsequently adopted by the Treaties. It will be discussed further in Chapter 5, § 4.

§5.2 SUBSIDIARITY

This principle of subsidiarity is defined by Article 5(3), first paragraph TEU, which states:

> Under the principle of subsidiarity, in areas which do not fall within its exclusive competence, the Union shall act only if and in so far as the objectives of the proposed action cannot be sufficiently achieved by the Member States, either at central level or at regional and local level, but can rather, by reason of the scale or effects of the proposed action, be better achieved at Union level.

This wording makes clear that there are two requirements which must both be satisfied before action at the Union level will be justified: it must not be possible for the objectives to be sufficiently achieved by the Member States, *and* the circumstances must be such that they could be better achieved at Union level. Thus, if the objectives could be sufficiently achieved at Member State level, it would not be enough that they could be achieved even better by action at Union level.

Even if the European Union has the competence to act, it should not do so unless there is a specific reason why action at Union level is preferable to action at national, regional, or local level. This specific reason must relate to the scale or effects of the proposed action.

[56] This occurred in 1993, when the Treaty on European Union 1992 came into force. A new provision was inserted into the EC Treaty (now the TFEU) establishing subsidiarity as a principle of EU law: see the second paragraph of Art. 5 [3b] EC as amended by the Treaty on European Union. For the background, see the Commission document entitled 'The Principle of Subsidiarity', Com. Doc. SEC(92) 1990, 27 October 1992; and 'Overall Approach to the Application by the Council of the Subsidiarity Principle and Article 3b of the Treaty on European Union', Annex 1 to Part A of the *Conclusions of the Presidency*, European Council in Edinburgh, 11–12 December 1992. Subsidiarity had previously been applied in a limited area (the environment) by the Single European Act 1986 (see Art. 174(4) [130r(4)] EC as inserted by the Single European Act). The relevant provisions have now been moved to the Treaty on European Union; perhaps an indication that subsidiarity (together with conferral and proportionality) have constitutional significance.

[57] See Emiliou, 'Subsidiarity: An Effective Barrier against "the Enterprises of Ambition"?' (1992) 17 ELRev. 383 at 388–91. Its origin seems to lie in doctrines of the Catholic Church.

[58] Its genealogy may be traced back through the Preamble (last recital) and Art. 12 of the draft Treaty establishing the European Union adopted by the European Parliament on 14 February 1984 (OJ 1984, C77/33) and the Commission's *Report on European Union*, 1975 (EC Bull., Supplement 5/75).

In other words, the principle contains a built-in bias in favour of action at the lowest possible level. If action at a level below that of the Union will attain results that are at least equally good, the Union must not act. However, since the principle is concerned with the situation where there is a choice between action at the Union and sub-Union (national, regional, or local) levels, it can apply only when the Union does not have exclusive competence (on the concepts of exclusive and shared competence, see § 3).

§5.3 PROPORTIONALITY

The principle of subsidiarity lays down rules as to when a joint competence should be exercised by the European Union, and when it should be exercised at a sub-Union level. Proportionality, on the other hand, is concerned with the form and content of the measure, which must not 'exceed what is necessary to achieve the objectives of the Treaties'.[59] In other words, the principle comes into play only once it is settled that the action will take place at Union level. Its purpose is to ensure that the Union measure does not go further than is required. Thus, it also has the objective of imposing restraint on the Union. Both principles could be regarded as a response to the perception in the past that the Union was 'legislation happy', making laws where none were needed and poking its nose into matters that were none of its business, one of the causes of the anti-European feeling that keeps coming to the surface in referendums and elections.

§5.4 PROCEDURE

The Protocol on the Application of the Principles of Subsidiarity and Proportionality is an attempt to ensure that these principles are taken seriously. Its most striking feature is that it confers a significant role on the national Parliaments, perhaps on the ground that they have the greatest interest in curbing excessive activity on the part of the Union.

The first rule is that (except in cases of exceptional urgency) the Commission must consult widely before proposing legislative acts.[60] This is something that any reasonable public authority would do anyway.

The second rule, laid down in Article 4 of the Protocol, is that draft legislative acts[61] and other documents that form part of the legislative process must be notified to the national Parliaments. Draft legislative acts must be justified with regard to subsidiarity and proportionality.[62] They should contain a detailed statement making it possible to appraise compliance with the two principles. The reasons for concluding that the objective can be better achieved at Union level must be substantiated by qualitative

[59] Art. 5(4) TEU. [60] Art. 2 of the Protocol.

[61] Art. 3 of the Protocol defines 'draft legislative acts' widely to mean proposals from the Commission, initiatives from a group of Member States, initiatives from the European Parliament, requests from the Court of Justice, recommendations from the European Central Bank and requests from the European Investment Bank for the adoption of a legislative act. [62] Art. 5 of the Protocol.

and, wherever possible, quantitative indicators. Draft legislative acts must take account of the need for any burden imposed by the measure to be minimized and to be commensurate with the objective to be achieved.[63]

Under the third rule, laid down by Article 6 of the Protocol, any national Parliament or any chamber of a national Parliament may, within eight weeks from the date of transmission of a draft legislative act, send to the Presidents of the European Parliament, the Council, and the Commission a reasoned opinion stating why it considers that the draft in question does not comply with the principle of subsidiarity.[64]

We now come to an interesting innovation. Each national Parliament is given two votes. In the case of a bicameral system, each chamber – in the United Kingdom, for example, the House of Commons and the House of Lords – has one vote. Where reasoned opinions on a draft legislative act's non-compliance with the principle of subsidiarity represent at least one-third of all the votes, the draft legislative act must be reviewed.[65] After such review, its author (usually the Commission) may decide to maintain, amend, or withdraw the draft. Reasons must be given.[66]

Under the ordinary legislative procedure (explained in § 1.2), further consequences ensue where reasoned opinions on non-compliance represent at least a simple majority of the votes allocated to the national Parliaments. If the Commission decides to maintain its proposal, it must produce a reasoned opinion explaining why it considers that the proposal complies with the principle of subsidiarity. This reasoned opinion, as well as the reasoned opinions of the national Parliaments, must be submitted to the Union legislator for consideration. ('Union legislator' means the European Parliament and the Council.) Before concluding the first reading in the legislative procedure, the legislator must consider whether the proposal is compatible with the principle of subsidiarity, taking particular account of the reasons expressed by the national Parliaments as well as the Commission. If, by a majority of 55 per cent of the members of the Council, or a majority of the votes cast in the European Parliament, the legislator is of the opinion that the proposal is not compatible with the principle of subsidiarity, the proposal will not be given further consideration.

[63] This is a classic statement of one aspect of proportionality: see Chap. 5, § 4.

[64] In appropriate cases, the President of the Council must forward it to the national governments and other Union institutions: Art. 6, second and third paras.

[65] The threshold is a quarter of the votes where the draft is submitted under Art. 76 TFEU.

[66] This procedure was used for the first time in 2012 when reasoned opinions were issued by a sufficient number of national Parliaments to satisfy the requirement that at least one-third of the votes must be negative. The measure in question was a draft regulation on the right to strike in transnational labour disputes. After considering the opinions of the national Parliaments, the Commission decided to withdraw the draft, though not (it said) because it infringed the principle of subsidiarity but because of political opposition in the Council and the European Parliament. An interesting feature of the affair is that most of the objections raised by the national Parliaments were on grounds other than subsidiarity. For an enlightening discussion, see Fabbrini and Granat, '"Yellow Card, But No Foul": The Role of the National Parliaments under the Subsidiarity Protocol and the Commission Proposal for an EU Regulation on the Right to Strike' (2013) 50 CMLRev. 115, in which the authors argue that, though the draft may have been problematic on other grounds, it was consistent with the principle of subsidiarity.

The following points should be noted. First, a measure is killed if *either* the Council *or* the European Parliament rejects it: it is not necessary that they should both do so. Secondly, the Council does not vote under the 'qualified-majority' system (see Chapter 1, § 3.3). For this purpose, each Member State has one vote. If there are (as at present) twenty-eight Member States, sixteen must vote against the draft act. It does not matter if they are the sixteen smallest Member States: all are equal for this purpose. Thirdly, there does not have to be a majority of members (absolute majority) in the European Parliament: a majority of votes is enough. As explained in Chapter 1, § 9, this is an important difference.

§5.5 JUDICIAL REVIEW FOR INFRINGEMENT OF SUBSIDIARITY

Legal principles such as subsidiarity and proportionality are unlikely to be effective unless measures that infringe them can be struck down by the European Court. As explained earlier (in § 5.1), the principle of proportionality was originally developed by the European Court as a general principle of Union law, and the Court has for many years been willing to annul legal acts that run counter to it. This will be discussed in Chapter 5, § 4. Subsidiarity is in a different position, and Article 8 of the Protocol contains special provisions concerning actions to annul legislative acts on grounds of non-compliance with subsidiarity. The first paragraph of Article 8 provides:

> The Court of Justice of the European Union shall have jurisdiction in actions on grounds of infringement of the principle of subsidiarity by a legislative act, brought in accordance with the rules laid down in Article 263 of the Treaty on the Functioning of the European Union[67] by Member States, or notified by them in accordance with their legal order on behalf of their national Parliament or a chamber thereof.

The first part of this paragraph does little except to make clear that legislative acts are subject to judicial review for infringement of subsidiarity, something that was already generally accepted. What is interesting is the last part of the provision, the part that reads 'or notified by them in accordance with their legal order on behalf of their national Parliament or a chamber thereof'.

This suggests that judicial review proceedings can be brought on behalf of a national Parliament or a chamber of a national Parliament. However, its meaning is not clear. If a national Parliament or a chamber wants to challenge a legislative act before the European Court, is the relevant national Government *obliged* to 'notify' the Court. If so, this provision is a major innovation, since it would (in effect) give the national Parliaments and chambers standing (the right to bring proceedings) before the European Court, something they did not have previously. On the other hand, if the national Government is not obliged to act on behalf of the national Parliament or chamber (but merely has the right to do so if it wants), it would add nothing new: Member States have always had the

[67] Art. 263 TFEU is the general provision on judicial review of legal acts.

right to bring proceedings before the European Court and there is no reason why they should not do so on behalf of some other body. Perhaps the phrase 'in accordance with their legal order' means that national law will decide this question. If this is so, the effect of the provision could vary from one Member State to another.

The second paragraph of Article 8 of the Protocol provides:

> In accordance with the rules laid down in the said Article [Article 263], the Committee of the Regions may also bring such actions against legislative acts for the adoption of which the Treaty on the Functioning of the European Union provides that it be consulted.

This could be regarded as clarifying Article 265 TFEU, which gives the Committee of the Regions and certain other EU bodies the right to bring actions before the European Court for the purpose of 'protecting their prerogatives'. It makes clear that, if the Committee has the right to be consulted on a legislative act, it also has the right to challenge it before the Court on the ground that it infringes the principle of subsidiarity. Since subsidiarity is intended to protect the rights of regional and local bodies, as well as national Parliaments, this makes sense. Although regional and local bodies cannot themselves bring a challenge, the EU body intended to represent them can do so, provided it had the right to be consulted in the first place.

In order to challenge a Union measure on the ground of subsidiarity, an applicant must establish the objectives of the measure and show that those objectives could be sufficiently (or equally well) attained through action by the Member States. Both of these requirements present difficulties. Most measures adopted by the Union have a number of objectives, some general and some specific. If any one of the objectives could be better attained by Union action, the European Court would probably regard that as sufficient to justify the measure (though it might be prepared to strike down clearly severable parts which did not fulfil the requirements of subsidiarity).

In practice, it will almost always be possible to formulate the objectives of the measure in different ways. In defending the measure, the Commission or the Council will argue for a formulation which requires Union action. One can even expect that the preamble and wording of the measure might be drafted so as to facilitate this.

In such a situation, everything will depend on the European Court. It will formulate the objectives of the measure; and it will decide whether they can be better achieved by Union action. All these questions involve so many imponderables that it will almost always be possible for the Court, if it wishes, to find grounds for upholding the measure. As a result, the effectiveness of subsidiarity will depend, to a considerable extent, on the attitude and policy of the European Court.

So far the European Court has not struck down any legislation on the ground of subsidiarity.[68] There is, however, a case which is of interest in this regard. This is the *Tobacco Advertising* case,[69] in which Germany brought proceedings before the

[68] There have been several cases in which the issue has arisen: see, for example, *United Kingdom v. Council*, Case C-84/94, [1996] ECR I-5755 (paras 46 *et seq.*).

[69] *Germany v. European Parliament and Council*, Case C-376/98, [2000] ECR I-8419.

European Court to annul a directive that imposed a general ban on the advertising or sponsorship of tobacco products in the European Union. Germany put forward various grounds for its claim, including subsidiarity, but the only ground considered by the Court was that the directive was outside the powers of the Union (lack of competence, or *ultra vires* in English legal terminology).[70] The directive was declared invalid on this ground. What is interesting is that the reasoning of the Court, though directed towards the question whether the measure was within the powers of the Union, was also pertinent to a subsidiarity-analysis: it was not concerned with the question whether a ban on tobacco advertising would be a good thing, but with the question whether it should be imposed at the Union level. The only justification for this would be that uniformity was desirable. The Court accepted that, in certain limited instances, a uniform rule would be desirable. However, in general this would not be the case; so the directive was declared invalid.

§5.6 CONCLUSIONS

Despite the impressive intellectual structure created by the Treaties, it is not yet clear whether subsidiarity will have a significant impact in practice. This will depend on the attitude of the main Union institutions, particularly the European Court.

§6 DELEGATION OF POWERS

So far we have been considering the powers granted to the Union institutions by the Treaties; the next question is the extent to which these powers may be delegated either to other Union institutions or to outside bodies.

§6.1 WHAT IS DELEGATION?

From a formal point of view, a delegation takes place whenever the authority granted a power by the Treaty conveys it to some other body. This definition is not, however, wholly satisfactory, since the formal position may not always correspond with the real situation: a formal delegation may be made without any real transfer of responsibility; or, conversely, formal power may remain with the delegating authority but real power may pass out of its hands.

In order to decide whether a real delegation has taken place, one must consider a number of questions. First, is the delegate granted a wide discretion or is the exercise of the power made subject to rules laid down by the delegating authority which are so restrictive that the delegate's role is merely executive? In this case the 'delegation' will be of little practical significance, since the way the power is exercised will not be affected.

[70] In present-day terminology, one would say that the principle of conferral was the issue.

Secondly, can the delegating authority exercise effective control over the delegate? This may be done in various ways. For example, it may be provided that the decision of the delegate will not come into force until it has been confirmed by the delegating authority; or the latter may be given the power to rescind it, provided it acts within a given period. This power might be exercisable by the delegating authority on its own initiative or on an appeal to it by some person or body affected by the decision. In Union law, controls of this nature are applicable when powers are delegated by the Council to the Commission.

Thirdly, one must consider whether the powers granted to a body are actually exercised by that body or whether the real decision is taken elsewhere. For example, the formal decision may be taken by the delegating authority and the role of the delegate may be confined to making proposals; but if the delegating authority never questions these proposals and merely rubber-stamps them, a *de facto* delegation will have taken place. Likewise, powers of control that are not in practice exercised are of little real significance.

Any effective system of administrative law must take all these factors into account in deciding whether a delegation has taken place. It must also be understood that a delegation is not a question of all or nothing: it is often a matter of degree. The practical significance of the delegation will depend on the extent to which real power has been transferred.

§6.2 DELEGATION TO THE COMMISSION

This is dealt with in Article 290 TFEU, which reads:

1. A legislative act may delegate to the Commission the power to adopt non-legislative acts of general application to supplement or amend certain non-essential elements of the legislative act.
   The objectives, content, scope and duration of the delegation of power shall be explicitly defined in the legislative acts. The essential elements of an area shall be reserved for the legislative act and accordingly shall not be the subject of a delegation of power.
2. Legislative acts shall explicitly lay down the conditions to which the delegation is subject; these conditions may be as follows:
   (a) the European Parliament or the Council may decide to revoke the delegation;
   (b) the delegated act may enter into force only if no objection has been expressed by the European Parliament or the Council within a period set by the legislative act.

   For the purposes of (a) and (b), the European Parliament shall act by a majority of its component members, and the Council by a qualified majority.
3. The adjective 'delegated' shall be inserted in the title of delegated acts.

The following points should be noted. First, though the act delegating the power is a legislative act, the act adopted under that power is, under the system of procedural classification brought in by the Treaty of Lisbon (explained in § 1.2), a non-legislative act. Secondly, though the Commission may be given the power to supplement or amend the legislative act, that applies only to 'non-essential elements'. Essential elements cannot be supplemented or amended.[71] Thirdly, the delegation may be subject to conditions. The conditions that apply in any given case will depend on the provisions of the delegating act. Article 230 specifies two conditions that may be imposed, but it is not clear whether others may be imposed instead of, or in addition to, these.

Although Article 230 TFEU as it now stands is worded differently from the provisions that applied previously, there has been a long history of delegation to the Commission. In the course of this, the European Court has decided a number of cases, some of which are still relevant today.

The *Köster* case[72] arose as follows. Acting under what was then Article 43(2) EEC (which empowered the Council to legislate in the field of agriculture), the Council passed a regulation setting out the general principles for the organization of a common market in cereals. This regulation also made provision for the detailed rules to be laid down in measures to be adopted by the Commission. Two objections to this were raised. First, it was pointed out that where measures were enacted by the Council under Article 43(2), the opinion of the European Parliament had to be obtained; but when the power was delegated to the Commission, no provision for this was made. Thus, the effect of the delegation was to deprive the Parliament of its right to be consulted. The Court, however, ruled that it is not necessary for all the details of regulations concerning agriculture to be enacted according to the procedure laid down in Article 43(2). It was sufficient if the general principles governing the question were set out in a measure adopted under this procedure: the details could then be laid down under a different procedure, either by the Council itself or by the Commission.

This case is the origin of the distinction, now incorporated into Article 290 TFEU, between laying down general principles (essential elements) and detailed implementation. Then, as now, only the latter may be delegated. However, the Court has shown itself prepared to give a wide interpretation to this concept. For example, in the *Chemiefarma* case,[73] the Council adopted a regulation under Article 87 EEC which provided for fines to be levied by the Commission on firms guilty of a violation of the Union competition provisions. Article 19 of this regulation stated that firms accused of such a violation should be granted a hearing before the Commission. Article 24 delegated to the Commission the power to make detailed rules governing the procedure at such a hearing. In the case, it was objected that this entailed the power to legislate and went beyond the concept of 'implementation'. The Court held, however,

[71] For what constitutes an essential element, see *European Parliament v. Council*, Case C-355/10, 5 September 2012 (Grand Chamber), in which the European Court said (at para. 65 of the judgment) that if exercise of the power requires 'political choices falling within the responsibilities of the European Union', an essential element is involved. Though this case was decided under the law existing prior to the Lisbon Treaty, its reasoning would apply under the new provisions.

[72] *Einfuhr- und Vorratsstelle v. Köster*, Case 25/70, [1970] ECR 1161.

[73] *Chemiefarma v. Commission*, Case 41/69, [1970] ECR 661.

that the concept of implementation includes the adoption of regulations (provisions of a legislative character). This was confirmed in *Commission v. Council*,[74] in which the European Court stated that for this purpose the concept of implementation comprises 'both the drawing up of implementing rules and the application of those rules to specific cases by means of acts of individual application'. Moreover, in an earlier case, *Rey Soda*,[75] the European Court said that the concept of implementation must be given a wide interpretation and in the sphere of agriculture the Council may confer on the Commission 'wide powers of discretion and action'.[76] In a more recent case, however, the European Court has said that if the exercise of the power requires 'political choices falling within the responsibilities of the European Union', the essential elements of the measure are involved and delegation is not possible.[77]

It is possible to conclude, therefore, that extensive discretionary powers may be delegated to the Commission, provided the empowering provision lays down the essential elements of the measure.

§6.3 DELEGATION TO OTHER UNION INSTITUTIONS

Today, the Treaties do not specifically refer to the delegation of powers to a Union institution other than the Commission; however, in the past, the European Court has said that the same principles apply.[78]

§6.4 DELEGATION TO OUTSIDE BODIES[79]

The leading case on delegation to bodies other than those created by EU law is the *Meroni* case.[80] This concerned the scrap-iron equalization fund which had been set up by the High Authority (Commission) under the ECSC in an attempt to deal with the scrap shortage in the 1950s. The idea was to subsidize imported scrap in order to bring its price down to the level of Union scrap; the subsidies were to be paid for by a levy on all scrap users. Two bodies were set up to run the scheme, the *Office Commun des Consommateurs de Ferrailles*, which arranged the imports, and the *Caisse de Péréquation des Ferrailles Importées*, which imposed the levy and distributed the subsidies. Both bodies were incorporated as co-operatives under Belgian law.

[74] Case 16/88, [1989] ECR 3457 (para. 11 of the judgment).

[75] *Rey Soda v. Cassa Conguaglio Zucchero*, Case 23/75, [1975] ECR 1279.

[76] See paras 10 and 11 of the judgment.

[77] *European Parliament v. Council*, Case C-355/10, 5 September 2012 (para. 65 of the judgment) (Grand Chamber).

[78] See *Einfuhr- und Vorratsstelle v. Köster*, Case 25/70, [1970] ECR 1161 at para. 6 of the judgment. See, further, *Commission v. Council*, Case 16/88, [1989] ECR 3457 (para. 10 of the judgment); *European Parliament v. Council*, Case 417/93, [1995] ECR I-1185. On the delegation of powers by the Commission to one of its members, see *AKZO Chemie v. Commission*, Case 5/85, [1986] ECR 2585 (paras 28–40).

[79] By 'outside bodies', we mean bodies not created by Union law. Such bodies are different from the bodies, offices, and agencies discussed in Chap. 1, § 8: the latter are all created by Union law.

[80] *Meroni v. High Authority*, Case 9/56, [1958] ECR 133. The relevant part of the judgment is section III.

The scheme was set up by a general decision of the High Authority which granted the two organizations their powers. There were, however, a number of ways in which the High Authority could control their activities. First, though the *Caisse* had the power to assess levy payments due from a particular firm and to issue a demand for the sum in question, it could not enforce its claims directly: if the firm failed to pay, the *Caisse* had to request the High Authority to take a decision having executive force. Secondly, both organizations had the power to take decisions only if the members of their governing bodies were unanimous; failing this, the matter would be decided by the High Authority itself. Thirdly, all meetings of the two organizations were attended by a representative of the High Authority who had the power to declare that any decision taken by them would be conditional on the High Authority's approval. The High Authority also had the power to call a meeting of either organization and lay proposals before it; if the proposals were not accepted within ten days, the High Authority could itself put the proposals into effect.

On paper, these powers of control appear extensive; however, according to evidence given by the High Authority in the case, they were rarely exercised. In practice the organizations had a large measure of independence.

The way the case arose was as follows. The *Caisse* had asked Meroni, an Italian steel manufacturer, to inform it of the quantity of scrap it had used, so that the *Caisse* could assess the levy payments due. Meroni failed to do this and the *Caisse* therefore told Meroni that it would make estimates of the relevant figures and assess the levy on that basis. Meroni still refused to co-operate; so the *Caisse* sent a demand for payment on the basis of the estimates. When Meroni failed to pay, the High Authority, at the request of the *Caisse*, took a decision demanding payment. Under Article 92 ECSC, this decision would be enforceable against Meroni through the Italian courts; Meroni therefore brought proceedings in the European Court to have it set aside. One of the arguments put forward was that the whole scrap equalization scheme involved an unlawful delegation of powers and was consequently invalid.

The first question the Court had to consider was whether there really had been a delegation of power to collect the levy, since the decision subject to challenge was that of the High Authority. It was, however, admitted by the High Authority that it never questioned assessments made by the *Caisse*: all it did was to rubber-stamp the *Caisse*'s decision. The Court therefore held that effective decision-making power had been delegated. The next question was whether the delegation was lawful. The Court held, on three separate grounds, that it was not. First, the Court held that the High Authority had attempted to transfer wider powers than it possessed itself. By this it meant that certain obligations and restrictions which applied when the High Authority itself acted were not applicable to the *Caisse* and *Office Commun*: for example, the High Authority was obliged by the Treaty to give reasons for its decisions but this obligation was not imposed on the two organizations.[81]

[81] The Court also felt that decisions made by the two organizations would be immune from judicial review, but a later case established that this is not so: see *SNUPAT v. High Authority*, Cases 32–3/58, [1959] ECR 127.

The second ground given by the Court was that the High Authority decision delegating powers to the two organizations did not expressly give them the power to assess the levy on the basis of an estimate of scrap used. One might have thought that this would have been covered by the doctrine of implied powers (narrow formulation),[82] but the Court ruled that a delegation of powers can never be implied. Even if the High Authority had been entitled to delegate this power, an express decision would have been necessary.

The third ground given by the Court was by far the most important: it concerned the question whether the High Authority had any power to delegate at all. The Court ruled that the High Authority possessed only very limited power to delegate to outside bodies: clearly defined executive powers could be delegated, provided their exercise was subject to strict rules based on objective criteria; but discretionary powers involving extensive freedom of judgment could not be delegated. This distinction between discretionary and non-discretionary (ministerial) powers is, of course, known to English administrative law and its adoption here may be justified on the ground that the authors of the Treaties were prepared to grant extensive discretionary powers to the Commission because they had confidence in it; they might not have been prepared to see these same powers exercised by an outside body not subject to the safeguards applicable to the Commission itself.

The outcome of all this was that the High Authority decision addressed to Meroni demanding payment of the levy was quashed because it was based on a decision of the *Caisse* made under an illegal delegation of powers.[83] In view of the Court's ruling on this point, the scrap equalization scheme had to be extensively restructured.

One may conclude from this case that there is an important difference between a delegation to the Commission and a delegation to an outside body: wide discretionary powers may be delegated in the former case but not in the latter.

§6.5 DELEGATION TO MEMBER STATES

In view of the special position of national governments in the EU structure, it is desirable to give separate treatment to the question of delegation to Member States. At the outset it is necessary to emphasize the distinction between a delegation of powers and a direction to a Member State to exercise its own powers in a particular way. The latter is very common: one form of Union act – the directive – was designed for just this purpose. Delegation of powers, on the other hand, is comparatively rare. The reason is that it is not generally necessary for powers to be transferred to Member States: they normally possess sufficient powers in their own right. If, however, Member States have given up their powers in a particular area in favour of the Union, it will be possible for powers to be transferred back to them by means of a delegation.

[82] See § 2.2.

[83] The Court also gave other grounds for its decision which were not concerned with the question of delegation.

The leading case on the topic is *Rey Soda*.[84] This was concerned with the common organization of the market in sugar, which had been brought about by Council Regulation 1009/67. In previous cases, the European Court had laid down the principle that when the market in a particular product is brought under a common organization, the Member States lose their powers to regulate it, except as regards the implementation of EU rules.[85] Under Regulation 1009/67, the Commission was given power to take measures to prevent disturbances in the market as a result of alterations in the price level. Acting under this provision, the Commission passed a regulation delegating to Italy the power to take measures to prevent disturbances on the Italian market as a result of the increase on 1 July 1974 in the price of sugar expressed in Italian lire. The Italian Government exercised this power by passing a decree imposing a levy on sugar stockholders. The validity of this measure was challenged in the Italian courts and the European Court had to decide on the validity of the sub-delegation to the Italian Government.

The European Court ruled that the delegation by the Council to the Commission was valid, but the sub-delegation to the Italian Government was not. This ruling illustrates vividly the difference in the legal principles governing a delegation within the European Union and a delegation to an outside body. The Court upheld the delegation to the Commission on the ground that, since the general principles had been laid down by Council Regulation 1009/67, it was legitimate to entrust the Commission with the task of implementation, even though this involved conferring wide discretionary powers on it. But the Commission had no power to delegate these discretionary powers to the Italian Government: only strictly defined powers of execution could be sub-delegated. From this it seems that the same principle applies in the case of a delegation to a Member State as in the case of a delegation to a body such as the *Caisse*.

§6.6 IMPLEMENTING POWERS

Article 291 TFEU concerns the implementation (putting into effect) of EU acts. Article 291(1) imposes a duty on Member States to adopt measures of national law to implement legally binding EU acts. For the reasons explained earlier, this would not normally entail any delegation of power: the Member States would use their own legislative power.

Article 291(2) provides that, where uniform conditions for implementing legally binding EU acts are needed, those acts will confer implementing powers on the Commission, or, in 'duly justified specific cases',[86] on the Council. These 'implementing powers' are in reality a form of delegation, though they are not regarded as such by the relevant Treaty provisions. Under the Treaties, they are distinguished from delegation by reason of their purpose: if their purpose is to implement the original act, they will

[84] *Rey Soda v. Cassa Conguaglio Zucchero*, Case 23/75, [1975] ECR 1279.

[85] See *per* Advocate General Mayras, *ibid.* at 1317–18.

[86] And in the cases provided for in Arts 24 and 26 TEU. Both these latter Articles concern the common foreign and security policy.

be regarded as 'implementing powers' and fall under Article 291 TFEU; if their purpose is to amend or supplement the original act, they will be regarded as a delegation in terms of Article 290 TFEU.[87]

Special rules are laid down in Regulation 182/2011[88] to govern the mechanisms which apply when implementing acts are adopted by the Commission.[89] If the original act (referred to in the Regulation as the 'basic act') so requires, the adoption of implementing acts by the Commission will be subject to control by the Member States. This may take one of two forms: the 'advisory' procedure and the 'examination' procedure.[90] Under both procedures, the Commission is assisted by a committee composed of representatives of the Member States and chaired by a Commission representative.[91] A draft of the implementing act is submitted to the committee, which gives its opinion within a time limit specified by the chairman. There is also an appeal committee.

Under the advisory procedure, the committee will give its opinion, if necessary after taking a vote. This is done by a simple majority of its members. The opinion is not binding, but the Commission must take the 'utmost account' of it and of the discussion in the committee.[92]

The committee has greater powers under the examination procedure. Here the committee votes according to the qualified-majority system laid down in Article 16(4) and (5) TFEU.[93] If the committee delivers a positive opinion, the Commission will adopt the act; if it delivers no opinion, the Commission may adopt it;[94] if it delivers a negative opinion, the Commission may not adopt it, though the chairman may submit either an amended version to the committee or the original version to the appeal committee.[95] In the latter case, the appeal committee will deliver its opinion by qualified-majority voting. If it delivers a positive opinion, the Commission will adopt the act; if it delivers no opinion, the Commission may adopt it;[96] if it delivers a negative opinion, the Commission may not adopt it.[97]

§6.7 CONCLUSIONS

An important feature of the law in this area is the distinction between delegation to the Commission, which may involve wide discretionary power, and delegation to outside

[87] In some cases, the difference between these concepts may be a subtle one: see Craig, 'Delegated Acts, Implementing Acts and the New Comitology Regulation' (2011) 36 ELRev. 671 at pp. 672–7.

[88] OJ 2011, L 55/13.

[89] See Craig, 'Delegated Acts' (n. 87), especially at pp. 677–87.

[90] Art. 2 of the Regulation lays down guidelines as to when each procedure should be used. Thus, the examination procedure will apply to 'implementing acts of general scope' or to programmes with 'substantial implications'. As will be appreciated, these distinctions are, to say the least, vague and fuzzy.

[91] The Commission representative has no vote.

[92] Art. 4 of the Regulation.

[93] See Chap. 1, § 3.3.

[94] There are certain exceptions to this.

[95] For special provisions which apply in particular circumstances, see Art. 5(4) and (5) of the Regulation.

[96] For an exception, see Art. 6(4) of the Regulation.

[97] Special rules, laid down in Arts 7 and 8 of the Regulation, apply in exceptional cases and in cases of urgency.

bodies (including Member States), which may be only of a limited nature. Another feature is the distinction between delegation as understood by Article 290 TFEU and implementation as understood by Article 291 TFEU. In the latter case, the Member States may retain a substantial degree of control through the committee system. This could be justified on the ground that, generally speaking, implementation of Union law is a matter for the Member States. It is only where uniformity is needed that the power of implementation is given to the Commission. Where this takes place, the committee system ensures that – provided they agree – the Member States can control what the Commission does.

§7 FORM

The main requirements of form for legal acts laid down by the Treaties are, first, a reference to any proposals, initiatives, recommendations, requests, or opinions (we shall refer to all these as 'preliminary acts') required by the Treaties; secondly, a statement of reasons; and, thirdly, signature by the appropriate person. We will consider each requirement separately.

§7.1 PRELIMINARY ACTS

The first requirement is laid down in Article 296(2) TFEU, which provides (in part): 'Legal acts... shall refer to any proposals, initiatives, recommendations, requests or opinions required by the Treaties.' All that is necessary under this provision is that the legal act should contain a reference to the preliminary act: it is not necessary to specify its contents or to deal with any points raised in it.[98]

§7.2 REASONS

Article 296(2) TFEU also lays down an obligation to give reasons. It provides: 'Legal acts shall state the reasons on which they are based.'

The purpose of this requirement was explained by the European Court in the *Brennwein* case (*Germany v. Commission*):[99]

> In imposing upon the Commission the obligation to state reasons for its decisions, Article 190 [the forerunner of Article 296(2) TFEU] is not taking mere formal considerations into account but seeks to give an opportunity to the parties of defending their rights, to the Court of exercising its supervisory functions and to Member States and to all interested nationals of ascertaining the circumstances in which the Commission has applied the Treaty.

[98] See *ISA v. High Authority*, Case 4/54, [1955] ECR 91 at 100. See also Lauwaars, *Lawfulness and Legal Force of Community Decisions* (1973), p. 151.

[99] Case 24/62, [1963] ECR 63 at 69. See also *REWE Handelsgesellschaft Nord v. Hauptzollamt Kiel*, Case 158/80, [1981] ECR 1805 at para. 25 of the judgment.

What the Court meant by this was as follows. As regards the parties, reasons will help them in two ways: if they know why the enacting authority[100] adopted the act in question, they will be able to address representations to it to persuade it to change its mind; they will also be in a better position to decide whether to bring legal proceedings to have it set aside. As regards the Court, a statement of reasons will be of assistance in deciding on the validity of the act; while third parties (including Member States) will find it useful to know the policies followed by the enacting authority so that they can appreciate the way the power is likely to be exercised in the future. Furthermore, if draft legal acts (proposals) contain a statement of reasons, the enacting institution – for example, the Council or the European Parliament – will itself be forced to consider exactly why it is adopting the act, and this might induce it to make modifications.[101]

In discussing the effect of the requirement of reasoning, two questions must be considered: the scope of the provision (to which acts does it apply?), and its content (what constitutes sufficient reasoning?). As far as the scope is concerned, the answer is given in Article 296(2) TFEU itself: it applies to all legal acts. A legal act is an act purporting to have legal effects, a concept discussed in greater detail in Chapter 11.[102] It makes no difference whether the institution in question is acting under a power conferred by the Treaties or a power delegated to it by another institution.[103]

If a Union institution delegates a power to some outside body to adopt legal acts, the delegate must be made subject to the same requirement of reasoning as the delegating authority. This follows from the decision in the *Meroni* case[104] (discussed in § 6.4), where the Court said that a Union institution cannot delegate a greater power than it possesses itself and that consequently any requirements that apply when the delegating authority exercises the power must also be imposed on the delegate. Failure to do this renders the delegation invalid. It will be remembered that in the *Meroni* case the Court specifically mentioned the requirement of reasoning.[105]

The next question is what constitutes sufficient reasons. The objectives which the requirement of reasoning is intended to serve were set out earlier. It would seem clear, as a matter of general principle, that the test for the sufficiency of the reasons given in a particular case should be derived from these objectives: the reasons given for an act are sufficient if, but only if, they permit the attainment of these objectives.[106] To do this, they must at the very least set out the factual background which the author of the act regards as relevant; they must specify the Treaty provision (or other source of

[100] In *Germany v. Commission* the enacting authority was the Commission, but the Court's statement would apply equally where it was some other institution.

[101] See Lauwaars, *Lawfulness and Legal Force of Community Decisions* (1973), p. 153.

[102] Prior to the Treaty of Lisbon, the obligation to give reasons applied only to regulations, directives, and decisions adopted by the Council or Commission, and to such acts adopted by the Parliament and Council jointly: see Art. 249 EC, as it stood at the time. For this reason, the European Court held in the *ERTA* case, *Commission v. Council*, Case 22/70, [1971] ECR 263 (paras 97 and 98 of the judgment) (discussed in § 1.1), that the requirement of reasoning did not apply to the act *sui generis* in issue there. Under the law as it stands today, this case would be decided differently.

[103] *Schwarze*, Case 16/65, [1965] ECR 877 at 887.

[104] *Meroni v. High Authority*, Case 9/56, [1958] ECR 133.

[105] See *ibid.* at 171.

[106] See Lauwaars, *Lawfulness and Legal Force of Community Decisions* (1973), p. 156.

legal authority) under which the act was adopted (its legal basis);[107] they must state the objectives which the act is designed to attain; and they should state why, in the opinion of the enacting authority, it is desirable to attain these objectives.

An important rule laid down by the European Court is that the degree of specificity required depends on the nature of the act in question: in the case of an act of a truly normative nature, affecting general categories of persons (the normal type of regulation), it is sufficient if the reasoning is limited to broad outlines; in the case of an individual act, affecting only a specific person (the normal type of decision), on the other hand, more detail is required. The reason for this distinction is that an act of a legislative nature, by its very nature, is of general application. The circumstances in which it might possibly apply can never be fully known in advance; consequently, it would be impractical to expect a high degree of specificity. An individual act, however, applies only to a particular case. All the relevant facts are known and it is therefore possible to give much fuller reasons.

An indication of what is required in the case of an act of a normative nature was given by the judgment of the European Court in the *Beus* case:[108]

> The extent of the requirement laid down by Article 190 of the Treaty [the forerunner of Article 296(2) TFEU] to state the reasons on which measures are based, depends on the nature of the measure in question. It is a question in the present case of a regulation, that is to say, a measure intended to have general application, the preamble to which may be confined to indicating the general situation which led to its adoption, on the one hand, and the general objectives which it is intended to achieve on the other.
>
> Consequently, it is not possible to require that it should set out the various facts, which are often very numerous and complex, on the basis of which the regulation was adopted, or *a fortiori* that it should provide a more or less complete evaluation of those facts.

An example of what the Court expects in the case of an individual act is provided by the *Brennwein* case (*Germany v. Commission*).[109] Brennwein is an alcoholic drink distilled from wine. Large quantities were produced in Germany and most of the wine was imported from outside the Union. When the common external tariff came into operation there was a substantial increase in the duty on this wine and the German Government took the view that this posed a threat to the industry. They therefore asked the Commission for a quota of 450,000 hectolitres to be imported at the old rate of duty. The Commission took a decision granting only 100,000 hectolitres. The key passage in its reasoning was as follows:[110]

> On the basis of the existing information it has been possible to ascertain that the production of the wines in question within the Union is amply sufficient. The grant of a tariff quota of the volume requested might therefore lead to serious disturbances of the market in the products in question...

[107] *Commission v. Council (Tariff Preferences)*, Case 45/86, [1987] ECR 1493. However, failure to refer to a precise provision will not result in the nullity of the act if other parts of the act make clear what its legal basis was: see para. 12 of the judgment.

[108] Case 5/67, [1968] ECR 83 at 95; see also *Barge v. High Authority*, Case 18/62, [1963] ECR 259 at 280.

[109] Case 24/62, [1963] ECR 63.

[110] Taken from the opinion of Advocate General Roemer, at p. 72.

The Court held that this was insufficient. Instead of referring merely to 'the existing information', the Commission should have been more specific and given an indication of the evolution and size of the surpluses within the Union; secondly, it should have specified what the 'serious disturbances' were and shown why they would have resulted from the granting of the request. The decision was therefore quashed.

May the enacting authority incorporate by reference reasons given in another instrument? This happens quite often, especially in the case of agricultural measures fixing the levels of levies and refunds. These are usually changed at short notice and it is common for the measure fixing the new rate to refer back to a previous measure in which the full criteria are set out. The practice of incorporating reasons by reference has been accepted by the European Court in a number of cases.[111] In the *Schwarze* case,[112] for example, the Court upheld a Commission decision fixing the free-at-frontier price of barley, even though it contained very little reasoning, because it included a reference to a previous decision which set out the general considerations applicable to the fixing of these prices. The Court stated that less strict criteria should be applied in cases of this kind in view of the short period of time within which the Commission must act, the confidentiality of the data on which their decisions are based, and the administrative difficulties which would result if detailed reasoning were required in every case.

In *Papiers Peints de Belgique v. Commission*,[113] on the other hand, the Commission had taken a decision imposing fines on a number of companies for breach of EU competition (anti-trust) law. The reasoning referred to a judgment of the European Court in a previous case. The Court held that this was insufficient: a decision which merely follows established policy may refer to the reasons given in a previous case, but a decision which breaks new ground – as was the case here – must be fully reasoned.

This shows that incorporation by reference is permissible only in certain cases. It is suggested that, where it is allowed, the reference should always be to a published document, or, where the measure itself need not be published, to a document available to all interested parties.[114] In deciding who are to be regarded as interested parties, one should remember the Court's statement that one of the purposes of the requirement of reasoning is to enable third parties to know the policies which the Union institutions pursue and the way in which they interpret their powers.[115]

Should insufficient reasoning be excused if interested parties are subsequently informed what the enacting authority's reasons were? Against such a principle one could argue that Article 296(2) TFEU clearly provides that legal acts 'shall state the reasons on which they are based': allowing incorporation by reference is stretching Article 296(2) to its limit; an *ex post facto* statement can in no sense be regarded as

[111] See Lauwaars, *Lawfulness and Legal Force of Community Decisions* (1973), pp. 161–2 for a summary of the cases; note that incorporation by reference was rejected in *Dalmas v. High Authority*, Case 1/63, [1963] ECR 303 (discussed by Lauwaars at p. 161) but accepted again in later cases.

[112] Case 16/65, [1965] ECR 877.

[113] Case 73/74, [1975] ECR 1491.

[114] Lauwaars, *Lawfulness and Legal Force of Community Decisions* (1973), p. 163.

[115] See earlier discussion.

compliance. On the other hand, however, it might be said that to insist on the letter of Article 296(2), when the reasons are in fact known, would serve no purpose.

In the *Brennwein* case[116] the Court appeared not to regard it as sufficient that the Commission provided the relevant data in Court; however, in the *Schwarze* case[117] the Court accepted that, in certain circumstances, the requirement of reasoning will be satisfied if the parties are supplied with the information once judicial proceedings have been commenced. Although the kind of decision in issue justified a relaxation of the requirement, it is hard to accept that Article 296(2) has been satisfied when the party must wait not only until after the promulgation of the measure before being given the reasons, but must first commence legal proceedings. According to the Court,[118] one of the purposes of the requirement of reasoning is to enable the parties to defend their rights; but they will frequently not be in a position to know whether they ought to take legal action until they have seen the reasons. Moreover, the requirement is also supposed to protect third parties: they cannot be expected to commence proceedings just in order to see the reasons.[119]

A more acceptable compromise between administrative and legal requirements is to be found in *Michel v. European Parliament*,[120] a case concerning the rejection of an application to take part in the selection procedure for appointment to the staff of the Parliament. Here the Court annulled the decision, though the applicant had been informed of the reasons during the court proceedings. The Court stated that the reasons must in principle be given at the same time as the decision, but relaxed this requirement in view of the large number of applications (1,455 out of 1,740 were rejected). It held that the selection board was obliged to set out in the letter of rejection only the general criteria applied, but if the candidate asked for the particular reasons that led to his rejection, these must be supplied within the time limit for commencing legal proceedings.

It will be evident from what has been said that the degree of detail required depends to a large extent on the circumstances of the case. Consequently, it is impossible to lay down precise rules as to what constitutes sufficient reasoning. It is, however, worth asking whether the rather ambitious objectives set out by the European Court in the *Brennwein* case are usually attained. As has been seen, the normal standards are of necessity relaxed in certain cases: in these circumstances the interests of third parties,

[116] See n. 109. [117] See n. 112.

[118] See the quotation from the *Brennwein* case (n. 110), set out earlier in this section.

[119] Other cases in which information given privately to a party has been taken into account by the Court are *Netherlands v. Commission*, Case 13/72, [1973] ECR 27 and *De Wendel v. Commission*, Case 29/67, [1968] ECR 263.

[120] Case 195/80, [1981] ECR 2861. See also *Bonu v. Council*, Case 89/79, [1980] ECR 553 at para. 6 of the judgment; and *European Parliament v. Innamorati*, Case C-254/95 P, [1996] ECR I-3423 at paras 21–34, where the European Court held that, while reasons must be given for a decision rejecting an application to take part in a selection test, reasons need not be given for the marks awarded to a candidate in such a test, nor are the examiners required to inform candidates of the criteria used in marking such tests.

and sometimes even of those directly involved, are liable to suffer. But are the objectives met even where these special circumstances do not exist?

The most serious problem is that the objectives set out by the Court will not be achieved unless the reasons given are the real ones. It has, however, been said that in the everyday practice of the Commission the substantive provisions of measures are drawn up first and the reasons are added afterwards by the legal service.[121] (In one case, the Secretariat of the Council even went so far as to change the statement of reasons after the measure had been adopted, but the Court regarded this as overstepping the mark and declared the measure invalid.)[122] In these circumstances there is a danger that the real reasons will not always be given: the legal service may be tempted to 'dress up' the measure by giving more acceptable reasons than those which the Commission actually had in mind. In this situation the requirement of reasons would degenerate into an empty formality.

One can conclude that, while the requirement of reasoning undoubtedly serves a useful purpose, the objectives set out in the *Brennwein* case are not always fully attained.

§7.3 SIGNATURE

Article 297 TFEU contains rules on the signature of legal acts. Legislative acts adopted under the ordinary legislative procedure must be signed by the President of the European Parliament and by the President of the Council. Legislative acts adopted under a special legislative procedure must be signed by the President of the institution which adopted them. Non-legislative acts adopted in the form of regulations, directives, or decisions[123] must be signed by the President of the institution which adopted them.

§8 PUBLICATION, NOTIFICATION, AND ENTRY INTO FORCE

Legislative acts must be published in the Official Journal. They enter into force on the date specified in them or, in the absence thereof, on the twentieth day following that of their publication.[124] Regulations and directives which are addressed to all Member States, as well as decisions which do not specify to whom they are addressed, must be published in the Official Journal.[125] They enter into force on the date specified in them or, in the absence thereof, on the twentieth day following that of their publication.[126]

[121] Hen, 'La motivation des actes des institutions communautaires' (1977) 13 CDE 49 at 54 and 90.

[122] *United Kingdom v. Council*, Case 131/86, [1988] ECR 905 (paras 31–39 of the judgment).

[123] In the case of decisions, this applies only when they do not specify to whom they are addressed.

[124] Art. 297(1), third para., TFEU.

[125] On the consequences of failure to publish, see *Skoma-Lux*, Case C-161/06, [2007] ECR I-10841 and *Heinrich*, Case C-345/06, [2009] I-1659; see Chap. 11, § 4.

[126] Art. 297(2), second para., TFEU.

Other directives, and decisions which specify to whom they are addressed, must be notified to those to whom they are addressed and take effect upon such notification.[127]

Publication and notification are not, however, constitutive requirements: an act which has not been published or notified is nevertheless an act. Failure to publish or notify does not affect its existence, but only its legal consequences. This was decided by the European Court in a number of cases concerning a provision under which the High Authority was empowered to make decisions only up to a certain date. The decisions in question had been made before this date, but had been notified to the addressees afterwards. The Court held they were valid.[128] In a similar case concerning a regulation, it was held that the validity of the measure was not affected by the fact that publication took place after the date in question.[129]

FURTHER READING

Items are listed in date order, the most recent being at the end.

Lenaerts, 'Regulating the Regulatory Process: "Delegation of Powers" in the European Union' (1993) 18 ELRev. 23.

Bermann, 'Taking Subsidiarity Seriously: Federalism in the European Union and the United States' (1994) 94 *Columbia Law Review* 331.

Emiliou, 'Opening Pandora's Box: The Legal Basis of Union Measures before the Court of Justice' (1994) 19 ELRev. 488.

Emiliou, 'Subsidiarity: Panacea or Fig Leaf?', in David O'Keeffe and Patrick M Twomey (eds), *Legal Issues of the Maastricht Treaty* (1994), p. 65.

Schilling, 'A New Dimension of Subsidiarity: Subsidiarity as a Rule and a Principle' (1994) 14 YEL 203.

Steiner, 'Subsidiarity under the Maastricht Treaty', in David O'Keeffe and Patrick M Twomey (eds), *Legal Issues of the Maastricht Treaty* (1994), p. 49.

Toth, 'A Legal Analysis of Subsidiarity', in David O'Keeffe and Patrick M Twomey (eds), *Legal Issues of the Maastricht Treaty* (1994), p. 37.

Toth, 'Is Subsidiarity Justiciable?' (1994) 14 ELRev. 268.

Dashwood, 'The Limits of European Union Powers' (1996) 21 ELRev. 113.

Dashwood, 'The Constitution of the European Union after Nice: Law-Making Procedures' (2001) 26 ELRev. 215.

A Estella, *The Principle of Subsidiarity and its Critique* (2002).

Von Bogdany, Arndt, and Blast, 'Legal Instruments in European Union Law and their Reform: A Systematic Approach on an Empirical Basis' (2004) 23 YEL 91.

[127] Art. 297(2), third para., TFEU.

[128] See Lauwaars, *Lawfulness and Legal Force of Community Decisions* (1973), pp. 166–7 and the cases cited there.

[129] *Hauptzollamt Bielefeld v. König*, Case 185/73, [1974] ECR 607 (paras 5–8 of the judgment). It has also been held that irregularities in the procedure for notification of a decision do not constitute a ground for its annulment: *ICI v. Commission*, Case 48/69, [1972] ECR 619 at 652 at paras 39–44 of the judgment.

WEATHERILL, 'Competence Creep and Competence Control' (2004) 23 YEL 1.

SACHA PRECHAL, *Directives in EU Law*, 2nd edn (2006).

SCHÜTZE, 'Lisbon and the Federal Order of Competences: A Prospective Analysis' (2008) 33 ELRev. 709.

DRIESSEN, 'Delegated Legislation after the Treaty of Lisbon: An Analysis of Article 290 TFEU' (2010) 35 ELRev. 837.

KLAMERT, 'Conflicts of Legal Basis: No Legality and No Basis but a Bright Future under the Lisbon Treaty?' (2010) 35 ELRev. 497.

CRAIG, 'Delegated Acts, Implementing Acts and the New Comitology Regulation' (2011) 36 ELRev. 671.

KIIVER, 'The Early-Warning System for the Principle of Subsidiary: The National Parliament as a *Conseil d'Etat* for Europe' (2011) 36 ELRev. 98.

BAST, 'New Categories of Acts after the Lisbon Reform: Dynamics of Parliamentarization in EU Law' (2012) 49 CMLRev. 885.

FABBRINI AND GRANAT, '"Yellow Card, But No Foul": The Role of the National Parliaments under the Subsidiarity Protocol and the Commission Proposal for an EU Regulation on the Right to Strike' (2013) 50 CMLRev. 115.

5

HUMAN RIGHTS AND GENERAL PRINCIPLES OF LAW

§1 INTRODUCTION

General principles of law are a major source of Union law. Until recently, they constituted the main – perhaps the sole – basis on which EU human rights law has been developed. However, since the coming into force of the Treaty of Lisbon, the European Union is required to apply to become a Party to the European Convention on Human Rights (ECHR), and legal effect has been given to the European Union's own Charter of Fundamental Rights; so human rights now have an independent foundation in Union law. Nevertheless, the theory of general principles of law will continue to be important for other reasons. In this chapter, we discuss general principles of law as a source of Union law; we also discuss human rights as they were developed as general principles of law and as they will continue on the basis of the new legal texts.

In what way are 'general principles' a source of law? In answering this question, it is desirable to look for a moment at a problem of judicial psychology. In no legal system is it possible for legislation or other written sources of law to provide an answer to every question which comes before the courts. The judges are therefore obliged to create rules of law to decide the issues before them; but if their law-creating role becomes too apparent, they may be accused of going beyond their proper function and trespassing on the domain of the legislature. How are they to resolve this dilemma? In England the courts have traditionally resorted to the myth of the common law, the age-old tradition of customary law which, by a fiction, was regarded as being both immemorial and within the special cognizance of the judges. The European Court, on the other hand, has utilized general principles of law to give an appearance of objectivity to its judgments: if a ruling can be shown to be derived from a principle of sufficient generality as to command common assent, it is thought that a firm legal foundation for the judgment will have been provided. For this reason, the European Court has developed a doctrine that rules of EU law may be derived, not only from treaties and legislation, but also from the general principles of law.[1]

[1] It must not be forgotten that 'general principles of law' are also one of the sources of international law, recognized in Art. 38(1)(c) of the Statute of the International Court of Justice. Unlike the Statute of the International

What is the origin of these general principles? They are derived from various sources, but the most important are the EU Treaties and the legal systems of the Member States. In the former case, the Court declares that a specific provision in one of the Treaties is an application of some more general principle which is not itself laid down in the Treaty. This is then applied in its own right as a general principle of law. An example of this is Article 18 TFEU [12/6 EC], which prohibits all discrimination based on nationality between EU citizens as regards matters within the scope of the Treaty. This, together with other texts, has been used by the Court as the foundation for a general doctrine of equality which forbids arbitrary discrimination on any ground (discussed in § 5).

Another example, *Meroni v. High Authority*,[2] is based on the ECSC Treaty. This Treaty has now expired, but the case retains its value as an example of judicial reasoning. Article 36 ECSC provided that in an appeal against a fine or penalty, the applicant could claim that the measure he had contravened was invalid. In *Meroni*, the applicant wished to invoke this plea in a case involving not a fine, but a levy (tax). Article 36 could not apply, but the Court held that it was a particular application of the general principle that all legislative measures may be challenged indirectly. This general principle was then applied to the case at hand so as to allow the applicant to challenge the measure.

It will be noticed that this reasoning involves two stages: the first is inductive, in which the Court derives a general principle from specific provisions in the Treaty; the second is deductive – here the Court arrives at a solution to the particular issue by applying the general principle. It should be stressed that when the Court acts in this way, the legal source of its decision is not the Treaty but the general principle.

When the Court looks to national law for inspiration, it is not necessary that the principle should be accepted by the legal systems of all the Member States. It would be sufficient if the principle were generally accepted by the legal systems of most Member States, or if it was in conformity with a trend in the Member States, so that one could say that the national legal systems were developing towards it.[3] It must again be emphasized, however, that whatever the factual origin of the principle, it is applied by the European Court as a principle of EU law, not national law.

It should also be mentioned that the Treaties themselves provide some justification for recourse to general principles as a source of law. First, there is Article 19 TEU [220/164 EC], the first paragraph of which states: 'The Court of Justice of the European Union…shall ensure that in the interpretation and application of the Treaties the law is observed.' It is usually thought that here the word 'law' must refer to something over

Court, however, the EU Treaties contain no reference to general principles of law as a general source of EU law. Their adoption by the European Court as such a source may, therefore, have been inspired by the role they play in international law. See, further, Akehurst, 'The Application of General Principles of Law by the Court of Justice of the European Communities' [1981] BYIL 29.

[2] Case 9/56, [1958] ECR 133.

[3] See *Hoogovens v. High Authority*, Case 14/61, [1962] ECR 253 at 283–4, where Advocate General Lagrange said that the Court is not content to adopt the common denominator between the different systems but 'chooses from each of the Member States those solutions which, having regard to the objects of the Treaty, appear to it to be the best'.

and above the Treaty itself; if correct, this means that Article 19 not only entitles, but also obliges, the Court to take general principles into account.

There is a more specific provision in Article 263 TFEU [230/173 EC]. This Article lays down (among other things) the grounds on which an EU act may be annulled by the Court. One of these grounds is 'infringement of the Treaties or of any rule of law relating to their application'. The phrase 'any rule of law relating to their application' must refer to something other than the Treaties themselves and it has been used by the Court as the basis for the doctrine that an EU act may be quashed for infringement of a general principle of law.

The third Treaty provision is Article 340 (second paragraph) TFEU [288/215 (second paragraph) EC]. This is concerned with non-contractual liability (tort) and it expressly provides that the liability of the European Union is based on 'the general principles common to the laws of the Member States'. This is discussed in detail in Chapter 16; all that need be said here is that, in spite of the wording of the provision, the Court is prepared to apply principles of law even if they are not found in the legal system of every Member State. In other words, it adopts the same free and independent approach to the elaboration of its case-law as in those areas where there is no express Treaty obligation to apply general principles of law.

The general principles of law are, therefore, an independent source of law and there can be little doubt that the Court would have applied them even if none of the Treaty provisions mentioned previously had existed. It should not, however, be thought that the Court always makes express reference to general principles whenever it propounds new rules of law. Sometimes it simply states a rule without any express indication of its source; or it may give a justification based on policy or the general requirements of the EU legal system. However, if a formal source for such rules were required, it could always be found either on the basis of a wide interpretation of a written text or on the basis of the general principles.

What general principles has the Court so far adopted? It is impossible to enumerate them all, but some of the more important will now be discussed.

§2 FUNDAMENTAL HUMAN RIGHTS

§2.1 DEVELOPMENT OF THE EU CONCEPT

In spite of their importance in the world today, fundamental human rights were not mentioned in the original Treaties and it was only later that they came to play a significant role in EU law. Moreover, it is probably fair to say that the conversion of the European Court to a specific doctrine of human rights has been more a matter of expediency than conviction. How this came about is as follows.

One of the most strongly pursued objectives of the European Court has always been to ensure the effectiveness of EU law and this in turn has led to the doctrine of the supremacy of EU law over national law, a doctrine which the European Court has upheld with the greatest vigour. By and large, this doctrine has been accepted by the national courts; however, since the early days of European integration, German lawyers have had doubts as to whether EU law should prevail over the provisions of the German Constitution (*Grundgesetz*), especially those concerning fundamental human rights. There has been no difficulty in Germany regarding the supremacy of EU law over ordinary German law, including statutes of the Federal Parliament. However, all German laws, including federal statutes, are subordinate to the Constitution; and there is a special Federal Constitutional Court (*Bundesverfassungsgericht*) which has power to determine the constitutionality of legislation. Since their own national legislation had to comply with the principles of the Constitution, it was hardly surprising that some German lawyers took the view that EU law could not apply in Germany if it violated the fundamental human rights provisions of the *Grundgesetz*. The strong attachment of German lawyers to the concept of fundamental law, and especially fundamental human rights, is, of course, understandable in the light of German history.

In the 1960s, the argument that EU law should comply with the fundamental human rights provisions of the *Grundgesetz* was frequently put forward by German litigants both in German courts[4] and in the European Court. At first the European Court was unsympathetic.[5] However, it was soon apparent that the German courts found the doctrine very persuasive, and it became imperative for the European Court to take action to head off a possible 'rebellion'. The solution it adopted was to proclaim an EU concept of human rights and to make clear that it would itself annul any provision of EU law contrary to human rights.

The case in which the European Court announced the new doctrine was *Stauder v. City of Ulm*.[6] This concerned an EU scheme to provide cheap butter for recipients of welfare benefits. The applicant received war victims' welfare benefits in Germany and was therefore entitled to the cheap butter; however, he objected to the fact that he was obliged to present a coupon bearing his name and address in order to obtain the butter: he maintained that it was a humiliation to have to reveal his identity, and argued that this constituted a violation of his fundamental human rights. He therefore claimed that the EU decision in question was invalid in so far as it contained this requirement. The action was originally brought before the German courts and a reference was made to the European Court.

The European Court held that, on a proper interpretation, the EU measure did not require the recipient's name to appear on the coupon.[7] It then continued:[8] 'Interpreted in this way the provision at issue contains nothing capable of prejudicing the fundamental human rights enshrined in the general principles of Community [Union] law and protected by the Court.' This recognized that fundamental human rights are a general principle of EU law.

[4] For summaries of the German cases, see Brinkhorst and Schermers, *Judicial Remedies in the European Communities* (1969), pp. 143–54 and *Supplement* (1972), pp. 72–7.

[5] See *Stork v. High Authority*, Case 1/58, [1959] ECR 17 at 26; and *Geitling v. High Authority*, Cases 36–8, 40/59, [1960] ECR 423 at 438.

[6] Case 29/69, [1969] ECR 419.

[7] This aspect of the case was discussed in Chap. 2, § 6.1.

[8] Para. 7 of the judgment.

Next came the *Internationale Handelsgesellschaft* case,[9] which concerned the Common Agricultural Policy. In order to control the market in certain agricultural products, a system had been introduced under which exports were permitted only if the exporter first obtained an export licence. When application was made for the licence, the exporter had to deposit a sum of money which would be forfeit if he failed to make the export during the period of validity of the licence. The applicants in this case, however, claimed that the whole system was invalid as being contrary to fundamental human rights. One principle invoked was that of proportionality. This is a doctrine of German constitutional law under which public authorities may impose on the citizen only those obligations which are necessary for attaining the public objective in question.[10] It was argued in the German *Verwaltungsgericht* (administrative court), where the proceedings commenced, that the relevant EU measure was invalid for violating the German Constitution, and the question of its validity was referred to the European Court.

The European Court first stated that the validity of EU measures cannot be judged according to the rules or concepts of national law: only EU criteria may be applied. Consequently, even a violation of the fundamental human rights provisions of a Member State's constitution could not impair the validity of an EU provision. Having said this, however, the Court then sweetened the pill by adding:[11]

> However, an examination should be made as to whether or not any analogous guarantee inherent in Community [Union] law has been disregarded. In fact, respect for fundamental rights forms an integral part of the general principles of law protected by the Court of Justice. The protection of such rights, whilst inspired by the constitutional traditions common to the Member States, must be ensured within the framework of the structure and objectives of the Community. It must therefore be ascertained, in the light of the doubts expressed by the Verwaltungsgericht, whether the system of deposits has infringed rights of a fundamental nature, respect for which must be ensured in the Community legal system.

The Court then examined the system in detail but concluded that no fundamental right had been violated by it.

It will be noticed that the *dictum* just quoted goes beyond that in the *Stauder* case in one important respect: it states that the concept of human rights applied by the Court, while deriving its validity solely from EU law, is nevertheless 'inspired' by national constitutional traditions.

A further step was taken in *Nold v. Commission*.[12] This concerned a Commission decision under the ECSC Treaty which provided that coal wholesalers could not buy Ruhr coal direct from the selling agency unless they agreed to purchase a certain minimum quantity. Nold was a Ruhr wholesaler who was not in a position to meet this requirement and consequently had to deal with an intermediary. He claimed that the decision was a violation of his fundamental human rights, partly because it deprived

[9] Case 11/70, [1970] ECR 1125. See also *EVGF v. Köster*, Case 25/70, [1970] ECR 1161 at para. 22 of the judgment.

[10] This doctrine has actually been adopted by the European Court as a general principle in its own right: see § 4.

[11] At 1134.

[12] Case 4/73, [1974] ECR 491.

him of a property right and partly because it infringed his right to the free pursuit of an economic activity. He therefore brought proceedings before the European Court under Article 33 ECSC for the annulment of the decision.

The Court appeared to recognize the two rights as principles of EU law, but held that they must not be regarded as absolute and unqualified: they are subject to limitations 'justified by the overall objectives pursued by the Community [Union]', and 'mere commercial interests or opportunities' are outside their scope. No infringement had therefore taken place.

In the course of its judgment, the European Court made the following statement:[13]

> As the Court has already stated, fundamental rights form an integral part of the general principles of law, the observance of which it ensures. In safeguarding these rights, the Court is bound to draw inspiration from constitutional traditions common to the Member States, and it cannot therefore uphold measures which are incompatible with fundamental rights recognised and protected by the constitutions of those States.
>
> Similarly, international Treaties for the protection of human rights on which the Member States have collaborated or of which they are signatories, can supply guidelines which should be followed within the framework of Community [Union] law.

This goes beyond the statement in the *Handelsgesellschaft* case in two respects: first, it makes clear that an EU measure in conflict with fundamental rights will be annulled; secondly, it reveals a new source of 'inspiration' for these rights – international treaties.

The cases discussed show that the Court's approach to fundamental rights is a little different from its approach to other general principles of law. The reason is that the acceptance of an express doctrine of fundamental rights was prompted by the desire to persuade the German courts to accept the supremacy of EU law even in the case of an alleged conflict with the fundamental-rights provisions of the *Grundgesetz*. In view of this, national provisions are likely to be much more influential than in the case of other general principles. However, the European Court will never admit to applying national law as such; this is why it puts forward the notion that the EU concept of fundamental rights is merely 'inspired' by the philosophical concepts underlying the national provisions. It follows that there is no rule of law that a particular right will be accepted as fundamental by the European Court just because it is protected in the constitutions of some of the Member States, or even a majority of them.[14] As was said extra-judicially by a member of the European Court, Judge Mancini:

> ...the Court does not have to go looking for maximum, minimum or average standards. The yardstick by which it measures the approaches adopted by the various legal systems derives

[13] At 507.

[14] Some authorities take a different view. They argue that any right constitutionally protected in even one Member State must, as a matter of law, be accepted as a fundamental right at the EU level. See *per* Advocate General Warner, *IRCA*, Case 7/76, [1976] ECR 1213 at 1237, who reasoned as follows: European Union law owes its existence to a partial transfer of sovereignty by the Member States to the European Union; but since a Member State cannot be regarded as having included in that transfer the power to legislate contrary to rights protected by its constitution, it must be assumed that the European Union has no power to infringe rights embodied in the constitution of *any* Member State. A similar view has been expressed by Schermers, 'The European Communities Bound by Fundamental Human Rights' (1990) 27 CMLRev. 249 at 253–5. The European Court has not, however, accepted this argument.

> from the spirit of the Treaty and from the requirements of a Community which is in the process of being built up.[15]

In other words, it all depends on the policy of the European Court. If the right in question were generally accepted throughout the European Union and did not prejudice fundamental EU aims, it is probable that the Court would, as a matter of policy, accept it as a fundamental right under EU law, even if it was constitutionally protected in only one Member State. The position would be different, however, if it was controversial.

Abortion is the best example of a controversial right. The right to life of the unborn is constitutionally protected in Ireland[16] and, as a result, abortion is prohibited there.[17] The right enjoys more limited constitutional protection in Germany.[18] In many other Member States, however, the right of a pregnant woman to choose whether to give birth or have an abortion, though not constitutionally protected,[19] is strongly supported by public opinion. In these circumstances, for the European Court to accept either the right to life of the unborn or the right to choose as a fundamental right would cause intense hostility in one part of the European Union or another. The appropriate course, therefore, is to let each Member State decide for itself.

The issue came before the European Court in *SPUC v. Grogan*,[20] a case in which a private organization, the Society for the Protection of Unborn Children, brought legal proceedings before the Irish courts to prevent student unions in Ireland from publicizing the addresses of British abortion clinics. The Society based its case on the provision of the Irish Constitution upholding the right to life of the unborn.[21] The students raised a defence under EU law: they argued that abortion was a service within the terms of the Treaties and that EU law therefore prohibited Ireland from placing restrictions on the right of Irish residents to have abortions in another Member State. The European Court accepted that abortion clinics perform a service for the purpose of EU law if their activities are legal in the Member State where they are located. Subject to certain exceptions, this would normally mean that they could publicize their activities in other Member States.[22] However, the Court held that the defendants could not benefit from this right because they

[15] Mancini, 'Safeguarding Human Rights: The Role of the Court of Justice of the European Communities' (Johns Hopkins University, Bologna, Occasional Paper 62, March 1990), quoted in Phelan, 'Right to Life of the Unborn *v.* Promotion of Trade in Services: The European Court of Justice and the Normative Shaping of the European Union' (1992) 55 MLR 670 at 674.

[16] See Art. 40.3.3 of the Constitution of Ireland.

[17] There is an exception where there is a real and substantial risk to the life, as distinct from the health, of the mother.

[18] See the decision of the *Bundesverfassungsgericht* of 28 May 1993, *Entscheidungen des Bundesverfassungsgerichts* 39, 1 [44]; see Forder, 'Abortion: A Constitutional Problem in European Perspective' (1994) 1 *Maastricht Journal of European and Comparative Law* 56.

[19] The only Western country in which abortion rights are constitutionally protected appears to be the United States: see *Roe v. Wade*, 410 US 113 (1973), a case somewhat battered in recent times, but still good law.

[20] Case C-159/90, [1991] ECR I-4685.

[21] Art. 40.3.3.

[22] See *GB-INN0-BM*, Case C-362/88, [1990] ECR I-667. This case concerned free movement of goods, but the same principle probably applies to services: see para. 25 of the judgment in *SPUC v. Grogan* (see n. 20).

were not acting on behalf of the abortion clinics: they were simply trying to help their fellow students.

It was argued by the Society that abortion cannot be regarded as a service for EU purposes because it is immoral. The Court refused to accept this. It said that it could not substitute its judgment for that of the Member State in which the abortion clinics were situated. It has been criticized for this;[23] but if it had accepted the argument, it would have meant that Ireland's anti-abortion views would have been forced on other Member States: British abortion clinics would not have been entitled to benefit from EU law even when receiving patients from Member States where abortion is legal.

On the other hand, it would be equally wrong if EU law had the effect of undermining the Irish Constitution in so far as it operates in Ireland. Even if one ignores developments which took place subsequent to the judgment,[24] however, it is doubtful whether it could have this effect. If British abortion clinics had sought to advertise in Ireland in contravention of Irish law, they could have been prevented from doing so under the public policy proviso contained in Article 52 TFEU [46/56 EC].[25] Resort to the proviso would have been precluded only if the right to an abortion had been held by the European Court to constitute a fundamental human right, an unlikely eventuality.

International treaties constitute the second source of 'inspiration' for the EU concept of fundamental human rights. If an EU measure were contrary to a human right embodied in a treaty to which a Member State was a party, the Member State might be unwilling to apply the measure in its territory for fear of breaching the treaty.[26] For this reason, what was said previously regarding constitutionally protected rights applies also to rights protected by treaties.

[23] See, for example, Phelan, 'Right to Life of the Unborn *v.* Promotion of Trade in Services: The European Court of Justice and the Normative Shaping of the European Union' (1992) 55 MLR 670.

[24] A Protocol attached to the Treaty on European Union and to the Treaties establishing the European Communities subsequently provided that nothing in any of the Treaties would affect the application in Ireland of Art. 40.3.3 of the Irish Constitution (the provision on the right to life of the unborn); however, a subsequent Declaration adopted on 1 May 1992 at a meeting in Guimares, Portugal, stated, as a 'legal interpretation', that it was the intention of the Member States that this Protocol would not limit freedom to travel between Member States or, in accordance with conditions laid down in conformity with EU law by Irish legislation, freedom to obtain or make available in Ireland information relating to services lawfully available in other Member States. Following a referendum held on 25 November 1992, the Irish Constitution was amended by the addition of provisions specifying that Art. 40.3.3 did not limit freedom to travel to another State or freedom to obtain or make available (subject to such conditions as may be laid down by law) information relating to services available in other States. As a result of these developments, there is probably no longer any conflict between the Irish Constitution and EU law in this regard, provided Irish legislation concerning information on abortion services available in other Member States does not infringe EU law. This is unlikely to be the case in view of the public policy proviso in Art. 52(1) TFEU [46(1)/56(1) EC].

[25] This applies to services by virtue of Art. 62 TFEU [55/66 EC]. It allows Member States to make exceptions to EU rights on grounds of public policy. Each Member State decides its public policy for itself: *Adoui and Cornuaille*, Cases 115–16/81, [1982] ECR 1665 (para. 8 of the judgment).

[26] If the Member State became a party to the human rights treaty before it joined the European Union, it would not be obliged to apply EU law to the extent that it conflicted with the previous treaty: see Art. 351 TFEU [307/234 EC], which provides that rights and obligations arising from such treaties 'shall not be affected by the provisions of this Treaty'. This provision, which does not apply where all the other parties to the treaty are EU Member States, does not, however, require the European Union to uphold the right: it merely requires the Union not to prevent the Member State from upholding it.

The most important treaty in this respect is the European Convention for the Protection of Human Rights and Fundamental Freedoms (ECHR). All the Member States are parties to it and there is no doubt that the rights protected by it are EU human rights. The European Court has made express reference to it on a number of occasions.[27] Other treaties to which it has referred include the European Social Charter of 18 November 1961 and Convention 111 of the International Labour Organization (25 June 1958).[28]

In spite of all its efforts, the European Court's attempt to head off a revolt by the German courts was not immediately successful. In the *Internationale Handelsgesellschaft* case,[29] the German *Verwaltungsgericht* was not satisfied with the European Court's ruling and it proceeded to request a ruling from the German Constitutional Court. The Constitutional Court stated that, in the absence of a codified catalogue of human rights in EU law, it was impossible to decide whether the EU standard of human rights was adequate in terms of that laid down by the *Grundgesetz*; consequently, it was not prepared to accept the European Court's ruling as conclusive. It then examined the question itself and concluded that the EU measure in question did not violate the fundamental-rights provisions of the *Grundgesetz*. However, it affirmed the supremacy of the latter and alluded to the possibility that EU measures might be declared inapplicable in Germany if they violated these provisions. It was only in 1986, in the *Wünsche Handelsgesellschaft* case,[30] that the Constitutional Court announced that it would no longer review EU measures to ensure that they did not infringe human rights. It was content to leave this to the European Court.[31]

Attempts to enhance the protection of human rights have also been made by the political institutions of the European Union.[32] In 1976 the Commission submitted a report[33] to the European Parliament in which it expressed the belief that the best level of protection

[27] See, for example, *Rutili*, Case 36/75, [1975] ECR 1219 (what restrictions may be placed on human rights); *Hauer v. Rheinland-Pfalz*, Case 44/79, [1979] ECR 3727 (First Protocol: right to property); *Pecastaing v. Belgium*, Case 98/79, [1980] ECR 691 (Art. 6: right to a fair hearing); *Valsabbia v. Commission*, Case 154/78, [1980] ECR 907 (First Protocol); *National Panasonic v. Commission*, Case 136/79, [1980] ECR 2033 (Art. 8: privacy – respect for home and correspondence); *Musique Diffusion Française v. Commission*, Cases 100–3/80, [1983] ECR 1825 (Art. 6: right to a fair hearing); *R. v. Kirk*, Case 63/83, [1984] ECR 2689 (Art. 7: non-retroactivity of penal provisions); *Johnston v. Chief Constable of the RUC*, Case 222/84, [1986] ECR 1651 (Arts 6 and 13: right to a legal remedy); *Hoechst v. Commission*, Cases 46/87, 227/88, [1989] ECR 2859; *Dow Benelux v. Commission*, Case 85/87, [1989] ECR 3137, and *Dow Chemical Ibérica v. Commission*, Cases 97–9/87, [1989] ECR 3165 (Art. 8(1): inviolability of the home); *ERT*, Case C-260/89, [1991] ECR I-2925 (Art. 10(1): freedom of expression); *SPUC v. Grogan*, Case C-159/90, [1991] ECR I-4685 (Art. 10(1): freedom of expression); *X v. Commission*, Case C-404/92 P, [1994] ECR I-4737 (Art. 8: respect for private life – testing for AIDS).

[28] *Defrenne v. Sabena*, Case 149/77, [1978] ECR 1365 at para. 28 of the judgment.

[29] *Bundesverfassungsgericht*, 29 May 1974, [1974] 2 CMLR 540.

[30] Decision of 22 October 1986, [1987] 3 CMLR 225.

[31] During this period the Constitutional Court never actually found any provision of EU law to be contrary to the *Grundgesetz*. For a fuller discussion of these cases, see Chap. 8, § 3.

[32] For a full list of statements, declarations, and other political instruments adopted by the EU institutions and the Member States, see the European Court's Opinion in the *ECHR* case, Opinion 2/94, [1996] ECR I-1759 at 1768–9.

[33] 'The Protection of Fundamental Rights in the European Community', EC Bull., Supp. 5/76.

would be provided by the European Court through its doctrine of general principles of law, the flexibility of which would ensure that the law kept pace with changing needs. The Commission also called for a Joint Declaration by the three political institutions of the European Union (the Commission, the Council, and the European Parliament) affirming their commitment to fundamental rights; this was made in 1977.[34] In it, the three institutions stressed the importance they attached to fundamental rights, as derived in particular from the constitutions of the Member States and the ECHR, and pledged to respect them in the exercise of their powers. No attempt was made to specify the rights in question. In 1986, there was a Joint Declaration against Racism and Xenophobia[35] by the same three institutions, and in 1989 the European Parliament adopted its own Declaration of Fundamental Rights and Freedoms, which spelt out in detail the rights which the Parliament thought should be protected.[36] None of these instruments has the force of law, though it is possible that the European Court may 'draw inspiration' from them.

Subsequently, provisions on human rights were embodied in the Treaties themselves. In addition to general references to fundamental rights in the Preambles to the Single European Act and the Treaty on European Union,[37] Article 6(2) [F(2)] TEU, in its original form, expressly required the Union to respect fundamental rights as general principles of Union (Community) law. Reference was made to the ECHR and the constitutional traditions common to the Member States.

This merely restated what the European Court had decided; nevertheless, it indicated the Member States' approval and support. In addition, amendments brought in by the Treaty of Amsterdam specified that respect for human rights was a precondition for joining the European Union[38] and that a Member State which persistently disregarded them might have some of its rights under the Treaties suspended.[39]

§2.2 THE EUROPEAN CONVENTION ON HUMAN RIGHTS

In a report published in 1979, the Commission proposed that the European Union should formally adhere to the ECHR.[40] This proposal was renewed in 1990: the Commission thought it was anomalous that, while acts of the Member States were subject to scrutiny by

[34] Joint Declaration by the European Parliament, the Council and the Commission, 5 April 1977, OJ 1977, C103/1.

[35] Joint Declaration of the European Parliament, the Council and the Commission against Racism and Xenophobia, 11 June 1986, OJ 1986, C 158/1.

[36] Declaration of Fundamental Rights and Freedoms of 1989, OJ 1989, C 120/51; EC Bull. 4/1989. It is not clear from the text of the Declaration, which was adopted 'in the name of the peoples of Europe', whether the European Parliament intended that it should apply only to the European Union or whether it was also addressed to the Member States. Art. 25 provides that it applies 'in the field of application of Community [Union] law'. This suggests that it might apply to Member States, but only when they are acting within this field. If this is the case, some of its provisions – for example, Art. 23, which abolishes the death penalty – seem hardly relevant. As regards the rights covered, in addition to those usually found in such instruments, there are some of a less traditional nature – for example, the right to social welfare (Art. 15); there is also a statement (Art. 24) that consumer protection and the protection of the environment 'shall form an integral part of Community policy'.

[37] An amendment to the latter under the Treaty of Amsterdam added a reference to fundamental social rights.

[38] Arts 49 and 6(1) TEU, as they were formulated at the time. See Chap. 3, § 1.3.

[39] Arts 7 TEU and 309 EC, as they then stood. See Chap. 3, § 1.4.

[40] 'Accession of the Communities to the European Convention on Human Rights', EC Bull., Supp. 2/79.

the organs set up under the ECHR, the acts of the European Union were not. Although it recognized the value of the European Court's work in developing an EU doctrine of human rights and acknowledged that the European Court drew inspiration from the ECHR, it nevertheless felt that a danger existed that EU acts could infringe the rights protected under the ECHR, or that those rights might be interpreted in different ways by the European Court and by the European Court of Human Rights (the court set up under the ECHR).[41]

In response to this, the Council decided to ascertain from the European Court whether it was legally possible for the European Union to become a party to the ECHR. An Opinion was sought under the procedure laid down in Article 218 TFEU [300/228 EC], a procedure which will be explained in Chapter 6, § 3.[42]

In its Opinion, the Court ruled that the European Union had no power to accede to the ECHR without an amendment to the Treaties.[43] The grounds of the decision will be discussed in Chapter 6, § 2.3; all that need be said here is that the Court's ruling, while not unjustifiable, was remarkable for its detached and sober analysis of the law: the Court's normal enthusiasm for expanding the powers of the European Union was conspicuous by its absence. It seems that it did not relish the prospect of a rival court – the European Court of Human Rights – having the final word on human rights in the European Union.[44]

This decision constituted a setback for those who wanted the European Union to join the ECHR. When the proposed Constitution of the EU was drawn up, it contained the necessary provision; but this fell by the wayside when the Constitution was rejected. Finally, more than thirty years after the idea was first put forward, the Treaty of Lisbon gave the go-ahead: as amended, Article 6(2) TEU provides for the European Union to accede to the ECHR.

The European Union then applied to join the Human Rights Convention. As the Union is not a State (or a member of the Council of Europe, the parent body of the ECHR), the Convention had to be modified to permit its accession.[45] In addition, the special requirements of the Union had to be accommodated. Negotiations began soon after the Treaty of Lisbon entered into force, and in 2013 a draft Accession Agreement was drawn up.[46] This will now have to go to the European Court to obtain its approval.[47] If this is given, the text will have to be adopted by unanimity in the Council, and the

41 See Press Release IP (90) 892, 31 October 1990.

42 For further discussion, see the House of Lords Select Committee on the European Communities, 71st Report, *Human Rights* (HL 362, 1979/80); see also McBride and Brown, 'The United Kingdom, the European Community and the European Convention on Human Rights' (1981) 1 YEL 167.

43 Opinion 2/94, [1996] ECR I-1759.

44 For a discussion of this decision, see Toth, 'The European Union and Human Rights: The Way Forward' (1997) 34 CMLRev. 491.

45 See Protocol No. 14 (in force on 1 June 2010), which amends Art. 59 of the ECHR to allow the European Union to accede to it.

46 See *Fifth Negotiation Meeting between the CDDH Ad Hoc Negotiation Group and the European Commission on the Accession of the European Union to the European Convention on Human Rights (Final Report to the CDDH)*, Council of Europe document 47+1(2013)008rev2, Strasbourg, 10 June 2013.

47 The European Court and the European Court of Human Rights have themselves held a series of discussions, the fruits of which were set out in a joint communication by the presidents of the two courts (24 January

consent of the European Parliament will have to be obtained. After this, the Agreement will have to be approved by each Member State in accordance with its constitutional requirements.[48] Only then will it go into force.

One of the major problems in the negotiations was how responsibility for violations of the Convention would be divided between the European Union and its Member States. The principle is easy enough to state: the Union should be responsible for violations within its sphere of competence and the Member States should be responsible for violations within theirs. The difficulty is that the line of demarcation between these two spheres is by no means easy to draw. Since only the European Court can authoritatively rule where it should be drawn in any particular case, the European Court of Human Rights could find itself in a difficult situation if the victim of an alleged human rights violation brought proceedings in the European Court of Human Rights against an EU Member State, and it was argued by that State that it was not liable because the matter fell within the competence of the Union.

This problem would be especially acute if the alleged infringement was an act of a Member State, but the Member State was obliged to do what it did by virtue of EU law.[49] The problem would also occur where an Article in one of the constitutive Treaties of the Union was claimed to be contrary to human rights. The proceedings might be brought against the Union; however, since the Treaties are acts of the Member States, the Union is not responsible for what they contain, nor could it strike down or amend the offending provision. Only the Member States could do that.

The draft Accession Agreement of 2013 solves the problem by proposing that the Convention should be amended to introduce a new concept – that of a 'co-respondent'.[50] A co-respondent will be a party to the proceedings and will be bound by the judgment. If the proceedings are brought against an EU Member State, the European

2011); see also *Discussion Document of the Court of Justice of the European Union on Certain Aspects of the Accession of the European Union to the European Convention for the Protection of Human Rights and Fundamental Freedoms* (5 May 2010). Both documents are available at http://curia.europa.eu/jcms/jcms/P_64268/. The most important concern of the European Court seems to be to ensure that, where an EU measure is challenged on human rights grounds, the matter should come to it before going to the ECtHR: see paras 9 and 12 of the *Discussion Document*. This is presumably to give the European Court the opportunity to pronounce on the correct interpretation of the measure.

48 The Accession Agreement will also have to be approved by the European Court of Human Rights and by the Parliamentary Assembly of the Council of Europe.

49 This is a problem which has arisen in the past: can a State Party to the Convention avoid liability by saying that it was obliged to act as it did by reason of a treaty which it concluded with other States? For the often inconsistent rulings given by the (old) Human Rights Commission and the European Court of Human Rights, see: the *CFDT* (*Confédération Française Démocratique du Travail*) case, Application No. 8030/77, Decision of 10 July 1978, 13 Decisions and Reports 213 (European Commission of Human Rights); *M & Co.*, Application No. 13258/87, Decision of 2 February 1990, 64 Decisions and Reports 138; *Matthews v. United Kingdom* (1999) 28 EHRR 361 (discussed in Chapter 3, § 4.3); *Bosphorus Hava Yollari Turizm Ve Ticaret Anonim Sirketi v. Ireland*[49] [2006] 42 EHRR 1 (30 June 2005) (the key reasoning is in paras 149–58); *MSS v. Belgium and Greece*, 21 January 2011 (appeal 30696/09) (Grand Chamber). The judgment in the *Matthews* case put the United Kingdom in a difficult situation, since it required the UK to act against a provision of EU law which probably has treaty status in the EU legal system. Luckily, the European Court took an indulgent view: *Spain v. United Kingdom*, Case C-145/04, [2006] ECR I-7917 (Grand Chamber).

50 See Art. 3 of the Accession Agreement, amending Art. 36 of the Convention.

Union will be able to become a co-respondent if the claim raises the question whether a provision of Union law is contrary to the Convention. This would apply in particular where the alleged violation of the Convention is an act of a Member State which was required by Union law. Where proceedings are brought against the European Union, a Member State of the Union could become a co-respondent if the claim raises the question whether a provision of one of the constitutive Treaties[51] is compatible with the Convention. Under this system, the European Court of Human Rights could give judgment against both parties – respondent and co-respondent – and the division of liability between them could be resolved elsewhere.

Article 6 TEU, after providing (in paragraph 2) for the European Union to accede to the ECHR, goes on to state (in paragraph 3) that fundamental rights, as guaranteed by the ECHR, and as they result from the constitutional traditions common to the Member States, constitute general principles of EU law. This makes clear that the work of the European Court over the last forty years in building up an EU concept of human rights will not be lost once the Union joins the ECHR. So, in future there will be two foundations on which EU human rights law will rest: general principles of law and the ECHR as a binding instrument. In fact, there is a third foundation: the European Union's own Charter of Fundamental Rights. This will be discussed later, in § 2.3. The significance of all this is that the European Union's accession to the ECHR will not entail any diminution of human rights protection in the Union: the European Court will be able, if it wishes, to use the concept of general principles of law (and the Charter) to go further than the European Court of Human Rights. So, in theory at least, the Union should enjoy the best of both worlds.

§2.3 THE CHARTER OF FUNDAMENTAL RIGHTS

On 7 December 2000, the European Parliament, the Council, and the Commission 'solemnly proclaimed' the Charter of Fundamental Rights of the European Union, the European Union's own human rights text.[52] Originally, the Charter had no legal force, but this was changed by the Treaty of Lisbon: Article 6(1) TEU now gives the Charter the same legal value as the EU Treaties. Since then, the Charter has been frequently cited by the European Court.

The existence of two human rights texts could create problems, since the Charter, though similar to the ECHR, goes beyond it in a number of ways – for example, it gives protection (more extensive in some cases than in others) to various rights of a social nature. These include the right to education (Article 14), the right to engage in work (Article 15), the rights of the elderly (Article 25), the right of access to a free placement service (for job seekers) (Article 29), and the right of access to health care (Article 35).

[51] The actual words of Art. 3 of the Accession Agreement refer to the TEU, the TFEU, or 'any other provision having the same legal value pursuant to those instruments'.

[52] OJ 2000, C 364.

To prevent a clash, it was provided in Article 52(3) of the Charter:

> In so far as this Charter contains rights which correspond to rights guaranteed by the Convention for the Protection of Human Rights and Fundamental Freedoms, the meaning and scope of those rights shall be the same as those laid down by the said Convention. This provision shall not prevent Union law providing more extensive protection.

This makes clear that where the Charter covers the same rights as the Convention, the interpretation and scope of those rights as laid down by the Human Rights Court will also apply to the Charter. To this extent, the Charter will add nothing to the Convention. However, the final sentence of Article 52(3) allows the European Court to give more extensive protection to the rights in question than the Human Rights Court, even though it cannot alter their content. Moreover, Article 52(3) does not apply to rights that find no counterpart in the Convention. In the case of these rights, the European Court will have unfettered power to determine their meaning and scope.

Since the EU Treaties themselves contain provisions for the protection of certain human rights, there could also be a clash between the Charter and the Treaties. To solve this, Article 52(2) provides that rights recognized by the Charter which are based on the EU Treaties must be exercised under the conditions and within the limits defined by those Treaties.

§2.4 DO EU HUMAN RIGHTS BIND THE MEMBER STATES?

In all the cases considered so far, human rights have been applied by the European Court against the European Union, either to interpret or strike down EU measures. To what extent is the EU concept of human rights binding on the Member States? For a long time, the answer appeared to be that it had no direct application at all.[53] It has now become clear, however, that there are a number of situations in which EU law requires Member States to respect human rights (and possibly other general principles of EU law).

First, and most obviously, Member States will be indirectly bound by the EU concept of human rights whenever that concept is used to interpret provisions in the Treaties or EU legislation. This has always been the case. Secondly, where such a provision grants rights to individuals, but those rights are subject to a proviso allowing derogations on grounds such as public policy,[54] any derogations thus made by the national Governments must not violate the EU concept of human rights.[55]

Thirdly, when Member States implement EU rules – for example, by passing legislation – they are bound by human rights as understood in EU law.[56]

[53] See *Defrenne v. Sabena*, Case 149/77, [1978] ECR 1365. For unsuccessful attempts prior to the Human Rights Act to invoke the ECHR in the British courts on the ground that it was part of EU law, see *Allgemeine Gold und Silberscheideanstalt v. Commissioners of Customs and Excise* [1978] 2 CMLR 292, affirmed [1980] QB 390 (CA); *Surjit Kaur v. Lord Advocate* [1980] 3 CMLR 79 (Court of Session). See further Drzemczewski, 'The Domestic Application of the European Human Rights Convention as European Law' (1981) 30 ICLQ 118.

[54] Such provisos are numerous in the Treaties.

[55] *ERT*, Case C-260/89, [1991] ECR I-2925 (para. 43 of the judgment); see also *Rutili v. Minister of the Interior*, Case 36/75, [1975] ECR 1219 (paras 31 and 32 of the judgment). The European Court has no power to strike down national legislation, but if it ruled that such legislation was contrary to EU law, the national court would be bound by such a ruling.

[56] *Wachauf*, Case 5/88, [1989] ECR 2609 (para. 19 of the judgment). It is not clear whether national implementing legislation must be struck down by the national courts if it infringes human rights, or merely that it

In addition to these rules, there are *dicta* by the European Court that Member States are also bound by the EU concept of human rights whenever they act within the scope of EU law. The Court has said that, when national legislation enters the field of application of EU law, the European Court must provide the national court with all the elements of interpretation necessary to enable the latter to assess the compatibility of the legislation with fundamental rights.[57] The implication is that the national court will be obliged to strike down, or not to apply, the national legislation if it fails the test. This could occur in those areas where national legislation is permitted only if justified under principles laid down by EU law.[58] In areas outside the scope of EU law, on the other hand, Member States are not bound by the EU concept of human rights.[59]

When the EU Charter of Fundamental Rights was adopted, there were fears on the part of some Member States (especially the United Kingdom) that it would indirectly extend the scope of EU human rights law and impose it on the Member States. These fears were addressed in Article 51(1) of the Charter, which provides:

> The provisions of this Charter are addressed to the institutions and bodies of the Union with due regard for the principle of subsidiarity and to the Member States only when they are implementing Union law.

This makes clear that the Charter does not apply to the Member States, except when they are implementing EU law. In addition, Article 51(2) states that the Charter does not establish any new power or task for the Union, or modify powers and tasks defined by the Treaties. So the giving of legal effect to the Charter is unlikely to extend the scope of EU human rights law with regard to the Member States.

§2.5 HUMAN RIGHTS AS A JUSTIFICATION FOR INFRINGING EU LAW

Can human rights constitute a justification for what would otherwise be an infringement of EU law? This question first arose in *Schmidberger v. Austria*,[60] in which

must, if possible, be interpreted so as not to infringe human rights. The European Court said in the *Wachauf* case that Member States must 'as far as possible' apply EU rules in accordance with the requirements of human rights, a formulation repeated in *Bostock*, Case C-2/92, [1994] ECR I-955 (para. 16 of the judgment). This might suggest that the second alternative is correct. Of course, if the national implementing legislation was based on an incorrect interpretation of the EU rule, it might be invalid as a matter of national law.

[57] *ERT* (see n. 55) (at para. 42 of the judgment); *SPUC v. Grogan*, Case C-159/90, [1991] ECR I-4685 (at para. 31 of the judgment).

[58] In *Konstantinidis*, Case C-168/91, [1993] ECR I-1191 at 1211–13, it was argued by Advocate General Jacobs that, where the victim is an immigrant from another EU country, *any* infringement of human rights is a matter for EU law: his reason was that EU citizens would be less willing to move to another Member State if their human rights might be infringed there. The Court did not, however, accept this argument.

[59] This was expressly stated in the *dicta* in *ERT* (see n. 55) and *SPUC v. Grogan* (see n. 57). See also *Demirel*, Case 12/86, [1987] ECR 3719 at para. 28 of the judgment; *Kremzow*, Case C-299/95, [1997] ECR I-2629. However, a Member State which persistently disregards human rights may have some of its rights under the Treaties suspended: Arts 7 TEU, 354 TFEU [309 EC] (discussed in Chap. 3, § 1.4).

[60] Case C-112/00, [2003] ECR I-5659.

environmentalists had blocked a vital motorway through the Austrian Alps as part of a protest against pollution caused by the heavy trucks moving along it. The organizers gave the Austrian authorities advance notice of the demonstration, which lasted approximately thirty hours. The authorities decided not to ban the demonstration. They considered that it constituted a legitimate exercise of the rights of free expression and free assembly as guaranteed by the ECHR and the Austrian Constitution.

Schmidberger, a German company which carried goods between Germany and Italy on the motorway, claimed that the demonstration infringed its rights under EU law. It sued the Austrian Government for damages in an Austrian court, arguing that the Government was responsible. On a reference to the European Court, the latter held that free movement of goods is a basic EU right that must be protected by Member States. This meant that the Austrian Government would incur liability for its failure to keep the motorway open, unless it could show that its decision was justified. The right of free movement of goods is not absolute under EU law, but must be balanced against other considerations. The right of free expression must also be balanced against other interests. The Court held that, in balancing the two rights, the national Government has a wide measure of discretion. Since the Austrian Government had taken all reasonable steps to minimize disruption – the closure was widely publicized in advance and alternative routes designated – the Court held that no infringement of EU law had occurred.

The important point to note is the wide measure of discretion enjoyed by national Governments. The Court did not say that it considered the closure of the motorway to be justified, but rather that the decision of the national Government fell within the latter's area of discretion.

This was made even clearer in a later case. In *Omega*,[61] the German authorities had prohibited a German company from operating an establishment, known as a 'laserdrome', in which participants played at killing other participants by shooting them with lasers. The lasers were supplied by a British company, with which the German company had concluded a franchise agreement, thus raising issues of EU law. The German authorities had closed the 'laserdrome' on human rights grounds: they considered simulated killing an affront to human dignity, a principle enshrined in the German Constitution. The European Court accepted this justification, even though similar establishments operate freely in other Member States.

§2.6 HUMAN RIGHTS LAW MEETS INTERNATIONAL LAW

Since human rights law is, to a significant extent, derived from international law, it might be thought that international law would be especially favourable to human rights. Unfortunately, this is not always the case. Treaties – including human rights instruments such as the ECHR – are the outcome of the political forces operating at a particular time among the States in question. These may be either favourable or unfavourable to

[61] Case C-36/02, [2004] ECR I-9609.

human rights. When the ECHR was adopted, they were favourable – at least, in Europe. However, things can change.

Such a change occurred when Muslim fundamentalists attacked various targets in the United States on 11 September 2001. This had severe repercussions on the entire world system. Not only was the United States the most powerful country in the world, with many allies and client States, but none of the major powers had any reason to be sympathetic towards fundamentalist Islam. These included all the permanent members of the UN Security Council – the United States itself, Britain and France (both American allies), and China and Russia (both having problems of their own with Muslim minorities). So when the United States asked the Security Council to take harsh measures against Islamists, the others were ready to agree. Moreover, they were not disposed to allow human rights to stand in the way.

They adopted a Resolution[62] designed to ensure that the assets of persons or organizations deemed sympathetic to Islamic terrorism were frozen. A committee of the Security Council was established to draw up lists of such persons and organizations. The suspects were not allowed to defend themselves; indeed, they were not even told their names were under consideration. It is not entirely clear on what basis names were put on the list, but it seems to have been done on the say-so of major Governments. The evidence was not made public. It may have been obtained under torture; it may have been obtained from persons with a grudge against the person concerned; or it may have rested simply on a hunch. We have no way of knowing. However, once a person's name was on the list, all States were required to freeze that person's assets.[63]

The victims of this procedure were eventually given the right to make representations to the Security Council committee through their national Governments, but it was not easy for them to prove their innocence, since they were never told the grounds on which they were adjudged to be guilty. Moreover, the committee acted more on a political basis than a legal basis, and a decision to remove a name from the list could be vetoed by any member of the committee. The end result was that, in this instance, international law was the enemy of human rights, not its friend.

At this point, the European Union became involved. Since the fight against terrorism fell under the Common Foreign and Security Policy (CFSP), the matter was first dealt with in this context. Common Positions were adopted calling for action. These were put into effect by EU regulations requiring Member States to freeze the assets of all persons and organizations on the Security Council list.

One such person was Mr Kadi, who lived in Saudi Arabia but had assets in Sweden. He brought proceedings under what was then Article 230 EC (now Article 263 TFEU) to annul the relevant EU regulation in so far as it applied to him. He put forward various grounds including infringement of his human rights, in particular the right to a fair trial and the right to property.

[62] Resolution 1267 of 1999. This was the first of a series of Resolutions.

[63] In order to demonstrate its humanity, the Security Council made it possible for the victims to apply to the relevant national Government for permission to obtain the release from their bank accounts or savings accounts of enough money to buy food and other necessities.

The proceedings came before the General Court (then called the 'Court of First Instance').[64] It dismissed the action on the ground that, under international law, obligations imposed by the UN Security Council are binding on all UN Members,[65] and override all other obligations, including obligations under treaties past, present, or future.[66] So, in the event of a conflict between their obligations under a Security Council Resolution and their obligations under the EU Treaties (including EU human rights obligations), they are obliged under international law to give priority to the former.[67] Although the European Union is not itself bound by the Security Council Resolutions under international law – it is not a Member of the UN – it nevertheless cannot require the Member States to do anything contrary to their obligations under the UN Charter: the Member States became Parties to the UN Charter before the EU Treaties;[68] so the first paragraph of what was then Article 307 EC (now Article 351 TFEU, discussed in Chapter 3, § 4.2) requires the Union not to prevent the Member States from fulfilling their obligations under the Security Council Resolution.

This judgment was reversed by the European Court,[69] which asserted the independence of the EU legal system from international law, ruling that EU law has its own hierarchy of norms (rules as to which instrument prevails in the event of a conflict) (see Chapter 3, § 4.4). In a robust statement of principle, it declared:[70]

> ... the obligations imposed by an international agreement cannot have the effect of prejudicing the constitutional principles of the EC Treaty [now the TFEU], which include the principle that all Community [Union] acts must respect fundamental rights, that respect constituting a condition of their lawfulness which it is for the Court to review in the framework of the complete system of legal remedies established by the Treaty.

This demolished the arguments on which the General Court had based its judgment.

The European Court then considered whether the contested EU regulation should be annulled. It held that the EU authority in question should have communicated to the persons concerned the grounds on which their names had been included in the list so that they could, within the time limits laid down by EU law, decide whether to bring legal proceedings and, if they did, to be in a position to make an effective challenge.[71] The fact that their names were already on the Security Council list did not affect the matter, since they had not been given a hearing by the Security Council or its committee. The European Court accepted that security considerations placed limitations

[64] *Kadi v. Council and Commission ('Kadi I')*, Case T-315/01, [2005] ECR II-3649.

[65] Arts 41 and 48(2) of the UN Charter.

[66] Art. 103 of the UN Charter. All EU Member States are Members of the UN.

[67] There was an exception to this (*jus cogens*) but the General Court held that this did not apply in the present case.

[68] Germany was an exception, but its duty to carry out its obligations under the Charter followed from certain other international agreements that predated the EC Treaty.

[69] *Kadi v. Council and Commission ('Kadi I')*, Cases C-402/05 P and 415/05 P, [2008] ECR I-6351.

[70] Para. 285 of the judgment.

[71] The ECJ said that the persons concerned do not have to be informed before their names are put on the list because they might take steps to frustrate the measure. They must, however, be told as soon as possible afterwards.

on what the applicants could be told, but this did not mean that measures of this kind could escape all review. The EU court before which proceedings are brought could apply techniques which accommodate, on the one hand, legitimate security concerns about the nature and sources of information taken into account in the adoption of the act concerned and, on the other, the need to accord the individual a sufficient measure of procedural justice.[72] Since none of this had happened, the contested regulation was annulled in so far as it concerned the applicants.

However, since grounds might nevertheless exist to justify the measures, the European Court suspended the annulment for a limited period.

The UN Sanctions Committee then provided a document setting out its 'reasons' for putting Mr Kadi on the list. This contained no evidence, but consisted solely of vague and unsubstantiated allegations. It was passed to the Commission, which gave it to Mr Kadi. He was invited to put his case. Mr Kadi asked to see the evidence against him. The Commission showed him no evidence, probably because it had none.

The Commission then took measures to continue the sanctions against him. In 2010, the General Court annulled the relevant regulation in so far as it applied to Mr Kadi.[73] This was affirmed by the European Court in 2013, shortly after the Sanctions Committee had itself removed Mr Kadi from the list.[74] So in the end, justice prevailed – at least, as far as Mr Kadi was concerned.

§3 LEGAL CERTAINTY

Legal certainty – sometimes referred to as 'legal security' (*sécurité juridique*, in French) – is another important principle. It is a wide concept which cannot easily be explained in a few words, though predictability is probably the core aspect of it. The general idea of legal certainty is of course recognized by most legal systems; however, in EU law it plays a much more concrete role in the form of various sub-concepts which are regarded as applications of it. The most important of these are non-retroactivity, vested rights, and legitimate expectations.

§3.1 RETROACTIVITY AND VESTED RIGHTS

'Retroactivity' is a term often used by lawyers but rarely defined. On analysis it soon becomes apparent that it is used to cover at least two distinct concepts. The first, which may be called 'true retroactivity', consists in the application of a new rule of law to an act or transaction which was completed before the rule came into force. The second concept, which will be referred to as 'quasi-retroactivity', occurs when a new rule of law

[72] See para. 344 of the judgment. For the subsequent application of these principles to proceedings in Member State courts, see *ZZ*, Case C-300/11, 4 June 2013 (Grand Chamber).

[73] *Kadi v. Commission ('Kadi II')*, Case T-85/09, [2010] ECR II-5177.

[74] *Commission v. Kadi ('Kadi II')*, Case C-584/10 P (18 July 2013) (Grand Chamber).

is applied to an act or transaction in the process of completion.[75] Since the foundation of these concepts is the distinction between completed and pending transactions, it will be useful to give examples of each.

As the first example one may take a law imposing a customs duty on imported goods. Let us assume that the obligation to pay arises when the goods cross the frontier. Now, if a law is passed increasing the duty and it is provided that the new duty will apply to goods which crossed the frontier before the new law came into force, this will be a case of true retroactivity. Assume, however, that the new duty applies only to goods crossing the frontier after the law comes into force but it applies even if the importer was legally committed to import them before it came into force, for example by virtue of a contract. This will be a case of quasi-retroactivity.

As a second example one may take the granting of a licence by a public authority to a private citizen. If, after it has been granted, the authority withdraws it in circumstances such that the licensee is deemed never to have had a licence, one would have a case of true retroactivity. However, if it is withdrawn only for the future, but the withdrawal takes place before the expiration of its period of validity, one could say that this was a case of quasi-retroactivity.

These examples will make clear that true retroactivity can often cause severe injustice to the individual. In both examples given, one would say that the action of the public authority was unacceptable in the absence of special circumstances. In the case of quasi-retroactivity, the injustice is much less; but nevertheless it could be quite considerable in some circumstances. The importer might have calculated his profit margins on the assumption that the rate of duty would remain constant and he might face a loss if he is obliged to absorb the new duty. Likewise, the licensee might have committed himself to a capital outlay on the assumption that the licence would remain in force for its stated period of validity. In both cases of quasi-retroactivity, however, the injustice lies not so much in the fact of retroactivity as in the fact that the legitimate expectations of the person concerned have been upset. This will occur if he had reasonable grounds for assuming that the legal position would remain unchanged and he acted to his detriment on that assumption.

The concept of vested rights is normally no more than another aspect of retroactivity. A provision which destroys vested rights will usually be retroactive in the strict sense: in fact, one could say that one test of whether a law is truly retroactive is whether it affects vested rights. The problem with this formulation, however, is that it raises two very difficult questions: what constitutes a right for this purpose, and when such a right should be regarded as vested.[76]

[75] See *per* Advocate General Roemer in *Westzucker*, Case 1/73, [1973] ECR 723 at 739. See also *Gardner & Co v. Cone* [1928] Ch. 995, *per* Maugham J. at 966. See further Letemendia, 'La rétroactivité en droit communautaire' (1977) 13 CDE 518 at 518–19.

[76] See, for example, in *Westzucker*, Case 1/73, [1973] ECR 723, where it could be argued that, when Westzucker obtained an advance fixing certificate subject to the condition that the amount of the export refund would automatically be adjusted if the intervention price changed, he obtained a vested right to an increased refund in the event of an increase in the intervention price; the better view, however, is that the right was not vested until either the intervention price was increased or he actually exported the sugar.

In EU law, there are two rules on true retroactivity: first, there is a rule of interpretation that, in the absence of a clear provision, legislation is presumed not to be retroactive;[77] secondly, there is a substantive rule that prohibits retroactivity in general, but allows exceptions where the purpose of the measure could not otherwise be achieved, provided the legitimate expectations of those concerned are respected.[78]

An example of the first rule is provided by *Société pour l'Exportation des Sucres v. Commission*,[79] where the Commission had passed a regulation taking away the right of exporters to obtain cancellation of their export licences. The regulation was made on 30 June 1976 and was published in an issue of the Official Journal which was dated 1 July 1976 and which should have been published on that date. However, it was delayed by a strike and appeared only on 2 July. On 1 July the applicant applied for the cancellation of certain licences, but this was refused on the basis of the regulation. The Court, however, interpreted the regulation as coming into force only on the date of actual publication (2 July), so that it did not apply to the applicant. This ruling was given in spite of the fact that the regulation expressly stated that it would enter into force on 1 July: the Court presumably considered that the Commission would not have included this provision if it had known that publication would be delayed; in other words, there was no intention to apply the regulation retroactively.

Amylum v. Council[80] is an example of the second rule. Here, a regulation imposing a system of quotas and levies on producers of isoglucose (a kind of sugar) had been annulled in previous proceedings because the European Parliament had not been consulted. The Council then passed another regulation (after consulting the Parliament) which reimposed the system with retroactive effect. Proceedings were brought to annul the new regulation, but the Court held that the requirements for retroactivity had been met: the purpose of the regulation was to ensure that isoglucose producers were subject to the same production system as other sugar producers and this would not be the case if the regulation were not backdated; the legitimate expectations of the isoglucose producers had been respected since, in the circumstances of the case, they had good reason to expect the retrospective reimposition of the system. The regulation was therefore upheld.[81]

[77] See *Kalsbeek v. Sociale Verzekeringsbank*, Case 100/63, [1964] ECR 565 at 575; *per* Advocate General Mayras in *Commission v. Germany*, Case 70/72, [1973] ECR 813 at 844; and *per* Advocate General Warner in *IRCA*, Case 7/76, [1976] ECR 1213 at 1237–9. This principle does not apply to procedural provisions: *Salumi*, Cases 212–17/80, [1981] ECR 2735.

[78] *Amylum v. Council*, Case 108/81, [1982] ECR 3107 at paras 4–17 of the judgment; *Racke*, Case 98/78, [1979] ECR 69 at para. 20; *Rewe-Zentrale des Lebensmittel-Großhandels*, Case 37/70, [1971] ECR 23, paras 17–19. See also *per* Advocate General Roemer in *Westzucker*, Case 1/73, [1973] ECR 723 at 739; *IRCA*, Case 7/76, [1976] ECR 1213, where the Court held that true retroactivity was not involved at all, but the Advocate General considered that it was.

[79] Case 88/76, [1977] ECR 709.

[80] Case 108/81, [1982] ECR 3107.

[81] This decision is not without disquieting implications, not least because it established the validity of a regulation which entirely nullified the effect of the Court's judgment in the earlier case.

§3.2 LEGITIMATE EXPECTATIONS

The principle of legitimate expectations is a concept derived from German law, where it is known as *Vertrauensschutz.* This was originally translated into English as 'protection of legitimate confidence', a phrase which corresponds more closely to the original German and to the French '*protection de la confiance légitime*'. It was, however, thought that this might be misleading in English; so 'legitimate expectations' is now generally used.[82] According to this principle, EU measures must not (in the absence of an overriding matter of public interest) violate the legitimate expectations of those concerned. It is the foundation of a rule of interpretation[83] as well as a ground for annulment of an EU measure;[84] most often, however, it is used as the basis for an action for damages for non-contractual liability (tort).

What constitutes a legitimate expectation? In answering this, a number of points must be considered. First of all, an expectation is not legitimate unless it is reasonable: the question here is whether a prudent person would have had the expectation. In deciding this, one must take all the circumstances into account: for example, in the case of a measure affecting grain dealers, one must ask whether a prudent dealer of reasonable knowledge and experience would have relied on the expectation; if he would not, the expectation is not legitimate.[85]

There is also a rule that if the person concerned was not acting in the normal course of business but was trying to take advantage of a weakness in the EU system to make a speculative profit, his expectations should not be regarded as legitimate: he should realize that the authorities will take the swiftest possible action to plug the loophole. This is well illustrated by *EVGF v. Mackprang*,[86] a case concerned with the intervention system for grain, under which the intervention agencies were obliged to buy grain at the intervention price. Grain could be offered to the intervention agencies in different places and there was usually no advantage to the seller in choosing one rather than another. Normally the product would be offered at the marketing centre nearest to where it was produced. However, in early 1969 there was a fall in the forward rate for the French franc in anticipation of its devaluation, and it became profitable for German grain dealers to buy grain in France in order to resell it to the German intervention agency, the EVGF. This threatened to exhaust the agency's storage capacity and bring about a collapse of the intervention system in Germany. To meet this threat, the Commission adopted a decision authorizing the German Government to confine intervention purchases of wheat and barley to German-grown products. The decision

[82] See Usher, 'The Influence of National Concepts on Decisions of the European Court' (1976) 1 ELRev. 359 at 363.

[83] *Deuka v. EVGF*, Case 78/74, [1975] ECR 421, a case where, as in *Société pour l'Exportation des Sucres v. Commission*, Case 88/76, [1977] ECR 709, the Court adopted a strained interpretation of the provision in order to protect the rights of the persons concerned without having to annul the measure.

[84] See *Töpfer v. Commission*, Case 112/77, [1978] ECR 1019.

[85] See, for example, *Union Nationale des Coopératives Agricoles de Céréales*, Cases 95–8/74, 15, 100/75, [1975] ECR 1615; *Union Malt*, Cases 44–51/77, [1978] ECR 57; and *Lührs*, Case 78/77, [1978] ECR 169.

[86] Case 2/75, [1975] ECR 607.

was made on 8 May and came into force on the same day; it expressly stated that it would not apply to cereals offered to the agency before it came into force.

Mackprang was a German grain dealer who had bought wheat in France with the object of importing it into Germany and selling it to the German agency. On 8 May most of the wheat was aboard ships and barges in transit to Germany and Mackprang could not make a valid offer of this wheat because there was a rule that grain could not validly be offered while it was still in transit. When it did arrive, the agency refused to buy it and Mackprang brought proceedings in the German courts claiming that he had had a legitimate expectation, when he bought the grain and arranged for shipment, that he would be able to sell it to the agency.

However, when a reference to the European Court was made, it was pointed out by Advocate General Warner that the importation of the wheat was not part of normal EU trade but was a speculative transaction of a kind which the EU provisions setting up the system had not been designed to assist. It was possible to profit from transactions of this kind only in an abnormal situation such as that resulting from the fall of the French franc. Advocate General Warner then continued:[87]

> No trader who was exploiting that situation in order to make out of the system profits that the system was never designed to bestow on him could legitimately rely on the persistence of the situation. On the contrary, the only reasonable expectation that such a trader could have was that the competent authorities would act as swiftly as possible to bring the situation to an end.

This view was accepted by the Court, which stated that the application of the Commission decision to cereals in transit to Germany was not an infringement of the principle of legitimate expectations but 'a justified precaution against purely speculative activities.'[88]

Where the principle of protection of legitimate expectations is used as the foundation for an action for damages, the applicant must prove not only that he had an expectation which was legitimate in the previously mentioned sense, but also that he acted in reliance on it and suffered loss as a result of the EU measure. He will then be able to obtain damages under Article 340, paragraph 2 TFEU [288/215, paragraph 2 EC], unless the EU measure is justifiable by reason of an overriding matter of public interest. The leading case on this is *CNTA v. Commission*,[89] which is considered in detail in Chapter 16, § 4.3.

One of the best examples of the protection of legitimate expectations is a case which at first sight appears not to involve retroactivity. This is *Commission v. Council* (first *Staff Salaries* case),[90] where the Commission brought proceedings against the Council because it felt that the latter had not given Union staff a sufficient increase in pay. Staff pay was governed by Article 65 of the Staff Regulations which provided for an annual review of staff salaries by the Council in the light of a report prepared by the Commission. In determining the level of pay, the Council was required to take a

[87] [1975] ECR 607 at 623. [88] At para. 4 of the judgment. [89] Case 74/74, [1975] ECR 533.
[90] Case 81/72, [1973] ECR 575.

number of factors into account, including inflation and salary increases in the public services of the Member States. In the past, serious friction had arisen as a result of disagreement as to how these factors should be measured. Protracted negotiations then took place between the Council, the Commission, and the staff associations, and a formula was eventually devised to settle the matter. This formula was embodied in a Council decision made in March 1972 and was stated to be applicable for a period of three years. When the next salary increase took place, however, the Council laid down new scales which the Commission regarded as being in breach of the formula.

The Court had to decide whether the decision containing the pay formula was legally binding on the Council. The Advocate General took the view that it was not, since a similar decision would not, in his opinion, be binding in the national legal systems. The Court, however, decided that the decision was binding. It held that, in view of the employer–employee relationship between the Council and the staff, the latter had a reasonable expectation that the Council would abide by its undertaking regarding the formula. The new pay scales were, therefore, invalid in so far as they conflicted with it.

§3.3 REVOCATION OF DECISIONS

The principle of legal certainty also imposes limits on the extent to which an individual legal act (decision) may be withdrawn. If it is lawful and valid, it may never be withdrawn retroactively, and may not be withdrawn prospectively if it provides otherwise (for example, a decision appointing a person to a post until retirement age).[91] If it is unlawful, it may always be revoked prospectively;[92] whether it may be revoked retrospectively depends on various considerations which involve balancing the public interest in legality against the private interest in legal certainty;[93] unreasonable delay on the part of the EU authority may also be a factor.[94]

§4 PROPORTIONALITY

As we have seen (Chapter 4, § 5), proportionality has now been embodied in the EU Treaties; however, it was originally developed by the European Court as a general principle of law. It is also an import from Germany, where it is called *Verhältnismässigkeit* and it is regarded as underlying certain provisions of the German Constitution. Its constitutional aspect has already been mentioned in connection with fundamental human rights, and it was in the *Internationale Handelsgesellschaft* case (discussed in

[91] *Algera v. Common Assembly*, Cases 7/56, 3–7/57, [1957] ECR 39.

[92] See *Algera* (n. 91); see also *Simon v. Court of Justice*, Case 15/60, [1961] ECR 115; *Elz v. Commission*, Case 56/75, [1976] ECR 1097; and *Herpels v. Commission*, Case 54/77, [1978] ECR 585 (at para. 38 of the judgment).

[93] *SNUPAT v. High Authority*, Cases 42, 49/59, [1961] ECR 53; *Hoogovens v. High Authority*, Case 14/61, [1962] ECR 253; *Lemmerz-Werke v. High Authority*, Case 111/63, [1965] ECR 677.

[94] *Consorzio Cooperative d'Abruzzo v. Commission*, Case 15/85, [1987] ECR 1005.

§ 2.1) that it first made an impact on EU law, though some earlier cases could be said to have applied it in a somewhat broader sense.[95]

According to the principle of proportionality, a public authority may not impose obligations on a citizen except to the extent to which they are strictly necessary in the public interest to attain the purpose of the measure.[96] If the burdens imposed are clearly out of proportion to the object in view, the measure will be annulled.[97] This requires that there exist a reasonable relationship between the end and the means. It implies both that the means must be reasonably likely to bring about the objective, and that the detriment to those adversely affected must not be disproportionate to the benefit to the public. It is to some extent analogous to the English concept of reasonableness.

Proportionality is particularly important in the sphere of economic law, since this frequently involves imposing taxes, levies, charges, or duties on businessmen in the hope of achieving economic objectives. The application of proportionality in such a situation as this is well illustrated by the *Skimmed-Milk Powder* case[98] where the Council had sought to reduce the surplus of skimmed-milk powder in the European Union by forcing animal-feed producers to incorporate it in their product in place of the normal protein element, soya. The drawback of this scheme was that skimmed-milk powder was approximately three times more expensive than soya. In consequence, the European Court held that the regulation embodying the scheme was invalid, partly because it was discriminatory, and partly because it offended against the principle of proportionality: the imposition of the obligation to purchase skimmed-milk powder was not necessary in order to diminish the surplus.[99]

The most striking point about the doctrine of proportionality is that it leaves a great deal to the judgment of the Court. Is the measure reasonably likely to attain its objective? Does it impose disproportionate burdens on those concerned? These are clearly questions on which opinions may frequently differ. The Court will not, of course, interfere unless there is a clear and obvious infringement of the principle; nevertheless, it is not always easy to predict when the Court will consider that this has occurred.

§5 EQUALITY

The principle of equality finds expression in a number of provisions in the Treaties: Article 18 TFEU [12/6 EC], as has already been mentioned, prohibits discrimination on grounds of nationality; Article 40(2) TFEU [34(2)/40(3) EC] prohibits

[95] See, for example, *Fédéchar v. High Authority*, Case 8/55, [1956] ECR 292 at 299.

[96] See *per* Advocate General Dutheillet de Lamothe in *Internationale Handelsgesellschaft*, Case 11/70, [1970] ECR 1125 at 1146.

[97] See *Balkan-Import-Export*, Case 5/73, [1973] ECR 1091 at 1112, in which the Court stated that it was not satisfied the measure in question imposed burdens which were 'manifestly out of proportion to the object in view'. See also the German decision, *Re Export of Oat Flakes* [1969] CMLR 85 at 91.

[98] *Bela-Mühle Josef Bergman v. Grows-Farm*, Case 114/76, [1977] ECR 1211; see also Case 116/76 and Cases 119, 120/76 at 1247 and 1269 respectively.

[99] Case 114/76 at para. 7 of the judgment; Case 116/76 at para. 24; and Cases 119, 120/76 at para. 7.

discrimination between producers and consumers in connection with agriculture; and Article 157 TFEU [141/119 EC] establishes the principle of equal pay for equal work irrespective of sex. The European Court has, however, gone beyond these specific provisions by holding that there is a general principle of non-discrimination in EU law.[100] This does not mean that EU institutions must treat everyone alike, but that there must be no arbitrary distinctions between different groups within the Union.[101]

The *Skimmed-Milk Powder* case (discussed in § 4) was partly decided on the basis of this principle, especially as formulated in Article 40(2) TFEU [34(2)/40(3) EC]: the effect of making animal-feed producers use skimmed-milk powder was to increase the price of animal feed, and this harmed all livestock breeders; the benefits of the policy were, on the other hand, felt only by dairy farmers. Thus the policy worked in a discriminatory fashion between different categories of farmers.

In *Sabbatini v. European Parliament*,[102] the Court established sex equality as a general principle of law. This case concerned a female EU official who was denied a certain allowance because she was not the 'head of the family'. The relevant provision defined this concept in such a way as to make it possible for a woman to be regarded as head of the family only in very exceptional circumstances, for example if her husband was incapacitated by illness. The provision was, therefore, discriminatory and, despite the views of the Advocate General, the Court held that it could not stand.

The Court went a step further in *Airola v. Commission*,[103] where the discriminatory provision was part of national law. Here, the applicant had lost her allowance because she had acquired Italian nationality on marriage to an Italian. Under Italian law, a foreign woman who married an Italian man automatically acquired Italian nationality, even if this was not her wish; but this rule did not apply to a foreign man marrying an Italian woman. EU law had simply given effect to Italian law for the purpose of a rule which provided that an expatriation allowance would not be paid if the official acquired the nationality of the country where she worked. But the European Court ruled that EU law could not take account of nationality acquired involuntarily under a discriminatory provision of national law.[104]

The question of religious discrimination came before the Court in *Prais v. Council*.[105] This concerned a woman of Jewish faith who wished to obtain a post as an EU official. In her application she did not mention her religion. However, when she was informed that she would have to sit a competitive examination on a particular day, she told the

[100] See *Frilli v. Belgium*, Case 1/72, [1972] ECR 457 at para. 19 of the judgment and *Sotgiu v. Deutsche Bundespost*, Case 152/73, [1974] ECR 153 at para. 11 of the judgment; see also *ECSC v. Ferriere Sant'Anna*, Case 168/82, [1983] ECR 1681.

[101] See *Hauts Fourneaux et Aciéries Belges v. High Authority*, Case 8/57, [1958] ECR 245 at 256–7; and *Union des Minotiers de la Champagne v. France*, Case 11/74, [1974] ECR 877 at para. 22 of the judgment.

[102] Case 20/71, [1972] ECR 345.

[103] Case 21/74, [1975] ECR 221. For a somewhat different situation, see *Van den Broeck v. Commission*, Case 37/74, [1975] ECR 235; see also *Devred v. Commission*, Case 257/78, [1979] ECR 3767.

[104] For a case involving discrimination against men, see *Razzouk and Beydoun v. Commission*, Cases 75, 117/82, [1984] ECR 1509 (pension rights for husbands of deceased EU officials).

[105] Case 130/75, [1976] ECR 1589.

Council that the day in question was a Jewish festival and she would be unable to attend. She asked the Council to allow her to sit on an alternative date, but this was refused on the ground that it was essential for all candidates to sit the examination on the same date. It was too late to change the date of the examination as the arrangements had been completed. The examination was duly held and Mrs Prais did not attend. Another candidate was appointed.

She then brought proceedings in the European Court to annul the decision to hold the examination on a Jewish festival and to annul the result of the competition; she also asked for damages. She based her case partly on Article 27 of the Staff Regulations, which provided that officials must be selected without reference to race, creed, or sex, and partly on what she claimed was a general principle of EU law prohibiting religious discrimination. The defendant accepted that freedom of religion was a general principle of EU law, but maintained that its action did not constitute a violation of it.

It should be noted that the appointing authority had not been guilty of religious discrimination in the ordinary meaning of the term: there was no evidence that it knew that the date in question was a Jewish festival when it originally scheduled the examination and it had certainly had no wish to create difficulties for the applicant. She, however, argued that subjective intention was not the only matter: if procedures were in fact adopted which put any candidate at a disadvantage by reason of her religion, her religious freedom had been violated.

The Court held that the appointing authority was not under an obligation to avoid holding an examination on a religious holiday if it had not been informed of the fact before the date was fixed. For this reason, Mrs Prais lost her case. However, it went on to state that if the appointing authority is informed in advance, it should take the religious difficulties of candidates into account and endeavour to avoid holding the examination on that date. This means that, even if informed in advance, the authority is not absolutely barred from choosing such a date: but it must give reasonable weight to the desirability of not doing so and should avoid it if reasonably practicable.[106]

§6 THE RIGHT TO A HEARING

This principle is of interest because it was the first example of the European Court drawing on English law in the elaboration of its general principles. The case in which this occurred was *Transocean Marine Paint Association v. Commission*,[107] which concerned EU competition law. This prohibits agreements which restrict competition, but provision is made for the Commission to grant exemptions in particular cases. The agreement establishing the Transocean Marine Paint Association was *prima facie* contrary to the Treaty; so an application was made to the Commission for exemption. This was

[106] For a similar decision in the English courts, see *Ostreicher v. Secretary of State* [1978] 1 WLR 810; [1978] 3 All ER 82 (CA); see also *Ahmad v. ILEA* [1977] 3 WLR 396; [1978] 1 All ER 574 (CA).

[107] Case 17/74, [1974] ECR 1063.

initially granted, subject to conditions, for a period of ten years. When the Association applied for renewal, it was told by the Commission of certain new conditions that the Commission had in mind and was given the opportunity to make representations. It was not, however, adequately informed of one condition which was in fact imposed.

For various reasons the Association objected to this condition and it brought proceedings to quash the decision granting the exemption, in so far as it imposed the condition. It put forward various grounds of invalidity but a breach of the principle of *audi alteram partem* was not one of them. It was Advocate General Warner who proposed that the case should be decided on this basis. He argued that the right to a hearing was a general principle of EU law and that it was binding on the Commission even in the absence of a specific legislative provision. He reached this conclusion after a survey of the national legal systems, in which he pointed out the important role that natural justice plays in England and was able to show that it also applies in most other Member States, though often in a less developed form.

This view was accepted by the Court, which held that there is a general rule of EU law that 'a person whose interests are perceptibly affected by a decision taken by a public authority must be given the opportunity to make his point of view known'.[108] The Court said that this rule requires that the persons concerned be clearly informed in advance of the essential features of any conditions the Commission intends to impose. Because this had not been done in the case, the condition was annulled.

Since this case, the European Court has developed a general doctrine of what it calls 'the rights of the defence',[109] a rather unhappy term for what English lawyers know as the principles of natural justice and what American lawyers call due process.[110] Besides the right to a fair hearing,[111] this also covers such rights as that of legal representation, the privileged nature of communications between lawyer and client (discussed later), and non-self-incrimination.[112]

[108] At para. 15 of the judgment. It is interesting to note that in the later case of *Mollet v. Commission*, Case 75/77, [1978] ECR 897, the Court spoke of a 'measure which is liable gravely to prejudice the interests of an individual' (para. 21), a narrower formulation than that in the *Transocean* case.

[109] This is a literal translation of the French expression, '*les droits de la défense*'. There is, however, no reason to believe that it is limited to the defendant: it could apply equally to the applicant (claimant).

[110] *Michelin v. Commission*, Case 322/81, [1983] ECR 3461 (para. 7 of the judgment); *Hoechst v. Commission*, Cases 46/87, 227/88, [1989] ECR 2859.

[111] For later developments, see *Oslizlok v. Commission*, Case 34/77, [1978] ECR 1099; *Hoffmann-La Roche v. Commission*, Case 85/76, [1979] ECR 461; and *Musique Diffusion Française v. Commission*, Cases 100–3/80, [1983] ECR 1825 at paras 6–36 of the judgment; *Fiskano v. Commission*, Case C-135/92, [1994] ECR I-2885; see also, Ehlermann and Oldekop, 'Due Process in Administrative Procedure' in FIDE, Reports of the 8th Congress, 1978, vol. III, 11-1 at 11-3 to 11-17; and Korah, 'The Rights of the Defence in Administrative Proceedings under Community Law' [1980] CLP 73. In *Al-Jubail Fertilizer v. Council*, Case C-49/88, [1991] ECR I-3187, the principle was applied to anti-dumping proceedings and in *Belgium v. Commission*, Case C-142/87, [1990] ECR I-959, to State aids. In the latter case, the European Court ruled that an infringement of the right to a hearing will not result in an annulment unless it is established that, had it not been for the infringement, the outcome of the procedure might have been different (para. 48 of the judgment).

[112] *Orkem v. Commission*, Case 374/87, [1989] ECR 3283.

§7 LEGAL PROFESSIONAL PRIVILEGE

The privileged nature of communications between lawyer and client was first recognized as a general principle in *A. M. & S. v. Commission.*[113] The issue arose when Commission inspectors arrived one day at the office of a British company and demanded to see its business records. This inspection was part of a general investigation into alleged anti-competitive practices in the zinc industry. It was carried out under an EU measure, Article 14 of Regulation 17, which made no mention of legal privilege. The company nevertheless refused to hand over certain documents on the ground that they were privileged. The Commission took a decision requiring the production of the documents and the company brought proceedings before the European Court to annul the decision.

The Court held that the confidentiality of written communications between lawyer and client, which was generally recognized in the legal systems of the Member States, would be upheld in EU law subject to two conditions: the communication must be for the purpose of the client's 'rights of defence'[114] and the lawyer[115] must be in private practice, not an employee of the client. This latter rule has been criticized as unfair to companies employing in-house lawyers, but it was reaffirmed in 2010.[116]

The procedure laid down by the European Court is as follows. If a client wishes to claim privilege, he must – without revealing the contents of the document – give the Commission sufficient information to demonstrate that the conditions have been satisfied. If the Commission does not accept this, it will take a decision requiring production of the document and, if necessary, impose a penalty for failure to comply, normally a periodic fine of a given amount for each day that the client fails to hand over the document. The client can then challenge this decision before the Court, which will decide the issue, if necessary after inspecting the document.[117] The mere initiation of annulment proceedings will not suspend the decision but the Court may, if it thinks fit, make an interlocutory order to this effect.

[113] Case 155/79, [1982] ECR 1575.

[114] See para. 21 of the judgment. This phrase appears to be the best the translator could come up with for the French '*[le] droit de la défense du client*', which shows that, though the English version of the judgment was supposed to be the authentic one, English having been the language of the case, in reality it was no more than a translation from the French.

[115] The Court adopted the definition of 'lawyer' contained in Directive 77/249, OJ 1977, L 78/17, which covers lawyers admitted in other Member States, but not non-EU lawyers, a fact which has been criticized by American lawyers in view of the fact that American courts have extended the attorney-client privilege to non-American lawyers: see Barsade, 'The Effect of EC Regulations upon the Ability of US Lawyers to Establish a Pan-European Practice' (1994) 28 *International Lawyer* 313 at 323–4.

[116] *Akzo Nobel Chemicals Ltd*, Case C-550/07 P, [2010] ECR I-8301.

[117] In the *A. M. & S.* case, the Court held that the documents in question were entitled to protection.

FURTHER READING

Items are listed in date order, the most recent being at the end.

WEILER, 'Eurocracy and Distrust: Some Questions Concerning the Role of the European Court of Justice in the Protection of Fundamental Human Rights within the Legal Order of the European Communities' (1986) 61 *Washington Law Review* 1103.

SCHERMERS, 'The European Communities Bound by Fundamental Human Rights' (1990) 27 CMLRev. 249.

DE BÚRCA, 'The Principle of Proportionality and its Application in EC Law' (1993) 13 YEL 105.

LENAERTS, 'Fundamental Rights in the European Union' (2000) 25 ELRev. 575.

WEILER, 'Does the EU Truly Need a Charter of Rights?' (2000) 6 ELJ 95.

DE BÚRCA, 'The Drafting of the European Charter of Fundamental Rights' (2001) 26 ELRev. 126.

GOLDSMITH, 'A Charter of Rights, Freedoms and Principles' (2001) 38 CMLRev. 1202.

LENAERTS AND DE SMIJTER, 'A Bill of Rights for the EU' (2001) 38 CMLRev. 273.

VON BOGDANDY, 'The EU as a Human Rights Organization' (2001) 38 CMLRev. 1307.

DOUGLAS-SCOTT, 'The Charter of Fundamental Rights as a Constitutional Document' [2004] EHRLR 37.

ANDREW WILLIAMS, *EU Human Rights Policies: A Study in Irony* (2005).

DOUGLAS-SCOTT, 'A Tale of Two Courts: Luxembourg, Strasbourg and the Growing European Human Rights *Acquis*' (2006) 43 CMLRev. 629.

TAKIS TRIDIMAS, *The General Principles of EC Law*, 2nd edn (2006).

ALMQVIST, 'A Human Rights Critique of European Judicial Review: Counter Terrorism Sanctions' (2008) 57 ICLQ 303.

HALBERSTAM AND STEIN, 'The United Nations, the European Union, and the King of Sweden: Economic Sanctions and Individual Rights in a Plural World Order' (2009) 46 CMLRev. 13.

HARPAZ, 'The European Court of Justice and its Relations with the European Court of Human Rights: The Quest for Enhanced Reliance, Coherence and Legitimacy' (2009) 46 CMLRev. 105.

KUNOY AND DAWES, 'Plate Tectonics in Luxembourg: The *Ménage à Trois* between EC Law, International Law and the European Convention on Human Rights Following the UN Sanctions Cases' (2009) 46 CMLRev. 73.

TRIDIMAS AND GUTIÉRREZ-FONS, 'EU Law, International Law and Economic Sanctions against Terrorism: The Judiciary in Distress?' (2009) 32 *Fordham Journal of International Law* 901.

LENAERTS AND GUTIÉRREZ-FONS, 'The Constitutional Allocation of Powers and General Principles of EU Law' (2010) 47 CMLRev. 1629.

LOCK, 'Accession to the ECHR: Implications for Judicial Review in Strasbourg' (2010) 35 ELRev. 777.

JACQUÉ, 'The Accession of the European Union to the European Convention on Human Rights and Fundamental Freedoms' (2011) 48 CMLRev. 995.

LOCK, 'End of an Epic? The Draft Agreement on the EU's Accession to the ECHR' (2012) 31, YEL 162.

6

AGREEMENTS WITH THIRD COUNTRIES

§1 INTRODUCTION

§1.1 INTERNATIONAL AGREEMENTS AS A SOURCE OF UNION LAW

In some ways international agreements are an anomalous source of EU law. The constitutive Treaties are acts of the Member States; regulations, decisions, etc., are acts of the European Union itself; general principles of law are the creation of the European Court; but international agreements have their origin outside the Union legal order and are, in part, the acts of non-member States. However, they have effects in Union law and are applied by the European Court, which has declared them to be 'an integral part of Community [Union] law'.[1] In spite of their origin, therefore, they may be regarded as a true source of Union law.

§1.2 LEGAL PERSONALITY

An international organization cannot conclude international agreements unless it has legal personality under international law. In the past, the Treaties conferred legal personality on the European Community (now abolished),[2] but not the European Union.[3] This was changed by the Treaty of Lisbon, which now gives the Union legal personality.[4] However, it is not enough that the Union possesses legal personality in international law: it also has to have treaty-making power (competence).

§1.3 EXCLUSIVE AND SHARED COMPETENCE

As is the case with all the European Union's powers, treaty-making competence in a given area may be exclusive (in which case the Member States are prohibited from

[1] *Haegeman v. Belgium*, Case 181/73, [1974] ECR 449 at para. 5 of the judgment.

[2] Art. 281 [210] EC. The EAEC Treaty conferred it on the EAEC: see Art. 184 EAEC.

[3] In spite of this, the Union concluded an international agreement with the Federal Republic of Yugoslavia in 2001. See Council Decision 2001/352/CFSP of 9 April 2001, OJ 2001, L 125, p. 1.

[4] Art. 47 TEU.

concluding treaties in that area) or shared (concurrent). In the latter case, both the Union and the Member States may conclude treaties; nevertheless, the Member States may exercise their competence only to the extent that the Union has not done so (see the principles regarding legislative competence discussed in Chapter 4, § 3).

§1.4 KINDS OF AGREEMENTS

International agreements forming part of Union law may be divided into three categories. The first consists of agreements between the European Union (acting alone) and one or more non-member States.[5] This method may be used where the subject matter of the agreement falls wholly within the treaty-making competence of the Union.

The second category consists of 'mixed' agreements, i.e., agreements between, on the one side, the Union and the Member States acting jointly and, on the other side, the non-member States.[6] Such agreements are used when the subject matter falls partly within the competence of the Union and partly within that of the Member States; it may also be used in cases of shared (concurrent) competence, though there is no legal requirement for this.

The third category consists of agreements between the Member States (acting alone) and non-member States. Such agreements can bind the Union and form part of Union law, but this occurs only in special circumstances.

Of the three, mixed agreements create the greatest problems. They first have to be ratified by each Member State according to its constitutional requirements; then they are approved by the Council on behalf of the Union. This means that one Member State can hold up ratification for all the others. The State in question may be one with no interest in the subject matter of the agreement; yet it could delay the conclusion of the agreement for years, causing problems for Member States for which the agreement is important. This cannot occur if the Member States act on their own – those that are interested can go ahead without being held back by the others – or if the Union acts alone (in which case, ratification by the Member States is not necessary).

§2 THE TREATY-MAKING POWERS OF THE UNION

§2.1 THE PRINCIPLE OF CONFERRAL

Under the principle of conferral (discussed in Chapter 4, § 2), the European Union enjoys only those powers (competences) conferred on it by the Treaties. In the past, the Treaties conferred few treaty-making powers. Tariff and trade agreements were the main exception.

[5] They may also be concluded with other international organizations.

[6] There is no express provision for mixed agreements in the TEU or TFEU, but such an agreement was approved by the European Court in the *Natural Rubber Agreement* case, Opinion 1/78, [1979] ECR 2871. Such agreements are referred to in Art. 102 of the EAEC Treaty. Mixed agreements are often used to enable the Union and the Member States to join international organizations. On the division of voting rights between the Union and the Member States in such cases, see *Commission v. Council* (*FAO* case), Case C-25/94, [1996] ECR I-1469.

However, the European Court stepped in and, in a series of cases of great interest and importance, held that the Union possessed implied treaty-making powers. This greatly extended its competence. Subsequently, the Treaty of Lisbon adopted the principles on which these cases were based.[7] For this reason, these powers can no longer be called 'implied'; nevertheless, they are of a different nature from powers of the kind originally conferred by the Treaties (which we shall refer to as 'primary' powers), since they are derived from other provisions of the Treaties and often come into existence only when EU legislation is enacted. We shall call them 'secondary' powers. They will be considered in § 2.3.

§2.2 PRIMARY POWERS

Primary powers are treaty-making powers expressly conferred on the Union to enable it to carry out its functions in a particular area. Subjects covered include:[8]

- relationships with neighbouring countries;[9]
- the common foreign and security policy;[10]
- migration (readmission of immigrants to their countries of origin);[11]
- international trade and commerce;[12] and
- association with the Union.[13]

These powers complement the legislative competences granted by the Treaties. Their nature as exclusive, shared, or supplementary is governed by the same principles as apply to legislative competences (outlined in Chapter 4, § 3).

§2.3 SECONDARY POWERS: THE COURT'S INITIATIVE

As already mentioned, the secondary treaty-making powers of the European Union were originally developed by the European Court under the theory of implied powers. The story begins in the 1960s.

For a long time, there were two rival theories regarding the European Union's power to conclude treaties. On the one hand, it was argued that the treaty-making power of the Union – its external competence – should reflect its internal competence. According to this doctrine of 'parallelism', as it was sometimes called, it would be illogical for the Union to have internal law-making power with regard to a topic and yet be unable to conclude international agreements in that field. Therefore, argued the proponents of this doctrine, the Union must be regarded not only as having those treaty-making powers expressly granted to it in the Treaties, but must also have such powers with regard to any topic which falls within its internal competence. This was justified on the basis of the theory of implied powers.

[7] Arts 216(1) and 3(2) TFEU.

[8] See also Arts 186 TFEU (research and technological development); 191(4) TFEU (environment); 209(2) TFEU (development co-operation); and 219 TFEU (monetary matters).

[9] Art. 8(2) TEU. [10] Art. 37 TEU. [11] Art. 79(3) TFEU. [12] Art. 207 TFEU.

[13] Art. 217 TFEU.

In the beginning, the Member States rejected this doctrine: they took the view that the Union possessed only such external powers as were expressly granted to it by the Treaties (what we have called 'primary' powers).[14] This standpoint was supported by comparing the EEC Treaty (as it originally stood) with the EAEC Treaty: Article 228 EEC (later Article 300 EC), the general provision covering all treaty-making by the EEC, began with the words: 'Where *this Treaty provides* for the conclusion of agreements . . .',[15] thus suggesting that it was only in the case of an express provision that the Union could conclude international agreements. Article 101 EAEC, on the other hand, stated: 'The Community [Union] may, within the limits of its powers and jurisdiction, enter into obligations by concluding agreements or contracts with a third State.' This implies that wherever the Union had internal competence with regard to a given matter, it would also have power to enter into international agreements with regard to that matter. The contrast between these two provisions was all the more significant in view of the fact that the two Treaties were drafted at the same time and in many instances contained identical provisions. It is hard to avoid the conclusion, therefore, that the authors of the Treaties originally intended the European Union (at the time, known as the EEC) to have considerably more restricted treaty-making powers than the EAEC.[16]

The first legal action between the Council and the Commission regarding the question was the *ERTA* case, decided in 1971.[17] The history of this dispute goes back to 1962 when five of the then six Member States, together with some other European countries, signed an agreement to harmonize social provisions relating to road transport. This agreement, normally known as the first ERTA (European Road Transport Agreement), never came into force, since it was not ratified by a sufficient number of contracting States. In 1967, negotiations started for a second ERTA and these were also conducted by the Member States. In 1969, however, the Council enacted a regulation covering much the same ground within the internal competence of the Union. The Member States were nevertheless still anxious to regulate the matter on a wider basis and they decided to continue the negotiations for a second ERTA.

On 20 March 1970, the Council met to discuss the matter and decided that the negotiations would be carried on by the Member States, which would become Parties to the new ERTA. It was agreed that the Member States would co-ordinate their positions and the Member State holding the presidency of the Council would act as spokesman. The Commission objected to this: it felt that it should have a role to play in view of the fact that the subject matter of the negotiations had already been regulated internally

[14] For further discussion of the disputes that took place at this time, see Costonis, 'The Treaty-Making Power of the European Economic Union' (1968) 5 CMLRev. 421; Bot, 'Negotiating Union Agreements: Procedure and Practice' (1970) 7 CMLRev. 286; Leopold, 'External Relations Power of EEC in Theory and in Practice' (1977) 26 ICLQ 54.

[15] Emphasis added.

[16] When the EAEC Treaty was concluded, the Member States were much less advanced in nuclear technology than the United States, and the authors of the Treaty probably thought that international agreements would be required to obtain technology and materials; they may also have believed that international agreements would be needed to deal with the security aspects of atomic energy.

[17] *Commission v. Council* (*ERTA* case), Case 22/70, [1971] ECR 263.

on a Union basis by the 1969 Regulation. In May 1970, it therefore brought legal action against the Council in the European Court to annul the Council resolution entrusting the conduct of the negotiations entirely to the Member States. On 1 July 1970, agreement on the new ERTA was reached and the text was declared open for signature; before the Court gave judgment, at least some of the Member States had signed it.

The jurisdictional aspects of this case have already been considered: it will be remembered that the Court eventually decided that the application was admissible since the Council resolution constituted a legal act *sui generis*.[18] As far as the substance was concerned, the main point was whether the Member States or the Union had power to enter into the agreement. This in turn depended on whether the Union had any treaty-making powers beyond those expressly granted by the Treaties.

In its judgment, the Court said that to determine the authority (competence) of the Union to conclude international agreements, it was necessary to consider the 'whole scheme of the Treaty' as well as its substantive provisions. It then went on to say, in paragraphs 16 to 19 of its judgment:

> 16. Such authority arises not only from an express conferment by the Treaty… but may equally flow from other provisions of the Treaty and from measures adopted, within the framework of those provisions, by the Union institutions.
>
> 17. In particular, each time the Union, with a view to implementing a common policy envisaged by the Treaty, adopts provisions laying down common rules, whatever form these may take, the Member States no longer have the right, acting individually or even collectively, to undertake obligations with third countries which affect those rules.
>
> 18. As and when such common rules come into being, the Union alone is in a position to assume and carry out contractual obligations towards third countries affecting the whole sphere of application of the Union legal system.
>
> 19. With regard to the implementation of the provisions of the Treaty the system of internal Union measures may not therefore be separated from that of external relations.

This, of course, constitutes approval of the doctrine of 'parallelism'; it is, however, expressed in a particular form. The vital element bringing about a transfer of treaty-making power from the Member States to the Union is the adoption by the Union of provisions laying down rules which might be affected if the Member States entered into treaties with regard to the subject matter in question.[19]

[18] See Chap. 4, § 1.1.

[19] See also paras 66, 82, and, especially, 84 of the judgment. In para. 84 the Court expressly said that power was conferred on the Union as a result of the 1969 Regulation. There is also, however, a different (and somewhat inconsistent) strand of reasoning in paras 23–27 of the judgment. This could be interpreted as meaning (though it does not expressly say) that the provisions of the Treaty giving the Union internal competence in the area of transport gave it an implied treaty-making power which existed irrespective of internal measures, a view which the Court seems to have adopted subsequently in the *WTO* case, Opinion 1/94, [1994] ECR I-5267 at para. 76 of the judgment. This power appears to be concurrent with that of the Member States until such time as internal measures are adopted: see the *WTO* case at para. 77 of the judgment, where the Court said: 'Only in so far as common rules have been established at internal level does the external competence of the Union become exclusive.' See, further, Dashwood and Heliskoski, 'The Classic Authorities Revisited', in Alan Dashwood and Christophe Hillion (eds), *The General Law of EC External Relations* (2000), p. 3 at pp. 7–9 *et seq*. If this interpretation of the *ERTA* case is correct, it means that subsequent developments were foreshadowed in it.

Having enunciated this new principle, the Court then applied it to the facts of the case. It noted that the adoption of a common transport policy is one of the objectives laid down in Part One of the Treaty and that common rules for the attainment of this objective had been laid down in the 1969 Regulation. It followed from this that the Union obtained treaty-making power in the area covered by the 1969 Regulation when it came into force on 1 October 1969. This automatically entailed the loss of such power on the part of the Member States.

One might have thought that the consequence of this would have been that the Commission should have negotiated the agreement on behalf of the Union. It must not be forgotten, however, that the negotiations for the second ERTA were based on the first ERTA: the idea was merely to make such modifications as were necessary to secure its acceptance. The negotiations taken up again in 1967 were, therefore, a continuation of those which resulted in the first ERTA in 1962. Consequently, a considerable part of the negotiations had been carried out before the transfer of treaty-making power in 1969. In the circumstances, it would not have been fair to third countries if the negotiating procedure, and indeed the parties to the negotiations, had been changed at that point. In such a situation, said the Court, the Council and Commission should have agreed between themselves on appropriate methods of co-operation to ensure the most effective way of defending the Union's interests. Clearly, no such agreement was reached. The Court therefore concluded that the Council had not violated the Treaty in deciding that the negotiations would continue to be conducted by the Member States. Technically, therefore, the Commission lost the case: in reality, of course, it won a victory, as explained later.

The Court's ruling in the *ERTA* case can be fully understood only if one analyses it from a policy point of view. What the Court was intent on doing was enhancing the Union's powers and thus reversing the previous trend away from Commission involvement in international negotiations. It did not, however, wish to jeopardize the agreement which had been reached on the second ERTA by ruling that it had to be renegotiated by the Commission: this would have upset the other Parties and damaged the international reputation of the European Union. The Court therefore had to find a way of upholding the Commission's contention in principle, without applying it to the facts of the case. It did this by holding that the Union gained treaty-making power only in 1969 when the internal measure came into effect.

The same result could, however, have been achieved by ruling that the enactment of the regulation did not *confer* power on the Union but merely *deprived* the Member States of power. This could be justified by the adoption of the doctrine of parallelism in its strong form by saying that the existence of an internal power automatically implies an external power, but this power does not become exclusive until it is exercised either internally or externally. Before this, the Member States would have concurrent powers. The outcome of the *ERTA* case would have been the same, but the Commission's position in future cases would have been stronger. It is possible that this is what the Court meant in the *ERTA* case, but if it was, it failed to make itself clear.[20]

[20] See the previous note.

The next step came in the *North-East Atlantic Fisheries Convention (Kramer)* case.[21] The Convention was an international agreement entered into by seven of the then nine Member States and several non-member States for the purpose of ensuring the conservation of fish stocks in the North-East Atlantic. A Fisheries Commission was set up under it, and this had the power to make recommendations for conservation measures if there was a two-thirds majority in favour. These were binding on each Party to the Convention unless it rejected the recommendation within a given period. Such a recommendation had been made concerning sole and plaice, and this became binding under the terms of the Convention. The Netherlands, which was a Party to the Convention, then enacted national measures to implement the recommendation, and these included criminal provisions. The case arose when certain Dutch fishermen were prosecuted in a Dutch court for breach of these provisions. They argued that the Member States had no power to enter into the Convention and the Dutch legislation was therefore contrary to Union law. This raised the question whether the Convention fell within the exclusive competence of the Union.

The position regarding fisheries was that the European Union had internal power but at the relevant time had not exercised that power for the purpose of conservation. However, conservation of fish in international waters is rather a special case, since it is normally feasible to proceed only by way of international measures: there is no point in imposing quotas on Union fishermen if non-Union fishermen are subject to no restrictions. It is hardly surprising, therefore, that the European Court held that the Union had treaty-making power in the area. However, it went on to rule that until the Union exercised its powers – one assumes either internally or externally – the Member States had concurrent powers. Consequently, the Dutch measure was not contrary to Union law.

In the *North-East Atlantic Fisheries Convention* case, the European Court appears to have taken the position that the mere existence of an internal power can give rise to an external power, even if no internal measures have in fact been adopted; nevertheless, this could be regarded as applying only in the special case of fisheries conservation. In the *Inland Waterway Vessels*[22] case, however, the Court made clear that it was laying down a general principle. After stating that the grant of internal power to attain a specific objective implies the authority to enter into international agreements where these are necessary for the attainment of that objective, it continued: 'This is particularly so in all cases in which internal power has already been used… it is, however, not limited to that eventuality.'[23] It went on to say:[24]

> …the power to bind the Union *vis-à-vis* third countries nevertheless flows by implication from the provisions of the Treaty creating the internal power and in so far as the participation of the Union in the international agreement is, as here, necessary for the attainment of one of the objectives of the Union.

[21] Cases 3, 4, 6/76, [1976] ECR 1279. This case was preceded by the *Local Cost Standard* case, Opinion 1/75, [1975] ECR 1355, which did not, however, significantly develop the law on the point under consideration.

[22] Opinion 1/76 on *The Laying-Up Fund for Inland Waterway Vessels*, [1977] ECR 741.

[23] Paras 3 and 4 of the Court's reasoning. [24] Para. 4.

This new principle, which has been called the principle of 'complementarity',[25] seems to be that an implied external power may result from an express internal power where the purpose for which the latter was given cannot be fully attained without the former.

The *Inland Waterway Vessels* case is also interesting because it throws light on two other matters. The case concerned an international agreement for the regulation of vessels on the Rhine–Moselle waterway system. The Union had internal competence in the area and could have dealt with the problem by means of a regulation. However, the Swiss were major users of the waterway and, as they had to be included in the scheme, action on the international level was necessary.

The solution chosen was a mixed agreement to which the Parties were the Union, Switzerland, and six of the Member States. The six contracting Member States were the three Benelux countries, Germany, France, and the United Kingdom. The reason these Member States participated in their individual capacities was that the waterways in question were already subject to two international conventions, the Mannheim Convention of 1868 and the Luxembourg Convention of 1956, and there was a potential conflict between certain provisions of the new agreement and the two earlier Conventions. The six participating Member States were all Parties to one or other of the earlier Conventions and they undertook in the agreement to make the necessary amendments to those Conventions.

On the basis of the Court's earlier decisions, one might have thought that there would have been no problem regarding the participation of the Member States. These cases hold that the implied powers of the Union are not exclusive until they have been exercised. In the *Inland Waterway Vessels* case, the Court did indeed accept the participation of the Member States; however, there is a suggestion that this was only because their intervention was necessary to secure the required amendments to the earlier Conventions. After referring to the necessity of amending the Conventions, the Court said: 'The participation of these States in the Agreement must be considered as being solely for this purpose and not as necessary for the attainment of other features of the system.'[26] It was for this reason, said the Court, that the participation of the six Member States 'is not such as to encroach on the external power of the Union'.[27] This suggests that the Court might not have accepted the participation of the Member States if these special circumstances had not been present.

The main question in the case was something much more fundamental than either of the issues already discussed. The agreement set up an organization called the 'Laying-Up Fund for Inland Waterway Vessels', which was modelled on the European Union itself. According to the Statute of the Fund, it was an international public institution with legal personality. Its organs were a Supervisory Board (analogous to the Council), a Board of Management (analogous to the Commission), and a court, the Fund Tribunal. The Supervisory Board was to consist of one representative of each

[25] Dashwood and Heliskoski, 'The Classic Authorities Revisited' in Alan Dashwood and Christophe Hillion (eds), *The General Law of EC External Relations* (2000), p. 3 at pp. 9 *et seq.* [26] At para. 7. [27] *Ibid.*

Member State except Ireland (which did not wish to be represented) and one representative of Switzerland; the (non-voting) chairman was to be a representative of the Commission. Voting was normally to be by a simple majority, but there was a provision that the majority had to contain the votes of at least three of the States with the greatest interest in the Fund (Belgium, Germany, France, the Netherlands, and Switzerland). The Board of Management was to consist of persons appointed by the same five States together with Luxembourg; but representation was not to be equal: Germany and the Netherlands were to have four members each, Luxembourg one, and the others two each. Decisions were to be taken by a two-thirds majority.

It was provided that the Fund was to have the power, within the very narrow limits of its competence, to enact measures having direct effect in all Member States of the Union as well as in Switzerland.

The Fund Tribunal was to consist of one judge from each of the six Member States that were Parties to the agreement and one from Switzerland. The intention was that the six Union judges would be appointed by the European Court from among its own members. The jurisdiction of the Tribunal was to be similar to that of the European Court and it was to have the power to give preliminary rulings on references from national courts in the European Union or Switzerland.

It will be seen from this that the Fund was a supranational organization like the Union itself. Could the European Union join another Union? In its Opinion, the European Court held that it was possible for the Union to set up a public international institution of this kind, but it found the structure of the Fund unacceptable. In particular, it considered that the Member States played too great a role – it felt that the Union institutions should have been given more say in the running of the Fund – and it thought that it was wrong for some Member States to be given powers that were not given to others. It also took objection to the fact that the Union judges on the Tribunal were to be appointed from among the judges of the European Court. The reason for this latter objection was that the agreement setting up the Fund was itself part of Union law and might have had to be interpreted by the European Court: if some judges of the European Court had already given a ruling on it in their capacity as members of the Fund Tribunal, they would be precluded from sitting when the issue came before the European Court. This might make it impossible for the European Court to find a quorum.

The interesting point about this opinion is that none of the points to which the European Court objected was an essential characteristic of a supranational organization. It follows from this that, if the right structure were chosen, the Union might be able to become a member of such a body.[28]

In the cases discussed so far, the European Court followed a consistent policy of enhancing the powers of the Union and restricting those of the Member States. Some subsequent judgments, however, show a more balanced attitude.

[28] For a fuller discussion of the case, see Hartley (1977) 2 ELRev. 275.

The first was the *WTO* case.[29] It concerned a group of agreements – the Multilateral Agreements on Trade in Goods, the General Agreement on Trade in Services (GATS), and the Agreement on Trade-Related Aspects of Intellectual Property Rights (TRIPs) – annexed to the Agreement Establishing the World Trade Organization ('WTO Agreement'). These were signed by the Member States as well as the European Union. The Commission considered that exclusive competence lay with the Union, but the Member States took the view that competence was shared: they thought the instruments should take effect as mixed agreements (see § 1.4).

The Commission then brought proceedings before the Court under what is now Article 218(11) TFEU (then Article 228(6) EC) for an opinion as to whether sole competence rested with the Union. Various arguments were advanced. These were successful in part, but the European Court ruled that some aspects of GATS and TRIPs fell outside the exclusive treaty-making powers of the Union. With regard to these instruments, the Union and the Member States were jointly competent.[30]

The *WTO* case, and the Court's later opinion in the *OECD* case,[31] have clarified the law as to when the Union's implied treaty-making powers (under the doctrine of parallelism) are exclusive. It is now settled that the mere existence of an internal power in the relevant area does not automatically result in exclusivity.[32] There are, however, two cases in which the Union's power *is* exclusive.[33] The first is where the Union has adopted internal legislation in the relevant area which could be affected by the agreement. This would be the case where, for example, the agreement would require the internal rules to be amended. It seems that exclusivity may also result where the Union adopts internal legislation which purports to effect a complete harmonization of the area – thus indicating an intention to take it over – even if there would be no direct clash with the agreement. The second case is where internal legislation expressly empowers the Union to negotiate with non-member States.

In the *WTO* case, the Commission argued that the power is also exclusive where this is necessary for the attainment of one of the objectives of the Union. As was pointed out earlier in connection with the *North-East Atlantic Fisheries Convention* case, there are some instances where it is not possible for the Union to act first on the internal level: it is only through international action that the objective can be achieved. It could be argued that in such instances, even before the Union has acted, the Member States should be precluded from entering into international agreements if these would prejudice future Union action. The Court, however, made conflicting statements on this

[29] Opinion 1/94, [1994] ECR I-5267. See, further, Opinion 1/08 (GATS), [2009] ECR I-11129 (Grand Chamber).

[30] The concept of joint competence or shared competence – the Court uses both terms in the *WTO* case – is ambiguous. Does it mean that *either* the Union *or* the Member States may act alone, or that *neither* may act alone? These are clearly two different concepts. In the *North-East Atlantic Fisheries Convention* case, it seems that *either* the Member States *or* the Union could have acted alone to conclude the agreement; in the *WTO* case, on the other hand, it seems clear that the Member States could not have acted on their own. It also seems that the Union could not have done so.

[31] Opinion 2/92, [1995] ECR I-521.

[32] See paras 77, 88, and 89 of the judgment in the *WTO* case, and para. 31 of the judgment in the *OECD* case.

[33] See paras 95 and 96 of the judgment in the *WTO* case and paras 31–33 of the judgment in the *OECD* case.

point: in paragraph 85 of the judgment in the *WTO* case it said (with reference to the *Inland Waterway Vessels* case and the *North-East Atlantic Fisheries Convention* case) that, where it is not possible to act first on the internal level, 'external powers may be exercised, and thus *become* exclusive, without any internal legislation having first been adopted',[34] a statement which suggests that the power is not exclusive until exercised; in paragraph 89, on the other hand, it said, 'Save where internal powers can only be effectively exercised at the same time as external powers (see Opinion 1/76 and paragraph 85 ...), internal competence can give rise to exclusive external competence only if it is exercised', a statement implying that, in such cases, it is exclusive *before* being exercised. Perhaps the judges were themselves divided on the issue. However, the first of these statements was repeated in the *OECD* case,[35] while the second was not. Since the Court held in the *North-East Atlantic Fisheries Convention* case that, even where it is not possible to act first on the internal level, external competence remains concurrent until exercised, this must still be regarded as the law, though the conflicting *dicta* in the *WTO* case serve as a warning that the Court may change its mind.

Another case in which the Court displayed its new-found restraint was *France v. Commission.*[36] Here the Commission had both negotiated and *concluded* an agreement with the United States on co-operation in the enforcement of competition (antitrust) law. Under the Treaty provision laying down the general procedure for concluding international agreements (then Article 228 EC, now Article 218 TFEU, discussed later, in § 3), the Commission negotiates international agreements, but they must be concluded by the Council. France brought proceedings to annul the agreement (or the Commission decision to conclude it) on the ground that the procedure violated Article 228 EC. In its defence, the Commission advanced an interesting variant of the doctrine of parallelism: it argued that since it had internal competence to enforce EU competition law, it should have external competence to conclude agreements in this area. It also claimed that, since the main provisions of the agreement required it to do no more than keep the American authorities informed of its activities, it could carry out the agreement without the assistance of the Council.

The Court refused to accept this argument. It first held that only the Union, and not an institution of the Union such as the Commission, could be a party to an international agreement. It then rejected the parallelism argument:[37]

> Even though the Commission has the power, internally, to take individual decisions applying the rules of competition, a field covered by the Agreement, that internal power is not such as to alter the allocation of powers between the Union institutions with regard to the conclusion of international agreements, which is determined by Article 228 of the Treaty.

In other words, the doctrine of parallelism applies only between the Union and the Member States, not between the Council and the Commission.

[34] Emphasis added. [35] At para. 32 of the judgment. [36] Case C-327/91, [1994] ECR I-3641.
[37] Para. 41 of the judgment.

Finally, something should be said about the application of the doctrine of parallelism with regard to Article 352 TFEU. As will be remembered from the discussion in Chapter 4, § 2.3, this is a provision which gives the Union the power to adopt measures where the Treaties have *not* provided the necessary powers, provided that action is necessary to attain one of the objectives set out in the Treaties. If the doctrine of parallelism was applied with regard to this provision, wide treaty-making powers would result.

In the *ECHR* case,[38] it was argued that this enabled the European Union to accede to the European Convention on Human Rights. However, the Court held that Article 352 (then Article 235 EC) cannot be used for the adoption of a measure that would have constitutional significance. Adherence to the ECHR would have had such significance, not least because it would place the European Court of Human Rights above the European Court in matters of human rights. The European Court, therefore, held that the Union lacked competence to adhere to the Convention, unless the EC Treaty was first amended.[39] However, this would not appear to exclude resort to Article 352 with regard to agreements that do not have constitutional significance.[40]

§2.4 THE TREATY OF LISBON

The cases discussed previously were all decided before the Treaty of Lisbon. In that Treaty, the Member States tried to clarify and codify the principles developed by the European Court in those cases. The results are to be found in Articles 216(1) and 3(2) TFEU. The former provides:

> The Union may conclude an agreement with one or more third countries or international organisations where the Treaties so provide or where the conclusion of an agreement is necessary in order to achieve, within the framework of the Union's policies, one of the objectives referred to in the Treaties, or is provided for in a legally binding Union act or is likely to affect common rules or alter their scope.

The first part of this provision (up to 'where the Treaties so provide') deals with what we have called 'primary' treaty-making powers and reproduces the content of the former provision, Article 228 [300] EC; however, the remainder is new. It provides that the Union has treaty-making power in three additional cases:

- where the conclusion of the agreement is necessary in order to achieve, within the framework of the Union's policies, one of the objectives referred to in the Treaties;
- where the conclusion of the agreement is provided for in a legally binding Union act; or
- where the conclusion of the agreement is likely to affect common rules or alter their scope.

[38] Opinion 2/94, [1996] ECR I-1759.

[39] For later cases in which the Court reverted to its previous policy of expanding Union competence and restricting that of the Member States, see the '*Open Skies*' cases, for example, *Commission v. United Kingdom*, Case C-466/98, [2002] ECR I-9427; *Lugano Convention Case*, Opinion 1/03, [2006] ECR I-1145.

[40] In fact, the Union had already concluded a number of agreements under Art. 308 TFEU [266 EC] long before the *ECHR* case arose – for example, the Convention for the Prevention of Marine Pollution from Land-Based Sources, signed in Paris on 4 June 1974, OJ 1975, L 194/6.

The wording of the first head is based on Article 352 TFEU. However, there is no requirement that other provisions of the Treaties should not have provided the necessary powers; consequently, it covers both the case where there is an express internal power and the case where there is not. This is based on the theory of 'parallelism' in a broad form as adopted in the case-law discussed previously.

The second head allows the Union to confer treaty-making power on itself by adopting a legal act to this effect. This act must of course fall within the competence of the Union as discussed in Chapter 4, § 3. This could be useful where it is desired to make clear that the Union has the power to enter into a particular kind of agreement. It might also specify how the agreement is to be concluded.

The third head will apply in particular where the Union has already exercised its powers (either internally or in an earlier international agreement) and the new agreement would affect the earlier instrument. The *ERTA* case would be an example.

Article 216(1) TFEU does not indicate whether these powers are exclusive or shared; this is specified by Article 3(2) TFEU, which provides that the Union has exclusive competence for the conclusion of an international agreement when:

- its conclusion is provided for in a legislative act of the Union;
- its conclusion is necessary to enable the Union to exercise its internal competence; or
- in so far as its conclusion may affect common rules or alter their scope.

The first head of this provision is similar to the second head of Article 216(1); however, it is narrower since it refers to a legislative act, not just any legally binding act. The meaning of this concept was explained in Chapter 4, § 1.2: it is a legal act adopted by legislative procedure. Where the power to conclude a treaty is conferred by a non-legislative act, it will be shared.

The second head in Article 3(2) is similar to the first head in Article 216(1); however, it too seems narrower: it appears to refer to the situation where it is not possible to exercise the internal competence without first (or at the same time) concluding an international agreement. Conservation of marine resources might be an example, as explained when the *North-East Atlantic Fisheries Convention* case was discussed earlier.[41]

The third head of Article 3(2) seems identical with the third head of Article 216(1); this too follows from the Court's case-law.

§2.5 CONCLUSIONS

The authors of the original EEC Treaty probably intended the EEC to have relatively limited treaty-making powers (in contrast to the EAEC, which was intended all along to have wide powers). In the 1970s, however, the Commission decided to increase those powers by resorting to legal action, knowing that it could count on the Court for

[41] In that case, however, the European Court held that power was shared. It seems that there would be a different result if the same question arose again today.

support. The result is that the powers of the Union (Community) were considerably extended, and those of the Member States were reduced.

The series of cases by which this has been achieved is also of interest as an example of the law-making strategy of the Court. This can best be characterized as a 'step-by-step' approach: the first step, taken in the *ERTA* case, was regarded at the time as very bold – *Le Monde* published an article on 27 April 1971 asking whether the Court had exceeded its jurisdiction – but the Court nevertheless went ahead with the second step – hesitantly in the *North-East Atlantic Fisheries Convention* case and firmly in the *Inland Waterway Vessels* case: what seemed bold in 1971 had been discarded as insufficient by 1977. Thirty years later, when the Treaty of Lisbon was adopted, the Member States had come round to the Court's way of thinking; so they gave the European Union what we have called 'secondary' treaty-making powers, which allowed it to exercise the same wide competence that the EAEC had enjoyed all along.

§3 TREATY-MAKING PROCEDURE

General provisions regarding the procedure to be adopted for the negotiation and conclusion of international agreements are laid down by Article 218 TFEU [300/228 EC]. The procedure starts when the Commission makes a recommendation to the Council that negotiations should begin.[42] If the Council adopts a decision authorizing this, it will nominate the European Union's negotiator or the head of the Union's negotiating team. The Council may issue directives to the negotiator or designate a special committee which has to be consulted during the course of the negotiations. This is to enable the Council to keep a check on what is happening and to ensure that the negotiator is keeping to the directives and not doing anything against the interests of the Union.

If the negotiations are successful, the agreement will be signed on behalf of the Union. It then has to be concluded by the Union. The decision to sign the agreement[43] and the decision to conclude it are taken by the Council on a proposal from the negotiator.

Except where the agreement relates exclusively to the common foreign and security policy, the European Parliament must either be consulted or give its consent. In certain specified areas – for example, agreements with important budgetary implications and agreements covering matters where the Parliament's consent would have to be obtained for the enactment of internal legislation – its consent must be obtained before the agreement is concluded. Its consent must also be obtained for the agreement under which the Union joins the ECHR. In all other cases,[44] the European Parliament must be consulted.[45]

[42] Where the proposed agreement relates exclusively or principally to the common foreign and security policy, the High Representative of the Union for Foreign Affairs and Security Policy makes the recommendation.

[43] This may involve its provisional application before entry into force.

[44] Except where the agreement relates exclusively to the common foreign and security policy.

[45] See Chap. 1, § 1.8 for a discussion of what consultation entails.

Where the European Parliament has to give its consent, it may – if the matter is urgent – agree with the Council upon a time limit. The European Parliament is not obliged to agree, and the Treaty does not say what happens if it does not agree, or if it agrees and does not give its consent within the specified period. There is no indication that the Council may conclude the agreement without its consent.

Where the European Parliament merely has to be consulted, the Council may set a time limit within which the European Parliament must give its opinion. The Treaty[46] states that if the European Parliament does not give its opinion within the time limit, the Council can go ahead without it. If such a rule did not exist, the European Parliament could turn a right to be consulted into a right to veto the agreement by the simple expedient of delaying indefinitely.

The Council generally acts by a qualified majority throughout the treaty-making procedure. However, in certain specified cases – for example, where unanimity would be required for internal legislation – it must be unanimous. In the case of the agreement for the Union's accession to the ECHR, the Council will have to be unanimous and the Member States will all have to give their approval in accordance with their respective constitutional requirements. The decision concluding the agreement will not come into force until this has taken place.[47]

Where the European Union wants to suspend an agreement that has already been concluded, the decision is taken by the Council on a proposal from the Commission or the High Representative of the Union for Foreign Affairs and Security Policy.

Although the European Parliament's most important powers come into operation only after the agreement has been negotiated, the Treaties require the Parliament to be fully informed at all stages of the procedure. The relevant committee will usually be told that the Council proposes to open negotiations and the European Parliament may hold a debate on the issue. During the course of the negotiations, confidential briefings will be given to the committee by the Commission. The European Parliament is thus able to exert influence on the course of the negotiations. This influence will be especially strong in those cases where the agreement cannot be concluded without its consent, since it can threaten to veto the agreement if its wishes are not taken into account.

Article 207 TFEU [133/113 EC] contains special rules on the conclusion of agreements concerning the common commercial policy.[48] Such agreements are negotiated by the Commission. Article 207 provides that the Commission must obtain the authorization of the Council to open negotiations; these are conducted in consultation with a special committee appointed by the Council. The Council also has the power to issue directives to the Commission. The Commission must report regularly to the special committee and to the European Parliament. If the negotiations are successful,

[46] Art. 218(6)(b) TFEU.

[47] This opens up the possibility of one Member State holding up accession for years by stubbornly refusing to ratify.

[48] There are also special rules regarding agreements on foreign-exchange and monetary matters, see Art. 219 TFEU [111/109 EC].

the agreement is concluded by the Council. In general, the Council acts by a qualified majority; however, unanimity is required in certain specified cases.

§4 LEGAL PROCEEDINGS

A special legal procedure is laid down by Article 218(11) TFEU [300(6)/228(6) EC], which provides:

> A Member State, the European Parliament, the Council or the Commission may obtain the opinion of the Court of Justice as to whether an agreement envisaged is compatible with the Treaties. Where the opinion of the Court is adverse, the agreement envisaged may not enter into force unless it is amended or the Treaties are revised.

This provision applies to all agreements to which the European Union is to be a Party. In essence, it provides a power of judicial review, but this takes place before the conclusion of the agreement[49] and is given in the form of an opinion.[50] This opinion, despite its name, has legal consequences: if it is adverse, the agreement cannot enter into force unless it is amended to meet the objections of the European Court, or the EU Treaties are amended to permit the Union to conclude the agreement.[51] Since the procedure for amending the Treaty is cumbersome,[52] an adverse opinion will normally prevent the conclusion of the agreement.[53] If the Court's objections are comparatively minor, however, it may be possible – if the other Parties are willing – to revise the agreement in accordance with the Court's judgment.

There can be no doubt that the object of this procedure as envisaged by the authors of the Treaty was to prevent the Union from entering into agreements which are incompatible with the Treaty. The Court, however, has allowed the Commission to use it for quite a different purpose: to prevent the Member States from encroaching on the competence of the Union. The *Natural Rubber Agreement* case[54] is a good example. The International Agreement on Natural Rubber was a draft agreement drawn up within the framework of UNCTAD. On the Union side, the negotiations had initially been conducted jointly by the Commission and the national Governments, and

[49] Normally the agreement will have been negotiated, but not concluded. If the agreement is concluded by the time it comes to give its opinion, the Court will not give a ruling: Opinion 3/94 (*Bananas* case) [1995] ECR I-4577. In such a case, the appropriate remedy for a Member State or EU institution that wished to contest the agreement would be to bring proceedings under Art. 263 TFEU [230/173 EC] to annul the decision of the Council to conclude it: *ibid.*, para. 22 of the judgment. In the *ECHR* case, Opinion 2/94, [1996] ECR I-1759, the Court was willing to give a ruling on whether the Union had *competence* to accede to the European Convention on Human Rights, even though negotiations had not been commenced; it was not, however, willing to give a ruling on whether accession would be *compatible* with the EU Treaties. This was because, though the provisions of the Convention were known, there was no indication of the terms on which the Union would adhere to it.

[50] For this reason, an application under this provision will not be called, for example, 'Case 1/76', but 'Opinion 1/76'.

[51] This procedure is similar to that under Art. 54 of the French Constitution.

[52] For a discussion of this procedure, see Chap. 3, § 1.2.

[53] The European Convention on Human Rights is an exception.

[54] Opinion 1/78, [1979] ECR 2871.

it was intended by the latter that both the Union and the Member States should be Parties. The Commission, however, felt that the matter came within the exclusive competence of the Union – it maintained that it was covered by the power to conclude trade agreements – and considered that the Member States should not participate in the negotiations.

In some ways the situation was similar to that in the *ERTA* case,[55] but here the Commission decided to use a different legal remedy: it brought an application under Article 218(11) TFEU [300(6)/228(6) EC] and asked the Court for an opinion as to whether it would be compatible with the Treaty for the proposed agreement to be concluded in the mixed form. Since it was not disputed that the Union would be a Party to the agreement, the issue before the Court was the participation of the Member States. The Member States protested at the use of the procedure for this purpose, but the Court held the application admissible, though it eventually gave an opinion which was not wholly in favour of the Commission. It held that the Member States could be Parties if, but only if, it was eventually agreed that the scheme would be financed out of national funds. Until this question was decided, the Member States could continue to participate in the negotiations.

The *ILO Convention 170* case[56] is an even more striking example. This concerned a convention on safety in the use of chemicals at work, which had been drawn up under the auspices of the International Labour Organization. The Commission claimed that it fell under the exclusive competence of the Union; several Member States disputed this.

The Commission brought the matter before the Court under the procedure laid down by Article 218(11) TFEU [300(6)/228(6) EC]. The striking fact about the case was that, as the European Union was not a member of the ILO,[57] it was not in a position to conclude the Convention: only the Member States could have done so. Since Article 218(11) TFEU [300(6)/228(6) EC] applies only where the agreement is to be concluded by the Union, the German and Dutch Governments challenged the jurisdiction of the Court.

The Court solved the problem by ignoring it. It stated that its opinion was concerned only with the question whether the Union had exclusive competence under Union law, not whether the ILO rules permitted the Union to conclude the Convention.[58] This was a fair point, but it was not the point made by the German and Dutch Governments: they had argued that the procedure under Article 218(11) TFEU [300(6)/228(6) EC] can be used only where the agreement is to be concluded by the Union, something which would admittedly not have occurred in the case before

[55] The procedural aspects of this case were discussed in Chap. 4, § 1.1. In the *ERTA* case the Commission could not have invoked Art. 218(11) TFEU [300(6)/228(6) EC], since that provision applies only where the Union is to be a Party to the agreement.

[56] Opinion 2/91, [1993] ECR I-1061.

[57] It only had observer status.

[58] It suggested that, if necessary, the Union's external competence could be exercised through the medium of the Member States acting jointly in the Union's interest.

the Court. Nevertheless, the Court held that the jurisdictional requirements of Article 218(11) TFEU [300(6)/228(6) EC] were satisfied.[59]

Certain features of the procedure under Article 218(11) are rather unusual.[60] The Council, the Commission, and the Member States may submit written observations, but there is no public hearing. All the Advocates General give opinions in a closed session; these are not published. The Court then gives judgment in the normal way, and this is published.

§5 ACTS OF INSTITUTIONS ESTABLISHED BY AGREEMENTS WITH THIRD COUNTRIES

International agreements entered into by the European Union sometimes set up institutional structures.[61] Association councils under association agreements are an example. If these organs have power under the agreement to adopt legally binding acts, can those acts constitute part of the Union legal system? According to the European Court, they can: decisions of the Association Council under the Association Agreement between Turkey and the European Union have been held to constitute 'an integral part of the Union legal system'.[62]

It seems that such decisions are regarded as in some sense partaking of the legal nature of the agreement under which the organ which adopted them was set up.

§6 INTERNATIONAL AGREEMENTS AND THE UNION LEGAL SYSTEM

The legal effect of international agreements with non-member States must be looked at on three levels: the international level, the Union level, and the national level. The effect of an agreement on the international level depends on whether there is a binding obligation between the Union (or the Member States), on the one hand, and the non-member State, on the other. This is decided by international law. At this level, the only way in which Union law could come into play would be if international law referred a particular issue to it.

The effect of an international agreement within the Union legal system, however, is for Union law to decide. It must determine whether international agreements are a

[59] In the end, the Court ruled that the subject matter of the Convention did not fall within exclusive Union competence.

[60] See the Rules of Procedure of the Court of Justice, Arts 107 and 108.

[61] The consent of the European Parliament must be obtained before such agreements may be concluded: Art. 218(6)(a)(iii) TFEU.

[62] *Greece v. Commission*, Case 30/88, [1989] ECR 3711 (para. 13 of the judgment). See also *Sevince*, Case C-192/89, [1990] ECR I-3461; *Deutsche Shell*, Case C-188/91, [1993] ECR I-363.

source of law within the Union legal order, and it can lay down the terms and conditions of that recognition.

The effect of an international agreement at the national level depends on national law. However, when the Member States concluded the Union Treaties, they gave the European Court jurisdiction to interpret those Treaties.[63] Acting under this jurisdiction, the European Court has ruled that the Union Treaties require the Member States to give effect to many provisions of Union law in their legal systems. The courts of the Member States accept that the Member States are under an obligation to give such effect to Union law. Subject to certain limitations, the national legal systems give to provisions of Union law the effect that Union law requires.[64] In this indirect way, therefore, Union law has a large role to play in determining the effect in the national legal systems of those provisions of treaties with non-member States that form part of the Union legal system.

The effect of a treaty obviously depends in part on its validity: a treaty can have no legal effects if it is invalid. A ruling by the European Court that an international agreement with a non-member State was invalid under international law would not be binding on non-member States. However, it would apply within the Union legal system and would determine whether the agreement would be applied as part of EU law.[65]

Even if the agreement was valid under international law, the European Court might still refuse to apply it, either because it was not the kind of agreement which it was prepared to enforce, or because it violated a principle of Union law. It is these questions that will now be considered; in doing so, a distinction will sometimes have to be drawn between the three kinds of international agreement – those concluded by the Union alone, those concluded by the Member States within the general scope of the Union Treaties, and those concluded jointly by the Union and the Member States (mixed agreements). We first consider the effect of the agreement on the Union.

§7 BINDING THE UNION

§7.1 AGREEMENTS CONCLUDED BY THE UNION

Article 216(2) TFEU [300(7)/228(7) EC] provides that international agreements concluded by the European Union are binding on the institutions of the Union. This is, of course, obvious and would be the case even if it were not expressly so provided by the Treaty.

[63] Art. 267 TFEU [234/177 EC]. [64] On these limitations, see Chap. 8.

[65] In deciding this question, the European Court should apply international law: see Pescatore, 'Les relations extérieures des Communautés européennes' (1961) (II) 103 *Recueil des cours de l'Académie de Droit International de la Haye* 1 at 127–8; and *per* Advocate General Mayras in the third *International Fruit Company* case, Cases 21–4/72, [1972] ECR 1219 at 1234.

§7.2 AGREEMENTS CONCLUDED BY THE MEMBER STATES

The European Court has, however, also held that international agreements concluded by the Member States can bind the Union. The leading case is the third *International Fruit Company* case,[66] in which the question arose whether the Union was bound by the General Agreement on Tariffs and Trade (GATT). This was the original GATT, which was concluded before the establishment of the European Community (Union). All the Member States were Parties to it. It was concerned, as its name suggests, with tariffs and trade, and thus fell within the area in which the Union subsequently came to have primary treaty-making power. The case arose after the establishment of the Union.

The European Court held that the Union was bound by it. The key paragraph of its judgment reads:[67]

> ...in so far as under the EEC Treaty the Community [Union] has assumed the powers previously exercised by Member States in the area governed by the General Agreement, the provisions of that agreement have the effect of binding the Community [Union].

In a later case,[68] the Court said that, as regards the fulfilment of commitments under GATT, the Union had 'replaced' the Member States.[69] Although the word 'succession' was not used by the Court, this seems to be the principle on which the case was based.

It is not entirely clear in exactly what circumstances the Union will become bound by agreements entered into by the Member States alone but, according to Advocate General Capotorti, four conditions are necessary: first, the agreement must have been concluded prior to the original EEC Treaty and all the Member States must have been Parties to it when the EEC Treaty was concluded; secondly, it must have been the wish of the Member States to pledge the Union to observe the agreement, the aims of which must be shared by the Union; thirdly, action must have been taken by the Union institutions within the framework of the agreement; and fourthly, the other Parties to the agreement must have recognized that powers had been transferred to the Union with regard to the subject matter of the agreement.[70] It remains to be seen whether the Court will adopt these principles.

The position is different where the Union does not take over the rights and obligations of Member States towards third countries. Where the agreement was concluded prior to the original EEC Treaty (or, in the case of an agreement concluded by a new Member State, prior to its accession), the Union, though not bound by the agreement,

[66] Cases 21–4/72, [1972] ECR 1219. See also *Schlüter*, Case 9/73, [1973] ECR 1135 and *Nederlandse Spoorwegen*, Case 38/75, [1975] ECR 1439. In the latter case, it was held that the Union was bound by two Conventions of 15 December 1950 on customs tariffs.

[67] Para. 18 of the judgment.

[68] *Nederlandse Spoorwegen*, Case 38/75, [1975] ECR 1439 (paras 16 and 21 of the judgment). See also *SPI*, Cases 267–9/81, [1983] ECR 801 (paras 17–19 of the judgment).

[69] When the original GATT was superseded by the WTO Agreement (and its associated instruments) the Union became a Party, along with the Member States.

[70] *Procureur Général v. Arbelaiz-Emazabel*, Case 181/80, [1981] ECR 2961 at 2987; see also *Attorney General v. Burgoa*, Case 812/79, [1980] ECR 2787 at 2815–16. For a recent reconsideration of these issues, see *Intertanko*, Case C-308/06, [2008] ECR I-4057 (Grand Chamber).

would nevertheless be under an obligation not to impede the fulfilment by the Member States which were Parties to the agreement of their obligations under it.[71] This rule, which applies even if only one Member State is a Party, follows from Article 351 TFEU [307/234 EC] (discussed in Chapter 3, § 4.2). Article 351 TFEU does not, however, give the earlier treaty any greater effect than it would have had if the EU Treaties had not been concluded; in particular, it does not require Member States to give direct effect to it,[72] though it does not prevent them from doing so.

The position of the Union with regard to agreements covered by Article 351 TFEU must be distinguished from its position under agreements to which it becomes a Party by succession under the principle laid down in the *International Fruit Company* case, discussed earlier. In the latter case, the Union is bound by the agreement and is responsible to the non-member States for its fulfilment. The agreement is part of the Union legal system. In the former case, the Union is not bound by the agreement and is not responsible to the non-member States for its fulfilment. This is the responsibility of the Member States which are Parties to it. The agreement is not part of the Union legal system, though the powers of the Union are restricted by it.

According to its terms, Article 351 does not apply to agreements concluded after the original EEC Treaty came into existence by countries that were already Member States when they concluded the agreement. In principle, however, a similar rule should apply where the subject matter of the agreement was not within the exclusive competence of the Union at the time when it was concluded: since the Member States that concluded the agreement would have been entirely within their rights in doing so, it would be wrong if the other Parties had their rights under it impaired because the subject matter subsequently came within the exclusive competence of the Union.[73]

If the subject matter *was* within the Union's exclusive competence when the agreement was concluded, the European Court would probably consider that the Union's powers were not restricted by it. Whether the agreement was valid at the international level would be a matter for international law.

§7.3 MIXED AGREEMENTS

Mixed agreements raise particular difficulties. This form of agreement has to be used where the subject matter falls partly within the competence of the European Union and partly within that of the Member States; it is also often used where part or all of the subject matter falls within an area of shared (concurrent) competence – in other words,

[71] *Attorney General v. Burgoa*, Case 812/79, [1980] ECR 2961 (para. 10 of the judgment).

[72] *Attorney General v. Burgoa*, Case 812/79, [1980] ECR 2787 (para. 10 of the judgment and para. 2 of the ruling). On the meaning of 'direct effect', see Chap. 7.

[73] A more difficult question is whether such agreements could ever be binding on the Union under the 'succession' principle laid down in the *International Fruit Company* case. The European Court has never suggested that they might; however, if they cannot, the strange result would ensue that the Union would not be bound by the European Road Transport Agreement, the agreement which was in issue in the *ERTA* case, discussed earlier, in § 2.3.

an area within which either the Union or the Member States could have concluded the agreement on their own.

It is clear that the Union is bound by all parts of a mixed agreement that fall within its competence, whether or not those parts also fall within the competence of the Member States (shared competence).[74] A more difficult question is whether the Union is bound by those parts of the agreement that are outside its competence. It is suggested that it should not be; otherwise, the conclusion of the agreement would constitute an amendment to the Union Treaties, which is surely not what would have been intended.[75] If this is correct, those parts of the agreement within the exclusive competence of the Member States would not form part of the Union legal system.

This reasoning seems to be in accord with that of the European Court. In *Hermès v. FHT*,[76] the Court had to decide whether it had jurisdiction to interpret Article 50 of TRIPs, a mixed agreement concluded jointly by the Union and the Member States as part of the WTO Agreement (see § 2.3). Article 50 is concerned with provisional measures for the protection of intellectual-property rights. The Court held that it did have jurisdiction. The reason was that a Union measure, Regulation 40/94,[77] entered into force shortly before TRIPs was signed. Article 99 of this Regulation was concerned with provisional measures for the protection of Union trade marks. It provides that an application may be made to the courts of a Member State for such provisional measures as are available under the law of that Member State for the protection of national trade marks. Since Article 50 of TRIPs has an effect on national measures available for the protection of trade marks, it has an indirect effect on the protection of Union trade marks. On these flimsy and insubstantial grounds the Court held that it had jurisdiction to interpret Article 50 of TRIPs when a Union trade mark was in issue.[78] The *Hermès* case concerned a trade mark, though not a Union trade mark. However, the Court thought that it would be undesirable if Article 50 were interpreted in one way when a Union trade mark was in issue and in another way when a non-Union trade mark was in issue. So it held that it had jurisdiction in the latter case as well.

Article 50 of TRIPs was again before the Court in *Dior v. Tuk Consultancy*.[79] This time the Court had to decide whether it had jurisdiction to interpret Article 50 when

[74] *Commission v. France*, Case C-239/03, [2004] ECR I-9325, paras 23–25 of the judgment; *Commission v. Ireland*, C-13/00, [2002] ECR I-2943, para. 14 of the judgment; *Demirel*, Case 12/86, [1987] ECR 3719, para. 9 of the judgment.

[75] Pietri, 'La valeur juridique des accords liant la CEE' (1976) 12 RTDE 50 at 75. See also Ehlermann in O'Keeffe and Schermers (eds), *Mixed Agreements* (1983), p. 18.

[76] Case C-53/96, [1998] ECR I-3603. The Court's reasoning in this case is not very clear, but it is clarified in the *Dior* case (see text accompanying n. 79).

[77] OJ 1994 L 11, p. 1.

[78] If the European Court's argument were valid, it would have had jurisdiction to interpret national law on provisional measures to protect trade marks, which it clearly does not. A stronger argument in favour of the Court's position would be to regard Reg. 40/94 as conferring international competence on the Union under the *ERTA* doctrine (discussed earlier, in § 2.3), though this argument is not very satisfactory in view of the limited scope of Art. 99.

[79] Cases C-300, 392/98, [2000] ECR I-11307.

the right in issue was not a trade mark, but an industrial design. It applied the same reasoning: it held that it would be undesirable if Article 50 was interpreted differently depending on whether it was being applied to a trade mark or to some other right.

The Court was also asked to decide on the effect of Article 50. Was the national court obliged to apply it to the case before it? On this, the Court gave a ruling[80] with regard to the field within the competence of the Union,[81] but refused to do so in so far as Article 50 applied outside that field. This was a matter to be decided by the national courts under national law.

One can conclude from this that provisions of mixed agreements that fall within the exclusive competence of the Member States do not form part of the Union legal system. It seems that the European Court has jurisdiction to interpret them only if there is some special reason.

§8 BINDING THE MEMBER STATES

Article 216(2) TFEU [300(7)/228(7) EC] provides that agreements concluded by the European Union are binding on the Member States. Agreements concluded by the Member States which subsequently became binding on the Union would, of course, continue to bind the Member States as well. All agreements binding on the Union are consequently binding on the Member States.

§9 EFFECT

§9.1 GENERAL PRINCIPLES

When might the European Court refuse to give effect to an international agreement on the ground that it was contrary to Union law? At the present time, one cannot lay down any hard and fast rules, but a few general observations may be made. In the *ERTA* case, the Court drew a distinction between the capacity of the European Union to enter into international agreements and its authority to do so. If the agreement was outside the authority of the Union, its conclusion would be contrary to Union law, and a ruling on this point could be obtained under Article 218(11) TFEU. This procedure, however, can be used only before the conclusion of the agreement. If no application is made under Article 218(11) TFEU and the question arises after it is concluded, the Court would not necessarily apply the same test. In particular, it is unlikely that the

[80] It held that it was not directly effective, but it should, as far as possible, be taken into account by national courts when interpreting national law ('indirect effect', explained in Chap. 7, § 4.8).

[81] It said that the test is whether the Union has already legislated in the field in question. Para. 47 of the judgment suggests that this field might be trade marks in general, rather than just EU trade marks.

agreement would be held invalid or inapplicable on the ground that the wrong negotiating procedure was used.

The Court has said that the Union has the capacity to enter into international agreements 'over the whole field of objectives defined in Part One of the Treaty'.[82] If the agreement was outside the capacity of the Union it might be of no effect in the Union legal system. Even if it came within this area, however, it could not be applied in the Union legal system if it directly conflicted with a provision in one of the constitutive Treaties: the powers of the Union come from the Treaties and they must be subject to the provisions of the Treaties.[83] The position would be the same if the international agreement was contrary to a general principle of law.[84] If it conflicted with a Union act, on the other hand, the agreement would be valid: in the third *International Fruit Company* case, this was expressly stated by Advocate General Mayras[85] and is implicit in the judgment of the Court. One may therefore conclude that an international agreement entered into by the Union will be of no effect within the Union legal system if it is outside the capacity of the Union or if it conflicts with one of the constituent Treaties or with a general principle of law.[86] It must again be stressed, however, that this relates solely to the effect of the agreement in the Union legal system, not under international law.

§9.2 PROCEEDINGS IN NATIONAL COURTS

As we shall see in Chapter 7, international agreements which are binding on the Union, and therefore part of the Union legal system, have to be applied by national courts if they are directly effective. In such a case, they will override provisions of national law that conflict with them.

The position is similar where the conflict is with a Union act. In the third *International Fruit Company* case,[87] the European Court held that a Union act may be challenged in a national court on the ground that it is contrary to an international agreement which is binding on the Union. Again, this applies only if the agreement is directly effective.[88]

82 *ERTA*, Case 22/70, [1971] ECR 263 (para. 14 of the judgment).

83 *Kadi v. Council and Commission ('Kadi I')*, Cases C-402/05 P and 415/05 P, [2008] ECR I-6351, paras 305–308 of the judgment. See also Pescatore, 'Les relations extérieures des Communautés européennes' (1961) (II) 103 *Recueil des cours de l'Académie de Droit International de la Haye* 1 at 127.

84 *Kadi v. Council and Commission ('Kadi I')*, Cases C-402/05 P and 415/05 P, [2008] ECR I-6351, paras 305–308 of the judgment.

85 [1972] ECR 1219 at 1233–4. Where a directly effective agreement conflicts with a Union act, the act will be invalid if it was subsequent to the agreement, and would probably be regarded as suspended if it was prior to it.

86 Such a question might come before the Court on a preliminary reference from a national court or in an enforcement action against a Member State (if the Member State is accused of violating the agreement). See also Pietri, 'La valeur juridique des accords liant la Communauté économique européenne' (1976) 12 RTDE 50 and 194 at 207–14.

87 Cases 21–4/72, [1972] ECR 1219.

88 *Van Parys*, Case C-377/02, [2005] ECR I-1465.

§9.3 PROCEEDINGS IN THE EUROPEAN COURT

In *Germany v. Council* (*Bananas* case),[89] the Court held that the same rule applies if the challenge is made in the European Court: a conflict between a Union act and an international agreement affects the validity of the former only if the latter is directly effective. Thus, an international agreement that is not directly effective under Union law cannot form the basis for a challenge to the validity of a Union act in proceedings under Article 263 TFEU; nor can it give rise to an action in tort against the Union under the second paragraph of Article 340 TFEU [288/215 EC].[90] The only exceptions are where the Union act was intended to give effect to an obligation under the international agreement in question[91] or where the Union act expressly refers to the agreement.[92]

FURTHER READING

Items are listed in date order, the most recent being at the end.

SCHERMERS, 'Community Law and International Law' (1975) 12 CMLRev. 77.

MEESSEN, 'The Application of Rules of Public International Law within Community Law' (1976) 13 CMLRev. 485.

JEAN GROUX AND PHILIPPE MANIN, *The European Communities in the International Order* (1985).

CHURCHILL AND FOSTER, 'European Community Law and Prior Treaty Obligations of Member States: The Spanish Fishermen's Cases' (1987) 36 ICLQ 504.

CHEYNE, 'International Agreements and the European Community Legal System' (1994) 19 ELRev. 581.

TRIDIMAS AND EECKHOUT, 'The External Competence of the Community and the Case-Law of the Court of Justice: Principle versus Pragmatism' (1994) 14 YEL 143.

WEISS, 'Succession of States in Respect of Treaties Concluded by the European Communities' (1994) 10 SEW 661.

SACK, 'The European Community's Membership of International Organizations' (1995) 32 CMLRev. 1227.

I MACLEOD, ID HENDRY, AND STEPHEN HYETT, *The External Relations of the European Community* (1996).

NEUWAHL, 'Shared Powers or Shared Incompetence? More on Mixity' (1996) 33 CMLRev. 667.

ALAN DASHWOOD AND CHRISTOPHE HILLION, *The General Law of EC External Relations* (2000).

SCHÜTZE, 'Parallel External Powers in the European Community: From "Cubist" Perspectives Towards "Naturalist" Constitutional Principles?' (2004) 23 YEL 225.

[89] Case C-280/93, [1994] ECR I-4973; see also *Portugal v. Council*, Case C-149/96, [1999] ECR I-8395; *Intertanko*, Case C-308/06, [2008] ECR I-4057.

[90] *Biret International v. Council*, Case C-93/02 P, [2003] ECR I-10497. It makes no difference if the WTO DSB has given a ruling: *FIAMM v. Council and Commission*, Cases C-120–121/06 P, [2008] ECR I-6513.

[91] *Nakajima v. Council*, Case C-69/89, [1991] ECR I-2069.

[92] *FEDIOL v. Commission*, Case 70/87, [1989] ECR 1781.

KUIJPER AND BRONCKERS, 'WTO Law in the European Court of Justice' (2005) 42 CMLRev. 1313.

BRONCKERS, 'The Relationship of the EC Courts with other International Tribunals: Non-Committal, Respectful or Submissive?' (2007) 44 CMLRev. 601.

HOFFMEISTER, 'Outsider or Frontrunner? Recent Developments under International and European Law on the Status of the European Union in International Organizations and Treaty Bodies' (2007) 44 CMLRev. 41.

MARISE CREMONA (ED.), *Developments in EU External Relations Law* (2008).

PIET EECKHOUT, *EU External Relations Law*, 2nd edn (2011).

PART III

UNION LAW AND THE MEMBER STATES

INTRODUCTION

This Part is concerned with the relationship between Union law and national law, in particular with the extent to which provisions of Union law must be applied by national courts.

In what circumstances is a provision of one legal system applicable in another? This depends on the relationship between the two systems. If one is dependent on the other (in the sense that it derives its validity from it), the question of transfer must be determined by the primary system. It can decide whether provisions of the one system can apply in the other and, if they do, in what circumstances this will occur. If, on the other hand, neither system is dependent on the other, each system decides for itself whether provisions of the other can be transferred to it.

This will be clear from two examples. Assume, first, that the United Kingdom decides to give home rule to a territory under its jurisdiction. It sets up a regional assembly with law-making powers and creates a system of courts for that territory. Clearly, UK law determines whether, and in what circumstances, provisions of UK law apply in the dependent legal system. It also decides whether, and in what circumstances, provisions of the dependent system apply in the UK system. This is because UK law is the primary system: it created the regional system and gave it its validity.

Now contrast the position where each system is independent of the other. Let us take the relationship between English and French law. The question whether a provision of French law should be applied in the English legal system depends on English law. It is the English rules of conflict of laws that determine whether a rule of French law will be applied by an English court to determine, for example, the validity of a marriage celebrated in France. French law cannot decide whether a rule of French law is part of the English legal system and must be applied by the English courts. Likewise, English law cannot decide whether a rule of English law is part of the French legal system. This is because each system is autonomous.

These principles also govern the relationship between international law and national law. Since these two systems are independent of each other,[1] the question whether a provision of international law applies in national law must depend on the latter. This is indeed the case. The law of each country decides to what extent international law has effect as part of the legal system of that country.[2]

Since Union law is based on a set of treaties, the important issue for our purposes is the application of a treaty in the domestic law of the States that are parties to it. If a treaty (or a provision in it) applies in the legal system of such a State without that State

[1] This may be rejected by theorists who follow the monist view of international law, but it accords with the actual, real-life relationship between the two systems.

[2] See Francis G. Jacobs and Shelly Roberts (eds), *The Effect of Treaties in Domestic Law* (1987), at p. xxiv (introduction by Jacobs, based on studies of individual countries in later parts of the book).

having to adopt any legislation specifically providing for the application of that treaty, the treaty is said to be 'directly effective' or to have 'direct effect'. A treaty that is directly effective is automatically part of the legal system of the State in question. If, on the other hand, it is not directly effective, it cannot be applied in the domestic law of that State without the adoption of legislation to make provision for this.

When States sign a treaty, they normally agree to achieve a certain result, but reserve to themselves the right to determine the means by which this will be brought about. If the desired result involves an alteration of their law, their law decides whether this will follow automatically from the treaty (direct effect) or whether legislation will be necessary. In certain States (sometimes called 'monist'), direct effect is possible;[3] in others (sometimes called 'dualist') it is not.[4] In both cases, however, it is by virtue of the law of the State in question that the treaty is applied: in a 'monist' country, it is the rule permitting the direct application of treaties (a rule that may be anything from a judge-made principle to a constitutional provision); in a 'dualist' country, it is the legislation passed to give effect to the particular treaty in question. In this latter case, the legislation may take various forms. At one end of the spectrum, it may simply amend national law to bring it into line with the treaty, possibly without even referring to it. At the other end, it may provide that the treaty (contained in a Schedule to the legislation) will have the force of law in the country concerned.[5] In this last situation, the only real difference between a 'dualist' and a 'monist' country is that in the former there is a separate legislative measure each time a treaty has to be applied in the domestic legal system, while in the latter there is one measure providing for the application of all future treaties.[6]

Since Member State law is not dependent on Union law – it does not derive its validity from it – Union law cannot apply in the legal systems of the Member States unless

[3] This does not mean that every treaty will be directly effective: the law of the State in question specifies the requirements for direct effect. Frequently, it must be shown that the treaty is self-executing. This concept was explained as long ago as 1829 by the United States Supreme Court in *Foster and Elam v. Neilson* 2 Pet. 253 at 314, where it distinguished a treaty provision which 'operates of itself, without the aid of any legislative provision' from a provision in which one of the parties 'engages to perform a particular act'. In the former case, the treaty provision is self-executing; in the latter, it is not.

[4] The distinction between the 'monist' and 'dualist' approaches is actually more complex and far-reaching than this, since it concerns the overall relationship between international and domestic law. In adopting these terms, we are not, however, raising these wider questions: we are simply using the terms as handy tags to denote the two approaches set out in the text. Even if the terms are used in this limited sense, however, the statements in the text are still something of an over-simplification: see Jacobs in Jacobs and Roberts (n. 2), pp. xxiv–xxvi.

[5] For an example of this latter method, see s. 2(1) of the Carriage of Goods by Sea Act 1971, which provides that the Hague-Visby Rules (an international agreement) will have the force of law in the United Kingdom. For a more detailed discussion of the position in the United Kingdom, see Higgins in Jacobs and Roberts (n. 2), at pp. 126–9.

[6] Even though the United Kingdom is a 'dualist' country, legislation adopted to give effect to a treaty will, if possible, be interpreted in such a way as to conform to the treaty: *James Buchanan & Co. Ltd v. Babco Forwarding and Shipping (UK) Ltd* [1978] AC 141; *Fothergill v. Monarch Airlines Ltd* [1981] AC 251. This rule can apply even if the UK legislation does not refer to the treaty, provided it is shown that the legislation was passed to give effect to it.

Member State law says so: no rule of Union law can itself bring this about.[7] However, as we shall see in Chapter 7, some provisions of the Treaties provide, and others have been interpreted by the European Court as providing, that Union law must in certain cases have direct application in the legal systems of the Member States. This means that, unlike the position in most treaties, the parties to the EU Treaties agreed not only to achieve a certain result, but also agreed on the means by which this would be brought about (direct effect). In other words, all the Member States undertook to adopt the 'monist' position in certain cases. Though unusual, such a provision is in no any way contrary to international law.[8]

Having undertaken this, the Member States then had to carry it out. In the case of the 'monist' countries, the rule of national law making general provision for direct effect – the rule making that country 'monist'– was sufficient; in the case of 'dualist' countries, on the other hand, a special rule had to be adopted for the purpose. In the United Kingdom, this was section 2(1) of the European Communities Act 1972, which states that all provisions of Union law (including those to be adopted in the future) that under Union law are to be given direct effect will be directly effective in the United Kingdom. It is only by virtue of this provision that Union law is directly effective in the United Kingdom. Thus, while the obligation to give direct effect to certain provisions of Union law stems from the Treaties, the *carrying out* of that obligation is a matter for national law. A detailed discussion of the way in which these obligations have been carried out in various Member States is provided in Chapter 8.

If a provision of one legal system is applied in another, it may conflict with a provision of the latter. When this occurs, the principles discussed previously must determine which prevails. Thus, where an international treaty is applied in the legal system of one of the parties to it, the question whether the treaty overrides national law must be determined by the law of that State. In the case of a 'monist' country, the rule providing for the direct effect of treaties may also indicate their position in the legal hierarchy; otherwise, there will usually be a judge-made rule. In the United States, for example, a treaty that is self-executing (directly effective)[9] has the same position in the legal hierarchy as a federal statute: it prevails over earlier federal statutes but is subordinate to later ones.[10] This is a judge-made rule, though it is partly derived from Article VI,

[7] Thus in *Thoburn v. Sunderland District Council* [2002] 3 WLR 247, Laws LJ said that the relationship between the United Kingdom and the European Union depends on UK law, not EU law (para. 69, proposition 4). See also *Brunner v. European Union Treaty, Bundesverfassungsgericht*, decision of 12 October 1993, [1994] 1 CMLR 57; (1994) 33 ILM 388; 89 BVerfGE 155, in which the German Constitutional Court stated that Union law applies in Germany only because the German laws ratifying the Union Treaties said that it would (para. 55 in the CMLR text). There was a similar ruling by the Danish Supreme Court in *Carlsen v. Rasmussen* [1999] 3 CMLR 854.

[8] See Jackson in Jacobs and Roberts (n. 2), p. 154; see also Plender, 'The European Court as an International Tribunal' [1983] CLJ 279 at 287–8; compare the Advisory Opinion of the Permanent Court of International Justice in the *Danzig Railway Officials* case (1928) PCIJ Ser. B No. 15.

[9] Not all international agreements count as 'treaties' in the United States, and not all 'treaties' are self-executing. For the details, see Jackson in Jacobs and Roberts (n. 2), pp 142–59.

[10] Jackson (n. 2), p. 162. For further details, see *ibid.*, pp 159–64.

section 2, of the United States Constitution. In the Netherlands, on the other hand, the Constitution provides that directly effective treaties prevail over both prior and subsequent legislation.[11]

In the case of a 'dualist' country (such as the United Kingdom), the status of a treaty depends on the instrument by which it was given legal effect. If words from a treaty are incorporated into a statute (either with, or without, a reference to the treaty), they take effect as part of that statute: it is the statute, not the treaty, that is applied. If there is a conflict with another legal provision, the conflict is not between the treaty and the other provision, but between the statute and the other provision. The normal rules determine which prevails. If, on the other hand, the statute says that the treaty has the force of law, it makes sense to say that the treaty itself is being applied. Nevertheless, it is applied only because the statute says so; consequently, the status of the treaty is the same as that of the statute. In both cases, therefore, the position of the treaty in the legal hierarchy depends on that of the legislation by which it was given effect. If this was a statute, it will prevail over earlier statutes, but not over later ones. If it was subordinate legislation, it will have the same status as that legislation.[12] These rules can, however, be changed if the legislation which gave effect to the treaty so provides. The Human Rights Act 1998 is an example: though it gives (limited) effect to the European Convention on Human Rights (ECHR) in the domestic law of the United Kingdom, it provides that the Convention does not prevail over *any* UK legislation, either subsequent or prior.[13]

These rules do not normally prevent States from carrying out their treaty obligations. Since most treaties merely require the parties to achieve a given result, the status of the treaty in their domestic law does not matter as long as the result is achieved. The fact that the treaty could be overridden by later legislation is not a breach of the obligations under it, provided this does not in fact occur. If it occurs inadvertently, the matter can be put right as soon as the conflict is evident. For example, the United Kingdom was a party to the ECHR for many years before the Human Rights Act 1998 came into force. Whenever it appeared, perhaps in a judgment of the European Court of Human Rights, that UK law conflicted with a provision of the Convention, the position was rectified by the amendment of the offending legislation.

There is no provision in the EU Treaties stating that Union law prevails over Member State law. It could, however, be argued that Article 288 TFEU [249/189 EC], which provides that regulations are directly applicable, implies that they should be given at least a certain degree of supremacy.[14] The numerous statements by the European Court that directly effective Union law prevails over Member State law, both prior and subsequent, are based on the proposition that this is what the Member States (implicitly) agreed when they signed the Treaties.[15]

[11] See Schermers in Jacobs and Roberts (n. 2), pp 112–14.

[12] The status of subordinate legislation normally depends on that of the statute under which it was adopted.

[13] See ss 3 and 4. [14] *Costa v. ENEL*, Case 6/64, [1963] ECR 585 at 594.

[15] See *Costa v. ENEL* (n. 14).

Have the Member States carried out this agreement? Here we have a problem. As we have seen, Union provisions can have effect in Member States only by virtue of Member State law,[16] and the extent to which they prevail over domestic law also depends on a rule of Member State law. However, all rules of Member State law derive their validity from the national constitution: consequently, they cannot be valid if the constitution declares them invalid. Since the rule providing for the supremacy of Union law is itself a rule of Member State law, its validity too depends on the national constitution. This means that the supremacy of Union law in a country always depends, in the last analysis, on the constitution of that country. If the constitution imposes limits on such supremacy, there is no way in which those limits can be avoided – unless the constitution itself is amended.

This is most obvious in those countries with written constitutions. In Germany, for example, the Constitutional Court has stated expressly that Union law applies in Germany only because the Treaties were approved by the German Parliament. Since the German Parliament is subject to the Constitution, it could not grant the Union any powers that conflicted with the Constitution. Although the Constitution permits Germany to confer powers on an international organization like the Union, those powers must not be open-ended: they have to be defined in advance. This means that the Union cannot be given the power to extend its powers, what the Germans call *Kompetenz-Kompetenz*. The German Constitutional Court has, therefore, ruled that any Union measure that contravenes this principle would be inapplicable in Germany.[17] The Danish Supreme Court has reached a similar conclusion.[18] Section 20 of the Danish Constitution permits the delegation of powers to an international organization, but this too requires that they be defined in advance. The Supreme Court, therefore, held that if a Union measure went beyond the powers conferred on the Union, the Danish courts would declare it inapplicable in Denmark. In both Germany and Denmark, the national courts would be the ones to decide.

Similar views have been expressed by courts in other Member States (though they have not always been so clearly formulated). So far, it has always been possible to solve the problems that have arisen. Sometimes a constitutional amendment or new legislation is required. If this is not possible,[19] the Member States would have to work together to find a solution, possibly by amending Union law. The adoption of human rights as a general principle of Union law, as explained in Chapter 5, shows that the European Court is prepared to play its part.

[16] For the United Kingdom, see the European Union Act 2011, s. 18.

[17] *Brunner v. European Union Treaty*, Federal Constitutional Court *(Bundesverfassungsgericht)*, decision of 12 October 1993, [1994] 1 CMLR 57.

[18] *Carlsen v. Rasmussen*, Danish Supreme Court (*Højesteret*), judgment of 6 April 1998, [1999] 3 CMLR 854.

[19] Certain provisions of the German Constitution cannot be amended: *Grundgesetz*, Art. 79(3); moreover, in both Germany and in other Member States, it might be politically impossible to obtain the necessary majority to amend the Constitution.

FURTHER READING

Items are listed in date order, the most recent being at the end.

John Usher, *European Union Law and National Law. The Irreversible Transfer?* (1981).

Pellet, 'Les Fondements Juridiques Internationaux du Droit Communautaire' (1997) V(2) *Collected Courses of the Academy of European Law* 193.

Hartley, 'The Constitutional Foundations of the European Union' (2001) 117 LQR 225.

7

DIRECT EFFECT AND NATIONAL REMEDIES

The purpose of this chapter is to consider the rules laid down by the European Court on the obligations of the Member States under Union law to give direct effect to provisions of Union law. The way in which and the extent to which these obligations are carried out in different Member States are considered in Chapter 8.

§1 THE PRINCIPLE OF DIRECT EFFECT

§1.1 BASIC IDEAS

Direct effect was explained in the Introduction to this Part. If direct effect is given to a provision of Union law, that provision is applied by the national court as part of the law of the land. No rule of national law *specifically* referring to it is necessary. As we saw in the Introduction, however, a rule of national law making general provision for direct effect *is* necessary.

The *Van Gend en Loos*[1] case was the first decision by the European Court on direct effect; it is also one of the most important judgments ever handed down by the Court. The case arose when a private firm sought to invoke Union law against the Dutch customs authorities in proceedings in a Dutch tribunal. The tribunal made a reference to the European Court. The main issue was whether Article 12 of the EEC Treaty was directly effective. As it stood at the time,[2] the Article read:

> Member States shall refrain from introducing between themselves any new customs duties on imports or exports or any charges having equivalent effect, and from increasing those which they already apply in their trade with each other.

It will be noticed that this provision was addressed to Member States: it imposed an obligation on them but did not expressly grant any corresponding right to individuals to import goods free from any new customs duties; nor did it state explicitly that any such duty would be invalid. For these reasons, one might have thought that it was not directly effective. The European Court, however, took the view that a provision is not prevented from being directly effective merely because it is addressed to Member States and does not expressly confer rights on private individuals.[3]

[1] Case 26/62, [1963] ECR 1. [2] It has since been replaced.

[3] For an affirmation of this, see *Defrenne v. Sabena*, Case 43/75, [1976] ECR 455 at para. 31 of the judgment.

The Court instead laid down a different test:[4]

> The wording of Article 12 contains a clear and unconditional prohibition which is not a positive but a negative obligation. This obligation, moreover, is not qualified by any reservation on the part of states which would make its implementation conditional upon a positive legislative measure enacted under national law. The very nature of this prohibition makes it ideally adapted to produce direct effects in the legal relationship between Member States and their subjects.

In later cases, this test has been modified and refined. The suggestion that only negative obligations (prohibitions) may be directly effective has been dropped and the test may now be stated succinctly as follows:[5]

1. the provision must be clear and unambiguous;
2. it must be unconditional;
3. its operation must not be dependent on further action being taken by Union or national authorities.

§1.2 CLEAR AND UNAMBIGUOUS

Clarity and unambiguity are striven for by every legal draftsman; frequently, however, they are not attained. This is particularly true in the case of instruments which have to be agreed to by a number of different parties with conflicting interests, as is the case both with the constitutive Treaties and Union legislation. Like many provisions of national law, Union law is often unclear and ambiguous. This does not in itself, however, prevent its being directly effective: the European Court is there to interpret it and once this has been done the ambiguities will be resolved.

The difficulty, therefore, is not so much ambiguity, as generality and lack of precision. If the provision merely lays down a general objective or policy to be pursued, without specifying the appropriate means to attain it, it can hardly be regarded as a legal rule suitable for application by a court of law. In such cases, further legislation is necessary before it can become operative.

A good example of such a provision is Article 4(3) TEU, which states:

> Pursuant to the principle of sincere cooperation, the Union and the Member States shall, in full mutual respect, assist each other in carrying out tasks which flow from the Treaties.
>
> The Member States shall take any appropriate measure, general or particular, to ensure fulfilment of the obligations arising out of the Treaties or resulting from the acts of the institutions of the Union.
>
> The Member States shall facilitate the achievement of the Union's tasks and refrain from any measure which could jeopardise the attainment of the Union's objectives.

[4] *Van Gend en Loos* (n. 1) at 13.

[5] See Dashwood, 'The Principle of Direct Effect in European Community Law' (1978) 16 JCMS 229 at 231 *et seq.*

This is far too general to be directly effective by itself, though it might be suitable for application in conjunction with some other provision which spelled out more clearly what Member States were required to do, or not to do.[6]

The degree of precision that is necessary will of course vary according to the situation. A provision imposing obligations on private citizens should have a higher degree of precision than a measure granting rights to individuals against national authorities. In the case of criminal law, a particularly high degree of precision is essential. Thus, for example, if a Union regulation required Member States to enact measures imposing criminal penalties for breach of Union law, one could hardly imagine the European Court holding that a new crime had been established by virtue of the direct effect of the regulation if a Member State had failed to enact the required measures.

§1.3 UNCONDITIONAL

A Union provision will not be prevented from being directly effective merely because the rights it grants are dependent on some objective factor or event: once the condition is satisfied, there is no reason why the provision should not be enforced by the national courts. What is meant by the requirement of unconditionality is rather that the right must not be dependent on something within the control of some independent authority, such as a Union institution, or the Member State itself. In particular, it must not be dependent on the judgment or discretion of any such body.

An example of a situation where the judgment or discretion of a Union institution is involved is furnished by Articles 107–109 TFEU. These concern State aid which distorts competition by favouring certain enterprises or products at the expense of others. This is stated by Article 107(1) to be 'incompatible with the internal market' where it affects trade between Member States; certain exceptions are provided by subsequent provisions. It might be thought that this was sufficiently definite to be directly effective; however, Article 108(2) makes provision for the Commission to decide whether any such aid infringes the provisions of Article 107 and to order the offending Member State to terminate it within a period of time laid down by the Commission. Moreover, Article 108(2) allows the Council to authorize any aid which might otherwise be regarded as contrary to the Treaty and, where an application is made to the Council for this purpose, any Commission proceedings must be suspended. In view of this, it is clear that Article 107(1) cannot have been intended to be directly effective: the prohibition it contains is conditional on the decisions of the Council and Commission.[7]

[6] However, in *Schlüter*, Case 9/73, [1973] ECR 1135 at para. 39 of its judgment, the European Court held that Art. 5 EEC, the predecessor of Art. 4(3) TEU, was not directly effective, even when combined with what was then Art. 107 EEC. See also *Hurd v. Jones (Inspector of Taxes)*, Case 44/84, [1986] ECR 29 at paras 47 and 48 of the judgment.

[7] See *Capolongo*, Case 77/72, [1973] ECR 611 at paras 4–6, where the Court held that, at least as regards systems of aid in operation at the time when the Treaty went into effect, Art. 107(1) TFEU (then Art. 92(1) EEC) was not directly effective in the absence of a decision under Art. 108(2) TFEU (93(2) EEC).

An extreme example of a right dependent on the discretion of a Member State would be a provision stating: 'Each Member State shall, in so far as it considers it desirable...' This obviously could not be directly effective: if the Member State failed to take the action in question, it could always argue that it did not consider it desirable to do so.

A more limited, but still significant, discretion is that which exists where Union law requires the attainment of an objective but allows the Member States to choose the means. If there are a number of quite different ways in which the objective could be attained, the discretion given to the Member States may prevent the provision from being directly effective.[8]

An example is a Union provision[9] adopted in 1976 (now replaced), which required Member States to give effect to the principle of equal treatment for men and women as regards access to employment. Among other things, the provision obliged Member States to provide a legal remedy for the victims of discrimination. In the *Von Colson* case[10] a woman who had been refused a job because of her sex argued that Union law gave her a directly effective right to demand that the court order the employer to appoint her to the post. The European Court, however, held that there were several ways in which Member States could fulfil the obligation to provide a legal remedy: for example, the victim of discrimination could be given the right to demand appointment or she could be given the right to claim damages. Any effective remedy would constitute compliance with the obligation. The discretion given to the Member States consequently prevented the obligation from being directly effective.

A different kind of discretion is given in the so-called 'safeguard' clauses which occur quite frequently in different parts of the Treaty. The normal pattern is for the Treaty to grant rights, but allow the Member States to restrict these rights in special cases, it being understood that it is for the Member State concerned to decide whether the situation justifies recourse to the safeguard clause.

One example of this is Article 45(3) TFEU, which grants workers the right of free movement between Member States but provides that this right is 'subject to limitations justified on grounds of public policy, public security, or public health'. Since it is the national authorities who decide what the requirements of public policy, etc. are, it will be appreciated that this provision makes the right to immigrate subject to a condition dependent on the judgment of the Member State. For example, if a Government decides that the activities of a certain organization are against public policy, it will be entitled to invoke the proviso so as to prevent members of that organization from entering the country.

[8] However, if the individual would be entitled to certain minimum rights whichever way the Member State exercised its discretion, the provision might be directly effective to that extent: *Francovich v. Italy*, Cases C-6, 9/90, [1991] ECR I-5357 at paras 15–21 of the judgment.

[9] The provision is contained in a directive, Directive 76/207, OJ 1976, L 39/40. As will be seen later, directives can be directly effective only where they are invoked against the State, as was the case in *Von Colson* (see n. 10).

[10] *Von Colson and Kamann v. Land Nordrhein-Westfalen*, Case 14/83, [1984] ECR 1891.

In view of this, one would have thought that the right of free movement granted by Article 45(3) TFEU was conditional and that, as a discretionary element is present, it could not be directly effective. In *Van Duyn v. Home Office*,[11] however, the European Court rejected this argument. The case concerned a Dutchwoman who wanted to enter the United Kingdom to take up a post with the Church of Scientology. Scientology might, perhaps, be described as a 'fringe religion': it is strongly supported by its adherents but disapproved of by the more established religious bodies. Some years previously, the British Government had reached the conclusion that Scientology was harmful to the mental health of those involved and adopted a policy of discouraging it, though it was not made illegal. One consequence of this was that immigration permission was normally refused to known Scientologists.

When Miss Van Duyn arrived in England, she was refused permission to enter, and this was justified on the basis of the public policy proviso. She then brought legal proceedings in the English courts to challenge this decision, and one question which arose was whether Article 45(3) TFEU (then Article 48(3) EEC) was directly effective. A reference was made to the European Court for a ruling on the issue and it was argued that the discretionary element eliminated the possibility of direct effect. The Court rejected this on the ground that the application of the proviso is 'subject to judicial control'. By this it seemed to be referring to the fact that decisions of the national authorities based on the proviso are subject to judicial review in the courts of the Member States.[12]

The difference between the situation in the *Von Colson* case and that in the *Van Duyn* case seems to be that, in the former, the Member States had a discretion as to how they would give effect to the right, while, in the latter, the right was provided by Union law and the Member States were merely given a limited power to restrict it in certain circumstances. In the former case, the right was incomplete until the Member State had acted; in the latter case, it was not.

§1.4 NOT DEPENDENT ON FURTHER ACTION

If the Union provision states that the rights it grants will come into effect when further action of a legislative or executive nature has been taken by the Union or the Member States, it would seem reasonable to hold that it cannot have direct effect until that action is taken. In accordance with its general policy, however, the European Court has sought to whittle this requirement down to its very minimum. It has done this by laying down a rule that, if the Union provision gives a time limit for its implementation, it can become directly effective if not implemented by the deadline.

Article 119 EEC, as it originally stood, provides an example. It stated:

> Each Member State shall during the first stage ensure and subsequently maintain the application of the principle that men and women should receive equal pay for equal work.

[11] Case 41/74, [1974] ECR 1337 at para. 7 of the judgment.

[12] This was required by Art. 8 of Directive 64/221, OJ (Spec. Ed.) 1963/64, p. 117.

This clearly envisaged action by the Member States to bring the principle into operation, but it laid down a deadline: the end of the first stage. The Court therefore held in the second *Defrenne* case[13] that the requirement of further action did not prevent it from being directly effective thereafter.

In practice, this modification of the original rule to a large extent nullifies it, since almost all Union provisions requiring further action contain a time limit. In such cases, the only consequence of the requirement is that direct effect is postponed until the deadline has passed.

§1.5 CONCLUSIONS

The rulings of the European Court on direct effect are a good example of the Court's strategy in introducing new legal principles: in the first case in which this question arose – the *Van Gend en Loos* case – it used language which suggested that there was a fairly stringent test and that direct effect, at least in the case of Treaty provisions, was a rather rare phenomenon. Once the principle was accepted, however, the requirements were cut down: the rule regarding negative obligations was dropped and the requirements that the obligations must be unconditional and not dependent on further action were considerably qualified. The result is that direct effect may now be regarded as the norm rather than the exception.

One can, in fact, say that the test is of an essentially practical nature: it lays down the minimum conditions for the application of almost any legal rule. In other words, the test is really one of feasibility: if the provision lends itself to judicial application, it will almost certainly be declared directly effective; only where direct effect would create serious practical problems is it likely that the provision will be held not to be directly effective.[14]

The previous comments concern direct effect in general. It is now desirable to change the focus of the discussion and give separate consideration to provisions derived from each of the various sources of Union law.

§2 TREATY PROVISIONS

There is no statement in any of the Treaties as to whether Treaty provisions are directly effective. It is in fact probable that the authors of the Treaties assumed that the question of direct effect would be decided by national courts according to the criteria of national law. If this is correct, the European Court's assumption of jurisdiction in this matter, as well as the liberal criteria it has adopted, constitutes a development of the greatest importance.

[13] *Defrenne v. Sabena*, Case 43/75, [1976] ECR 455.

[14] *Banks*, Case C-128/92, [1994] ECR I-1209 at 1237 (*per* Advocate General van Gerven). See also Pescatore, 'The Doctrine of "Direct Effect": An Infant Disease of Community Law' (1983) 8 ELRev. 155, especially at 174–7.

§3 REGULATIONS

Article 288 TFEU [249/189 EC] states that a regulation is 'directly applicable in all Member States'. The authors of the Treaties probably intended 'directly applicable' to mean the same thing as 'directly effective'. Since there is no similar statement regarding other kinds of Union legislation, or regarding the Treaties themselves, it seems likely that they intended that regulations, and only regulations, would be directly effective. The Court has ruled, however, that other Union instruments are also capable of having direct effect. This has given rise to the problem of reconciling the Court's ruling with the wording of the Treaties, a problem which has caused much concern to legal writers,[15] though not (apparently) to the Court itself. The dilemma is as follows: if one interprets 'directly applicable' to mean the same thing as 'directly effective',[16] it would seem to follow that only regulations can be directly effective. If, on the other hand, one treats the two terms as meaning something different, one has to find a suitable meaning for 'directly applicable', a meaning that refers to some quality possessed by regulations but not by other instruments of Union law.[17] This in turn causes other problems because, though such features undoubtedly exist, they are neither clear-cut nor important enough to warrant a special provision in the Treaty, especially when the Treaty does not (it is assumed) make express provision for direct effect. In fact, the whole debate is sterile, since the sole purpose of drawing a distinction between the two terms is to rebut the accusation that the Court is acting contrary to the Treaties: it does not lead to any better understanding of the law.[18] The best solution, therefore, is to bypass these semantic issues and proceed directly to the concrete features of the different instruments. This will now be done.

In view of Article 288 TFEU, it might be thought that regulations were always directly effective. Very frequently this is the case – but it is not always so.[19] Take, for

[15] For a summary of the different views, see Steiner, 'Direct Applicability in EEC Law – A Chameleon Concept' (1982) 98 LQR 229.

[16] See Bebr, 'Directly Applicable Provisions of Community Law: The Development of a Community Concept' (1970) 19 ICLQ 257, *passim* and especially at 266–7; and Toth, *Legal Protection of Individuals in the European Communities* (1978), I, p. 119, note 1.

[17] This theory was first put forward by JA Winter in an article entitled 'Direct Applicability and Direct Effect: Two Distinct and Different Concepts in Community Law' (1972) 9 CMLRev. 425. He makes the distinction between the two terms clear at pp. 425–6 and again at pp. 435–6, though paradoxically he himself sometimes uses 'direct applicability' as if it meant 'direct effect': see, for example, at pp. 427 *et seq*. Other authors who regard the two terms as having different meanings include Dashwood, 'The Principle of Direct Effect in European Community Law' (1978) 16 JCMS 229 at 230, and Brinkhorst (1971) 8 CMLRev. 380 at 390–1.

[18] At the time when these developments were taking place, the Court seemed to use the two terms as meaning the same thing: see Pescatore, 'The Doctrine of "Direct Effect": An Infant Disease of Community Law' (1983) 8 ELRev. 155, note 2. Pescatore was one of the leading judges on the European Court at the time in question.

[19] See *per* Advocate General Warner in *Galli*, Case 31/74, [1975] ECR 47 at 70 and in *Steinike und Weinlig v. Germany*, Case 78/76, [1977] ECR 595 at 583; and *per* Advocate General Reischl in *Ratti*, Case 148/78, [1979] ECR 1629 *passim*.

example, Regulation 1463/70[20] (now repealed). This was concerned with the introduction of recording equipment (tachographs) in commercial vehicles, and Article 4 stated that the use of this equipment would be compulsory from a given date. Article 21(1)[21] then provided:

> Member States shall, in good time and after consulting the Commission, adopt such laws, regulations or administrative provisions as may be necessary for the implementation of this Regulation.
>
> Such measures shall cover, *inter alia*, the reorganization of, procedure for, and means of carrying out, checks on compliance and the penalties to be imposed in case of breach.

This provision clearly could not have been directly effective; in particular, it could not have created a new criminal offence – that of driving a commercial vehicle without a tachograph. It was far too vague: it did not state exactly what would constitute the offence, who would be regarded as responsible (owner or driver), what the penalties would be, or what defences would be available.

Since regulations are normally directly effective, there is usually no need for the enactment of national legislation to give effect to them. The European Court has moreover laid down a general rule that, except where they are necessary, national implementing measures are improper.[22] The reason for this is that the Court does not want the Union nature of the provision to be obscured: it must be clearly applied as a provision of Union law, not of national law. In particular, the Court seems concerned about three matters. First, if the provisions of the regulation were enacted as part of a national measure, it might be thought that they took effect from the date of the national measure, rather than that of the Union measure: this could mean that the provisions would not come into force on the same date in all the Member States. Secondly, there is a danger that, when the Union provisions were transformed into national law, subtle changes would be made in their content to suit national interests: in this way the uniformity of Union law would be jeopardized. Thirdly, national implementation could prejudice the European Court's jurisdiction to give a ruling on the interpretation and validity of the measure under the procedure for a preliminary reference.[23] It is true that the Court has expressly stated that its jurisdiction cannot be affected by national implementation measures;[24] nevertheless, it is conceivable that some national courts

[20] OJ 1970 (Spec. Ed.) 482.

[21] Art. 21 was renumbered Art. 23 with effect from 1 January 1978 by Art. II of Regulation 2828/77, OJ 1977, L 334/5.

[22] This rule is often justified on the ground that, under Art. 288 TFEU, regulations are directly applicable. This could, therefore, indicate an appropriate meaning to give to 'directly applicable' if one wanted to distinguish it from 'directly effective', but this would then mean that not all regulations were directly applicable, which would conflict not only with Art. 288 TFEU, but also with the opinion of Advocate General Warner in *R v. Secretary of State for Home Affairs, ex parte Santillo*, Case 131/79, [1980] ECR 1585 at 1608. Moreover, the European Court has said that the fact that regulations are directly applicable does not mean that they cannot contain provisions empowering Member States to pass implementing measures: *Eridania*, Case 230/78, [1979] ECR 2749 at para. 34 of the judgment.

[23] See *Variola*, Case 34/73, [1973] ECR 981 at para. 11 of the judgment.

[24] *Ibid.*

might be less ready to make a reference to the European Court if the Union provisions were incorporated in a national measure.

The doctrine that national measures are improper was first laid down in 1973 in *Commission v. Italy*.[25] This case concerned a Union plan to counter the over-production of dairy products by the introduction of a premium for the slaughter of cows. The Italian Government had passed a decree which stated that the provisions of the relevant regulations were 'deemed to be included' in it and then proceeded to reproduce them together with certain procedural provisions of a national character.

Enforcement proceedings were taken against Italy, both because it had failed to bring the scheme into operation on time, and because certain aspects of it had not been put into effect at all. In the course of its judgment, the Court made the following comments concerning the enactment of the national decree:[26]

> By following this procedure, the Italian Government has brought into doubt both the legal nature of the applicable provisions and the date of their coming into force.
>
> According to the terms of Articles 189 [now 288 TFEU] and 191 [now 297 TFEU] of the Treaty, Regulations are, as such, directly applicable in all Member States and come into force solely by virtue of their publication in the *Official Journal* of the Communities, as from the date specified in them, or in the absence thereof, as from the date provided in the Treaty.
>
> Consequently, all methods of implementation are contrary to the Treaty which would have the result of creating an obstacle to the direct effect of Union Regulations and of jeopardizing their simultaneous and uniform application in the whole of the Union.

The Court went on to point out that in one respect the Italian decree had departed from the terms of Union law in that it had failed to take into account an extension of the time allowed for slaughter under a later regulation. It then concluded:[27]

> The default of the Italian Republic has thus been established by reason not only of the delay in putting the system into effect but also of the manner of giving effect to it provided by the decree.

The rule that national measures are improper is subject to exceptions in a number of situations. The first and most obvious exception is where the regulation itself expressly requires the Member States to take action to implement it: this was the case with Article 21 of the tachograph regulation discussed previously. Here, implementing measures are not only permitted, they are obligatory: when the United Kingdom failed to implement Article 21, it was ordered to do so by the European Court.[28]

Secondly, there may be cases in which, though the regulation does not expressly require implementation, it may impliedly permit it. This would be the case where the terms of the regulation are rather vague and provision for its detailed application is desirable. It appears that in such a case national measures will be permissible, provided they are not incompatible with the provisions of the regulation.[29]

[25] Case 39/72, [1973] ECR 101. [26] Para. 17. [27] Para. 18.
[28] *Commission v. United Kingdom*, Case 128/78, [1979] ECR 419.
[29] See *Bussone*, Case 31/78, [1978] ECR 2429 at para. 32 of the judgment.

Whether national measures are permissible in other circumstances is uncertain. One situation in which they would serve a useful function is where national provisions purport to codify the law in a particular area and thus give a complete statement of all the relevant legal rules. If a regulation impinges on that area, so that in certain cases rights may be derived from it, it might be desirable in the interests of clarity, certainty, and legislative 'tidiness' for those aspects of the issue governed by the regulation to be repeated in the national provision.

§4 DIRECTIVES

§4.1 THE TREATIES

Whatever the position may be regarding other Union measures, there is little doubt that the authors of the Treaties did not intend directives to be directly effective. This view, which was generally accepted in the early days of the Union, follows from the concept of a directive as laid down in the Treaties: Article 288 TFEU [249/189 EC] pointedly refrains from declaring directives directly applicable. Moreover, it states that a directive is binding only 'as to the result to be achieved' but leaves 'the choice of form and methods' to the national authorities. In other words, the directive lays down an objective and leaves it to the Member States to achieve that objective according to such means as they might think fit. This clearly implies that legislative measures will be taken by the national authorities and that, though the result must be the same in all Member States, the details of the legislation may vary: this is the essence of the distinction between regulations and directives. In these circumstances, one might have thought, there could be no possibility of directives having direct effect.

§4.2 THE FIRST STEP

The European Court, however, decided otherwise. The first tentative step was taken in two cases decided within a couple of months of each other in 1970, *Grad*[30] and *SACE*.[31] In both these cases, the role of the directive was limited to setting the date when a provision in another instrument would come into force.[32] The European Court held that this fact did not prevent the provision in the other instrument from being directly effective. It was only in a limited sense, therefore, that the directives in these cases were themselves directly effective.

[30] Case 9/70, [1970] ECR 825. [31] Case 33/70, [1970] ECR 1213.

[32] In *SACE* the provision was contained in the Treaty; in *Grad* it was in a decision. The ruling in the latter case that a decision can be directly effective may be thought of as foreshadowing that in the *Van Duyn* case (see n. 33).

§4.3 THE NEW PRINCIPLE

This reasoning might have suggested that these were special cases; any such illusions were, however, dispelled when the Court decided the *Van Duyn* case in 1974.[33] The facts have already been outlined in § 1.3, where it was mentioned that the Court held Article 45(3) TFEU (then Article 48(3) EEC) to be directly effective. This, however, was only one issue in the case; the Court was also asked whether Article 3(1) of Directive 64/221[34] was directly effective. The purpose of this directive was to limit the discretion of Member States when they invoked the public policy proviso under Article 45(3) TFEU, and Article 3(1) lays down that such measures must be 'based exclusively on the personal conduct of the individual concerned'. It was argued on behalf of Miss Van Duyn that this provision was directly effective and that she could therefore rely on it before the English court: she maintained that the only ground the Home Office had for refusing her admission to the United Kingdom was her membership of the Church of Scientology, and she contended that this did not constitute 'personal conduct' in terms of Article 3(1).

This was, of course, a different situation from that in the previous cases: here the very essence of the right was laid down in the directive. There could be no question of a 'special case': the Court was obliged to decide, as a matter of general principle, whether a directive could have direct effect. The UK Government argued that it could not, basing its argument on the provisions of Article 288 TFEU (then 189 EEC) mentioned earlier. The European Court, however, held that directives can be directly effective.

The Court gave three arguments in support of this conclusion. The first was that it would be incompatible with the binding effect attributed to a directive in Article 288 TFEU (189 EEC) to exclude in principle the possibility of direct effect. This argument is unsound: it is quite possible for a measure to be fully binding at the international level without its being enforceable in national courts by private individuals. In such a case it could be enforced by means of an action brought in the European Court by the Commission or by another Member State.

The second argument was much stronger. This, however, was a policy argument, not a legal one. It was that the *practical effectiveness* ('*effet utile*', in French) of the measure would be greater if individuals were entitled to invoke it before the national courts. This will be considered further later.

The third argument was based on Article 267 TFEU (then 177 EEC). This is the provision which governs references from national courts to the European Court (see Chapter 9). It grants the Court jurisdiction to give preliminary rulings on, among other things, the validity and interpretation of 'acts of the institutions . . . of the Union'. The exact meaning of this phrase will be considered in Chapter 9; there can, however, be no doubt that it includes decisions and directives as well as regulations. The Court argued that this implies that all such acts can be directly effective.

[33] Case 41/74, [1974] ECR 1337. [34] OJ 1963/64 (Spec. Ed.) 117.

The Court's argument, however, assumes that a national court might require a preliminary ruling only in the case of a directly effective provision. This is not so: if a Union provision which is not directly effective is implemented by a national measure, the validity and interpretation of the latter might – under *national* law – depend on the validity and interpretation of the former. As will be shown in Chapter 8, § 7.4, this is the case in the United Kingdom. Consequently, a national court might very well require a preliminary ruling on the validity and interpretation of a Union provision which was not directly effective: the European Court has itself said that this is permissible.[35] It may also be required as a matter of Union law by virtue of the doctrine of 'indirect effect' (discussed in § 4.8). Consequently, no inference can be drawn from the terms of Article 267 TFEU.[36]

The strongest argument of a legal, or quasi-legal, nature is in fact one that was not even mentioned in the *Van Duyn* case. This is an argument derived from the English doctrine of equity and similar principles in civil law systems.[37] The problem in the *Van Duyn* case was that the UK Government had done nothing to implement Article 3(1) of the directive: there was no British provision stating that entry could be refused only on the basis of the personal conduct of the would-be immigrant. If the directive had been implemented, there would have been no difficulty: Miss Van Duyn could have relied on the British provision. In effect, therefore, the UK Government was seeking to deny her a right on the ground of its own failure to implement the directive. This could bring into play the principle that no one should profit from his own wrongdoing. In other words, Miss Van Duyn's rights should have been regarded as being no less than they would have been if the UK Government had fulfilled its obligation to implement the directive. This would have entailed allowing her to invoke the provisions of the directive in the English courts.

The idea that the direct effect of directives can be justified on the ground that it prevents a Member State from taking advantage of its own wrongdoing was first put to the Court by an Englishman, Advocate General Warner, in 1977, three years after the *Van Duyn* case was decided.[38] It was adopted by the Court in 1979.[39] Today, the other arguments have been quietly dropped and the 'equity' argument is now routinely put forward by the Court as the official justification.[40]

Whatever one may think about these arguments, there can be no doubt that it was on policy grounds that the Court decided to proclaim the new doctrine: the argument of *effectiveness* was what really won the day. The fact of the matter is that Member States

[35] *Mazzalai*, Case 111/75, [1976] ECR 657 at 665.

[36] It is interesting to note that this argument has been abandoned in subsequent cases: see, for example, *Verbond van Nederlandse Ondernemingen*, Case 51/76, [1977] ECR 113 at paras 20–24 of the judgment.

[37] See *per* Advocate General van Gerven in *Barber*, Case C-262/88, [1990] ECR I-1889, note 34, where the civil law principle of *nemo auditur propriam turpitudinem allegans* is contrasted with the common law doctrine of estoppel.

[38] *Enka*, Case 38/77, [1977] ECR 2203 at 2226.

[39] *Ratti*, Case 148/78, [1979] ECR 1629 at para. 22 of the judgment.

[40] See, for example, *Faccini Dori v. Recreb*, Case C-91/92, [1994] ECR I-3325 at para. 22 of the judgment; *Arcaro*, Case C-168/95, [1996] ECR I-4705 at para. 36 of the judgment.

were (and still are) remiss in implementing directives,[41] and it was this that persuaded the Court to act. Without direct effect, a directive can be enforced only by means of an enforcement action brought in the European Court by the Commission (or by another Member State). The difficulty is that – for reasons of manpower, if for no others – the Commission is able to handle only a small number of such cases each year: it would be quite impossible for them to bring proceedings with regard to every directive which had not been fully implemented. In some cases, moreover, pressure may be brought against the Commission to dissuade it from taking action. By declaring a directive directly effective, on the other hand, the Court can open the way for individuals to enforce it in the national courts. This has the added advantage both of shielding the Commission from political pressure and of casting on the national courts the burden of ensuring compliance.

§4.4 THE IMPORTANCE OF THE DEADLINE

In the *Van Duyn* case the time limit for the implementation of the directive had long since passed; the significance of this date was not therefore given much emphasis. The *Ratti* case,[42] however, shows that it is in fact crucial. This concerned two directives dealing with the packaging and labelling of solvents and varnishes respectively. The first, Directive 73/173,[43] was adopted on 4 June 1973 and required Member States to implement its provisions by 8 December 1974; the second, Directive 77/728,[44] was adopted on 7 November 1977 and laid down a deadline of 9 November 1979.

Mr Ratti was an Italian who ran a firm selling both solvents and varnishes in Italy. The firm decided that it would package and label its products so as to comply with the two directives, even though neither had been implemented in Italy. The matter was, however, covered by an Italian law passed in 1963 which applied to both products and was in some ways more lenient than the directives, but in other ways stricter. When the firm put its products on the market, Ratti was prosecuted for failure to comply with the provisions of the Italian law. At the relevant time, the deadline for implementation of the first directive had expired but that for the second had not. Ratti admitted that he had not complied with the Italian law but argued that compliance with the directives was sufficient.

The court in Milan, before which the prosecution had been brought, made a reference to the European Court for a ruling on whether the directives were directly effective. The European Court held that a directive can become directly effective only when

[41] The Netherlands is generally regarded as one of the most conscientious of the Member States, yet a study by two Dutch authors at roughly the same time as the *Van Duyn* decision shows that even the Dutch had a bad record in this regard. Of the ninety-four directives chosen for examination, almost two-thirds (sixty) were not implemented on time: Maas and Bentvelsen, 'De tijdige uitvoering van EEG-richtlijnen in Nederland' [1978] *Bestuurswetenschappen* 443 at 446. If this was the state of affairs in the Netherlands, things were probably even worse in some other countries.

[42] Case 148/78, [1979] ECR 1629. For an illuminating comment, see Usher (1979) 4 ELRev. 268.

[43] OJ 1973, L 189/7.

[44] OJ 1977, L 303/23.

the deadline for implementation has expired; therefore, the first directive was directly effective, but the second was not. The Court held that this result was not affected by the fact that some of the varnishes had been imported from Germany, which had already implemented the second directive, and were therefore packaged and labelled in accordance with it. The result was that Union law afforded Ratti a defence to the charges relating to the solvents, but not those concerning the varnishes.

This case shows that a directive which has not been implemented cannot become directly effective before the expiry of the time limit,[45] but this does not mean that it has no effects at all. In *Inter-Environnement Wallonie v. Région Wallonne*,[46] the European Court held that, in the period between the adoption of the directive and the expiry of the deadline, Member States must not enact any legislation that could seriously compromise the attainment of the result required by the directive. A later case, *Mangold*,[47] (discussed in § 4.6) could be seen as extending this principle so as to prohibit any retrograde legislation during the period for implementation, even if it does not prevent implementation by the deadline. However, though this was the view put forward by Advocate General Sharpston in a later case,[48] the Court did not accept it;[49] so it seems that the principle does not extend so far. *Mangold* must be regarded as confined to its own rather special facts (explained in § 4.6).

§4.5 DIFFERENCES BETWEEN DIRECTIVES AND REGULATIONS

The granting of direct effect to directives has probably done more than any other initiative by the European Court to enhance the effectiveness of Union law. Yet there has been a price to pay: the distinction between regulations and directives has been blurred and the structure of the Treaty deformed. This, in turn, has provoked a reaction at the national level.[50] The question must therefore be asked to what extent significant differences between directives and regulations still remain.

Some differences have already been mentioned. First of all, there is the date on which direct effect comes into operation: a regulation can be directly effective as soon as it comes into force, but a directive cannot be directly effective before the expiry of the time limit for implementation.

A second difference is that Member States are not normally either required or permitted to pass national legislation giving effect to the provisions of a regulation; in the case of a directive, on the other hand, there is the much-vaunted right to choose the

[45] For the position where, after it has expired, the deadline is postponed, see *Kloppenburg*, Case 70/83, [1984] ECR 1075.

[46] Case C-129/96, [1997] ECR I-7411.

[47] Case C-144/04, 25 November 2005 (Grand Chamber).

[48] *Stichting Zuid-Hollandse Mileufederatie*, Case C-138/05, [2006] ECR I-8339 at para. 86 of the Opinion.

[49] *Ibid.* at paras 39–48 of the judgment. Moreover, in *Adeneler*, Case C-212/04, [2006] ECR I-6057, also a decision of a Grand Chamber, the Court cited *Mangold* simply as authority for the principle in *Inter-Environnement Wallonie v. Région Wallonne*: see para. 121 of the judgment in *Adeneler*. See also *Bartsch v. Bosch und Siemens*, Case C-427/06, [2008] ECR I-7245.

[50] See Chap. 8.

'form and methods' by which the objective of the directive will be attained.[51] There is no doubt that this applies even where the directive is directly effective; however, in such a case the discretion enjoyed by Member States could be severely restricted.

There are two reasons for this. First, the Union institutions long ago adopted the habit of enacting directives with provisions every bit as detailed and precise as those to be found in a regulation.[52] Moreover, the Court has developed a doctrine that the area of choice left to the Member States regarding the 'form and methods' of implementation depends on the objective to be achieved: in some cases, the objective will be such that this diminishes to vanishing point. For example, in *Enka v. Inspecteur der Invoerrechten en Accijnzen*[53] the Court stated that in the case of customs legislation absolute uniformity may be necessary. It therefore held that the relevant provision of the directive in issue had to be reproduced in exactly the same way in the implementing legislation of each Member State.[54] In such a situation, implementation is, from the Member State's point of view, an empty exercise.[55]

It is, of course, true that there are many cases in which a real discretion will exist. It must not be forgotten, however, that some regulations have to be implemented and sometimes Member States will enjoy a significant discretion in this case as well. The tachograph regulation (discussed in § 3) was a case in point: the powers of inspection, the details of criminal procedure, and the maximum penalty were all matters which, within certain limits, could be determined by the Member States.

Another possible difference which has sometimes been suggested is that, while direct effect is the normal characteristic of a regulation, it is exceptional in the case of a directive.[56]

From a purely theoretical point of view, this is obviously true: if the Member States carry out their obligations under Union law, there will never be occasion for a directive to have direct effect. In practice, of course, Member States do not always implement directives as they should: from the practical point of view, therefore, the important question is whether a provision is less likely to be declared directly effective simply because it is contained in a directive, rather than in a regulation.

In the *Van Duyn* case[57] the European Court said that, while regulations 'may by their very nature have direct effects', directives 'have no automatic direct effect'.[58] This suggests that such a difference does indeed exist. However, the test applied to directives is exactly the same as that adopted in the case of Treaty provisions and, though the

[51] Art. 288 TFEU.

[52] Compare, for example, Directive 75/34, OJ 1975, L 14/10, with Regulation 1251/70, OJ (Spec. Ed.) 1970 (II), p. 402.

[53] Case 38/77, [1977] ECR 2203 at paras 11–18.

[54] For a less strict attitude, see *Commission v. Italy*, Case 363/85, [1987] ECR 1733.

[55] It is an exercise which must nevertheless be gone through. The Member State cannot rely on the direct effect of the directive to excuse its failure to implement it: see *Commission v. Belgium*, Case 102/79, [1980] ECR 1473 at para. 12 of the judgment.

[56] See Brinkhorst (1971) 8 CMLRev. 380 at 390; Dashwood, 'The Principle of Direct Effect in European Community Law' (1978) 16 JCMS 229 at 241; and *per* Advocate General Reischl in *Ratti*, Case 148/78, [1979] ECR 1629 at 1650 and 1653–4.

[57] Case 41/74, [1974] ECR 1337.

[58] At paras 12 and 13 of the judgment.

Court gave very careful scrutiny to the provision in issue in the *Van Duyn* case, it has subsequently shown itself prepared to declare whole groups of directives directly effective *en bloc*, without even listing them individually, much less attempting to examine their provisions in order to see whether they comply with the requirements for direct effect.[59] It is, therefore, hard to discern any practical difference between regulations and directives on this point.

The differences discussed so far have shown themselves to be rather insubstantial; there is, however, one difference which is of great significance. This is that, according to the Court, directives are not capable of imposing *obligations* on individuals.

§4.6 VERTICAL AND HORIZONTAL DIRECT EFFECT

There is no doubt that both regulations and Treaty provisions are able not only to confer rights on private individuals, but also to impose obligations on them.[60] However, the European Court has stated, many times over, that directives can only confer rights on individuals (against the State); they cannot impose obligations on individuals (in favour of the State or other individuals). Put another way, directives are capable of only 'vertical' direct effect; unlike regulations and Treaty provisions, they are not capable of 'horizontal' direct effect.

The question whether it is possible for directives to have horizontal direct effect was controversial for many years. The writers were divided on the question;[61] two Advocates General came out against the possibility;[62] the Court gave hints that it shared this view;[63] finally, in *Marshall v. Southampton and South West Hampshire Area Health Authority (Teaching)*,[64] the Court stated explicitly that a directive 'may not of itself impose obligations on an individual' and that 'a provision of a directive may not be relied on as such against such a person.'[65]

This was not, however, the end of the matter: some time later, a campaign appears to have been mounted by a group of Advocates General to have the decision in *Marshall* reversed. Two of them argued, in cases in which the point was not actually in issue, that

[59] In *Watson and Belmann*, Case 118/75, [1976] ECR 1185, the Court said that all measures adopted by the Union in application of what were then Arts 48–66 EEC were directly effective: see the first paragraph of its formal ruling.

[60] As far as regulations are concerned, this follows from the terms of Art. 288 TFEU, which state that regulations have general application. In the second *Defrenne* case, Case 43/75, [1976] ECR 455, the Court held that Treaty provisions can also have this effect. This has since been confirmed in numerous cases.

[61] See the list in Easson, 'Can Directives Impose Obligations on Individuals?' (1979) 4 ELRev. 67 at 70, note 24.

[62] Advocate General Reischl in *Ratti*, Case 148/78, [1979] ECR 1629 at 1650; and (more clearly) Advocate General Slynn in *Becker*, Case 8/81, [1982] ECR 53 at 81.

[63] See, for example, *Becker* (n. 62), at paras 17–26 of the judgment.

[64] Case 152/84, [1986] ECR 723.

[65] Para. 48 of the judgment. See also *Kolpinghuis Nijmegen*, Case 80/86, [1987] ECR 3969, in which the European Court held that a Member State cannot rely on the direct effect of a (non-implemented) directive in criminal proceedings against an individual; see, further, *Pretore di Salò v. X*, Case 14/86, [1987] ECR 2545.

directives *should* be capable of horizontal direct effect.[66] When the point finally arose for decision in *Faccini Dori v. Recreb*,[67] a third Advocate General[68] took the same view; the Court, however, reaffirmed its earlier position. Since this was a Full Court, consisting of thirteen judges, it should have been possible to regard the matter as settled.[69]

This has not, however, been the case. Although the Court continues to pay lip service to the principle that directives are incapable of horizontal direct effect, and indeed actually applies it in many cases, there are other cases in which it is not applied. Unfortunately, it is not easy to find any feature that distinguishes the two sets of cases.

The first case to consider is *CIA Security v. Signalson and Securitel.*[70] It concerned a Belgian law passed in 1990, which provided that security firms had to obtain authorization from the Government. A decree adopted in 1991 stated that alarm systems could not be sold unless approved by a government committee. An EU directive (Directive 83/189),[71] however, provided that all 'technical regulations' had to be notified to the Commission and, in certain circumstances, could not come into force for specified periods. Neither the law nor the decree had been notified.

CIA Security, Signalson, and Securitel were all security firms. The latter two claimed that CIA Security's alarm systems did not meet Belgian requirements. CIA Security brought proceedings in Belgium for an order preventing them from making such statements. The defendants tried to justify their statement by claiming that CIA Security had not been authorized under the law of 1990 and that its alarm systems had not been approved under the decree of 1991; they counterclaimed for an order that CIA Security cease trading. CIA Security responded by arguing that since the two measures had not been notified as required by the directive, the court could not apply them.

A reference was made to the European Court, which ruled that the law of 1990 was not a technical regulation and did not, therefore, have to be notified. The 1991 decree, on the other hand, should have been notified. The European Court ruled that, as a result, the Belgian court could not apply the decree.

Since all the companies concerned were private parties, it could be argued that this constituted horizontal direct effect: the effect of the directive was to prevent Signalson, and Securitel from relying on the 1991 decree in the proceedings against CIA Security. However, there is another point of view. The decree imposed an obligation on an individual: it precluded him from selling an alarm system that had not been approved. If a public authority had sought to enforce the decree, CIA Security could have invoked the directive as a defence. This would have been a case of vertical direct effect, since CIA Security would have been claiming a right against the State. Did it make a difference if a private party was trying to enforce the decree? Views may differ on this. However,

[66] Advocate General van Gerven in the second *Marshall* case, *Marshall v. Southampton and South West Hampshire Area Health Authority (Teaching) (No. 2)*, Case C-271/91, [1993] ECR I-4367; and Advocate General Jacobs in *Vaneetveld*, Case C-316/93, [1994] ECR I-763.

[67] Case C-91/92, [1994] ECR I-3325.

[68] Advocate General Lenz.

[69] For a possible exception with regard to remedies, see *Draehmpaehl v. Urania Immobilienservice*, Case C-180/95, [1997] ECR I-2195.

[70] Case C-194/94, [1996] ECR I-2201.

[71] OJ 1983 L 109/8, subsequently replaced by Directive 98/34, OJ 1998 L 204/37.

the decree was a measure intended to benefit the public, and it would normally be enforced by a public authority. If a private party seeks to enforce such a measure, it could be argued that the defendant should not be in a weaker position than he would be if the measure were enforced by a public authority.

Directive 83/189 was again before the Court in *Unilever Italia v. Central Food*.[72] The parties were two Italian companies. Unilever Italia had sold a consignment of olive oil to Central Food. The latter refused to pay on the ground that the oil did not comply with Italian legislation. The legislation constituted a 'technical regulation' in terms of the directive. It had been notified, but its promulgation was an infringement of a provision in the directive under which such legislation could not be brought into force for a specified period. For this reason, Unilever Italia, which had brought proceedings before an Italian court, claimed that the court could not apply the legislation in deciding whether the olive oil complied with Italian law.

The European Court agreed. It held that the principle laid down in *Faccini Dori* does not apply to technical regulations brought into force contrary to Directive 83/189. The reason it gave was that Directive 83/189 lays down a procedural bar to the adoption of national legislation, while the directive in *Faccini Dori* required Member States to adopt positive rules granting rights to, and imposing obligations on, individuals.[73]

In *Lemmens*,[74] a case decided after *CIA Security* but before *Unilever Italia*, a motorist convicted of drunken driving sought to have his conviction overturned on the ground that the breathalyser on which he had been tested was based on national regulations which should have, but had not, been notified under Directive 83/189. The European Court, however, rejected his argument: it restricted the *CIA Security* principle to cases where the application of the national regulations would hinder the use or marketing of a product not in conformity with them.

Unilever Italia was of course such a case; nevertheless, it could be criticized on the ground that it introduces uncertainty into the law: private parties might not know whether the requirements of Directive 83/189 had been satisfied.[75] This point was strongly made by the Advocate General in the case (Advocate General Jacobs), who said:[76]

> 111. In my view, a failure to notify (which may happen very frequently, given the vast range of measures potentially within the scope of the directive, and which may of course be inadvertent) cannot be treated as having far-reaching effects on contractual relations between individuals. In substance the effect would be that, solely on the basis of such failures by Member States, courts would be obliged to find a breach of contract.
>
> 112. Such consequences would be contrary to principles fundamental to our legal systems, and contrary in particular to fundamental requirements of legal certainty. There may be

[72] Case C-443/98, [2000] ECR I-7535.

[73] Paras 50 and 51 of the judgment.

[74] Case C-226/97, [1998] ECR I-3711.

[75] See Weatherill, 'Breach of Directives and Breach of Contract' (2001) 26 ELRev. 177. For further cases and further analysis, see the articles by Lackhoff, Hilson, Lenz, and Dougan in 'Further Reading', at the end of this chapter.

[76] Paras 111 and 112 of the Opinion.

> uncertainty as to whether the measure is a technical regulation and whether it required notification; uncertainty, in the absence of any provisions laying down a transparent procedure, as to whether it has in fact been notified; uncertainty, where a national regulation or parts of it are disapplied, as to what legal regime is to replace the disapplied measures; uncertainty as to the appropriate remedies for the breach of contract, in the absence of fault in either party. Moreover, such consequences would follow whether or not the technical regulation was an obstacle to the free movement of goods, and even where it facilitated such freedom of movement. I can see no basis for giving such consequences to a failure to notify.

This is a powerful criticism of the judgment the Court was about to deliver.

Subsequent cases have further muddied the waters, causing problems for those trying to make sense of the law. One theory is that of 'triangular' relationships.[77] It is said that an exception exists where there is a relationship between an individual and the State which also affects a second individual. In such a case, the first individual may rely on the direct effect of a directive against the State, even though this might have adverse repercussions on the other individual.

Wells provides an example.[78] In this case, the owners of a quarry in England applied for development consent. The matter went to the Secretary of State. A neighbouring landowner brought proceedings (in England) against the Secretary of State, claiming that he should apply the provisions of an EU directive, something that would have been detrimental to the interests of the quarry owners. On a reference to the European Court, the United Kingdom argued that acceptance of the neighbouring landowner's claim would allow one individual to use a directive to deprive other individuals (the quarry owners) of their rights. After restating the principle that directives cannot have horizontal direct effect, the Court said:

> On the other hand, mere adverse repercussions on the rights of third parties, even if the repercussions are certain, do not justify preventing an individual from invoking the provisions of a directive against the Member State concerned.[79]

So it ruled that the directive could be invoked by the claimant.

This accords with the theory of 'triangular situations', but it involves an extension of the concept of vertical direct effect. In the classic cases, an individual was invoking a directive to claim a freedom or immunity against the State: he wanted to defend himself against a criminal charge, to avoid paying tax, or to enter the country. In a case such as *Wells*, on the other hand, the individual was using a directive to require the State to deprive another individual of the freedom to develop his land. Moreover, such a 'repercussion' was not incidental or unintended: it was the whole purpose of the exercise.

A second theory is based on the distinction between an 'exclusionary effect' and a 'substitution effect'.[80] The former occurs when a directive has the negative effect

[77] Lackhoff and Nyssens, 'Direct Effect of Directives in Triangular Situations' (1998) 23 ELRev. 397.

[78] Case C-201/02, [2004] ECR I-723.

[79] Paras 55–57 of the judgment.

[80] See *per* Advocate General Saggio in *Oceano Grupo Editorial v. Rocio Murciano Quintero*, Cases C-240–44/98, [2000] ECR 1-4941, at paras 37–39 of the Opinion.

of eliminating national legislation – for example, because it was not notified to the Commission; the latter has the positive effect of imposing rules laid down in the directive. According to the theory, the inapplicability of the national legislation may be relied on by one individual against another, while the positive effect of the new rules cannot. Both *CIA Security* and *Unilever Italia* could be regarded as examples of a purely 'exclusionary' effect.

Though useful, these theories[81] do not fully explain all the cases. *Pfeiffer*[82] is an example. This was a case concerning maximum permitted hours of work. The Union had adopted a directive (the Working Time Directive),[83] Article 6 of which established the principle that no one may be required to work more than forty-eight hours per week (on average), though there were certain exceptions. Paragraph 3 of the German legislation transposing this directive, the *Arbeitsgesetz*, established maximum working hours, but provided (in paragraph 7) for an exception in the case of emergency workers (such as ambulance crews) who spend significant periods of time on standby, waiting for a call.

Pfeiffer and his colleagues worked for the German Red Cross as emergency workers, operating ambulances and similar vehicles. The contract under which they were employed required them to work more than forty-eight hours a week. The Red Cross considered that this was justified under paragraph 7 of the *Arbeitsgesetz*. Pfeiffer objected and sued the Red Cross in a German court. He argued that paragraph 7 was contrary to the directive. Since the Red Cross is not a State organization, this meant that he was claiming that the relevant provisions of the directive had horizontal direct effect.

The German court referred the issue to the European Court, which ruled that paragraph 7 of the *Arbeitsgesetz* was indeed contrary to the directive. The relevant provision of the directive (Article 6) fulfilled the requirements for direct effect. The Court therefore ruled that it had vertical direct effect. It did not, however, have horizontal direct effect; consequently, it could not be invoked by Pfeiffer against the Red Cross.[84]

This seems to conflict with the second theory. All Pfeiffer wanted was for paragraph 7 of the *Arbeitsgesetz* to be ruled inapplicable. Then, paragraph 3 of the *Arbeitsgesetz* would apply to his case. This was all he needed to win. In other words, his claim involved only an 'exclusionary effect', not a 'substitution effect'.[85]

In its judgment, the Court did not mention *CIA Security* or *Unilever Italia*. The ruling could, however, be reconciled with these cases on the basis that, in them, the directive imposed a procedural bar to the application of the national legislation, while in

[81] Both theories must be applied, since cases like *Wells* involve a 'substitution effect' and are not, therefore, covered by the second theory.

[82] Cases C-397–403/01, [2004] ECR I-8835. For a comment, see Prechal (2005) 42 CMLRev. 1445.

[83] Directive 93/104, OJ 1993 L 307, p. 18.

[84] Paras 107–110 of the judgment.

[85] For another case that seems to conflict with the theory, see *Berlusconi*, Cases C-387/02, 391/02, and 403/02, [2005] ECR I-3565.

Pfeiffer the national legislation conflicted with a substantive provision in the directive.[86] The Court did not, however, justify its decision on this basis; it simply referred to the classic cases on horizontal direct effect.[87]

Pfeiffer was a judgment of a Grand Chamber of the Court and might, therefore, be regarded as having special authority. A year later, however, another Grand Chamber (with a somewhat different composition) reached a different conclusion. This was in *Mangold*,[88] which concerned the interaction of two other aspects of employment law: fixed-term employment contracts and discrimination on grounds of age. The former are regarded as undesirable on the ground that they create insecurity, and an EU Framework Agreement, which had been put into effect by Council Directive 1999/70,[89] imposed restrictions on them. However, older workers who lose their job often find it difficult to get another one. One possible solution is to make an exception in their case with regard to fixed-term contracts: if fixed-term contracts are made lawful for older workers, employers might be more willing to give them work. However, this could be regarded as condoning discrimination on grounds of age, something that was contrary to another EU directive, Directive 2000/78.[90] It was these difficult problems that constituted the background to the *Mangold* case.

German law had a general rule prohibiting fixed-term employment contracts unless there was 'objective justification', a concept explained in the legislation.[91] However, the Law of 23 December 2002, which came into force on 1 January 2003, provided that objective justification was not necessary if the worker was aged 58 or over; moreover, it went on to say that, up until 31 December 2006, fixed-term contracts without objective justification would be permitted for workers aged 52 or over when the contract began. This was intended to combat the unemployment crisis in Germany by making it easier for older workers to find a job.

The case concerned an employment contract between an employer, Mr Helm, and an employee, Mr Mangold. The contract was for a fixed term: it began on 1 July 2003 and ended on 28 February 2004. When it commenced, Mr Mangold was 56 years of age. The contract (rather surprisingly)[92] stated that there was no objective justification for the fixed term other than the employee's age. Mangold then sued Helm in a German court, claiming that the provision limiting the term of the contract was contrary to Directive 2000/78. The German court referred the matter to the European Court.

Now, there was one obvious and easy answer to the question. In the case of Germany, the deadline for implementing Directive 2000/78 was 2 December 2006. The contract began and ended before that date. As we saw earlier, the European Court held in the

[86] This was the ground on which the Court based its judgment in *Unilever Italia*.

[87] *Marshall* and *Faccini Dori*, though it also cited *Wells*.

[88] Case C-144/04, [2005] ECR I-9981.

[89] OJ 1999 L 175, p. 34.

[90] OJ 2000 L 303, p. 16.

[91] The legislation was extremely complicated: what follows is intended to convey the gist of it.

[92] The contract was fairly obviously contrived to provide a test case. As we shall see in Chap. 9, § 4, there have been occasions in the past (most notably the two *Foglia v. Novello* cases) in which the European Court has held that it has no jurisdiction to decide references in such circumstances. In *Mangold*, however, it refused to be deterred by these considerations.

Ratti case that direct effect cannot arise until after the deadline; so the directive should have been irrelevant to the proceedings in the case. Admittedly, the European Court qualified this in the *Inter-Environnement Wallonie* case[93] by saying that, during the period before the deadline, a Member State must not adopt measures that seriously compromise the attainment of the result prescribed by the directive. However, it is doubtful whether a national provision due to expire twenty-nine days after the deadline could be said to 'seriously compromise' the attainment of the result to be achieved.

The Court sought to meet this objection by pointing out that the deadline for implementation was originally 2 December 2003. Member States were, however, entitled to an additional three years if they so requested. Germany had made such a request; so its deadline was 2 December 2006. However, the directive contained a provision that where a Member State availed itself of this right, it had to report annually to the Commission on the progress it had made. This, the Court said, implied that it could not adopt legislation that constituted a retrograde step. It also said that some workers, including Mangold himself, would be over 58 by the time the deadline expired and would, therefore, be caught by the general rule that fixed-term contracts were permitted without objective justification if the worker was aged 58 or above. For these reasons, the Court concluded that the fact that the deadline had not expired was irrelevant.

This, however, still left the question of horizontal direct effect, since Mangold and Helm were both private parties. The Advocate General held that the directive could not be applied for this reason.[94] The Court, however, ignored the issue: it simply ruled that the directive had to be applied by the German court. No mention was made of *Pfeiffer*.[95]

The judgment gives one the feeling that the European Court had got out of its depth. Indeed, the *Common Market Law Review* ran an editorial on the *Mangold* case under the heading 'Horizontal direct effect – A law of diminishing coherence?'[96] This contained scathing criticism of the Court's reasoning.[97]

In 2010, the Court tried to clarify the position. This was in *Kücükdeveci v. Swedex*,[98] another case on age discrimination in employment – this time, discrimination against younger people. As in *Mangold*, the parties were both private individuals, an employer (Swedex) and an employee (Kücükdeveci). When the facts arose, the time limit for implementation of the directive had expired; so the problem of the deadline did not arise. Again the case was decided by a Grand Chamber.

In its judgment, the Court first said (at paragraph 21) that non-discrimination on grounds of age is a general principle of EU law.[99] This general principle was given

[93] Case C-129/96, [1997] ECR I-7411. [94] Paras 104–111 of the Opinion.

[95] *Mangold* was also a case of 'exclusionary effect': if the special provision in the law of 23 December 2002 was rendered inapplicable, the general rule would apply under which the age limit was 58. However, the Court made no attempt to explain its ruling on this ground. [96] (2006) 43 CMLRev. 1.

[97] The compatibility of *Mangold* with established case-law of the Court also seems to have worried other members of the Court: see *per* Advocate General Kokott in *Commission v. Ireland*, Case C-418/04, [2007] ECR I-10947, at para. 89, note 58 of her Opinion. [98] Case C-555/07, [2010] ECR I-365.

[99] It cited *Mangold* and Art. 21(1) of the Charter of Fundamental Rights of the European Union, given treaty effect by Art. 6(1) TEU.

expression by Directive 2000/78; nevertheless, it was the general principle – not the directive alone – which was in issue in the case. It then reaffirmed the principle that a directive cannot have horizontal direct effect, saying (at paragraph 46 of the judgment):

> ...where proceedings between individuals are concerned, the Court has consistently held that a directive cannot of itself impose obligations on an individual and cannot therefore be relied on as such against an individual [citing *Marshall*; *Faccini Dori*; and *Pfeiffer*].

It then went on to say that, where a provision of national law infringes the EU principle of non-discrimination on the ground of age, that provision of national law must, as far as possible, be interpreted by Member State courts in accordance with EU law. In the case before the Court, the national court had said that this was not possible. The European Court then continued:

> 50 It must be recalled here that... Directive 2000/78 merely gives expression to, but does not lay down, the principle of equal treatment in employment and occupation, and that the principle of non-discrimination on grounds of age is a general principle of European Union law in that it constitutes a specific application of the general principle of equal treatment (see, to that effect, *Mangold*, paragraphs 74 to 76).
>
> 51 In those circumstances, it [is] for the national court, hearing a dispute involving the principle of non-discrimination on grounds of age as given expression in Directive 2000/78, to provide, within the limits of its jurisdiction, the legal protection which individuals derive from European Union law and to ensure the full effectiveness of that law, disapplying if need be any provision of national legislation contrary to that principle (see, to that effect, *Mangold*, paragraph 77).

The answer seems to be, therefore, that the horizontal direct effect of directives was not in issue in the case because the principle of non-discrimination in employment is a general principle of EU law. It was this general principle that was applied horizontally, not the directive. All the directive did was to 'give expression' to the general principle. Without this, the general principle would have been too vague and general to be directly effective. Thus, though a directive cannot 'of itself' or 'as such'[100] impose obligations on an individual, it can have the effect of converting a general principle of law that would otherwise have had no direct effect into something with both vertical and horizontal direct effect. Another way of saying the same thing would be that a directive can have horizontal direct effect where it gives expression to a general principle of EU law.

One can conclude from this that the general rule that directives have no horizontal direct effect continues to apply; nevertheless, there are a number of exceptions, some rather ill defined. One exception is that a directive giving expression to a general principle of EU law is capable of horizontal direct effect.

§4.7 THE 'STATE'

Since, in at least some situations, directives can be directly effective only against the State, we must next consider what exactly constitutes the 'State'. The first question

[100] See para. 46 of the judgment, quoted earlier.

is whether it matters in what capacity the State is acting. In the *Marshall* case the European Court held that it does not: it is not necessary that it should be exercising governmental powers (for example, collecting taxes); vertical direct effect applies even if it is entering into an ordinary private-law transaction, such as a contract of employment. In both cases 'it is necessary to prevent the State from taking advantage of its own failure to comply with Union law'.[101]

The second question is exactly what bodies are regarded as being part of the State. In the *Marshall* case, Advocate General Slynn said that 'State' must be taken broadly, as including all organs of the State. In matters of employment, it covers the employees of such organs and not just the central civil service.[102] The Court itself seemed to use the terms 'State' and 'public authority' interchangeably. In the *Marshall* case the claimant was an employee of an Area Health Authority, which the Court of Appeal had described as 'an emanation of the State'. It was clearly covered. Nevertheless, other bodies could present more difficult problems.

In later cases, the European Court has tried to clarify matters. In *Johnston v. Chief Constable of the RUC*,[103] it held that the chief constable of a UK police force is, when acting in his official capacity, an emanation of the State.[104] He cannot take advantage of the failure of the State to comply with Union law. In *Fratelli Costanzo v. Comune di Milano*,[105] it held that a local authority is also part of the State for this purpose.[106] In neither case, it should be noted, could the body in question be regarded as in any way responsible for the Government's failure to implement the directive;[107] nevertheless, both are clearly public authorities.

In *Foster v. British Gas*,[108] the European Court was faced with a more difficult question: was British Gas part of the State before it was privatized? This question was referred to the European Court by the House of Lords in a case in which the facts were similar to those in the *Marshall* case.

The first ruling made by the Court concerned the division of jurisdiction between it and the national courts: it held that it had jurisdiction to determine the categories of persons against whom a directive may be directly effective; the national courts, on the other hand, decide whether a particular body falls into one of those categories. In other words, the European Court lays down the rules and the national courts apply them to the facts of the case.

[101] At para. 49 of the judgment.

[102] Case 152/84, [1986] ECR 723.

[103] Case 222/84, [1986] ECR 1651.

[104] Para. 56 of the judgment.

[105] Case 103/88, [1989] ECR 1839.

[106] In *Rienks*, Case 5/83, [1983] ECR 4233, a case decided before *Marshall*, the European Court appeared to hold that a directive can be directly effective against the governing body of a profession in so far as the latter is 'entrusted with a public duty' (para. 10 of the judgment). The facts were, however, rather special: the public duty was the enrolment of a practitioner on a professional register, and the case was a criminal prosecution for illegal practice. Compare *R v. Royal Pharmaceutical Society*, Cases 266–7/87, [1989] ECR 1295.

[107] See *per* Advocate General van Gerven in *Foster v. British Gas* (see n. 108) at I-3330.

[108] Case C-188/89, [1990] ECR I-3313.

Next came the question of substance. In keeping with its ruling on the jurisdictional point, the Court did not decide directly whether a nationalized industry is to be regarded as part of the State. Instead, it laid down a general formula:

> ...a body, whatever its legal form, which has been made responsible, pursuant to a measure adopted by the State, for providing a public service under the control of the State and has for that purpose special powers beyond those which result from the normal rules applicable in relations between individuals is included in any event among the bodies against which the provisions of a directive capable of having direct effect may be relied upon.

This test consists of four elements. First, the body must provide a public service; secondly, it must do so pursuant to a measure adopted by the State; thirdly; it must do so under the control of the State; and fourthly, it must possess special powers beyond those normally applicable in relations between individuals. Each of these is important.

The first element would seem to exclude a government-owned industry that carries on normal commercial activities, for example an engineering company. The second would seem to rule out a charity created by some private act like a will or trust deed, even if it provides a public service (unless it is part of the State system).[109] The third element might seem to exclude privatized industries, but the English High Court has held otherwise: in *Griffin v. South West Water Services*[110] it ruled that a privatized water company was part of the State for the purpose of direct effect;[111] the third element might also be thought to exclude the holder of an independent public office, such as the chief constable of a police force, but, as we have seen, this is also not the case.[112] The fourth element requires that the body should possess special powers of a governmental nature. This, too, would normally exclude private charities (unless they were given special powers), as well as commercial companies even if government owned. It must, however, be kept in mind that the European Court has a history of whittling down requirements for the application of Union law – the general rules for the direct effect of directives are an example in point – and one should not be surprised if it did so here too. In any event, it seems that the Court does not necessarily regard the *Foster* formula as being the exclusive test: bodies not covered may be included on some other basis.[113]

When the *Foster* case came back to the House of Lords, the test was applied to the facts of the case.[114] The first and second elements were present, since British Gas was

[109] As to which see *NUT v. St Mary's School* [1997] 3 CMLR 630; [1997] ICR 334 (CA).

[110] [1995] IRLR 15.

[111] The court held that the test is not whether the body providing the service (the privatized water company) is subject to the control of the State, but whether the *public service* is under the control of the State.

[112] *Johnston v. Chief Constable of the RUC*, Case 222/84, [1986] ECR 1651.

[113] This is indicated by the phrase 'in any event' in the quotation. In *Doughty v. Rolls-Royce* (see n. 118), the Court of Appeal held that the test was not intended to provide the answer to every category of case; nevertheless, it said that, in a case of the same general type as *Foster*, the formula must always be the starting point and would usually be the finishing point: if every element was present, it would require something very unusual to produce the result that the body was not an emanation of the State; conversely, if one element was not present, it would need the addition of something else not contemplated by the formula before it could be so regarded.

[114] [1991] 2 AC 306.

given by statute the duty of maintaining an efficient system of gas supply for Great Britain.[115] The element of State control was also present, since the minister had statutory authority to give directions to British Gas.[116] The fourth element was held to be present since British Gas was given a monopoly in the supply of gas.[117] As a result, the House of Lords held that British Gas, when a nationalized industry, was an emanation of the State for the purpose in question.

In *Doughty v. Rolls-Royce*,[118] the English Court of Appeal had to determine whether Rolls-Royce plc was an emanation of the State. The facts were similar to those in *Foster*, except that Rolls-Royce plc was a commercial company, though all its shares were held by nominees of the Crown. Was this sufficient to make it part of the State? The Court of Appeal held that it was not. It was prepared to assume, for the purpose of argument, that the element of State control was present, but it held that Rolls-Royce did not provide a public service; there was no relevant statute or other measure adopted by the State; nor did it enjoy any special powers. The fact that it produced military equipment, much of which was sold to the State, was not enough: such sales were made at arm's length on a commercial basis.

In *NUT v. St Mary's School*,[119] on the other hand, the Court of Appeal held that the governing body of a voluntary aided school *was* an emanation of the State, thus enabling teachers who had lost their jobs at the school to rely on an EU directive in proceedings against it. St Mary's was a Church of England school which voluntarily decided to join the State system and to accept financial aid from the local education authority. Once it did this, it became an emanation of the State for the purpose of direct effect, since it was providing a public service on behalf of the State.

The granting of direct effect to directives is not the only purpose in Union law for which it is necessary to determine exactly what constitutes the State. Similar problems arise when Article 45(4) TFEU [39(4)/48(4) EC] is invoked. Article 45 TFEU is concerned with the rights of migrant workers. Article 45(2) prohibits all discrimination based on nationality against workers from another Member State, but Article 45(4) lays down an exception: it provides that the provisions of Article 45 do not apply to 'employment in the public service'. Clearly, employment in the public service is a similar concept to employment by the State, though possibly wider. The European Court, however, has given it a *narrower* definition. It seems to cover only those officials who exercise governmental powers or policy-making functions. Nurses in public hospitals are excluded;[120] nor can there be much doubt that most – if not all – employees of nationalized industries are also excluded. Thus neither Ms Foster nor Ms Doughty

[115] Gas Act 1972, s. 2(1).

[116] *Ibid.*, ss 4 and 7. The fact that the government did not have day-to-day control over British Gas was held by the House of Lords to be irrelevant.

[117] The Gas Act 1972, s. 29 prohibited any person other than British Gas from supplying gas to any premises.

[118] [1992] ICR 538; [1992] IRLR 126; *The Times*, 14 January 1992.

[119] [1997] 3 CMLR 630; [1997] ICR 334 (CA).

[120] *Commission v. Belgium*, Case 149/79, [1980] ECR 3881 and [1982] ECR 1845.

would have been regarded as employed in the public service for the purpose of Article 45(4). This shows that, in the hands of the European Court, the meaning of concepts such as 'the State' changes to fit the purpose for which they are employed. Where a narrow meaning enhances the effectiveness of Union law, such a meaning will be adopted; where the opposite is the case, a broad meaning will be given.[121]

The European Court's acceptance of the principle that directives cannot impose obligations on individuals may be viewed as a tactical retreat occasioned by the adverse reaction in certain quarters to the whole concept of granting direct effect to directives.[122]

In view of the Court's deep commitment to the policy of promoting the effectiveness of Union law, it was inevitable that it would seek other means of recovering the lost ground. The wide meaning given to the concept of the State is part of this strategy. Two other developments, which make the distinction between vertical and horizontal direct effect of less practical importance, are what is sometimes called 'indirect effect', and the possibility of an action for damages against the Government of a Member State for failure to implement a directive. These will now be considered.

§4.8 INDIRECT EFFECT

The term 'indirect effect', though not used by the European Court, is a handy label for the doctrine that Union provisions, even if not directly effective, must be taken into account by national courts when interpreting national legislation. It is also called the doctrine of 'consistent interpretation'. It is applied mainly (though not exclusively)[123] to directives, which, as we have seen, cannot always impose obligations directly on individuals. It thus provides a back-door route by which something approaching the same result may be attained under the guise of interpretation.[124]

[121] Compare *per* Advocate General van Gerven in *Foster* (see n. 108) at I-3334–6.

[122] See, for example, the decision of the French *Conseil d'Etat* in the *Cohn-Bendit* case (discussed in Chap. 8, § 5) and the decision of the German *Bundesfinanzhof* in the *Kloppenburg* case (Chap. 8, § 3).

[123] In *Grimaldi*, Case C-322/88, [1989] ECR 4407, the European Court held that recommendations (which have no binding force) must be taken into account by national courts when interpreting national or Union legislation. There is no doubt that the same would apply with regard to any Union instrument that is not directly effective. Thus, a directive can have indirect effect even if it is not vertically directly effective: *R v. Ministry of Agriculture, ex parte Hedley Lomas*, Case C-5/94, [1996] ECR I-2553, *per* Advocate General Léger at para. 64 of his Opinion; *Dekker*, Case C-177/88, [1990] ECR I-3941, *per* Advocate General Darmon at para. 15 of his Opinion.

[124] In *R v. Ministry of Agriculture, ex parte Hedley Lomas*, Case C-5/94, [1996] ECR I-2553, Advocate General Léger said at para. 64 of his Opinion, that a directive can have indirect effect even before the time limit for implementation has expired, a proposition which he claimed was supported by para. 15 of the judgment in *Kolpinghuis Nijmegen*, Case 80/86, [1987] ECR 3969. This, however, is a misreading of the judgment. *Kolpinghuis Nijmegen* was a reference from a Dutch court in which the European Court was asked to answer four questions. In the first two, the Court was asked whether a directive could be horizontally directly effective: the Court replied that it could not. The third was whether a directive could have indirect effect in a criminal case: the Court replied that it could not have indirect effect where this would be against the interests of the accused (by making him liable or by aggravating his liability). The fourth question was whether the answers to the first three questions would be any different if the time limit for implementation of the directive had not yet

The doctrine originated in *Von Colson and Kamann v. Land Nordrhein-Westfalen*,[125] a case concerning a directive on sex discrimination. In the course of its judgment, the Court said: 'It is for the national court to interpret and apply the legislation adopted for the implementation of the directive in conformity with the requirements of Union law, in so far as it is given discretion to do so under national law.'[126]

This is an entirely reasonable requirement. If legislation is passed to implement a directive, it may be assumed that the national legislature intended the legislation to give full effect to the directive and it is right that it should be interpreted with this in mind.[127] Moreover, the European Court made clear that national courts were not being asked to go beyond what was permitted under national law.

Subsequently, the same doctrine was applied to national legislation not adopted to implement the directive,[128] indeed which was passed *before* the directive. This was in *Marleasing*,[129] a case which arose out of proceedings in a Spanish court. The Spanish Civil Code provides that contracts have no legal effect if they are without a cause or have an illegal cause,[130] and it was argued, on the basis of this provision, that a contract leading to the incorporation of a Spanish company was void, since it lacked cause, was a sham transaction, and was entered into in order to defraud the creditors of another company. It was therefore claimed that the incorporation of the company was a nullity. A Union directive, however, gives an exhaustive list of the grounds on which the incorporation of a company may be declared void, and the lack of a legal cause is not one of them. There was thus a potential conflict between the provisions of the Spanish Civil Code and those of the directive, which had not been implemented in Spain. The Spanish court asked the European Court whether the directive was directly effective. As the parties to the case were all private, this raised the question of horizontal direct effect.

expired: the Court answered this (in para. 15) by saying, first, that the answers to the first two questions would not be affected, and, secondly, by saying: 'As regards the third question concerning the limits which Union law might impose on the obligation or power of the national court to interpret the rules of its national law in the light of the directive, it makes no difference whether or not the period prescribed for implementation has expired.' Since the Court had said in its answer to the third question that indirect effect can never operate against the interests of the accused, it is obvious that this limit on indirect effect would apply *a fortiori* if the deadline had not expired. The Court's statement cannot, therefore, be taken as authority for the proposition that, in other situations, indirect effect operates even before expiry of the deadline.

[125] Case 14/83, [1984] ECR 1891.

[126] Para. 28 of the judgment, reproduced in the final sentence of para. 3 of the Ruling.

[127] This principle is applied in English law with regard to legislation passed to give effect, not only to a Union obligation, but also to obligations under other international treaties: see, for example, *per* Lord Diplock in *Garland v. British Rail Engineering* [1983] 2 AC 751 at 771.

[128] There is a hint to this effect in para. 26 of the judgment in the *Von Colson* case (see n. 125) and in para. 12 of the judgment in *Kolpinghuis Nijmegen*, Case 80/86, [1987] ECR 3969; but see the opinion of Advocate General Slynn in the *Marshall* case, in which he said (at 733) that he was not satisfied that Union law obliged national courts to construe prior legislation in conformity with a directive.

[129] Case C-106/89, [1990] ECR I-4135.

[130] The concept of 'cause' (*causa* in Latin) has played an important role in the history of civilian legal systems and is found in several modern codes. It is not an easy concept to explain in a few words, but it is to some extent analogous to the purpose or object of the contract.

In answer to the question, the European Court reaffirmed the ruling in *Marshall*, that a directive cannot directly impose obligations on a private party. However, it then went on to consider the doctrine of indirect effect. It extended the principle in the *Von Colson* case to apply to national legislation passed before the directive, thus making it possible for the doctrine to apply to the relevant provisions of the Spanish Civil Code. Moreover, it said that the national law had to be interpreted so as to preclude the declaration of nullity of a company other than on the grounds permitted by the directive, thus implying that the national court had no option but to reach that result.

This suggests that the result envisaged by the directive must be attained irrespective of whether or not there is any doubt as to the meaning of the national provision and irrespective of whether or not the words of that provision could reasonably bear the meaning required by the directive. This, however, would no longer constitute interpretation – it would create horizontal direct effect under another name – and in *Webb v. EMO Air Cargo*[131] the House of Lords made clear that it did not accept such a reading of *Marleasing*. It said:[132]

> It is to be observed that the provision of Spanish law in issue in that case was of a general character capable of being construed either widely or narrowly. It did not refer specifically to the grounds upon which the nullity of a public limited company might be ordered. If it had done so, and had included among such grounds the case where the company had been formed with the purpose of defrauding creditors of one of the corporations, the Spanish court would have been entitled and bound to give effect to it notwithstanding the terms of the Directive. As the European Court of Justice said, a national court must construe a domestic law to accord with the terms of a Directive in the same field only if it is possible to do so.[133] That means that the domestic law must be open to an interpretation consistent with the Directive whether or not it is also open to an interpretation inconsistent with it.

The House of Lords then made a reference to the European Court under Article 267 TFEU (then Article 177 EEC) for a preliminary ruling on the interpretation of the directive in issue. The European Court gave the ruling without commenting on the passage quoted.[134] By that time, however, the European Court, sitting as a thirteen-judge Full Court, had already ruled (in a case decided after the House of Lords had made the reference) that the obligation to interpret national legislation in accordance with Union law applies only in so far as such an interpretation is possible.[135] The wide reading of the judgment in *Marleasing*

[131] [1993] 1 WLR 49 (HL).

[132] At 60, *per* Lord Keith of Kinked, with whom Lords Griffiths, Browne-Wilkinson, Mustill, and Slynn of Hadley agreed. Lord Slynn, it should be remembered, had, until a short while before, himself been a judge on the European Court.

[133] The phrase 'as far as possible' occurs in para. 8 of the judgment in *Marleasing*. It is not, however, repeated in later paragraphs nor is it to be found in the actual Ruling.

[134] *Webb v. EMO Air Cargo*, Case C-32/93, [1994] ECR 3567.

[135] *Faccini Dori v. Recreb*, Case C-91/92, [1994] ECR I-3325 at para. 26 of the judgment.

is, therefore, wrong. Whether this was a misunderstanding all along,[136] or whether the Court was testing the waters and decided to pull back, is not known.[137]

Even in its restrained form, the doctrine of indirect effect is a powerful tool for bringing national law into line. It nevertheless generates great uncertainty since it is hard to know how unclear national law must be for indirect effect to operate. Reasonably enough, English courts seem more willing to interpret a national provision in accordance with Union law when it was passed to give effect to Union law than when it was not.[138]

For some years, there has been speculation as to whether indirect effect can apply to a directive before the expiry of the deadline for its implementation. This controversy has now been settled by the decision of a Grand Chamber of the European Court in *Adeneler*,[139] in which it said that indirect effect in its full sense applies only after the expiry of the deadline. Before this date, national courts are required only to interpret national legislation (as far as possible) in accordance with the doctrine in *Inter-Environnement Wallonie v. Région Wallonne.*[140] This case was discussed earlier (in § 4.4): it will be remembered that it held that, in the period between the adoption of the directive and the expiry of the deadline, Member States must not enact any legislation that could seriously compromise the attainment of the result required by the

[136] It appears from the opinion of Advocate General van Gerven that Spanish law was in fact far from clear on the point. The Spanish statute on company law did not state the grounds on which the incorporation of a company could be declared void, and it was on the basis of legal literature that it was contended that the contract provisions of the Code should be applied by analogy. If this was so, the statements by the Court could perhaps be justified by the facts of the case. For further analysis of *Marleasing*, see De Búrca, 'Giving Effect to European Community Directives' (1992) 55 MLR 215; Mead, 'The Obligation to Apply European Law: Is *Duke* Dead?' (1991) 16 ELRev. 490; Greenwood, 'Effect of EC Directives in National Law' [1992] CLJ 3 at 4–5; Maltby, '*Marleasing*: What is All the Fuss About?' (1993) 109 LQR 301.

[137] In more recent years, the European Court seems to be doing everything within its power to emphasize the importance of indirect effect, though it never forgets to include the words 'so far as possible' in its rulings. See, for example, *Pfeiffer*, Cases C-397–403/01, [2004] ECR I-8835 (discussed earlier), at paras 110–119 of the judgment.

[138] In *Duke v. Reliance Systems* [1988] AC 618, a case decided before *Marleasing*, Lord Templeman refused to 'distort the meaning of a domestic statute so as to conform with Community law which is not directly applicable' (at 641); see also *Finnegan v. Clowney Youth Training Programme* [1990] 2 AC 407. In *Litster v. Forth Dry Dock & Engineering Co.* [1990] 1 AC 546, on the other hand, the House of Lords was prepared to imply words into British legislation passed to implement a directive in order to make it conform to the directive. After the European Court had given its ruling on the interpretation of the directive in *Webb v. Emo Air Cargo*, the House of Lords interpreted the British legislation in conformity with the directive, even though, had it not been for the directive, it would have interpreted it differently: see *Webb v. EMO Air Cargo (No. 2)* [1995] 1 WLR 1454 (HL). For a discussion of these cases, see Craig, 'Directives: Direct Effect, Indirect Effect and the Construction of National Legislation' (1997) 22 ELRev. 519 at 530–3. For a Scottish case in which the Inner House of the Court of Session said that the interpretation of national regulations enacted to implement a directive can be affected by the directive only to the extent that there is an ambiguity in the regulations which can be resolved by reference to the directive, see *Stirling District Council v. Allan*, 1995 SC 420 at 424; [1995] IRLR 301 at 303 (para. 10). The European Court has also stated that the duty to interpret national legislation so as to be consistent with a directive arises *a fortiori* where the legislation in question was passed to give effect to the directive: *Pfeiffer*, Cases C-397–403/01, [2004] ECR I-8835 (discussed earlier), at para. 112 of the judgment.

[139] *Adeneler*, Case C-212/04, [2006] ECR I-6057.

[140] Case C-129/96, [1997] ECR I-7411.

directive. During this period, therefore, national legislation must (as far as possible) be interpreted so as to avoid this.[141]

Finally, a word should be said about criminal proceedings. If a directive is capable of direct effect, it can be invoked by the accused: this would constitute vertical direct effect;[142] on the other hand, it cannot be invoked by the prosecution against the accused: this would constitute horizontal direct effect.[143] Moreover, the European Court has held that a directive cannot have indirect effect in criminal proceedings in so far as this would make the accused guilty where he would otherwise have been acquitted, or where it would aggravate his guilt;[144] however, there is no reason why a directive which does not have (vertical) direct effect should not have indirect effect where this would benefit the accused.

§4.9 GOVERNMENTAL LIABILITY FOR NON-IMPLEMENTATION

Another way in which the European Court has tried to regain the ground lost in *Marshall* has been to develop the doctrine that a person who has suffered loss as a result of the failure of a national government to implement a directive may bring proceedings in tort in the national courts against the Government. However, as this is a general doctrine, applying to other infringements of Union law as well, it will be considered separately in § 11.

§5 DECISIONS

The next question is whether an EU decision can have direct effect. It might be thought that this question was of only limited importance, since it was said previously that a decision was an executive act: the rights created by such an act would only rarely be invoked in the national courts. In fact, however, the Union institutions have not felt themselves precluded from adopting decisions of a legislative character: some of these are similar to directives and require Member States to take action in order to achieve a stated objective; others lay down general rules rather like regulations.

141 *Adeneler*, at paras 107–124 (especially para. 123) of the judgment. Though *Mangold* was cited, there was no suggestion that it had widened the principle laid down in *Inter-Environnement Wallonie v. Région Wallonne*: see para. 121 of the judgment. For further discussion, see Klamert, 'Judicial Implementation of Directives and Anticipatory Indirect Effect: Connecting the Dots' (2006) 43 CMLRev. 1251.

142 This occurred in *Ratti*, Case 148/78, [1979] ECR 1629 (with regard to the directive for which the deadline had already expired).

143 *Pretore di Salò v. X*, Case 14/86, [1987] ECR 2545; *Kolpinghuis Nijmegen*, Case 80/86, [1987] ECR 3969 (the first two questions); *Arcaro*, Case C-168/95, [1996] ECR I-4705 (the second question).

144 *Kolpinghuis Nijmegen* (see n. 143) (the third question); *Arcaro* (see n. 143) (the third question, especially para. 42 of the judgment). For the possibility that this paragraph might impose limitations on indirect effect even outside the criminal area, see Craig, 'Directives: Direct Effect, Indirect Effect and the Construction of National Legislation' (1997) 22 ELRev. 519 at 526–8.

In view of the Court's rulings in the case of directives, it would have been surprising if it had not also declared that decisions can be directly effective. In fact, this occurred first: the *Grad* case,[145] in which the European Court decided that decisions can be directly effective, was decided some four years before the *Van Duyn* case.[146] The reasons given were the same.

Most of the comments made previously with regard to directives apply also to decisions. Of course, a decision is different from a directive, in that it can be addressed to an individual as well as a Member State. However, in view of what the Court said in the *Marshall* case,[147] it would seem that a decision can impose a directly effective obligation only on the addressee.[148] Where the decision is addressed to a Member State, it cannot be horizontally directly effective.[149]

§6 GENERAL PRINCIPLES OF LAW

Until the decision of the European Court in *Mangold*, it was assumed by everyone that general principles of law, being inherently amorphous and uncertain, have no direct effect. The decision in *Mangold* could be regarded as casting doubt on this. However, as explained in *Kücükdeveci* (§ 4.6), all that *Mangold* does is to lay down the rule that a general principle of law can have direct effect if a directive (or, one assumes, some other instrument) gives expression to it. This is the same thing as saying that a directive can have horizontal direct effect if it gives expression to a general principle of law. So general principles of law have no direct effect in themselves.

§7 AGREEMENTS WITH THIRD COUNTRIES

Agreements with non-member States are obviously in a different category from the Union Treaties and Union legislation. In particular, it might be thought that there would be a lack of balance and reciprocity if they were directly effective in the Union countries but not in the other countries. This argument appears originally to have had some influence,[150] but it was subsequently rejected by the European Court, at least with regard to association agreements and bilateral trade agreements.[151] The position now is that such agreements – whether they are intended to establish a special regime giving greater rights to the third country than to the Union,[152] or are intended to be

[145] Case 9/70, [1970] ECR 825. [146] See § 1.3. [147] See § 4.6.

[148] According to Art. 288 TFEU, a decision is binding only on the person (or persons) to whom it is addressed.

[149] But see *per* Advocate General Reischl in *Unil-It*, Case 30/75, [1975] ECR 1419 at 1434.

[150] *Bresciani*, Case 87/75, [1976] ECR 129 at 148–9 (*per* Advocate General Trabucchi) and para. 22 of the judgment; *Polydor*, Case 270/80, [1982] ECR 329 at 355 (*per* Advocate General Rozès).

[151] *Kupferberg* (discussed later). [152] *Bresciani* (see n. 150).

reciprocal[153] – can be directly effective in the courts of the Member States of the Union, even if they are not directly effective in the non-member State. The test appears to be the same as for the Union Treaties.

This is the case, irrespective of whether the agreement is concluded (on the Union side) by the Union alone, as occurred in *Kupferberg*,[154] or by the Union and the Member States acting together (mixed agreement), as occurred in *Bresciani*.[155] In the latter case, however, national law will determine the effect of those parts of the agreement that are outside the treaty-making competence of the Union.[156]

With regard to agreements concluded by the Member States alone which become binding on the Union by succession (such as the old GATT), the European Court appears to accept the possibility of direct effect in principle, though in practice it has always ruled against it.[157]

In *Kupferberg*,[158] it was argued that a German tax on wine could not apply to imports from Portugal (before Portugal joined the Union) because it conflicted with a provision in the Free Trade Agreement between the Union and Portugal. This raised the question whether the relevant provision of the Free Trade Agreement was directly effective in Germany. The European Court held that this question could not be left to the national law of each Member State because a uniform solution throughout the Union was desirable. So Union law had to decide,[159] and the Court held, after examining the provision, that it was directly effective. The fact that it was probably not directly effective in Portugal was regarded as irrelevant.[160]

The result is that non-Union businessmen selling in the Union could have a more effective means of enforcing the agreement than Union businessmen exporting to the foreign country. However, the European Court has also made clear that provisions in agreements with non-member States are not necessarily to be given the same wide and policy-oriented interpretation that is given to the EU Treaties. This is so even if, as is often the case, the agreement reproduces almost exactly the wording of a provision in the EU Treaties.[161]

The reason the European Court has adopted this strategy appears to be as follows. When the Union enters into an agreement with a non-member State, it is under an obligation to ensure that the agreement is carried out. Frequently, however, the

153 *Kupferberg* (discussed later). 154 See later. 155 See n. 150.

156 *Dior v. Tuk Consultancy*, Cases C-300, 392/98, [2000] ECR I-11307 (discussed in Chap. 6, § 7.3).

157 See *International Fruit Company*, Cases 21–4/72, [1972] ECR 1219; *Schlüter*, Case 9/73, [1973] ECR 1135; *SPI*, Cases 267–9/81, [1983] ECR 801.

158 Case 104/81, [1982] ECR 3641. See also *Sevince*, Case C-192/89, [1990] ECR I-3461; *Demirel*, Case 12/86, [1987] ECR 3719; *Kziber*, Case C-18/90, [1991] ECR I-199.

159 But the European Court said, at para. 17 of its judgment, that if the agreement itself provides whether or not it is to be directly effective, that will be decisive. Such provisions are not, however, normal, and there was no such provision in the agreement with Portugal. In the absence of such a provision, the European Court will decide the question according to its own criteria.

160 See para. 18 of the judgment.

161 *Polydor*, Case 270/80, [1982] ECR 329; *Kupferberg* (see n. 158) at paras 28–31 of the judgment. This means that the same words can mean one thing in the EU Treaties and another in an agreement with a third country.

implementation of the agreement on the Union side will depend on the Member States. The Union could, therefore, be embarrassed in its relations with the non-member State, if the Member States failed to give effect to the agreement.

Agreements between the Union and a non-member State are, of course, binding on the Member States,[162] and an action under Article 258 TFEU[163] could be brought against any Member State which failed to abide by them. But this is a cumbersome remedy. By making such agreements directly effective, the European Court has established an easy means of enforcement. At the same time, by refusing to apply its normal method of interpretation to such agreements, it has ensured that non-member States will not be given too great an advantage.

Different considerations have prevailed in the case of the GATT, now part of the WTO Agreement.[164] The old GATT was held not to be directly effective on the ground that its provisions were too flexible.[165] It seems to have been thought that parties to GATT had the option either of obeying GATT rules or of accepting that other parties could take countervailing action.[166] The fact that other parties did not regard the Agreement as directly effective was also relevant.[167] It appears to have been thought that if the Agreement were held to be directly effective in the Union, this would put the Union at a disadvantage since the Union could not take unilateral action when other parties violated the Agreement.[168]

Whatever justification there might have been for this attitude under the old GATT, it might have been thought that the position would be different under the WTO Agreement, which has a much stronger enforcement system. Nevertheless, in *Portugal v. Council*,[169] the European Court held that the position had not altered. In particular, the Court seemed to be unwilling to 'deprive the legislative or executive organs of the Union of the scope for manœuvre enjoyed by their counterparts in the Union's trading partners'.[170] This ruling has attracted criticism;[171] however, though hardly consistent with the Court's claim to uphold the rule of law, it is nevertheless understandable from the political point of view.[172] Subsequently, the Court has held that it makes no difference if there has been a ruling of the Dispute Settlement Body of the WTO holding the

[162] Art. 216(2) TFEU. [163] See Chap. 10.

[164] *Portugal v. Council*, Case C-149/96, [1999] ECR I-8395, para. 42 of the judgment.

[165] See *International Fruit Company*, Cases 21–4/72, [1972] ECR 1219; *Schlüter*, Case 9/73, [1973] ECR 1135; *SPI*, Cases 267–9/81, [1983] ECR 801.

[166] See *per* Advocate General Reischl in *SPI*, Cases 267–9/81, [1983] ECR 801 at 838, referring to his opinion in *SIOT*, Case 266/81, [1983] ECR at 790.

[167] See *SIOT* (n. 185) at 791. See also *Portugal v. Council* (see n. 164) at paras 43–45 of the judgment.

[168] See *per* Advocate General Reischl in *SPI* referring to his opinion in *SIOT* (n. 185) at 791.

[169] Case C-149/96, [1999] ECR I-8395. [170] At para. 46 of the judgment.

[171] See, for example, Griller, 'Judicial Enforceability of WTO Law in the European Union' (2000) 3 *Journal of International Economic Law* 441. See also Petersmann, 'European and International Constitutional Law: Time for Promoting "Cosmopolitan Democracy" in the WTO' in Gráinne de Búrca and Joanne Scott (eds), *The EU and the WTO: Legal and Constitutional Issues* (2001) 81.

[172] See Peers, 'Fundamental Right or Political Whim? WTO Law and the European Court of Justice' in Gráinne de Búrca and Joanne Scott (eds), *The EU and the WTO: Legal and Constitutional Issues* (2001) 111.

Union measure contrary to the GATT;[173] nor is it possible for an importer to sue the Union in tort for damages: this too has been blocked by the Court.[174] The same political arguments apply in all these cases.

§8 ACTS OF INSTITUTIONS ESTABLISHED BY AGREEMENTS WITH THIRD COUNTRIES

Agreements with third countries sometimes establish institutions, such as councils of association under association agreements. In *Sevince*,[175] the European Court held that acts (decisions) adopted by such institutions can be directly effective in the Union if they comply with the same requirements as those that apply to agreements between the Union and non-member States.

§9 THE SUPREMACY OF UNION LAW AND THE RESTRICTION OF NATIONAL POWERS

It is a basic rule of Union law that (subject to one exception)[176] a directly effective provision of Union law always prevails over a provision of national law. This rule, which is not found in any of the Treaties but has been proclaimed with great emphasis by the Court, applies irrespective of the nature of the Union provision (constitutive Treaty, Union act, or agreement with a non-member State) or that of the national provision (constitution, statute, or subordinate legislation); it also applies irrespective of whether the Union provision came before, or after, the national provision: in all cases the national provision must give way to Union law.[177]

The second *Simmenthal* case[178] provides a good example. The facts were simple: Simmenthal imported some beef from France into Italy and was made to pay a fee for a public health inspection when the meat crossed the frontier. This was laid down by an Italian law passed in 1970; it was, however, contrary to the EU Treaties and two Union regulations passed in 1964 and 1968 respectively. The case began in an Italian court where two points were raised by the Italian authorities: first, that the Italian law must prevail because it was passed *after* the two Union regulations; and, secondly, that even if the Italian law conflicted with Italy's treaty obligations, it had to be applied by

[173] *Van Parys*, Case C-377/02, [2005] ECR I-1465 (Grand Chamber).

[174] *FIAMM v. Council and Commission*, Cases C-120–121/06 P, [2008] ECR I-6513; *Biret International v. Council*, Case C-93/02 P, [2003] ECR I-10497. For a comment on *Biret*, see Thies (2004) 41 CMLRev. 1661.

[175] Case C-192/89, [1990] ECR I-3461.

[176] The only exception is where the national provision is necessary to give effect to obligations under an international agreement entered into by the Member State before it became a party to the relevant Union Treaty: see *Levy*, Case C-158/91, [1993] ECR I-4287 (discussed in Chap. 3, § 4.2).

[177] For a succinct survey of the relevant case law, see the opinion of Advocate General Reischl in the *Simmenthal* case, Case 106/77, [1978] ECR 629 at 651–2.

[178] Case 106/77, [1978] ECR 629.

the Italian courts until such time as it had been declared unconstitutional by the Italian Constitutional Court. This latter contention was based on a principle of Italian constitutional law according to which questions concerning the constitutionality of Italian laws had to be determined by the Constitutional Court. A reference was made to the European Court to obtain a ruling on these issues.

The European Court held that it was the duty of a national court to give full effect to the Union provisions and not to apply any conflicting provision of national legislation, even if it had been adopted subsequently. It also held that it should not wait for the national law to be set aside either by a constitutional court or by the legislature. The key passages in the judgment deserve to be quoted in full:[179]

> Furthermore, in accordance with the principle of the precedence of Community law, the relationship between provisions of the Treaty and directly applicable measures of the institutions on the one hand and the national law of the Member States on the other is such that those provisions and measures not only by their entry into force render automatically inapplicable any conflicting provision of current national law but – in so far as they are an integral part of, and take precedence in, the legal order applicable in the territory of each of the Member States – also preclude the valid adoption of new national legislative measures to the extent to which they would be incompatible with Community provisions.
>
> Indeed any recognition that national legislative measures which encroach upon the field within which the Community exercises its legislative power or which are otherwise incompatible with the provisions of Community law had any legal effect would amount to a corresponding denial of the effectiveness of obligations undertaken unconditionally and irrevocably by Member States pursuant to the Treaty and would thus imperil the very foundations of the Community.

Three points about this should be noted: the Court's statement is limited to Treaty provisions and 'directly applicable measures of the institutions'; secondly, it does not state that conflicting national provisions are void, but merely that they are 'inapplicable'; and, thirdly, the second paragraph is concerned not only with national legislation which conflicts directly with a Union provision, but also with national laws which 'encroach upon the field within which the Union exercises its legislative power'.

As regards the first point, it is obvious that a Union provision will prevail over national legislation only if the Union provision is directly effective. The use by the Court of the term 'directly applicable' does not indicate that the principle of supremacy is limited to regulations: to the extent that they are directly effective, directives and decisions will also prevail over inconsistent national legislation. The *Ratti*[180] and *Marshall*[181] cases are both examples of the supremacy of directives over national legislation – provided the right contained in the directive is invoked against the State. It is equally clear from the cases discussed earlier, in § 7,[182] that a directly effective provision in an international agreement will prevail over inconsistent national legislation.

[179] Paras 17 and 18 of the judgment. [180] Case 148/78, [1979] ECR 1629, discussed in § 4.4.
[181] Case 152/84, [1986] ECR 723, discussed in § 4.6.
[182] See, for example, *Bresciani*, Case 87/75, [1976] ECR 129.

The significance of the second point is that there is, according to the European Court, a positive obligation on Member States to repeal conflicting national legislation, even though it is inapplicable. This was laid down in the *French Merchant Seamen* case,[183] which concerned a French law which provided that a certain proportion of the crew on French merchant ships had to be of French nationality. This was plainly in conflict with Union law, and enforcement proceedings under Article 258 TFEU [226/169 EC] were brought against France. The French Government argued that the French law was not in fact applied and that, since under Union law it was inapplicable, the continued existence of the law did not constitute a violation of the Treaty. The European Court held, however, that the failure to repeal the law created 'an ambiguous state of affairs' which would make Union seamen uncertain 'as to the possibilities available to them of relying on Union law'.[184] Judgment was therefore given against France.

The discussion so far has been concerned with the situation where there is a direct conflict between Union and national law; however, the significance of the third point is that the powers of Member States can be limited even where the conflict is only indirect or potential. Although the position is not entirely clear, it seems that this can occur in certain situations. For example, in the field of agriculture, if the Union has introduced a common organization of the market for a given product, the Member States are precluded from adopting any measures which 'might undermine or create exceptions to it'.[185]

§10 REMEDIES AND PROCEDURE IN NATIONAL COURTS[186]

As a general rule, Union law does not provide remedies for the infringement of rights it confers: this is left to national law.[187] Although Member States do not necessarily have to create new remedies for Union purposes, all remedies normally available under national law must be open to litigants seeking to enforce claims under Union law. Such litigants must be able to enjoy these remedies on terms that are no less favourable than those that apply to litigants with claims under national law: there must be no discrimination.[188]

[183] *Commission v. France*, Case 167/73, [1974] ECR 359.

[184] See para. 41 of the judgment.

[185] See *Pigs Marketing Board v. Redmond*, Case 83/78, [1978] ECR 2347 at para. 56 of the judgment. For a detailed discussion of the cases in this area, see Baumann, 'Common Organizations of the Market and National Law' (1977) 14 CMLRev. 303 and Usher, 'The Effects of Common Organizations and Policies on the Powers of a Member State' (1977) 2 ELRev. 428.

[186] For a recent examination of these questions by a Grand Chamber of the Court, see *Unibet*, Case C-432/05, [2007] ECR I-2271.

[187] National law also normally governs questions of evidence and procedure. These include such matters as the appropriate court or tribunal to hear the case, time limits for commencing proceedings, and the burden of proof: *Rewe-Zentralfinanz*, Case 33/76, [1976] ECR 1989; *Comet v. Produktschap voor Siergewassen*, Case 45/76, [1976] ECR 2043; *Deutsche Milchkontor v. Germany*, Cases 205–15/82, [1983] ECR 2633.

[188] *Comet v. Produktschap voor Siergewassen* (see n. 187) at para. 13 of the judgment; *Deutsche Milchkontor v. Germany* (see n. 187) at para. 23 of the judgment; *BP Supergas*, Case C-62/93, [1995] ECR I-1883.

This has been made clear by the European Court in numerous cases. For example, in *Rewe v. Hauptzollamt Kiel*[189] it said:

> ...it was not intended to create new remedies in the national courts to ensure the observance of Community law other than those already laid down by national law. On the other hand the system of legal protection established by the Treaty, as set out in Article 177 [267] in particular, implies that it must be possible for every type of action provided for by national law to be available for the purpose of ensuring observance of Community provisions having direct effect, on the same conditions concerning the admissibility and procedure as would apply were it a question of ensuring observance of national law.[190]

The principle of equal availability of national remedies is, however, subject to the overriding principle that Member States must ensure that there is an *effective* remedy for the enforcement of Union rights. In particular, if the application of the normal national remedies would mean that it was impossible, or excessively difficult, in practice to enforce the Union right, the Member State is obliged to create special remedies.[191]

Thus in *Von Colson and Kamann v. Land Nordrhein-Westfalen*,[192] a case concerning a directive on sex discrimination, the European Court said:[193]

> Although...full implementation of the directive does not require any specific form of sanction for unlawful discrimination, it does entail that that sanction be such as to guarantee real and effective judicial protection. Moreover, it must also have a real deterrent effect on the employer. It follows that where a Member State chooses to penalize the breach of the prohibition of discrimination by the award of compensation, that compensation must in any event be adequate in relation to the damage sustained.[194]

There are some special situations in which the European Court will itself take action to ensure that an appropriate remedy is available. Four examples will be given. The first

[189] Case 158/80, [1981] ECR 1805. [190] Para. 44 of the judgment.

[191] In *Emmott*, Case C-208/90, [1991] ECR I-4269, the European Court held that, until a directive has been properly implemented, the defaulting Member State cannot rely on national time limits for bringing legal proceedings to claim rights arising under it. However, two later cases, *Steenhorst-Neerings*, Case C-338/91, [1993] ECR I-5475 and *Johnson v. Chief Adjudication Officer*, Case C-410/92, [1994] ECR I-5483 held the opposite. In *Steenhorst-Neerings* the Court purported to distinguish *Emmott* on the facts, though in *Johnson* Advocate General Gulmann had some difficulty 'at first glance' in understanding what the difference was (at 5498–9). It seems that the *Emmott* rule will now apply only where the time-bar has the result of depriving the claimant of *any* opportunity of relying on the directive: para. 26 of the judgment in *Johnson*; *Ansaldo Energia*, Cases C-279–281/96, [1998] ECR I-5025 at paras 19–21 of the judgment. This could be regarded as an application of the general rule that it must not be impossible in practice to obtain a remedy (but see Hoskins, 'Tilting the Balance: Supremacy and National Procedural Rules' (1996) 21 ELRev. 365 at 371–2, where it is suggested that *Emmott* should be overruled). See, further, *Biggs v. Somerset County Council* [1966] ICR 364 (CA).

[192] Case 14/83, [1984] ECR 1891. [193] Para. 23 of the judgment.

[194] On the extent to which national procedural rules may be applied to prevent parties in proceedings before appellate courts from raising new issues based on Union law, see, *Van Schijndel*, Cases C-430, 431/93, [1995] ECR I-4705 and *Peterbroeck v. Belgium*, Case C-312/93, [1995] ECR I-4599, two cases in which the European Court gave seemingly conflicting judgments on the same day. For trenchant criticism of the judgment that the Court was about to deliver in *Peterbroeck*, see the Opinion of Advocate General Jacobs in that case. These two cases are discussed in the 5th edition of this book at pp. 230–2.

is *UNECTEF v. Heylens*,[195] where the European Court laid down the rule that a decision by a national authority rejecting a claim under Union law must be reasoned and subject to judicial review in the national courts even, it seems, if this is not normally the case under the relevant national legal system.

The second example is *R v. Secretary of State for Transport, ex parte Factortame (No. 2).*[196] This case arose when Spanish fishing interests transferred ownership of their boats to British-registered companies in order to fish under the British fishing quota. British fishermen objected, and the United Kingdom passed legislation to prevent it.[197] The Spaniards challenged the legislation in the British courts, and the Divisional Court made a reference to the European Court to determine whether the legislation was contrary to Union law.

At the time, the European Court normally took between one and two years to decide such cases; so this would have meant that the Spanish boats would have been idle for a significant period. The Spaniards therefore applied for an interim injunction to preclude the Government from enforcing the British statute until the European Court had given its ruling. This was granted by the Divisional Court, but rescinded by the Court of Appeal, a decision upheld by the House of Lords, which ruled that, under UK law, there was no power to grant an injunction against the Crown to suspend the application of an Act of Parliament.[198] The House of Lords itself then made a reference to the European Court on the question of remedies: did Union law require that interim injunctions against the Crown should be available to litigants claiming rights under Union law?

The questions referred by the House of Lords were actually decided by the European Court before those referred by the Divisional Court.[199] The European Court ruled that where, in a case involving Union law, a national court considers that the sole obstacle to the granting of interim relief is a rule of national law, Union law requires it to set aside that rule.

The House of Lords had asked the European Court whether, in the situation before it, Union law either required or empowered a national court to grant interim relief. The European Court did not directly answer this question, but it seems implicit in its ruling that national courts are not required to grant interim relief in all cases where the validity of national legislation is subject to challenge on the basis of Union law. Rather, the position seems to be that the same criteria must be applied as would apply under national law if there was no question of suspending national legislation: the normal rules for interim injunctions must be extended to apply against the Crown.[200]

[195] Case 222/86, [1987] ECR 4097.

[196] Case C-213/89, [1990] ECR I-2433; [1990] 3 WLR 818.

[197] The Merchant Shipping Act 1988, Part II; the Merchant Shipping (Registration of Fishing Vessels) Regulations 1988 (SI 1988/1926). The purpose of this legislation was to ensure that boats could not fly the British flag unless they had a genuine link with the United Kingdom. This was to be achieved by laying down new requirements for registration – for example, that boats owned by a company could not be registered unless 75% of the shares in the company were held by British citizens resident and domiciled in the United Kingdom.

[198] *R v. Secretary of State for Transport, ex parte Factortame* [1990] 2 AC 85.

[199] These were decided soon afterwards: *R v. Secretary of State for Transport, ex parte Factortame (No. 3)*, Case C-221/89, [1991] ECR I-3905.

[200] See *R v. Secretary of State for Transport, ex parte Factortame (No. 2)* [1990] 3 WLR 856, where, after a careful consideration of the matter, the House of Lords decided to grant the injunction. See, further, *R v. HM*

The third example is the second *Marshall* case.[201] This was a sequel to the case in which the European Court held that directives do not have horizontal direct effect. Ms Marshall was a woman employed by the National Health Service in England, who had been forced to retire shortly after reaching the age of 60, when, if she had been a man, she could have continued working until the age of 65. Her action had originally been brought in an industrial tribunal and when the case was remitted to the industrial tribunal after the European Court's judgment, the question of compensation arose. The industrial tribunal considered that the appropriate sum was £19,405, an amount which included interest. This gave rise to two difficulties: first, there was an upper limit under English law to the amount of compensation that could be awarded in such proceedings (at the relevant time, this stood at £6,250); secondly, it was uncertain whether industrial tribunals had the power to grant interest. In a second reference to the European Court, the latter ruled that neither restriction could apply where Union law formed the basis of the claim. Thus, there can be no *a priori* limit to the amount of damages recoverable in such a case, and the national court or tribunal must be free to award interest according to the normal national rules.

The fourth example concerns the liability in tort of national governments for failure to obey Union law. But this is so important a topic that it requires separate consideration.

§11 GOVERNMENTAL LIABILITY IN TORT

§11.1 THE FIRST STEP: *FRANCOVICH*

The *Francovich*[202] case opened a new chapter in the European Court's campaign to make Union law more effective. The case concerned an EU directive intended to ensure

Treasury, ex parte British Telecommunications, The Times, 2 December 1993 (CA). It is interesting to note that, shortly after the *Factortame* decision, the European Court laid down rules for the granting of interim relief by national courts where the validity of a national measure implementing Union law is challenged on the ground that the Union provision it implements is invalid (*Zuckerfabrik Süderdithmarschen*, Cases C-143/88, 92/89, [1991] ECR I-415). These rules, which concern the temporary suspension of the national measure while a decision by the European Court is pending on the validity of the Union provision, are not dissimilar to the normal English rules for interim relief, which were applied by the House of Lords in the *Factortame* case (see the start of this note) when it granted the interim injunction. In both cases, there must be a serious doubt as to the validity of the measure (Union or English, as the case may be), damages must not be an adequate remedy, and the balance between the public interest and the interest of the applicant must come down in favour of the latter. See, further, *Giloy*, Case C-130/95, [1997] ECR I-4291. For the suspension of a Union measure by a national court pending a reference to the European Court, see *Atlanta Fruchthandelsgesellschaft* (*Bananas* case), Case C-465/93, [1995] ECR I-3761. National courts cannot, however, grant interim measures where the Union *fails* to act, since in such cases they cannot make a reference to the European Court under Art. 267 TFEU [234/177 EC]: *Port*, Case C-68/95, [1996] ECR I-6065.

[201] *Marshall v. Southampton and South West Hampshire Area Health Authority (Teaching) (No. 2)*, Case C-271/91, [1993] ECR I-4367.

[202] *Francovich v. Italy*, Cases C-6, 9/90, [1991] ECR I-5357.

that full payment of salary arrears is received by employees if their employer becomes insolvent. This was to be achieved through the establishment in each Member State of 'guarantee institutions', which had to be financed by the employers but had to be independent of them, and not subject to claims by their creditors. The directive should have been implemented by 23 October 1983. Italy failed to adopt the necessary legislation and the Commission brought a successful action against it under Article 258 TFEU [226/169 EC].[203] In spite of this, there was still no action to implement the directive.

A group of employees, who had been unable to obtain arrears of pay from their employers, then sued the Italian Government, claiming either the sums payable under the directive or damages for its non-implementation. The Italian court hearing the case referred the matter to the European Court, which ruled that the directive was not directly effective, since the guarantee institutions were not established by the directive but were to be set up by the Member States: the Italian Government could not itself be regarded as the guarantee institution merely because it had not implemented the directive. The first argument put forward by the employees therefore failed.

The European Court, however, ruled in their favour on the second argument. It held that there is a general principle inherent in the Treaty that a Member State is liable to compensate individuals for loss caused to them as a result of a violation of Union law for which the Member State is responsible. It based this holding on the same policy argument as was used to justify the doctrine of direct effect: the effectiveness of Union law would be prejudiced and the protection of the rights of individuals weakened if such a rule did not exist.[204] In other words, the principle exists because it is in the interests of the Union that it should exist.[205]

Having established the existence of the principle, the Court next laid down the requirements for its application. In the case of non-implementation of a directive, three requirements must be satisfied. First, the result to be achieved under the directive must involve the conferring of rights on individuals; secondly, those rights must be identifiable from the provisions of the directive; and thirdly, there must be a causal link between the violation of Union law by the Member State and the loss suffered by the applicant. National law determines the procedural details, but the national rules must not be less favourable to the applicant than those applicable to similar claims under national law, nor must they make it impossible (or excessively difficult) in practice for a remedy to be obtained.

The failure of the Italian Government to implement the directive had already been established by the judgment of the European Court in the earlier case; the result to be achieved under the directive involved the conferring of rights on individuals and

[203] *Commission v. Italy*, Case 22/87, [1989] ECR 143.

[204] It also invoked what was then Art. 5 EEC (now Art. 4(3), second para., TEU), which requires the Member States to take all appropriate measures to ensure the fulfilment of Union obligations. This provision too has been used to justify the principle of direct effect.

[205] For further discussion, see Trevor C Hartley, *Constitutional Problems of the European Union* (1999), pp. 59–65.

the nature of these rights could be determined from the provisions of the directive.[206] Therefore, all the requirements were fulfilled. The case was sent back to the Italian court for it to provide an appropriate remedy.[207]

§11.2 FURTHER DEVELOPMENT: *FACTORTAME*

The principle laid down was potentially of great significance, but just how significant was not appreciated until its full scope was revealed in later cases. The first of these were two cases based on different facts which were joined for the purpose of proceedings before the European Court, *Brasserie du Pêcheur v. Germany* and *R v. Secretary for Transport, ex parte Factortame*,[208] the former being a reference from Germany and the latter from England.

The facts in the *Factortame* case were set out in § 10: it will be remembered that a British Act of Parliament had been passed to prevent Spanish fishermen from registering their boats as British. The European Court subsequently held that this was contrary to Union law.[209] Because it took some time for the European Court to give this ruling (and for it to decide that an interim injunction should be granted), the Spaniards incurred considerable losses for which they claimed compensation from the British Government. They argued that, since the passing of the Act of Parliament was an infringement of Union law, the British Government was liable in tort for any harm that resulted. The Government replied that the legislation had been passed in good faith to meet what it regarded as a problem: the legislation had been suspended when the European Court ruled that it had to be suspended, and repealed when the Court ruled that it had to be repealed.

Unlike the situation in *Francovich*, the provision which Britain had violated was not a directive, but a Treaty provision which was directly effective. This, the Court ruled, did not prevent liability from arising.[210] It was argued that there could be no liability where the wrongful act – the passing of the statute – had been committed by a national legislature: the Court rejected this.[211] It also held that a prior ruling by the European Court was not a necessary precondition for liability.[212]

[206] This had been established by the Court in an earlier part of its judgment when it was considering the question of direct effect: it had found that in this respect the directive was sufficiently clear and precise to be directly effective.

[207] For at least some of the claimants, this was not immediately forthcoming: see *Bonifaci v. INPS*, Cases C-94/95 and 95/95, [1997] ECR I-3969; *Palmisani v. INPS*, Case C-261/95, [1997] ECR I-4025; *Maso v. INPS and Italy*, Case C-373/95, [1997] ECR I-4051.

[208] Cases C-46/93 and 48/93, [1996] ECR I-1029; [1996] 2 WLR 506.

[209] *R v. Secretary of State for Transport, ex parte Factortame (No. 3)*, Case C-221/89, [1991] ECR I-3905.

[210] Paras 18–23 of the judgment.

[211] Para. 36 of the judgment and para. 1 of the Ruling.

[212] Para. 95 of the judgment and para. 5 of the Ruling. It will be remembered that in *Francovich* the European Court had previously ruled that Italy was in default, but the Italian Government had taken no steps to comply with the judgment.

The general principles concerning national remedies – equal availability and effectiveness – are still applicable,[213] but Union law now goes much further than national law – certainly than English law – in providing a remedy in tort. This could be regarded as an application of the principle of effectiveness,[214] but what is really involved is the creation of a new remedy.

As regards the circumstances in which Member States incur liability, the European Court said that the principles to be applied cannot, in the absence of special justification, differ from those governing the liability of the Union.[215] The latter will be discussed in Chapter 16, but their most remarkable feature is that it is extremely difficult in practice for an applicant ever to obtain damages. According to Advocate General Tesauro, speaking in 1995, only eight awards had ever been made.[216] However, the European Court clearly does not intend to interpret the law in the same way when it is applied to the Member States: in five of the first six cases to come before it, it indicated that the Member State should be liable.[217]

In principle, all that has to be done to establish liability is to show that the Member State has violated Union law: it is not necessary to prove deliberate wrongdoing or even negligence.[218] However, one of the rules applied to the Union is that, in a legislative context characterized by the exercise of a wide discretion, the Union cannot incur liability unless the institution concerned has manifestly and gravely disregarded the limits on the exercise of its powers.[219] Where they enjoy a similar discretion, the same principle applies to Member States.[220] In establishing whether a national Government manifestly and gravely disregarded the limits to its discretion, the factors which must, according to the European Court, be taken into consideration include the following:

> ... the clarity and precision of the rule breached, the measure of discretion left by that rule to the national or Community [Union] authorities, whether the infringement and the damage caused was intentional or involuntary, whether any error of law was excusable or inexcusable, the fact that the position taken by a Community institution may have contributed towards

[213] The Court said, for example, that the English remedy of exemplary damages must be available for a violation of Union (Community) law in the same circumstances in which it would apply to a violation of English law.

[214] The European Court seems to take this view: see paras 39 and 52 of the judgment.

[215] Para. 42 of the judgment.

[216] See his Opinion in *Brasserie du Pêcheur* and *Factortame*, [1996] ECR at 1101, note 65.

[217] Although the final outcome rests with the national courts, the European Court indicated in all the cases in question what it thought the result should be. The five cases in which it considered that the State should be liable are: *Francovich v. Italy*, Cases C-6/90 and C-9/90, [1991] ECR I-5357; *Brasserie du Pêcheur v. Germany*, Case C-46/93 (in part) and *R v. Secretary for Transport, ex parte Factortame*, Case C-48/93 (joined cases) [1996] ECR 1209; *R v. Ministry of Agriculture, ex parte Hedley Lomas*, Case C-5/94, [1996] ECR I-2553; and *Dillenkofer v. Germany*, Cases C-178, 179, 188–190/94, [1996] ECR I-4845. The case in which it considered that there should be no liability was *R v. HM Treasury, ex parte British Telecommunications*, Case C-392/93, [1996] ECR I-1631. For a later case in which the European Court did not indicate whether it thought there should be liability, see *R v. Secretary of State for Social Security, ex parte Sutton*, Case C-66/95, [1997] ECR I-2163.

[218] See paras 75–80 of the judgment and para. 3 of the Ruling.

[219] See Chap. 16, § 4.

[220] Para. 47 of the judgment.

the omission, and the adoption or retention of national measures or practices contrary to Community law.[221]

The European Court said that the national courts have sole jurisdiction to apply these principles and to characterize the breaches of Union law at issue.[222] In spite of this, however, it went on to indicate what it thought the result should be in each of the two cases. It considered that both cases fell into the 'wide discretion' category; so the test outlined previously had to be applied. In *Brasserie du Pêcheur*, there were two separate violations of Union law: the Court indicated that one was difficult to regard as an excusable error, but the position was less clear with regard to the other.[223] The violation of Union law that had occurred in *Factortame* was, in the Court's view, sufficiently serious for the British Government to incur liability.[224]

While the question of liability depends on Union law, the other aspects of the tort – for example, causation and damages – are governed by national law, provided that it is not impossible or excessively difficult for a remedy to be obtained.[225]

§11.3 MALTREATMENT OF ANIMALS: *HEDLEY LOMAS*

The next case to come before the Court was *R v. Ministry of Agriculture, ex parte Hedley Lomas*[226] which arose out of a ban imposed by the British Government in 1990 on the export of animals for slaughter in Spain. The reason for the ban was that it was believed that the animals would suffer unnecessarily in Spanish abattoirs. This problem had been around for some years and in 1974 the Union had adopted a directive[227] to deal with it. The directive, which was supposed to be the first step towards a general Union policy against cruelty, required Member States to ensure that animals were stunned before slaughter. In Spain, the Government gave effect to this by adopting legislation making stunning obligatory, but there was no provision for any penalty if stunning did not take place.

On the basis of information obtained from various sources – including an animal welfare organization in Spain – the British Ministry of Agriculture concluded that the directive and the Spanish legislation were being ignored in a significant number of abattoirs in Spain. Some abattoirs did not even possess stunning equipment. It was for this reason that the ban on live exports to Spain was adopted. The ban was based on what is now Article 36 TFEU [Article 30/36 EC], which permits Member States to restrict exports on grounds of, *inter alia*, public morality, public policy, and the

[221] Para. 56 of the judgment. The Court went on to say (para. 57) that, on any view, the breach of Union (Community) law will be sufficiently serious if it has persisted despite a judgment finding the infringement in question to be established.

[222] Para. 58.

[223] In the end, the *Bundesgerichtshof* (German Supreme Court) held that the latter was the determinative one; so it ruled that Germany was not liable: BGH, EuZW 1996, 761.

[224] The British courts subsequently held that the Crown was liable to pay damages: *R v. Secretary for Transport, ex parte Factortame (No. 5)* [1999] 3 WLR 1062; [1999] 4 All ER 906; [1999] 3 CMLR 597 (HL).

[225] On these matters, see *Bonifaci v. INPS*, Cases C-94 and 95/95, [1997] ECR I-3969; *Palmisani v. INPS*, Case C-261/95, [1997] ECR I-4025; *Maso v. INPS and Italy*, Case C-373/95, [1997] ECR I-4051.

[226] Case C-5/94, [1996] ECR I-2553.

[227] Directive 74/557, OJ 1974 L 316/10.

protection of the health and life of animals – grounds that might have appeared wide enough to cover the case.

As a result of complaints addressed to it in 1990, the Commission had entered into discussions with the Spanish authorities on the lack of enforcement of the directive. The latter gave certain assurances; the Commission then dropped the matter. In July 1992, it informed the British Government that it considered that the export ban could not be justified under Article 36.

The British Government lifted the export ban as from 1 January 1993, following a meeting between the Chief Veterinary Officer of the United Kingdom and his opposite number in Spain to devise a procedure to ensure that all animals exported from the United Kingdom were sent only to abattoirs certified by the Spanish authorities as conforming to the provisions of the directive.

Shortly before the ban was lifted (in October 1992), Hedley Lomas applied for a licence for the live export of sheep destined for slaughter in a named abattoir in Spain. Hedley Lomas claimed that the abattoir in question conformed to the provisions of the directive and the British Government had no proof to the contrary. Nevertheless, the licence was refused. Hedley Lomas then brought proceedings in the English courts for a declaration that the refusal was contrary to Union law, and for damages. The English court made a reference to the European Court.

The European Court first considered whether the export ban was justified by virtue of Article 36. Although Britain had no proof that every abattoir in Spain was violating the directive, it considered that there was a significant risk that animals exported to Spain would suffer. It regarded the risk as sufficient to justify the ban. This might have seemed reasonable, since the prevention of unnecessary suffering during slaughter was one of the objectives of the directive. However, instead of making the export ban legitimate in Union eyes, the directive made it illegitimate. The reason, according to the European Court, was that when a problem is recognized by the Union and dealt with in a Union measure, it is taken out of the hands of the Member States and becomes a Union matter. Member State action is no longer permitted; only the Union can take action. The fact that the Union action is ineffective does not seem to make any difference. Britain had no right to act. Member States, said the Court, must trust each other. Although this general principle had been applied in previous cases and the British Government should perhaps have known about it, as applied to the facts of the case it led to the paradoxical result that the directive, which was supposed to benefit animals, actually made things worse. If it had not existed, the ban might have been upheld under Article 36.

Having determined that the ban was contrary to Union law, the Court turned to the question of damages. It repeated the principles laid down previously and considered their application to the facts of the case. Though it reached no final conclusion – this was a matter for the English courts – it made clear that it thought the British Government should be liable. Although Article 36 gave the Government a margin of discretion, this was considerably reduced, if it did not entirely disappear, once the directive had been adopted. In such a situation, *any* violation of Union law would result in liability.

§11.4 THE TRANSPOSITION OF DIRECTIVES

Two cases on the transposition of directives should also be mentioned. These are *Dillenkofer v. Germany*,[228] and *R v. HM Treasury, ex parte British Telecommunications*.[229] In the former, the German Government had failed entirely to implement a directive by the deadline: the European Court held that this in itself was enough to produce liability.[230] In the latter, the British Government had implemented the directive, but had done so incorrectly because it had misunderstood what the directive required. The European Court held that this mistake was excusable, since the directive was reasonably capable of bearing the construction given to it by the British Government; so no liability arose.

§11.5 INCORRECT DECISIONS BY JUDGES

In 2003, the European Court gave a judgment that produced a sense of shock in some quarters: it held that, in certain situations, an incorrect ruling by a national court on a point of Union law can give rise to liability in tort under the *Francovich* principle. The liability is not that of the judges as individuals, but of the State. Nevertheless, the ruling could be regarded as conflicting with the principle of judicial independence.[231]

The case was *Köbler v. Austria*,[232] and the facts were as follows. Under Austrian legislation, professors who had completed fifteen years' service were entitled to a special length-of-service increment. However, the service had to be in Austrian universities. Professor Köbler was a professor at an Austrian university. He had not completed fifteen years' service in Austrian universities, but he had done so if his combined service in universities in Austria and other Union countries was taken into account. He argued that it was contrary to Union law to make the increment dependent on service only at Austrian universities; so he brought proceedings for a ruling that he was entitled to the increment.

The case came on appeal before the *Verwaltungsgerichtshof*, the highest administrative court in Austria. That court initially took the view that the increment was not a loyalty bonus, but a normal component of salary. It made a reference to the European Court for a ruling as to whether such an increment was compatible with Union law if it distinguished between service in Austria and elsewhere in the Union. The Registrar of the European Court asked it whether it wished to maintain its request for a ruling

[228] Cases C-178, 179, 188–190/94, [1996] ECR I-4845.

[229] Case C-392/93, [1996] ECR I-1631; [1996] 3 WLR 203. See also *Denkavit Internationaal v. Bundesamt für Finanzen*, Cases C-283, 291 and 292/94, [1996] ECR I-5063.

[230] The directive was intended to protect travellers whose tour-provider had become bankrupt, and the German Government was obliged to compensate a large number of people as a result of the European Court's ruling.

[231] The principle of *res judicata* is not affected: the original judgment, which may have been between two private individuals, still stands, but the Government has to pay compensation to the party who suffered loss.

[232] Case C-224/01, [2003] ECR I-10239. See also *Traghetti del Mediterraneo v. Italy*, Case C-173/03, [2006] ECR I-5177.

in view of an earlier judgment of the European Court which appeared to cover the point.[233] This case held that such an increment was not compatible with Union law. The *Verwaltungsgerichtshof* then withdrew the request for a reference. However, at the same time it reversed its earlier ruling that the increment was not a loyalty bonus. It then decided that the earlier judgment of the European Court was not applicable and decided the case against Professor Köbler. There was no appeal against this judgment.

Professor Köbler next brought an action for damages against the Austrian Government in an ordinary civil court, the *Landesgericht für Zivilrechtssachen Wien* (Vienna Civil Court). He argued that the *Verwaltungsgerichtshof* had infringed Union law by giving judgment against him, and that Austria was liable in tort for this infringement of Union law. The Vienna Civil Court made a reference to the European Court.

The European Court held that the *Francovich* principle applies to all organs of the State, including the judiciary.[234] However, it sweetened the pill by saying that, in the latter case, liability would arise only 'in the exceptional case where the court has manifestly infringed the applicable law'.[235] It made clear, however, that a deliberate refusal to follow Union law would result in liability.[236] The European Court then applied these principles to the facts of the case. It held that the *Verwaltungsgerichtshof* had given a decision contrary to Union law, but that it was not sufficiently serious to result in liability. So Professor Köbler lost his case.

§11.6 CONCLUSIONS

The European Court clearly hopes that the *Francovich* principle will make Union law more effective. However, those countries that show least respect for Union law in general are unlikely to show any greater respect for this remedy, the application of which will always remain in the hands of the national courts.[237] So the remedy is likely to be least effective in those countries where it is most needed.

233 *Schöning-Kougebetopoulou*, Case C-15/96, [1998] ECR I-47.

234 It pointed out that such a principle also applies under international law – for example, under the ECHR.

235 Para. 53 of the judgment.

236 Para. 55 of the judgment.

237 A study published in 2001 (Tridimas, 'Liability for Breach of Community Law: Growing Up and Mellowing Down?' (2001) 38 CMLRev. 301) indicates that, except for *Francovich* itself, all the cases that had, up to that point, come before the European Court came from Germany, Austria, Sweden, Denmark, or the United Kingdom, countries with a fairly good record for respecting Union law: see, in addition to the cases just mentioned in the text, *Norbrook Laboratories v. Ministry of Agriculture*, Case C-127/95, [1998] ECR I-1531; *Brinkmann Tabakfabriken v. Skatteministeriet* (Denmark), Case C-319/96, [1998] ECR I-5255; *Konle v. Austria*, Case C-302/97, [1999] ECR I-3099; *Andersson v. Sweden*, Case C-321/97, [1999] ECR I-3551; *Rechberger v. Austria*, Case C-140/97, [1999] ECR I-3499; *Haim v. Kassenzahnärztliche Vereinigung Nordrhein* (Germany), Case C-424/97, [2000] ECR I-5123. This suggests that courts in some Member States are simply not sending cases to the European Court. This is confirmed by a later study, Lock, 'Is Private Enforcement of EU Law through State Liability a Myth? An Assessment 20 Years after *Francovich*' (2012) 49 CMLRev. 1675, which covers the period up to the end of 2011. It finds that almost half the references on liability under *Francovich* (sixteen out of thirty-three) were from just two countries: England and Germany (*ibid.* at p. 1678). Again, these were two countries with a fairly good record as regards obeying EU law.

FURTHER READING

Items are listed in date order, the most recent being at the end.

Curtin, 'Directives: The Effectiveness of Judicial Protection of Individual Rights' (1990) 27 CMLRev. 709.

Curtin, 'The Province of Government: Delimiting the Direct Effect of Directives in the Common Law Context' (1990) 15 ELRev. 195.

Steiner, 'Coming to Terms with EEC Directives' (1990) 106 LQR 144.

Craig, 'Once upon a Time in the West: Direct Effect and the Federalization of EEC Law' (1992) 12 OJLS 453.

Maltby, '*Marleasing*: What is All the Fuss About?' (1993) 109 LQR 301.

Steiner, 'From Direct Effects to *Francovich*: Shifting Means of Enforcement of Community Law' (1993) 18 ELRev. 3.

Van Gerven, 'Non-Contractual Liability of Member States, Community Institutions and Individuals for Breaches of Community Law' (1994) 1 *Maastricht Journal of European and Comparative Law* 6.

Plaza Martin, 'Furthering the Effectiveness of EC Directives and the Judicial Protection of Individual Rights Thereunder' (1994) 43 ICLQ 26.

Eleftheriadis, 'The Direct Effect of Community Law: Conceptual Issues' (1996) 16 YEL 205.

Van Gerven, 'Bridging the Unbridgeable: Community and National Tort Laws after *Francovich* and *Brasserie*' (1996) 45 ICLQ 507.

Harlow, '*Francovich* and the Problem of the Disobedient State' (1996) 2 ELJ 199.

Hoskins, 'Tilting the Balance: Supremacy and National Procedural Rules' (1996) 21 ELRev. 365.

Convery, 'State Liability in the United Kingdom after *Brasserie du Pêcheur*' (1997) 34 CMLRev. 603.

Craig, 'Directives: Direct Effect, Indirect Effect and the Construction of National Legislation' (1997) 22 ELRev. 519.

Craig, 'Once More unto the Breach; the Community, the State and Damages Liability' (1997) 113 LQR 67.

Downes, 'Trawling for a Remedy: State Liability under Community Law' (1997) 17 *Legal Studies* 286.

Eeckhout, 'The Domestic Legal Status of the WTO Agreement: Interconnecting Legal Systems' (1997) 34 CMLRev. 11.

Himsworth, 'Things Fall Apart: The Harmonization of Community Judicial Procedural Protection Revisited' (1997) 22 ELRev. 291.

Lackhoff and Nyssens, 'Direct Effect of Directives in Triangular Situations' (1998) 23 ELRev. 397.

Hilson and Downes, 'Making Sense of Rights: Community Rights in EC Law' (1999) 24 ELRev. 121.

Dougan, 'The "Disguised" Vertical Direct Effect of Directives?' [2000] CLJ 586.

Lenz, Tynes, and Young, 'Horizontal What? Back to Basics' (2000) 25 ELRev. 509.

Prechal, 'Does Direct Effect Still Matter?' (2000) 37 CMLRev. 1047.

Tridimas, 'Enforcing Community Rights in National Courts: Some Recent Developments' in David O'Keeffe and Antonio Bavasso (eds), *Judicial Review in European Union Law: Liber Amicorum Gordon Slynn* (2000), p. 465.

Weatherill, 'A Case Study in Judicial Activism in the 1990s: The Status before National Courts of Measures Wrongfully Unnotified to the Commission' in David O'Keeffe and Antonio Bavasso (eds), *Judicial Review in European Union Law: Liber Amicorum Gordon Slynn* (2000), Chap. 31.

PEERS, 'Fundamental Right or Political Whim? WTO Law and the European Court of Justice' in Gráinne de Búrca and Joanne Scott (eds), *The EU and the WTO: Legal and Constitutional Issues* (2001).

TRIDIMAS, 'Liability for Breach of Community Law: Growing Up and Mellowing Down?' (2001) 38 CMLRev. 301.

WEATHERILL, 'Breach of Directives and Breach of Contract' (2001) 26 ELRev. 177.

ANAGNOSTARAS, 'State Liability and Alternative Courses of Action: How Independent Can an Autonomous Remedy Be?' (2002) 21 YEL 355.

DAVIES, 'Bananas, Private Challenges, the Courts and the Legislature' (2002) 21 YEL 299.

KLABBERS, 'International Law in Community Law: The Law and Politics of Direct Effect' (2002) 21 YEL 263.

TRIDIMAS, 'Black, White and Shades of Grey: Horizontality of Directives Revisited' (2002) 21 YEL 327.

KREMER, 'Liability for Breach of European Community Law: An Analysis of the New Remedy in the Light of English and German Law' (2003) 22 YEL 203.

WATTEL, '*Köbler, CILFIT* and *Welthgrove*: We Can't Go on Meeting Like This' (2004) 41 CMLRev. 177.

DRAKE, 'Twenty Years after *Von Colson*: The Impact of "Indirect Effect" on the Protection of the Individual's Community Rights' (2005) 30 ELRev. 329.

ANAGNOSTARAS, 'Erroneous Judgments and the Prospect of Damages: The Scope of the Principle of Governmental Liability for Judicial Breaches' (2006) 31 ELRev. 735.

DAVIS, 'Liability in Damages for a Breach of Community Law: Some Reflections on the Question of Who to Sue and the Concept of the "State"' (2006) 31 ELRev. 69.

KLAMERT, 'Judicial Implementation of Directives and Anticipatory Indirect Effect: Connecting the Dots' (2006) 43 CMLRev. 1251.

DASHWOOD, 'From *Van Duyn* to *Mangold* via *Marshall*: Reducing Direct Effect to Absurdity?' (2006–07) 9 *The Cambridge Yearbook of European Legal Studies* 81

DOUGAN, 'When Worlds Collide! Competing Visions of the Relationship between Direct Effect and Supremacy' (2007) 44 CMLRev. 931.

GRANGER, 'National Applications of *Francovich* and the Construction of a European Administrative *Jus Commune*' (2007) 32 ELRev. 157.

NASSIMPIAN, '... And We Keep on Meeting: (De-)Fragmenting State Liability' (2007) 32 ELRev. 819.

ANAGNOSTARAS, 'The Incomplete State of Community Harmonization in the Provision of Interim Protection by the National Courts' (2008) 33 ELRev. 586.

WARD, 'Do unto Others as You Would Have Them Do unto You: *Willy Kempter* and the Duty to Raise EC Law in National Litigation' (2008) 33 ELRev. 739.

BEUTLER, 'State Liability for Breaches of Community Law by National Courts: Is the Requirement of a Manifest Infringement of the Applicable Law an Insurmountable Obstacle?' (2009) 46 CMLRev. 773.

ANDREA BIONDI AND MARTIN FARLEY, *The Right to Damages in European Law* (2009).

CRAIG, 'The Legal Effect of Directives: Policy, Rules and Exceptions' (2009) 34 ELRev. 349.

ARNULL, 'The Principle of Effective Judicial Protection in EU Law: An Unruly Horse?' (2011) 36 ELRev. 51.

MUIR, 'Of Ages in – and Edges of – EU Law' (2011) 48 CMLRev. 39.

LOCK, 'Is Private Enforcement of EU Law through State Liability a Myth? An Assessment 20 Years after *Francovich*' (2012) 49 CMLRev. 1675.

8

THE NATIONAL RESPONSE

§1 INTRODUCTION

In the previous Chapter the relationship between Union law and national law was discussed from the Union side. The rules we considered were what the European Court thinks the Member States accepted when they signed the EU Treaties. In this chapter, we will consider how the Member States have responded to these demands.

We saw in the Introduction to Part III that some countries (called 'monist' for convenience) have provisions in their legal systems (usually in their constitutions) permitting international agreements to have direct effect in certain cases. Where there is a conflict with national law, some monist countries – for example, the Netherlands – will recognize the supremacy of the treaty. Such countries have a ready-made mechanism for giving effect to Union law.

Another possibility is for the Member State to transfer powers to the Union. This solution can be adopted even by countries which apply the dualist approach to international law. Express provision for the transfer of powers to international organizations is found in Article 24(1) of the German Constitution and Article 20 of the Danish Constitution. There is a similar provision in Article 67 of the Dutch Constitution: the Netherlands can therefore apply the Treaties on the basis of the monist theory, or it can give effect to Union legislation under the terms of Article 67. In Italy, the constitutional position appears at first sight to be less clear-cut, but Article 11 of the Constitution, which authorizes such limitations of sovereignty as may be necessary to ensure peace and justice between nations, has been pressed into service to provide the constitutional foundation for Italian membership of the Union.[1]

A further possibility is to amend the constitution to provide for Union membership. This was done in Ireland, where the Constitution was amended to provide that nothing in it would prevent Union measures from having the force of law in Ireland.[2] Germany and France have also amended their Constitutions, though this was not originally necessary.

[1] See the *Frontini* case, *Corte Costituzionale*, 27 December 1973, [1974] 2 CMLR 372 at 384–5 (para. 7 of the judgment).

[2] Third Amendment to the Constitution.

Not being in a position to adopt a constitutional amendment, the United Kingdom passed a simple Act of Parliament, the European Communities Act 1972, which made provision for the direct effect and supremacy of Union law.

Thus each Member State has found its own way of giving effect to Union law. In all cases, however, Union law has effect in the State concerned only because the law of that State so provides. As a result, it can have effect only to the extent that the national constitution permits. Moreover, although the European Court likes to talk as if the transfer was irreversible,[3] the process could always be reversed, though in the case of some countries a constitutional amendment may be required.

We shall now consider selected countries in more detail.[4] The discussion that follows will focus on only the most important issues.

§2 BELGIUM

The particular interest of Belgium lies in the fact that its constitution contained no statement that international treaties have direct effect and override national law, and it was originally unclear whether it adopted the monist or dualist theory of international law. The Belgian courts therefore had to face the challenge of Union law without the support of an appropriate constitutional provision.

The test came in *Minister for Economic Affairs v. Fromagerie Franco-Suisse 'Le Ski'*.[5] A number of royal decrees had imposed import duties on dairy products which the respondent had been obliged to pay. However, in enforcement proceedings brought by the Commission under what is now Article 258 TFEU (then Article 169 EEC) against Belgium and Luxembourg, the European Court had declared these duties to be contrary to the Treaties.[6] They were then abolished, but the Belgian Parliament passed a statute providing that money already paid could not be recovered. The respondent objected to this and instituted legal proceedings in the Belgian courts to recover the duties it had paid. It won a judgment in its favour in the Brussels *Cour d'Appel* and the Minister appealed to the *Cour de Cassation*, the highest civil court in the country.

Two main arguments were put forward by the Minister. First, he referred to the fact that, when Belgium joined the Union, a statute was passed by the Belgian Parliament ratifying the Treaties. The effect of the Treaties in Belgium was, he argued, dependent on that statute: since the statute prohibiting recovery of the money was passed subsequent to it, the latter must prevail over the former and, therefore, over the Treaties as well: a later law always prevails over an earlier one.

[3] See *Costa v. ENEL*, Case 6/64, [1964] ECR 585 at 594, where it said that the Member States had agreed to 'a permanent limitation of their sovereign rights'.

[4] For the Czech Republic, where the Czech Constitutional Court has refused to apply a judgment of the European Court, see Komarek, 'Playing with Matches: the Czech Constitutional Court Declares a Judgment of the Court of Justice of the EU Ultra Vires' (2012) 8 *European Constitutional Law Review* 323.

[5] *Cour de Cassation*, Belgium, 21 May 1971, [1972] CMLR 330.

[6] *Commission v. Luxembourg and Belgium*, Cases 90, 91/63, [1964] ECR 625.

The second argument put forward was that the judgment of the *Cour d'Appel* had violated a provision of the Belgian Constitution according to which only the Belgian Parliament may determine the constitutionality of a statute: the courts have no right to annul any Act of Parliament. It will be noticed that both these arguments are very pertinent to the British situation.

The *Cour de Cassation* dismissed the appeal and upheld the right of the respondent to reclaim the money. It met the first argument by declaring that when the Belgian Parliament passes a statute to ratify a treaty, that statute is merely the constitutionally prescribed method of giving assent to a treaty entered into by the Crown: the treaty does not take effect in Belgian law as part of the statute, but as a treaty. In other words, the Court declared in this case that Belgium was a monist country. Consequently, the conflict was not between two statutes, but between two instruments of a fundamentally different nature: a treaty and a statute. The Court then continued:[7]

> The rule that a statute repeals a previous statute in so far as there is a conflict between the two, does not apply in the case of a conflict between a treaty and a statute.
>
> In the event of a conflict between a norm of domestic law and a norm of international law which produces direct effects in the internal legal system, the rule established by the treaty shall prevail. The primacy of the treaty results from the very nature of international treaty law.
>
> This is *a fortiori* the case when a conflict exists, as in the present case, between a norm of internal law and a norm of Community [Union] law.
>
> The reason is that the treaties which have created Community law have instituted a new legal system in whose favour the Member States have restricted the exercise of their sovereign powers in the areas determined by those treaties.

It concluded that since the EU Treaty provision violated by the royal decrees was directly effective, it was the duty of the courts to uphold it, even when it was in conflict with a statute.

The second argument of the Minister was met by stating that the *Cour d'Appel* had not annulled the law prohibiting recovery but had merely declared its operation suspended to the extent of the conflict. This could be regarded as a distinction without any real difference: but once the monist position is accepted, it necessarily follows that the courts must have the power to disregard national legislation when it conflicts with a directly effective treaty provision. The truly innovative part of the judgment, therefore, was the acceptance of the monist doctrine as a part of Belgian law.

This judgment was satisfactory from the point of view of Union law. It would not, however, be of much assistance to the British courts if they had to face a similar problem, since it is quite firmly established that the United Kingdom is a dualist country: when the British Parliament passes a statute to give effect to a treaty, the courts apply the treaty only because they are required to do so by the statute: in the United Kingdom the conflict *is* between two statutes.

[7] [1972] CMLR 330 at 373.

§3 GERMANY

Germany emerged from defeat in the Second World War with a Constitution giving significantly more protection to fundamental human rights than those of many other Member States. This has created special problems with regard to Union law: can Union measures take effect in Germany even if they are contrary to fundamental human rights as understood in Germany?

The best-known case is the decision of the Constitutional Court in *Internationale Handelsgesellschaft v. EVGF*.[8] The background to this case was considered in Chapter 5, § 2.1: it will be remembered that the plaintiff had asked a German administrative court to annul a decision of the EVGF (an administrative agency in Germany) based on two Union regulations; it argued that the regulations should not be applied in Germany on the ground that they were contrary to the fundamental human rights provisions of the German Constitution. The administrative court first made a reference to the European Court, which ruled that the validity of Union provisions should be determined according to Union law, not national constitutional law, and that the provisions in question did not violate the Union concept of human rights.[9]

This was not, however, the end of the matter: the administrative court next made a reference to the Federal Constitutional Court (*Bundesverfassungsgericht*) for a ruling on whether the regulations were contrary to the fundamental human rights provisions of the German Constitution. Before considering this question, the Constitutional Court had to decide whether the reference was admissible: in other words, whether Union measures were subject to the German Constitution.

The first question considered by the Constitutional Court was the relationship between German constitutional law and Union law. It took the view that Union law 'is neither a component part of the national legal system nor international law, but forms an independent system of law flowing from an autonomous legal source'[10] and concluded from this that the two legal systems were independent of each other.

The Constitutional Court next pointed out that the Union lacked a directly elected Parliament[11] to which the Union organs with legislative powers were responsible on a political level and that it also lacked a 'codified catalogue of fundamental rights' comparable to that in the German Constitution. It concluded that until such time as Union protection for fundamental rights measured up to that in the German Constitution, Union measures would be subject to the fundamental rights provisions of the German Constitution.

[8] *Bundesverfassungsgericht*, 29 May 1974, [1974] 2 CMLR 540.

[9] Case 11/70, [1970] ECR 1125.

[10] [1974] 2 CMLR 540 at 549 (para. 19 of the judgment).

[11] At the time when the case was decided the European Parliament was not directly elected.

Having thus decided the question of its own jurisdiction, the Constitutional Court next considered the substantive issue: it ruled that the Union measures in issue were not contrary to the German Constitution.

This case therefore represented a potential, rather than an actual, rebellion. In fact the Constitutional Court never found any Union measure to be contrary to the German Constitution and, after hinting at a new approach in 1979,[12] it finally ruled in 1986 that the protection of human rights in the Union had developed sufficiently to meet the requirements of the German Constitution. This occurred in the *Wünsche Handelsgesellschaft* case,[13] where the Constitutional Court stated that, provided the general level of protection of human rights under Union law remained adequate by German standards, it would no longer entertain proceedings to test Union measures against the human rights provisions of the *Grundgesetz*. Later cases have made clear, however, that the application of Union law in Germany is still subject to the *Grundgesetz*. If the European Court failed to give sufficient protection to human rights as defined in the *Grundgesetz*, the Constitutional Court would itself have to take up the task again.[14]

This also follows from the amendment to the Constitution made in 1992 to make better provision for Germany's membership of the European Union. The amended Article 23(1) permits the transfer of sovereign powers to the Union, but this is subject to certain basic principles of the German Constitution, including those relating to fundamental rights.[15]

Problems have also been caused by the refusal of the Federal Tax Court (*Bundesfinanzhof*) to accept the direct effect of directives. It should be explained that in Germany there are no fewer than five separate court systems: in addition to the ordinary courts, there are specialized courts dealing with tax, labour, social security, and administrative matters. Each of these court systems is headed by a federal supreme court, the Federal Tax Court being at the top of the tax court system. Each system is independent of the others, so that the Federal Tax Court is not bound by the rulings of, for example, the Federal Administrative Court and *vice versa*. On constitutional matters, however, all courts are subject to the rulings of the Federal Constitutional Court.

[12] *Steinike und Weinlig*, 25 July 1979, [1980] 2 CMLR 531 at 537 (para. 12).

[13] Decision of 22 October 1986, [1987] 3 CMLR 225. The most important developments, in the eyes of the Constitutional Court, were the further elaboration by the European Court of its doctrine of fundamental rights, especially the significance now attached to the constitutions of the Member States, and the Joint Declaration of 5 April 1977 of the Parliament, the Council, and the Commission.

[14] See, for example, the decision of the Constitutional Court of 12 May 1989 in the *Tobacco Advertising* case, Case 2 BvQ 3/89, [1990] 1 CMLR 570, in which the Constitutional Court pointed out that a directive infringing fundamental human rights as understood in EU law could be brought before the European Court. It added, however, that if this proved inadequate to protect the constitutional standards considered unconditional by the German Constitution, recourse could be had to the Constitutional Court. It also said that German legislation to implement a directive would be subject to constitutional review. See also the *Brunner* case (German 'Maastricht' case), discussed later.

[15] Art. 23(1) of the *Grundgesetz*, referring to Art. 79(3).

The problem regarding the direct effect of directives arose when Germany was tardy in implementing an EU directive dealing with VAT. Certain provisions of this directive gave tax exemptions which were not recognized by the relevant German law. Could a taxpayer claim an exemption on the basis of the directive, even though it conflicted with German legislation?[16] In two cases, decided in 1981[17] and 1985[18] respectively, the Federal Tax Court held that this was not possible.

The two cases were similar, but the second was more interesting since the judgment of the Federal Tax Court directly contradicted a ruling given by the European Court at an earlier stage of the proceedings in the case.[19] This was the *Kloppenburg* case, in which a lower tax court, the *Niedersächsisches Finanzgericht*, had referred the question to the European Court and been told that the relevant provision of the directive was directly effective. The lower tax court then ruled in favour of the taxpayer. The tax authorities appealed, and the Federal Tax Court reversed the lower court's judgment.

Its reasoning started from the premise that Union law could have effect in Germany only to the extent that Germany had transferred legislative powers to the Union. This transfer, permitted by Article 24(1) of the German Constitution, was limited by the terms of the EEC Treaty, which in the case of tax matters gave the Union the power to adopt only directives. According to what is now Article 288 TFEU (then Article 189 EEC), directives leave the Member States free to choose the form and methods of giving effect to them; so national implementing legislation is necessary for the provisions of a directive to have the force of law in the Member States. From this the Federal Tax Court concluded that directives can never have direct effect, an argument not lacking in legal logic. It supported this conclusion with references to both the *travaux préparatoires* to the EEC Treaty (in which the German Government had said that a directive cannot directly bind an individual in the absence of national legislation) and the decision of the French *Conseil d'Etat* in the *Cohn-Bendit* case (discussed later, in § 5). The Federal Tax Court did not allow itself to be deflected by the European Court's ruling: it said that the latter's jurisdiction under what is now Article 267 TFEU (then Article 177 EEC) was limited to Union law and that it did not have the power to determine which law should be applied by national courts. It also stated that the preliminary reference procedure could not be used to extend the legislative jurisdiction of the Union beyond that laid down in the Treaties.

The matter did not rest there, however, because the taxpayer, Ms Kloppenburg, then brought proceedings before the Federal Constitutional Court, which ruled that the Federal Tax Court had acted unconstitutionally: it should either have followed the ruling of the European Court or made a second reference. The third paragraph of Article 267 TFEU [177 EEC] states that a court 'against whose decision there is no judicial

[16] Since the defendant was the State, the issue was one of vertical direct effect only.

[17] *Bundesfinanzhof*, decision of 16 July 1981, [1982] 1 CMLR 527.

[18] *Bundesfinanzhof*, decision of 25 April 1985 (VR 123/84), *Entscheidungen des Bundesfinanzhofes* 143 at 383 (noted by Crossland, (1986) 11 ELRev. 473 at 476–9).

[19] *Kloppenburg*, Case 70/83, [1984] ECR 1075.

remedy' is obliged to make a reference when its judgment depends on a question of Union law. The Federal Tax Court was such a court; therefore its failure to make the reference (or follow the ruling in the earlier reference) was a violation of Article 267 TFEU [177 EEC]. The reason this violation of the Treaties also constituted a violation of the German Constitution was that Article 101(1) of the latter guarantees that no one shall be deprived of his 'lawful judge'. This provision, which protects the right of the citizen to have his case heard by the lawfully constituted court having jurisdiction in the matter, was intended to prevent the establishment of special courts, which might be less impartial than the ordinary courts. The Constitutional Court had already held in the *Wünsche Handelsgesellschaft* case (discussed previously) that the European Court is a 'lawful judge' in terms of Article 101(1). By deliberately refusing to make a reference to the European Court, the Federal Tax Court had deprived Ms Kloppenburg of her 'lawful judge'. Its judgment was therefore annulled.[20]

Another challenge to the Union arose in 1993 when a group of Germans headed by Manfred Brunner, a former official at the Commission, asked the Constitutional Court to rule on the constitutionality of Germany's ratification of the Treaty on European Union. The Constitutional Court held the application admissible, but eventually dismissed it.[21] Reported in English as *Brunner v. European Union Treaty*,[22] this judgment is of great importance for some of the statements it contains.

First, the Constitutional Court said it will continue to guarantee the effective protection of basic rights, as against the Union, for the inhabitants of Germany. It said, however, that it will do this in co-operation with the European Court, a statement which appears to mean that the latter will have the task of reviewing Union measures on a case-by-case basis and the former will restrict itself to a more general role.[23]

The Constitutional Court next considered the legal nature of the Union and classified it as a 'union of States' (*Staatenbund*), not a federal State (*Bundesstaat*). The Union, it said, is intended to provide for an ever closer union of the peoples of Europe (the latter being organized through States); it is not a State based on a single nation.[24] As such, the Union derives its authority from the Member States and can have no greater powers than those conferred on it. The Member States, in a memorable phrase, are the 'masters of the Treaties' ('*Herren der Verträge*'). Germany, it said, remains a sovereign State.[25]

It follows from this that the Union cannot take for itself greater powers than those granted by the Treaties. If it did so, the resulting legislation would be legally invalid in Germany, and the German Government would be constitutionally prohibited from

[20] *Bundesverfassungsgericht*, decision of 8 April 1987 (2 BvR 687/85), [1987] RIW 878; [1988] 3 CMLR 1.

[21] The delay meant, however, that Germany was the last Member State to ratify.

[22] *Bundesverfassungsgericht*, decision of 12 October 1993, [1994] 1 CMLR 57. For the German text, see 2 BvR 2134/92 and 2 BvR 2159/92. The background and significance of the case are explained in Foster, 'The German Constitution and EC Membership' [1994] PL 392.

[23] Para. B(2)(b) of the judgment; para. 13, p. 79 of the CMLR.

[24] Para. C II of the judgment; para. 51, p. 89 of the CMLR.

[25] Para. C II(1) of the judgment; para. 55, p. 91 of the CMLR.

applying it. The Constitutional Court reserved to itself the power of reviewing Union legislation to ensure that it stays within the bounds of the powers conferred on the Union.[26] It also made clear that there are limits to the extent to which the European Court can extend the powers of the Union through its judgments.[27]

This last statement is perhaps the most important because it asserts the right of the *Bundesverfassungsgericht*, rather than the European Court, to act as ultimate arbiter on the division of power between the Union and the Member States. The courts of the other Member States no doubt take the same view, but the *Bundesverfassungsgericht* was the first to express it so clearly.

In a subsequent decision (18 July 2005), the *Bundesverfassungsgericht* held that the German legislation giving effect to the EU third-pillar framework decision on the European Arrest Warrant[28] was invalid because it was contrary to the constitutional provision forbidding the extradition of German citizens.[29] This provision is contained in Article 16(2) of the *Grundgesetz*. Originally, it was stated in absolute terms, but an amendment adopted in 2000[30] made provision for exceptions in the case of extradition to other EU States or international tribunals, provided the principles of the rule of law (*rechtsstaatliche Grundsätze*) were guaranteed. The Constitutional Court held, however, that any such exception was subject to the constitutional principle of proportionality. The German legislation had not complied with this principle; so it had to be struck down.[31] It is, however, clear from the judgment that effect could be given to the EU framework decision in Germany if this was done in the appropriate manner. Consequently, the case does not constitute a rejection of the Union decision itself.

In June 2009, the German Constitutional Court had to decide whether the Treaty of Lisbon was compatible with the German Constitution.[32] In a judgment which reaffirmed the principles laid down in earlier cases, it held that it was. Democracy is one of the principles of the German Constitution, and it was argued that the European Union was not democratic enough to comply with this principle. The Constitutional Court accepted that the Union did not meet the standard of democracy required for a State – in part, because the voting rights of citizens of different Member States were not equal (see Chapter 1, § 1.1) – but it said that this was not the appropriate standard

[26] Para. C I(3) of the judgment; para. 49, p. 89 of the CMLR.

[27] Para. C II(3)(b) of the judgment; para. 99, p. 105 of the CMLR. The Constitutional Court said the same thing (though less assertively) in the *Kloppenburg* case (discussed earlier), [1988] 3 CMLR 1, para. 6, p. 13; para. 19, p. 18; and para. 21, p. 19. Some of the other statements in *Brunner* were also first made in *Kloppenburg*.

[28] Council Framework Decision 2002/584/JHA, OJ 2002, L 190/1.

[29] 2 BvR 2236/04: see http://www.bundesverfassungsgericht.de/en/decisions/rs20050718_2bvr223604en.html (English translation). For a comment, see Hinarejos Parga, (2006) 43 CMLRev. 583.

[30] This was the 47th Amendment to the Constitution.

[31] An additional ground was that a decision of the German Government granting an extradition order was not subject to judicial review. Unlike the Polish Constitutional Court in its decision on the constitutionality of implementing legislation for the same EU framework decision (discussed later, in § 6), the German Constitutional Court did not suspend the effect of its decision to enable the necessary amendments to be made.

[32] *Bundesverfassungsgericht*, decision of 30 June 2009, available at http://www.bverfg.de (click on the Union Jack for the English version).

to apply: the principle of democracy would continue to be satisfied through the right of the German people to vote in elections for the German Parliament.[33]

One can see from this that the German Constitutional Court is not prepared to allow the Union to decide for itself what its powers are. Union law, in the opinion of the Constitutional Court, applies in Germany only because the German Constitution permits it to apply. It is the German Constitution, as interpreted by the Constitutional Court, that determines the extent to which Union law applies in Germany.

§4 DENMARK

The Danish 'Maastricht' decision, *Carlsen v. Rasmussen*,[34] in many ways covers the same ground as the German one; however, the relative brevity of the Court's reasoning and the less abstract language in which it is expressed mean that the judgment is easier for foreign lawyers to understand. The case also began with a legal action by a group of citizens to challenge ratification of the Treaty on European Union.

The provision of the Danish Constitution permitting Denmark's membership of the Union is section 20, which states that powers may be delegated to an authority 'to an extent specified by statute', a requirement that precludes the delegation of unlimited or undefined powers. The appellants argued that the powers delegated to the Union under the Treaty on European Union were too ill-defined to satisfy the requirements of section 20. In particular, they referred to the open-ended nature of the Council's legislative power under what is now Article 352 TFEU (discussed in Chapter 4, § 2.3) and the law-making activities of the European Court.

The Danish Supreme Court rejected these arguments and held that Denmark could ratify the Treaty on European Union. It began its reasoning by stating that section 20 does not permit an international organization (such as the Union) to be given power to adopt legal acts or to make decisions that are contrary to the provisions of the Danish Constitution.[35] Secondly, it made clear that an international organization cannot be permitted to determine for itself what its powers are.[36]

Having specified the requirements of the Constitution, the Supreme Court next considered whether they had been met. It first noted that the EU Treaties were based on the principle of conferral, the principle that the Union possesses only those powers given to it by the Treaties (see Chapter 4, § 2). It then turned its attention to what is now Article 352 TFEU. The Supreme Court gave a fairly restrictive interpretation to this provision, partly on the basis of a passage from the European Court's judgment

[33] It reaffirmed that *Kompetenz-Kompetenz* (the power of an entity to extend its powers, or conclusively determine the extent of its powers) cannot be conferred on the European Union.

[34] Danish Supreme Court, judgment of 6 April 1998, Case I 361/1997, [1999] 3 CMLR 854 (English translation).

[35] Section 9.2 of the judgment.

[36] *Ibid.* It is not, however, necessary that the powers should be specified so precisely that there is no room left for discretion or interpretation.

in the *ECHR* case.[37] It concluded that, if what is now Article 352 was applied no more widely than this, the requirements of section 20 of the Danish Constitution would be satisfied. If an attempt were made to apply it on a wider basis, the Danish Government would be obliged to veto the proposed legislation.[38]

The Supreme Court next dealt with the argument that the European Court's methods of 'interpreting' Union law were contrary to section 20 of the Danish Constitution. It indicated that it was prepared to allow the European Court a great deal of latitude: it was in fact prepared to accept the European Court's law-making activities, provided these remained within the scope of the EU Treaties.[39] The Supreme Court recognized that the European Court had been given jurisdiction to rule on the validity of Union acts; as a consequence, it said, Danish courts cannot declare Union acts inapplicable in Denmark without first referring the question of their validity to the European Court. The European Court's ruling on such questions should, in general, be accepted by Danish courts. However, the Supreme Court held that the requirement of specificity in section 20 of the Danish Constitution meant that Danish courts cannot be deprived of their right to judge for themselves whether EU acts go beyond the powers conferred on the Union. Consequently, if the European Court held the act valid, the Danish courts could in exceptional situations nevertheless hold it inapplicable in Denmark. The same applies, said the Supreme Court, to legal principles derived from the case-law of the European Court.[40]

On these grounds, the Supreme Court ruled that neither the open-ended nature of what is now Article 352 TFEU nor the law-making activities of the European Court rendered Danish ratification of the Treaty on European Union unconstitutional.[41] This judgment allows Denmark to give effect to Union law, but nevertheless makes clear that the Danish courts retain their power to ensure that the Union does not go beyond the Treaties.

§5 FRANCE

Since it was provided in Article 55 of the French Constitution that international treaties have authority superior to that of any national law, one might have assumed that the application of Union law would have raised no problems in France. However, this has not always been entirely true.

It should be explained at the outset that there are two separate court systems in France: the ordinary (judicial) courts, which deal with civil and criminal matters, and the administrative courts, which hear cases where action on the part of the

[37] Opinion 2/94, [1996] ECR I-1759 (para. 30 of the Opinion). This case was discussed in Chap. 4, § 2.3.

[38] Measures may be adopted under Art. 352 TFEU only if the members of the Council are unanimous.

[39] See the last paragraph of section 9.5 of the judgment.

[40] Section 9.6 of the judgment.

[41] Section 9.7 of the judgment.

administration is subject to challenge.[42] The administrative courts may also annul legislative measures enacted by the executive. The highest court in the judicial order is the *Cour de Cassation*; while the *Conseil d'Etat* is the supreme administrative court. These two court systems have very different traditions, and one of the most notable features of the French response to Union law has been the difference in attitude displayed by the judicial and administrative courts, especially by the *Cour de Cassation* and the *Conseil d'Etat*, the former being more willing to meet the demands of the European Court than the latter.

What obstacles have there been to the application of Union law in France? The most important have been the traditional reluctance of all French courts to question the validity of a statute – the French courts (judicial and administrative) cannot review statutes (*lois*) to determine their constitutionality[43] – and the reluctance of the judicial courts to query acts of the administration, whether legislative or executive. In particular, this has made it difficult for them to refuse to apply a French statute (*loi*) when it conflicts with Union law. A second obstacle has been that Article 55 of the Constitution makes the supremacy of treaties over national legislation subject to a proviso: the treaty in question must be applied by the other party. This could be regarded as making the application of Union law in France contingent on its application in other Member States.

The first major case in the *Cour de Cassation* was *Directeur Général des Douanes v. Société Vabre & Société Weigel*,[44] decided in 1975. Vabre had imported a product into France from another Member State and had been required to pay customs duties under a French statute passed subsequent to the EU Treaties. Proceedings were brought to reclaim the money. The Paris *Cour d'Appel* upheld the claim on the ground that the EU Treaties prevailed even over a subsequent statute;[45] a further appeal was taken to the *Cour de Cassation*, where it was argued by the Director-General of Customs that the Paris *Cour d'Appel* had arrogated to itself the right to determine the constitutionality of a statute and this it could not do. He also pointed out that under Article 55 of the French Constitution a treaty is applicable in France only if the other country also applies it: no attempt had been made to ascertain whether the Netherlands, the country from which the product had been imported, met this condition of reciprocity. He therefore concluded that Article 55 could not be invoked to provide a basis for the application of the EU Treaties in the case.

The *Cour de Cassation* rejected these arguments and upheld the judgment of the Paris *Cour d'Appel*. In reply to the first argument of the Director-General, the *Cour de Cassation* stated that the Union Treaties had created a separate legal order which was

[42] The division of jurisdiction between the two sets of courts is actually much more complicated than this.

[43] Draft legislation may, however, be reviewed by the *Conseil Constitutionnel* (Constitutional Council) before enactment, to determine whether it is in accordance with the Constitution. In special circumstances, the *Conseil Constitutionnel* may review statutes after enactment.

[44] *Cour de Cassation*, 24 May 1975, [1975] 2 CMLR 336.

[45] 7 July 1973, [1975] 2 CMLR 336.

binding on the national courts. The second argument was rejected on the ground that what is now Article 259 TFEU (then Article 170 EEC) grants each Member State the right to bring legal proceedings in the European Court against any other Member State which fails to apply the Treaties. Since there is thus a legal procedure to remedy any lack of reciprocity, this could not constitute a ground for not applying the Treaties. This judgment did a great deal to put Union law on a secure footing in France.

In the administrative courts, on the other hand, the story was rather different. Over a considerable period, the *Conseil d'Etat* and the *tribunaux administratifs* had been less willing to find acceptable solutions. In the *Semoules* case,[46] decided in 1968, the *Conseil* refused to accept the supremacy of a Union regulation over a French statute passed subsequent to the regulation, a position maintained in several later cases.[47] It was only in 1989 that the *Conseil d'Etat* abandoned this position.[48]

Directives have caused even greater difficulties. The starting point for any discussion must be the *Cohn-Bendit* case.[49] Cohn-Bendit was a German citizen who was resident in France. He was a student of sociology at a French University and became one of the leaders of the student revolt of May 1968. On 24 May 1968, the French Minister of the Interior (equivalent to the Home Secretary) issued a deportation order against him. He therefore had to leave.

Some years later, Cohn-Bendit wanted to return to France to take up an offer of employment. He asked the Minister to rescind the deportation order, but this was refused, without any proper reason being given. Cohn-Bendit challenged this refusal in proceedings brought before the Paris *Tribunal Administratif*: he argued that the Minister's refusal was contrary to EU law and invoked Article 6 of Directive 64/221.[50] The *Tribunal Administratif* made a reference to the European Court for the interpretation of the relevant provisions and stayed the proceedings until an answer was received.

By making this order, the *Tribunal Administratif* implicitly recognized that the directive could be invoked by Cohn-Bendit.

The Minister refused to accept this and appealed to the *Conseil d'Etat* against the order of reference. Shortly before judgment was given, however, the Minister revoked the deportation order. One might have thought that this would have been the end of the matter, but the *Conseil d'Etat* went ahead and delivered a surprising judgment: it allowed the appeal on the ground that, under the EU Treaties, directives cannot be

[46] *Conseil d'Etat*, 1 March 1968, [1970] CMLR 395. In this case the *Conseil* appeared to accept the view of the *Commissaire du gouvernement* (analogous to an Advocate General in the European Court) that French courts cannot refuse to apply a statute because it conflicts with a treaty. For a fuller discussion of the attitude of the French administrative courts towards EU law at this time, see Weiss, 'Self-Executing Treaties and Directly Applicable EEC Law in French Courts' (1979) 1 LIEI 51 at 69–71 and 73–4.

[47] See, for example, *Conseil d'Etat*, 22 October 1979, [1980] AJDA 39.

[48] *Nicolo, Conseil d'Etat*, 20 October 1989, [1990] 1 CMLR 173. For a full and informative discussion of the case, see Manin, 'The *Nicolo* Case of the *Conseil d'Etat*: French Constitutional Law and the Supreme Administrative Court's Acceptance of the Primacy of Union Law over Subsequent National Statute Law' (1991) 28 CMLRev. 499. See also *Conseil d'Etat*, 24 September 1990 (*Boisdet*) [1991] 1 CMLR 3.

[49] *Conseil d'Etat*, 22 December 1978, Dalloz, 1979, 155.

[50] OJ (Spec. Ed.) 1963/64, p. 17.

invoked by individuals in the national courts in order to challenge an individual administrative decision; Cohn-Bendit could not, therefore, invoke Directive 64/221 before the court. The interpretation of the directive was consequently irrelevant to the proceedings.

Although there are good reasons for thinking that the authors of the Treaties did not intend directives to have direct effect,[51] the doctrine of the (vertical) direct effect of directives had been firmly established by the date of the *Cohn-Bendit* judgment[52] and the *Conseil* was perfectly well aware of it. This judgment was a clear and deliberate act of defiance: by rejecting the authority of the European Court, the *Conseil d'Etat* had struck a blow at the foundations of the Union.

Over the following years, however, the *Conseil d'Etat* gradually softened its position by creating more and more exceptions to its ruling in the *Cohn-Bendit* case.[53] Finally, in 2009, it abandoned its previous approach and fell into line with the European Court.[54]

The position of Union law in France was put in a new perspective by amendments[55] to the French Constitution adopted in order to permit France to ratify the Treaty on European Union.[56] They were necessitated by a judgment of the *Conseil Constitutionnel*,[57] which declared certain provisions of the Treaty on European Union[58] to be incompatible with the French Constitution.[59] The most important amendment was the addition to the Constitution of Title XIV,[60] which made provision for French membership of the European Union.[61]

Once the Constitution had been amended, the Treaty on European Union could have been ratified by statute; instead, however, President Mitterrand decided to call a referendum. This almost resulted in disaster for him. In the end, however, there was a narrow majority in favour of ratification, which duly took place.[62]

[51] See Chap. 7, § 4.1.

[52] It had also been clearly laid down that Directive 64/221 was directly effective: see, for example, *Van Duyn v. Home Office*, Case 41/74, [1974] ECR 1337; *Bonsignore*, Case 67/74, [1975] ECR 297; *Rutili*, Case 36/75, [1975] ECR 1219; *Royer*, Case 48/75, [1976] ECR 497; and *Watson and Belmann*, Case 118/75, [1976] ECR 1185.

[53] For the details, see Tatham, 'Effect of European Union Directives in France: The Development of the *Cohn-Bendit* Jurisprudence' (1991) 40 ICLQ 907; Simon, 'Le Conseil d'Etat et les directives communautaires: Du gallicanisme à l'orthodoxie' [1992] RTDE 265; Mehdi, 'French Supreme Courts and European Union Law: Between Historical Compromise and Accepted Loyalty' (2011) 48 CMLRev. 439.

[54] *Conseil d'Etat, Assemblée*, 30 October 2009, *Dame Perreux, No. 298348.*

[55] No referendum was needed for these amendments; instead, a joint sitting of both Houses of Parliament was held to adopt them. This had to be done by a three-fifths majority.

[56] See Oliver, 'The French Constitution and the Treaty of Maastricht' (1994) 43 ICLQ 1.

[57] Decision of 9 April 1992, [1993] 3 CMLR 345.

[58] These concerned the right of EU citizens resident in France to vote in municipal elections; the provisions on economic and monetary union; and qualified-majority voting in the Council on the non-member States whose citizens had to be in possession of a visa when entering a Member State from outside the Union.

[59] Decisions of the *Conseil Constitutionnel* (in French) may be found at http://www.conseil-constitutionnel.fr/.

[60] For the full text in French, see Oliver, 'The French Constitution and the Treaty of Maastricht' (1994) 43 ICLQ 1 at 24–5.

[61] It dealt expressly with the provisions of the Treaty on European Union which had been ruled incompatible with the French Constitution.

[62] Further attempts to block ratification were rejected by the *Conseil Constitutionnel*: decision of 2 September 1992 (Case 92–312, [1992] JORF 12095) and decision of 23 September 1992 (Case 92–313, [1992] JORF 13337).

Despite the fact that it was the French who first initiated the European project, EU law has not always had an easy time in France.[63] In the end, however, the French courts have usually accepted the requirements of the European Court.

§6 POLAND

Poland is a former Soviet-bloc country which now has a democratic Constitution. The Constitution provides for a Constitutional Court, which has the power to rule on the constitutionality of Polish legislation and Government decisions. Acting under this power, it has given a number of rulings of relevance to the European Union.[64]

The fullest analysis of the relationship between Union law and Polish law is to be found in the decision of 11 May 2005 on the constitutionality of Poland's membership of the European Union.[65] Although it held Poland's membership constitutional, the Constitutional Court made clear that the Polish Constitution is supreme law in Poland. Union law has effect in Poland only by virtue of, and to the extent permitted by, the Polish Constitution.[66] However, the Constitution requires Poland to respect provisions of international law binding on Poland.[67] If a conflict arose between Union law and the Polish Constitution, it could not be solved by giving Union law precedence over the Polish Constitution. Possible solutions would be for Poland to amend the Constitution, for the Union to amend the relevant Union provision, or for Poland to withdraw from the Union. The Constitutional Court also said that the Member States retain the right to decide whether, when Union organs adopt legal acts, they are acting within the powers conferred on them by the Treaties and in accordance with the principles of subsidiarity and proportionality. If they are not, Union law would not have precedence over Polish law in Poland.

In a judgment given a few weeks earlier, that of 27 April 2005,[68] the Constitutional Court held that Polish legislation enacted to give effect to the EU framework decision

[63] See also the series of cases on MCAs: *Conseil d'Etat*, 26 July 1985, (*Maïseries de Beauce*) [1985] *Recueil des Décisions du Conseil d'Etat* 233; [1985] AJDA 615, [1986] RTDE 158; *Conseil d'Etat*, 13 June 1986, [1986] RTDE 533. Compare *Cour de Cassation*, 10 December 1986, [1986] RTDE 195. For a discussion of these cases, see the seventh edition of this book, pp. 273–5.

[64] These include Cases K 11/03, K 33/03, K 15/04, K 18/04, K 24/04, and P 1/05. English translations and summaries of decisions of the Polish Constitutional Court may be found at http://www.trybunal.gov.pl/eng/summaries/wstep_gb.htm.

[65] Case K 18/04 (at http://www.trybunal.gov.pl/eng/summaries/wstep_gb.htm). Paras 6–16 of the English language summary contain the most important points.

[66] The Constitutional Court said that Poland could denounce the EU Treaties under the conditions laid down by international law as expressed in the 1969 Vienna Convention on the Law of Treaties.

[67] This means that Polish courts should interpret Polish law, as far as possible, so as not to conflict with EU law. The Constitutional Court said that a reciprocal duty rested on the European Court to be sympathetically disposed towards national legal systems.

[68] Case P 1/05 (at http://www.trybunal.gov.pl/eng/summaries/wstep_gb.htm). For a comment, see Leczykiewicz, (2006) 43 CMLRev. 1181. The decision of the German Constitutional Court on the same issue is discussed in § 3.

on the European Arrest Warrant was invalid. It ruled that the legislation was contrary to the constitutional provision prohibiting the extradition of Polish citizens. However, it suspended the effect of its decision for eighteen months to give the Government the opportunity to amend the Constitution. This shows that the Constitutional Court is sensitive to the needs of the European Union and will do what it can, within the limits of what is constitutionally possible, to ensure that Poland meets her Union obligations.[69]

§7 THE UNITED KINGDOM

Since the United Kingdom has a largely unwritten constitution, provision for membership of the European Union could not be made by means of a constitutional amendment (as was done in the Republic of Ireland). Moreover, the attitude of the United Kingdom towards international law is strictly dualist: there is no general rule of law allowing treaties to take effect in the internal legal system. So this route could not be used to give effect to the EU Treaties. These problems could be, and were, overcome by means of a special Act of Parliament. However, none of this could affect the principle of the Sovereignty of Parliament, the fundamental doctrine of the British Constitution.

§7.1 THE EUROPEAN COMMUNITIES ACT

The European Communities Act 1972 was passed by Parliament to make provision for Britain's membership of the European Communities (now the European Union). An Act of Parliament was necessary for a number of purposes, but above all to make Union law applicable in the national legal system: without the European Communities Act, the EU Treaties and EU legislation – though binding on the United Kingdom at the international level – would have been of no effect internally. This was made clear by Lord Denning MR in the following *dictum* from *McWhirter v. Attorney-General*,[70] a case decided before the Act had been passed:

> Even though the Treaty of Rome has been signed, it has no effect, so far as these Courts are concerned, until it is made an Act of Parliament. Once it is implemented by an Act of Parliament, these Courts must go by the Act of Parliament.

This shows that the doctrine adopted by the Belgian *Cour de Cassation* in the *Fromagerie 'Le Ski'* case[71] does not apply in the United Kingdom: the European Communities Act 1972 is not merely the means by which Parliament gave assent to the Treaties (something which is not strictly necessary in British constitutional law);[72] it also provides the

[69] For further details, see Lazowski, 'Half Full and Half Empty Glass: The Application of EU Law in Poland' (2011) 48 CMLRev. 503.

[70] [1972] CMLR 882 at 886.

[71] See § 2.

[72] It is, however, normal practice (and possibly a constitutional convention) for treaties requiring ratification by the Crown to be laid before Parliament twenty-one days before they are ratified (the 'Ponsonby Rule'): see (1924) 171 H.C. Debates, cols 2001–2004.

legal foundation for the direct effect of Union law in the United Kingdom. Because of this, the provisions of the Act are of special importance.

§7.2 THE UNION TREATIES

Section 1(2) of the European Communities Act 1972 defines what is meant by 'the Treaties', the most important being listed by name.[73] This list is similar to the list of constitutive Treaties given in Chapter 3, § 1.1, but it includes instruments, such as certain Council decisions of a constitutional nature, which are not, strictly speaking, treaties. Treaties entered into *by* the Union (with or without the participation of the Member States) are included. The EEA Treaty is expressly mentioned. Treaties entered into by the Member States which are ancillary to any of the other Treaties are also covered.

It is provided by section 1(3) that an Order in Council may declare that a treaty falls within the definition, and such a declaration is conclusive. An Order in Council is not, however, necessary: an agreement which falls within the definition will be so regarded, even without a declaration. There is, however, one exception: a post-accession treaty *entered into by the United Kingdom* (other than a pre-accession treaty to which the United Kingdom accedes on terms settled on or before 22 January 1972)[74] will not be covered unless it is so specified in an Order in Council of which a draft has been approved by resolution of each House of Parliament.[75]

This provision gives Parliament control over three classes of agreement:[76] first, it covers agreements concluded by the Member States between themselves – new constitutive Treaties (including treaties amending or supplementing existing constitutive Treaties – for example, the Treaty of Lisbon), subsidiary conventions, and acts of the representatives of the Governments of the Member States meeting in the Council (in so far as these constitute international agreements); secondly, it applies to so-called 'mixed agreements' (agreements between, on the one side, the Union and the Member States, and, on the other, third countries); and thirdly, it could apply to agreements between the Member States and third countries which are binding on the Union and consequently part of Union law (assuming this is possible). The result is that the Government cannot enter into a new Union Treaty without the approval of Parliament. This brings the United Kingdom into line with the other Member States.

[73] The list is regularly updated as new treaties are concluded.

[74] See Art. 3(1) of the Act of Accession: agreements falling within Art. 3(2) would not come within this exception as the terms had to be agreed to at a later date.

[75] For an (unsuccessful) attempt by a private citizen to prevent an agreement between the Member States from being so specified, see *R v. HM Treasury, ex parte Smedley* [1985] QB 657 (CA).

[76] In one special case, Parliament must give its approval by statute: under the European Parliamentary Elections Act 2002, s. 12, it is stated that no treaty providing for any increase in the powers of the European Parliament may be ratified by the United Kingdom unless it has been approved by Act of Parliament.

§7.3 DIRECT EFFECT

Section 2(1) of the European Communities Act 1972 makes provision for the direct effect of Union law in the United Kingdom. It reads as follows:

> All such rights, powers, liabilities, obligations and restrictions from time to time created or arising by or under the Treaties, and all such remedies and procedures from time to time provided for by or under the Treaties, as in accordance with the Treaties are without further enactment to be given legal effect or used in the United Kingdom shall be recognised and available in law, and be enforced, allowed and followed accordingly; and the expression 'enforceable EU right'[77] and similar expressions shall be read as referring to one to which this subsection applies.

Three comments may be made about this: first, it provides for the direct effect of both the Union Treaties (as previously defined) and Union legislation ('rights… created or arising… *under*[78] the Treaties'); secondly, it includes future Union law ('from time to time created'); and thirdly, it makes clear that Union law determines whether a particular provision is directly effective ('as *in accordance with the Treaties*[79] are without further enactment to be given legal effect').

In view of the wide definition given to the 'Treaties', section 2(1) covers all forms of written Union law. The only provisions of Union law which might not be covered are the general principles of law; but as these apply only when some other instrument gives expression to them, they do not have direct effect in themselves.[80]

§7.4 IMPLEMENTATION

Section 2(2) makes provision for the implementation of Union law by means of subordinate legislation. The measure must be in the form of a statutory instrument[81] and must be approved by Parliament.[82]

This power may be used for the following purposes:

- implementing any EU obligation of the United Kingdom;
- enabling any such obligation to be implemented;
- enabling any rights enjoyed, or to be enjoyed, by the United Kingdom under, or by virtue of, the Treaties to be exercised;
- dealing with matters arising out of, or related to, any such obligation or rights, or the coming into force, or the operation from time to time, of the foregoing.

'EU obligation' means an obligation 'created or arising by or under the Treaties'.[83] It follows from this that the power is dependent on the existence of a right or obligation

[77] As amended by the European Union (Amendment) Act 2008, Sch. 1(1), para. 1.

[78] Emphasis added. [79] Emphasis added. [80] See Chap. 7, § 6. [81] Sch. 2, para. 2(1).

[82] If the instrument has not been approved in draft by each House of Parliament, it will be subject to annulment by negative resolution of either House: European Communities Act 1972, Sch. 2, para. 2(2).

[83] Sch. 1, Part II.

under the Treaties (as previously defined) or under Union legislation,[84] and can be used only for purposes subordinate to such right or obligation. Consequently, if the British Government uses this power to implement a Union provision but misconstrues that provision so that the implementing measure goes beyond the provision, the implementing measure may be ruled *ultra vires* by the British courts. Where the Union provision turns out to be invalid, there will of course be no EU obligation to implement; therefore, the implementing measure will be even more clearly invalid.[85] It follows from this that, in order to determine the validity of the implementing measure under British law, the British court may have to make a reference to the European Court under Article 267 TFEU in order to obtain a ruling on the interpretation or validity of the Union provision. This will be the case even where the Union provision is not directly effective.

It is provided by section 2(4) of the Act that implementing measures made under section 2(2) may include 'any such provision (of any such extent) as might be made by Act of Parliament'.[86] There are, however, four things which are expressly prohibited. These are specified in Schedule 2, paragraph 1, which provides that the power may not be used:

(a) to impose or increase taxation;
(b) to enact retroactive legislation;
(c) to sub-delegate legislative power (except to make rules of procedure for any court or tribunal);
(d) to create any new criminal offence punishable with imprisonment for more than two years or punishable on summary conviction with imprisonment for more than three months or with a fine of more than [an amount specified in Schedule 2].

If it is necessary to do any of these things to implement Union law, an Act of Parliament will have to be passed.

§7.5 ENFORCEMENT OF JUDGMENTS

The European Communities (Enforcement of Community Judgments) Order 1972,[87] which was made under section 2(4) of the European Communities Act 1972, makes provision for the enforcement in the United Kingdom of judgments of the European Court, and of decisions of the Council or Commission imposing fines or penalties.

[84] A right or obligation under EU legislation would constitute a right or obligation arising 'under' the Treaties.

[85] *R v. Minister of Agriculture, ex parte Fédération Européenne de la Santé Animale* [1988] 3 CMLR 661, English High Court.

[86] It is not entirely clear what the purpose of this provision is, but it is possible that it was intended to exclude the common law presumptions applicable to delegated legislation (other than those given statutory force in Sch. 2, para. 1). On the effect of measures under s. 2(2), see *Thoburn v. Sunderland City Council* [2002] EWHC 195; [2002] 3 WLR 247; [2002] 1 CMLR 50 (DC), discussed in § 7.6.

[87] SI 1972/1590 (as amended).

The judgment or decision must be registered by the High Court (after the Secretary of State has appended an enforcement order) and is then enforced in the same way as an ordinary High Court judgment.

§7.6 SUPREMACY OF UNION LAW

Section 2(4) of the European Communities Act 1972 also provides that 'any enactment passed or to be passed, other than one contained in this Part of this Act, shall be construed and have effect subject to the foregoing provisions of this section'. Now, the foregoing provisions of section 2 include section 2(1), which states that directly effective EU law must be recognized and enforced in the United Kingdom; consequently, it seems that Parliament intended that all Acts of Parliament, both past and future, should be subordinated to Union law.[88] This view is strengthened by section 3(1), which states that any question as to the 'effect' of any of the Treaties or of Union legislation must be decided 'in accordance with the principles of any relevant decision of the European Court…' One such principle is, of course, that of the supremacy of Union law.

There is no doubt that these provisions are effective as regards UK legislation passed prior to the European Communities Act: Parliament can obviously state that all previous legislation is subject to the provisions of a new statute. The same applies to delegated legislation made under a statute passed prior to the European Communities Act, even if the delegated legislation itself was adopted after the European Communities Act: the force and effect of delegated legislation can never be greater than that of the empowering statute itself.

The real problem concerns statutes passed after the European Communities Act. It is true that, under section 2(4), these are also subject to Union law; however, the principle of the Sovereignty of Parliament intrudes at this point and limits the effectiveness of this provision. The doctrine of the Sovereignty of Parliament is the fundamental principle of the British Constitution: it states that there are no legal limits to the legislative power of Parliament, except that Parliament cannot limit its own powers for the future. It follows from this that section 2(4) must be ineffective if it was intended to deprive Parliament of the power to pass legislation which would override Union law: Parliament is constitutionally unable to deprive itself of this power.

This does not, however, mean that post-accession Acts of Parliament prevail over Union law in the absence of express words to this effect. Section 2(4) could be regarded as laying down a rule of interpretation – and in view of the United Kingdom's membership of the European Union, it is a very strong rule – that Parliament is to be presumed not to intend any future statute to override Union law. Thus in *R v. Secretary of State for Transport, ex parte Factortame*,[89] the House of Lords said that section 2(4) of the European Communities Act has the same effect as if a section were incorporated in

[88] For a more detailed discussion of this topic, see the contribution by Clarke and Sufrin, listed under 'Further Reading'.

[89] [1990] 2 AC 85.

every subsequent Act of Parliament, expressly stating that the provisions of the latter were to be without prejudice to directly effective Union law.[90] Consequently, Union law will always prevail unless Parliament clearly and expressly states in a future Act that the latter is to override Union law. This, of course, would constitute a repudiation of the Treaties and would lay the United Kingdom open to proceedings in the European Court for violation of a Treaty obligation. Responsibility would then rest with Parliament, not with the courts. The position was clearly expressed by Lord Denning MR in *Macarthys Ltd v. Smith*[91] where he said:

> If the time should come when Parliament deliberately passes an Act with the intention of repudiating the Treaty or any provision in it or intentionally of acting inconsistently with it and says so in express terms then I should have thought that it would be the duty of our courts to follow the statute of our Parliament. I do not however envisage any such situation... Unless there is such an intentional and express repudiation of the Treaty, it is our duty to give priority to the Treaty.[92]

This means that ultimate sovereignty still rests with Parliament: Union law prevails only because Parliament wants it to prevail. Parliament could always repeal the European Communities Act and then Union law would cease to have effect in the United Kingdom.

This same result was reached by a slightly different route in the judgment of the Divisional Court in *Thoburn v. Sunderland City Council*.[93] The issue was whether subordinate legislation adopted in 1994 under section 2(2) of the European Communities Act to implement a directive could repeal the Weights and Measures Act 1985, an Act of Parliament passed after the European Communities Act. The Divisional Court held that it could. It rejected the argument that the 1985 Act had impliedly repealed the European Communities Act to the extent that the latter permitted the adoption of subordinate legislation that was inconsistent with it. It did so, however, on the ground that the European Communities Act was a constitutional statute and that, as such, it could be repealed only by express words. This is by virtue of the common law, not by virtue of EU law.

In the course of his judgment, Laws LJ, made the following comment about the relationship between EU law and British law:

> Thus there is nothing in the [European Communities Act] which allows the [European Court], or any other institutions of the EU, to touch or qualify the conditions of Parliament's legislative

[90] *Per* Lord Bridge at 140.

[91] [1979] 3 All ER 325 at 329. See also *per* Lawton LJ at 334. In subsequent proceedings in the same case, Lord Denning made the point even more forcefully: see [1981] 1 All ER 111 at 120. For an earlier statement by Lord Denning, see *Shields v. E. Coomes (Holdings) Ltd* [1979] 1 All ER 456 at 461–2; [1978] 1 WLR 1408 at 1414 (CA).

[92] In *Garland v. British Rail Engineering Ltd* [1983] 2 AC 751; [1982] 2 All ER 402; [1982] 2 WLR 918, the House of Lords expressly refrained from considering the correctness of this approach. It was sufficient for the purposes of that case to affirm that post-accession statutes should, if reasonably capable of bearing such a meaning, be construed so as to be consistent with EU law. See also *National Smokeless Fuels Ltd v. IRC* [1986] 3 CMLR 227; but see *Duke v. GEC Reliance* [1988] 1 All ER 626 (HL).

[93] [2002] EWHC 195; [2002] 3 WLR 247; [2002] 1 CMLR 50 (DC).

> supremacy in the United Kingdom. Not because the legislature chose not to allow it; because by our law it could not allow it. That being so, the legislative and judicial institutions of the EU cannot intrude upon those conditions. The British Parliament has not the authority to authorise any such thing. Being sovereign, it cannot abandon its sovereignty. Accordingly there are no circumstances in which the jurisprudence of the [European Court] can elevate Community [Union] law to a status within the corpus of English domestic law to which it could not aspire by any route of English law itself. This is, of course, the traditional doctrine of sovereignty. If it is to be modified, it certainly cannot be done by the incorporation of external texts. The conditions of Parliament's legislative supremacy in the United Kingdom necessarily remain in the United Kingdom's hands.

He went on to make clear that the relationship between the United Kingdom and the European Union depends on UK law, not EU law.[94]

This was put beyond doubt when the British Parliament passed the European Union Act 2011, section 18 of which provides that directly effective EU law is applicable in the United Kingdom only because the European Communities Act (or some other Act of Parliament) so provides.[95] In other words, EU law applies in the United Kingdom because the United Kingdom makes it applicable, not because the European Union does so.[96]

§8 CONCLUSIONS

What has been said in this chapter makes clear that there is a divergence between the European Court and the courts of the Member States as to the basis on which Union law is to be applied in the Member States. For the Member State courts, the national Constitution is the supreme legal instrument. Its validity is regarded as axiomatic: it cannot be questioned on the basis of any other legal instrument. They, therefore, look at Union law in terms of their national Constitutions. They apply it to the extent that their Constitutions make provision for its application. The European Court, on the other hand, starts with the EU Treaties. It regards their validity as axiomatic and – in theory, at least – demands unquestioning obedience.

This difference could lead to serious consequences. In practice, however, the two sides have taken pains to ensure that the system works without major difficulties.

[94] Para. 69, proposition 4.

[95] The Act also provides that there must be a referendum in the United Kingdom before the Government agrees to any amendment to the EU Treaties (or to an EU decision) that would transfer powers from the United Kingdom to the Union; there must also be an Act of Parliament before the Government agrees to certain specified decisions in the Council or the European Council.

[96] It might be argued that if (as is maintained in this book) the United Kingdom has never ceased to be sovereign, section 18 is superfluous; if, on the other hand, the United Kingdom has lost its sovereignty to the European Union, nothing the British Parliament does can alter that fact. From one point of view this is true. However, section 18 makes the British position clear, and will be followed by British courts and British executive authorities. It is important for that reason.

Thus, the Member State courts have in general interpreted their law and Constitutions so as to meet the reasonable requirements of the Union, while the European Court, for its part, has been careful to moderate its demands where it appeared likely that the national courts would not accept them. It has even gone so far as to create new rules of Union law for this purpose.[97] The result has been a fairly satisfactory *modus vivendi*.

FURTHER READING

Items are listed in date order, the most recent being at the end.

Mitchell, Kuipers and Gall, 'Constitutional Aspects of the Treaty and Legislation Relating to British Membership' (1972) 9 CMLRev. 134.

trindade, 'Parliamentary Sovereignty and the Primacy of Community Law' (1972) 35 MLR 375.

Wade, 'Sovereignty and the European Communities' (1972) 88 LQR 1.

Maresceau, 'The Effect of Community Agreements in the UK under the European Communities Act 1972' (1979) 28 ICLQ 241.

Clarke and Sufrin, 'Constitutional Conundrums: The Impact of the United Kingdom's Membership of the Communities on Constitutional Theory' in Furmston *et al.* (eds), *The Effect on English Domestic Law of Membership of the European Communities and of Ratification of the European Convention on Human Rights* (1983), p. 32.

Koopmans, 'Receptivity and its Limits: The Dutch Case' in St John Bates *et al.* (eds), *In Memoriam J. D. B. Mitchell* (1983), p. 91.

Ganshof van der Meersch, 'Community Law and the Belgian Constitution' in St John Bates *et al.* (eds), *In Memoriam J. D. B. Mitchell* (1983), p. 74.

La Pergola and Del Duca, 'Community Law and the Italian Constitution' (1985) 79 Am. J. Int. L. 598.

Petriccione, 'Italy: Supremacy of Community Law over National Law' (1986) 11 ELRev. 320.

Simon, 'L'effet dans le temps des arrêts préjudiciels de la CEE: enjeu ou prétexte d'une nouvelle guerre des juges?' in *Liber Amicorum P. Pescatore* (1987).

Gaja, 'New Developments in a Continuing Story: The Relationship between EEC Law and Italian Law' (1990) 27 CMLRev. 83.

Schermers, 'The Scales in Balance: National Constitutional Court v. Court of Justice' (1990) 27 CMLRev. 97.

Roth, 'The Application of Community Law in West Germany: 1980–1990' (1991) 28 CMLRev. 137 (especially at 137–45).

Foster, 'The German Constitution and EC Membership' [1994] PL 392.

Herdegen, 'Maastricht and the German Constitutional Court: Constitutional Restraints for an "Ever Closer Union"' (1994) 31 CMLRev. 233.

Oliver, 'The French Constitution and the Treaty of Maastricht' (1994) 43 ICLQ 1.

Roseren, 'The Application of Community Law by French Courts from 1982 to 1993' (1994) 31 CMLRev. 315.

Tomlinson, 'Reception of Community Law in France' (1995) 1 CJEL 183.

[97] The 'discovery' that fundamental human rights constitute a general principle of law is the most notable example: see Chap. 5, § 2.1.

Maganaris, 'The Principle of Supremacy of Community Law – The Greek Challenge' (1998) 23 ELRev. 179.

Mouthaan, 'France: Amending the Amended Constitution' (1998) 23 ELRev. 592.

Høegh, 'The Danish Maastricht Judgment' (1999) 24 ELRev. 80.

Maganaris, 'The Principle of Supremacy of Community Law in Greece – From Direct Challenge to Non-Application' (1999) 24 ELRev. 426.

Schilling, 'The Court of Justice's Revolution: Its Effects and the Conditions for its Consummation. What Europe Can Learn from Fiji' (2002) 27 ELRev. 445.

Albi and Van Elsuwege, 'The EU Constitution, National Constitutions and Sovereignty: An Assessment of a "European Constitutional Order"' (2004) 29 ELRev. 741.

Beck, 'The Problem of *Kompetenz Kompetenz*: A Conflict between Right and Right in which There Is No *Praetor*' (2005) 30 ELRev. 42.

Claes, 'Constitutionalising Europe at its Source. The "European Clauses" in the National Constitutions: Evolution and Typology' (2005) 24 YEL 81.

Phelan, 'Can Ireland Legislate Contrary to EC Law?' (2008) 33 ELRev. 530.

Doukas, 'The Verdict of the German Federal Constitutional Court on the Lisbon Treaty: Not Guilty, but Don't Do it again' (2009) 34 ELRev. 866.

Arnull, 'The Law Lords and the European Union: Swimming with the Incoming Tide' (2010) 35 ELRev. 57.

Phelan, 'Political Self-control and European Constitution: The Assumption of National Political Loyalty to European Obligations as the Solution to the *Lex Posterior* Problem of EC Law in the National Legal Orders' (2010) 16 ELJ 253.

Craig, 'The ECJ and *Ultra Vires* Action: A Conceptual Analysis' (2011) 48 CMLRev. 395.

Craig, 'The European Union Act 2011: Locks, Limits and Legality' (2011) 48 CMLRev. 191

Lazowski, 'Half Full and Half Empty Glass: The Application of EU Law in Poland' (2011) 48 CMLRev. 503.

Mehdi, 'French Supreme Courts and European Union Law: Between Historical Compromise and Accepted Loyalty' (2011) 48 CMLRev. 439.

Payandeh, 'Constitutional Review of EU Law after *Honeywell:* Contextualizing the Relationship between the German Constitutional Court and the EU Court of Justice' (2011) 48 CMLRev. 9.

Komarek, 'Playing with Matches: the Czech Constitutional Court Declares a Judgment of the Court of Justice of the EU Ultra Vires' (2012) 8 European Constitutional Law Review 323.

9

PRELIMINARY REFERENCES

§1 INTRODUCTION

The preliminary reference procedure is one of the most original features of the Union system. Although the idea of giving an international court jurisdiction of this kind had been around for a long time,[1] the European Court seems to have been the first international court actually to be granted it. Subsequently, jurisdiction of a similar kind has been conferred on the Benelux Court, the Andean Court of Justice, and the EFTA Court, the last having jurisdiction only to give advisory opinions.[2]

There are two major differences between an appeal and a reference. First, in the case of an appeal the initiative lies with the parties: the party who is dissatisfied with the court's judgment decides whether to appeal and then takes the necessary procedural steps. The court *a quo* normally has no further say in the matter and cannot prevent the appeal from being lodged.[3] Secondly, the appeal court decides the *case* (even though the appeal may be on limited grounds only) and it has the power to set aside the decision of the court *a quo*; normally it can then substitute its own decision for that of the lower court.[4] These features are not found in the procedure for a preliminary reference: the court *a quo* decides whether the reference should be made, and only specific issues are referred to the European Court. Once it has decided these, the European Court remits the case to the national court for a final decision.

This procedure puts the European Court in a weaker position than would be normal for the supreme court in a federation. It suggests that the national courts are not subordinate to the European Court, but co-equal: the relationship is not one of hierarchy, but of co-operation.

[1] Plender, 'The European Court as an International Tribunal' [1983] CLJ 279 at 284. See also Lauterpacht, 'Decisions of Municipal Courts as a Source of International Law' (1929) 10 BYIL 65 at 94–5, where it was suggested that the Permanent Court of International Justice might one day be given jurisdiction to hear references from national courts.

[2] On the Benelux Court, see Art. 6 of the Treaty establishing the Benelux Court, 1965 (in force on 1 January 1974); on the Andean Court, see Arts 28–31 of the Treaty creating the Court of Justice of the Cartagena Agreement, 1979, (1979) 18 ILM 1203; on the EFTA Court, see Art. 34 of the Agreement between the EFTA States on the establishment of a Surveillance Authority and a Court of Justice, OJ 1994, L 344.

[3] In some cases, however, the parties may appeal only with the leave of the court *a quo* or the appeal court.

[4] In some Continental countries, for example, France, the position is different in the case of an appeal in cassation: if the Court of Cassation allows the appeal, it quashes the lower court's judgment and then sends the case to another *Cour d'Appel* – not the one from which the appeal came – for a new decision.

The relevant provision is Article 267 TFEU [234/177 EC], which reads:

> The Court of Justice of the European Union shall have jurisdiction to give preliminary rulings concerning:
>
> (a) the interpretation of the Treaties;
>
> (b) the validity and interpretation of acts of the institutions, bodies, offices or agencies of the Union;[5]
>
> Where such a question is raised before any court or tribunal of a Member State, that court or tribunal may, if it considers that a decision on the question is necessary to enable it to give judgment, request the Court to give a ruling thereon.
>
> Where any such question is raised in a case pending before a court or tribunal of a Member State against whose decisions there is no judicial remedy under national law, that court or tribunal shall bring the matter before the Court.
>
> If such a question is raised in a case pending before a court or tribunal of a Member State with regard to a person in custody, the Court of Justice of the European Union shall act with the minimum of delay.

There are a number of comments that may be made about this provision.

§1.1 MEANING OF 'COURT'

Article 267 TFEU states that the reference is made to the 'Court of Justice of the European Union'. It will be remembered from what was said at the beginning of Chapter 2 that this term covers both the Court of Justice (usually known as the 'European Court') and the General Court (previously the Court of First Instance). Theoretically, therefore, this could allow references to be made to the General Court, as well as to the European Court. So far, however, no provision has been made for this; so all references go to the European Court.

§1.2 ENTITIES COVERED

Sub-paragraph (b) of Article 267 TFEU covers acts of the 'institutions, bodies, offices or agencies' of the Union (for ease of reference, the bodies, offices and agencies of the Union will henceforth be called 'Union entities'). There are seven Union institutions (listed at the beginning of Chapter 1); the meaning of 'bodies, offices or agencies of the Union' was considered in Chapter 1, § 8. Acts of any of these institutions or entities will be covered. What they have in common is that they were created by Union law. Entities created by Member State law – for example, government departments, public

[5] This is how the Consolidated Version of the Treaties is printed in the Official Journal. There should of course be a full stop, not a semi-colon, at this point. The mistake was probably made because there was previously a third sub-paragraph, numbered '(c)', that referred to the statutes of bodies established by the Council. This third sub-paragraph had no point and has now been deleted.

corporations or local government authorities – will not be covered, even when acting under EU law.[6]

§1.3 ISSUES COVERED

It will be seen from the text of Article 267 TFEU that questions both of interpretation and validity may be referred: references for interpretation may be made with regard both to the Treaties and to acts of Union institutions or entities, but references for a ruling on validity may be made only in the case of the latter. Since the Treaties are, in a sense, the constitution of the Union, it is understandable that their validity cannot be challenged in terms of the Union legal order.

One of the most important issues that may be referred is that of the *effect* of a Union provision (a Treaty provision or an act of a Union institution or entity). The direct effect of Union provisions is treated by the European Court as a matter of interpretation, since the Member States are regarded as having agreed to it when they signed the Treaties. The result is that three issues may be referred for a ruling – interpretation, effect, and validity – though the latter applies only in certain cases. Questions of fact and of national law may not be referred, nor may the European Court rule on the *application* of the law to the particular case – though the exact borderline between interpretation and application is at the best of times uncertain (see § 7).

§2 WHICH PROVISIONS MAY BE REFERRED?

Article 267 TFEU covers two kinds of provision: (a) the Treaties; (b) acts of Union institutions or entities. Its effect can best be considered by looking in turn at each of the sources of Union law.

§2.1 THE TREATIES

The words 'the Treaties' in sub-paragraph (a) of Article 267 TFEU cover the Treaty on European Union and the Treaty on the Functioning of the European Union, as they exist at any given time.[7] However, as we saw in Chapter 1, § 7.1, the jurisdiction of the Court is largely excluded in the area of the Common Foreign and Security Policy.

[6] Thus, it has been held that Art. 267 TFEU (then Art. 177 EEC) does not cover international agreements concluded by national organizations to give effect to a directive: *Demouche*, Case 152/83, [1987] ECR 3833, a case concerning an agreement between national motor insurance bureaux on the 'green card' system. The wording of the Article has changed since this case (Art. 177 EEC did not refer to 'bodies, offices or agencies') but there is no doubt that the result would be the same today.

[7] With regard to the instruments by which new Member States accede to the Union, see, for example, Art. 1(3) of the Treaty of Accession 1972, which brings that Treaty and the Act of Accession annexed to it within the scope of Art. 267 TFEU (then Art. 177 EEC).

§2.2 SUBSIDIARY CONVENTIONS

Even if adopted to attain objectives set out in the EU Treaties, subsidiary conventions cannot be regarded as forming part of the Treaties; therefore, they are not covered by the words 'the Treaties' in sub-paragraph (a) of Article 267 TFEU.[8] However, the convention might itself make provision for preliminary references to the European Court.

§2.3 ACTS OF THE REPRESENTATIVES OF THE MEMBER STATES

By definition, these are not acts of Union institutions or entities but acts of the Member States; so they are excluded from sub-paragraph (b); nor are they part of the Treaties. Consequently, they fall outside Article 267 TFEU, and cannot be referred to the European Court. This is not very significant, however, because national courts would not normally have occasion to consider them.

§2.4 UNION ACTS

Acts of Union institutions and what we have called 'Union entities' (see § 1.2) are covered by sub-paragraph (b) of Article 267 TFEU. This refers simply to 'acts': it is not necessary that the act be directly effective. As was explained in Chapter 8, § 7.4, a national court might have good reason for referring an act that was not directly effective for a ruling on its validity or interpretation.[9] It follows from this that all binding acts are covered, including acts *sui generis*.[10] Non-binding acts, such as recommendations or opinions, are none the less 'acts'[11] and may also be referred:[12] national courts must take them into account when interpreting national and Union measures.[13]

§2.5 GENERAL PRINCIPLES OF LAW

According to the Treaty, these cannot form the subject matter of a reference, as they are neither part of the Treaties nor Union acts. However, if a national court referred a

[8] See *Hurd v. Jones*, Case 44/84, [1986] ECR 29, in which the European Court held that the agreements between the Member States setting up European Schools in various Union countries were not covered by Art. 267 TFEU (then Art. 177 EEC).

[9] In *Haaga*, Case 32/74, [1974] ECR 1201, a German court asked for a reference on a directive which was not directly effective, in order to elucidate the meaning of a national implementing measure; the European Court had no hesitation in giving the ruling. See also *Mazzalai*, Case 111/75, [1976] ECR 657 at 665.

[10] It was held in the *ERTA* case (*Commission v. Council*, Case 22/70, [1971] ECR 263) that an act *sui generis* is an 'act' for the purpose of Art. 263 [230/173 EC] (see Chap. 4, § 1.1); consequently, it must also be an 'act' for the purpose of Art. 267 TFEU.

[11] This follows by implication from Art. 263 TFEU, which speaks of 'acts…other than recommendations and opinions'.

[12] *Grimaldi*, Case C-322/88, [1989] ECR 4407, a case dealing with recommendations.

[13] *Ibid.*

provision of one of the Treaties or a Union act, the European Court would also interpret any general principle of law that was relevant to the provision referred.

§2.6 AGREEMENTS WITH NON-MEMBER STATES

Since these are clearly not part of the Treaties, they will be covered only if they are regarded as acts of Union institutions (or Union entities). As has already been explained, agreements between the Union and non-member States are normally concluded by the Council:[14] in the *Haegeman* case,[15] the European Court seized on this as a ground for regarding such agreements as Union acts. The Court therefore ruled that the Association Agreement between the Union and Greece (before Greece joined the Union) was covered by sub-paragraph (b) of Article 267 TFEU (then Article 177 EEC).

Is this view justified? First, it should be pointed out that there is a distinction between an international agreement and a national measure passed by one of the Contracting Parties to conclude or ratify the agreement: the latter is simply the constitutionally required method of giving assent to the agreement. In the *Haegeman* case the Court mentioned that the Association Agreement had been concluded by means of a Council decision. However, it was not the Council decision that the Court interpreted, but the agreement itself. The two should not be confused.[16]

It should also be noted that the party to the agreement on the Union side is the Union itself, not the Council.[17] Such agreements, therefore, do not constitute acts of an *institution* (or entity) of the Union, as required by sub-paragraph (b) of Article 267 TFEU: they are acts of the Union. Even if one takes the view that one cannot distinguish the Union from its institutions and entities, moreover, it is still doubtful whether agreements are covered by sub-paragraph (b) of Article 267 TFEU: this provision was surely intended to apply to unilateral acts, not bilateral acts such as international agreements.[18]

14 See Chap. 6, § 3. 15 Case 181/73, [1974] ECR 449.

16 See *France v. Commission*, Case C-327/91, [1994] ECR I-3641 at paras 13–17 of the judgment, where the Court held that the appropriate subject matter of an action under Art. 263 TFEU (then Art. 173 EEC) – a provision which gives the Court jurisdiction to annul acts of the Council and Commission – is the decision to conclude the agreement, not the agreement itself.

17 *France v. Commission* (see n. 16) at para. 24 of the judgment.

18 This is the view of Advocate General Trabucchi, who said in *Bresciani*, Case 87/75, [1976] ECR 129 at 147, that a convention is of necessity a bilateral or multilateral legal instrument, and, as such, 'does not lend itself to identification with the acts of the Community executive, which are inherently unilateral'. Advocate General Trabucchi concluded that the *Haegeman* judgment therefore means that, in Union law, international agreements are not binding on private individuals as such, but only by virtue of an act of a Union institution (i.e., the decision or regulation formally concluding the agreement). It appears from this that the Advocate General regards the Union as adopting an essentially dualist approach to international law. This seems to be the only way in which the European Court's judgment in *Haegeman* can be justified; but the view that the Union adopts a dualist approach to international law does not seem consistent with the general tenor of the Court's judgments, especially its decision in the *SPI* case (see n. 20), nor does it seem to be borne out by the wording of the decisions or regulations themselves.

Whatever view one takes of the *Haegeman* case, there can be no doubt that its reasoning can apply only if the Union formally becomes a party to the agreement by means of an act of one of its institutions. This would seem to exclude the possibility that the European Court could take jurisdiction under Article 267 TFEU to interpret an international agreement such as the original General Agreement on Tariffs and Trade (old GATT), to which the Union did not formally adhere, even though the European Court has held that the Union became bound by it because it succeeded to the rights and obligations under it of the Member States.[19] Yet the European Court, in one of the most blatantly policy-based judgments it has ever given, has ruled that the GATT *is* covered by Article 267 TFEU.

This occurred in the *SPI* case,[20] where the Italian *Corte Suprema di Cassazione* expressly asked the European Court whether the old GATT fell within the scope of Article 267 TFEU (then Article 177 EEC).[21] The European Court's answer was not based on the wording of Article 267 TFEU [177 EEC], which it did not even quote, but on pure policy.[22] It started with the proposition that the GATT, like all agreements binding on the Union, should receive a uniform interpretation throughout the Union: any divergence in its application in the different Member States would compromise the unity of the Union's common commercial policy and create distortions in trade within the Union. The Court then characterized its jurisdiction under Article 267 TFEU [177 EEC] on a functional basis: it referred to it as 'the jurisdiction conferred upon the Court in order to ensure the uniform interpretation of Union law'.[23] It was then able to conclude that Article 267 TFEU [177 EEC] must cover the GATT.[24]

The Court's rhetoric in this case was beguiling, but it should not be allowed to obscure the nature of the Court's reasoning. The Court was saying, quite simply, that because it would be desirable for the GATT to be covered by Article 267 TFEU [177 EEC], therefore it *is* covered. This is the reasoning of politics, not law.[25]

It should be noted that the Court stated in the *Haegeman* case that it had jurisdiction to interpret the agreement *within the framework of Union law*;[26] it also said that the agreement constituted an act of a Union institution *in so far as it concerned the Union*.[27] These phrases indicate that the Court was interpreting the agreement only in so far as it applied as part of Union law, and was not claiming that its interpretation was binding

[19] See Chap. 6, § 7.2.

[20] Cases 267–9/81, [1983] ECR 801. See also *Singer and Geigy*, Cases 290–1/81, [1983] ECR 847.

[21] This was in a reference under Art. 267 TFEU [177 EEC]. Since it involved the interpretation of the Treaties, this question was itself covered by Art. 267 TFEU [177 EEC].

[22] The relevant passages are contained in paras 14–19 of the judgment. [23] Para. 15.

[24] The Court stated that this was the case only from 1 July 1968, the date on which the Common Customs Tariff came into force in the Union. (It was on this date that, according to the Court, the Union took the place of the Member States with regard to the GATT.) Prior to this date, only the national courts could interpret the GATT.

[25] For an acknowledgement that criticism of the case is justified, see *R v. Secretary of State for the Home Department, ex parte Evans Medical* (*Generics* case), Case C-324/93, [1995] ECR I-563 *per* Advocate General Lenz at 581 (para. 40 of his Opinion).

[26] Para. 6 of the judgment. [27] Para. 4 of the judgment.

on the other party to the agreement. This is clearly right: if the other Contracting State felt that the European Court had misinterpreted the agreement and that as a result it was not being properly applied on the Union side, it would be entitled to complain that the Union was failing in its obligations under the agreement and, if this produced no results, to resort to the remedies available under international law.

The Association Agreement with Greece, which featured in the *Haegeman* case, was concluded jointly by the Union and the Member States on the one side, and by Greece on the other (mixed agreement). This was because it was considered to fall partly within the treaty-making competence of the Union and partly within that of the Member States. Later cases show that the European Court has jurisdiction to interpret a mixed agreement only with regard to those provisions falling within Union competence, unless there is some special reason for going beyond this.[28] In the absence of such a reason, provisions falling within the exclusive competence of the Member States cannot be considered by the European Court.

Where the international agreement as a whole is not binding on the Union, the European Court has no jurisdiction to interpret it, even if one of the Member States is a party to it and it conflicts with one of the Union Treaties. Thus in *Levy*[29] it was argued that France could not give effect to a directive on sex equality,[30] which required the repeal of French legislation prohibiting women from working at night, because the legislation had been passed to implement an international convention[31] to which France was a party. Since the convention had been entered into by France before it became a party to the EEC Treaty (the Treaty originally establishing the EEC, now the European Union), the provisions of the convention prevailed over those of the EEC Treaty to the extent to which they were incompatible.[32] The correct interpretation of the convention was, therefore, central to the proceedings; nevertheless, the European Court held that only the national court could decide this.[33]

§2.7 ACTS OF INSTITUTIONS ESTABLISHED BY AGREEMENTS WITH NON-MEMBER STATES

The Association Agreement with Turkey provides for the setting up of a Council of Association, which has the power to adopt decisions. In *Sevince*,[34] the European

[28] See *Hermès v. FHT*, Case C-53/96, [1998] ECR I-3603; *Dior v. Tuk Consultancy*, Cases C-300, 392/98, [2000] ECR I-11307, both discussed in Chap. 6, § 7.3.

[29] Case C-158/91, [1993] ECR I-4287. The case was a criminal prosecution against an employer for having employed twenty-three women on night work contrary to Art. L 213–1 of the French Labour Code (discussed further in Chap. 3, § 4.2). See also *R v. Secretary of State for the Home Department, ex parte Evans Medical* (*Generics* case), Case C-324/93, [1995] ECR I-563 at paras 27–30 of the judgment.

[30] Directive 76/207.

[31] ILO Convention No. 89, prohibiting night work for women.

[32] Art. 351 TFEU [307/234 EC].

[33] It was also necessary to consider whether the convention was repealed or modified by subsequent conventions between the same parties. This, too, had to be determined by the national court.

[34] Case C-192/89, [1990] ECR I-3461. See also *Deutsche Shell*, Case C-188/91, [1993] ECR I-363, where the European Court held that it had jurisdiction to decide on the interpretation of 'arrangements' adopted by the

Court held that it has jurisdiction to give preliminary rulings on the interpretation of such decisions: its argument appears to be that its jurisdiction to interpret agreements with non-member States in some way extends to the acts of institutions set up by such agreements. This nicely illustrates the hollowness of the Court's reasoning: even if agreements with non-member States were regarded as acts of an institution of the Union, how can acts of institutions set up by such agreements be acts of a Union institution?[35]

§2.8 NATIONAL PROVISIONS BASED ON UNION LAW

It sometimes happens that a provision of national law refers to a provision of Union law or is in some way based on it. In such a case, Union law may, by reason of national law, apply beyond its intended scope. When the national court applies the national provision, it may, therefore, need to know the correct interpretation of the Union provision. Does the European Court have jurisdiction to interpret the Union provision in such a case?

An example is provided by the *Dzodzi* case,[36] which concerned a woman of Togolese nationality, Mrs Dzodzi, who married a Belgian citizen. Since the husband had never exercised his right under Union law to migrate to another Union country, Union law did not apply to the case and Mrs Dzodzi could claim no right under it to reside in Belgium. If, on the other hand, she had been married to a citizen of another Union country who had availed himself of his Union right to reside in Belgium, Union law would have given her the right to reside there.

It seems that the Belgians thought it wrong that the wife of a citizen of another Union country should have more rights in Belgium than the wife of a Belgian citizen; consequently, legislation was passed to extend to the wives of Belgian citizens the rights given by Union law to the wives of citizens of other Union countries. As a result, Mrs Dzodzi was, under Belgian law, entitled to reside in Belgium if, under Union law, she would have had such a right if she had been married to a citizen of another Union country. The Belgian court therefore asked the European Court, in a reference under Article 267 TFEU (then Article 177 EEC), whether she would have had a right of residence in Belgium if she had been married to a citizen of another Member State. The European Court decided that it had jurisdiction to interpret the relevant Union provisions in order to answer the question.[37]

Joint Committee set up under the Convention on a Common Transit Procedure, even though the 'arrangements' were not legally binding.

[35] At the time this case was decided, sub-para. (b) of Art. 267 TFEU (then Art. 177 EEC), did not cover acts of bodies, offices, or agencies of the Union; so to reach its decision, the Court had to treat acts of the Council of Association as acts of a Union institution. Under the present wording of Art. 267 TFEU, it could be argued that the Council was a body, office, or agency of the Union. Even this, however, is hard to accept, since the Council was established by an international agreement, a bilateral act under international law, not by a normal Union act.

[36] *Dzodzi*, Cases C-297/88, 197/89, [1990] ECR I-3763.

[37] See also *Gmurzynska-Bscher*, Case C-231/89, [1990] ECR I-4003, in which rights under German tax law depended on provisions of the EC Common Customs Tariff. In both cases, Advocate General Darmon took the view that the European Court had no jurisdiction.

Similar rulings were given in a number of later cases,[38] but a different approach was adopted in *Kleinwort Benson v. City of Glasgow District Council*,[39] a reference by the English Court of Appeal. The case concerned a subsidiary convention, the Brussels Convention of 1968 on Jurisdiction and the Enforcement of Judgments in Civil and Commercial Matters (now no longer in force among the Member States), which laid down rules as to when a court in one Member State could take jurisdiction over a defendant domiciled in another. References to the European Court to interpret the Convention were governed by a Protocol of 3 June 1971, which was similar to Article 267 TFEU.

The case concerned jurisdiction as between England and Scotland. Since this was internal to a Member State, it was not covered by the Convention. However, the British legislation which gave effect to the Convention, the Civil Jurisdiction and Judgments Act 1982, laid down a slightly modified version (contained in Schedule 4) which applied as between different parts of the United Kingdom.[40] The provisions before the Court of Appeal were Article 5(1) and Article 5(3) of Schedule 4, the wording of which was substantially the same as the equivalent provisions in the Convention. Under section 16(3) of the Act, UK courts were obliged, when interpreting Schedule 4, to have regard to decisions of the European Court as to the meaning of the equivalent provisions of the Convention. The Court of Appeal, therefore, asked the European Court to give a ruling on the interpretation of Articles 5(1) and 5(3) of the Convention.

The European Court held that it had no jurisdiction to do this. The reason it gave was that the Convention did not apply *as such* to the facts of the case, since the national legislation had not made a direct and unconditional reference to it and UK courts were not absolutely bound by the European Court's rulings. This the Court regarded as unacceptable; so it refused to rule.[41]

In subsequent cases, in which the Union provision did apply as such, the Court has returned to its previous practice of giving a ruling.[42]

[38] *Tomatis*, Case C-384/89, [1991] ECR I-127; *Federconsorzi*, Case C-88/91, [1992] ECR I-4035; *Fournier*, Case C-73/89, [1992] ECR I-5621. In *Federconsorzi*, the Union provision applied, not by virtue of national legislation, but by virtue of a contract, and in *Fournier*, the Court was asked to interpret a term of an agreement which reproduced the provisions of a directive. In both cases, the European Court nevertheless interpreted the provision in question.

[39] Case C-346/93, [1995] ECR I-615.

[40] Schedule 4 is printed in such a way that it is possible to tell at a glance where it differs from the Convention.

[41] The Court seems to be extremely sensitive about giving rulings which are not absolutely binding: see the first *EEA* case, Opinion 1/91, [1991] ECR I-6079 at para. 61 of the judgment.

[42] *Giloy*, Case C-130/95, [1997] ECR I-4291; *Leur-Bloem*, Case C-28/95, [1997] ECR I-4161. The Court did this despite a vigorous plea to the contrary by Advocate General Jacobs. See, further, *Adam*, Case C-267/99, [2001] ECR I-7467; *Kofisca Italia*, Case C-1/99, [2001] ECR I-207.

§3 WHICH COURTS ARE COVERED?

Article 267 TFEU draws a distinction between courts which *may* make a reference and those which *must* do so: the former are covered by the second paragraph and the latter by the third.

§3.1 POWER TO REFER

The second paragraph of Article 267 TFEU states that 'any court or tribunal of a Member State' may request a ruling. This, therefore, lays down two requirements: the body making the request must be a 'court' or 'tribunal' and it must be 'of a Member State'.[43]

What are the essential characteristics of a court or tribunal? It is generally recognized that this is a question which must be decided by Union law: it is not decisive whether the body is recognized as a court under national law.[44] It does not matter what the body is called: according to the European Court, the important question is whether it performs judicial functions.[45] The concept of a 'judicial function' is notoriously difficult to pin down, but one would normally regard a body as being judicial if it had power to give binding determinations of legal rights and obligations. Thus, it should be established by law; it should be permanent; its jurisdiction should be compulsory; its procedure should be *inter partes* (though this is not always required);[46] it should apply rules of law; and it should be independent.[47]

[43] The view has been put forward that a body may be entitled to make a reference even if it is not covered by the second paragraph of Art. 267 TFEU [234/177 EC]. The argument is that the second paragraph is not an exhaustive statement of the power to refer: the first paragraph should, according to this view, be regarded as independently conferring a power to make a reference: see Mok, 'Should the "First Paragraph" of Art. 177 of the EEC Treaty be Read as a Separate Clause?' (1967–68) 5 CMLRev. 458, where this theory is considered but ultimately rejected. There seems little doubt in fact that the drafters of the Treaty intended that the second and third paragraphs should define the scope of the general principle laid down in the first: a body that is not a court or tribunal would not, therefore, be covered.

[44] *Corbiau v. Administration des Contributions*, Case C-24/92, [1993] ECR I-1277 at para. 15 of the judgment; see also *per* Advocate General Gand in *Vaassen*, Case 61/65, [1966] ECR 261 at 281; *Miles v. European Schools*, Case C-196/09, [2011] ECR I-5105 at para. 37 of the judgment (Grand Chamber). It follows from this that the question whether a body is a court or tribunal for the purposes of Art. 267 TFEU may itself be referred to the European Court, either by the body in question or by another body, for example a court hearing an appeal against the first body's decision to refer or not to refer.

[45] *Politi v. Italy*, Case 43/71, [1971] ECR 1039 at para. 5; *Simmenthal*, Case 70/77, [1978] ECR 1453 at para. 9.

[46] See *Job Centre*, Case C-111/94, [1995] ECR I-3361 at para. 9 of the judgment; *Corsica Ferries*, Case C-18/93, [1994] ECR I-1783 at para. 12 of the judgment; *Birra Dreher v. Italian Finance Administration*, Case 162/73, [1974] ECR 201 at paras 2 and 3 of the judgment; *Politi v. Italy*, Case 43/71, [1971] ECR 1039; and *Hoffmann-La Roche v. Centrafarm*, Case 107/76, [1977] ECR 957 at para. 4 of the judgment. In *Dorsch Consult*, Case C-54/96, [1997] ECR I-4961 the European Court said that an adversarial procedure is not an absolute requirement (para. 31 of the judgment).

[47] *Garofalo*, Cases C-69–79/96, [1997] ECR I-5603; *Dorsch Consult*, Case C-54/96, [1997] ECR I-4961. The latter judgment contains a detailed discussion of these requirements. See also *Gabalfrisa*, Cases C-110–147/98, [2000] ECR I-1577 at paras 33–41 of the judgment.

The requirement of independence has given rise to seemingly conflicting decisions. The problem arises where an administrative body hears disputes between the citizen and the government. If the decision-making body is part of the relevant government department, it might be thought that it is not independent, especially if its members are appointed by the relevant minister and can be dismissed by that minister. In some cases, the European Court has held that such a body cannot make a reference: for example, it has held that if a taxpayer is in dispute with the revenue service, the director of that service cannot make a reference, even if he has the power to hear appeals from decisions of subordinate officials.[48]

In other cases, however, such a body *has* been allowed to make a reference.[49] The inconsistency of some of these decisions came under attack from Advocate General Colomer in *De Coster v. Collège des bourgmestre et échevins de Watermael-Boitsfort*,[50] who put forward a more structured and systematic approach based on the case-law of the European Court of Human Rights.[51] His proposal was not followed by the Court; nevertheless, the Court now seems to place more emphasis on independence.[52]

In addition to this, one would normally expect to find a procedure under which the determination was made on the basis of evidence and legal argument. However, although courts are normally concerned with declaring the rights of parties, they do have discretionary powers and to that extent exercise functions which might not be regarded as strictly judicial. Moreover, courts also hear non-contentious proceedings and do not always operate under normal adversarial procedure: the European Court has, in fact, held that a reference can be made in *ex parte* and interlocutory proceedings.[53] On the other hand, one would not usually regard a body as judicial if its functions were purely advisory, investigatory, or conciliatory, nor if they were legislative or executive.[54] In addition to these requirements, the body should enjoy some measure of official recognition: it should in some sense be part of the State machinery.

In *Nederlandse Spoorwegen*,[55] the European Court had to decide whether a body whose decisions were in theory only advisory came within the terms of the second paragraph of Article 267 TFEU (then Article 177 EEC). This was the Dutch *Raad van*

[48] *Corbiau v. Administration des Contributions*, Case C-24/92, [1993] ECR I-1277. See also *Criminal proceedings against X*, Cases C-74 and 129/95, [1996] ECR I-6609; *Almelo and ors*, Case C-393/92, [1994] ECR I-1477 at para. 21.

[49] *Gabalfrisa*, Cases C-110–147/98, [2000] ECR I-1577; *Köllensperger and Atzwanger*, Case C-103/97, [1999] ECR I-551; *Dorsch Consult*, Case C-54/96, [1997] ECR I-4961.

[50] Case C-17/00, [2001] ECR I-9445.

[51] See paras 11–118 of his Opinion.

[52] See *Schmid*, Case C-516/99, [2002] ECR I-4573.

[53] See *Politi v. Italy*, Case 43/71, [1971] ECR 1039; *Birra Dreher v. Italian Finance Administration*, Case 162/73, [1974] ECR 201.

[54] If the proceedings are non-contentious, a reference will normally be inadmissible: *Lutz GmbH*, Case C-182/00, [2002] ECR I-547; *HSB-Wohnbau GmbH*, Case C-86/00, [2001] ECR I-5353; *Salzmann*, Case C-178/99, [2001] ECR I-4421; *Victoria Film*, Case C-134/97, [1998] ECR I-7023; *Job Centre*, Case C-111/94, [1995] ECR I-3361.

[55] Case 36/73, [1973] ECR 1299. The jurisdictional problem was discussed by Advocate General Mayras at 1317–20. An interesting possibility raised by this case is whether the Parliamentary Commissioner for Administration in Britain could make a reference.

State (Council of State), which is in effect the supreme administrative court in the Netherlands. In strict law, however, the application for review is made to the Crown, which is advised by the *Raad van State*. Like the Privy Council, the *Raad van State* has a judicial committee which functions as a court and operates according to normal judicial procedure. The European Court had no difficulty in accepting the *Raad van State* as a court for the purpose of Article 267 TFEU, thus showing that the reality of the matter is more important than the theory. This does not, however, mean that a body whose decisions were in fact, as well as in theory, only advisory could make references to the European Court.[56]

The requirement of official authority has been considered by the European Court in several cases. The first is *Vaassen*,[57] which concerned a reference from a body in the Netherlands, officially described as an 'arbitration tribunal' (*scheidsgerecht*), which settled disputes regarding the pension fund for the mining industry. Although the pension scheme was set up privately by organizations representing employers and workers in the industry, it was approved both by the minister responsible for mining and the minister responsible for social security, the latter's approval being necessary for the purpose of obtaining exemption from the national social insurance scheme. This meant that any subsequent changes in the rules of the scheme also required ministerial approval. The members of the arbitration tribunal were appointed by the minister, and it operated according to adversarial procedure of the normal judicial type. By virtue of a regulation of the Council of the Mining Industry – a public body – all eligible persons were obliged to be members of the scheme, and any disputes concerning rights under the scheme had to be taken to the arbitration tribunal for decision. These features indicate that the *scheidsgerecht* was not really an arbitral body: as was pointed out by Advocate General Gand, it was 'a judicial body duly representing the power of the state, and settling as a matter of law disputes concerning the application of the insurance scheme'.[58] In these circumstances, it is hardly surprising that the European Court held that it was a court or tribunal within the meaning of Article 267 TFEU (then Article 177 EEC).

The *Broekmeulen* case[59] involved similar issues. It concerned a body in the Netherlands called the Appeals Committee for General Medicine. This body heard appeals from the General Practitioners Registration Committee, which registered GPs wishing to practise in the Netherlands. Both bodies were set up by the Royal Netherlands Society for the Promotion of Medicine. Though a private association of doctors, the Society had a large degree of control over the practice of medicine in the Netherlands and GPs

[56] However, in *Garofalo* (see n. 47), the European Court held that the Italian *Consiglio di Stato* (Council of State) is a court for this purpose, even when it is giving an opinion on an 'extraordinary petition'. Under this procedure, the final decision is that of the President of the Italian Republic. It seems that the opinion of the *Consiglio di Stato* is not absolutely binding; if the President departs from it, however, the matter must first be considered by the Council of Ministers. Moreover, the President must state the reasons why he did not follow the opinion.

[57] Case 61/65, [1966] ECR 261. [58] *Ibid.* at 282. [59] Case 246/80, [1981] ECR 2311.

were not recognized for the purposes of Dutch social security legislation unless they were registered with the society; so, from a practical point of view, it was impossible to practise without registration.

The Appeals Committee was constituted as follows: one-third of its members were appointed by the medical faculties of the Dutch universities, one-third by the Society, and one-third by the Dutch Government. It followed adversarial procedure and legal representation was allowed.[60] It was not, however, a court or tribunal under Dutch law; nevertheless the European Court held that it could make a reference under Article 267 TFEU (then Article 177 EEC).

Both these cases concerned bodies which enjoyed a significant degree of official recognition and to some extent carried out a public function. Where this is not the case, the situation will be different. Thus, the European Court has held that a private arbitrator, deriving his (or her) powers from an arbitration clause in a contract freely entered into by private parties, cannot make a reference under Article 267 TFEU, even though he is obliged to decide the case according to the law and his awards are enforceable through the judicial system.[61] It is also doubtful whether a purely domestic tribunal, operating under the rules of a private association, could make a reference unless some measure of official recognition was accorded to it.

The second requirement of the second paragraph of Article 267 TFEU is that the court or tribunal must be 'of a Member State', which suggests not only that the body should have official standing, but also that it should be *in* a Member State, or at least part of the judicial system of a Member State. This raises questions with regard to courts in dependencies of Member States. There can be little doubt that Article 267 TFEU applies to the courts of territories to which the EU Treaties apply in full, even if such territories are not an integral part of any Member State.[62] It also applies to the courts of territories to which the general institutional provisions of the Treaties apply, even if other parts of the Treaties do not apply.[63] Thus the courts of the Isle of Man are covered.[64] Advocate General Jacobs has gone further and suggested that Article 267 TFEU applies to the courts of territories to which any part of the Treaties applies, since such courts will need to obtain rulings from the European Court on those provisions.[65] It is likely that the Court will accept this, since it would otherwise be impossible to ensure the uniform interpretation and application of the Treaties, something to which the Court attaches great importance.[66]

[60] In some circumstances there might have been a right of appeal to the courts from its decisions, but no such appeal had ever been made.

[61] *Nordsee v. Reederei Mond*, Case 102/81, [1982] ECR 1095. The result of this ruling is that the only way in which a point of Union law raised in arbitration can be referred to the European Court is through an appeal to a court, which can then make the reference. For a case in which this occurred, see *Bulk Oil v. Sun International* [1984] 1 WLR 147 (CA). On the duties under Union law of a national court in such a situation, see *Eco Swiss v. Benetton International*, Case C-126/97, [1999] ECR I-3055.

[62] See, for example, territories to which the Treaty applies by virtue of Art. 355 TFEU.

[63] *Barr and Montrose Holdings*, Case C-355/89, [1991] ECR I-3479 at paras 6–10 of the judgment.

[64] *Ibid.* [65] *Ibid.* at 3493. [66] *Ibid.* at para. 9 of the judgment.

Foreign (non-Union) courts are clearly excluded, even if the State in which they sit is a Party to an association agreement with the Union;[67] it is also doubtful whether international courts, such as the European Court of Human Rights, come within the terms of the provision, though some may take a different view. On the other hand, there is a ruling by the European Court that a court, such as the Benelux Court,[68] that is common to a number of Member States may make a reference when it has to decide a point of Union law.[69] Such a court could perhaps be regarded as a joint court of the Member States in question, since certain points of law that would otherwise have been decided by their courts are decided by it.

In *Miles v. European Schools*,[70] the European Court held that it had no jurisdiction to rule on a reference for a preliminary ruling from the Complaints Board of the European Schools. The European Schools are a system of schools in different EU countries for the education of the children of EU officials. They operate under an international agreement, the European Schools Convention,[71] to which all the Member States and the Union are Parties. The Complaints Board was set up under this agreement to hear disputes concerning the application of the Convention to the persons covered by it. Its members are independent and it follows a judicial-type procedure. However, the European Court held that, though it satisfied the criteria for being regarded as a 'court or tribunal' within the meaning of Article 267 TFEU, it was not a court *of a Member State*. It distinguished the Benelux Court on the ground that the Benelux Court was a court common to a number of Member States and that the procedure before it was a step in the procedure before the national courts in the countries concerned. This was not true with regard to the Complaints Board. The Complaints Board is not a court common to a number of Member States, but a court of an international organization, which, despite the functional links it has with the Union, remains formally distinct from the Union and from the Member States.[72]

Where a body has the right to make a reference under Union law, it cannot be deprived of that right by national law. This is illustrated by the *Rheinmühlen* cases,[73]

[67] See *per* Advocate General Mischo in *Kaefer and Procacci*, Cases C-100, 101/89, [1990] ECR I-4647 at 4658. In this case, the European Court held that the *Tribunal Administratif* of Papeete, French Polynesia, was covered by Art. 267 TFEU (then Art. 177 EEC), since it was an integral part of the French judicial system.

[68] It was established under a Treaty of 1965 between Belgium, the Netherlands, and Luxembourg. It is composed of judges of the supreme courts of these three States. In certain cases, courts in the Benelux countries have to refer questions to it under a procedure similar to that for preliminary references to the European Court.

[69] *Parfums Christian Dior v. Evora*, Case C-337/95, [1997] ECR I-6013 at paras 15–31 of the judgment. What the European Court must have meant by this ruling is that, when they concluded the agreement setting up the Benelux Court, the Member States were obliged under the EC Treaty (as it then was) to require it to make references to the European Court on questions of Community (Union) law. If the point arose before it, the Benelux Court would have to interpret the agreement that created it in order to see whether, under *that* agreement, it did have such a power. It might well conclude that, since all the parties to the agreement were parties to the EC Treaty, they must have intended that their obligations under that Treaty would not be prejudiced by the agreement.

[70] Case C-196/09, [2011] ECR I-5105 (Grand Chamber).

[71] Concluded in Luxembourg on 21 June 1994, OJ 1994 L 212, p. 3.

[72] Para. 42 of the judgment.

[73] Cases 166/73, [1974] ECR 33 and 146/73; [1974] ECR 139.

which concerned an attempt by a German cereal exporter to obtain an export rebate under Union law. The *Hessisches Finanzgericht* (Hessian Tax Court) ruled against Rheinmühlen, which then appealed to the highest German court in these matters, the *Bundesfinanzhof* (Federal Tax Court). The *Bundesfinanzhof* quashed the judgment and held that Rheinmühlen was entitled at least to a rebate at a lesser rate. The case was then sent back to the *Hessisches Finanzgericht* for a decision on certain questions of fact.

Under German law, the Hessian court was bound by rulings of the Federal court on points of law. The *Hessisches Finanzgericht* was not, however, prepared to accept the ruling in this case, as questions of Union law were involved. It therefore made a reference to the European Court for an interpretation of the relevant provision; it also asked the European Court for a ruling on the question whether it is permissible for a lower court to make a reference when the case has been sent back to it by a higher court after an earlier judgment has been set aside.

Rheinmühlen then appealed to the *Bundesfinanzhof* against the Hessian court's order referring the case to the European Court and the *Bundesfinanzhof* itself made a reference to the European Court: it asked whether Article 267 TFEU (then Article 177 EEC) gives lower courts an unfettered right to refer, or whether it is subject to national provisions under which lower courts are bound by the judgments of superior courts. This was of course substantially the same as the second question referred by the Hessian court.

The European Court held that the power of a lower court to make a reference cannot be abrogated by a provision of national law: it stated that the lower court must be free to make a reference if it considers that the superior court's ruling could lead it to give judgment contrary to Union law. This means that national rules of *res judicata* do not apply to Union law. On all questions of Union law, including the question of supremacy, the European Court must be the final authority.

It is interesting to note that the Advocate General, Mr Warner, went even further: he suggested that there ought not even to be a right of appeal against an order for reference. In his view, such a right of appeal itself fettered the power of the lower court to make a reference. On this point, however, the European Court did not follow him. The position is, therefore, that national law cannot take away the right given in the second paragraph of Article 267 TFEU, but this does not prevent the lower court's order for reference from being quashed on appeal. The consequences of this are considered in § 6.3.

§3.2 OBLIGATION TO REFER

The third paragraph of Article 267 TFEU provides that a court or tribunal of a Member State 'against whose decisions there is no judicial remedy under national law' *must* make a reference. Two points of view exist as to the meaning of this phrase: according to the 'abstract theory', the only courts within the scope of the provision are those whose decisions are *as a general rule* not subject to appeal; according to the 'concrete theory', on the other hand, the important question is whether the court's decision *in the case in question* is subject to appeal. This distinction can be important where, for example, there is a right of appeal only if the sum of money in issue is more than a certain amount.

The wording of the third paragraph of Article 267 TFEU itself favours the abstract theory: if the authors of the Treaty had intended the decisive point to be whether there was a right of appeal in the particular case in question, they would not have put the word 'decisions' into the plural. The use of the plural suggests that the general position regarding appeals is the criterion. Another argument may be derived from considerations of legal policy: the reason rights of appeal are limited in certain cases is to prevent proceedings from becoming too drawn out and to keep costs within reasonable bounds. These objectives would be jeopardized if national courts were obliged to make a reference to Luxembourg even where the sum in issue was small or the case was generally of limited importance.

The policy of Union law, on the other hand, places great importance on maintaining uniformity of interpretation of Union provisions: this could be undermined if it were possible for a case involving Union law to run its course without a reference being made. Some of the most important judgments of the European Court have in fact been handed down in cases involving very small sums of money.[74]

There is an *obiter dictum* of the European Court supporting the concrete theory: this was in *Costa v. ENEL*,[75] a reference from a *giudice conciliatore* (magistrate) in Italy. Although the decisions of a *giudice conciliatore* are appealable in some cases, there was no right of appeal against the decision in the proceedings in question because the sum of money involved was so small. In the course of its judgment, the European Court said, with reference to Article 267 TFEU (then Article 177 EEC):[76] 'By the terms of this Article, however, national courts against whose decisions, *as in the present case*, there is no judicial remedy, must refer the matter to the Court of Justice.' This suggests that the European Court considered that the third paragraph of Article 267 TFEU [177 EEC] refers to the highest court in the case, rather than the highest court in the country.

On the other hand, the European Court's ruling in *Parfums Christian Dior v. Evora*[77] (discussed later) makes sense only if the abstract theory is correct. According to this judgment, the highest court of a Member State is obliged to refer questions of Union law to the European Court even if, in the particular case before it, it is required under national law to refer the same point to an international court, such as the Benelux Court (which, the European Court ruled, is also bound by the third paragraph of Article 267 TFEU [234/177 EC]).[78] In such a situation, the highest court in the Member State is not the highest court in the case; so this judgment presupposes that the abstract theory is

[74] In *Costa v. ENEL* (see n. 75), for example, the sum in dispute was less than £2.

[75] Case 6/64, [1964] ECR 585. [76] *Costa* (n. 75) at 592 (emphasis added).

[77] Case C-337/95, [1997] ECR I-6013.

[78] The European Court did, however, say that neither court was obliged to refer a point if the same point had already been referred by the other.

correct. However, since the case was not argued in these terms, it would be dangerous to place too much weight on this inference.[79]

Special difficulties arise with regard to the English Court of Appeal. If the abstract theory is correct, it is never bound to refer; but what if the concrete theory is correct? Decisions of the Court of Appeal may be taken on appeal to the Supreme Court only if the leave of either the Court of Appeal or the Supreme Court is obtained. Clearly, if the Court of Appeal is prepared to grant leave to appeal in a particular case, it would not be under an obligation to make a reference to the European Court: it would, on any theory, be outside the third paragraph of Article 267 TFEU. But what if it refuses leave to appeal?

Assuming that the concrete theory is correct, there are two possible solutions: on the one hand, it could be argued that, if a reference is appropriate and the Court of Appeal does not make it, it *must* grant leave to appeal to the Supreme Court.[80] If it does not, it would be in breach of the third paragraph of Article 267 TFEU. On the other hand, the position could be saved if the Supreme Court itself granted leave. In other words, if the Court of Appeal does not make a reference and refuses leave, the Supreme Court would be obliged to grant leave to appeal.[81]

The decision of the European Court in *Lyckeskog*,[82] a reference from a court of appeal in Sweden, answers these questions. In Sweden, there is a right of appeal from a court of appeal to the Swedish supreme court (*Högsta Domstolen*) only if the latter gives leave. The European Court held that a Swedish court of appeal is never obliged to make a reference: it seems that the right to petition the supreme court for leave is itself a judicial remedy. However, the supreme court must make a reference, either when considering whether to grant leave or (if it grants leave) when deciding the appeal. This implies that the English Court of Appeal is not obliged to make a reference, but the Supreme Court must do so, either when hearing the petition for leave to appeal[83] or when hearing the appeal.

Up to now it has been assumed that the question is simply one of appeal; but it will be remembered that the phrase in the Treaties is 'judicial remedy'. This clearly does not cover a non-judicial remedy, such as the prerogative of mercy, but would it cover judicial review? If the decision of a tribunal, though not subject to appeal, may be quashed in proceedings for judicial review, this should be regarded as constituting a 'judicial

[79] See, further, *per* Advocate General Capotorti in *Hoffmann-La Roche v. Centrafarm*, Case 107/76, [1977] ECR 957 at 979–80.

[80] See Jacobs and Durand, *References to the European Court* (1975), p. 163; and Jacobs, 'Which Courts and Tribunals are Bound to Refer to the European Court?' (1977) 2 ELRev. 119 at 121.

[81] See Jacobs (1977) 2 ELRev. 119 at 121.

[82] Case C-99/00, [2002] ECR I-4839; [2003] 1 WLR 9.

[83] It might be objected that, when the appellants are petitioning for leave to appeal, the case is not 'pending' before the Supreme Court, as required by the third para. of Article 267 TFEU. Perhaps, however, the 'case' is not the appeal itself but the application for leave to appeal: this certainly would be pending before the Supreme Court. Since the Supreme Court would grant leave if it considered that the Union point had been wrongly decided by the Court of Appeal, the decision to grant leave would depend on the point of Union law.

remedy', provided there is an unconditional right to obtain review and the review proceedings include a reconsideration of the point of EU law.[84]

What is the position where the judgment may be reconsidered in other proceedings? This occurs if an interim order is given in interlocutory proceedings: the order may not be subject to appeal in the interlocutory proceedings, but will be subject to review in the main action. The point arose in *Hoffmann-La Roche v. Centrafarm*,[85] in which the plaintiff had applied to the German courts for an interim order to prohibit the defendant from marketing pharmaceutical products with a particular trade mark. Centrafarm maintained that it had a right under Union law to market the products, but the court of first instance granted the order. On appeal, Centrafarm asked the *Oberlandesgericht* Karlsruhe to refer the relevant provisions of EU law to the European Court. The *Oberlandesgericht* was apparently unwilling to make the reference unless it was obliged to do so; it therefore referred three questions to the European Court: the first concerned the interpretation of the third paragraph of Article 267 TFEU (then Article 177 EEC) itself and was aimed at discovering whether it applied in interlocutory proceedings; the other two related to the substantive issues in the case, but the *Oberlandesgericht* stated that these were to be answered only if the ruling on the first question meant that a reference was obligatory. This rather unusual procedure could have caused the European Court some embarrassment; however, it dealt with the matter by confining the proceedings in the first instance to the question relating to Article 267 TFEU [177 EEC], the other two questions being left over for later consideration.

The judgment of the *Oberlandesgericht* was not subject to appeal within the context of the interlocutory proceedings, but was subject to review in the main proceedings. In other words, any ruling on a point of Union law made by the *Oberlandesgericht* could be challenged subsequently in the main proceedings. Under German law, the defendant could, moreover, compel the plaintiff to institute the main action. In view of this, it was fair to say that the judgment of the *Oberlandesgericht* was not final, except in a temporary sense.

The European Court began its judgment by expressly affirming that interlocutory proceedings are covered by the second paragraph of Article 267 TFEU [177 EEC]: the summary and urgent character of these proceedings does not deprive the court of the *power* to make a reference. This is clear enough (though it had been doubted by the German court); but what about the third paragraph of Article 267 TFEU [177 EEC]: does the possibility of review in the main action constitute a 'judicial remedy'?

In deciding this question, the Court started from the premise that the function of the third paragraph of Article 267 TFEU [177 EEC] 'is to prevent a body of national

[84] *Re a Holiday in Italy* [1975] 1 CMLR 184. See also *R v. National Insurance Commissioner, ex parte Warry*, Case 41/77, [1977] ECR 2085. For a detailed discussion of this question, see Jacobs, 'Which Courts and Tribunals Are Bound to Refer to the European Court?' (1977) 2 ELRev. 119.

[85] Case 107/76, [1977] ECR 957. For an enlightening comment, see Jacobs (1977) 2 ELRev. 354.

case law not in accord with the rules of Union law from coming into existence in any Member State'. This suggests that the important thing is that, *at some stage in the course of the national proceedings*, there should be an obligation to refer. In accordance with this, the Court therefore held that there is no obligation to make a reference in interlocutory proceedings for an interim order, even if there is no appeal against that decision in the context of those proceedings, provided the decision is subject to review in subsequent proceedings which may be instituted by, or at the request of, either party.

This last point is, of course, crucial: if the ruling cannot be reconsidered in the main proceedings, or if each party is not given the right to insist that those proceedings take place, the judgment in the interlocutory proceedings will not be subject to a 'judicial remedy'. It is of course true that in practice interlocutory orders are often allowed to stand. But this is because the losing party does not consider it worthwhile to contest the order further. The same thing happens in ordinary proceedings: a court gives a judgment which is subject to appeal, but the unsuccessful party decides not to appeal. In both cases, however, the party against whom judgment is given has the right to take the matter further.

What is the position where there is a remedy in an international court? This point arose in *Parfums Christian Dior v. Evora*[86] (discussed earlier). The case was referred to the European Court by the *Hoge Raad*, the highest court in the Netherlands, which wanted to know whether the highest court in a Member State is still obliged to refer questions to the European Court if it is also obliged to refer the same question to a court such as the Benelux Court. The European Court answered this by saying that *both* courts were obliged to refer questions of Union law to it. Since there is no appeal from the judgments of the Benelux Court, and those judgments are binding on the courts of the Benelux countries, it falls under the third paragraph of Article 267 TFEU and is, therefore, obliged to refer. However, the European Court went on to hold that since the *Hoge Raad* is the highest court in the Netherlands, it is also covered by the third paragraph of Article 267 TFEU [234/177 EC]. It seems, therefore, that a judicial remedy to a court outside the Member State in question does not absolve the highest court in that Member State from the obligation to refer.

§3.3 PRELIMINARY RULINGS ON VALIDITY

Under Article 41 of the ECSC Treaty (now expired), it was provided that the European Court had *exclusive* jurisdiction to rule on the validity of an act of the Commission or Council. This means that no national court could declare an ECSC act invalid. There is no equivalent provision under the EU Treaties, but the European Court has achieved the same result by judicial decision. This was in the *Foto-Frost*[87] case, where it said that, while national courts may declare a Union act valid, they have no power

[86] Case C-337/95, [1997] ECR I-6013.

[87] Case 314/85, [1987] ECR 4199.

to declare it invalid. The decision was justified on the basis of policy considerations, the desirability of safeguarding the uniform application of Union law being the most important.[88]

§4 HYPOTHETICAL QUESTIONS AND CONTRIVED PROCEEDINGS

The European Court has no jurisdiction to give rulings on hypothetical questions, even if the reference comes from a court or tribunal of a Member State. The issues referred to the Court must be in controversy in judicial proceedings. For this to be the case, three conditions should be fulfilled: there must be a dispute; that dispute must be the subject of proceedings before a body which has the power to resolve it in a legally binding way; and the questions put to the European Court must be in issue in those proceedings.

In the *Borker*[89] case, a member of the Paris Bar had been refused permission by a German court to appear before it. He considered that this was contrary to Union law and complained to the Paris Bar Council, which made a reference to the European Court. Since the Paris Bar Council has no jurisdiction to decide who can appear before a German court, the proceedings before it could not lead to a 'decision of a judicial nature'. The European Court therefore ruled that it could not accept the reference.[90]

The question of the nature of the proceedings sometimes also involves that of the appropriate point at which to make the reference, since the nature of the proceedings may undergo a change at a certain point – for example, from investigatory (administrative) to judicial. This can happen in criminal proceedings, where one might regard the judicial phase as commencing when a suspect is arrested, or perhaps when he is charged.

These issues arose in an Italian case known, revealingly, as *Pretore di Salò v. Persons Unknown*.[91] The proceedings began when Italian anglers, concerned at the high level of pollution in a river, complained to the local *Pretore*, who instituted criminal proceedings under Italian anti-pollution legislation against a person or persons unknown. (According to the European Court, a *Pretore* is a judge who combines the duties of public prosecutor and investigating judge.) The *Pretore* made a reference to the European Court on the interpretation of a directive that was relevant to the case.

[88] It is interesting to note that some years ago the European Court proposed that the Treaties should be amended to incorporate such a rule: see *Suggestions of the Court of Justice on European Union*, EC Bull., Supp. 9/75, p. 17 at 21. This proposal was not put into effect, and the Court apparently decided to take the necessary action itself.

[89] Case 138/80, [1980] ECR 1975. See also *Victoria Film*, Case C-134/97, [1998] ECR I-7023; *Job Centre*, Case C-111/94, [1995] ECR I-3361; *Greis Unterweger*, Case 318/85, [1985] ECR 955.

[90] The position would have been different if the Paris Bar Council had been dealing with a matter over which it did have jurisdiction. The right to appear before the Paris courts may well be such an issue.

[91] Case 14/86, [1987] ECR 2545. See also *Pretore of Cento v. A Person or Persons Unknown*, Case 110/76, [1977] ECR 851.

Since no one had so far been charged, it could have been (and was) argued that the reference was premature: the proceedings had not yet assumed a judicial character. The European Court, however, accepted the reference, saying that it is for the national court to decide when the reference should be made.[92]

The most controversial case on this issue is *Foglia v. Novello*.[93] This was a reference by an Italian court in an action between two Italians who had entered into a contract of sale requiring delivery of the goods in France. The contract provided that the buyer would not be responsible for the payment of any taxes imposed in contravention of Union law. The goods were duly delivered. The seller was required to pay a consumption tax in France and claimed reimbursement from the buyer. The latter refused on the ground that the tax was contrary to Union law. Thus the Italian courts were required to decide whether the French tax was in accordance with Union law.

There were in fact grounds for believing that the whole transaction was contrived in order to raise a test case. For this reason, the European Court refused to accept the reference, stating that there was no genuine dispute between the parties. The Italian court, which had to give judgment in the case, was unwilling to accept this and made a second reference; but the European Court remained adamant.[94]

This ruling could be criticized because, whatever the motives of the parties, the Italian court was faced with what, on the surface at least, was a genuine dispute. Moreover, the bringing of a test case is a recognized device for obtaining a ruling on a disputed question of law. For these reasons, the European Court has accepted references in several later cases, even though the proceedings appear to have been contrived specifically for the purpose of obtaining a ruling.[95]

In between the two rulings in *Foglia v. Novello*, two other references were made to the European Court by courts in Italy. In both these cases, *Chemial v. DAF*[96] and *Vinal v. Orbat*,[97] the facts were similar to those in *Foglia v. Novello*, except that the disputed tax was Italian, not French. In the first case, the Advocate General (Mr Mayras) regarded the case as covered by the decision in *Foglia v. Novello (No. 1)*, and urged the Court to refuse to give a ruling. In *Vinal v. Orbat*, however, a different Advocate General (Mr Reischl) said that the Court should accept the reference, first, because the action was not *manifestly* bogus and, secondly, because it was an *Italian* tax that was in issue. In both the cases, the Court accepted the reference, thus suggesting that it agreed with Advocate General Reischl's opinion. In fact it seems likely that the real reason for its decision in *Foglia v. Novello* was one of policy: it did not wish to offend France by allowing the lawfulness of its taxes to be challenged by such roundabout means, rather than by the more normal route of an

[92] This was in spite of the fact that, as the European Court recognized, some of the *Pretore*'s duties were not of a strictly judicial nature.

[93] Case 104/79, [1980] ECR 745. See also the earlier case of *Mattheus v. Doego*, Case 93/78, [1978] ECR 2203, where the parties to a private contract tried to make the European Court give a ruling on the admission of Spain and Portugal to the Union.

[94] Case 244/80, [1981] ECR 3045.

[95] See, for example, *Mangold*, Case C-144/04, [2005] ECR I-9981; *PreussenElektra*, Case C-379/98, [2001] ECR I-2099. The *Mangold* case was discussed in Chap. 7, § 4.6.

[96] Case 140/79, [1981] ECR 1.

[97] Case 46/80, [1981] ECR 77.

enforcement action under Article 258 TFEU [226/169 EC].[98] This view is supported by the fact that in *Foglia v. Novello (No. 2)* the Court said that special vigilance was required where the legislation of one Member State is subject to challenge in the courts of another Member State.[99]

Even if there is a genuine dispute, and genuinely judicial proceedings, the European Court may be asked to rule on questions which, though they are of great general interest, are not actually relevant to those proceedings. This may occur either because one of the parties manipulates the procedure in order to obtain a ruling on some general issue or because the national court wants to obtain a general clarification of the law. Since the early 1990s, the European Court has often refused to answer such questions.[100] It will also refuse to give a ruling if the referring court fails to provide it with sufficient information regarding the factual and legal background of the case.[101] Such information is needed by the Court to give an appropriate interpretation; it is also necessary to enable it to ascertain whether the question is genuinely relevant to the proceedings.[102]

§5 WHEN SHOULD A REFERENCE BE MADE?

Two separate, but related, questions must now be considered. First of all, in what circumstances does the power, or obligation, to refer come into existence? Secondly, where the court has the power to refer, but is not obliged to do so, how should it exercise its discretion? The first question concerns the law; the second relates to judicial policy.[103]

[98] Or by means of a reference from a *French* court.

[99] Para. 30 of the judgment in Case 244/80; see, however, Anderson, 'The Admissibility of Preliminary References' [1994] YEL 179 at 194–5, where it is pointed out that there are other cases in which the European Court has accepted a reference in such circumstances.

[100] See *Meilicke*, Case C-83/91, [1992] ECR I-4871; *Dias*, Case C-343/90, [1992] ECR I-4673. The judgment in the first of these cases was given by the Full Court, and that in the second by the Fifth Chamber; yet identical words were used in both cases to explain the Court's position, thus sending a clear signal to national courts (compare paras 21–25 of the judgment in the *Meilicke* case with paras 13–17 of the judgment in the *Dias* case). See also *Legros*, Case C-163/90, [1992] ECR I-4625, in which (despite the contrary view of the Advocate General) the Court refused to rule on a matter of great general importance, which was not strictly relevant to the issue before the national court, but which had been fully argued in the proceedings before the European Court.

[101] *Telemarsicabruzzo v. Circostel*, Cases C-320–2/90, [1993] ECR I-393; *Pretore di Genova v. Banchero*, Case C-157/92, [1993] ECR I-1085. Both these rulings were given by a Full Court (thirteen judges). See also *Laguillaumie*, Case C-116/00, [2000] ECR I-4979; *Lehtonen and Castors Braine*, Case C-176/96, [2000] ECR I-2681.

[102] For a general discussion of these questions, see Kennedy, 'First Steps towards a European Certiorari?' (1993) 18 ELRev. 121; Anderson, 'The Admissibility of Preliminary References' [1994] YEL 179; Barnard and Sharpston, 'The Changing Face of Article 177 References' (1997) 34 CMLRev. 1113, especially at 1127–57. For a full list of cases in which the new policy has been applied, see Barnard and Sharpston, 1126, note 67. For criticism of the European Court, see O'Keeffe, 'Is the Spirit of Article 177 under Attack? Preliminary References and Admissibility' (1998) 23 ELRev. 509. For more recent developments, see Tridimas, 'Knocking on Heaven's Door: Fragmentation, Efficiency and Defiance in the Preliminary Reference Procedure' (2003) 40 CMLRev. 9 at 21–6.

[103] On both these questions, see Jacobs, 'When to Refer to the European Court' (1974) 90 LQR 486.

§5.1 THE LAW

The first paragraph of Article 267 TFEU states which questions may be referred to the European Court; this has already been discussed. The second paragraph then provides that where 'such a question' is raised, the court may make a reference 'if it considers that a decision on the question is necessary to enable it to give judgment'. Here the phrase 'such a question' refers back to the first paragraph and means those questions of Union law covered by that provision. Consequently, there are two requisites which must be fulfilled before the second paragraph comes into operation: an appropriate question of Union law must be *raised* before the court; and a decision on that question must be *necessary* to enable it to give judgment.

At first sight it appears that, under the third paragraph of Article 267 TFEU, only the first requisite need be met: the third paragraph states merely that where 'any such question is raised', the court must refer the matter to the European Court. Here the phrase 'any such question' could be read as meaning the same thing as 'such a question' in the second paragraph and therefore referring back to the first paragraph. However, it would be absurd if a court were obliged to refer a question which was quite irrelevant to the proceedings; therefore, 'any such question' must refer back to the second paragraph and mean any question which falls within that provision, i.e., a question of Union law on which a decision is necessary to enable the court to give judgment.[104] It follows from this that the same two requisites apply under the third paragraph.

What is the meaning of these two requisites? The first could suggest that a reference cannot be made unless one or other of the parties has raised a point of Union law: the phrase 'raised *before* any court' could be read as precluding the court itself from raising the point of its own motion. This, however, seems an unduly restrictive interpretation and has been rejected by the European Court, which has ruled that a reference may be made by the national court of its own motion.[105]

The second requisite is that the national court must consider that a decision on the question is necessary to enable it to give judgment. Two points should be noted at the outset: it is not a *reference* to the European Court which must be necessary, but a *decision* on the question; secondly, the Treaty makes clear that this is a question for the national court to decide and, unless Union law is clearly inapplicable to the case[106] or the questions asked are clearly irrelevant to the issues before the national court,[107] the European Court will not question whether the reference is necessary.

[104] See *Bulmer v. Bollinger* [1974] Ch 401 at 421; [1974] 3 WLR 202 at 211–12; [1974] 2 All ER 1226 at 1234, *per* Lord Denning MR, and the decision of the Dutch *Hoge Raad* (the highest civil court in the Netherlands) in the *Reinvoorde* case, 7 April 1970, [1973] CMLR 175 at para. 20.

[105] *Salonia*, Case 126/80, [1981] ECR 1563 at para. 7 of the judgment; see also CPR 68.2(1)(a).

[106] See *Rijksdienst voor Werknemerspensioenen v. Vlaeminck*, Case 132/81, [1982] ECR 2953.

[107] *Meilicke*, Case C-83/91, [1992] ECR I-4871; *Dias*, Case C-343/90, [1992] ECR I-4673.

When is a decision necessary in order to give judgment? Clearly, the outcome of the case must be dependent on the decision: as Lord Denning has said,[108] if the Union point is decided in one way, judgment for one party must result; if it is decided in another way, judgment must be given for the other party. This does not, however, mean that everything must hinge on the Union point: it would be sufficient if the final judgment were in any way different, even if it were a question only of the measure of damages or terms of the order. If, on the other hand, the judgment would be exactly the same however the Union point was decided, a decision on it would not be necessary for the judgment.

What if the Union point would be conclusive only in certain circumstances? Two examples may be given of such a situation. Assume that one party bases his case exclusively on a provision of Union law, but that provision would be applicable only if certain contested facts are established. Before those facts have been established, the court cannot be certain whether a decision on the Union point is necessary or not: if the facts cannot be established, the outcome of the case would be the same irrespective of how the Union point was decided. Until evidence has been heard, therefore, the Union point is only potentially decisive.

The second example is a case where one party puts forward two quite separate grounds, each of which, if established, would make good his claim. If one ground is based on Union law and one on national law, the court cannot tell whether the Union point is decisive until it has decided the other point: if the party can win on that, it would not matter which way the Union point was decided; only if the national point goes against him, would the Union point become decisive.

The problem in both these situations is that, until the other matters have been decided, the Union point would dispose of the case only if it was decided in one particular way. In the first example, it would dispose of the case if it were decided against the person relying on Union law: in such a case, he would lose even if he succeeded in establishing his contentions of fact. In the second example, on the other hand, the Union point would dispose of the case only if it were decided in favour of the person relying on it: he would then win even if the other point went against him.

What should a court do in such a situation? It could be argued that the court cannot make a reference until the other matters have been decided: unless it does this, it cannot be certain that a decision on the Union point is really necessary.[109] This, however, is too restrictive an interpretation.[110] From a practical point of view, it might be much better in some cases to decide the Union point first. If it is fairly simple, but the other matters are complex, it could be less expensive and more expeditious to make an immediate reference

[108] In *Bulmer v. Bollinger* [1974] Ch 401 at 422; [1974] 3 WLR 202 at 212; [1974] 2 All ER 1226 at 1234; but see *Foglia v. Novello*, discussed in § 4.

[109] *Per* Lord Denning MR in *Bulmer v. Bollinger* [1974] Ch 401 at 423; [1974] 3 WLR 202 at 213; [1974] 2 All ER 1226 at 1235. In Lord Denning's view, the court should decide the facts before making the reference.

[110] Lord Denning's view to the contrary (see earlier) has been subject to widespread criticism and was not followed in *R v. Plymouth Justices, ex parte Rogers* [1982] 3 WLR 1; [1982] 2 All ER 175; [1982] 3 CMLR 221; see also *Polydor v. Harlequin Record Shops* [1980] 2 CMLR 413 (CA).

to the European Court. It is suggested, therefore, that 'necessary' should be interpreted to mean that the point *could* be decisive. In other words, it should be sufficient if a decision on the point is potentially decisive: it should not have to be proved that it would be decisive in all possible eventualities. If this interpretation is accepted, the national court would then be able to decide for itself when to make the reference.[111]

What is the position where the point has already been decided by the European Court in a previous case? The European Court has ruled that in such a case the national court is not obliged to make a reference even if it is a court against whose decisions there is no judicial remedy under national law.[112] In such a situation the point can be regarded as settled and the case would be exempted from the third paragraph of Article 267 TFEU: according to the European Court, the authority of the previous ruling would deprive the obligation under the third paragraph of Article 267 TFEU [177 EEC] of its purpose 'and thus empty it of its substance'.[113] However, the European Court is not bound by its own previous decisions, and if the national court thought that the previous judgment was wrong and wanted the European Court to reconsider the matter, it would be entitled to make the reference.[114] The existence of a previous ruling, therefore, removes the obligation to refer, but does not affect the power to refer.

Some lawyers push this argument further and apply the same rule where the Union provision is regarded as clear, even if the European Court has not ruled on it. This is the so-called '*acte clair*' doctrine, according to which a clear provision (*acte clair*) does not require 'interpretation' and therefore falls entirely outside the scope of Article 267 TFEU as a whole. If there is no doubt as to the meaning of the provision, it is argued, there can be no 'question' on which a decision is necessary: all the court has to do is to apply the provision.

This doctrine has something to recommend it from a common-sense point of view and has attracted the support of some eminent jurists.[115] However, it is a well-known fact that what is clear to one set of lawyers can be extremely doubtful to another set of lawyers. This is especially true where the two groups belong to different legal traditions or look at the law from different points of view. In the case of Union law in particular, the policy-oriented approach of the European Court can produce very different results from the more traditional methods of an English judge.

This controversy is important only with regard to the third paragraph of Article 267 TFEU: since a lower court is not in any case obliged to make a reference, it would be entitled to refrain from doing so on the ground that the provision is sufficiently clear. In the case of a court against whose decisions there is no judicial remedy, however, the

[111] As far as the English High Court is concerned, it is expressly stated in CPR 68.2(1)(a) that the order may be made at any stage in the proceedings.

[112] *Da Costa*, Cases 28–30/62, [1963] ECR 31 at 38; *CILFIT*, Case 283/81, [1982] ECR 3415 at paras 13–15.

[113] *Da Costa* (see n. 112). [114] *Ibid.*

[115] See, for example, Lagrange, 'The Theory of the *Acte Clair*: A Bone of Contention or a Source of Unity?' (1971) 8 CMLRev. 313.

question is crucial: is such a court exempted from the obligation to refer if it considers that the provision does not require interpretation?

In spite of its dangers, the *acte clair* doctrine has been fairly widely accepted by national courts in the Union,[116] and in 1982 it gained the approval of the European Court, though this approval was subject to so many conditions that one might think the Court was really trying to kill the idea.[117] The case in question was *CILFIT*,[118] where the European Court said that even a court covered by the third paragraph of Article 267 TFEU (then Article 177 EEC) is not obliged to make a reference where the answer is 'so obvious as to leave no scope for any reasonable doubt'.[119] It qualified this, however, by saying that the national court must be convinced that the answer would be equally obvious to a court in another Member State and to the European Court. In deciding whether the answer is obvious, the national court must compare the different versions of the text in the various Union languages. It must also bear in mind that legal concepts and terminology do not necessarily have the same meaning in Union law as in national law. The European Court concluded by saying that 'every provision of Union law must be placed in its context and interpreted in the light of the provisions of Union law as a whole, regard being had to the objectives thereof and to its state of evolution at the date on which the provision in question is to be applied'.[120] Put more simply, the national court must remember the European Court's habit of giving great weight to policy.

It is not hard to see that full compliance with these requirements is virtually impossible. In particular, the obligation to compare the text in its different linguistic versions could cause great difficulties. In the absence of expert evidence, an English court could not compare, for example, the Greek and Danish texts. The importance of this is, however, beyond doubt, since it can often happen that a text which appears straightforward in one language may be ambiguous (or mean something different) in another. An example in point is *Koschniske*,[121] in which a Dutch social security tribunal had to interpret a Union regulation which contained, in the Dutch text, the word '*echtgenote*'. The English version of the regulation uses the word 'spouse' and all the other texts use a word which can apply to both a husband and a wife; the Dutch word, however, can apply only to a woman: it means 'wife'. (The masculine form is '*echtgenoot*'.) The question before the Dutch tribunal was whether the term could cover a husband. On the

[116] The Commission has also expressed its acceptance of the doctrine: see European Parliament, Question 608/78, 31 January 1979, OJ 1979, C 28/9. Lord Denning gave the doctrine his approval in *Bulmer v. Bollinger* [1974] Ch 401 at 423; [1974] 3 WLR 202 at 213; [1974] 2 All ER 1226 at 1235, and it was applied in *SA Magnavision NV v. General Optical Council (No. 1)* [1987] 1 CMLR 887 and *(No. 2)* [1987] 2 CMLR 262; see also *R v. Secretary of State for Social Services, ex parte Bomore Medical Supplies* [1986] 1 CMLR 228 (CA). However, in *R v. Henn* [1980] 2 WLR 597 at 636–7; [1980] 2 All ER 166 at 196–7, the House of Lords went no further than to say that a reference need not be made where the point is covered by an 'established body of case law' of the European Court. It also stressed the pitfalls of applying English canons of statutory interpretation to Union law.

[117] See Rasmussen, 'The European Court's *Acte Clair* Strategy in *CILFIT*' (1984) 9 ELRev. 242.

[118] Case 283/81, [1982] ECR 3415.

[119] *Ibid.* at para. 16 of the judgment.

[120] Para. 20 of the judgment.

[121] Case 9/79, [1979] ECR 2717.

basis of the Dutch text alone, it might have seemed clear that it could not. Fortunately, the tribunal made a reference to the European Court which ruled, after considering all the versions of the provision, that it covered both a husband and a wife. If the tribunal had interpreted the provision for itself without considering the other versions of the text, it would have made a serious mistake.

§5.2 DISCRETION

A court has a discretion only if its decisions are subject to an appeal or other judicial remedy. Assuming this to be the case, how should the discretion be exercised?[122] This is, of course, a question for the national courts themselves, but among the factors which they may wish to take into consideration are the following. Should the facts be decided first? In many cases this will be desirable,[123] but in some it may be better to obtain a ruling from the European Court right at the outset: until that has been obtained, it might not be clear what facts *are* relevant.

Referring a case to Luxembourg will involve a considerable delay in the proceedings. In some cases a lower court might feel that the time factor is so important that it would be justified in deciding the point itself. However, if the case is taken on appeal, a reference may well be made in the end and the result might be that a final judgment takes even longer to obtain. In some interlocutory cases – for example, an application for an injunction pending trial – the best course might be for the court to grant the order and at the same time make the reference. This will protect the plaintiff's position while the Luxembourg proceedings are taking place.

The difficulty and importance of the point, as well as the expense of a reference compared to the amount at stake, will also be considered, though there have been cases where points of great public importance have been decided in actions involving only very small sums of money. The wishes of the parties will not be ignored, but it must be remembered that the decision to refer is that of the court, not the parties.

In *R v. International Stock Exchange, ex parte Else*,[124] Sir Thomas Bingham MR said that if the facts have been found, and the Union law issue is critical to the court's final decision, the appropriate course is ordinarily to refer the issue to the European Court

[122] For a general discussion, see *Bulmer v. Bollinger* [1974] Ch 401 at 423–4; [1974] 3 WLR 202 at 213–15; [1974] 2 All ER 1226 at 1235–6 (CA); *Church of Scientology of California v. Customs and Excise Commissioners* [1981] 1 All ER 1035 (CA); *R v. Plymouth Justices, ex parte Rogers* [1982] 3 WLR 1; [1982] 2 All ER 175; [1982] 3 CMLR 221; *Customs and Excise Commissioners v. Samex* [1983] 1 All ER 1042; [1983] 3 CMLR 194; *R v. International Stock Exchange, ex parte Else* [1993] QB 534; [1993] 2 WLR 70; [1993] 1 All ER 420 (CA); see also Jacobs, 'When to Refer to the European Court' (1974) 90 LQR 486. In *R v. Henn* [1980] 2 WLR 597 at 635; [1980] 2 All ER 166 at 196, the House of Lords said that in a criminal trial on indictment it will rarely be proper for the trial court to make a reference.

[123] See *Irish Creamery Milk Suppliers Association v. Ireland*, Cases 36, 71/80, [1981] ECR 735, where, however, the European Court stressed that it was for the national court to decide when to make the reference. See also the English cases cited in n. 122.

[124] [1993] QB 534; [1993] 2 WLR 70; [1993] 1 All ER 420 (CA).

unless the English court can with complete confidence resolve the issue itself.[125] This probably expresses the gist of the matter.[126]

§6 PROCEDURE

§6.1 ENGLISH COURTS

In England, provision for preliminary references has been made in the rules of procedure of the most important courts.[127] However, even where this is not the case, any court or tribunal covered by Article 267 TFEU may make a reference: its power to do so derives from the Treaty and section 2(1) of the European Communities Act 1972; the procedural details may be fixed by the court itself under its inherent power to regulate such matters.[128] The discussion which follows is based on the Civil Procedure Rules (CPR) Part 68,[129] which applies to the High Court and the Court of Appeal; similar provisions are applicable in the other courts for which special provision has been made, and CPR Part 68 would no doubt furnish a model for those courts and tribunals for which no special provision has been made.

It is expressly provided that an order for reference may be made by the court on application by either party, or of the court's own motion.[130] It is also expressly stated that it may be made at any stage of the proceedings;[131] thus there is no requirement in the CPR that the evidence must be heard before a reference may be made.

If the court decides to make the reference, the order will contain a schedule in which the request for a ruling and the questions asked will be set out. The proceedings will then be stayed (unless the court orders otherwise) until the European Court has given its ruling.[132] The Senior Master of the Supreme Court (Queen's Bench Division) will transmit the order to the European Court.[133]

If the point at issue is whether a British statute is incompatible with Union law, the court can suspend the operation of the statute while the reference is pending.[134] If the reference concerns the validity of a Union measure, the court can also suspend the operation of any British measure that is dependent on it.[135]

[125] [1993] 2 WLR at 76.

[126] For a suggestion that this way of putting it represents a change from the previous approach (in favour of a greater willingness to refer), see Walsh, 'The Appeal of an Article 177 EEC Referral' (1993) 56 MLR 881.

[127] For the High Court and Court of Appeal, see CPR Part 68.

[128] Jacobs and Durand, *References to the European Court* (1975), pp. 164 and 167.

[129] See also Practice Direction 68 and the European Court's 'Information Note on References by National Courts for Preliminary Rulings' included therein. The latter may also be found on the European Court's website.

[130] CPR 68.2(1).

[131] *Ibid.* A reference cannot, however, be made after delivery of judgment, even if the order of the court has not yet been drawn up: *SA Magnavision NV v. General Optical Council (No. 2)* [1987] 2 CMLR 262.

[132] CPR 68.4. [133] CPR 68.3(1) and Practice Direction 68, para. 2.1.

[134] *R v. Secretary of State for Transport, ex parte Factortame (No. 2)*, Case C-213/89, [1990] ECR I-2433; [1990] 3 WLR 818 (discussed in Chap. 7, § 10).

[135] *Zuckerfabrik Süderdithmarschen*, Cases C-143/88, 92/89, [1991] ECR I-415.

§6.2 THE REFERENCE

The form and content of the reference are covered by Practice Direction 68, supplementing CPR 68. Normally the order for reference will contain a brief summary of the facts of the case (in so far as these have already been established), an account of the procedure followed prior to the reference, the order sought by the claimant, the matters raised in defence, the main arguments of the parties on the Union point, and the reasons of the court for making the reference. Where national law is relevant, the national court should give a clear statement of the provisions in question: the European Court has no power to rule on national law, but a knowledge of the relevant national provisions may be useful in order to define the exact issues at stake.[136] It is important that the background of the reference should be fully explained: if insufficient detail is given, the European Court may refuse to entertain the proceedings.[137]

In proceedings for a preliminary reference, the European Court has no jurisdiction to rule on the *application* of Union law to the facts of the case: all it can do is to interpret Union law and, in the case of Union acts, rule on their validity. For this reason, the questions put to the European Court should be phrased in an abstract way: the Court should, for example, be asked whether a particular provision of Union law is to be interpreted as having a particular meaning, rather than asked whether it provides a defence to the charge in the case. The European Court, however, adopts a flexible approach and will not refuse to give a ruling on the ground that questions are improperly phrased: it will simply decide what questions should have been asked and then proceed on the basis that those are the questions referred. In this way it can get to the substance of the matter with the minimum of formality and delay.

§6.3 APPEALS AGAINST AN ORDER FOR REFERENCE

Is it legitimate for national law to provide for a right of appeal against an order for reference? In *Rheinmühlen*,[138] the European Court said that an order by a lower court to refer a question to the European Court is subject to appeal if provision for this is made by the law of the Member State in question. However, it said that even if, under the law of the Member State, the effect of lodging the appeal was to suspend the order for reference, it would still hear the case as long as the order for reference had not been 'revoked'. This statement could be regarded as ambiguous, since it was not clear whether it had to be revoked by the court making the reference or whether it could also be revoked by the appellate court. The ambiguity was resolved a few years later in *Simmenthal*,[139] where the European Court said that where there is an appeal against the

[136] See the European Court's 'Information Note on References by National Courts for Preliminary Rulings' (n. 129), para. 22.

[137] *Telemarsicabruzzo v. Circostel*, Cases C-320–2/90, [1993] ECR I-393; *Pretore di Genova v. Banchero*, Case C-157/92, [1993] ECR I-1085.

[138] Cases 146/73, [1974] ECR 139 at 147 (para. 3 of the judgment).

[139] Case 106/77, [1978] ECR 629 at para. 10 of the judgment.

order for reference, it would continue to hear the case 'so long as the reference has not been withdrawn by the court from which it emanates or has been quashed on appeal by a higher court'. This made clear that the proceedings before the European Court would be discontinued if the order for reference was set aside on appeal.

However, the European Court reconsidered the matter in *Cartesio Oktató és Szolgáltató bt*,[140] a reference from a court in Hungary. There, while affirming that an appeal may be brought against an order to refer (if national law so provides), it held that the outcome of the appeal cannot deprive the European Court of the power to hear the reference. No mention was made of the ruling to the contrary in *Simmenthal*.

The position now appears to be that if the order for reference is quashed on appeal, the reference will nevertheless be heard by the European Court unless the court making the reference decides to revoke it. The European Court made clear that, in deciding whether to revoke its order, the referring court is not bound by the decision of the appellate court: the referring court alone has the power to take the decision.[141]

The result is strange, to say the least. What is the point of an appeal if the reference will go ahead even if the order to refer is set aside? At most, the judgment of the appellate court will constitute mere advice to the lower court, which will have to decide for itself whether to take any notice of it.[142]

§6.4 THE EUROPEAN COURT

The procedure in the European Court was discussed in Chapter 2, § 5 (especially § 5.8). The parties – together with the Member States, the Commission, and, where one of its acts forms the subject matter of the proceedings, the Council – have the right to submit written observations and make oral submissions.[143] However, the issues before the Court are determined by the order for reference, and the role of the parties in this regard is limited to making suggestions to the Court as to how the reference should be interpreted. As was mentioned previously, the Court does not pay excessive regard to the exact wording of the questions submitted by the national court but tries rather to get to the heart of the matter. If the case can be disposed of without answering all the questions posed by the national court, the European Court will do this: for example, if the European Court is asked questions concerning the validity and interpretation of a Union measure, it will not concern itself with the interpretation if it holds the measure invalid.

The European Court has no jurisdiction to give rulings which bind the national court on questions of fact. Often it cannot decide the relevant points of law without some basis of fact, but it normally relies on the national court to supply this. For these reasons, the European Court is not normally required to make findings of fact in preliminary

[140] Case C-210/06, [2008] ECR I-9641 at paras 88–98 of the judgment (Grand Chamber).

[141] *Ibid.* at para. 97 of the judgment.

[142] For further discussion, see Broberg and Fenger, 'Preliminary References and a Right: But for Whom? The Extent to Which Preliminary Reference Decisions Can Be Subject to Appeal' (2011) 36 ELRev. 276.

[143] See Art. 23 of the Statute of the Court of Justice of the European Union, Protocol No. 3 to the EU Treaties.

references. There are, however, exceptions: for example, if the validity of a Union act is in issue, the Court may have to decide a question of fact in order to determine whether the Union act is valid. In this situation the Court will decide the question of fact according to its normal procedure – if necessary hearing witnesses – and then rule on the validity of the measure.[144] The national court is bound by the ruling on the point of validity, though not (presumably) on the findings of fact on which it was based.

In its judgment, the European Court will, after setting out the facts and background to the case, discuss the questions posed and give reasons for its rulings on the various issues. At the end of its judgment, it will give formal rulings on the questions asked, or state that certain questions do not require an answer.[145] As was mentioned previously, if the questions are put in an improper form, the Court will answer them as if they had been properly put. Sometimes two or more questions will be answered together. Occasionally the Court will answer more than was asked.

The final paragraph of Article 267 TFEU states that where the question referred concerns a person in custody, the Court must give its ruling with the minimum of delay. Article 23a of the Statute of the Court makes provision for an 'urgent' procedure and also for an 'expedited or accelerated' procedure. Under these procedures, time limits are shorter and the case may be decided without a submission from the Advocate General. In the case of the urgent procedure, there may be restrictions on the right to submit statements or written observations and, in cases of extreme urgency, the written stage of the procedure may be omitted.[146]

§7 INTERPRETATION AND APPLICATION

It has already been pointed out that the European Court has power to interpret Union law, but not to apply it to the facts of the case. The precise distinction between interpretation and application is, however, very elastic and the European Court appears to make use of this elasticity for its own purposes. Thus, if it is asked to interpret a Union provision, it may satisfy itself with a general indication of the provision's meaning and then state that it is a question of fact, to be decided by the national court, whether a particular case comes within its scope: in such a situation, the effective determination of the case rests with the national court. On the other hand, however, it might give such a precise and specific interpretation that the national court is left with nothing more to do, other than to give a formal judgment. Its choice between these two approaches seems to depend on policy (though one might surmise that the Court would incline

[144] See *per* Advocate General Warner in *EMI*, Case 51/75, [1976] ECR 811 at 854. A case in which such questions of fact had to be decided was *Milac*, Case 131/77, [1978] ECR 1041.

[145] The formal rulings must be interpreted in the light of the reasons: *Bosch*, Case 135/77, [1978] ECR 855 at para. 4.

[146] For an assessment of these procedures, see Barnard, 'The PPU: Is it Worth the Candle? An Early Assessment' (2009) 34 ELRev. 281. See also Chap. 2, § 5.8.

towards the first alternative if its members were unable to agree among themselves on the precise interpretation of the provision).

The distinction between these approaches may be made clear by two examples. The first is *Walrave and Koch v. Union Cycliste Internationale*,[147] which concerned motor-paced cycle racing. In this sport, one person rides ahead on a motorcycle and is followed by another on a racing bicycle, the former being called the 'pacer', and the latter the 'stayer'. The idea is that the pacer creates a slipstream and, if the stayer remains within it, he can achieve considerable speeds. The case arose because the body controlling the sport made a rule that pacer and stayer had to be of the same nationality. The two plaintiffs, who were both professional pacers, felt that the rule would make it difficult for them to obtain work. They therefore brought proceedings in a national court for a declaration that the rule was contrary to Union law. The Treaties prohibit discrimination against workers, self-employed persons, and providers of services, and the European Court, to which a reference was made under Article 267 TFEU (then Article 177 EEC), had no difficulty in finding that professional sportsmen were covered by the relevant provisions. However, it took the view that, notwithstanding the prohibition against discrimination, national teams could be selected on the basis of nationality. The question, therefore, was whether pacer and stayer constituted a team or whether the stayer was the only competitor and the pacer a mere auxiliary, like a trainer or coach. Instead of giving a clear answer, however, the European Court merely stated:[148] 'it is for the national court... to decide in particular whether in the sport in question the pacemaker and stayer do or do not constitute a team'. This left everything to the national court.

This may be contrasted with a case decided a year later, *Cristini v. SNCF*.[149] Under Article 7(2) of Regulation 1612/68 it is provided that a Union national working in another Member State is entitled to the same 'social advantages' as national workers in the country of immigration. A French court asked the European Court whether a French provision entitling large families[150] to a special card giving them the right to reduced fares on the French railways was a 'social advantage' within the meaning of the Regulation.

The European Court might have given some vague definition of a 'social advantage' and left it to the French court to decide whether this covered the French provision. Instead it went right to the point. After first disclaiming any power to 'apply the Community [Union] rule to a specific case', it stated:[151] 'Article 7(2) of Regulation (EEC) No. 1612/68 of the Council must be interpreted as meaning that the social advantages referred to by that provision include fares reduction cards issued by a national railway authority to large families.' This clearly left nothing more to be decided by the national court.

[147] Case 36/74, [1974] ECR 1405.
[148] *Ibid.* at para. 10 of the judgment.
[149] Case 32/75, [1975] ECR 1085.
[150] Families with three or more children under the age of 18.
[151] *Cristini* (n. 149) para. 19 of the judgment; see also the formal ruling.

§8 EFFECTS OF PRELIMINARY RULINGS

After the European Court has given judgment, the case is sent back to the national court which made the reference. The proceedings will then continue in the national court from the point at which they were suspended. The national court is not obliged to apply Union law – it may eventually decide the case on other grounds – but if it does apply it, it is bound by the European Court's ruling.[152]

What is the effect of the ruling in *subsequent* cases? As was mentioned earlier, if the same issue arises again in a later case in the courts of the Member State from which the reference was made, or in the courts of another Member State, the ruling may be applied again without its being necessary to make a new reference. This is so even if the court concerned is one from which there is no appeal. On the other hand, the court is not *precluded* from making a reference if it wishes. It might do this if it considers the previous ruling mistaken and would like the European Court to reconsider the matter. As no strict doctrine of precedent operates in Union law, the European Court could in theory overrule its previous decision; in practice, however, it would be very unlikely to do so, since individuals and courts in the Member States might have relied on it.

Are all courts and tribunals in Member States *bound* by the ruling unless and until it is overruled in a later judgment? It is suggested that this is the case: even if the court in question is not covered by the third paragraph of Article 267 TFEU, it should be obliged either to follow the ruling or to make a new reference.[153] It would be improper for it simply to depart from the ruling because it thought that it was wrong. This is certainly the position in the United Kingdom, where it is provided by section 3(1) of the European Communities Act 1972 that any question as to the meaning or effect of any of the Treaties, or as to the validity, meaning, or effect of any Union instrument, must, if not referred to the European Court for a ruling, be decided in accordance with the principles laid down by any relevant decision of the European Court.[154]

FURTHER READING

Items are listed in date order, the most recent being at the end.

Lagrange, 'The Theory of the *Acte Clair*: A Bone of Contention or a Source of Unity?' (1971) 8 CMLRev. 313.

Jacobs, 'When to Refer to the European Court' (1974) 90 LQR 486.

Barav, 'Preliminary Censorship? The Judgment of the European Court in *Foglia v. Novello*' (1980) 5 ELRev. 443.

Alexander and Grabandt, 'National Courts Entitled to Ask For Preliminary Rulings

[152] *Milch- Fett- und Eierkontor*, Case 29/68, [1969] ECR 165 at para. 3 of the judgment.

[153] For a general discussion of this question, see Trabucchi, 'L'effet "erga omnes" des décisions préjudicielles rendues par la Cour de justice des Communautés européennes' [1974] RTDE 56.

[154] The position regarding preliminary rulings on the validity of a Union act is discussed further in Chap. 14, § 7.

under Article 177 of the EEC Treaty: The Case Law of the Court of Justice' (1982) 19 CMLRev. 413.

BARAV, 'Imbroglio préjudiciel'[1982] RTDE 431.

BEBR, 'The Possible Implications of *Foglia v. Novello II*' (1982) 9 CMLRev. 421.

GRAY, 'Advisory Opinions and the European Court of Justice' (1983) 8 ELRev. 24.

DASHWOOD AND ARNULL, 'English Courts and Article 177 of the EEC Treaty' (1984) 4 YEL 255.

O'KEEFFE, 'Appeals against an Order to Refer under Article 177 of the EEC Treaty' (1984) 9 ELRev. 87.

RASMUSSEN, 'The European Court's *Acte Clair* Strategy in *CILFIT*' (1984) 9 ELRev. 242.

BEBR, 'Arbitration Tribunals and Article 177 of the EEC Treaty' (1985) 22 CMLRev. 489.

HENRY G SCHERMERS *ET AL.* (EDS), *Article 177 EEC: Experiences and Problems* (1987).

ARNULL, 'The Use and Abuse of Article 177 EEC' (1989) 52 MLR 622.

ARNULL, 'The Evolution of the Court's Jurisdiction under Article 177 EEC' (1993) 18 ELRev. 129.

ANDERSON, 'The Admissibility of Preliminary References' [1994] YEL 179.

STRASSER, 'Evolution and Effort: Docket Control and Preliminary References in the European Court of Justice' (1995/96) 2 CJEL 49.

BARNARD AND SHARPSTON, 'The Changing Face of Article 177 References' (1997) 34 CMLRev. 1113.

O'KEEFFE, 'Is the Spirit of Article 177 under Attack? Preliminary References and Admissibility' (1998) 23 ELRev. 509.

DAVID ANDERSON AND MARIE DEMETRIOU, *References to the European Court*, 2nd edn (2002).

TRIDIMAS, 'Knocking on Heaven's Door: Fragmentation, Efficiency and Defiance in the Preliminary Reference Procedure' (2003) 40 CMLRev. 9.

LEFEVRE, 'The Interpretation of Community Law by the Court of Justice in Areas of National Competence' (2004) 29 ELRev. 501.

WATTEL, 'Köbler, *CILFIT* and *Welthgrove*: We Can't Go on Meeting Like This' (2004) 41 CMLRev. 177.

ANAGNOSTARAS, 'Preliminary Problems and Jurisdiction Uncertainties: The Admissibility of Questions Referred by Bodies Performing Quasi-Judicial Functions' (2005) 30 ELRev. 878.

KOMÁREK, 'In the Court(s) We Trust? On the Need for Hierarchy and Differentiation in the Preliminary Ruling Procedure' (2007) 32 ELRev. 467.

BROBERG, '*Acte Clair* Revisited: Adapting the *Acte Clair* Criteria to the Demands of the Times' (2008) 45 CMLRev. 1383.

MORTEN BROBERG AND NIELS FENGER, *Preliminary References to the European Court of Justice* (2010).

BROBERG AND FENGER, 'Finding Light in the Darkness: On the Actual Application of the *acte clair* Doctrine' (2011) 30 YEL 180.

BROBERG AND FENGER, 'Preliminary References as a Right: But for Whom? The Extent to which Preliminary Reference Decisions can be Subject to Appeal' (2011) 36 ELRev. 276.

10

ENFORCEMENT ACTIONS

§1 INTRODUCTION

There are two ways in which Union law can be enforced against national Governments. The first is through action taken by private individuals in the national courts. This is possible through the application of the doctrine of direct effect, which works well in many circumstances. However, it applies only with regard to directly effective provisions – though the European Court is now prepared to hold most provisions directly effective – and then only if an individual or company whose interests are affected is prepared to take legal action. So far, the Commission has not itself brought proceedings in national courts in order to secure compliance with Union law, nor does it appear to be prepared to give financial assistance to would-be litigants for this purpose.

This way of proceeding is of great importance and will be valuable to the individual concerned; it is not, however, sufficient in itself to ensure the effectiveness of Union law in all cases. The second way in which Union law can be enforced against national Governments is by direct proceedings against the Member State concerned. Special provision is made for this in the Treaties and it was originally thought by many to be the only way in which Union law could be enforced.[1]

The relevant provisions are Articles 258–260 TFEU [226–228/169–171 EC]. In addition, there are certain special procedures which apply only in the case of violations of particular rules of Union law. The main examples are found in Articles 108(2) TFEU [88(2)/93(2) EC], 114(9) TFEU [95(9)/100a(4), third paragraph EC], 271 TFEU [237/180 EC], and 348, second paragraph TFEU [298, second paragraph/225, second paragraph EC]. These provisions lay down variants of the normal procedure, which replace the latter in the circumstances indicated.

The bulk of this chapter will be taken up with a discussion of the normal enforcement procedure against Member States – that is to say, the procedure initiated by the Commission under the general enforcement provisions mentioned previously: the rights of Member States and of private individuals to take action will be dealt with separately; the special enforcement procedures will be considered only incidentally.

[1] See, for example, the arguments advanced by the Dutch and Belgian Governments in *Van Gend en Loos*, Case 26/62, [1963] ECR 1.

§2 WHAT CONSTITUTES A VIOLATION?

§2.1 PROVISIONS COVERED

What constitutes a violation of Union law for the purpose of an enforcement action? According to the Treaties, proceedings may be brought only if a Member State has failed 'to fulfil an obligation under the Treaties': only a violation of such an obligation will provide the foundation for an enforcement action. What does this cover? Clearly, a violation of a provision in one of the Treaties would be included, although the European Court's jurisdiction with regard to the Common Foreign and Security Policy is largely excluded.[2]

A violation of an obligation contained in Union legislation enacted under one of the Treaties would be covered: violation of the legislation would constitute a violation of the Treaty provision empowering its enactment. The same would apply to a violation of a provision in an agreement between the European Union and a non-member State: this would be a violation of the Treaty provision under which the Union was empowered (expressly or impliedly) to conclude the agreement.[3] It would also be a violation of Article 216(2) TFEU, which states that international agreements concluded by the Union are binding on the Member States. Though more difficult to justify, it is probable that the European Court would regard an obligation as covered if it arose under an act of an institution set up by such an international agreement.[4]

It is hard to see how international agreements between the Member States (without the Union) and third countries could be covered, even if, as in the case of the old GATT, they are binding on the Union.[5] Article 216(2) would not apply in such a case, as it covers only 'agreements concluded by the Union'. However, in view of the disregard for the words of the Treaties displayed by the European Court in the *SPI*[6] case, one cannot rule out the possibility that it would hold these agreements to be covered by Article 258 TFEU.

What is the position with regard to an agreement concluded jointly by the Union and the Member States, on the one side, and one or more non-member States on the other? It will be remembered from the discussion in Chapter 6, § 1.4 that these 'mixed agreements' are normally entered into where the matters dealt with are thought to fall partly within the jurisdiction of the Union and partly within that of the Member States. If this is so, a breach by a Member State of an obligation under a mixed agreement could

[2] Art. 24(1), second sub-para., last sentence, TEU. See Chap. 1, § 7.1.

[3] First *EEA* case, Opinion 1/91, [1991] ECR I-6079 at para. 38; *Commission v. Germany*, Case C-61/94, [1996] ECR I-3989; *Commission v. Ireland*, Case C-13/00, [2002] ECR I-2943.

[4] The European Court has already held that such acts are part of the EU legal system and are covered by Art. 267 TFEU (then Art. 177 EEC): *Greece v. Commission*, Case 30/88, [1989] ECR 3711 at para. 13 of the judgment; the first *EEA* case (see n. 3) at para. 37; *Sevince*, Case C-192/89, [1990] ECR I-3461.

[5] See Chap. 6, § 7.2. [6] Cases 267–9/81, [1983] ECR 801.

form the subject matter of an enforcement action if the obligation fell within the jurisdiction of the Union, but should not do so otherwise.[7]

Agreements between the Member States themselves (other than the constitutive Treaties) pose similar problems. A decision of the representatives of the Governments of the Member States meeting in the Council cannot constitute an obligation under the Treaties if, on its true construction, it is no more than an international agreement in simplified form.[8] The same is true of subsidiary conventions.

Difficulties also arise with regard to obligations derived from general principles of law: unless they can be regarded as in some way inherent in the Treaties, they would not fall within the scope of an enforcement action.[9] This problem is not likely to arise very often. What could easily happen, however, is that a Member State might be bound by an express provision of Union law and the European Court might have recourse to a general principle of law in order to interpret the provision: in this situation the general principle would be indirectly applicable to the Member State and a breach of it would also constitute a violation of the express provision. In such a case, of course, no difficulties would arise.

§2.2 VIOLATIONS BY THE LEGISLATURE OR JUDICIARY OF A MEMBER STATE

What is the position where the violation of Union law is the result of action (or failure to act) on the part of the national legislature or courts? For example, the national Parliament may fail to pass legislation introduced by the Government to give effect to a Union obligation, or it may insist on enacting legislation contrary to Union law. A violation by the courts could take a number of forms: they could refuse to give direct effect to a provision of Union law; they could refuse to make a reference to the European Court even where bound to do so under the third paragraph of Article 267; or they could refuse to accept that Union law overrides national law in the event of conflict. Is the national Government responsible for these violations?

The short answer to this question is that, although the national Government appears before the European Court in enforcement actions, the actual defendant is the State, not the Government.[10] Since the legislature and judiciary are organs of the State just as much as the Government is, there is no reason in principle why a violation of Union law by the legislature or courts should not engage the responsibility of the State in the same way as a violation by the executive. There have, in fact, been cases in which

[7] *Commission v. France*, Case C-239/03, [2004] ECR I-9325, paras 23–31 of the judgment.

[8] See Chap. 3, § 3.

[9] It should, however, be noted that both Mertens de Wilmars and Verougstraete, 'Proceedings against Member States for Failure to Fulfil Their Obligations' (1970) 7 CMLRev. 385 at 388 (para. 5) and Barav, 'Failure of Member States to Fulfil Their Obligations under Community Law' (1975) 12 CMLRev. 368 at 377 consider that general principles of law are covered, though neither gives any satisfactory reasons to support this opinion.

[10] See *per* Advocate General Warner in *Cremonini*, Case 815/79, [1980] ECR 3583 at 3621–2, and in *R v. Bouchereau*, Case 30/77, [1977] ECR 1999 at 2020. There appears to be one exception to this, *Commission v.*

national legislation was required in order to comply with Union law and the national Government introduced a bill and did all in its power to secure its enactment, but the national legislature failed to pass it: in these cases the national Government argued before the European Court that it was absolved from responsibility for the violation of Union law as it had done everything it could to get the measure approved. The Court, however, rejected these arguments on the ground just given.[11]

Similar arguments can be used in the case of the judiciary, but so far no enforcement action has been brought for a violation of Union law by national courts, though – as was shown in Chapter 8 – there have been several occasions on which such violations occurred.[12] In practice, the Commission has shown itself loath to institute proceedings in such cases.[13] It seems that this is partly because the independence of the judiciary might appear to be undermined by such proceedings and partly because the effective application of Union law depends to a great extent on the co-operation of the national courts. This is normally given, but if relations between the European Court and the national courts were soured by proceedings in which the former appeared to sit in judgment over the latter, the national judges might change their attitude.

The European Court has also ruled that constitutional difficulties are no excuse for a failure to fulfil an obligation under the Treaties.[14] If the defendant Member State is a federation, it will not constitute a defence to show that the violation was due to the action of a constituent state, such as a German *Land*.[15] The same rule would apply with regard to a violation by the legislature, executive, or judiciary of a dependency of a Member State, provided it was covered by the Treaties. Thus the United Kingdom

Government of the Italian Republic, Case 16/69, [1969] ECR 377, but this was probably a mistake. The Court itself gave judgment against the 'Italian Republic', not the Italian Government.

[11] See *Commission v. Belgium*, Case 77/69, [1970] ECR 237 and *Commission v. Italy*, Case 8/70, [1970] ECR 961. In the former case the Court said that a Member State is responsible even for the actions of 'a constitutionally independent institution' (para. 15 of the judgment): this phrase could cover the courts as well as the legislature.

[12] Notably by the French *Conseil d'Etat*.

[13] Proceedings against Germany were apparently commenced after the decision of the *Bundesverfassungsgericht* in the *Internationale Handelsgesellschaft* case but they were not pursued: *Europe*, 27 December 1974, No. 1657, p. 9. When the French *Conseil d'Etat* refused to make a reference to the European Court in the *Semoules* case (1 March 1968, [1970] CMLR 395), the Commission evidently considered whether action under Art. 258 (then Art. 169 EEC) should be taken against France: see the Commission's replies to Parliamentary Questions 28/68 (OJ 1968, C 71/1) and 349/69 (OJ 1970, C 20/4). In *Meyer-Burckhardt v. Commission*, Case 9/75, [1975] ECR 1171 at 1187, Advocate General Warner said that proceedings can be brought under Art. 258 [169 EEC] where a national court covered by the third paragraph of Art. 267 [177 EEC] fails to make a preliminary reference when required to do so by that provision; but he made clear that the Commission has a discretion whether or not to initiate the procedure and said that proceedings should 'not lightly be undertaken'. For references to the views of writers on this question, see Barav, 'Failure of Member States to Fulfil Their Obligations Under Community Law' (1975) 12 CMLRev. 369 at 379–80.

[14] See *Commission v. Italy*, Case 100/77, [1978] ECR 879 at para. 21 of the judgment.

[15] See *Casagrande v. Munich*, Case 9/74, [1974] ECR 773: this was a reference under Art. 267 [177 EEC], but the European Court made clear that Union law is binding at all levels in a Member State. The position would be the same in the case of a violation by a local authority.

would be liable for a violation by Gibraltar, the Channel Islands, or the Isle of Man, to the extent to which Union law applies to them.

§2.3 VIOLATION BY POPULAR ACTION

Violation of Union law by popular action is a problem of a somewhat different nature. This has occurred mainly in France, where farmers have blocked imports of agricultural produce from other Member States by ambushing the trucks bringing it into the country. The French police have been notoriously reluctant to intervene in such cases, leaving the drivers almost entirely at the mercy of their attackers. For many years, nothing was done about this. In 1985, the Commission wrote a formal letter of complaint to the French Government. In August 1995, it brought proceedings before the Court, claiming that France's failure to take effective measures to prevent such occurrences was a violation of the Treaty.

In December 1997, the Full Court (thirteen judges) ruled against France.[16] It held that France had violated Article 34 TFEU (then Article 30 EC) coupled with Article 4(3) TEU (then Article 5 EC). The former prohibits restrictions on imports of goods; the latter requires Member States to take all appropriate measures to ensure the fulfilment of their Treaty obligations. Although the Court was prepared to accept that, in specific instances, inaction might be excused if there was a threat to public order of such magnitude that the Member State could not cope with its consequences, France had failed to establish that this was the case in any of the instances in question.

This was an important judgment. As the Court pointed out, the mere threat of such attacks could be enough to deter producers in other Member States from exporting to France. Compensation for those actually attacked is not, therefore, enough.

§3 THE ADMINISTRATIVE STAGE

§3.1 INTRODUCTION

The proceedings in enforcement actions consist of two stages: an administrative stage and a judicial stage. The administrative stage is covered by the first paragraph of Article 258 TFEU, which provides:

> If the Commission considers that a Member State has failed to fulfil an obligation under the Treaties, it shall deliver a reasoned opinion on the matter after giving the State concerned the opportunity to submit its observations.

The use of the word 'shall' in this provision suggests that the Commission is under an obligation to deliver the opinion. (This contrasts with the second paragraph, where it is stated that, if the Member State does not comply with the opinion, the Commission

[16] *Commission v. France*, Case C-265/95, [1997] ECR I-6959.

'may' bring the matter before the European Court.) However, this obligation can arise only if two conditions are fulfilled: the Commission must consider that a breach has taken place and the Member State must have been given an opportunity to submit its observations.

The structure of the Treaty provision suggests that the normal order of events will be: first, the Commission concludes that a violation has taken place; then it allows observations to be submitted; and finally it delivers the opinion. However, no reasonable administrative authority would reach a definite conclusion on a matter as important as this until *after* it had considered the Member State's observations: it is an essential part of the *audi alteram partem* doctrine that the hearing must precede the decision. Therefore, the correct order of events should be: first the observations; then the conclusion that there has been a violation; and finally the delivery of the opinion. However, the Commission would not ask the Member State for its observations unless it had reason to believe that a breach might have taken place. Therefore, the formal request for observations must itself be preceded by a preliminary determination that a violation appears to have occurred.

In fact, the whole administrative stage can be subdivided into two distinct phases: the informal phase and the formal phase. In the informal phase, the Commission investigates a possible breach and considers whether there is sufficient evidence to justify the commencement of formal proceedings.[17] This informal investigation will be conducted with discretion, and the Commission will try to avoid press publicity. Informal discussions with the Member State will be held in an attempt to ascertain the facts and to reach a settlement. Only when the Commission feels that the factual and legal issues have been fully investigated will it consider whether to move on to the formal phase. It will then decide either that further proceedings are not warranted, in which case the matter will be at an end, or it will decide that sufficient evidence of a violation exists to justify the commencement of the formal phase.

The formal phase will begin with a formal request to the Member State to submit its observations (known as a 'letter of formal notice'). This formal communication specifies what the Member State is alleged to have done wrong and which rule of Union law has been infringed;[18] it will also lay down a time limit for the submission of observations.[19] Further discussions may take place after the Member State's observations have

[17] Member States are obliged under Art. 4(3) TEU [10/5 EC] to co-operate with the Commission in its investigations. Failure to do so may itself result in proceedings under Art. 258 [169 EEC]: *Commission v. Greece*, Case 240/86, [1988] ECR 1835. Any information requested must, therefore, be handed over within a reasonable time.

[18] The Member State must be told in clear terms, either in the formal communication or at an earlier stage, exactly what the allegations against it are; otherwise the whole proceedings could be nullified: see *Commission v. Denmark*, Case 211/81, [1982] ECR 4547 at paras 5–12 of the judgment; see also *Commission v. Italy*, Case 309/84, [1986] ECR 599; *Commission v. Denmark*, Case C-52/90, [1992] ECR I-2187. The formal notice must refer to an existing violation of Union law, not a possible future one: *Commission v. Netherlands*, Case C-341/97, [2000] ECR I-6611.

[19] This time limit must be reasonable; otherwise, subsequent court proceedings will be dismissed as inadmissible: *Commission v. Belgium*, Case 293/85, [1988] ECR 305. What is reasonable depends on the facts of the case.

been received: the Commission is always anxious to reach an amicable settlement, if this is possible. Only when it becomes clear that the Member State is not prepared voluntarily to accept the Commission position, will the Commission issue the reasoned opinion formally recording the violation.

§3.2 COMMISSION DISCRETION

Must the Commission issue a formal opinion to record every failure to observe the Treaties that comes to its notice? Or does it have a discretion as to which cases it will pursue? As was shown earlier, the Treaty suggests that the Commission has no discretion once it has concluded that a violation has taken place. However, it was also shown that the Commission will normally reach such a conclusion only after a fairly complex procedure of investigation and consultation has taken place. Before this has happened, the Commission will not be in a position to reach a definite conclusion; and before such a conclusion is reached, the obligation to deliver the opinion or take the decision will not arise.

The important question, therefore, is whether there is any obligation on the Commission to set the investigatory procedure in motion whenever it appears, either on the basis of information arising in the course of the Commission's normal operations or as a result of representations made by some outside person or body, that there are reasonable grounds for believing that a violation might have occurred. Article 258 TFEU contains no direct statement that such an obligation exists. It would not, however, be unreasonable to take the view that an implied obligation exists to consider with an open mind whether investigations should begin. This view is supported by Article 17(1) TEU, which provides that the Commission 'shall ensure the application of the Treaties, and of measures adopted by the institutions pursuant to them'.

Before considering the existence and limits of any obligation that may exist regarding the setting in motion of the enforcement procedure, however, it would be desirable to turn for a moment from legal principle to practicalities. First, it should be noted that a large number of contraventions of Union law take place. Many directives are implemented by the Member States only after the time limit has expired.[20] When implementation does take place, it is not always wholly satisfactory. The scope for enforcement actions is therefore very large: since the Commission has only limited staff available, it is not possible for it to investigate every suspected violation.

Secondly, there is a tendency for national Governments to resent the initiation of enforcement proceedings against them. As was once said by Advocate General Roemer,[21] this procedure puts the Member State's prestige in issue: no one likes to be accused of having broken the law. Since the Union mechanism functions only if there

[20] See the various reports submitted by the Commission to the European Parliament on the implementation of Union law.

[21] *Commission v. France*, Case 7/71, [1971] ECR 1003 at 1026.

is mutual trust and goodwill between the Member States and Union institutions, excessive resort to enforcement actions might do more harm than good.

In view of these considerations, it would be unreasonable to hold that there is an absolute obligation on the Commission to commence enforcement proceedings in every case where a violation may have occurred. On the other hand, however, it would be wrong to assume that there is no obligation at all. The true position seems to be that the Commission has a discretion but is also subject to a duty. The duty is to take the most appropriate action to ensure that Union law is obeyed; the discretion concerns the determination of what is most appropriate in the circumstances.[22] This discretion must, however, be exercised according to the correct criteria.

In *Commission v. France*[23] (*EAEC* case) Advocate General Roemer indicated some of the situations in which the Commission might be justified in not initiating the enforcement procedure: where there is a possibility that an amicable settlement may be achieved if formal proceedings are delayed; where the effects of the violation are only minor; where there is a major political crisis which could be aggravated if proceedings are commenced with regard to matters of secondary importance; and where there is a possibility that the Union provision in issue might be altered in the near future. These are only examples: the basic principle is that the Commission must balance the harm caused by non-compliance against the embarrassment and inconvenience that could result from bringing proceedings.

Events in October 2010 provide a graphic illustration of the political circumstances which can influence the Commission. On President Sarkozy's orders, the French police had moved against Roma (Gypsy) camps in France. Many Roma were deported to their home countries, mostly Romania and Bulgaria. Since the Roma were EU citizens exercising their EU rights of free movement,[24] these deportations ran up against EU law. The French claimed to be acting under the rule that Member States may deport EU migrants on grounds of public policy. However, EU law provides that such actions must be based exclusively on the personal conduct of the individual concerned.[25] Being a member of a particular ethnic group does not constitute personal conduct.

Members of the French Government told Viviane Reding, EU Commissioner for Justice, Fundamental Rights and Citizenship, that the Roma were not being targeted as a group. Shortly thereafter, however, a French Government circular came to light which showed that the French Government was doing exactly that. Ms Reding reacted strongly, and seemed to accuse the French of misleading her. She compared the deportations to those carried out by the Nazis, and said she expected legal proceedings to be brought against France.

The French Government then went on the offensive and accused her of insulting France. This belligerency paid off: when the Commission discussed the matter, they refused to support Ms Reding and she had to back down. No proceedings were brought with regard

[22] *Commission v. France* (see n. 21) at para. 5 of the judgment.

[23] *Commission v. France* (see n. 21) at 1025.

[24] See Art. 20(2)(a) TFEU.

[25] Art. 27(2), Directive 2004/38, OJ 2004, L 158/77.

to the Roma. Since it is hard to doubt that France had infringed EU law, this loss of nerve on the part of the Commission shows that a powerful and aggressive Member State, enjoying at least passive support from other Member States, can bully the Commission into submission. Ethnic minorities will no doubt conclude that there is no point in looking to the Commission for protection, at least if no other Member State is willing to support them.[26]

§3.3 RECORDING THE VIOLATION

After it has considered any observations submitted by the Member State within the time limit laid down in the request, the Commission must decide whether a violation has occurred. If it considers that it has, it will record this infringement in a reasoned opinion. The main function of the opinion is to specify exactly what the Member State has done wrong. If the matter subsequently goes to the European Court, the opinion serves as a definition of the issues before the Court: the Commission cannot raise any violations which are not set out in it.[27] The reasons given by the Commission will help the Member State to prepare its case before the Court. They should be sufficient to enable the Member State to know precisely why the Commission thinks it has infringed the Treaty.

The Commission has to set a time limit within which the Member State must end the violation,[28] and it cannot bring legal proceedings until this has expired.[29] The time limit thus gives the Member State a period of grace within which it is protected from the threat of legal proceedings.[30] The reasoned opinion also specifies what action may be taken by the Member State to end its infringement. However, as the opinion is merely declaratory – it simply records a violation – the Commission cannot impose any new obligation on the Member State:[31] the Member State can therefore choose what measures it takes, so long as the infringement is in fact terminated.

§3.4 TIME LIMIT FOR COMMISSION ACTION

There is no time limit for the initiation of proceedings or for the delivery of the reasoned opinion: it falls within the Commission's discretion to decide when to act. This is

[26] Romania and Bulgaria kept a low profile.

[27] *Commission v. Belgium*, Case 298/86, [1988] ECR 4343 at paras 9–11 of the judgment.

[28] This must be reasonable. If it is too short, the subsequent application to the Court will be dismissed as inadmissible: *Commission v. Belgium*, Case 293/85, [1988] ECR 305. What is reasonable depends on all the circumstances.

[29] Art. 258, second para., TFEU. If legal proceedings are brought, the onus is on the Commission to prove that the violation was not rectified before the expiry of the time limit: *Commission v. Belgium*, Case 298/86, [1988] ECR 4343 at para. 15 of the judgment.

[30] The reasoned opinion cannot, however, affect the rights of third parties. A finding that no violation occurred does not preclude proceedings in the national courts by private individuals, nor does it prevent the European Court from ruling against the Member State in a reference from a national court under Art. 267 TFEU [177 EEC]: see *Essevi*, Cases 142–3/80, [1981] ECR 1413 at paras 13–18 of the judgment.

[31] See *Netherlands v. High Authority*, Case 25/59, [1960] ECR 355 at 373–5. This case concerned the ECSC Treaty; the position is even clearer under the EU Treaties, since the reasoned opinion is not legally binding.

illustrated by a case under Article 141 EAEC, which is the EAEC (Euratom) equivalent of Article 258 TFEU. The case was *Commission v. France*,[32] which concerned Title II, Chapter VI of the EAEC Treaty, which contained various provisions designed to ensure that all users of nuclear fuels in the Union could obtain reasonable supplies. A special Supply Agency was set up to control the supply of nuclear materials. The French Government, however, took the view that these provisions lapsed after seven years, as they had not been confirmed by the Council under Article 76(2) EAEC. In 1965, it informed French undertakings that the provisions of Chapter VI were no longer applicable: the French Government itself ceased to comply with them. In particular, it did not inform the Supply Agency of contracts it had concluded for the procurement and supply of nuclear materials. The Commission considered, however, that Chapter VI was still in force, and in 1970 it commenced proceedings under Article 141: France was invited to submit observations; a reasoned opinion was given declaring France guilty of a violation of the Treaty; and, after France had failed to comply with it within the period laid down, an action was instituted before the European Court.

One argument put forward by the French Government was that the proceedings had been started too late. It maintained that it had made its views known in 1965 and that it was not open to the Commission to wait so long before bringing the action. The Court rejected this contention. It held:[33]

> The action for a declaration that a State has failed to fulfil an obligation provided for by Article 141 of the Treaty, does not have to be brought within a predetermined period, since, by reason of its nature and purpose, this procedure involves a power on the part of the Commission to consider the most appropriate means and time-limits for the purposes of putting an end to any contraventions of the Treaty.

The action was therefore declared admissible;[34] the Court went on to hold that Chapter VI had not lapsed: it gave judgment against France.

§3.5 CONSEQUENCES OF PROCEDURAL DEFECTS

It will be seen from what has been said that there are a number of procedural requirements which must be complied with by the Commission: the Member State must be given a fair opportunity to submit its observations (this involves both giving it sufficient information regarding the case it must meet and allowing a reasonable time for the observations to be communicated); the opinion must be properly reasoned; and the Member State must be given a reasonable period to end its violation. If the Commission violates one of these requirements, the Member State may raise the procedural infringement in any subsequent proceedings before the Court. If it is sufficiently serious, it will

[32] Case 7/71, [1971] ECR 1003. [33] Para. 5 of the judgment.

[34] The Court's ruling that no time limit exists with regard to proceedings by the Commission against a Member State contrasts with its decision to create such a time limit in the case of proceedings by a Member State against the Commission: see *Netherlands v. Commission*, Case 59/70, [1971] ECR 639, discussed later.

constitute a bar to the action, since the procedural requirements laid down in the Treaty are essential preconditions for the admissibility of an enforcement action.[35]

§4 THE JUDICIAL STAGE

The delivery of the reasoned opinion marks the end of the administrative stage. Next comes the judicial stage, where the matter is put before the European Court for a final ruling. There is no deadline for the commencement of the action, but, as we have seen, the Commission must wait until the expiry of the time limit in its reasoned opinion.[36]

The Court has full (plenary) jurisdiction to consider all the issues. The proceedings are not a review of the opinion: the Court considers *de novo* whether the violation has occurred. As will be seen in Chapter 15, the powers of the Court in review proceedings are restricted: it may annul the measure in question on limited grounds only; its power to review the Commission's evaluation of a situation is restricted; and the only remedy it can grant is a declaration of invalidity: it cannot substitute its decision for that of the Commission. These restrictions do not apply when the Court exercises plenary jurisdiction.

However, the scope of the proceedings is limited to the infringements specified in the reasoned opinion: the Commission cannot raise new allegations before the Court.[37] Proceedings cannot be brought if the breach is terminated before the deadline laid down in the reasoned opinion,[38] but what happens if it is terminated after the

[35] In *Commission v. Italy*, Case 7/61, [1961] ECR 317, the Court appeared to consider an allegation that the opinion did not contain sufficient reasons as relating to the admissibility of the enforcement action; and in *Commission v. Italy*, Case 31/69, [1970] ECR 25, the Court said that the opportunity to submit observations was 'an essential procedural requirement' (para. 13 of the judgment); see also *Commission v. Germany*, Case 325/82, [1984] ECR 777 at para. 8 of the judgment; *Commission v. Belgium*, Case 293/85, [1988] ECR 305; *Commission v. Denmark*, Case C-52/90, [1992] ECR I-2187. In *Commission v. Netherlands*, Case C-341/97, [2000] 6611, the Court held the proceedings inadmissible because the formal notice was defective, since, at the time when it was issued, the Member State had not committed the violation.

[36] The European Court cannot extend or reduce the time limit set by the Commission: *Commission v. Italy*, Case 28/81, [1981] ECR 2577.

[37] See, for example, *Commission v. Italy*, Case 166/82, [1984] ECR 459 at para. 16 of the judgment. However, if the Commission is seeking to establish that the Member State is guilty of a general and persistent failure to abide by Union law (a concept discussed later), it can introduce evidence of further specific violations (in addition to those given in the reasoned opinion) in order to show that the failure is general and persistent: see *Commission v. Ireland*, Case C-494/01, [2005] ECR I-3331 at paras 37–38 of the judgment (Grand Chamber). These further allegations will not lead to a judgment that the Member State is guilty of further specific violations, but may lead to a judgment that it is guilty of a general and persistent failure to comply with Union law. This latter allegation must, of course, be made in the reasoned opinion.

[38] However, there is an exception if, in addition to alleging various specific violations, the Commission also claims that the Member State is guilty of a general and persistent failure to abide by Union law (see n. 37). Here, a specific violation that ended before the deadline may still be used as evidence of a general and persistent failure, even though it can no longer lead directly to a judgment against the Member State: see *Commission v. Ireland*, Case C-494/01, [2005] ECR I-3331 (Grand Chamber) at paras 29–32 of the judgment.

deadline but before judgment is given? This occurred in *Commission v. Italy*[39] (*Pork Imports* case) where the Court ruled that it did not constitute a bar to the action.[40] Proceedings cannot, on the other hand, be brought regarding a violation which had not occurred when the Commission invited the Member State to submit its observations, even though the Commission may have had reason to believe that it was contemplated.[41]

It is no defence to argue that the Commission or Council is also in breach of the Treaty with regard to the same subject matter, or that the act complained of was in retaliation for a comparable violation by another Member State.[42] Nor may a Member State complain that other Member States were doing exactly the same thing and no proceedings were brought against them.[43] In general, the Court, though willing to consider policy issues, is not impressed by technical, legalistic defences.

If the Court finds the allegations proved, it will give judgment against the Member State. This takes the form of a declaration that the Member State has failed to fulfil an obligation under the Treaty. The Court will, of course, specify what act or omission is the source of the violation. The Court has no power specifically to order the Member State to do, or not to do, something;[44] nor, if the violation takes the form of national legislation contrary to Union law, can it declare the legislation invalid.[45] This does not, however, mean that the Member State is not obliged to comply with the judgment. The first paragraph of Article 260 TFEU [228/171 EC] states:

> If the Court of Justice of the European Union finds that a Member State has failed to fulfil an obligation under the Treaties, the State shall be required to take the necessary measures to comply with the judgment of the Court.

[39] Case 7/61, [1961] ECR 317 at 326.

[40] There are various reasons why the Commission might wish to continue with the action: for example, it might want to obtain a ruling to clarify the matter in case the violation is repeated at a later stage. In practice, however, it will usually drop the proceedings once the breach has been remedied.

[41] See *Commission v. Italy*, Case 31/69, [1970] ECR 25 at paras 11–14 of the judgment; see also *Commission v. Italy*, Case 309/84, [1986] ECR 599.

[42] See *Commission v. Luxembourg and Belgium*, Cases 90, 91/63, [1964] ECR 625 at 631, where it was held that failure by the Union to carry out its obligations does not justify the Member States' taking the law into their own hands, and *Steinike und Weinlig*, Case 78/76, [1977] ECR 595, where the Court held that a breach by a Member State of an obligation under the Treaties cannot be justified by the fact that other Member States have also failed to fulfil the obligation in question (para. 24 of the judgment). *Commission v. France*, Case 26/69, [1970] ECR 565, suggests, however, that a Member State might be excused if it was not engaged in an act of retaliation but, through no fault of its own, was forced into violating the Treaties by a wrongful act on the part of the Union.

[43] See *Germany v. Commission*, Cases 52, 55/65, [1966] ECR 159 at 170–2.

[44] This does not apply in the case of interim measures (discussed later, in § 7). The Court might, of course, try to help the Member State by suggesting ways in which it could bring the violation to an end.

[45] In *Commission v. Italy* (second *Art Treasures* case), Case 48/71, [1972] ECR 527 at paras 7–9 of the judgment, the Court emphasized that national authorities should not apply national legislation that is incompatible with Union law: this, of course, is a simple reiteration of the doctrines of direct effect and the supremacy of Union law discussed in Chap. 7.

This makes clear that the judgment, though declaratory in nature, is binding: the Member State is obliged to terminate the violation found by the Court, though it can choose the way in which this will be done.

§5 REMEDIES WHERE THE COMMISSION FAILS TO ACT

It was said previously that the Commission has a discretion as to whether to set the enforcement procedure in motion, but there is a duty to exercise that discretion properly. What remedies exist if the Commission fails in that duty?

Under the ECSC Treaty (now expired) it was possible for either another Member State or a private party with sufficient standing to bring an action for failure to act under Article 33 ECSC.[46] This was because, instead of giving a reasoned opinion, the Commission adopted a reasoned decision, which constituted a reviewable act[47] for the purpose of Article 35 ECSC. This remedy is not available under the EU Treaties, because a reasoned opinion, unlike a reasoned decision under the ECSC Treaty, is not legally binding and hence not a reviewable act. Even if it were, a private individual could not challenge it because he would lack standing:[48] if given, the opinion would not be addressed to him, nor would it concern him directly and individually; consequently, an omission or refusal to give an opinion (or to take any of the preceding steps) cannot be challenged under Article 263 TFEU [230/173 EC] or Article 265 TFEU [232/175 EC].[49] This is not important as far as Member States are concerned, since Article 259 TFEU gives Member States the right to bring proceedings themselves. Private individuals, on the other hand, are in a much less advantageous position than they were under the ECSC Treaty.

Are any other remedies available? In *Vloeberghs v. High Authority*,[50] another case under the ECSC Treaty, Vloeberghs, a Belgian coal dealer, suffered loss because the French Government refused to allow the entry into France of a consignment of coal

[46] *De Gezamenlijke Steenkolenmijnen in Limburg v. High Authority*, Case 17/57, [1959] ECR 1; *Groupement des Industries Sidérurgiques Luxembourgeoises v. High Authority*, Cases 7, 9/54, [1956] ECR 175.

[47] This concept is discussed in Chap. 11.

[48] The rules for standing were less strict under the ECSC Treaty than they are under the EU Treaties.

[49] *Lütticke v. Commission*, Case 48/65, [1966] ECR 19; *Commission v. France*, Cases 6, 11/69, [1969] ECR 523 (paras 35–37 of the judgment); *Star Fruit v. Commission*, Case 247/87, [1989] ECR 291 (para. 13 of the judgment); *Emrich v. Commission*, Case C-371/89, [1990] ECR I-1555; *Sonito v. Commission*, Case C-87/89, [1990] ECR I-1981 (paras 5–7 of the judgment); *Asia Motor France v. Commission*, Case C-72/90, [1990] ECR I-2181; *Asia Motor France v. Commission*, Case C-29/92, [1992] ECR I-3935; *Bundesverband der Bilanzbuchhalter v. Commission*, Case C-107/95 P, [1997] ECR I-947. For the possibility that there might be exceptional situations in which an individual may be able to bring proceedings against a refusal by the Commission to adopt a decision under the special procedure laid down in Art. 106(3) TFEU (then Art. 90(3) EC), see *Bundesverband der Bilanzbuchhalter v. Commission*, Case C-107/95 P, [1997] ECR I-947 at para. 25 of the judgment.

[50] Cases 9, 12/60, [1961] ECR 197.

which Vloeberghs had imported into Belgium from outside the Union. He maintained that the French had violated the Treaty and asked the Commission to take action under Article 88 ECSC, the equivalent of Article 258 TFEU. The Commission refused. Vloeberghs then brought an action for damages against the Commission and claimed compensation for the loss he had suffered through not being able to export the coal to France.[51] He lost the action in the end, but there was no suggestion in the case that such actions are not available in principle.

Can actions in tort (or 'non-contractual liability', as it is called in Union terminology) be brought under the EU Treaties? In principle, there seems to be no reason why the position should be any different from that under the ECSC Treaty: the distinction between an opinion and a decision is not relevant in actions for damages. In *Denkavit v. Commission*,[52] a private firm sued the Commission for damages for loss caused by the fact that deliveries of feeding-stuffs had been stopped at the Italian frontier. The Italian authorities had done this on the ground that the potassium nitrate content of the feeding-stuffs was higher than that permitted under an 'urgent note' which had been issued by the Italian Minister of Health a year previously. Denkavit claimed that the 'urgent note' violated the Treaty and that the Commission was partly to blame for the situation, as it had acted too slowly in taking measures to require Italy to revoke the note.

The Advocate General, Mr Mayras, was unsympathetic to this claim.[53] The Court, however, did not dismiss it out of hand but considered it on its merits: it eventually concluded that the Commission's tardiness – it did eventually take action – was excused by the legal uncertainties and scientific doubts which existed at the time. The Court said, however, that the 'urgent note' constituted an obstacle to trade between Member States and that it was 'necessary to consider whether the Commission, by conduct for which there was no justification, did not improperly contribute to the maintenance of that obstacle and thereby incur liability'.[54] This suggests that in principle such an action can be brought. Subsequently, however, the Court seems to have turned against the idea: in *Asia Motor France v. Commission*,[55] it declared the action inadmissible on the ground that the Commission is not under a duty to commence proceedings under Article 258 TFEU (then Article 169 EEC).[56]

[51] He was unable to use the procedure under Art. 35 ECSC because, as a coal dealer and not a coal producer, he lacked standing under Arts 33 and 35 ECSC.

[52] Case 14/78, [1978] ECR 2497.

[53] See *ibid.* at 2515–16.

[54] *Ibid.* at para. 8 of the judgment. See also *Lütticke v. Commission*, Case 4/69, [1971] ECR 325; see further *Société d'Initiatives et de Coopération Agricoles v. Commission*, Case 114/83, [1984] ECR 2589; *GAARM v. Commission*, Case 289/83, [1984] ECR 4295.

[55] Case C-72/90, [1990] ECR I-2181.

[56] Para. 13 of the judgment. In an earlier case, *Meyer-Burckhardt v. Commission*, Case 9/75, [1975] ECR 1171 at 1190, Advocate General Warner came down against the possibility of such an action on the ground that it would be wrong for the Court to decide whether a Member State had infringed the Treaties if that State was not a party to the proceedings and did not enjoy the safeguards provided for in Art. 258 (then Art. 169 EEC).

§6 ACTIONS BY MEMBER STATES

Article 259 TFEU [227/170 EC] permits enforcement actions to be brought by a Member State. This reads as follows:

> A Member State which considers that another Member State has failed to fulfil an obligation under the Treaties may bring the matter before the Court of Justice of the European Union.
>
> Before a Member State brings an action against another Member State for an alleged infringement of an obligation under the Treaties, it shall bring the matter before the Commission.
>
> The Commission shall deliver a reasoned opinion after each of the States concerned has been given the opportunity to submit its own case and its observations on the other party's case both orally and in writing.
>
> If the Commission has not delivered an opinion within three months of the date on which the matter was brought before it, the absence of such opinion shall not prevent the matter from being brought before the Court.

The first steps under this procedure are clear enough. The applicant requests the Commission to deliver a reasoned opinion on the alleged infringement. The Commission must comply with this request within three months; otherwise the applicant may commence proceedings before the Court without waiting for the opinion. The procedure before the Commission is similar to that under Article 258 TFEU but the rights of the Member States are more extensive: each party is entitled both to present its own case and to comment on that of the other party; moreover, these proceedings are both written and oral.[57]

It is less clear exactly what happens after the opinion has been given – assuming that it is duly given within the three-month period. There are several possibilities. Assume, first, that the opinion is to the effect that there has been no infringement: is this the end of the matter or may the applicant persist in its claim and bring the case before the Court? It would seem that it can:[58] the first paragraph of Article 259 TFEU gives Member States a general right to bring proceedings. This is qualified by the second paragraph, which lays down a procedural condition, but this condition is satisfied once the matter has been 'brought before the Commission' and the latter has been given an opportunity (three months) to deliver its opinion: there is no requirement that the opinion must be favourable to the applicant's case. Once the opinion has been given, the procedural conditions are satisfied and the general right in the first paragraph then has full application.[59]

[57] The English text is ambiguous as to whether the words 'both orally and in writing' in the third para. of Art. 259 apply only to the observations on the other party's case or also to the submission of the Member State's own case. The French text, however, makes clear that it applies to both. It reads: '*La Commission émet un avis motivé après que les Etats intéressés aient été mis en mesure de présenter contradictoirement leurs observations écrites et orales.*'

[58] Mertens de Wilmars and Verougstraete (1970) 7 CMLRev. 385 at 393.

[59] There is no time limit for bringing the action.

What happens if the opinion is that the defendant has committed a breach? There is no statement in the Treaties that the opinion must set a time limit within which the defendant must cease the violation. Could this be implied by analogy with Article 258 TFEU? Some writers consider this to be so,[60] but it is hard to see what function such a time limit would serve, since the applicant would not be obliged to wait for the expiration of the period before going to the Court.

Further difficulties could arise if the Commission upholds the applicant's claim only in part. Say, for example, the applicant alleges that the defendant has broken the Treaty in three ways, but the Commission rejects two of these complaints and upholds only the third: if the defendant then complies with the opinion, can the applicant nevertheless go to the Court with regard to the first two complaints? If the applicant can go to the Court when the opinion is wholly against the applicant – as was suggested earlier – it would be strange if it could not do the same when the opinion is partly in its favour and partly against it. It seems, therefore, that the defendant cannot necessarily obtain immunity from legal action by complying with the opinion, as it can under Article 258. This means that the opinion has little significance under Article 259, except as an indication to the Court of how the Commission views the matter.[61]

As was mentioned previously, the procedure under Article 259 TFEU is little used. The first case under it to go to judgment was an action (under what was then Article 170 EEC) brought by France against the United Kingdom in which it was claimed that certain fish conservation measures adopted by the United Kingdom were contrary to the Treaty. The Commission was asked by France to give an opinion and, after the parties had put forward their views in writing, it held a hearing at which the parties could present their cases orally. It then gave an opinion which stated that the United Kingdom had infringed the Treaty. (No time limit was set for ending the infringement nor were any suggestions made as to what action would be sufficient to bring this about.) France then took the matter before the Court and the Commission applied for leave to intervene in support of France. This was granted. The hearing then proceeded in the normal way; judgment was given against the United Kingdom.[62]

§7 INTERIM MEASURES

When Member States break the Treaty – as they sometimes do quite consciously – they usually intend their action to be only temporary: they know they will have to come into line eventually but try to put it off as long as possible. They therefore play for time in their negotiations with the Commission, and the Commission tries to hurry the procedure along. In such a situation, the ability to apply for an interim order from the Court is a useful weapon.

[60] Mertens de Wilmars and Verougstraete (see n. 58), p. 393.

[61] It is possible, however, that the Commission might feel obliged to intervene in the Court proceedings in support of its opinion, as it did in *France v. United Kingdom* (see n. 62).

[62] *France v. United Kingdom*, Case 141/78, [1979] ECR 2923.

The relevant provision is Article 279 TFEU, which provides:

> The Court of Justice of the European Union may in any cases before it prescribe any necessary interim measures.

This rather uninformative provision gives no indication of what kinds of interim measures may be prescribed, but it has come to be accepted that something in the nature of an English interlocutory injunction can be granted.

Despite initial doubts,[63] it was established in *Commission v. United Kingdom* (*Pig Producers*)[64] that such a remedy is available against a Member State. There are three main considerations which the Court will take into account when deciding whether to grant it.[65] First, it will consider the likelihood of the proceedings being successful: no order will be made if the claim in the main action is manifestly unfounded. Secondly, it must be shown that the need for the order is urgent.[66] Thirdly, the Commission will normally be required to demonstrate that irreparable damage to the Union interest will occur if the order is not given, but the defendant may attempt to show that irreparable damage to its interests will ensue if the order is granted.[67]

Commission v. Germany[68] (*Road Tax* case) illustrates the application of these principles. Germany had introduced a tax on heavy goods vehicles using German roads which, it was alleged, applied in a way that was unfair to carriers from other Member States. The Commission brought enforcement proceedings against Germany under Article 258 (then Article 169 EEC) and applied for an interim order suspending application of the tax until the Court had given judgment. Five other Member States intervened in support of the Commission. As he was entitled to do under the Court's Rules of Procedure, the President of the Court granted the application on a temporary basis even before Germany had been able to put its case. He then referred the matter to the Court,[69] which was obliged to give it priority over all other cases.[70]

[63] In enforcement actions, the judgment takes the form of a declaration that the Member State has failed to fulfil an obligation under the Treaties: the Court does not expressly order the Member State to do anything, though Art. 260 requires the Member State to take the 'necessary measures' to comply with the judgment. If the final judgment is only declaratory, it might be asked, can the Court grant an interim order specifically requiring the Member State to do something?

[64] Cases 31, 53/77 R, [1977] ECR 921. See also *Commission v. Ireland*, Case 61/77 R, [1977] ECR 937; *Commission v. Italy*, Case 154/85 R, [1985] ECR 1753; *Commission v. Belgium*, Case 293/85 R, [1985] ECR 3521.

[65] See *per* Advocate General Mayras in *Commission v. United Kingdom*, Cases 31, 53/77 R, [1977] ECR 921 at 931–5 and *per* Advocate General Reischl in *Commission v. Ireland*, Case 61/77 R, [1977] ECR 937 at 953–4.

[66] In *Commission v. Ireland*, however, Advocate General Reischl took the view that the mere fact that the Irish measures were actually being applied was sufficient to establish the requisite degree of urgency (at 954).

[67] For the application of these principles to the special procedure under Art. 348 TFEU [298/225 EC], see *Commission v. Greece* (*Macedonia* case), Case 120/94 R, [1994] ECR I-3037.

[68] Case C-195/90 R, [1990] ECR I-3351.

[69] It seems rather strange that the President should both make an order himself – in effect, an 'interim' interim order, since it applied only until the Court made a 'final' interim order – *and* refer it to the Court. The Rules of Procedure made no provision for this: the first para. of Art. 85 stated simply that the President 'shall *either* decide on the application himself *or* refer it to the Court' (emphasis added). The reason, presumably, was that the matter was thought too urgent to be delayed until the Court could deal with it, but too politically delicate for the President to decide it alone.

[70] The Court acted fast: its order was made exactly two weeks after that of the President.

In its judgment, the Court first examined the substantive claim and concluded that the Commission had established a *prima facie* case of sufficient strength to justify an interim order. It next considered whether there was a risk that a subsequent award of damages would not constitute sufficient compensation for the harm suffered by carriers from other Member States. It concluded that such a risk existed, since some of the carriers might be driven into bankruptcy. Germany argued that it would suffer irreparable damage if the tax *were* suspended, since there would be no way in which it could recover the lost revenue. The Court, however, rejected this argument on the ground that the interim order would only restore the *status quo* before the tax was introduced, a ground that raises a number of unanswered questions. It also rejected Germany's demand that the Commission should lodge security for half a billion Deutschmarks to provide it with compensation, should the final judgment be in Germany's favour: the Court held that the lodging of security, for which there was provision in the Rules of Procedure,[71] is not to be required unless there is a risk of non-payment as a result of insolvency, an unlikely contingency in the case of the Union. An interim order was therefore made in virtually the same terms as those of the President.[72]

§8 RESTITUTION AND DAMAGES

If the delinquent Member State could be forced to undo its action, delaying tactics would serve no purpose. In some situations this might be impossible, but if the violation consisted of an illegal subsidy or an unlawful tax, restitution might be feasible. This could occur under national law simply as a result of the Court's judgment in the enforcement action: for example, the European Court's decision in *Commission v. Luxembourg and Belgium*[73] that import duties imposed by the Belgian Government were a violation of Union law was followed by a successful action by importers to reclaim money already paid.[74] (Such actions are, of course, based on the doctrine of direct effect and could succeed even without enforcement proceedings having been brought; where this is the position, a reference will normally be made to the European Court under Article 267.)

In some cases, however, national law will make no provision for restitution. Where this is so, can the Member State be forced to repay or reclaim the money by means of the procedure under Articles 258–260? The difficulty here is that a judgment under Article 258 does no more than declare that the defendant Member State has failed to fulfil an obligation under the Treaty: as was mentioned previously, it does not (except in

[71] Art. 86(2).

[72] See also *Commission v. Austria*, Case C-320/03 R, [2003] ECR I-7929, [2003] ECR I-11665, [2004] ECR I-3593; *Commission v. Malta*, Case C-76/08 R, [2008] ECR I-64.

[73] Cases 90, 91/63, [1964] ECR 625.

[74] *Minister for Economic Affairs v. Fromagerie Franco-Suisse 'Le Ski', Cour de Cassation*, Belgium, 21 May 1971, [1972] CMLR 330.

the case of interim measures) order the Member State to take any specific action. Article 260 requires the Member State to take 'the necessary measures to comply with the judgment of the Court', but it is generally assumed that it is for the Member State itself to decide what these are. Although it must end its infringement, it is not clear to what extent Article 260 obliges the Member State to attempt to undo its past misconduct.

One possibility would be for the Commission to request the Member State to repay or reclaim the money. If it refused, new enforcement proceedings could be commenced for a breach of Article 260: in this way, the Court could be asked to rule on the matter. So far, however, the Commission has not resorted to this procedure.

The only cases in which the Commission has required restitution concern illegal State aid, which is not covered by Articles 258–260 but falls under a special procedure laid down by Articles 108 and 109 TFEU. The first case in which this occurred was *Commission v. Germany*[75] (*Kohlegesetz*). The German Government had made provision for certain investment grants which the Commission regarded as contrary to the Treaties. On 17 February 1971, the Commission adopted a decision requiring Germany to cease paying the grants: the German Government complied, but only after a certain period of time. The Commission regarded this delay as unacceptable and brought proceedings under Article 108 TFEU (then Article 93 EEC): it asked the Court not only for a declaration that Germany had failed to comply with the decision of 17 February 1971, but also for a ruling that it was obliged to obtain repayment of grants made after the promulgation of the decision.

The German Government objected to the admissibility of this second claim but the Court overruled the objection. The Court pointed out that the Commission has the power, when it rules that an aid is contrary to the Treaty, to require the Member State to abolish or alter it: this is specifically stated by Article 108(2) TFEU (then Article 93(2) EEC). It then said: 'To be of practical effect, this abolition or modification may include an obligation to require repayment of aid granted in breach of the Treaty, so that in the absence of measures for recovery, the Commission may bring the matter before the Court.'[76]

It might be thought that this applied only under the special procedure laid down by Article 108 [93 EEC], but the Court went out of its way to dispel any such idea: it expressly said that, in an action under Articles 258–260 (then Articles 169–171 EEC), the Commission can apply for a declaration that 'in omitting to take specific measures' the Member State has failed to fulfil an obligation under the Treaty. It then continued:[77]

> Since the aim of the Treaty is to achieve the practical elimination of infringements and the consequences thereof, past and future, it is a matter for the Community authorities whose task it is to ensure that the requirements of the Treaty are observed to determine the extent to which the obligation of the Member State concerned may be specified in the reasoned opinions or decisions delivered under Articles 169 and 93(2) respectively and in applications addressed to the Court.

[75] Case 70/72, [1973] ECR 813. [76] *Ibid.* at para. 13 of the judgment. [77] *Ibid.*

This suggests that in its decision (under Article 108 [93 EEC]) or reasoned opinion (under Article 258 [169 EEC]) the Commission may specify what remedial measures are required: failure to carry these out would itself be a breach of the Treaties. For example, the Commission could say in its reasoned opinion that the Member State had violated the Treaty (i) by applying an illegal tax and (ii) by not repaying money already collected. If the Member State refused to comply, the Court could grant a declaration in similar terms.

In *Commission v. Germany*, the Court decided in the end that the Commission had failed to establish its case; so the order sought by the Commission was not granted. Nevertheless, the judgment clearly establishes the principle. In spite of this, however, the Commission for many years made no further attempt to obtain restitution. Then in 1980 it announced a change of policy regarding State aid to industry: it said that in future it would require repayment of aid granted in violation of Union law.[78] After a somewhat shaky start,[79] this new policy became firmly established.[80] It has, however, been applied only to state aid: the Commission has never accepted the Court's invitation to adopt a similar policy in proceedings under Article 258.

Where the Treaty violation consists of, say, an import ban, there can be no question of restitution. Could the procedure under Articles 258–260 be used to make a Member State pay damages? In the course of the dispute over the French Government's refusal to obey the Court's judgment in the *Sheepmeat* case (discussed later, in § 10), the British Government spoke of the possibility of obtaining damages. It could perhaps be argued that failure to compensate British exporters was itself a violation of the Treaty, either because there is an independent obligation to compensate the victims of illegal acts, or because of Article 260. When the dispute was settled, however, the claim for damages was dropped.[81] It is uncertain, therefore, whether damages can be obtained in this way. On the other hand, as we saw in Chapter 7, § 11, it is open to claimants who have suffered loss as a result of a Member State's violation of Union law to bring proceedings for damages in the national courts. The case in which this was established, *Francovich v. Italy*,[82] did in fact arise following a judgment against Italy under Article 258, but, as we saw, the right to bring proceedings is not dependent on such a judgment.[83]

[78] See OJ 1983, C 318/3.

[79] The first time the policy was put to the test, something rather strange occurred: a Commission decision was adopted requiring Belgium to reclaim illegal aid granted to a factory making wall coverings (Decision 82/312, OJ 1982, L 138/18); some months later, however, a 'corrigendum' was published deleting the provisions requiring repayment (OJ 1982, L 289/35). So Belgium did not have to reclaim the aid.

[80] See the line of cases beginning with *Commission v. Belgium*, Case 52/84, [1986] ECR 89. For a discussion of the rules laid down by these cases, see Priess, 'Recovery of Illegal State Aid: An Overview of Recent Developments in the Case Law' (1996) 33 CMLRev. 69. See now Art. 14 of Reg. 659/1999, OJ 1999 L 83.

[81] The request for damages was made to the Commission. The idea was that the Commission would ask the Court to make a declaration that France's failure to pay compensation was a violation of the Treaty. The sum claimed was approximately £20 million: see *The Times*, 11 January 1980.

[82] Cases C-6, 9/90, [1991] ECR I-5357.

[83] If the national courts persistently failed to grant a remedy, proceedings could be brought in the European Court under Art. 258; however, as was mentioned earlier, the Commission is reluctant to bring proceedings for a violation of Union law by national courts and one would not expect it to do so unless the failure was blatant.

§9 THE NORTH–SOUTH GRADIENT

Is there any pattern to the violations of EU law recorded against Member States? Are some more likely to break the law than others? Research done towards the end of the 1990s showed that this was indeed the case.[84] In fact, there was a remarkably consistent pattern. By ranking Member States according to the number of violations recorded against them in a given year, it was possible to show that the position of individual Member States in the 'league table' remained remarkably constant over the years, suggesting that underlying factors (probably of a cultural nature) are at work. The research, which was carried out before the former Communist-bloc countries joined the Union, showed that – at least, up until then – there was a clearly discernible North–South gradient: Denmark, Sweden, and Finland almost always stood at the top, being the States showing the highest level of respect for Union law, while Greece, Italy, and France usually came at the bottom.[85] No comparable research seems to have been done for subsequent periods, but one would expect to see the same forces at work, with one group of countries consistently occupying the top positions and another group consistently occupying the bottom positions.

§10 COMPLIANCE

Unfortunately, compliance with the Court's judgments is by no means automatic; sometimes, it can take years.[86] In this section, we consider the problem of non-compliance.

§10.1 DEFYING THE COURT

When Member States fail to obey judgments against them, they usually take care not to inflame the situation by making outspoken public statements. In one case, however, the Government of the Member State in question openly and publicly defied the Court, hoping thereby to gain an advantage in domestic politics. This occurred in the late 1970s in the notorious *Sheepmeat* case, which began when France (with some justification on legal and social grounds) refused to admit imports of lamb and mutton from other Member States, principally Britain. The Commission brought proceedings, and in due course the Court gave judgment against France.[87] The French Government, however, made clear that it would not comply with the judgment until the Council agreed to a Union support system which would protect French farmers, a measure

[84] Trevor C Hartley, *Constitutional Problems of the European Union* (1999), Chap. 6.

[85] Spain and Portugal ranked higher than their geographical position would suggest, while France ranked lower.

[86] In one case, *Commission v. Italy*, Case 79/72, [1973] ECR 667, the judgment had still not been obeyed after ten years: HAH Audretsch, *Supervision in European Community Law*, 2nd edn (1986), pp. 395–6.

[87] *Commission v. France*, Case 232/78, [1979] ECR 2729.

blocked by Britain. It was thus using its refusal to comply with the judgment as a bargaining counter to obtain a Union subsidy for its sheep farmers.

The Commission then brought new proceedings (on the ground that the failure to obey the judgment was an independent infringement of Union law) and applied for an interim order requiring France to admit British lamb without restrictions. Surprisingly, this was rejected by the Court on the ground that it would substantially duplicate the previous judgment and would not, therefore, be 'necessary', as required by Article 279 TFEU (then Article 186 EEC).[88] In fact, one suspects that the Court, knowing that any order it gave would be ignored, decided that it would be better to save what was left of its tattered authority by refusing the order.

In the end, the case never went to a final judgment: Britain agreed to a Union regime for lamb and mutton in exchange for concessions on its budgetary claims; France then lifted the ban on imports. The case must be regarded as a victory for France, and shows that, for a powerful and determined Member State, defiance of the Court can sometimes pay off.

§10.2 FINES

When the *Sheepmeat* case was decided, there was no provision in the relevant Treaty (then the EEC Treaty) for sanctions against a Member State for disobeying a judgment.[89] Today, the Court can impose a fine. This is possible under an amendment to Article 260 TFEU brought in by the Treaty on European Union in 1993.[90] The procedure is the same as that for bringing a new action under Article 258. If the Commission considers that a Member State has not complied with a judgment of the Court, it issues a reasoned opinion after giving the Member State the opportunity to submit its observations. The opinion must specify the points on which the Member State has not complied with the judgment and must lay down a time limit for compliance. If the Member State does not fall into line within the time limit, the Commission may bring the case before the Court. When it does so, the Commission may specify the amount of the lump-sum fine or penalty payment that it considers appropriate. (A penalty payment, generally called a 'periodic penalty payment', is a payment of a specified amount for each day, or other period of time, that elapses[91] until compliance takes place.) The Court is not obliged to follow the Commission's proposal, though it takes it into account.

88 Cases 24, 97/80 R, [1980] ECR 1319.

89 The only provision for sanctions was contained in Art. 88 of the ECSC Treaty (now expired). This provided that money payable to the delinquent Member State could be withheld, or other Member States permitted to take action 'to correct the effects of the infringement'. The Commission authorized these sanctions but the assent of the Council (acting by a two-thirds majority) had to be obtained. In fact, no sanctions were ever imposed during the fifty years in which the ECSC Treaty was in operation.

90 This was adopted at the suggestion of the United Kingdom, following a proposal made by the European Court: Kilbey, 'Financial Penalties under Article 228(2) EC: Excessive Complexity?' (2007) 44 CMLRev. 743 at 745; *Financial Times*, 6 February 1991.

91 Time runs from the date on which the judgment was originally served on the recalcitrant Member State.

On 6 July 1996, the Commission issued a communication setting out the criteria it intended to apply in asking the Court to impose monetary penalties.[92] This was subsequently replaced, first by a communication issued in 1997,[93] and then by one issued in 2005.[94] In the 1996 communication, the Commission said that a periodic penalty payment would normally be more appropriate than a lump sum.[95] However, the Commission has since come round to the view that it will often be appropriate to ask the Court for both.[96]

The problem is that some Member States continue with the infringement until the penalty is about to be imposed and then comply with the judgment just in time to avoid having to pay it. Since the enforcement procedure (like all ECJ procedures) moves slowly, this could easily be five to ten years from the date on which the Commission first notified the national Government that it considered that the Member State had infringed Union law. A periodic penalty payment applies only in the future (after the second judgment); so it does nothing to deter such conduct. The new idea is that the lump sum will penalize the infringement between the date of the first judgment and that of the second; the periodic penalty will penalize the continuing infringement after the second judgment.

In the past, the Commission would withdraw the action for the penalty if the Member State put an end to the infringement after the Court was seised but before judgment was given; now, it will continue the action, but ask only for a lump sum.[97]

In calculating the amount of the penalty to be proposed, the Commission takes three factors into account: the seriousness of the infringement, its duration, and the need to deter future infringements. The seriousness of the infringement is determined on the basis of the importance of the Union rule infringed, and the effect of the infringement on the interests of the European Union and of individuals. To ensure a deterrent effect, the penalty is higher if there is a risk of a repetition, or if there has been a repetition.

The Commission has adopted a formula for calculating the amount of the periodic penalty it will propose,[98] though it reserves the right to depart from it if there is good reason to do so. It starts with a rather arbitrary sum of money, the 'standard flat-rate amount'. In 2005, this was €600 per day.[99] This is multiplied by two coefficients, the first (with a minimum value of 1 and a maximum of 20) reflecting the seriousness of the infringement, and the second (with a minimum value of 1 and a maximum of 3) reflecting its duration. To achieve deterrence, the result will be multiplied by a factor reflecting the ability of the Member State to pay (based on its GDP) and the

[92] OJ 1996, C 242/6. [93] OJ 1997, C 63/2. [94] SEC(2005)1658. This is available online.

[95] *Ibid.*, para. 4.

[96] This follows from the case of *Commission v. France*, Case C-304/02, discussed below.

[97] This happened for the first time in *Commission v. France*, Case C-121/07, [2008] ECR I-9159, in which a lump sum penalty of €10 million was imposed.

[98] SEC(2005)1658. There is a similar formula for a lump sum.

[99] It is subject to revision to take account of inflation. This was supposed to take place every three years, but so far it has not occurred, mainly because of the economic crisis.

number of votes it commands in the Council. This ranges from 0.36 for Malta to 25.40 for Germany.

Almost seven years after the system was first introduced, a fine was imposed for the first time. The country concerned was Greece. In 1992, the Court gave judgment against Greece for failure to implement a directive on environmental pollution.[100] Greece did nothing to comply and further proceedings were commenced in 1995. The Court gave judgment in July 2000.[101] It imposed a fine of €20,000 per day, an extremely small sum, even smaller than the €24,600 proposed by the Commission.[102]

Since this case, the Commission has been sparing in the use of its power to bring applications before the Court. In 2003, the Court imposed an annual penalty on Spain in a case concerning pollution of the sea,[103] and in 2005 it imposed a lump-sum fine *and* a periodic penalty payment on France in a case concerning conservation of fish, even though the Commission had asked only for a periodic penalty payment.[104] The Court's judgment is lacking in clarity, but it seems that the lump sum was intended to punish France for past behaviour; the periodic penalty was to ensure future compliance.[105] This at least is how the Commission has interpreted the judgment: it was on the basis of this case that the Commission introduced its new policy of asking for both a lump sum and a periodic penalty.[106]

Since then, judgments imposing fines have been given at the rate of about one a year. The sums involved have almost always been small.[107]

§10.3 FIXING THE PENALTY IN ADVANCE

The Treaty of Lisbon brought in a new procedure under which it is possible, in certain cases, for the penalty to be fixed in the original judgment.[108] This is laid down in Article 260(3) TFEU, which applies where a Member State fails to transpose (implement) a

[100] *Commission v. Greece*, Case C-45/91, [1992] ECR I-2509.

[101] *Commission v. Greece*, Case C-387/97, [2000] ECR I-5047.

[102] Greece paid this fine until the Commission concluded, in July 2001, that it had complied with the judgment. This means that it took almost exactly a year from the date of the second judgment (almost nine years from the date of the original judgment) for Greece to comply.

[103] *Commission v. Spain*, Case 278/01, [2003] ECR I-14141. The fine was fixed at an annual amount of €624,150 for each 1 per cent of the total area that remained polluted.

[104] *Commission v. France*, Case C-304/02, [2005] ECR I-6263 (Grand Chamber). For discussion of this case, see Kilbey, 'Financial Penalties under Article 228(2) EC: Excessive Complexity?' (2007) 44 CMLRev. 743 at 749–50.

[105] The lump sum was only €20 million. The periodic penalty was €57,761,250 for every six months during which France had not complied.

[106] See earlier.

[107] See *Commission v. France*, Case C-177/04, [2006] ECR I-2461 (periodic penalty of €31,650 per day); *Commission v. Italy*, Case C-119/04, [2006] ECR I-6885 (no penalty); *Commission v. Portugal*, Case C-70/06, 10 January 2008 (periodic penalty of €19, 392 per day); *Commission v. France*, Case C-121/07, 9 December 2008 (lump sum of €10 million; no periodic penalty); *Commission v. Greece*, Case C-369/07, 7 July 2009 (Grand Chamber) (lump sum of €2 million and periodic penalty of €16,000 per day).

[108] See Wennerås, 'Sanctions against Member States under Article 260 TFEU: Alive, but not Kicking?' (2012) 49 CMLRev. 145 at 165–70.

directive which was adopted under a legislative procedure.[109] Under Article 260(3), the Commission may, in the proceedings to establish the *original* violation, specify the amount of the lump sum or penalty payment to be paid by the Member State. The second paragraph of Article 260(3) TFEU then provides:

> If the Court finds that there is an infringement it may impose a lump sum or penalty payment on the Member State concerned not exceeding the amount specified by the Commission. The payment obligation shall take effect on the date set by the Court in its judgment.

This appears to mean that the Court can set the level of the fine in advance and it will then apply automatically if the Member State does not comply with the judgment by the date specified.[110]

§10.4 GENERAL AND PERSISTENT INFRINGEMENTS

Another development occurred in 2005, when the European Court gave judgment in *Commission v. Ireland*.[111] This concerned illegal dumping of waste (rubbish) by private individuals in Ireland. The Irish Government was accused of violating Union law by failing to take adequate steps to prevent it. The innovative features of the case were, first, that the Commission brought proceedings for a large number of specific instances in one action; and, secondly, that it asked the Court to find not only that Ireland had violated Union law in those specific instances, but also that it was guilty of a general and persistent failure to comply with Union law. This latter claim was based on the contention that the Irish Government had failed to put adequate legal and administrative mechanisms in place to ensure that illegal dumping did not occur. The Court agreed with the Commission. It held that Ireland had failed to take the measures necessary to ensure the correct implementation of the relevant directive. The significance of this is that it will not be enough for Ireland to rectify the various specific instances of illegal dumping in order to comply with the judgment; it will also be necessary for it to show that it has taken the necessary steps to ensure that the directive is enforced in general.[112]

§10.5 CONCLUSIONS

Enforcing Union law has always been problematic. Since the Union institutions have no means of direct enforcement – there are no Union bailiffs, policemen, or soldiers

[109] On the meaning of 'legislative procedure', see Chap. 4, § 1.2.

[110] It is assumed that the date set by the court must be *after* the judgment (so that the Member State cannot be punished for violating Union law prior to the judgment) and that it will be given a reasonable period within which to transpose the directive.

[111] Case C-494/01, [2005] ECR I-3331 (Grand Chamber).

[112] For a general discussion of this case, see Wennerås, 'A New Dawn for Commission Enforcement under Articles 226 and 228 EC: General and Persistent (GAP) Infringements, Lump Sums and Penalty Payments' (2006) 43 CMLRev. 31 at 33–50.

to arrest members of the national Government – they must rely in the last resort on political pressure from other Member States. The extent to which this will be applied depends on the circumstances. As we have seen, Member States sometimes demand a *quid pro quo* for complying with a judgment.

The policy of imposing fines has had only limited success. The sums involved are small and they cannot be a great deterrent.[113] However, if the fines were large enough to have a serious effect on the economy of the State concerned, Member States might refuse to pay. In the case of a small Member State that obtained more from the Union budget than it paid in, it might be possible to deduct the amount of the fine from money owing to it; however, in the case of a large and powerful Member State that was a net contributor to the Union budget, this might be a dangerous tactic. It is possibly for this reason that the Commission asks the Court to impose a fine only in a small number of cases and, when it does, specifies only modest sums of money.

FURTHER READING

Items are listed in date order, the most recent being at the end.

Evans, 'The Enforcement Procedure of Article 169 EEC: Commission Discretion' (1979) 4 ELRev. 442.

Gray, 'Interim Measures of Protection in the European Court' (1979) 4 ELRev. 80.

HAH Audretsch, *Supervision in European Community Law*, 2nd edn (1986).

Dashwood and White, 'Enforcement Actions under Articles 169 and 170 EEC' (1989) 14 ELRev. 388.

Bonnie, 'Commission Discretion under Article 171(2) EC' (1998) 23 ELRev. 537.

Alberto Gil Ibañez, *The Administrative Supervision and Enforcement of EC Law: Powers, Procedures and Limits* (1999).

Theodossiou, 'An Analysis of the Recent Response of the Community to Non-Compliance with Court of Justice Judgments' (2002) 27 ELRev. 25.

Harlow and Rawlings, 'Accountability and Law Enforcement: The Centralised EU Infringement Procedure' (2006) 32 ELRev. 447.

Wennerås, 'A New Dawn for Commission Enforcement under Articles 226 and 228 EC: General and Persistent (GAP) Infringements, Lump Sums and Penalty Payments' (2006) 43 CMLRev. 31.

Kilbey, 'Financial Penalties under Article 228(2) EC: Excessive Complexity?' (2007) 44 CMLRev. 743.

Andersen, 'Procedural Overview and Substantive Comments on Articles 226 and 228 EC' (2008) 27 YEL 121.

Kilbey, 'The Interpretation of Article 260 TFEU' (2010) 35 ELRev. 370.

Prete and Smulders, 'The Coming of Age of Infringement Proceedings' (2010) 47 CMLRev. 9.

[113] See Nicolaides and Suren, 'The Rule of Law in the EU: What the Numbers Say' EIPASCOPE 2007/1 33 at 37 (available online), who conclude that when a Member State does not want to comply, it can escape punishment for about a decade.

Stine Andersen, *The Enforcement of EU Law: The Role of the European Commission* (2012).

Editorial, 'A Revival of the Commission's Role as Guardian of the Treaties?' (2012) 49 CMLRev. 1553.

Wennerås, 'Sanctions against Member States under Article 260 TFEU: Alive, but not Kicking?' (2012) 49 CMLRev. 145.

PART IV

ADMINISTRATIVE LAW

INTRODUCTION

The Rule of Law is fundamental to all systems of constitutional law. It is so fundamental, in fact, that if it does not exist in at least its most basic form – that governmental authorities not only enforce the law but are also bound by it themselves – there can be no constitutional law. Constitutional law is, after all, the system of legal rules regulating governmental authority and the relations between citizens and the State.

The Rule of Law in this basic sense is, of course, a principle of the European Union. However, if the concept is to attain its full realization, more is required than this. In addition, the legality of governmental action should be subject to determination by an independent, impartial adjudicatory body – in short, by a court. In the Union, the appropriate body is the European Court. How far may the Court pass judgment on the actions of the Union authorities? This raises the question whether the Union possesses a system of administrative law to provide the citizen with a remedy in the event of a legal dispute with the Union. This involves three main issues: whether the European Court may review (and, if necessary, quash) Union measures; whether it may require the Union to act where its failure to act is a violation of the law; and, finally, whether it is possible to enforce obligations in contract, restitution, and tort against the Union.

With regard to the first issue, a distinction must be made between a direct challenge and an indirect challenge to a Union act. The object in the former is to obtain a declaration of invalidity. The object of the latter, on the other hand, is something quite different, and the validity of the act arises for decision only because the main question before the court depends on it: the challenge to the act is merely a preliminary step in a procedure leading to a decision on a different issue.

This distinction is important as regards the way the proceedings are instituted. As might be expected, a declaration of invalidity can be obtained only in proceedings specially instituted for this purpose under the relevant provision in the Treaties. In the case of an indirect challenge, on the other hand, the direct object of the proceedings is, and must be, something other than the determination of the validity of the act. In other words, an indirect challenge is made when the act in question is applicable to, or otherwise relevant in, proceedings concerned with something else, and it is argued that the act should not be applied, on the ground that it is invalid. The court will then consider its validity. If it finds the act invalid, it will refuse to apply it. The purpose of making an indirect challenge, then, is to induce the court not to apply the act to the proceedings.

An important point to note is that, while a direct challenge can be made only before the European Court, an indirect challenge may be made both before a national court and before the European Court. If it is made before a national court, the question of the validity of the act will be referred to the European Court for a preliminary ruling.

It will be seen from this that there are three procedural mechanisms or 'avenues of review' by which the question of validity can be brought before a court: a direct challenge before the European Court; an indirect challenge before the European Court; and an indirect challenge before a national court. However, an essential principle is that, whatever avenue of review is used, the *substantive* question before the Court is always the same: the validity of the act.

If proceedings are brought to quash a Union act (direct challenge) the first question that must be considered is jurisdiction. Closely related to this is the concept of *locus standi* (standing). Jurisdiction is concerned with the power of the Court to hear the case. Looked at from the point of view of the applicant, *locus standi* relates to his right to bring the proceedings, his right to appear before the Court and put his case to it. In other words, if there is an admittedly unlawful act, the question still arises of who has the right to ask the Court to quash it.

However, if one looks at it from the point of view of the Court, it appears as an aspect of jurisdiction: does the Court have the power to hear proceedings brought by *this* applicant? Thus, from the Court's point of view one can distinguish two kinds of jurisdiction. The first is concerned with the Court's power to hear a case concerning a particular subject matter. This is jurisdiction *ratione materiae* (regarding the subject matter). The second, otherwise known as *locus standi*, is jurisdiction *ratione personae* (regarding the person who is bringing the proceedings). There is also a third kind of jurisdiction: jurisdiction *ratione temporis* (regarding the time of the proceedings). This is concerned with the question: can the Court hear proceedings brought *at this time*? The importance of this is that there are strict time limits for bringing proceedings: if the application is too late, the Court will not be able to hear it. The time limit in annulment actions before the Court is two months.

The second issue mentioned previously concerns an unlawful failure to act. In one sense, a remedy for failure to act is simply the reverse of an annulment action. In fact, however, the matter is more complicated. If an annulment action is successful, the Court will declare the act void; but if proceedings for failure to adopt an act are successful, the Court merely declares that the defendant's failure is contrary to the Treaties: it cannot declare the act adopted. For this reason, an indirect challenge is not possible in the case of inaction: in collateral proceedings, the Court cannot be asked to decide the case on the basis that the act in question has been adopted. This means that the remedies open to the individual are more restricted in the case of a failure to act.

The third issue concerns the enforcement of Union obligations, in particular the right to obtain damages from the Union.

These are the matters that will be considered in this final Part of the book.

FURTHER READING

Items are listed in date order, the most recent being at the end.

Jürgen Schwarze, *European Administrative Law*, rev. edn (2006).

Angela Ward, *Judicial Review and the Rights of Private Parties in EU Law*, 2nd edn (2007).

Paul Craig, *EU Administrative Law*, 2nd edn, (2012).

Carol Harlow, *Accountability in the European Union*, 2nd edn (2012).

11

REVIEWABLE ACTS

§1 INTRODUCTION

The first question concerns jurisdiction *ratione materiae*: over what matters does the Court have jurisdiction? Review proceedings are brought for a particular purpose: to have the Court *declare a Union act void*. This is laid down in Articles 263 TFEU [230/173 EC] and 264 TFEU [231/174 EC]. The first paragraph of Article 263 provides:

> The Court of Justice of the European Union shall review the legality of legislative acts, of acts of the Council, of the Commission and of the European Central Bank, other than recommendations and opinions, and of acts of the European Parliament and of the European Council intended to produce legal effects *vis-à-vis* third parties. It shall also review the legality of acts of bodies, offices or agencies of the Union intended to produce legal effects *vis-à-vis* third parties.

And Article 264 states:

> If the action is well founded, the Court of Justice shall declare the act concerned to be void.

The question to be considered, therefore, is: what kinds of acts may the Court declare void?

In Union law there is no procedure equivalent to the English action for a declaration (or injunction). The Court cannot consider the legal position of the applicant in the abstract. If the action is brought under Article 263, the applicant must find some 'act' to be the subject matter of the proceedings: he can then ask the Court to declare it void. Without this, the Court lacks jurisdiction *ratione materiae*.

The text just quoted shows that Article 263 applies to three classes of acts:

1. legislative acts;
2. acts of the Council, Commission, and European Central Bank 'other than recommendations and opinions'; and
3. acts of the European Parliament, the European Council[1] and of bodies, offices, and agencies of the Union 'intended to produce legal effects *vis-à-vis* third parties'.[2]

[1] For the distinction between the Council and the European Council, see Chap. 1, § 2.

[2] The original version of this provision – in Art. 173 EEC – covered only 'acts of the Council and the Commission other than recommendations and opinions'. Since then, there has been an expansion of the kinds of measures that are subject to judicial review and the bodies against which proceedings may be brought.

If we ignore for a moment the author of the act, it will be seen that the acts subject to review – what we call 'reviewable acts' – fall into three classes:

- legislative acts;
- acts other than recommendations and opinions;
- acts intended to produce legal effects *vis-à-vis* third parties.

The important point to note about these classes of legal acts is that they are all intended to produce legal effects or – to say the same thing in different words – they are intended to be legally binding. As has been affirmed by the European Court on many occasions, legal effect is an essential characteristic of a reviewable act.[3]

The best way to see this is to look at the list in Article 288 TFEU [249/189 EC] of acts that may be adopted by the Union institutions. These are:

1. regulations;
2. directives;
3. decisions;
4. recommendations; and
5. opinions.

According to the definitions in Article 288 TFEU, regulations, directives, and decisions are all legally binding, while recommendations and opinions are stated to have 'no binding force'.

The first class of reviewable acts specified in Article 263 consists of 'legislative acts'. Article 289 TFEU provides that these must take the form of a regulation, directive, or decision. These are legally binding. The second class consists of acts other than recommendations and opinions: these too are legally binding. The third class consists of 'acts intended to produce legal effects *vis-à-vis* third parties'. By definition, these are intended to be legally binding.

The requirement of legal effect has always been regarded as essential by the European Court: if an act has no legal effect, it is not reviewable. Indeed, the Court has gone further. In the *ERTA* case,[4] the European Court held that a legally binding act that does not fall into any of the categories specified in what is now Article 288 TFEU (then Article 189 EEC) is also reviewable. Prior to this case, it was thought that every act that is legally binding must be a regulation, directive, or decision. For reasons explained in Chapter 4, § 1.1, the European Court decided that this is not the case. The result is that such acts – usually referred to as 'acts *sui generis*' – are also reviewable under what is now the first paragraph of Article 263 TFEU (then Article 173 EEC). The result is that

[3] See, for example, *Italy v. Commission*, Case 151/88, [1989] ECR 1255; see further *Deutsche Post and Germany v. Commission*, Case C-463/10 P, [2011] ECR I-9639 at paras 36–38 and cases cited therein.

[4] *Commission v. Council*, Case 22/70, [1971] ECR 263.

any legally binding act is reviewable under Article 263 TFEU, provided it is adopted by the appropriate authority.

It is not necessary that the act should be expressly adopted pursuant to provisions of one of the Treaties.[5] As is shown by the Court's decisions discussed later, any statement intended to produce legal effects, even if contained in a letter or other such document, can constitute a reviewable act: it is not necessary for it to be in the form of a regulation, directive, or decision.

What does 'having legal effects' mean? This is not always an easy question to answer. However, as a starting point, one might say that an act has legal effects if it alters the legal position of some person. A person's legal position is the sum total of his legal rights and obligations (in a broad sense). In other words, to have legal effects, an act must produce a change in somebody's rights or obligations.[6]

§2 THE *NOORDWIJKS CEMENT ACCOORD* CASE

A good illustration of the way this principle applies is the *Noordwijks Cement Accoord* case.[7] In order to grasp the issues in this case it is necessary to have some understanding of the Union law relating to competition. At the time of the case, the relevant provision was Article 85 EEC (now Article 101 TFEU). Paragraph 1 of this prohibits agreements between undertakings which restrict competition. In order to give it teeth, the Council adopted Regulation 17, which imposed fines on undertakings guilty of violating the provision. It was, however, realized that not all restrictive agreements are bad; so provision was made in Article 85(3) EEC (now Article 101(3) TFEU) for exemptions to be granted to agreements that were economically beneficial. Such exemptions were granted by the Commission after an examination of the agreement in question.

Under the procedure established by Regulation 17, a restrictive agreement had to be notified to the Commission, which then had the task of deciding whether it violated the provisions of Article 85(1). If it did not, there was no problem. If it did, the Commission had to decide whether an exemption under Article 85(3) should be granted. It was only if the Commission refused to grant an exemption that the firms concerned were liable to be fined.

The problem with this procedure was that it might take a considerable time for the Commission to reach a decision on these two points. What were the firms to do in the meantime? If they decided not to operate the agreement, which might eventually be held lawful, they would suffer commercially. But if they carried out the agreement and it was finally held unlawful, they might be subject to fines. This difficulty

[5] *Parliament v. Council*, Case C-316/91, [1994] ECR I-625 at para. 9 of the judgment.

[6] In the case of acts falling into the third class mentioned earlier, Art. 263 TFEU expressly provides that the legal effects must apply *vis-à-vis* third parties. This is no doubt true in the other cases as well: the act must produce a change in the legal rights or obligations of some person other than the author of the act.

[7] Cases 8–11/66, [1967] ECR 75.

was understood by the authors of Regulation 17, and it was therefore provided in Article 15(5) of the Regulation that undertakings would enjoy immunity from fines from the time when the agreement was notified until the Commission reached its decision. This, of course, gave the firms full protection; but it appears to have been thought too favourable to them. So it was provided in Article 15(6) of the Regulation that the immunity would cease to apply once the Commission had informed the firms, *after a preliminary examination*, that the agreement appeared to violate Article 85(1) and that there appeared to be no grounds to justify an exemption under Article 85(3). Once the firms received this communication, they continued to operate the agreement at their own risk: if eventually it was held to be lawful, well and good; otherwise, they would be subject to fines.

In the *Noordwijks Cement Accoord* case the companies concerned had notified their agreement to the Commission. In due course they received a letter under Article 15(6) of Regulation 17. It stated:

> The Commission subjected the agreement in question to a provisional examination. It reached the conclusion that the conditions of the application of Article 85(1) of the Treaty were met and that application of Article 85(3) to the said agreement, in the form in which it was notified, was not justified.

The letter then went on to inform the companies that the immunity from fines would cease as from the receipt of the letter. The companies concerned brought proceedings under Article 263 (then Article 173 EEC) to quash the decision contained in the letter.

The Commission argued that the proceedings were inadmissible because the Court had no jurisdiction *ratione materiae*: no 'act' was in existence which could be quashed. The letter, they said, contained a mere *opinion* by the Commission, which would be subject to reconsideration and which was not legally binding. It was not, therefore, a reviewable act.

The Court rejected this contention. After pointing out that the effect of the decision was to remove the immunity provided by Article 15(5), it stated:[8]

> This measure deprived them of the advantages of a legal situation which Article 15(5) attached to the notification of the agreement, and exposed them to a grave financial risk. Thus the said measure affected the interests of the undertakings by bringing about a distinct change in their legal position. It is unequivocally a measure which produces legal effects touching the interest of the undertakings concerned and which is binding on them. It thus constitutes not a mere opinion but a decision.

The proceedings were therefore held to be admissible.

This judgment shows that it is sufficient if the act has only a contingent effect on the legal position of those concerned.[9] The immunity taken away by the decision was in the nature of an insurance policy: if in the end the agreement was held not to infringe Article 85, the immunity would – with hindsight – turn out to have been unnecessary.

[8] *Ibid.* at 91.

[9] See also *Deshormes v. Commission*, Case 17/78, [1979] ECR 189 at paras 8–17 of the judgment.

Only if this was not the case would the applicants' legal rights have been affected by the decision.

§3 PROBLEM CASES

In most cases, it will be fairly obvious whether or not an act has legal effects. Some examples have already been given. However, there are a number of difficult cases that have been brought to light in judgments of the European Court. This Section is devoted to a discussion of them.

First, if a legal act merely confirms a previous act, it does not change anyone's legal position. It has no legal effects.[10] This does not apply, however, if the later act goes beyond the first one and creates new rights or obligations,[11] or if, after the adoption of the first act, there has been a fundamental change in the circumstances such that the legal effects of the first act are modified.[12] In particular, this will be the case where the judgment of a court obliges the authority to reconsider the first act.[13] It should also be said that, where the Council confirms a decision taken by COREPER, the definitive act is that of the Council. Therefore, the Council's decision is a reviewable act.[14]

Secondly, the European Court has said that an act is not reviewable if it has only internal effects.[15] By this it means that if the act affects only the internal organization or operation of the institution which adopted it, third parties cannot challenge it.[16] The principle has been applied mainly to acts of the European Parliament[17] and is now expressly set out in Article 263.[18] It is not always easy, however, to draw the line between a purely internal act and one that affects third parties.[19]

[10] See *SNUPAT v. High Authority*, Cases 42, 49/59, [1961] ECR 53 at 75–6.

[11] See, for example, *France v. Commission*, Case C-325/91, [1993] ECR I-3283; *France v. Commission*, Case C-303/90, [1991] ECR I-5315. In the first of these cases a 'communication' and in the second a 'code of practice' were held to be reviewable acts, since they sought to impose rights and obligations beyond those contained in the principal measure to which they applied. See also *France v. Commission*, Case C-57/95, [1997] ECR I-1627.

[12] See *ERTA*, Case 22/70, [1971] ECR 263 at para. 66 of the judgment and *per* Advocate General de Lamothe at 286.

[13] *SNUPAT v. High Authority* (see n. 10).

[14] *Commission v. Council* (*FAO* case), Case C-25/94, [1996] ECR I-1469 at paras 22–28.

[15] *Group of the European Right v. Parliament*, Case 78/85, [1988] ECR 1753; *Les Verts v. Parliament*, Case 190/84, [1988] ECR 1017; *France v. Parliament*, Cases 358/85, 51/86, [1988] ECR 4821 at para. 17 of the judgment. These cases concerned, respectively, a decision that a motion to set up an inquiry into Fascism was admissible, decisions implementing the budget, and a decision to hold an urgent debate on a particular topic.

[16] This does not prevent a member of the staff of the institution from challenging the act if it affects his legal rights.

[17] It may to some extent be based on the concept of parliamentary sovereignty or autonomy.

[18] Art. 263 states that such acts can be challenged only if they are 'intended to produce legal effects *vis-à-vis* third parties'. This provision, which was added by the Treaty on European Union, incorporates into the Treaty a principle first laid down by the European Court in *Les Verts v. Parliament*, Case 294/83, [1986] ECR 1339 at para. 25 of the judgment.

[19] See, for example, *France v. Commission*, Case C-366/88, [1990] ECR I-3571, a case concerning internal instructions by the Commission to its officials as to how they should exercise certain powers. The Court held that the instructions were reviewable because they affected the rights of third parties.

Difficult problems arise where an authority adopts an act which binds it as to how it will act in the future. Since this may deprive it of a power – the power to act differently – it can affect the legal position of those who would benefit from the exercise of the power. The matter is difficult, however, because the authority may be able to revoke the act. Nevertheless, if the authority is bound by the act until it is revoked, it should probably be regarded as reviewable.

An example of this is the case of *Lassalle v. European Parliament*.[20] In this case, Lassalle, a Union official on the staff of the European Parliament, brought proceedings[21] to annul a notice of vacancy for the post of Head of Division in the division in which he worked. The notice specified that one of the qualifications for the post was a 'perfect knowledge of Italian'. There was no actual reason why the holder of the post had to have a perfect knowledge of Italian and this was, in fact, a disguised way of saying the job was reserved for an Italian national. This requirement would have precluded Lassalle from being a candidate and he therefore wished to have the notice quashed. The admissibility of the application was not in fact contested by the defendant and was not therefore discussed in detail by the Court. However, the Advocate General stated:[22]

> ...the notice of vacancy in this instance contains various conditions which limit the choice which the administration will have eventually to make. In short, it is limiting its choice in advance and, in so doing, is taking a decision which, when published, has an immediate adverse effect on servants who, like the applicant, do not fulfil one or other of the required conditions...

The notice was, therefore, a reviewable act.

Though theoretically different, cases in which an authority merely makes a statement as to how it will exercise its powers in future are often hard to distinguish in practice from those in which it adopts an act which binds it in this regard. As was pointed out earlier, one of the defects of Union law is that it has no equivalent to the English action for a declaration. The European Court has, however, tried to alleviate this by ruling that a statement of future intention can be a reviewable act. Strictly speaking, this would be the case only if the authority was bound by its statement; however, this could have undesirable consequences, as the persons concerned might be deprived of a remedy.

The case of *Fédération Charbonnière de Belgique v. High Authority*[23] provides an example. In this case, the Commission wrote to the Belgian Government and told it

[20] Case 15/63, [1964] ECR 31. See also *Küster v. European Parliament*, Case 79/74, [1975] ECR 725 at paras 4–8 of the judgment and *De Roubaix v. Commission*, Case 25/77, [1978] ECR 1081 at paras 6–9 of the judgment.

[21] The proceedings were brought under Art. 91 of the Staff Regulations (Regulation 31/1962, JO 1962, p. 1385): see Art. 179 EEC as it stood at the time. The issue, however, was the same as under what is now Art. 263 TFEU.

[22] At 41.

[23] Case 8/55, [1956] ECR 245. This case was decided under the ECSC Treaty (now expired), but the principle is the same.

that continued grants of equalization aid for the Belgian coalfields would be conditional on the Belgian Government taking certain steps. This obviously meant that the subsidies would be withdrawn if the steps were not taken. Strictly speaking, nobody's legal rights were affected because the Commission was not (presumably) bound by its statement. Yet it was obviously desirable that the mining companies should be allowed to obtain a ruling on the validity of the Commission's decision as soon as it was made, rather than making them wait to see what action the Commission took if the Belgian Government refused to comply. A declaration would have been the appropriate remedy. In the absence of such a remedy, the Court had to characterize the Commission's letter as a reviewable act. This is what it did. It justified its ruling as follows:[24]

> In its letter of 28 May 1955 the High Authority accepted that equalization aid must be accompanied by a series of measures to be adopted by the Belgian Government. Furthermore, it considers that the Belgian Government ought to apply four measures, indicated at points (a), (b), (c) and (d). The action referred to under (d) is, therefore, one of the series of measures which the Belgian Government would be obliged to take if the circumstances so required. The High Authority has thus unequivocally determined the attitude which it has decided to take henceforth should the circumstances mentioned under point 2(d) of the letter arise. In other words, it has laid down a rule to be applied if necessary. It must therefore be seen as a decision within the meaning of Article 14 of the Treaty.

Another example is the case of *Algera v. Common Assembly*.[25] The applicants were all officials of the Common Assembly of the ECSC who had been appointed on fixed-term contracts. When the Staff Regulations for Union (then Community) employees were adopted, the applicants were offered permanent appointments under these regulations. They were, however, unwilling to accept the gradings they were offered. A letter was written to them on behalf of the Assembly noting their rejection of their gradings and stating that if they continued in this attitude they would be regarded as only temporary employees and would lose various benefits. The Court held that this letter constituted a reviewable act because it specified with all necessary precision what action the Common Assembly intended to take if the applicants continued to refuse the grading offered.[26]

The European Court has in fact adopted a general doctrine that any statement as to the action that will be taken in the future is a reviewable act, provided it is definite and unequivocal. The fact that such a statement is not legally binding appears to be immaterial. It is obviously desirable that the persons affected should be able to test the legality of the action proposed and they are entitled to assume that the authority means what it says. Thus, though such a statement of intention may not strictly speaking be a legal act, it is desirable on policy grounds that it should be treated as such in the absence of provision for an action to obtain a declaration.

[24] *Ibid.* at 257. [25] Cases 7/56, 3–7/57, [1957] ECR 39. [26] *Ibid.* at 54.

In view of these earlier cases, it is hard to understand the judgment of the European Court in *United Kingdom v. Commission*,[27] a case concerning the awarding of contracts to companies to provide services to Third World countries under an EU aid programme.[28] Companies bidding for contracts were required to submit applications to the Commission, which drew up a short-list. The problem arose when the Commission announced that in doing this it would take into account the nationality of the company concerned. The idea was that contracts should, as far as possible, be shared out among companies in each Member State according to the money contributed to the aid programme by the Member State in question: it seems that a company could be excluded from the short-list if too many other companies from the same Member State had already been awarded contracts.

The Commission partly abandoned this policy, and then took a decision to apply it fully again. This decision was challenged by the United Kingdom,[29] which argued that it had legal effects, since it could lead to the exclusion of a company from the short-list. The Court, however, rejected this on the ground that the legal effects were produced, not by the decision itself, but by the drawing up of the short-lists.[30] The United Kingdom's challenge was therefore inadmissible.

This ruling seems unfortunate. Even if the Commission's policy could be challenged in the course of proceedings to annul the decision to exclude a particular company from the short-list, it would be difficult in practice to prove that a company had been excluded for this reason. Moreover, such proceedings would provide an effective remedy only if the selection process were frozen until the Court had given its ruling. This could result in a two-year delay in the provision of aid. It would have been far more sensible for the Court to have decided the question of principle as soon as the Commission announced its new policy.[31]

Another problem arises where the procedure laid down for taking a decision involves a number of steps, each step being itself a sort of preliminary decision. It might, for example, be required that, before the final decision is taken, the opinion of certain bodies should be obtained. The question is whether each of these preliminary decisions should be regarded as a reviewable act or whether they should be regarded as being subsumed in the final decision. From an analytical point of view, the correct answer to this question might depend on the exact requirements of the law. If it is provided merely

[27] Case 114/86, [1988] ECR 5289.

[28] The Second ACP–EEC Convention of Lomé, 1979.

[29] The United Kingdom was supported by the Netherlands; Italy intervened in support of the Commission.

[30] The Court sought to reinforce its conclusion by pointing out that the lists were not always settled entirely in conformity with the criteria adopted by the Commission. It is hard to see how this is relevant: even if the criteria were applied on only some occasions, they could still affect the rights of applicants.

[31] See the Opinion of Advocate General Lenz, who took the view that the proceedings were admissible and that the decision should be annulled. It is possible that the Court deliberately declared the application inadmissible so that it could avoid having to give a ruling on the substance. It is likely that the Commission's policy was supported by the majority of the Member States; so if the Court had declared it unlawful, it would have offended those States. On the other hand, if it had upheld it, this would have created a precedent which could have caused problems in cases where Member States were accused of discriminating on grounds of nationality.

that the opinion of a certain body must be *taken into account* by the authority making the final decision, it might seem that the preliminary decision does not affect anyone's legal position and is not, therefore, a reviewable act. If, on the other hand, the law states that the authority making the final decision cannot decide in a certain way unless some other body gives a favourable opinion, the preliminary decision will restrict the power of the body giving the final decision. In such a case the preliminary decision should be regarded as a reviewable act.

This, however, is not the view which has been taken by the Court. In the case of *Huber v. Commission*[32] the Court had to consider a problem concerned with the establishment of a Union official. Under the Staff Regulations, the opinion of the Establishment Board had first to be obtained. It was moreover provided that the decision-making authority, the Committee of Chairmen, could not establish an official unless the report of the Establishment Board was favourable. In *Huber v. Commission* the report was unfavourable and the Advocate General stated that, since the appointing authority was legally precluded from establishing an official if the report of the Establishment Board was unfavourable, this report was a reviewable act.[33] It took away the power to establish from the Committee of Chairmen and thus put an end to the official's chances of establishment. The Court, however, rejected this opinion and held that the report was not a reviewable act, on the ground that it was not separable from the final decision.[34]

This ruling is questionable from the legal point of view but it probably did little harm on the facts of the case since the Court made clear that the report could be challenged in the course of proceedings to annul the final decision. Moreover, the applicant would benefit in one respect, since the time limit for bringing the proceedings would begin only on the date of the final decision. The result of this and subsequent cases is that preliminary decisions of this kind are not reviewable in their own right.[35] To come within this rule, the preliminary decision must not affect the applicant's rights independently of the final decision. Its only legal consequences must be its effects on the final decision,[36] and it must be possible to challenge it in the course of a challenge to the final decision.[37]

One of the best known cases is *IBM v. Commission*,[38] another decision under EU competition law. The Commission decided to open proceedings against IBM for abuse of a dominant position and it wrote IBM a letter informing it of this and inviting it to put its case. A statement of objections, specifying what IBM was alleged to have done, was enclosed. This communication was a necessary preliminary to any decision

[32] Case 78/63, [1964] ECR 367. This was also a case under the Staff Regulations. The issue, however, was the same as under Art. 263 TFEU.

[33] *Ibid.* at 383. [34] *Ibid.* at 375–6.

[35] See also *Weighardt v. EAEC Commission*, Case 11/64, [1965] ECR 285 at 298; *Bossi v. Commission*, Case 346/87, [1989] ECR 303 at para. 23 of the judgment; *Marcopoulos v. European Court of Justice*, Cases T-32, 39/89, [1990] ECR II-281 at paras 20–23 of the judgment.

[36] In the *Noordwijks Cement Accoord* case (see n. 7 and accompanying text) the Commission argued that the decision in its letter was a mere preliminary decision, but the Court rejected this because the decision had immediate legal consequences which were independent of the final decision.

[37] *Deutsche Post and Germany v. Commission*, Case C-463/10 P, [2011] ECR I-9639 at paras 50–54, especially paras 53–54. [38] Case 60/81, [1981] ECR 2639.

against a defendant in such proceedings. IBM, however, objected to the proceedings on a number of grounds extrinsic to the substance of the case. In particular, it alleged that the statement of objections lacked clarity (it said that it had no clear idea what it was alleged to have done), that the decision to bring proceedings had not been taken by the Commissioners themselves but by an official, and that the proceedings were contrary to international law because the Commission was attempting to apply Union law extraterritorially. There were obviously great advantages in obtaining a decision on these points before the substance of the action was dealt with; so IBM brought an annulment action against the decision to commence proceedings and against the statement of objections.

The Court, however, held that these were not reviewable acts: they were mere preliminary decisions which could be challenged only in the course of a review of the final decision. The Court justified this on the ground that the consequences of the decision to bring proceedings were either wholly favourable to IBM (for example, it precluded proceedings by the national authorities) or merely paved the way for later steps in the procedure.[39]

This judgment may have been correct in terms of the previous case-law of the Court, but it had unfortunate consequences for IBM because it meant that IBM had to incur the great expense of fighting the case on the merits before it could raise its preliminary objections.[40]

Another case in which the Commission raised the 'preliminary decision' argument was *AKZO Chemie v. Commission*.[41] This was also a competition case, in which the Commission decided to show certain documents to the complainant. The company against which the proceedings had been brought, AKZO, claimed that the documents contained confidential information which it did not want business rivals to see; it therefore brought an annulment action against the Commission's decision to show the documents to the complainant. This time, the Court held the proceedings admissible: the decision directly affected AKZO's right to confidentiality, independently of

[39] On the other hand, a decision *not* to continue with an investigation initiated at the request of a complainant is a reviewable act since it is the final step in the procedure: it will not be followed by any other decision amenable to annulment proceedings by the complainant. See *SFEI v. Commission*, Case C-39/93P, [1994] ECR I-2681 (appeal from Case T-36/92, [1992] ECR II-2479), paras 27–28 of the judgment. See also *AKZO Chemie v. Commission*, Case 5/85, [1986] ECR 2585. On whether a notification under Art. 6 of Regulation 99/63 is a reviewable act, see *Guérin Automobiles v. Commission*, Case C-282/95, [1997] ECR I-1503 (appeal from Case T-186/94, [1995] ECR II-1753): the previous case-law is summarized by Advocate General Tesauro at paras 10–17 of his Opinion.

[40] For two other decisions along the same lines, see *Nashua Corporation v. Commission and Council*, Cases C-133, 150/87, [1990] ECR I-719 and *Gestetner Holdings v. Commission and Council*, Case C-156/87, [1990] ECR I-781, both of which concerned anti-dumping proceedings. The actions were brought to annul the refusal by the Commission to accept undertakings offered by the companies concerned: the Court held that this refusal was not a reviewable act, because the Commission plays only a preliminary role in the proceedings, the final decision being taken by the Council, which was not bound to adopt any proposal that might be put forward by the Commission. If the Council imposed an anti-dumping duty, the companies concerned could challenge the Commission's refusal in the context of a challenge to the regulation introducing the duty.

[41] Case 53/85, [1986] ECR 1965.

the final decision. Moreover, a right to challenge the decision on the documents in the course of a review of the final decision would not constitute an adequate remedy because by then the damage would already have been done.

The position was similar in *Italy v. Commission*,[42] a case on State aid to industry. Under Article 107 TFEU (then Article 92 EEC), such aid is deemed incompatible with the internal market (then the common market) if it distorts competition, though there are a number of exceptions. There is a distinction between aid that was already in existence when the EEC Treaty went into force and aid granted subsequently. The latter had to be notified to the Commission before it was put into effect. If, after a preliminary examination, the Commission considered that it appeared not to be compatible with the internal market, it set in motion a formal procedure to determine whether this was indeed the case. Once such a procedure had been begun, the Member State was not permitted to give the aid until a final decision had been taken. Aid granted contrary to this rule had to be recovered from the recipient, even if the final decision declared it legitimate.[43] In the case of existing aid, on the other hand, a decision by the Commission to open the procedure did not entail the suspension of the aid.

The case concerned aid which the Italian Government regarded as existing aid. The Commission, however, considered it to be new aid and took a decision to open the procedure. Since this affected the right of the recipient to receive the aid while the procedure was pending, the Court held, despite the protests of the Commission, that it was a reviewable act. It made clear, however, that the review would be limited to the question whether the aid was new, rather than existing: the question of its compatibility with the internal market would have to wait until the Commission had taken a final decision.

Finally, a word should be said about *NBV and NVB v. Commission*,[44] a case decided by the General Court (then the Court of First Instance). This was a competition case in which the applicants had applied to the Commission for negative clearance of an agreement.[45] This was granted. The decision which granted it stated that, although the agreement was inherently restrictive of competition, it was not contrary to Union law because it did not affect trade between Member States.[46] The applicants then brought proceedings to annul the part of the decision which said that the agreement was inherently restrictive of competition. Since they wanted to annul only that part, the question was whether *that part* had legal effects, and since it did not – any effects it might have had were negatived by the finding that the agreement did not affect trade between Member States – it was not a reviewable act. The application was therefore inadmissible.[47]

[42] Case C-47/91, [1992] ECR I-4145.

[43] *Fédération Nationale du Commerce Extérieur v. France*, Case C-354/90, [1991] ECR I-5505.

[44] Case T-138/89, [1992] ECR II-2181.

[45] Negative clearance is a decision that an agreement does not infringe Union law.

[46] Under Art. 81 [85] EC, agreements are within the scope of Union law only if there is a possibility that they will affect trade between Member States.

[47] For further cases on legal effect, see *Assicurazioni Generali v. Commission*, Case T-87/96, [1999] ECR II-203; *Coca-Cola v. Commission*, Cases T-125, 127/97, [2000] ECR II-1733; *Geotronics v. Commission*, Case

§4 VOID AND VOIDABLE ACTS

Up to now nothing has been said about the validity of acts. This is obviously important because it might be thought that an invalid act could have no legal effects. However, in Union law the general rule is that invalid acts are voidable, not void. In other words, they have legal effects unless and until the European Court sets them aside.[48] Since the question of jurisdiction is decided at the beginning of the hearing, it is clearly proper, in the case of a voidable act, to assume its validity for the purpose of deciding whether it has legal effects.

The rule that invalid acts are normally voidable and not void is important for another reason as well. It will be remembered that there is a short time period for bringing proceedings to quash an act. Once this has gone by, the act can no longer be annulled. An invalid act which is immune from review for this reason is not, however, the same as a valid act, since it may be subject to indirect challenge.[49] However, this right is limited; so for some purposes a voidable act which has not been annulled within the time limit has the same effect as a valid one.

The reason for the rule that invalid acts are merely voidable, and also for the short period within which a challenge may be brought, is said to be a desire to protect legal certainty. If an act of a public authority has the appearance of being valid, it is desirable that it should be treated as such unless and until it is annulled; and the period of uncertainty is restricted as much as possible by having a short time limit. However, if the act is quite patently and obviously invalid – for example, if it is made by an authority which could not possibly have had the power to make it – legal certainty is no longer in issue. In such a case the act may be regarded as being void: 'non-existent' in Union terminology.[50]

This has two important consequences. First, paradoxical as it may seem, the European Court will have no jurisdiction to quash it. Since it is non-existent, it can have no legal effects; therefore it is not a reviewable act. If proceedings are brought to annul such an 'act', the Court will declare them inadmissible: it will lack jurisdiction *ratione materiae*. This is quite logical, though it may seem strange to the Anglo-Saxon mind that an act which is vitiated by a significant but not obvious fault may, being merely voidable, be quashed by the Court; but that an 'act' which is patently invalid, being absolutely void, cannot be annulled. In practice, however, this is not as serious a drawback as it might appear since, if the Court gives a judgment stating that the case

C-395/95 P, [1997] ECR I-2271; *Ca'Pasta v. Commission*, Case C-359/98, [2000] ECR I-3977; *Reynolds Tobacco v. Commission*, Case 131/03 P, [2006] ECR I-7795. In this last case, the Court (Grand Chamber) held that a decision by the Commission to sue various tobacco companies in a US court (because they were allegedly involved in smuggling cigarettes into the European Union) was not a reviewable act because it did not produce legal effects. This is in line with *IBM v. Commission* (see n. 38).

[48] *Commission v. BASF*, Case C-137/92P, [1994] ECR I-2555 (appeal from Cases T-79/89 (etc.), [1992] ECR II-315) at para. 48 of the judgment of the European Court.

[49] See Chap. 14.

[50] *Commission v. BASF* (see n. 48), para. 49 of the judgment of the European Court.

is inadmissible because the 'act' is non-existent, the practical effect will be the same as a declaration of invalidity (and costs may even be granted to the applicant – who is technically the losing party – if he can show that the defendant was at fault in leading him to believe that the 'act' was in fact legally effective).[51]

The second consequence of the 'act' being non-existent is that the expiry of the time limit cannot give it even the shadow of validity. It is open to indirect challenge in all circumstances since, once it is shown to be non-existent, no court is entitled to take cognizance of it.[52] The passage of time can never confer validity on such an act.[53]

It is not easy to say precisely in what circumstances an act will be non-existent, but the European Court has said that the defects of the act must be particularly serious and obvious.[54] Normally, the invalidity of the act must be apparent on its face. In *Société des Usines à Tubes de la Sarre v. High Authority*[55] the European Court held that the absence of reasons renders an act non-existent. However, this has not been followed in later cases[56] and cannot now be regarded as good law. The two situations in which an act probably would be non-existent are where it is clearly and obviously *ultra vires*, for example if it deals with a subject matter completely outside the scope of the Treaties,[57] or if there are such major procedural defects in its enactment that it could not be said to have been adopted by the authority.

The latter situation was considered by the European Court in *Lemmerz-Werke v. High Authority*,[58] in which the Court had to decide whether certain letters constituted reviewable acts under the ECSC Treaty (now expired). The Commission (High Authority) had previously issued a general decision[59] (Decision 22/60) prescribing the form that decisions had to take.[60] One of the requirements was that the decision had to be signed by a member of the Commission on its behalf. The letters, which were signed merely by an official of the Commission, did not comply with these requirements and

[51] See *Lemmerz-Werke v. High Authority*, Cases 53–4/63, [1963] ECR 239 at 249. In this case the applicant had to pay a quarter of the costs and the defendant had to pay three-quarters. In the *Tubes de la Sarre* case (see n. 55), the applicant had to pay all the costs; but in *Commission v. BASF* (see n. 48), the General Court (Court of First Instance) ordered the defendant (Commission) to pay all the costs. On appeal, the European Court held that the decision was not non-existent, but it annulled it. It ordered the Commission to pay all the costs both in the General Court and on appeal.

[52] In *Commission v. BASF* (see n. 48), the General Court (Court of First Instance) said that a plea that an act is non-existent, being a matter of public interest, may be relied upon by the parties at any time during the proceedings and must be raised by the Court of its own motion (para. 68 of its judgment). This passage was quoted without comment by the European Court in the appeal (para. 16 of the judgment of the European Court).

[53] *Consorzio Cooperative d'Abruzzo v. Commission*, Case 15/85, [1987] ECR 1005 at para. 10 of the judgment.

[54] *Commission v. BASF* (see n. 48), para. 50 of the judgment of the European Court; *Consorzio Cooperative d'Abruzzo v. Commission* (see n. 53), para. 10 of the judgment. See further *Algera v. Common Assembly*, Cases 7/56, 3–7/57, [1957] ECR 39 at 60–1.

[55] Cases 1, 14/57, [1957] ECR 105.

[56] See, for example, *Nold v. High Authority*, Case 18/57, [1957] ECR 121, and the *Noordwijks Cement Accoord* case, Cases 8–11/66, [1967] ECR 75.

[57] *Commission v. France* (*Rediscount Rate*), Cases 6, 11/69, [1969] ECR 523.

[58] Cases 53, 54/63, [1963] ECR 239.

[59] Equivalent to a regulation under the EU Treaties.

[60] On this, see *Krupp v. Commission*, Cases 275/80, 24/81, [1981] ECR 2489; see also *National Carbonising v. Commission*, Cases 109, 114/75, [1977] ECR 381 at 388 *per* Advocate General Mayras.

the Court held that they did not constitute decisions and were not, therefore, reviewable. It gave its reasons as follows:[61]

> According to Article 14 [of the ECSC Treaty], decisions shall be taken by the High Authority, that is to say by its members sitting as a body. As such decisions are 'binding in their entirety' however, they must show that they are intended to have legal effects upon those to whom they are addressed.
>
> It follows from the natural meaning of the word that a decision marks the culmination of procedure within the High Authority, and is thus the definitive expression of its intentions.
>
> Finally, it is necessary for the legal protection of all those affected that they should be able to identify by its very form a decision which involves such serious legal consequences, in particular a compulsory time-limit for exercising the right of instituting proceedings against it. In particular, for a measure to amount to a decision, those to whom it is addressed must be enabled clearly to recognize that they are dealing with such a measure.
>
> It follows therefore from all these considerations that a decision must appear as a measure taken by the High Authority, acting as a body, intended to produce legal effects and constituting the culmination of a procedure within the High Authority, whereby the High Authority gives its final ruling in a form from which its nature can be identified.
>
> Any measure, therefore, which, in particular, does not appear to have been debated and adopted by the High Authority and authenticated by the signature of one of its members, cannot be regarded as a decision.

It is not easy to know to what extent the principles laid down in this passage are based on Decision 22/60 as distinct from the Treaty itself. The judgment was not expressly based on Decision 22/60, and the Court was careful to point out that the absence of a non-essential requirement of form will not prove fatal as long as the 'fundamental conditions underlying the concept of a decision within the meaning of the Treaty' are satisfied. This suggests that the judgment was, at least in part, independent of Decision 22/60. If this is so, it must now be regarded as a doubtful authority if it is to be understood as requiring the signature of a member of the Commission in all cases:[62] it would be unreasonable if the Commission could not delegate less important decision-making powers to its staff, and there have been a number of cases in which the Court has recognized that letters signed by Commission officials can constitute reviewable acts.[63]

[61] [1963] ECR at 248.

[62] The third para. of the quotation suggests that the Court may have intended the principle to apply only to decisions which involve 'serious legal consequences'.

[63] For instance, in the *Noordwijks Cement Accoord* case, Cases 8–11/66, [1967] ECR 75; see further Usher (1984) 9 ELRev. 261 at 262. It is interesting to note that in *Kohler v. Court of Auditors*, Cases 316/82, 40/83, [1984] ECR 641, a case under the Staff Regulations, the European Court held that an oral decision can be a reviewable act (see Usher, n. 63); and in *Air France v. Commission*, Case T-3/93, [1994] ECR II-121, the General Court (then the Court of First Instance) reached a similar conclusion in proceedings under Art. 263 TFEU (then Art. 173 EEC) (paras 55–60 of the judgment). In *AKZO Chemie v. Commission*, Case 5/85, [1986] ECR 2585, the Court held that measures of management or administration may be delegated by the Commission to a single Commissioner (paras 28–40 of the judgment); see also *VBVB v. Commission*, Cases 43, 63/82, [1984] ECR 19.

The leading case on this question is now *Commission v. BASF*.[64] This concerned a Commission decision which declared that a number of companies had infringed EU law by participating in a price-fixing arrangement. The companies, which had been fined by the Commission, brought proceedings before the General Court (Court of First Instance) to annul the decision. In the course of the hearing, the Commission admitted it was unable to produce an original copy of the decision, signed and duly authenticated as required by its Rules of Procedure. In fact, it seems likely that the Commissioners themselves did not agree on a precise text but only on the substance of the decision. In any event, the text had been significantly altered after the date on which it was supposed to have been adopted; moreover, the Dutch and Italian versions had been adopted by only a single Commissioner, who had acted after he had ceased to hold office.

The General Court began its judgment by stressing the importance of the rule that decisions cannot be altered after they have been adopted,[65] a rule it considered essential for legal certainty. It found that it was impossible to ascertain the precise content of the decision because the Commission had completely disregarded the authentication procedure laid down in its Rules of Procedure.[66] It was also impossible to know exactly when and by whom it had been adopted. For these reasons, the 'decision' was declared non-existent. The case went on appeal to the European Court, where it was held that the defects were not serious enough to render the decision non-existent; nevertheless, they were serious enough to render it voidable and it was duly annulled.

What is the position where the act is duly adopted, but deliberately not published? This occurred in the case of a Regulation dealing with airport security. Regulation 2320/2002,[67] adopted after the 9/11 attacks on targets in the United States, was intended to counter terrorist acts against passenger aircraft. An Annex concerned 'prohibited items' which passengers were not allowed to take on board. This was implemented by Commission Regulation 622/2003.[68] The effective provisions of this Regulation, which listed the prohibited items, were, however, contained in an Annex, which was deliberately kept secret.[69]

Could this secret legislation be invoked against passengers? The question arose in *Heinrich*, a case decided by a Grand Chamber of the European Court in 2009.[70] Since Article 297 TFEU (then Article 254 EC) requires all regulations to be published in the Official Journal, Advocate General Sharpston concluded that the unpublished

[64] Case C-137/92 P, [1994] ECR I-2555 (appeal from Cases T-79/89 (etc.), [1992] ECR II-315).

[65] This does not mean that they cannot be amended by a later decision: it just means that the text cannot be surreptitiously changed by an official (or even a Commissioner) without going though the procedure for adopting a new decision.

[66] Under Art. 12 of these Rules, the text of acts adopted by the Commission, authenticated by the signatures of the President and Secretary-General of the Commission, had to be annexed to the minutes recording their adoption.

[67] OJ 2002, L 355/1.

[68] OJ 2003, L 89/9, as amended by Commission Regulation 68/2004, OJ 2004, L 10/14.

[69] See Art. 3 of Regulation 622/2003.

[70] Case C-345/06, 10 March 2009. For a helpful Comment, see Bobek, (2009) 46 CMLRev. 2077.

Annex was non-existent. The Court, however, disagreed: it held that the Annex was valid but that it had no binding force in so far as it sought to impose obligations on individuals.[71]

§5 THE AUTHOR OF THE ACT

In addition to the requirement of legal effects, an act is reviewable only if it has been adopted by the appropriate Union institution or body. Article 263 TFEU permits review of the following:

1. legislative acts (which are adopted by the European Parliament and the Council acting together);
2. acts of the Council;
3. acts of the Commission;
4. acts of the European Central Bank;
5. acts of the European Parliament;
6. acts of the European Council;
7. acts of bodies, offices, or agencies of the Union.[72]

Prior to the Treaty on European Union (in force in 1993), only acts of the Council and Commission were subject to review. The European Court had, however, decided that acts of the European Parliament were also covered (provided they have legal effects *vis-à-vis* third parties)[73] and the relevant provision (then Article 230 EC, now Article 263 TFEU) was amended by the Treaty on European Union to give formal effect to this. The European Court has also held that acts of the Court of Auditors could be challenged,[74] but the Treaties were not amended to give formal effect to this.[75]

Review of acts adopted jointly by the European Parliament and the Council became possible for the first time as a result of the Treaty on European Union, which also provided for the creation of the European Central Bank. Review proceedings therefore had to be extended to apply to these two categories of acts as well.[76]

[71] Para. 71 of the judgment. On the position where the measure is published in some of the official languages of the Union but not in others, see *Skoma-Lux*, Case C-161/06, [2007] ECR I-10841.

[72] For the meaning of 'bodies, offices or agencies', see Chap. 1, § 8.

[73] *Parti Ecologiste – 'Les Verts' v. European Parliament*, Case 294/83, [1986] ECR 1339.

[74] *Maurissen v. Commission*, Cases 193 and 194/87, [1989] ECR 1045. The remarkable thing about this decision is that the Court did not discuss the issue, though the Advocate General did: see his Opinion at 1063–5.

[75] Since the coming into force of the Treaty of Lisbon, it might be argued that Art. 263 applies to the Court of Auditors on the basis that it is covered by the phrase 'bodies, offices or agencies of the Union', though this seems a little strange, since the Court of Auditors is an institution of the Union: Art. 13 TEU. The Court of Auditors is expressly mentioned (in the third para. of Art. 263) as entitled to *bring* proceedings.

[76] Art. 271 TFEU also allows acts of the Board of Governors and the Board of Directors of the European Investment Bank to be challenged in certain circumstances.

If the author of the act is not one of the bodies just listed, the act will not be reviewable. Thus, for example, an act of the representatives of the Governments of the Member States is not reviewable under Article 263 TFEU, even if the representatives were meeting in the Council.[77] The Court will not, however, look simply at the designation of the act: it will verify whether or not it was adopted by the body in question by considering its content and the circumstances in which it was adopted.[78]

What happens if a Union institution, the acts of which are reviewable, delegates power to some other body? Will the acts of this other body be reviewable? There will, of course, be no problem if the power is delegated to another Union institution whose acts are also reviewable. For example, if the Council delegates power to the Commission, the European Court will have jurisdiction to review any act adopted under the delegated power.[79]

What is the position where power is delegated to a body specially established by a Union institution? Until the Treaty of Lisbon came into force, this could have been a problem.[80] Now, however, the entity to which power is delegated, provided it is established under Union law, would be regarded as a body, office, or agency of the Union, and its acts would be reviewable under Article 263 TFEU, provided they were intended to produce legal effects *vis-à-vis* third parties.

Up to now it has been assumed that the act is a unilateral one, but what is the position if it is bilateral? For example, can an international agreement be a reviewable act? In *France v. Commission*,[81] the French Government brought proceedings under Article 263 TFEU (then Article 173 EEC) to challenge an international agreement on competition law concluded by the Commission with the United States. The Commission argued that an international agreement is not a reviewable act under Article 263, since it is bilateral. France argued that a bilateral act can be reviewable; alternatively, it maintained that the proceedings should be regarded as directed against the Commission decision authorizing the conclusion of the agreement. Advocate General Tesauro, after pointing out that an *obiter dictum* of the Court states that an international agreement can be a reviewable act,[82] said that it was of little importance whether the agreement itself or the decision to conclude it was the subject matter of the proceedings. The Court held that, since the agreement was intended to produce legal effects, 'the act whereby the Commission sought to conclude the Agreement' must be regarded as reviewable.[83] It ruled that France's action should be regarded as directed

[77] *European Parliament v. Council*, Cases C-181, 248/91, [1993] ECR I-3685. [78] *Ibid.*

[79] Nor will there be any problem if an institution, such as the Commission, delegates power to one of its members, since the decision will have been adopted in the name of the institution: *AKZO Chemie v. Commission*, Case 5/85, [1986] ECR 2585 at para. 36 of the judgment.

[80] But in *SNUPAT v. High Authority*, Cases 32, 33/58, [1959] ECR 127, a case decided under the ECSC Treaty (now expired), the Court held that legal acts adopted by an entity to which power is delegated by a Union institution are to be regarded for review purposes as acts of the delegating institution. In this case, the entity in question had been established under Belgian law.

[81] Case C-327/91, [1994] ECR I-3641.

[82] *Local Cost Standard* case, Opinion 1/75, [1975] ECR 1355 at 1361. [83] Para. 15 of the judgment.

against that act.[84] This could be seen as implicitly accepting that only a unilateral act can be reviewable.

FURTHER READING

Items are listed in date order, the most recent being at the end.

RH Lauwaars, *Lawfulness and Legal Force of Community Decisions* (1973) pp. 256–61.

Waelbroeck, 'La notion d'acte susceptible de recours dans la jurisprudence de la Cour de Justice des Communautés européennes' [1965] CDE 225.

[84] Para. 17 of the judgment.

12

LOCUS STANDI

§1 PRIVILEGED APPLICANTS

Under the second paragraph of Article 263 TFEU, the European Court has jurisdiction in actions for judicial review brought by a Member State, the European Parliament, the Council, or the Commission. Parties covered by this provision will be referred to as 'privileged applicants': they always have *locus standi* (standing) to challenge any reviewable act, even a decision addressed to someone else.[1] The exercise of this right is not conditional on the position taken, at the time the measure was adopted, by the institution or Member State bringing the action: even if they had some political or administrative means of challenging the act but did not avail themselves of it, they can still bring proceedings before the Court.[2]

Originally, the European Parliament had no *locus standi* under Article 263 (then Article 173 EEC). In the *Comitology* case,[3] the European Parliament claimed that it should benefit from the unlimited standing conferred on privileged applicants, but the Court rejected this. The Court also said that the European Parliament was not a 'legal person' within the meaning of what is now the fourth paragraph of Article 263 (then the second paragraph of Article 173 EEC), which meant that it could not bring any proceedings at all under Article 263. Subsequently, the Court had a change of heart and ruled in the *Chernobyl* case[4] that the European Parliament did have *locus standi* but on a limited basis: it could bring proceedings, but only to safeguard its prerogatives, and such proceedings could be founded only on submissions alleging the infringement of those prerogatives. This ruling, which might be regarded as a compromise between the provisions of the Treaties and the claims of the European Parliament,[5] was adopted by the Treaty on European Union. Subsequently, the Treaty of Nice put the European Parliament on a par with the other privileged applicants by abolishing the rule that it could bring proceedings only to protect its prerogatives, though the restricted form of

[1] See, for example, *Commission v. Council*, Case 45/86, [1987] ECR 1493 at para. 3 of the judgment; *United Kingdom v. Council*, Case 131/86, [1988] ECR 905 at para. 6 of the judgment; *Parliament v. Commission*, Case C-355/10, 5 September 2012 (Grand Chamber) at para. 37 of the judgment and cases cited therein.

[2] *Parliament v. Commission*, Case C-355/10, 5 September 2012 (Grand Chamber) at para. 38 of the judgment.

[3] *European Parliament v. Council*, Case 302/87, [1988] ECR 5615.

[4] *European Parliament v. Council*, Case C-70/88, [1990] ECR I-2041. This case actually concerned Art. 146 EAEC, but the two provisions were identical.

[5] On these aspects of the judgment, see Chap. 2, § 10.

standing originally conferred on the European Parliament still applies to certain other organs of the Union.

The position today is that the second paragraph of Article 263 covers the Member States, the European Parliament, the Council, and the Commission. They have full 'privileged' status. The third paragraph covers the Court of Auditors, the European Central Bank and the Committee of the Regions.[6] They have 'semi-privileged' status: they may bring proceedings only to protect their prerogatives.[7]

The justification for giving privileged applicants unlimited *locus standi* is that *every* Union act concerns them. This idea of universal interest is justified in the case of the three 'privileged' Union institutions by reason of their wide responsibilities; while the Member States, as the creators of the whole system, may equally be regarded as interested in everything it does. This explains why privileged status attaches only to the Parties to the Treaties – the Member States as such – and not to political sub-divisions of a Member State.[8] Scotland or Wales, for example, would not constitute privileged applicants, even if the subject matter of the measure under review was something within their jurisdiction.[9]

§2 NON-PRIVILEGED APPLICANTS: BASIC REQUIREMENTS

Applicants who do not fall into the 'privileged' or 'semi-privileged' categories are dealt with in the fourth paragraph[10] of Article 263 TFEU. This reads:

> Any natural or legal person may, under the conditions laid down in the first and second paragraphs, institute proceedings against an act addressed to that person or which is of direct and individual concern to them, and against a regulatory act which is of direct concern to them and does not entail implementing measures.

From this it will be seen that a non-privileged applicant can bring proceedings in three cases:

1. against an act addressed to him;
2. against an act of direct and individual concern to him; and

[6] The European Central Bank was brought in by the Treaty on European Union, the Court of Auditors by the Treaty of Amsterdam, and the Committee of the Regions by the Treaty of Lisbon.

[7] The case-law on what constituted an infringement of the Parliament's prerogatives will continue to apply to the Court of Auditors, the European Central Bank, and the Committee of the Regions. On this, see *European Parliament v. Council*, Case C-316/91, [1994] ECR I-625 at paras 10–19 of the judgment; *European Parliament v. Commission*, Case C-156/93, [1995] ECR I-2019 at paras 10–13 of the judgment.

[8] *Région Wallonne v. Commission*, Case C-95/97, [1997] ECR I-1787 at para. 6 of the judgment. See also *Regione Toscana v. Commission*, Case C-180/97, [1997] ECR I-5245.

[9] They could, however, constitute non-privileged applicants under the fourth paragraph of Art. 263: see *Regione Autonoma Friuli-Venezia v. Commission*, Case T-288/97, [1999] ECR II-1871.

[10] Prior to the Treaty on European Union, it was the second para.

3. against a regulatory act which is of direct concern to him and which does not entail implementing measures.

The logic of this is as follows. The first case concerns an act addressed to the applicant: this means that it must expressly state that he is the addressee. The reason for giving him standing in such a case is obvious. The second case concerns an act that is of direct and individual concern to the applicant. If he is both directly and individually concerned by an act, it might be said that he is a kind of *de facto* addressee: in essence, he is in the same situation as an addressee.[11]

The third case is new: it was made part of the Treaties by an amendment under the Treaty of Lisbon. It is intended to fill a gap that was thought to exist in the legal protection of the individual – a gap that would exist if there were no alternative means by which an applicant could obtain a ruling on the validity of a Union act.

§3 INDIVIDUAL CONCERN

The first question to consider is the meaning of individual concern. Over the years, this has given rise to a considerable body of case-law; unfortunately, however, the cases have not always been consistent. The best-known definition was given many years ago by the European Court in *Plaumann v. Commission*:[12]

> Persons other than those to whom a decision is addressed may only claim to be individually concerned if that decision affects them by reason of certain attributes which are peculiar to them or by reason of circumstances in which they are differentiated from all other persons and by virtue of these factors distinguishes them individually just as in the case of the person addressed. In the present case the applicant is affected by the disputed decision as an importer of clementines, that is to say, by reason of a commercial activity which may at any time be practised by any person and is not therefore such as to distinguish the applicant in relation to the contested decision as in the case of the addressee.

In this case, the act in question was a decision of the Commission addressed to the German Government refusing permission to lower the duty on imported clementines. The applicant was an importer of clementines. He was affected by the decision, but only as a member of a general class: any other importer of clementines would be affected in the same way. He was not, therefore, individually concerned and consequently lacked *locus standi* to bring the proceedings.

The test laid down in *Plaumann* has been refined and developed in later cases. Its most sophisticated version is the 'closed-category' test, under which an applicant can establish individual concern if he can show that he was affected by the measure as a

[11] See *Municipality of Differdange v. Commission*, Case 222/83, [1984] ECR 2889 at para. 9 of the judgment.

[12] Case 25/62, [1963] ECR 95 at 107.

member of a closed category.[13] A closed category is a class of persons the membership of which is fixed when the measure comes into force. It is distinguished from an open category, which is a class the membership of which is not fixed when the measure comes into force. Thus, if the measure applies only to persons who held an import licence during some period prior to the coming into force of the measure, the persons in question will be members of a closed category. If, on the other hand, it applies to anyone who wishes to import fruit in the future, it will apply to an open category of persons, since, when the measure comes into force, it will not be possible to know who will want to import fruit. This version gives greater precision than the original *Plaumann* test; however, though it has been applied by the Court in some cases, it has not been applied in others. This is one of the reasons why the case-law does not present a clear picture.

Another problem is that, until the Treaty of Lisbon came into force, there was an additional requirement for standing in the case of a non-privileged applicant: as well as proving that he was directly and individually concerned, he also had to show that the act in question was, in substance, a decision. This was because the Treaty provision granting the right to challenge an act of direct and individual concern to the applicant provided that the challenge could be brought only against 'a decision which, although in the form of a regulation or a decision addressed to another person, is of direct and individual concern' to the applicant. In applying this provision, the European Court always emphasized that it was not the form of the act that counted but its substance; in spite of this, however, it never treated an act in the form of a decision as anything other than a decision in substance. So, in practice, the requirement that the act had to be (in substance) a decision was applied only in cases in which it was in the form of a regulation or directive.

The test applied to determine whether an act was in substance a regulation (also known as a 'general act' or 'act of general application') was whether it applied to 'objectively determined situations' and produced 'legal effects for categories of persons regarded generally and in the abstract'.[14] The problem with this is that it is almost impossible to distinguish from the test for individual concern.[15] Thus, in *Confédération Nationale des Producteurs de Fruits et Légumes v. Commission*,[16] the Court said that the criterion for determining whether a measure was (in substance) a decision or a

[13] On who is affected by a measure, see *CIDA v. Commission*, Case 297/86, [1988] ECR 3531 (an unsuccessful candidate is affected by a decision appointing the successful candidates); see also *Apesco v. Commission*, Case 207/86, [1988] ECR 2151.

[14] See, for example, *Alusuisse v. Council and Commission*, Case 307/81, [1982] ECR 3463 at para. 9 of the judgment.

[15] In *Greek Canners v. Commission*, Case 250/81, [1982] ECR 3535 at 3544–5, Advocate General Slynn said that the two tests were 'analogous'. On the other hand, Advocate General Warner had said earlier, in the *Japanese Ball-Bearing* cases, Cases 113/77, etc. [1979] ECR 1185 at 1243, that the tests were separate and independent, a view repeated in *Calpak v. Commission*, Cases 789–90/79, [1980] ECR 1949 at 1970–1; see, further, Usher (1984) 9 ELRev. 263 at 264. For a detailed review of the Court's rulings on the subject, see the Opinion of Advocate General Jacobs in *Extramet Industrie v. Commission*, Case C-358/89, [1991] ECR I-2501 at 2515–19.

[16] Cases 16–17/62, [1962] ECR 471.

regulation was whether or not it was of individual concern to specific individuals. This ambiguity muddied the waters: when the Court denied standing to challenge an act that was not in the form of a decision, it sometimes did so on the ground that the act was not (in substance) a decision, and sometimes on the ground that there was no individual concern. The reason why it chose one of these grounds rather than the other has not always been easy to discern.

At the time, the distinction was not of great importance, since the result would have been the same whichever ground was chosen. Today, however, it makes a difference, since the fact that the act is not a decision is no longer a ground for denying standing. It is possible, however, that the cases in which, in the past, standing was denied on the ground that the act was not (in substance) a decision would today be decided – in the same way – on the ground that the applicant was not individually concerned.

Having made these preliminary points, we are now in a position to discuss the case-law. In doing so, a distinction will be introduced which has not been applied by the Court itself. This is between proceedings to annul acts of a quasi-judicial nature and proceedings to annul acts based purely on policy and discretion. The reason for making this distinction is that the Court has followed a markedly more liberal policy in cases falling into the former category. These cases are those in which the Union institution adopting the act is bound by clear rules, the final determination depends largely on questions of fact, and a semi-judicial procedure is followed. The main cases falling into this category concern competition, dumping, and State aid; they will be given separate treatment later, in § 4. First, we will deal with acts based on policy and discretion, many of which concern agriculture.

§3.1 SMALL GROUPS

The first situation to consider is where the measure is drafted in general terms but the persons affected, though members of a theoretically open category, in fact consist of a small and easily identifiable group. This situation arises quite frequently and the Court almost always denies *locus standi*. *KSH v. Council and Commission*[17] is an example. This concerned an act in the form of a regulation which applied to isoglucose, a form of sugar made from starch. The persons concerned were the producers of isoglucose. They were in theory a general class but in fact there were only very few of them. Their number was unlikely to increase, since heavy capital investment was necessary and some of the technology was protected by patents. It was probable that the relevant Union officials were aware of their identity. Nevertheless, the Court ruled that the producers had no *locus standi*. The reason given was that the measures were true regulations and not decisions in disguise.

[17] Case 101/76, [1977] ECR 797. See also *Buralux v. Council*, Case C-209/94 P, [1996] ECR I-615 at para. 29 of the judgment; *Campo Ebro v. Council*, Case T-472/93, [1995] ECR II-421 at paras 33–36 of the judgment (General Court (Court of First Instance)).

Spijker v. Commission[18] shows that the Court adopts the same approach where the act is in the form of a decision (addressed to someone other than the applicant). The case arose when the Commission adopted a decision addressed to the three Benelux countries, banning imports into those countries of brushes manufactured in China. The persons concerned – brush importers in the Benelux countries – were an open category, but the applicant was in fact the only person in the three countries who imported Chinese brushes. Moreover, there was evidence indicating that the decision was passed expressly to deal with him (he was suspected by the Dutch Government of having previously made a false declaration regarding the origin of the product). For these reasons, Advocate General Rozès considered that the applicant had *locus standi*; but the Court held that he was not individually concerned.

Binderer v. Commission[19] also appears rather unfair. Binderer, a firm of wine merchants, had asked the Commission whether Union law prohibited the use of certain German words to describe wines produced in Hungary and Yugoslavia. The Commission replied that it did not. Binderer then took steps to import the wines, but the Commission subsequently passed a regulation prohibiting the use of the terms in question. Binderer brought proceedings to annul the regulation but the Court held that Binderer lacked *locus standi*. It is true that Binderer was affected by the regulation only as a member of an open category – wine importers – but in view of the fact that Binderer had previously consulted the Commission and apparently relied on the Commission's reply, the Court might have found that Binderer had been sufficiently singled out to be given *locus standi*.[20]

§3.2 CLOSED CATEGORIES: DECISIONS

We will now consider cases in which the measure, though drafted in abstract terms, applies (in whole or in part) to a closed category of persons. We will first take acts in the form of a decision. *Toepfer v. Commission*,[21] decided in 1965, is an example. The applicants in this case were a group of German grain dealers who, on 1 October 1963, applied to the relevant German authority for import licences. There was a variable levy on imports and the applicable rate (in the circumstances of the case) was that prevailing when the application was made. On 1 October 1963 the rate was zero. The German authority realized, however, that because of a change in market conditions, the importers were likely to make large profits; so it decided to reject all applications until the levy rate had been increased. It therefore told the importers that their applications would be refused, and asked the Commission to confirm this decision. On the same day, the Commission raised the levy rate as from 2 October. On 3 October, the

[18] Case 231/82, [1983] ECR 2559. But for a more liberal decision, see *Control Data Belgium v. Commission*, Case 294/81, [1983] ECR 911.

[19] Case 147/83, [1985] ECR 257.

[20] For further authorities on the position of members of small groups, see *Antillean Rice Mills v. Council*, Case C-451/98, [2001] ECR I-8949 at para. 52 of the judgment and the cases cited therein.

[21] Cases 106–7/63, [1965] ECR 405.

Commission took a decision, addressed to Germany, confirming the ban with regard to applications made on 1–4 October, inclusive. The dealers brought proceedings to annul this decision.

The position here was that the category of persons affected by the decision was partly closed (those who had already applied) and partly open (those who would apply during the remainder of the period covered by the ban). The Court held that the dealers who had applied on 1 October were affected differently from the others because, if they had resubmitted their applications when the ban had expired, they would have had to pay the increased levy. From this the Court concluded that the 1 October applicants were individually concerned. This case is interesting because it shows that if a measure in the form of a decision affects an open category of persons, but contained within that open category there is a closed category the members of which are affected in a significantly different way, the latter will be individually concerned.

A similar result was reached in *Bock v. Commission*.[22] Bock applied to the relevant German authority for a permit to import Chinese mushrooms. The German authority told him that this would be refused as soon as authorization had been obtained from the Commission. The Commission then took a decision authorizing the refusal of import permits, including those for which applications had already been made. Bock asked the Court to annul only the provision applying the decision to such applications. Since the persons affected by this provision were a closed category, the Court held that Bock was individually concerned, though it was less clear than in the previous case that such persons were affected differently from later applicants.

The same point arose in *Piraiki-Patraiki v. Commission*,[23] decided in 1985. This concerned a Commission decision (based on Article 130 of the Greek Act of Accession) permitting France to impose restrictions on imports of cotton yarn from Greece. The decision was challenged by a number of Greek manufacturers, some of whom had entered into contracts to export cotton to France which had not been carried out when the decision was taken. The Court held that these exporters were individually concerned. It said that Article 130 imposed an obligation on the Commission to take the interests of such exporters into account and, since the Commission had not done so, it annulled the decision to the extent to which it applied to them.[24] If this obligation had not been imposed on the Commission, however, the fact that the decision applied to existing contracts would not have been enough to establish that the parties to those contracts were individually concerned.[25]

[22] Case 62/70, [1971] ECR 897. [23] Case 11/82, [1985] ECR 207.

[24] See, further, *Antillean Rice Mills v. Council*, Case C-451/98, [2001] ECR I-8949 at para. 57 of the judgment; *Antillean Rice Mills v. Commission*, Case C-390/95 P, [1999] ECR I-769 at para. 25 of the judgment.

[25] *Buralux v. Council*, Case C-209/94 P, [1996] ECR I-615 at paras 30–34 of the judgment.

§3.3 CLOSED CATEGORIES: REGULATIONS

We will now consider cases involving closed categories where the measure was in the form of a regulation. The earliest such case was *Compagnie Française Commerciale et Financière v. Commission*,[26] which was decided in 1970. Most of the provisions of the regulation in issue applied to open categories of persons, but one provision, which was of a transitional nature, only affected French exporters who had entered into contracts before 11 August 1969, had registered them with the French authorities by 18 August, but had not carried them out when the regulation was made on 22 August. Such persons were a closed category and their identity could have been ascertained by the Commission when it adopted the regulation. For this reason, Advocate General Roemer considered that the exporters had *locus standi* to challenge the provision in question, but the Court held that the measure, including the provision subject to challenge, was a true regulation, which could not be challenged by a private applicant.

The next case, *International Fruit Company v. Commission*,[27] concerned the procedure for importing apples from non-member States. Under this, importers had to apply in advance to the national authorities for an import licence. Each week, the national authorities would collate the applications made during the previous week and pass the details to the Commission. The Commission would then adopt a regulation laying down rules for deciding the applications in question. These measures concerned only a closed category of persons: those who had made applications during the preceding week. One such applicant brought annulment proceedings and the Court held that the relevant provision was in reality a bundle of decisions. The application was held admissible. In this case, the measure as a whole concerned a closed category, unlike in the previous case. It is also worth noting that once the Court had decided that the measure was really a decision, it affirmed individual concern without further discussion.

Four years later, in 1975, the Court decided *CAM v. Commission*,[28] in which the facts were almost indistinguishable from those in the *Compagnie Française* case. Advocate General Warner considered that the Court should follow its earlier ruling and therefore concluded that the application was inadmissible. The Court, however, decided to consider first the question of individual concern. It applied the closed-category test and, on finding this satisfied, held the application admissible. There was no express finding that the measure was a decision; the Court must have assumed that this followed from its finding on individual concern. The same approach was adopted in *Exportation des Sucres v. Commission*,[29] decided in 1977, and in *UNICME v. Council*,[30] decided in 1978. (In the latter case the regulation applied to an open category, and the application was consequently inadmissible, but the Court said that if direct and individual concern can be established, it is unnecessary to consider whether the measure is in substance a decision or a regulation.)[31]

26 Case 64/69, [1970] ECR 221.
27 Cases 41–4/70, [1971] ECR 411.
28 Case 100/74, [1975] ECR 1393.
29 Case 88/76, [1977] ECR 709.
30 Case 123/77, [1978] ECR 845.
31 See para. 7 of the judgment.

At this point it might have seemed that the law was settled: the *Compagnie Française* case could have been dismissed as an early aberration and one could have concluded that the closed-category test had triumphed. In succeeding cases, however, the Court swung back to the approach in the *Compagnie Française* case. The first such case was *Beauport v. Council and Commission*,[32] decided in 1979. Here, the entire regulation applied to a closed category: sugar refineries which had previously been allocated a sugar quota. Advocate General Warner considered that the measure was a disguised decision, but the Court ruled that it was a true regulation. Subject to a small number of exceptions, a similar approach was adopted throughout the 1980s: during this period, where the measure was in the form of a regulation and did not fall into the quasi-judicial category discussed later, the Court normally denied standing on the ground that the measure was a true regulation and did not concern itself with the question of individual concern.[33]

In the 1990s, a more liberal approach became the norm again. The first case was *Sofrimport v. Commission*,[34] which concerned Commission regulations imposing a temporary ban on imports of Chilean apples into the Union. The applicant was a French importer which had a consignment of apples in transit to Europe and had applied for an import licence on the day the ban was imposed. The Advocate General took the view that, on the basis of prior decisions of the Court,[35] the measures subject to challenge were true regulations; he therefore considered the application inadmissible. The Court, however, passed over the question whether the measures were true regulations and went straight to the question of individual concern. It applied the closed-category test and held that importers whose goods were in transit when the ban was adopted were sufficiently well defined in relation to other importers – by reason of the fact that a prior Council regulation required the Commission to take special account of their position – for them to be individually concerned,[36] though only to the extent

[32] Cases 103–9/78, [1979] ECR 17.

[33] See *Wagner v. Commission*, Case 162/78, [1979] ECR 3467; *Calpak v. Commission*, Cases 789–90/79, [1980] ECR 1949; *Moksel v. Commission*, Case 45/81, [1982] ECR 1129; *Deutz und Geldermann v. Council*, Case 26/86, [1987] ECR 941; *Asteris v. Commission*, Cases 97, 99, 193, 215/86, [1988] ECR 2181; *Abertal v. Commission*, Case C-213/91, [1993] ECR I-3265; *UCDV v. Commission*, Case C-244/88, [1989] ECR 3811; *Fédération Européenne de la Santé Animale v. Council*, Case 160/88R, [1988] ECR 4121; *Gibraltar v. Council*, Case C-298/89, [1993] ECR I-3605 (the last two cases concerned directives, but the Court's approach seemed to be the same). For further discussion, see Greaves, 'Locus Standi under Art. 173 EEC when Seeking Annulment of a Regulation' (1986) 11 ELRev. 119. There were a number of exceptions, but these involved special circumstances: see *Roquette v. Council*, Case 138/79, [1980] ECR 3333; *Agricola Commerciale Olio v. Commission* Case 232/81, [1984] ECR 3881; *Parti Ecologiste 'Les Verts' v. European Parliament*, Case 294/83, [1986] ECR 1339. See also *Salerno v. Commission and Council*, Cases 87, 130/77, 22/83, 9–10/84, [1985] ECR 2523 at paras 26–32 of the judgment (Case 22/83). This was a staff case concerning the re-employment of officials of an organization which was about to be dissolved.

[34] Case C-152/88, [1990] ECR I-2477.

[35] *Moksel v. Commission*, Case 45/81, [1982] ECR 1129; *UCDV v. Commission*, Case C-244/88, [1989] ECR 3811.

[36] If the regulation had not required the Commission to take special account of their position, they would not have been individually concerned: *Unifruit Hellas v. Commission*, Case T-489/93, [1994] ECR II-1201 at paras 24–28 of the judgment.

to which they challenged the measure with regard to its effect on products in transit. Sofrimport, the applicant in the case, fell into this category and the application was consequently admissible. The regulations were annulled in so far as they concerned products in transit.

This was followed by *Weddel v. Commission*,[37] a case on all fours with *International Fruit Company v. Commission*. It concerned importation of meat into the Union and the system was the same as that in *International Fruit*: importers lodged applications for permits and the Commission then adopted a regulation specifying to what extent they would be granted. On the facts of the case, a regulation adopted on 18 September 1987 applied to applications made on 1–10 September. Since it granted the applications only as to a very small percentage of the quantity requested, one applicant brought proceedings to annul it. The Court held the application admissible on the basis of the decision in *International Fruit*.[38]

In 1994, the Court decided *Codorniu v. Council*,[39] a decision of the Full Court that, until 2002, constituted the leading case. It concerned a Spanish company, Codorniu, which since 1924 had marketed one of its quality sparkling wines under the trademark '*Gran Cremant de Codorniu*'. However, in 1989 the Council passed a regulation which provided that the French word '*Crémant*', and its translations into other languages, could be used only for quality sparkling wines produced in France and Luxembourg. This would have meant that Codorniu would have been precluded from using the term. It therefore brought proceedings to annul the relevant provision of the regulation.

The Court ruled that the measure was a true regulation, but nevertheless held the application admissible on the ground that the applicant was individually concerned.[40] It might be thought that Codorniu, which was not the only Spanish producer who marketed quality sparkling wine under the designation '*Cremant*', might not have satisfied the *Plaumann* test. The Court held, however, that Codorniu was sufficiently singled out by virtue of the fact that, long before the regulation was adopted, it had registered a trade mark incorporating the word '*Cremant*'.

This case established that, if the applicant could demonstrate individual concern, it was not necessary to show that the measure was a true decision. It seemed to suggest, however, that individual concern did not automatically mean that the measure was a decision; rather that a non-privileged applicant could challenge a true regulation provided he could satisfy the *Plaumann* test.[41]

[37] Case C-354/87, [1990] ECR I-3847.

[38] The Court did not apply the abstract terminology test, but went straight to the question of direct and individual concern: see para. 18 of the judgment. See also *Emerald Meats v. Commission*, Cases C-106, 317/90, C-129/91, [1993] ECR I-209, in which the situation was similar and the admissibility of the proceedings was not contested.

[39] Case C-309/89, [1994] ECR I-1853.

[40] Paras 19–22 of the judgment.

[41] *Antillean Rice Mills v. Council*, Case C-451/98, [2001] ECR I-8949 at paras 43–46 of the judgment. See, further, Arnull, 'Private Applicants and the Action for Annulment since *Codorniu*' (2001) 38 CMLRev. 7 at 20–1 and the decisions of the General Court (Court of First Instance) cited therein.

Codorniu was the last case decided by the European Court before jurisdiction in actions by non-privileged parties was transferred to the General Court; since then, such cases have normally come before the European Court only on appeal. After *Codorniu*, there were many cases,[42] but no major developments until 2002, when the European Court decided *Unión de Pequeños Agricultores v. Council* (the *UPA* case),[43] a decision in which considerations of fundamental human rights played an important role.

It is generally accepted that, in order to comply with the requirements of human rights, the Union must provide everyone with an effective means of legal redress when his interests are affected by a Union provision alleged to be invalid.[44] Since, as we have seen, the standing of non-privileged applicants to bring annulment actions is severely restricted, this raises the question whether the other avenues of redress – proceedings in national courts followed by a reference to the European Court or actions in tort in the European Court – provide a satisfactory alternative.

In the *UPA* case, a Spanish organization representing small agricultural businesses challenged a Council regulation withdrawing subsidies and other benefits from olive oil producers. UPA admitted that the measure was a true regulation, and it was clear that the applicants lacked individual concern under the Court's previous case-law; nevertheless, UPA argued that, since it did not require implementation at national level, there was no way in which an action to challenge it could be brought before the national courts. It claimed that it would be denied a remedy if it was not allowed to bring a direct action.[45]

The General Court (then the Court of First Instance) held that UPA had no *locus standi*. UPA appealed to the European Court. The appeal was heard by a Full Court, thus indicating the Court's willingness to reconsider its case-law. In a lengthy and closely argued Opinion, Advocate General Jacobs concluded that the Court's existing case-law on *locus standi* was incompatible with the principle of effective judicial protection. He therefore proposed a radical revision of the law. He suggested that a non-privileged

[42] See, for example, *Greenpeace v. Council*, Case C-321/95 P, [1998] ECR I-1651 (affirming Case T-585/93, [1985] ECR II-2205); *CNPAAP v. Council*, Case C-87/95 P, [1996] ECR I-2003 (affirming Case T-116/94, [1995] ECR II-1); *Buralux v. Council*, Case C-209/94 P, [1996] ECR I-615 (affirming Case T-475/93, 17 May 1994, not published in the ECR); *Exporteurs in Levende Varkens v. Commission*, Cases T-481 and 484/93, [1995] ECR II-2941; *Terres Rouges v. Commission*, Case T-47/95, [1997] ECR II-481 at para. 43 of the judgment; *Antillean Rice Mills v. Commission*, Case C-390/95 P, [1999] ECR I-769 (affirming Cases T-480 and 483/93, [1995] ECR II-2305); *Antillean Rice Mills v. Council*, Case C-451/98, [2001] ECR I-8949. For cases in which the General Court (Court of First Instance) has specifically rejected the closed-category test, see *Roquette v. Council*, Case T-298/94, [1996] ECR II-1531; *Michailidis v. Commission*, Case T-100/94, [1998] ECR II-3115. See, further, Arnull, 'Private Applicants and the Action for Annulment since *Codorniu*' (2001) 38 CMLRev. 7 at 32 *et seq*.

[43] Case C-50/00 P, [2002] ECR I-6677.

[44] See Arts 6 and 13 of the European Convention on Human Rights and Art. 47 of the Charter of Fundamental Rights of the European Union.

[45] For earlier cases in which the Court alluded to the question of alternative remedies, see *Alusuisse v. Council and Commission*, Case 307/81, [1982] ECR 3463 at para. 13 of the judgment; *Spijker v. Commission*, Case 231/82, [1983] ECR 2559 at para. 11 of the judgment; *Allied Corporation v. Commission*, Cases 239, 275/82, [1984] ECR 1005 at para. 15 of the judgment; *Union Deutsche Lebensmittelwerke v. Commission*, Case 97/85, [1987] ECR 2265 at para. 12 of the judgment.

applicant should be regarded as individually concerned where, by reason of his particular circumstances, the measure has, or is liable to have, a substantial adverse effect on his interests.

The European Court rejected these arguments and upheld the interpretation of individual concern originally put forward in the *Plaumann* case. It accepted that individuals should have an effective means of redress, but said that this could be achieved through the national courts. If this was not possible, the fault lay with the Member States. It rejected the contention put forward by UPA that an applicant should be given standing to bring a direct action whenever he can demonstrate that a remedy does not exist in the national courts. This would require the European Court to decide difficult questions of national law, something on which it has no jurisdiction to give an authoritative ruling.

It is of interest that in 1995 the Court proposed to the Member States that the Treaty should be amended to increase the rights of non-privileged applicants.[46] The Member States did not, however, act on this suggestion. This is probably why the Court said in its judgment that if change is needed, it is for the Member States to effect it by amending the Treaty.[47]

The European Court did, however, clarify the law in one respect. It made clear that a non-privileged applicant could not challenge an act that was in substance a regulation.[48] It explained the decision in *Codorniu* by saying that a true regulation could, in certain circumstances, be of individual concern to certain non-privileged applicants and thus be 'in the nature of a decision in their regard'.[49] Thus, the fact that the measure was of individual concern to the applicant automatically meant that it was a decision. However, it was a decision only with regard to those who were individually concerned by it; otherwise, it retained its character as a regulation.[50]

[46] *Report of the Court of Justice on Certain Aspects of the Application of the Treaty on European Union*, Luxembourg, May 1995.

[47] Para. 47 of the judgment. [48] Para. 35 of the judgment. [49] Para. 36 of the judgment.

[50] After Advocate General Jacobs had given his Opinion in the *UPA* case but before the Court gave judgment, the General Court decided *Jégo-Quéré v. Commission*, Case T-177/01, [2002] ECR II-2365. This was a challenge against a Commission regulation prohibiting the use in specified waters of fishing nets with mesh below a certain size. The applicant was a fishing company that regularly fished in the waters in question using nets with a mesh below the minimum size. The Commission claimed that it had no standing. The General Court accepted that this was so under the existing case-law. The applicant, however, argued that if it was denied standing, it would be left without a remedy. Drawing inspiration from the Opinion of Advocate General Jacobs in the *UPA* case, the Court considered whether an action in the national courts would afford an adequate remedy. The only way this could be done appears to have been for the applicant deliberately to break the law and, when prosecuted, to plead the invalidity of the regulation as a defence. The Court considered that it was not acceptable that a person should have to break the law in order to obtain a remedy. It also regarded an action in tort as unsatisfactory. For these reasons, it held that an applicant should be regarded as having standing if the measure affects his legal position in a manner that is both definite and immediate, by restricting his rights or imposing obligations on him, a rule similar to that put forward by Advocate General Jacobs in the *UPA* case. It therefore held the application admissible. When the case went on appeal, the European Court reversed this decision: it said that the General Court's interpretation had the effect of 'removing all meaning' from the requirement of individual concern: Case C-263/02 P, [2004] ECR I-3425 at para. 28 of the judgment.

The *Codorniu* and *UPA* cases brought about an important change in the law. They established that the nature of the act subject to challenge – whether it is a (true) regulation or a decision in disguise – was no longer relevant for determining the standing of an applicant. As long as the applicant could show individual concern, it no longer mattered whether the act was a decision or regulation. Thus, when the Treaty of Lisbon abolished the requirement that the act subject to challenge had to be a decision (even if disguised as a regulation), it was doing no more than bringing the wording of Article 263 TFEU into line with the Court's case-law. *Any* reviewable act can now be challenged, provided the applicant is individually (and directly) concerned by it.

§4 QUASI-JUDICIAL DETERMINATIONS

We now consider individual concern with regard to quasi-judicial determinations. This concept is not recognized by the European Court; nevertheless, special considerations apply in such cases. An attempt was made earlier to explain what was meant by a 'quasi-judicial' determination. The core idea is that the determination is to a large extent made on the basis of objective considerations and is the culmination of a procedure which has judicial features. Such determinations are predominantly decisions of fact and law, rather than discretionary decisions. There are, moreover, persons who could be regarded as being, in some sense, parties to the proceedings. Once one acknowledges that someone is a 'party' to the proceedings which resulted in the determination, it is easy to conclude that he should have *locus standi* to challenge it.

§4.1 COMPETITION PROCEEDINGS

The first example is a decision whether a firm has violated Union competition law. The Treaties prohibit certain activities and the Commission has the task of ensuring compliance. The essence of the procedure is that the Commission first conducts an investigation and then holds a hearing at which the firm whose conduct is under consideration is invited to appear and present its case. Such a firm could therefore be regarded as the defendant. The determination takes the form of a decision addressed to it. The decision may exonerate the defendant or find that it has violated the law. In the latter case a fine may be imposed. Since the decision is addressed to the defendant, it can clearly challenge it under Article 263 TFEU.

What about the victim of the alleged malpractice? Union law allows anyone with a 'legitimate interest' to lodge a complaint with the Commission. Such a complainant is granted various procedural rights and may be entitled to participate in the hearing. Can a complainant bring proceedings under Article 263 to challenge the final determination if it exonerates the defendant?

This question came before the Court in 1977 in *Metro v. Commission*.[51] Metro was a self-service wholesaler dealing in electronic goods, which complained that another firm, SABA, was acting in violation of EU law because its conditions of sale, which applied to all its dealers, had the effect of precluding self-service wholesalers from distributing its products. The Commission investigated this complaint and took a decision exonerating SABA.

Metro wished to have this decision annulled. Since it was not the addressee of the decision (though it had been informed of it), Metro had to show that it was directly and individually concerned. One might have thought that it was not individually concerned since it was affected by the decision simply as a self-service wholesaler in electronic goods, a commercial activity which – in the words of the judgment in the *Plaumann* case – may at any time be practised by any person. The Court, however, held the proceedings admissible. It pointed out that the decision had been adopted as a result of Metro's complaint and said that it was in the interests of a 'satisfactory administration of justice' that anyone entitled to make a complaint should be allowed to institute proceedings against a decision dismissing the complaint. This case therefore establishes that in competition proceedings a complainant is regarded as individually concerned by the final decision even if it is affected by it in the same way as other members of an open category.[52]

§4.2 ANTI-DUMPING PROCEEDINGS

The second example concerns measures adopted in the course of anti-dumping proceedings. (Dumping is a form of unfair competition in international trade, usually involving selling in different markets at different prices, particularly exporting at a lower price than that applicable on the home market.) A special difficulty arises here because the normal remedy for dumping is an anti-dumping duty, which under Union law has to be imposed by regulation. Nevertheless, even prior to its ruling in *Codorniu*, the European Court was willing to allow non-privileged applicants to challenge such measures if they could establish individual concern.[53]

The procedure in anti-dumping cases is analogous to that in competition cases. The status of complainant is fully recognized and proceedings are not normally initiated without a complaint. The role of defendant is more ambiguous because anti-dumping duties are usually imposed on all goods of the relevant kind from the country in question. This means that all exporters of such goods in the foreign country, as well as importers in the

[51] Case 26/76, [1977] ECR 1875.

[52] See further *GEMA v. Commission*, Case 125/78, [1979] ECR 3173; *Demo-Studio Schmidt v. Commission*, Case 210/81, [1983] ECR 3045 at paras 10–16 of the judgment; *Metro v. Commission (No. 2)*, Case 75/84, [1986] ECR 3021; *BAT and Reynolds v. Commission*, Cases 142 and 156/84, [1987] ECR 4487 at paras 11–13 of the judgment and at 4546–9 of Advocate General Mancini's Opinion; *SFEI v. Commission*, Case C-39/93P, [1994] ECR I-2681; *Lord Bethell v. Commission*, Case 246/81, [1982] ECR 2277.

[53] *Alusuisse v. Commission*, Case 307/81, [1982] ECR 3463 at para. 9 of the judgment; *Allied Corporation v. Commission*, Cases 239, 275/82 [1984] ECR 1005 at para. 11 of the judgment (Full Court).

Union, could be regarded as having an interest in the proceedings. Public notice is given of the initiation of proceedings, and all exporters and importers known to be concerned are informed individually by the Commission. They have the right to make representations in writing and are normally entitled to make oral representations as well. The Commission usually invites them to give evidence and Commission inspectors may visit their plants. Firms that participate in the procedure in this way could be regarded as parties.

The first judgment to consider is that in the *Japanese Ball-Bearing* cases.[54] This concerned a challenge to a Council regulation imposing an anti-dumping duty on all ball-bearings manufactured in Japan. The duty was, however, suspended for as long as the four major producers (who were named in the regulation) carried out an undertaking to raise their prices. Did the four producers have *locus standi* to challenge the regulation? According to the normal principle, they were not individually concerned because they were affected by the regulation only as exporters of ball-bearings from Japan, an activity that could be practised by anyone. The Court nevertheless held that they had *locus standi* since they were named in the regulation, the purpose of which was to ensure that they carried out their undertakings.

The *Japanese Ball-Bearing* cases were concerned with a rather unusual situation, but *Allied Corporation v. Commission*[55] clarified and broadened the law. It established that exporters could challenge a regulation laying down an anti-dumping duty either if they were identified in the measure *or* if they were 'concerned by the preliminary investigations',[56] i.e., took part in the Commission investigation.[57]

Importers were originally in a less favourable position (possibly because they are normally the persons who pay the import duty and therefore have a remedy in the national courts): for a long time they were not accorded *locus standi* unless they were named in the regulation, the Commission used their retail prices as a basis for constructing the export price,[58] or they were associated with exporters on whose products duties were imposed (though possibly only if the export price had been calculated on the basis of their selling prices in the Union).[59] In their case, participation in the investigation was not sufficient.[60] In the 1990s, the Court seemed to be moving towards

[54] *NTN v. Council*, Case 113/77, [1979] ECR 1185; *ISO v. Council*, Case 118/77, [1979] ECR 1277; *Nippon Seiko v. Council and Commission*, Case 119/77, [1979] ECR 1303; *Koyo Seiko v. Council and Commission*, Case 120/77, [1979] ECR 1337; and *Nachi Fujikoshi v. Council*, Case 121/77, [1979] ECR 1363.

[55] Cases 239, 275/82, [1984] ECR 1005. See also *Toyo v. Council*, Case 240/84, [1987] ECR 1809 (another case involving Japanese ball-bearings).

[56] Para. 12 of the judgment.

[57] It is interesting that in the *Allied Corporation* case the Commission informed the Court that it was in favour of the exporters' actions being held admissible because otherwise Union exporters to the United States might not be allowed to challenge anti-dumping measures against their goods: see para. 9 of the judgment.

[58] Para. 15 of the judgment in the *Allied Corporation* case; *Sermes v. Commission*, Case 279/86, [1987] ECR 3109; *Frimodt Pedersen v. Commission*, Case 301/86, [1987] ECR 3123; *Nachi Europe*, Case C-239/99, [2001] ECR I-1197 at para. 21 of the judgment. For a fuller discussion of the law, see the Opinion of Advocate General Jacobs in *Extramet Industrie v. Commission*, Case C-358/89, [1991] ECR I-2501.

[59] *Canon v. Council*, Case 300/85, [1988] ECR 5731 at para. 8 of the judgment.

[60] *Nuova Ceam v. Commission*, Case 205/87, [1987] ECR 4427. See also *Alusuisse v. Council and Commission*, Case 307/81, [1982] ECR 3463 at paras 12 and 13 of the judgment.

a more liberal approach,[61] though it now seems that, outside the situations just mentioned, importers will be granted standing only in exceptional cases.[62]

Complainants have been treated more generously[63] (like exporters, they have no alternative remedies). *Timex v. Council and Commission*[64] concerned a regulation imposing an anti-dumping duty on mechanical watches from the Soviet Union. The proceedings had been initiated after a complaint by a British trade association on behalf of Timex, the only British manufacturer. Timex participated in the investigation and the duty was fixed in the light of the effect of the dumping on Timex, which was named in the preamble to the regulation. Timex, however, thought that the duty was too low and brought proceedings to annul the regulation. It was argued by the defendants that Timex was not individually concerned because it was affected only as a manufacturer of mechanical watches, an activity that may be carried on by anyone. However, the Court held that Timex had *locus standi*: the regulation was 'a decision which is of direct and individual concern to Timex'.[65]

§4.3 STATE AID

State aid which distorts competition is (generally speaking) contrary to Union law and the Treaties lay down a procedure for determining when a violation has occurred. This involves an investigation by the Commission, followed by a decision addressed to the Member State alleged to have granted the aid. That Member State can clearly challenge the decision under Article 263,[66] but what are the rights of a complainant? The status of complainant is not given formal recognition in the same way as in the case of competition and anti-dumping proceedings, but in practice competitors of the firms receiving the aid are allowed to participate in the investigations.

[61] *Extramet Industrie v. Commission*, Case C-358/89, [1991] ECR I-2501 (a decision of the Full Court). The Opinion of Advocate General Jacobs in this case puts the issues with great clarity. Unfortunately, the Court, though it followed his conclusions, was not prepared to accept his invitation to reassess its previous case-law. Further evidence of flexibility is to be found in the earlier case of *Nashua Corporation v. Commission and Council*, Cases C-133, 150/87, [1990] ECR I-719 at paras 12–21 of the judgment (also a decision of the Full Court). For a discussion of the whole question following the *Extramet* case, see Arnull, 'Challenging EC Anti-Dumping Regulations: The Problem of Admissibility' [1992] 2 ECLR 73.

[62] See *British Shoe Corporation Footwear Supplies v. Council*, Case T-598/97, [2002] ECR II-1155.

[63] *FEDIOL v. Commission*, Case 191/82, [1983] ECR 2913, establishes that a complainant has a remedy where the Commission fails to initiate proceedings.

[64] Case 264/82, [1985] ECR 849.

[65] Para. 16 of the judgment. In para. 12, however, the Court said that anti-dumping regulations are 'legislative in nature and scope, inasmuch as they apply to traders in general'.

[66] But firms receiving the aid and bodies involved in its distribution cannot, in the absence of special circumstances, challenge the decision: *DEFI v. Commission*, Case 282/85, [1986] ECR 2469 (where the statutory body administering the aid was held not to have *locus standi*); *Van der Kooy v. Commission*, Cases 67, 68, 70/85, [1988] ECR 219 (where it was held that individual recipients had no *locus standi*, but an organization representing them could challenge the decision since it had played a part in the proceedings and other special circumstances applied).

In *COFAZ v. Commission*,[67] COFAZ and three other French fertilizer producers complained through their trade association to the Commission that their Dutch competitors were receiving aid from the Dutch Government. The Commission initiated the procedure under EU law, and the French firms played some part in the proceedings. Eventually, the Commission concluded that no aid was involved and it took a decision, addressed to the Dutch Government, terminating the proceedings. COFAZ challenged this decision, but the Commission argued that it was not individually concerned because it was affected only in its capacity as a fertilizer producer. The Court, however, held the application admissible. It said that firms playing a part in the procedure comparable to that of a complainant should have *locus standi*, provided their position in the market was significantly affected by the aid. Subsequent cases have established that complainants also have standing where the decision was taken by the Commission without commencing the Treaty procedure.[68]

§4.4 CONCLUSIONS

The cases discussed show that where a quasi-judicial determination is challenged, the Court has adopted a more liberal attitude than in the case of a discretionary act. Not only did it accept ten years earlier that a non-privileged applicant could challenge a true regulation, but complainants and other persons who have played a part in the proceedings have been granted standing even though they have been affected by the measure only as members of an open category.

§5 THE TREATY OF LISBON

We are now in a position to consider the changes introduced by the Treaty of Lisbon. The first change was the abolition of the requirement that the act challenged must be a decision. As already explained, this was done in order to bring the words of the Treaty into line with the case-law of the European Court.

The second change was to give a non-privileged applicant the right to challenge 'a regulatory act which is of direct concern to him and which does not entail implementing measures'. The reason for this was that the requirement of individual concern, as interpreted by the European Court, seemed to preclude a direct challenge to Union

[67] Case 169/84, [1986] ECR 391. See also *ASPEC v. Commission*, Case T-435/93, [1995] ECR II-1281; *Ducros v. Commission*, Case T-149/95, [1997] ECR II-2031; *Gestevisión Telecinco v. Commission*, Case T-95/96, [1998] ECR II-3407.

[68] *Cook v. Commission*, Case C-198/91, [1993] ECR I-2487; *Matra v. Commission*, Case C-225/91, [1993] ECR I-3203; *CIRFS v. Commission*, Case C-313/90, [1993] ECR I-1125; *Spain v. Lenzing*, Case C-525/04 P, [2007] ECR I-9947 at paras 28–42 of the judgment. For further cases and a detailed discussion of standing in State aid cases, see Winter, 'The Rights of Complainants in State Aid Cases: Judicial Review of Commission Decisions Adopted under Article 88 (ex 93) EC' (1999) 36 CMLRev. 521. See also *Commission v. Kronoply and Kronotex*, Case C-83/09 P, [2011] ECR I-4441 (Grand Chamber).

acts even where there was no other remedy open to the applicant. This was the problem highlighted in the *UPA* case: if the applicant is not individually concerned by the Union act, and the act does not have to be implemented by a measure which he can challenge, there may be no way in which he can obtain a ruling from the Court on the validity of the act. It was to avoid this that the Treaty of Lisbon amended the fourth paragraph of Article 263 TFEU to allow a direct challenge to a regulatory act which does not entail implementing measures.

This new right will be discussed later; first, however, the present position regarding individual concern must be considered.

§5.1 INDIVIDUAL CONCERN AFTER LISBON

Individual concern is still an essential requirement unless the act subject to challenge is addressed to the applicant, or is a regulatory act that does not entail implementing measures. Except in these cases, the case-law discussed previously remains applicable. It is suggested, however, that the Court should regard the new regime introduced by the Treaty of Lisbon as an opportunity for ironing out the inconsistencies in the case-law which were revealed by the discussion in § 3. In view of the importance of safeguarding the judicial protection of the individual, a liberal approach should be adopted. So, it is proposed that an applicant should have standing:

- if he satisfies the closed-category test;
- if he played a part in the procedure leading up to the adoption of the act;[69]
- if he was in contact with the author of the act with regard to it before it was adopted; [70]
- if his situation was taken into account by the author of the act when it adopted it;[71] or
- if there are other circumstances that make it desirable to grant him standing.[72]

If this were done, the law would be both clearer and more in keeping with the requirements of a fair system of judicial review.

§5.2 REGULATORY ACTS THAT DO NOT ENTAIL IMPLEMENTING MEASURES

The words in the fourth paragraph of Article 263 TFEU giving non-privileged applicants the right to bring proceedings 'against a regulatory act which is of direct

[69] As in the quasi-judicial cases discussed earlier, in § 4.

[70] Contrary to what was decided in the *Binderer* case, discussed previously, in § 3.1.

[71] Contrary to what was decided in the *Spijker* case, discussed earlier, in § 3.1.

[72] Compare *Parti Ecologiste 'Les Verts' v. European Parliament*, Case 294/83, [1986] ECR 1339; *Agricola Commerciale Olio v. Commission*, Case 232/81, [1984] ECR 3881.

concern to them and does not entail implementing measures' were taken directly from the equivalent provision in the ill-fated Constitution for Europe. There are two problems.

The first is the meaning of 'regulatory act'. This is not a term mentioned anywhere else in the Treaties, nor was it mentioned anywhere else in the Constitution. However, the Constitution, like the Treaties, draws a distinction between legislative and non-legislative acts, and those involved in drawing up the Constitution seem to have assumed that regulatory acts were non-legislative acts of general application.[73]

This was the view taken in the first case on the matter, *Inuit Tapiriit Kanatami v. Parliament and Council*.[74] The case came initially before the General Court,[75] which held that a 'regulatory act' for the purpose of the fourth paragraph of Article 263 TFEU is an act of general application other than a legislative act. In the *Inuit* case, the act subject to challenge was a regulation of the Parliament and Council adopted, prior to the coming into force of the Treaty of Lisbon, under a procedure (co-decision) equivalent to the ordinary legislative procedure. The General Court held that, for this purpose, 'legislative act' is to be defined on the basis of the procedure under which it is adopted, not on a functional basis. It concluded, therefore, that since the act subject to challenge had been adopted under the ordinary legislative procedure, it constituted a legislative act, not a regulatory act; so it could be challenged only if the applicants proved direct and individual concern. It then proceeded to apply the *Plaumann* test and held that the applicants were not individually concerned. So the application was inadmissible. On appeal, this ruling was upheld by the European Court.

It will be seen from this case that two classes of acts are outside the scope of the new right of review: legislative acts (see Chapter 4, § 1.2) and acts which are not of 'general application'. In these cases, the applicant must either be the addressee of the act (not possible in the case of a legislative act) or directly and individually concerned by it.

The second case was another decision of the General Court, *Microban v. Commission*,[76] in which there does not seem to have been an appeal. In that case, the act subject to challenge was a Commission decision (addressed to the Member States) refusing to add a certain product to the list of additives which may be used in the manufacture of articles intended to come into contact with foodstuffs. Since the decision had been adopted under implementing powers delegated to the Commission, it did not constitute a 'legislative act' as defined earlier.[77]

[73] See Doc. CIG 4/04 of 6 October 2003, pp. 428–9 (Legal Experts Group at the Inter-Governmental Conference that adopted the Constitution); see also Secretariat of the European Convention, Final report of the discussion circle on the Court of Justice of 25 March 2003, CONV 636/03, para. 22, and Cover note from the Praesidium to the Convention of 12 May 2003, CONV 734/03, p. 20. Commission regulations would be the most common example. They are often adopted to implement legislative acts.

[74] Case C-583/11 P, 3 October 2013 (Grand Chamber).

[75] Case T-18/10, [2011] ECR II-5599 (order of 6 September 2011). For proceedings in the General Court on the substance of the claim (which did not deal with admissibility), see *Inuit Tapiriit Kanatami*, Case T-526/10, 25 April 2013.

[76] Case T-262/10, [2011] ECR II-7697 (25 October 2011).

[77] Para. 22 of the judgment.

The next question was whether it was of general application, the second requirement which, according to the *Inuit* case, has to be satisfied in order for it to constitute a 'regulatory act'. Here the General Court applied the test previously used to decide whether the challenged act was in substance a decision (an individual act).[78] This was discussed in § 3. It will be remembered that, under it, an act is regarded as being of general application if it applies to objectively determined situations and produces legal effects for categories of persons regarded generally and in the abstract. However, the function of the test is now reversed: previously, the applicant had to show that the act was *not* of general application; now he must show that it *is*.

In the *Microban* case, the act subject to challenge satisfied this test; so the Court held that it constituted a regulatory act. Since it did not require implementing measures, the applicants did not have to prove that they were individually concerned.

As regards direct concern, the General Court held that the concept of direct concern, as applicable in the amendments introduced by the Treaty of Lisbon, could not 'in any event' be subject to a more restrictive interpretation than the notion of direct concern as applied in the pre-Lisbon case-law. This test was satisfied; so the application was admissible. The Court went on to annul the decision.

It was said previously (in § 3) that the test for deciding whether an act is of general application is similar to that for deciding individual concern: if no one is individually concerned by it, it will be a general act. This means that if it is not of general application, it will almost certainly be of individual concern to *someone*. However, if the applicant is not such a person, he will not be able to challenge it.

So far, the Court has not given consideration to the meaning of 'implementing measure'. However, in view of the thinking behind the new provision, it should not be regarded as covering measures which cannot be challenged, either in the national courts or in the European Court. If the measure cannot be challenged, it will not provide an alternative means of obtaining a ruling on the validity of the original act.

§6 DIRECT CONCERN

A non-privileged applicant must establish direct concern in all cases unless he is the addressee of the act. This applies even with regard to regulatory acts that do not entail implementing measures. As might be expected, direct concern raises issues of cause and effect. The main situation in which it is important is where the effect of the decision on the applicant depends on the discretion of another person.[79] Thus if a Union

[78] Para. 23 of the judgment.

[79] Problems can also arise where the contested act is one giving aid to a competitor (*Eridania v. Commission*, Cases 10,18/68, [1969] ECR 459) or refusing to prevent a Member State from doing so (*COFAZ v. Commission*, Case 169/84, [1986] ECR 391). This in turn raises the question whether there must be an effect on the applicant's *rights*, or whether an effect on his *interests* is sufficient. Union law has not yet come to terms with this problem.

institution grants a discretionary power to another authority (for example, a Member State), the mere fact that the power would, if exercised, affect the applicant does not mean that he has *locus standi* to challenge the decision granting it: the interposition of an autonomous will between the decision and its effect on the applicant means that he is not *directly* concerned. Moreover, since a negative act is treated in the same way as a positive act for the purpose of jurisdiction, a decision by a Union institution refusing to grant a discretionary power cannot be challenged by those who would have been affected by its exercise, had it been granted.

The best case to illustrate these principles is *Alcan v. Commission*.[80] The facts in the *Alcan* case were that, under the relevant provisions, Member States could apply to the Commission for a quota of unwrought aluminium imports at a reduced rate of duty. In October 1968, the Belgian Government made a request for such a quota for the year 1968 and a request for an increased quota was made in December 1968. In May 1969, the Commission took a decision addressed to the Belgian Government rejecting the request. The question was whether the applicants, Alcan and two other aluminium refining companies in Belgium, could challenge this decision.

Two points about the situation should be noted: first, that if the quota had been granted, the Belgian Government would not have been obliged to allow the quantity of unwrought aluminium in question to be imported at the reduced rate. In other words, the Commission would merely have given an authorization: the Belgian Government would have had a discretion whether or not to make use of it. Secondly, since the Commission's decision was not made until May 1969, and the quota was for the year 1968, the effect of the authorization (if it had been given by the Commission and put into effect by the Belgian Government) would merely have been that companies which had imported aluminium in 1968 would have been able to claim a refund on duty paid by them. In view of this latter fact, Advocate General Gand considered that the applicants were individually concerned; but both he and the Court took the view that they were not directly concerned because, even if the authorization had been granted, the Belgian Government might have decided not to use it. It was probably unlikely, in the circumstances, that this would have happened – why would the Belgian Government have made the request if it had not intended making use of it? – but the possibility was enough to eliminate *locus standi*.

If, however, the power is not discretionary, or if it is exercised first and confirmed afterwards, those affected by its exercise will be directly concerned by the act conferring or confirming it. An example of the first situation is the *International Fruit Company* case (discussed earlier, in § 3.3). It will be remembered that, under the provisions then in force, persons wishing to import table apples were required to obtain an import permit from the national authorities. Each week the national authorities would inform the Commission of the number of applications for permits made to them during the

[80] Case 69/69, [1970] ECR 385. See also *Mannesmann-Röhrenwerke v. Commission*, Case 333/85, [1987] ECR 1381; *L'Etoile Commerciale v. Commission*, Cases 89, 91/86, [1987] ECR 3005; *Arposol v. Council*, Case 55/86, [1988] ECR 13.

preceding week. The Commission would then adopt an act (which the Court held to be a bundle of decisions, though it was in the form of a regulation) which laid down a formula for deciding how the applications should be dealt with. The national authorities then granted import permits on the basis of the formula. The Court held that, since the formula left no discretion to the national authorities, an applicant for a permit was directly concerned by the Commission's decision.

An example of the second situation is the *Toepfer* case (discussed earlier, in § 3.2), which also concerned import permits but the system in operation was different. Normally all applications had to be granted by the national authorities; but on this occasion the national authorities had decided to apply 'safeguard measures' and this entitled them to refuse applications, provided that their decision to apply the 'safeguard measures' was confirmed by the Commission. The applicant applied for a permit; the German authorities declared that safeguard measures were to be applied; the Commission confirmed this; and the applicant was then informed that his application was rejected. Since the Commission's decision confirming the measures was taken after the German authorities' decision to apply them, the applicant was, the Court held, directly concerned by the Commission's decision: at the time when it was taken, an independent will no longer stood between the decision and its effect on the applicant.[81]

A more difficult case relating to this problem is *Bock v. Commission*,[82] which concerned import permits for mushrooms. At the time in question, the German Government had a policy of excluding imports of mushrooms that originated in the People's Republic of China. It was not, however, easy to give effect to this policy when the mushrooms were already in free circulation in another Member State. For, although such imports could not be made without an import permit, the German authorities were obliged to grant such a permit within a reasonable time (normally four days) after the application, unless they first obtained authorization from the Commission to suspend the issue of permits.

In the case, Bock lodged his application for a permit on 4 September 1970. On 11 September, the German authorities told the Commission that they had received an application for an import permit for Chinese mushrooms, and they requested authorization to exclude imports of such mushrooms 'including the import envisaged by the import application in question'. On the same day, the German authorities informed Bock that his application would be rejected as soon as the Commission had given its authorization. On 15 September, the Commission made a decision addressed to the German Government authorizing the excluding of Chinese mushrooms, including those for which applications for import permits were pending.[83] Bock's application was

[81] The position might be different in the case of someone who applied for a permit *after* the Commission's decision was taken. Even if the Commission authorized the continuance of the 'safeguard measures' for a certain period of time subsequent to its decision, the national authorities would, presumably, retain the discretion to revoke them sooner.

[82] Case 62/70, [1971] ECR 897.

[83] There was some dispute as to the correct interpretation of this part of the decision but the Court held that this is what it meant.

then formally rejected. He brought proceedings to quash the decision in so far as it applied to applications already pending.

The Commission objected to the admissibility of the case on the ground that Bock was neither individually nor directly concerned. The Court, however, held the application was admissible. It considered Bock individually concerned because his application was lodged before the decision was made. In so far as the decision applied to such applications (and it was challenged only to the extent that it did), the persons affected were ascertainable (a closed category) when the decision was made. The Court also considered that Bock was directly concerned: the German authorities had already informed him that his application would be rejected as soon as authorization had been obtained and the authorization had been requested for precisely this purpose.

One might criticize this decision on the ground that the German authorities were, nevertheless, still legally entitled not to make use of the authorization. They had been given a discretionary power. It is true that they would not have asked for the power if they had not intended using it, and they clearly did intend using it with regard to Bock's application. But they could have changed their minds. After all, in the *Alcan* case one could have argued that the Belgian Government would not have asked for the authorization unless it had intended using it. Yet the Court held, in that case, that the applicant was not directly concerned.

These two cases are obviously very similar. However, there are two important differences between them. The first was that the German authorities had expressly told Bock that, if they obtained the authorization, it would be used to reject his application. There was no evidence that this was so in the *Alcan* case. The second difference was that in the *Alcan* case the Belgian Government had been acting in the interest of Alcan and the other importers in making the application. One might almost say that it had been acting on their behalf. Since the importers and the Member State were 'on the same side', so to speak, it would not have been unreasonable to regard the interests of the importers as sufficiently protected by the right of the Belgian Government to bring proceedings to set aside the decision. As it was a privileged applicant, there could have been no objections to the Belgian Government's *locus standi*. The fact that the Belgian Government did not bring an application suggests either that it did not consider it would meet with success or that it had changed its mind about the desirability of making use of the authorization. In the *Bock* case, on the other hand, the German Government was obviously acting against the interests of the importer. Bock could not look to his Government to bring an application to quash the decision. So if he had been refused *locus standi* there would have been no possibility that the legality of the decision would have been challenged (except in the somewhat unlikely circumstance of an application by another Member State, perhaps Holland, the country from which the import was to have been made).

The first distinguishing fact was recognized by the Court itself and is obviously relevant. The second was not alluded to by the Court, but it may have been influenced by it. It is obviously a factor of great practical importance, though it is hardly something that could have been expressly stated by the Court.

A later case, which is similar to *Bock* but goes further, is *Piraiki-Patraiki v. Commission.*[84] The facts of this case were outlined earlier, in § 3.2: it will be remembered that the Commission took a decision authorizing France to exclude Greek cotton yarn. Since France was not legally obliged to exercise the power, it could be argued that the Greek exporters who challenged the decision were not directly concerned by it. However, France was already exercising a very restrictive system of licences for such imports and the Court said that the possibility that France might decide not to make use of the authorization was 'entirely theoretical';[85] so the applicants were held to be directly concerned.[86] This is probably the Court's most liberal decision on the subject.[87]

Although the applicable rules are fairly clear, it is nevertheless hard to understand why an applicant's right to bring proceedings should hang on such fine distinctions. It is unfortunate that the authors of the Treaty of Lisbon did not reform the law in this regard as well.

FURTHER READING

Items are listed in date order, the most recent being at the end.

HARDING, 'The Private Interest in Challenging Union Action' (1980) 5 ELRev. 354.

RASMUSSEN, 'Why is Article 173 Interpreted against Private Plaintiffs?' (1980) 5 ELRev. 112.

G BEBR, *Development of Judicial Control of the European Communities* (1981).

GREAVES, 'Locus Standi under Article 173 EEC when Seeking Annulment of a Regulation' (1986) 11 ELRev. 119.

ARNULL, 'Challenging EC Anti-Dumping Regulations: The Problem of Admissibility' [1992] 2 ECLR 73.

HARLOW, 'Towards a Theory of Access for the European Court of Justice' (1992) 12 YEL 213.

CRAIG, 'Legality, Standing and Substantive Review in Union Law' (1994) 14 OJLS 507.

ARNULL, 'Private Applicants and the Action for Annulment under Article 173 of the EC Treaty' (1995) 32 CMLRev. 7.

GREAVES, 'The Nature and Binding Effect of Decisions under Article 189 EC' (1996) 21 ELRev. 3.

NEUWAHL, 'Article 173, Paragraph 4 EC: Past, Present and Possible Future' (1996) 21 ELRev. 17.

ARNULL, 'Private Applicants and the Action for Annulment since *Codorniu*' (2001) 38 CMLRev. 7.

USHER, 'Direct and Individual Concern – An Effective Remedy or a Conventional Solution?' (2003) 28 ELRev. 575.

WARD, 'Locus Standi under Article 230(4) of the EC Treaty: Crafting a Coherent Test for a "Wobbly Polity"' (2003) 22 YEL 45.

[84] Case 11/82, [1985] ECR 207. See also *ASPEC v. Commission*, Case T-435/93, [1995] ECR II-1281 at paras 60–61 of the judgment.

[85] Para. 9 of the judgment.

[86] See also *AIUFFASS v. Commission*, Case T-380/94, [1996] ECR II-2169 at paras 46 and 47 of the judgment.

[87] For later decisions of the Court of First Instance which display a restrictive attitude, see Arnull, 'Private Applicants and the Action for Annulment since *Codorniu*' (2001) 38 CMLRev. 7 at 25–30.

ENCHELMAIER, 'No-One Slips through the Net? Latest Developments, and Non-Developments, in the European Court of Justice's Jurisprudence on Art. 230(4) EC' (2005) 24 YEL 173.

KOCH, '*Locus Standi* of Private Applicants under the EU Constitution: Preserving Gaps in the Protection of Individuals' Right to an Effective Remedy' (2005) 30 ELRev. 511.

ANGELA WARD, *Judicial Review and the Rights of Private Parties in EU Law*, 2nd edn (2007).

BALTHASAR, 'Locus Standi Rules for Challenges to Regulatory Acts by Private Applicants: The New Article 263(4) TFEU' (2010) 35 ELRev. 542.

ALBORS-LLORENS, 'Remedies against the EU Institutions after Lisbon: An Era of Opportunity?' [2012] CLJ 507.

BAST, 'New Categories of Acts after the Lisbon Reform: Dynamics of Parliamentarization in EU Law' (2012) 49 CMLRev. 885 (pp. 898–907).

13

FAILURE TO ACT

§1 INTRODUCTION

A remedy for a wrongful failure to act is provided by Article 265 TFEU [232/175 EC], which reads as follows:

> Should the European Parliament, the European Council, the Council, the Commission or the European Central Bank, in infringement of the Treaties, fail to act, the Member States and the other institutions of the Union may bring an action before the Court of Justice of the European Union to have the infringement established. This Article shall apply, under the same conditions, to bodies, offices and agencies of the Union which fail to act.
>
> The action shall be admissible only if the institution, body, office or agency concerned has first been called upon to act. If, within two months of being so called upon, the institution, body, office or agency concerned has not defined its position, the action may be brought within a further period of two months.
>
> Any natural or legal person may, under the conditions laid down in the preceding paragraphs, complain to the Court that an institution, body, office or agency of the Union has failed to address to that person any act other than a recommendation or an opinion.

It will be noticed that this provision bears a fairly strong resemblance to Article 263 TFEU. The most obvious difference between the two Articles is that proceedings cannot be brought under Article 265 unless the applicant has first addressed a request for action to the defendant. The defendant must be given two months to comply and the action may then be brought within the following two months. Another difference is that only one ground of review is laid down by Article 265, while under Article 263 there are four. (The grounds of review under both Articles are discussed in Chapter 15.)

From a theoretical viewpoint, it is quite clear that proceedings to quash a legal act, and proceedings to require a public authority to take action, are two aspects of the same legal remedy. The similarities between the two sets of provisions in each of the Treaties indicate that the authors of the Treaties were well aware of this. It is no surprise, therefore, that the European Court has adopted this doctrine as a general principle. Thus, in *Chevalley v. Commission*[1] it was not clear whether the application should have been under Article 265 [175 EEC] or under Article 263 [173 EEC]. The action had originally been brought under Article 265 but, in the course of the hearing, the

[1] Case 15/70, [1970] ECR 975.

applicant had requested the Court to consider it as an application under either Article 265 or Article 263, depending on which the Court considered appropriate. In its judgment, however, the Court did not regard it as necessary to characterize the proceedings as being under either one or the other, since the two Articles 'merely prescribe one and the same method of recourse'.[2]

The principle that the two Articles are concerned with essentially the same remedy, which for the sake of brevity will henceforth be referred to as the 'unity principle', is not of merely theoretical interest but has a very important practical consequence. It implies that the conditions and limitations applicable to the remedy should be the same under the two procedures, except to the extent that different rules are a necessary consequence of the inherent differences between an act and a failure to act, between commission and omission. Subject to this exception, one would expect the applicant to have the same rights in proceedings under Article 265 as he has in proceedings under Article 263. Generally speaking, this is indeed the case, though, as we shall see later, there are some anomalies.

§2 NEGATIVE DECISIONS

A 'negative decision' is a decision of a public authority in which it decides not to act in a particular way. A rejection of a request is the most common example. From a strictly theoretical viewpoint, a negative decision would be a reviewable act – an act having legal effects – only if it was binding on the authority, in the sense that it precluded the authority, at least for a period, from changing its mind and taking the action in question. In such a situation, the authority will have lost the power to take the action in question. Where this is not the case, however, the decision will have no legal effects: in law the legal position of the authority and of the person making the request will be the same as before. Normally, of course, a negative decision is not binding on the authority making it.

It will, however, be remembered that the European Court has departed from strict theory by ruling that a statement by a Union institution on how it intends to act in the future, even if it is not legally binding on the institution, is to be regarded as a reviewable act if it is definite and unequivocal.[3] As was explained previously, this was

[2] Para. 6 of the judgment. For similar statements by Advocates General, see: *Mackprang v. Commission*, Case 15/71, [1971] ECR 797 at 802, *per* Advocate General Dutheillet de Lamothe; *Nordgetreide v. Commission*, Case 42/71, [1972] ECR 105 at 116, *per* Advocate General Roemer; *Compagnie d'Approvisionnement v. Commission*, Cases 9, 11/71, [1972] ECR 391 at 414, *per* Advocate General Dutheillet de Lamothe; and *Holtz & Willemsen v. Council*, Case 134/73, [1974] ECR 1 at 14, *per* Advocate General Reischl. However, in *European Parliament v. Council* (*Comitology* case), Case 302/87, [1988] ECR 5615 at para. 16 of the judgment, the Court said that there is 'no necessary link between the action for annulment and the action for failure to act'. For the special context in which this was said, see later, in § 3.

[3] See *Fédération Charbonnière de Belgique v. High Authority*, Case 8/55, [1956] ECR 245, discussed in Chap. 11, § 3.

necessitated by the absence in Union law of anything corresponding to the English action for a declaration. Were it not for this doctrine, it would be impossible for the legality of a proposed course of action to be challenged until it had actually been carried out.

Since a negative act is no more than a (negative) statement of future intention, it is not surprising that the European Court has adopted a general doctrine that a negative act which is sufficiently clear and precise constitutes a reviewable act, provided the act which the Union institution has refused to adopt would itself have been reviewable.[4] If, for example, the Commission informs a citizen that it will not address a decision to him, the citizen would be able to challenge the refusal in annulment proceedings, since the decision, if it had been taken, would have been reviewable.

A negative act is, moreover, classified for the purpose of *locus standi* in the same way as the positive act. Thus, if a private individual requests the Commission to adopt an act and the Commission refuses, the question whether the applicant has standing to challenge the negative decision containing the refusal depends on whether he would have had standing to challenge the act he had requested, if the Commission had adopted it.

This attitude makes sense if one realizes that a challenge to a negative act is in reality an application for a remedy for a failure to act; consequently, it is really directed at the defendant's failure to adopt the requested act and it is therefore right that questions of *locus standi*, as well as questions of reviewability, should be determined with reference to that act. This may be demonstrated by considering the effect of a judgment in favour of the applicant. A declaration by the Court that a negative act is invalid would be meaningless, were it not for the fact that the defendant must then adopt the act which it had previously refused to adopt. This follows from the first paragraph of Article 276 TFEU, which states:

> The institution whose act has been declared void or whose failure to act has been declared contrary to the Treaties shall be required to take the necessary measures to comply with the judgment of the Court of Justice of the European Union.

If the negative act has been quashed because the defendant had no right to refuse to take the action required, the 'necessary measures' would be the adoption of the act in question.

An action to annul a negative decision is, therefore, a remedy for failure to act; nevertheless, in form it is still an action to annul, and it is governed by Article 263 and not by Article 265 TFEU. The latter Article comes into play only when the defendant has not 'defined its position'. The meaning of this phrase must now be considered.

[4] *De Gezamenlijke Steenkolenmijnen in Limburg v. High Authority*, Case 30/59, [1961] ECR 1 at 15; *Lütticke v. Commission*, Case 48/65, [1966] ECR 19 at 31, *per* Advocate General Gand; *Irish Cement v. Commission*, Cases 166, 220/86, [1988] ECR 6473 at 6495–6, *per* Advocate General Darmon. See also *Buckl*, Cases C-15, 108/91, [1992] ECR I-6061 at paras 22 and 23 of the judgment; *Zunis Holding*, Case T-83/92, [1993] ECR II-1169 at para. 31 of the judgment.

§3 DEFINITION OF POSITION

One would have thought that any clear and definite answer to the request for action, including a total or partial refusal, would constitute a definition of position. Though it might seem strange that a remedy under Article 265 TFEU could be barred by an outright refusal, no problems will be caused as long as the refusal constitutes a negative decision which the applicant can challenge under Article 263 TFEU. This should normally be the case. Where it is not, however, serious difficulties could arise, since the applicant might be deprived of any remedy.

An example of a refusal to act that cannot be challenged under Article 263 concerns the European Parliament. The Parliament has always had standing as a privileged applicant under Article 265,[5] but, prior to the *Chernobyl* case,[6] it had no standing to bring an annulment action. This meant that if the Parliament brought proceedings under Article 265 and was met with a flat refusal, it could not challenge the refusal as a negative act. Consequently, if such a refusal were regarded as a definition of position for the purpose of Article 265, the Parliament's right to bring proceedings under that Article would be largely illusory.

The first time the question arose was in the *Transport* case,[7] in which the Parliament brought proceedings against the Council because the latter had failed to establish a common transport policy for the Union. The Court, however, avoided the issue by ruling that the somewhat equivocal reply given by the Council was not sufficiently clear to constitute a definition of position.[8]

The issue arose again in the *Comitology* case.[9] This was the case in which the Parliament argued that, in spite of the wording of what was then Article 173 EEC, it *was* entitled to bring proceedings under that provision. One of the most powerful arguments in favour of its position was that if it were not entitled to bring proceedings under Article 173 EEC, its admitted right of action under Article 175 EEC (now Article 265 TFEU) could be rendered nugatory by the simple expedient of an outright refusal.

Since the Court intended to deny the Parliament's claim, it had to meet this argument. It did so by rejecting the premise on which it was based. It stated: 'A refusal to act, however explicit it may be, can be brought before the Court under Article 175 since it does not put an end to the failure to act.'[10]

This must mean that even an explicit refusal does not constitute a definition of position. If this were accepted as a general proposition, however, two serious problems

[5] It is covered by the phrase 'the other institutions of the Union' in the first para. of Art. 265 TFEU (formerly Art. 175 EEC): *European Parliament v. Council* (*Transport*), Case 13/83, [1985] ECR 1513.

[6] *European Parliament v. Council*, Case C-70/88, [1990] ECR I-2041. Art. 263 now gives it this right.

[7] *European Parliament v. Council*, Case 13/83, [1985] ECR 1513.

[8] *Ibid.* at para. 25 of the judgment.

[9] *European Parliament v. Council*, Case 302/87, [1988] ECR 5615.

[10] *Ibid.* at para. 17 of the judgment.

would arise. The first is that it would be hard to see what *could* constitute a definition of position if a clear and explicit refusal does not do so. It could hardly have been the intention of the authors of the Treaty that the only way a defendant under Article 265 could define its position would be to agree to whatever was requested.

The second difficulty is that there have been several cases in which a statement by the defendant that it would not meet the request *has* been held by the Court to constitute a definition of position.[11] In none of them, however, was the applicant thereby deprived of a remedy which he would otherwise have had.[12] Perhaps it is only where this would be the case that a refusal will not be regarded as a definition of position.

The European Court subsequently modified its position on the Parliament's right of action under Article 173 EEC (now Article 263 TFEU) by ruling, in the *Chernobyl* case, that the Parliament *can* bring proceedings, though only for the purpose of protecting its prerogatives,[13] a rule subsequently embodied in the text of Article 263 by an amendment under the Treaty on European Union. The problem is now fully solved by the current text, which gives the Parliament the full rights of a privileged applicant.

§4 PARTIES TO THE PROCEEDINGS

The first paragraph of Article 265 TFEU makes provision for proceedings against the Parliament, the European Council, the Council, the Commission, and the European Central Bank, as well as bodies, offices, and agencies of the Union.[14]

As far as potential applicants are concerned, the first paragraph of Article 265 provides that the Member States and 'the other institutions of the Union' may bring proceedings.[15] These are all privileged applicants.

The third paragraph of Article 265 grants a limited right of action to non-privileged applicants. 'Any natural or legal person' may bring proceedings on this basis, subject to the rules on *locus standi*, which are discussed later, in §7.

§5 REVIEWABLE OMISSIONS

What kind of act may the Commission or Council be required to adopt by means of proceedings under Article 265 TFEU? In other words, what kind of omission is reviewable? This question is, of course, the negative equivalent of the question discussed in

[11] See, for example, *Lütticke v. Commission*, Case 48/65, [1966] ECR 19; *Nordgetreide v. Commission*, Case 42/71, [1972] ECR 105; *Irish Cement v. Commission*, Cases 166, 220/86, [1988] ECR 6473; *Buckl*, Cases C-15, 108/91, [1992] ECR I-6061; *Guérin Automobiles v. Commission*, Case C-282/95, [1997] ECR I-1503 (appeal from Case T-186/94, [1995] ECR II-1753).

[12] See the discussion of *Lütticke* and *Nordgetreide* in § 7.

[13] *European Parliament v. Council*, Case C-70/88, [1990] ECR I-2041.

[14] On the meaning of 'bodies, offices and agencies of the Union', see Chap. 1, § 8.

[15] There is a list of the institutions of the Union at the beginning of Chap. 1.

Chapter 11: what acts are reviewable? From the point of view of theory (unity principle), one would expect the answer to be that only an omission to adopt a reviewable act – an act having legal effects – would be reviewable under Article 265. In order to facilitate discussion, this view will henceforth be referred to as the 'narrow interpretation', while the view that other kinds of omissions are also reviewable will be called the 'wide interpretation'.

Article 265 refers in its first paragraph simply to a failure 'to act'. This contrasts with the first paragraph of Article 263 which applies to 'acts... other than recommendations or opinions'. Does the fact that non-binding acts (recommendations and opinions) are not expressly excluded in Article 265 mean that a failure to adopt such an act may be challenged by proceedings under Article 265? It could, of course, be argued that 'act' in Article 265 is impliedly limited to a reviewable act; but this could be countered by reference to the third paragraph of Article 265. This provision, which is concerned with proceedings by non-privileged applicants, refers to 'any act other than a recommendation or an opinion': if the word 'act' in the first paragraph is impliedly limited to a reviewable act, it would be unnecessary expressly to exclude a recommendation or an opinion in the third paragraph. It seems, therefore, that an analysis of the text lends support to the wide interpretation.

The objection to such a conclusion is that it conflicts with the unity principle: if the action to annul and the action for a remedy for failure to act are, as the European Court has confirmed, merely different aspects of the same remedy, how can the subject matter of the second be wider than that of the first?

In the *Draft Budget* case,[16] Advocate General Mischo came out explicitly in favour of the narrow interpretation. He said:[17]

> The decisive criterion is therefore that of the legal effects. Thus, a 'failure to act' within the meaning of Article 175 [265] may be constituted by the non-adoption by the Council or by the Commission of an act or measure, of whatever nature, form or description, which is capable of producing legal effects *vis-à-vis* third parties.

The case was an action brought under Article 265 TFEU (then Article 175 EEC) by the Parliament against the Council because the latter had failed to place the draft budget before the Parliament by the due date. The Council argued that the action was inadmissible because the draft budget was not a reviewable act – in its opinion, only the final budget would be reviewable – and consequently its failure to adopt it was not a reviewable omission in terms of Article 265. This argument was of course based on the narrow interpretation. In his Opinion, Advocate General Mischo accepted that the narrow interpretation was correct, but maintained that the draft budget *was* a reviewable act because it had legal effects. The Court did not decide the point. The Council had in fact adopted the draft budget within two months of being called on to act, and

[16] *European Parliament v. Council*, Case 377/87, [1988] ECR 4017; see also *Commission v. Council*, Case 383/87, [1988] ECR 4051.

[17] *European Parliament v. Council*, Case 377/87 at 4029 (para. 30).

the Court therefore concluded that the subject matter of the action (the failure to act) had ceased to exist. The final ruling was, 'The Court declares that there is no need for it to give a decision.'

This was not the end of the matter, however, because in the *Comitology* case[18] the Court stated that, as was 'shown' by its judgment in the *Draft Budget* case, an action for failure to act can be brought by the Parliament if the Council fails to adopt a draft budget. This, the Court said, establishes that an action under Article 265 can be brought by the Parliament for failure to adopt a measure that is not itself a reviewable act. It seems, therefore, that the Court now rejects the narrow interpretation, though its decision in the *Draft Budget* case is not an authority for this.

It should be said that the Court's statement in the *Comitology* case was made very much with a particular purpose in mind. The *Comitology* case, it will be remembered, was the case in which the Parliament argued that, in spite of the clear wording of the first paragraph of Article 173 EEC (now Article 263 TFEU) as it then stood, it should nevertheless be entitled to bring annulment proceedings as a privileged applicant. One of the arguments it put forward was that, since it had standing under Article 265, it would be illogical to deny it standing under Article 263. The Court replied to this by saying that there is 'no necessary link' between the two actions, and supported this assertion by saying that a non-reviewable act can constitute a reviewable omission. Since the Court was about to rule against the Parliament, it is possible that it was trying to sweeten the pill by expressly confirming the Parliament's right to bring proceedings under Article 265 in the case of a preliminary act such as a draft budget, a right which was actually left uncertain by the *Draft Budget* case. If this is correct, it is possible that the Court's adoption of the wide interpretation will apply only in the case of preliminary acts (discussed in the following sub-section).

§5.1 PRELIMINARY ACTS

A 'preliminary act' is the first step in the adoption of some other act. The concept was discussed in Chapter 11, § 3, where it was suggested that the reviewability of a preliminary act should depend on whether or not it has legal effects. For example, if the law provides that the final act cannot be adopted until some other body has been consulted, it would be wrong to regard the opinion of this other body as a reviewable act, since it is not binding on the authority empowered to adopt the final act. If, on the other hand, the final act can be adopted only if the other body gives its consent, then the 'opinion' of that other body would have legal effects and ought to be regarded as reviewable. However, as was pointed out in Chapter 11, the European Court has taken the view that, even in this case, such a preliminary act will not necessarily be a reviewable act. This does not normally have serious consequences, however, because the preliminary act may be reviewed in the context of proceedings to annul the final act.

[18] *European Parliament v. Council*, Case 302/87, [1988] ECR 5615.

Unfortunately, this will not always be possible in the case of a failure to act, particularly where the preliminary act is the responsibility of a different body from that empowered to adopt the final act: if proceedings are brought against the body responsible for the final act, it can raise the defence that it cannot adopt it until the preliminary act has been adopted; since the latter is not its responsibility, it could not be held to blame for the failure to act.

The draft budget has already been mentioned as an example of this problem. The Union's budget is adopted by the Parliament, but the Parliament can act only if the Council first adopts a draft budget. If the Council fails to make such a proposal, the Parliament is powerless to act. If Article 265 did not apply in such a case because (as was argued by the Council in the *Draft Budget* case) a draft budget is only a preliminary act, there would be no remedy open to the Parliament. It could not bring proceedings against the Council for failure to adopt a final budget, since the Parliament itself does this. It should also be noted that the Council cannot adopt the draft budget until the Commission draws up the preliminary draft budget. The same problem would arise if the Commission failed to do this. Moreover, the problem is not limited to the budget since most of the legal acts which the Council is empowered to adopt may be enacted only on the basis of a proposal from the Commission.

As was pointed out earlier, there are strong theoretical grounds for saying that drafts and proposals of this kind *are* reviewable acts. By adopting a draft budget, for example, the Council confers a power on the Parliament to adopt the final budget. This was the view of Advocate General Mischo in the *Draft Budget* case.[19] The same is true of a Commission proposal for a measure to be adopted by the Council. However, since the Court regards preliminary acts as non-reviewable under Article 263, it probably felt that it could not say they were reviewable for the purpose of Article 265. This, it is suggested, is why it ruled instead that a failure to act can include a failure to adopt a non-reviewable act.[20]

§5.2 FAILURE TO REPEAL AN ACT

Assume that a Union institution adopts a legal act and, after the time limit for challenging it in annulment proceedings has passed, the applicant requests the institution to repeal it on the ground that it violates Union law. If the Union institution

[19] See n. 17.

[20] For similar problems regarding the right of a complainant in EU competition procedure, see *GEMA v. Commission*, Case 125/78, [1979] ECR 3173; *Automec v. Commission (No. 2)*, Case T-24/90, [1992] ECR II-2223 at paras 71–82 of the judgment. For a helpful summary of the position, see the Opinion of Advocate General Tesauro in *Guérin Automobiles v. Commission*, Case C-282/95, [1997] ECR I-1503 (appeal from Case T-186/94, [1995] ECR II-1753) at paras 10–17. See also *Automec v. Commission (No. 1)*, Case T-64/89, [1990] ECR II-367 at paras 45–46 of the judgment. See further *Demo-Studio Schmidt v. Commission*, Case 210/81, [1983] ECR 3045 at paras 10–16 of the judgment; *BAT and Reynolds v. Commission*, Cases 142 and 156/84, [1987] ECR 4487 at paras 11–13 of the judgment; *SFEI v. Commission*, Case C-39/93 P, [1994] ECR I-2681 (appeal from Case T-36/92, [1992] ECR II-2479) at paras 27–33 of the judgment of the European Court.

does not comply with this request, may the applicant bring proceedings for a remedy for failure to act? In support of such an application it could be argued that, since all Union institutions are obliged to respect the law, there is a legal obligation to repeal any act which is inconsistent with Union law, even if the time limit for an annulment action has expired. Moreover, since the repealing act would clearly have legal effects, the controversy over the wide and the narrow interpretations would not affect the matter.

The European Court has, however, ruled that this cannot be done. The leading case is *Eridania v. Commission*,[21] in which an Italian sugar-refining concern brought proceedings to challenge three Commission decisions granting aid to its competitors. The applicant claimed that these decisions were illegal and requested the Commission to revoke them. When this request was not met, it brought two actions: first, proceedings under what was then Article 173 EEC (now Article 263 TFEU) to annul the decisions (Case 10/68); secondly, proceedings under what was then Article 175 EEC (now Article 265 TFEU) for a remedy for the Commission's failure to revoke the decisions (Case 18/68). These two actions were joined, and the Court decided them both in a single judgment. Case 10/68 was declared inadmissible because the applicant lacked *locus standi*: the decisions were not addressed to the applicant and the applicant was not, in the opinion of the Court, directly and individually concerned by them. Case 18/68 was also declared inadmissible. The reasoning of the Court was as follows:

> This application concerns the annulment of the implied decision of rejection resulting from the silence maintained by the Commission in respect of the request addressed to it by the applicants seeking the annulment or revocation of the three disputed decisions for illegality or otherwise because they are inappropriate.
>
> The action provided for in Article 175 [265 TFEU] is intended to establish an illegal omission as appears from that article, which refers to a failure to act 'in infringement of this Treaty' and from Article 176 [266 TFEU] which refers to a failure to act declared to be 'contrary to this Treaty'.
>
> Without stating under which provision of Union law the Commission was required to annul or to revoke the said decisions, the applicants have confined themselves to alleging that those decisions were adopted in infringement of the Treaty and that this fact alone would thus suffice to make the Commission's failure to act subject to the provisions of Article 175 [265 TFEU].
>
> The Treaty provides, however, particularly in Article 173 [263 TFEU], other methods of recourse by which an allegedly illegal Union measure may be disputed and if necessary annulled on the application of a duly qualified party.
>
> To admit, as the applicants wish to do, that the parties concerned could ask the institution from which the measure came to revoke it and, in the event of the Commission's failing to act, refer such failure to the Court as an illegal omission to deal with the matter would amount

[21] Cases 10, 18/68, [1969] ECR 459 at 482–3.

to providing them with a method of recourse parallel to that of Article 173 [263 TFEU], which would not be subject to the conditions laid down by the Treaty.

This application does not therefore satisfy the requirements of Article 175 [265 TFEU] of the Treaty and must thus be held to be inadmissible.

This does not mean that there is no obligation on Union institutions to repeal an invalid act: all the Court decided was that it had no jurisdiction to consider the question in proceedings brought under Article 175 EEC [265 TFEU]. The ruling was procedural, not substantive. This is also clear from the ruling in an earlier case under the ECSC Treaty, *Meroni v. High Authority*[22] (fifth *Meroni* case), in which the Court stated that 'an applicant cannot be permitted, by using the procedural artifice of an action for failure to act, to ask for the annulment of decisions which might have been declared void if proceedings had been instituted within the time limit laid down in the third paragraph of Article 33'.[23]

The Court's objection to the use, for this purpose, of proceedings for a remedy for failure to act is that it would allow a decision to be challenged after the expiry of the time limit for annulment actions. This is what the Court meant in the *Eridania* case when it said that, if this procedure were allowed, applicants would be provided with a method of recourse 'which would not be subject to the conditions laid down by the Treaty'. This cannot refer to the *locus standi* provisions, since these are the same in actions for a remedy for failure to act as in annulment actions (see § 7).

It is interesting to note in this connection that the *Eridania* case (Case 18/68) could in fact have been decided on the ground of *locus standi*. This was the ground on which the annulment action (Case 10/68) was decided; but the same reasoning could have been applied to the action for a remedy for failure to act. The third paragraph of Article 265 TFEU (then Article 175 EEC) allows a non-privileged applicant to bring proceedings only where the defendant has failed to address an act *to him*. The applicant's request in the *Eridania* case was for the revocation of the three decisions and this could have been done only by passing three further decisions revoking the earlier ones. These latter decisions would have been addressed to the same persons as the earlier ones, namely the recipients of the aid (the rival firms) and the Italian Government. Eridania was not, therefore, asking the Commission to address an act to it; moreover, since the original decisions were not – in the Court's view – of direct and individual concern to Eridania, the repealing decisions would also not have been of direct and individual concern to it. Consequently, it had no greater *locus standi* in the Article 265 proceedings than it had in the Article 263 proceedings.

It should also be pointed out that the rationale given by the Court is not entirely sound. The purpose of the short time limit in annulment actions is the protection of persons who have relied on the act in question – the principle of legal certainty – and it is to uphold this principle that the Court does not allow acts to be challenged by means of proceedings for a remedy for failure to act. However, where the act is repealed, the

[22] Cases 21–6/61, [1962] ECR 73 at 78.

[23] Art. 33 ECSC was the equivalent of Art. 263 TFEU.

interests of these persons could, in some cases at least, be protected by means of transitional provisions in the repealing measure. Moreover, it should be remembered that the repeal of an act need not be retroactive, while the annulment of an act normally has the effect of rendering it void *ab initio*. Consequently, repeal does not pose the same threat to legal certainty as annulment.

Whatever view one takes of this, there are some special situations in which it seems the Court *will* allow the action. One is where the act in question is originally quite valid, but subsequently becomes incompatible with Union law as a result of a later development. If this development takes place more than two months after the publication, or notification, of the act, it will not be possible to bring proceedings under Article 263 TFEU. In such a case, an action under Article 265 TFEU will be the only possibility, and it would be a particularly appropriate remedy since an act which was validly passed, but which subsequently became illegal, ought more properly to be repealed than annulled. A *dictum* by Advocate General Roemer in the *Eridania* case suggests that an exception might exist in such a case.[24]

A second such situation is where a judgment by the European Court annulling one act also requires the amendment or repeal of another. This was the situation in *Asteris v. Commission*,[25] which concerned aid to producers of tomato concentrates in Greece. In a judgment given in 1985,[26] the Court had annulled a regulation granting the aid for the marketing year 1983/84 on the ground that it was too little. The Commission then adopted a new regulation increasing the aid. This applied only to 1983/84, even though the reasoning of the judgment was equally applicable to other years. The measure dealing with the three years subsequent to 1983/84 had been adopted in 1984, over a year prior to the judgment. By the time the judgment was given, therefore, it was too late for Greece to commence proceedings to annul it under Article 263 (then Article 173 EEC). Instead it initiated the procedure under Article 265 (then Article 175 EEC) by asking the Commission to amend the regulation to bring it into line with the judgment. When the Commission refused, Greece brought proceedings to annul the refusal. The Court held the proceedings admissible and ruled that the refusal was void.

§6 THE REQUEST FOR ACTION

§6.1 GENERAL

The most important procedural difference between actions for a remedy for failure to act and annulment actions is that in the former case there is a special preliminary procedure which must be gone through before the application may be made to the

[24] [1969] ECR at 494. [25] Cases 97, 99, 193, 215/86, [1988] ECR 2181.
[26] *Greece v. Commission*, Case 192/83, [1985] ECR 2791.

European Court. This procedure consists of a formal request to the defendant to take action. The request must state clearly what action is required.[27] This is important since, when the case goes before the Court, the applicant can complain only that the defendant failed to take the action previously requested.

It must also be clear that the request is being made in terms of Article 265 TFEU, and that the applicant considers the defendant legally obliged to take the action required.[28] For this reason, 'request' is probably too mild a term to use: 'demand' might be more appropriate. It would be desirable, therefore, for the applicant to refer expressly to the Treaty or to state that legal proceedings will be taken if the required action is not forthcoming.

After the request for action has been made, the defendant institution has a period of two months to comply. Only if this period expires without action by the defendant may the application be made to the Court.[29] There is, however, a time limit for this application: it must be brought within two months. This time limit (which runs from the end of the initial two-month period) is very short, and the action will be declared inadmissible if it is brought either too early or too late. This could cause difficulties for the applicant if he is uncertain whether a particular communication made by him to the defendant constitutes a formal request for action or not: if he goes to Court and it transpires that it does not, his application will be declared inadmissible and he will have to pay costs; but if he fails to institute proceedings within the time limit and it is subsequently established that the communication *did* constitute a request for action, he will have lost the right to bring proceedings. (It is not clear whether he could start the procedure all over again with a new request for exactly the same action; the Court might hold that his right of action had been time-barred.)

What is the purpose of this special procedure? In answering this question it must be remembered that an important difference between an act and an omission is that, while one can say exactly what the contents of an act are and when it came into existence, this is not always so easy in the case of an omission. The function of the special procedure is to make good this deficiency: the omission is deemed to have taken place at the end of the first two-month period and its contents are defined by the terms of the request. The purpose of the procedure is, therefore, formally to put the defendant in default.[30]

[27] *Nuovo Campsider v. Commission*, Case 25/85, [1986] ECR 1531. [28] *Ibid.*

[29] Moreover, the European Court has held that a definition of position – in the case in question, an outright refusal – which takes place *after* the expiry of the two-month period, but before judgment, also puts an end to the action under Art. 265 (though it may open up an action under Art. 263): *Buckl*, Cases C-15, 108/91, [1992] ECR I-6061 at paras 13–18 of the judgment.

[30] There are, of course, some cases in which this is not necessary, for example where the law lays down both the content of the action and the date by which it must be performed. In these cases the only function of the procedure will be to give the defendant the opportunity to comply with the request before legal proceedings are brought.

§6.2 TIME LIMIT FOR MAKING REQUEST

It will be noticed that the Treaties lay down no time limit within which the request for action must be made. This is quite logical if one accepts that the failure to act is established only when the preliminary procedure has been completed. In spite of this, however, the European Court has stated, in *Netherlands v. Commission*[31] (a case under the ECSC Treaty), that the preliminary procedure must be initiated within a 'reasonable time'. The case arose in the following circumstances. The French Government had drawn up a plan for restructuring the iron and steel industry, which entailed low-interest Government loans to iron and steel producers. The French Government informed the Commission of this in September 1966 and the Commission had to consider whether the plan contravened the ECSC Treaty, especially Article 4(c), which prohibits State subsidies and aids. The Commission reached a provisional conclusion that the plan was not contrary to the Treaty and informed the other Member States of this in June 1967. The Dutch Government immediately expressed its reservations, and in April 1968 it requested the Commission to define its position further. After further consideration, the Commission reached a final conclusion that the plan did not violate Union law and it informed the Dutch Government of this on 9 December 1968. A year and a half later, on 24 June 1970, the Dutch Government made a formal request in terms of Article 35 ECSC (the equivalent of Article 265 TFEU) that the Commission take a decision under Article 88 ECSC (the equivalent of Article 258 TFEU) to the effect that the French plan involved violations of Union law; the Commission did not comply and the Netherlands then brought the action.[32]

The Court, however, held that the application was inadmissible because the period of eighteen months between the communication of 9 December 1968 and the request for action of 24 June 1970 was too great.[33] The Court began its reasoning by mentioning that Article 35 ECSC lays down no time limit for bringing the request for action. It then continued:[34]

> It follows, however, from the common purpose of Articles 33 and 35 that the requirements of legal certainty and of the continuity of Union action underlying the time-limits laid down for bringing proceedings under Article 33 must also be taken into account – having regard to the special difficulties which the silence of the competent authorities may involve for the interested parties – in the exercise of the rights conferred by Article 35.
>
> These requirements may not lead to such contradictory consequences as the duty to act within a short period in the first case and the absence of any limitation in time in the second.

[31] Case 59/70, [1971] ECR 639.

[32] The Dutch Government could not have challenged the Commission decision that the plan did not contravene Union law, since it was not a reviewable act: *De Gezamenlijke Steenkolenmijnen in Limburg v. High Authority*, Case 17/57, [1959] ECR 1.

[33] It is interesting to compare this with the decision in *Commission v. France (Euratom)*, Case 7/71, [1971] ECR 1003, decided a few months later, in which the Court refused to lay down a time limit where a *Member State* fails to comply with the Treaty: see para. 5 of the judgment and *per* Advocate General Roemer at 1026.

[34] [1971] ECR at 653.

> This view finds support in the system of time-limits in Article 35, which allows the Commission two months in which to define its position, and the interested party one month in which to institute proceedings before the Court.
>
> Thus it is implicit in the system of Articles 33 and 35 that the exercise of the right to raise the matter with the Commission may not be delayed indefinitely.
>
> If the interested parties are thus bound to observe a reasonable time-limit where the Commission remains silent, this is so *a fortiori* once it is clear that the Commission has decided to take no action.

It will be noticed that the Court purported to base its argument on the unity principle: if there is a time limit under Article 33 ECSC (the equivalent of Article 263 TFEU), there should also be one under Article 35 (the equivalent of Article 265 TFEU). However, there *was* a time limit under Article 35: this was the period within which the action had to be brought (one month under the ECSC Treaty). This ran, of course, from the end of the two-month period, that is from the date on which the defendant was formally deemed to be in default. The proposition that there must be a time limit for making the *request* can be deduced from the unity principle only if one accepts that the cause of action arises at some earlier date; but this cuts away the justification for the preliminary procedure.

The proposition accepted by the Court was considered by Advocate General Roemer. He rejected it on the ground that the adoption of a period of limitation of no specific length – that the request must be made within a reasonable time – was contrary to the principle of legal certainty.[35] How can the parties know where they stand if they cannot be sure how long the period of limitation is?

The principle of legal certainty was, of course, one of the principles invoked by the Court in support of its ruling. This was because the justification usually given for the short time limit under Article 33 ECSC and Article 263 TFEU is that, by annulling an apparently valid legal act, the Court could upset the legitimate expectations of persons who relied on it; therefore, in order to limit as much as possible the uncertainty caused by annulment actions, the period within which they may be brought should be as short as possible. However, as was pointed out earlier, the analogy between Articles 33 and 35 does not hold good at this point, since proceedings under Article 35 do not result in any *retrospective* change in the legal rights of the persons concerned: the annulment of a legal act invalidates it from the moment when it was adopted; but an order under Article 35 merely requires the defendant to adopt an act in the future. Such an act need not be retrospective.

§7 *LOCUS STANDI*

It will be remembered from Chapter 12 that, in proceedings under Article 263 TFEU, privileged applicants always have *locus standi*; non-privileged applicants, on the other

[35] [1971] ECR at 658.

hand, may challenge an act only in limited circumstances. The position under Article 265 TFEU is similar: privileged applicants always have *locus standi*; but non-privileged applicants have *locus standi* only where the defendant institution has 'failed to address' to them 'any act other than a recommendation or an opinion'.

In theory, the word 'act' in this provision should mean an act that is reviewable under Article 263: this would seem to follow from the unity principle laid down in the *Chevalley* case.[36] As we have seen, however, there is at least one situation in which this is not so: this is in the case of an act that is not regarded by the Court as reviewable because it is merely a step in the procedure and is not the definitive decision.

Under Article 265, an applicant can only complain that the defendant has failed to address an act to him. What is meant by 'address'? Must the act be formally addressed to him or is it sufficient if he is directly and individually concerned by it? It will be remembered from the discussion in Chapter 12 that the latter is sufficient under Article 263 TFEU, and it was said that in such a case the person concerned was a '*de facto*' addressee. If one accepts the unity principle, the same rule should apply under Article 265 TFEU and this would seem to follow from the *Chevalley* case. Moreover, although most of the texts of Article 265 are the same as the English, the Dutch and Italian texts suggest that this wider interpretation is legitimate: these texts state that a non-privileged applicant may bring proceedings where the defendant institution has failed to adopt an act other than a recommendation or opinion 'with respect to him'.

This wider view was strongly supported by Advocate General Dutheillet de Lamothe in *Mackprang v. Commission*.[37] In that case, the Commission had argued in favour of the narrow interpretation, i.e., that the act requested must be one which would be *formally addressed* to the applicant. Advocate General de Lamothe replied to this contention as follows:

> The Commission's argument on this point comes up against a very strong objection. If the concept of a measure against which individuals could bring proceedings were different in scope with regard to the application of Article 173 [263] from that with regard to the application of Article 175 [265] the result would be that, in certain cases, the existence or absence of a judicial remedy would depend on the actions of the Union authorities to which the request was submitted.
>
> If those authorities replied to the request either by accepting it or by rejecting it, the author of the request would be entitled to proceed under Article 173, even if he is not the addressee of the measure adopted or requested, provided that this measure is of direct and individual concern to him.
>
> On the other hand, if the Union authorities did not reply to the person concerned he would, according to the Commission's argument, be deprived of any method of recourse if he is not the addressee of the measure requested, *even if the latter is of direct and individual concern to him*.[38]

[36] See n. 1 and accompanying text.

[37] Case 15/71, [1971] ECR 797 at 807–8. But see *per* Advocate General Slynn in *Lord Bethell v. Commission*, Case 246/81, [1982] ECR 2277 at 2295–6 (and the statements by other Advocates General there cited).

[38] Emphasis in the original.

> It is obviously difficult to justify making the existence or absence of a judicial remedy depend on the action or inaction of the administrative body to which a request is submitted.

The Court did not rule on the question in *Mackprang v. Commission* and more than twenty years were to elapse before the matter was finally settled.[39] This was in *ENU v. Commission*,[40] a case under the EAEC Treaty.[41] ENU, a company producing a form of uranium, had asked the Commission to adopt a decision under Article 53 EAEC. When the Commission failed to do so, ENU brought proceedings under Article 148 EAEC (the equivalent of Article 265 TFEU). The Commission argued that ENU lacked standing because the decision would have been addressed to the EAEC supply agency, not to ENU. The Court, however, held that ENU would have been directly and individually concerned by the decision and that this was sufficient to give it standing. The application was admissible (and ultimately successful).

It follows, therefore, that a non-privileged applicant under Article 265 TFEU has *locus standi* either if the act requested would have been formally addressed to him or if he would have been the '*de facto*' addressee, i.e., if it would have concerned him directly and individually. This makes the position the same as under Article 263.

It was said earlier that it would be wrong if the applicant's right to obtain a remedy were affected by the fact that proceedings which began as an action under Article 265 were switched to an action under Article 263 because the defendant defined its position by refusing to comply with the request. So far at least, this does not seem to have occurred.[42]

Two cases which are sometimes thought to indicate that this could happen are *Lütticke v. Commission*[43] and *Nordgetreide v. Commission*.[44] The first concerned a private firm which considered that Germany had violated the Treaties. It requested the Commission to commence the procedure under Article 258 TFEU (then Article 169 EEC); but the Commission took the view that Germany had not infringed the Treaty and therefore refused to comply. The applicant then brought proceedings before the Court under Article 263 TFEU (then Article 173 EEC) to quash the negative decision of refusal; alternatively it asked for a remedy under Article 265 TFEU (then Article 175 EEC).

[39] But hints as to how the Court viewed the matter may be found in *Star Fruit v. Commission*, Case 247/87, [1989] ECR 291 at para. 13 of the judgment, and in *Lord Bethell v. Commission*, Case 246/81, [1982] ECR 2277, where the Court four times used phraseology suggesting acceptance of this wider view: it referred to the adoption of an act 'in relation to' the applicant (para. 13 of the judgment), 'in respect of' him (paras 15 and 16), and 'with regard to' him (para. 16).

[40] Case C-107/91, [1993] ECR I-599.

[41] See also *Port*, Case C-68/95, [1996] ECR I-6065 at paras 58–59 of the judgment; *Gestevisión Telecinco v. Commission*, Case T-95/96, [1998] ECR II-3407, at paras 58 *et seq.* of the judgment.

[42] At one time it was thought that *GEMA v. Commission*, Case 125/78, [1979] ECR 3173, revealed that this could occur in the field of competition law, but subsequent cases show that this is not the case: see, in particular, *Guérin Automobiles v. Commission*, Case C-282/95, [1997] ECR I-1503 (appeal from Case T-186/94, [1995] ECR II-1753).

[43] Case 48/65, [1966] ECR 19. See also *Star Fruit v. Commission*, Case 247/87, [1989] ECR 291.

[44] Case 42/71, [1972] ECR 105.

The Court held the application inadmissible. In so far as it was based on Article 263, it was inadmissible because the refusal to act was not a reviewable act. The reason for this was that no measure taken by the Commission during the preliminary procedure under Article 258 – neither the request to the Member State to submit its observations, nor the reasoned opinion – has any binding force. In other words, the acts which the applicant requested the Commission to perform were not reviewable acts; therefore, the Commission's refusal to perform them could not be a reviewable act. The application was also inadmissible in so far as it was based on Article 265, because the refusal constituted a definition of position.

This does not reveal a gap in the law, however, because the result would have been exactly the same if the Commission had remained silent instead of giving an express refusal. As we have seen, a private applicant, as was Lütticke, may bring proceedings under Article 265 TFEU only with regard to a failure by a Union institution to adopt an act which would have been addressed to it or which would have concerned it directly and individually. Since Lütticke had not asked the Commission to adopt such an act, its application would have been inadmissible irrespective of whether the Commission had defined its position or not.

In *Nordgetreide v. Commission* the applicant had requested the Commission to amend a regulation dealing with monetary compensatory amounts. The Commission refused to make the amendment and the applicant brought proceedings under Article 263 TFEU (then Article 173 EEC) to quash the refusal; alternatively, it asked for a remedy under Article 265 TFEU (then article 175 EEC). The Court stated that, since the measure to be amended was a regulation, the amending measure would also have to be a regulation. Such an amending measure would not have concerned the applicant directly and individually. Since it would have had no *locus standi* to challenge the act requested, it likewise had no *locus standi* to challenge the negative decision refusing to adopt it. The application was, therefore, declared inadmissible in so far as it was based on Article 263; in so far as it was based on Article 265, it was inadmissible because the Commission's refusal constituted a definition of position.

Here too, the position would have been exactly the same if the Commission had remained silent. *Nordgetreide* would still have lacked *locus standi* since it had not asked the Commission to adopt an act which would have been addressed to it or which would have concerned it directly and individually.

§8 FORM OF JUDGMENT

Under Article 263 TFEU the consequence of a successful action is that the provision in question is declared void by the Court. In proceedings under Article 265 TFEU, however, the Court has no power itself to adopt the act which the defendant wrongfully failed to pass: all it can do is to declare that the failure to act was contrary to the Treaty. However, Article 266 provides that the defendant institution 'shall be required to take the necessary measures to comply with the judgment of the Court of Justice'.

This obliges the defendant to take action; but it still retains such measure of discretion as to the form and content of the act as is granted to it under the provision requiring the act to be performed.

FURTHER READING

Items are listed in date order, the most recent being at the end.

BARAV, 'Considérations sur la spécificité du recours en carence en droit communautaire' [1975] RTDE 53.

TOTH, 'The Law as it Stands on the Appeal for Failure to Act' (1975) 2 LIEI 65.

ANGELA WARD, *Judicial Review and the Rights of Private Parties in EU Law*, 2nd edn (2007).

14

INDIRECT CHALLENGE

§1 INTRODUCTION

An indirect challenge to the validity of an act is a challenge made in the course of proceedings not instituted for that purpose. The object of the proceedings must be something other than the annulment of the act, and the court must have jurisdiction on some ground independent of the indirect challenge. The purpose of an indirect challenge is to require the court to decide the case on the basis that the act in question is invalid; consequently, the challenge may be made only if the act is relevant to the proceedings.[1] It follows as a matter of principle, therefore, that an act is susceptible to indirect challenge whenever it is relevant to the proceedings, but is not itself the subject matter of the proceedings.

Another name for an indirect challenge, often used by writers on Union law, is 'plea of illegality'. This indicates that a party to proceedings has contended that an act is illegal and therefore invalid.[2] It is a translation of the French term, *exception d'illégalité* (sometimes mistranslated as 'exception of illegality'). This term does not, however, convey the idea quite as well as 'indirect challenge', which expresses both the fact that the validity of the act is under attack and that the challenge is incidental to the primary object of the proceedings.

Since Union law is applied at the national level as well as at the Union level, an indirect challenge to a Union act may be brought in a national court as well as in the European Court. When this occurs, the question of the validity of the act is referred to the European Court under sub-paragraph (b) of the first paragraph of Article 267 TFEU. Once the European Court has made a ruling, the case goes back to the national court, which will give judgment on the basis of the decision of the European Court.

Some writers take the view that the issues involved where the European Court makes a decision under this procedure are fundamentally different from those where the indirect challenge is made in proceedings brought initially in the European Court.[3]

[1] See *Italy v. Commission*, Case 32/65, [1966] ECR 389.

[2] Most writers, however, use this term only where the challenge is made in proceedings brought in the European Court and not where it is made in a national court.

[3] See Bebr, 'Examen en validité au titre de l'article 177 du traité CEE et cohésion juridique de la Communauté' [1975] CDE 379 at 417–20. Many writers, however, accept the basic identity between the two cases: see Arendt, 'La procédure selon l'article 177 du traité instituant la Communauté Economique Européenne' (1965) 13 SEW 383 at 409; Mertens de Wilmars, 'La procédure suivant l'article 177 CEE' (1965) 13 SEW 437 at 444; for further references, see Bebr (above), p. 417, note 110.

This view derives some justification from the fact that different Treaty provisions are applicable and also from the fact that the relationship between Union law and national law is involved. However, at a more fundamental level the issues are identical, since the legal nature of an indirect challenge is the same, irrespective of the court in which it is brought. For this reason, the general principles of indirect challenge will be discussed in this chapter in the context of both kinds of procedure.

The possibility of an indirect challenge (which may, of course, be brought by either applicant or defendant) could arise in almost any proceedings in the European Court. Thus, in an annulment action under Article 263 TFEU, the validity of the act subject to direct challenge could depend on the validity of another act, and an indirect challenge could be made against the latter. For example, the former act might have been adopted on the basis of powers delegated by the latter. Other questions which could in theory depend on the validity of an act which is not itself the subject matter of the proceedings are: in an action under Article 265 TFEU for a remedy for failure to act, the obligation to act; in actions arising out of a contract (Article 272 TFEU), the validity of the contract; in actions in tort (Articles 268 and 340 TFEU), the lawfulness of the allegedly wrongful act; in enforcement actions against a Member State under Article 258 TFEU, the existence of the obligation which the Member State is alleged not to have fulfilled; and in appeals against penalties under Article 261 TFEU, the validity of the measure that the appellant is alleged to have violated. In a national court, the question could arise whenever Union law was relevant to the proceedings, for example when a party claims a right based on a directly effective Union measure or when a national measure is enacted in implementation of a Union measure.

The potential scope for indirect challenge is wide. The question to be considered in this chapter is whether it may be invoked whenever appropriate, or whether there are restrictions on its use. In particular, there is the question whether it should be regarded as available in all cases where it is not excluded by express enactment or whether it may be invoked only where there is express authorization in the Treaties.

§2 TREATY PROVISIONS

The Treaties contain two provisions dealing with indirect challenge. The first is Article 277 TFEU [241/184 EC], which reads:

> Notwithstanding the expiry of the period laid down in Article 263, sixth paragraph, any party may, in proceedings in which an act of general application adopted by an institution, body, office or agency of the Union is at issue, plead the grounds specified in Article 263, second paragraph, in order to invoke before the Court of Justice of the European Union the inapplicability of that act.

This is a classic description of an indirect challenge. The grounds of invalidity are exactly the same as in the case of a direct challenge. If successful, the effect of the challenge is that the act is not applied in the case in question.

Although Article 277 is expressed in general terms, it nevertheless contains two limitations: first – and most important – it applies only to acts of general application;[4] secondly, it applies only where the challenge is made in the course of proceedings in the European Court (this is not clear from the wording of Article 277 but was laid down by the European Court in *Wöhrmann v. Commission*).[5] The first of these restrictions raises fundamental issues which will be discussed later; the second, however, is easily explained by virtue of Article 267 TFEU.

Sub-paragraph (b) of the first paragraph of Article 267 is the second Treaty provision dealing with indirect challenge. It makes provision for national courts to refer to the European Court questions concerning 'the validity...of acts of the institutions, bodies, offices or agencies of the Union'. Since the national courts have no power to hear a direct challenge to the validity of Union acts, this must refer to an indirect challenge; it therefore implicitly accepts that an indirect challenge may be made before a national court. It should be noted that this provision does not lay down any limitations as to the kind of act that may be challenged, provided it is a Union act.

Cases decided under the ECSC Treaty establish that the right to make an indirect challenge is not dependent on an express Treaty provision: it is a general principle of law.[6] However, this general principle does not apply in all cases. The next question to consider is the scope of the principle and the restrictions to which it is subject.

§3 WHAT ACTS MAY BE CHALLENGED?

Here a distinction is generally made between acts of general application (also called 'normative' or 'general' acts) and individual acts. This distinction was discussed in Chapter 4, § 1.3, where classification of legal acts on the basis of their function was discussed. Acts of general application are acts that lay down general rules; individual acts are acts that decide particular cases. In principle, regulations are acts of general application; decisions are individual acts. However, it is not the form of the act which is decisive but its substance; therefore, an act in the form of a regulation may turn out to be, in substance, a decision (individual act), while an act in the form of a decision may actually be an act of general application.[7]

In view of Article 277 TFEU, there are no problems regarding an indirect challenge in the European Court to an act of general application. Moreover, there has never been any doubt that an act of general application is subject to indirect challenge in the national courts. This means that such acts are open to indirect challenge in all courts.

[4] Before amendments brought in by the Treaty of Lisbon, it applied only to regulations.

[5] Cases 31, 33/62, [1962] ECR 501.

[6] *Meroni v. High Authority*, Case 9/56, [1958] ECR 133; *Meroni v. High Authority*, Case 10/56, [1958] ECR 157; *Compagnie des Hauts Fourneaux de Chasse v. High Authority*, Case 15/57, [1958] ECR 211.

[7] *Simmenthal v. Commission*, Case 92/78, [1979] ECR 777 at paras 39–41 of the judgment.

In the case of individual acts, on the other hand, the position is more complex. In cases under the ECSC Treaty, it has been held that the addressee of an individual act may not challenge it indirectly in the European Court.[8] This applies just as much under the EU Treaties. Thus, for example, if a decision is addressed to a Member State under Article 106 TFEU (public undertakings)[9] or Article 108 TFEU (State aid)[10] and the Member State neither complies with it nor brings proceedings to annul it within the time limit laid down by Article 263 TFEU, it cannot thereafter challenge it indirectly in the course of an action against it under Article 258 TFEU or Article 108(2) TFEU.[11]

It is also clear that a person who is *not* the addressee of an individual act and does not have *locus standi* to challenge it directly may challenge the act indirectly in a national court: thus, for example, if the Commission addresses a decision to a Member State empowering it to take a certain action, and the Member State takes that action, a person affected by it may make an indirect challenge to the Commission decision in the course of proceedings brought in the national courts to challenge the validity of the action of the Member State.[12]

Until the beginning of 1994, this also appeared to be true if the person making the indirect challenge, though not the addressee of the act, could nevertheless have challenged it in a direct action in the European Court under Article 263 TFEU. There were two authorities. The first was the *Universität Hamburg*[13] case, in which the Court allowed the University of Hamburg to make an indirect challenge in the German courts against a decision which (though addressed to the German Government) concerned the University directly and individually and which could, therefore, have been challenged directly by it under Article 263 TFEU.[14] The reason the Court gave was that the University might not have been aware of the decision before the expiry of the time limit under Article 263 because the Commission was not obliged to inform the University or even to publish the decision; consequently, the University might not have been able to exercise its right to challenge the decision directly. This would be true in most cases where the decision was not addressed to the person concerned.

[8] *Dalmas v. High Authority*, Case 21/64, [1965] ECR 175; *Sideradria v. Commission*, Case 41/85, [1986] ECR 3917.

[9] *Commission v. Greece*, Case 226/87, [1988] ECR 3611.

[10] *Commission v. Belgium*, Case 156/77, [1978] ECR 1881; *Commission v. Greece*, Case C-183/91, [1993] ECR I-3131.

[11] The same was true where the proceedings were under Art. 88 ECSC (the equivalent of Art. 258 TFEU): *Germany v. High Authority (Railway Tariffs)*, Case 3/59, [1960] ECR 53.

[12] See, for example, *Gesellschaft für Getreidehandel v. EVGF*, Case 55/72, [1973] ECR 15. See also *Handelsvereniging Rotterdam*, Cases 73–4/63, [1964] ECR 1, especially *per* Advocate General Roemer at 20–2.

[13] Case 216/82, [1983] ECR 2771.

[14] This was established in the earlier case of *Control Data Belgium v. Commission*, Case 294/81, [1983] ECR 911.

The second authority was *Rau v. BALM*,[15] in which the European Court made the following statement:[16]

> It must be emphasised that there is nothing in Community law to prevent an action from being brought before a national court against a measure implementing a decision adopted by a Community institution where the conditions laid down by national law are satisfied. When such an action is brought, if the outcome of the dispute depends on the validity of that decision the national court may submit questions to the Court of Justice by way of a reference for a preliminary ruling, without there being any need to ascertain whether or not the plaintiff in the main proceedings has the possibility of challenging the decision directly before the Court.

In 1994, however, the European Court decided the *TWD* case.[17] This concerned a German company which had been given aid by the German authorities. The Commission subsequently took a decision addressed to Germany, which declared the aid incompatible with the Common Market and required the German Government to obtain its repayment. The German Government informed the company of the decision and told the company that it could challenge the decision in the European Court under Article 263 TFEU (then Article 173 EEC). The company did not do so.

Acting on the basis of the decision, the German Government then adopted a measure which would have had the effect of requiring the repayment of the aid. The company challenged this measure in the German courts, partly on the ground that the Commission decision on which it was based was invalid. The German court made a preliminary reference to the European Court asking, first, whether an indirect challenge is possible in such a situation and, secondly, whether the Commission decision was invalid. By the time the indirect challenge was made in the German court, the time limit for a direct challenge had expired.

Following the lead of Advocate General Jacobs, the European Court held that no indirect challenge could be made, since the company could 'without any doubt'[18] have challenged it directly under Article 263 TFEU [173 EEC].[19] On the other hand, however, the European Court confirmed that, where this is not the case, there is a general principle of law which 'confers upon any party to proceedings the right to challenge, for the purpose of obtaining the annulment of a decision of direct and individual concern to that party, the validity of previous acts of the institutions which form the legal basis of the decision which is being attacked...'.[20]

[15] Cases 133–6/85, [1987] ECR 2289.

[16] Para. 11 of the judgment.

[17] Case C-188/92, [1994] ECR I-833.

[18] Para. 24 of the judgment.

[19] It distinguished *Rau v. BALM* on the ground that in that case a direct challenge under Art. 263 (then Art. 173 EEC) was in fact pending when the reference was made.

[20] Para. 23 of the judgment. This had previously been laid down in *Simmenthal v. Commission*, Case 92/78, [1979] ECR 777 and has been confirmed in later cases, including *Pringle v. Government of Ireland*, Case C-370/12, 27 November 2012 (Full Court) at para. 39 of the judgment.

The position now is that a party with *locus standi* to make a direct challenge to an act may challenge it indirectly only if its *locus standi* is not beyond doubt.[21] In *Pringle v. Government of Ireland*,[22] the European Court put it as follows:

> ...the point must be made that the recognition of a party's right to plead the invalidity of an act of the Union presupposes that that party did not have the right to bring, under Article 263 TFEU, a direct action for the annulment of that act...Were it to be accepted that a party who beyond doubt had standing to institute proceedings under the fourth paragraph of Article 263 TFEU for the annulment of an act of the Union could, after the expiry of the time-limit for bringing proceedings laid down in the sixth paragraph of Article 263 TFEU, challenge before the national courts the validity of that act, that would amount to enabling the person concerned to circumvent the fact that that act is final as against him once the time-limit for his bringing an action has expired...

It follows *a fortiori* from these cases that the addressee of an individual act can never challenge it indirectly, either in the European Court or in the national courts.[23]

§4 WHO MAY MAKE THE CHALLENGE?

Are privileged applicants (the European Parliament, the Commission, the Council, and the Member States) ever entitled to make an indirect challenge, or are they precluded from doing so by virtue of their status, irrespective of the nature of the act involved? Since they have *locus standi* to challenge *any* reviewable act, it could be argued that they can never make an indirect challenge.

The question arose in *Italy v. Commission*.[24] Here, Italy brought proceedings under Article 263 TFEU (then Article 173 EEC) to quash a Council regulation, and also made an indirect challenge against two other regulations. The Commission questioned whether a Member State is entitled to make an indirect challenge, but Advocate General Roemer stated that a Member State should have the same rights as other applicants. He based his opinion on two arguments: first, Article 277 TFEU (then Article 184 EEC) is expressed in general terms and provides that 'any' party may make the challenge; and secondly, he said that the Member State might not have exercised its right to make a direct challenge because the defects in the regulation might not have

[21] For later cases, see *R v. Intervention Board for Agricultural Produce, ex parte Accrington Beef*, Case C-241/95, [1996] ECR I-6699 at paras 14–16 of the judgment; *Eurotunnel v. SeaFrance*, Case C-408/95, [1997] ECR I-6315 at paras 26–30 of the judgment; *Nachi Europe*, Case C-239/99, [2001] ECR I-1197 at paras 28–40 of the judgment; *E and F*, Case C-550/09, [2010] ECR I-6213 at paras 37–62 of the judgment; *Bolton Alimentari*, Case C-494/09, [2011] ECR I-647 at paras 20–25 of the judgment.

[22] Case C-370/12, 27 November 2012 (Full Court) at para. 41 of the judgment.

[23] *Wiljo v. Belgium*, Case C-178/95, [1997] ECR I-585. For earlier (inconclusive) cases on this point, see *De Bloos v. Bouyer*, Case 59/77, [1977] ECR 2359; *Commission v. Belgium*, Case 156/77, [1978] ECR 1881. For further discussion, see Wyatt, 'The Relationship between Actions for Annulment and References on Validity after *TWD Deggendorf*' in J Lonbay and A Biondi (eds), *Remedies for Breach of EC Law* (1997).

[24] Case 32/65, [1966] ECR 389.

been fully apparent until it was applied in a particular case.[25] The European Court did not deal with the point; it rejected the challenge on the ground that the regulations in question were not relevant to the issue before the Court.[26] The matter therefore remains unresolved.

§5 IN WHAT PROCEEDINGS MAY THE CHALLENGE BE MADE?

It was shown earlier that the theoretical conditions for an indirect challenge could occur in proceedings of almost any kind. Are there in fact any limitations on the proceedings in which the challenge may be made? So far, the European Court has allowed the challenge to be made in annulment actions, actions under Article 35 ECSC (the equivalent of Article 265 TFEU) for a remedy for failure to act,[27] staff actions under Article 270 TFEU (then Article 179 EEC),[28] enforcement actions under Article 258 TFEU (then 169 EEC),[29] and proceedings in a national court. There is no doubt that it may also be made in an appeal against a penalty: under the ECSC Treaty this was expressly covered by the third paragraph of Article 36. It appears, therefore, that an indirect challenge is not ruled out in any kind of proceedings.

§6 ON WHAT GROUNDS MAY THE CHALLENGE BE MADE?

Article 277 TFEU makes clear that where the challenge is made in the European Court the grounds of review are exactly the same as in the case of a direct challenge under Article 263 TFEU. At one time there was some doubt as to whether this was also true in the case of a challenge in the national courts in view of the fact that Article 267 TFEU speaks of the 'validity' of an act, while Article 263 uses the word 'legality'. Is there any difference between validity and legality? In the *Handelsvereniging Rotterdam* case,[30] it was suggested by the German Government in its observations that 'validity' had a

[25] *Ibid.* at 414.

[26] The Court did, however, repeat the words of Art. 277 (then Art. 184 EEC) ('any party may…') and some writers have taken this as an indication that the Court accepted the Advocate General's Opinion: see Barav, 'The Exception of Illegality in Community Law: A Critical Analysis' (1974) 11 CMLRev 366 at 372. This view, however, may involve reading too much into the judgment.

[27] *SNUPAT v. High Authority*, Cases 32–3/58, [1959] ECR 127 at 139.

[28] *Sabbatini v. European Parliament*, Case 20/71, [1972] ECR 345.

[29] See *Commission v. Germany*, Case 116/82, [1986] ECR 2519, where Germany was allowed without objection to make an indirect challenge to a regulation as a defence to an action against it under Art. 258 (then Art. 169 EEC). A Member State cannot, of course, make an indirect challenge to an individual act addressed to it.

[30] Cases 73–4/63, [1964] ECR 1.

much more restricted meaning than 'legality' and that in proceedings under Article 267 (then Article 177 EEC) the Court could consider only whether or not the act was non-existent (void) and not whether it might be merely voidable. (It will be remembered from the discussion in Chapter 11, § 4, that invalid Union acts are normally voidable and not void: the latter is the case only in very special circumstances where the act lacks any semblance of validity.)

This argument was rejected by Advocate General Roemer, who took the view that the same grounds of review apply as in the case of a direct challenge.[31] The Court did not specifically consider the problem but it has never given any indication that narrower grounds should be applied under Article 267, and in the third *International Fruit Company* case[32] it expressly stated that the grounds of review under Article 267 TFEU (then Article 177 EEC) cannot be restricted. One can conclude, therefore, that the grounds of review are identical in all cases.[33]

§7 THE EFFECT OF A SUCCESSFUL CHALLENGE

Since the purpose of an indirect challenge is to persuade the Court to decide the case before it on the basis that the act subject to the indirect challenge is invalid, it might be thought that a successful challenge could have no consequences beyond the case in question: unlike a ruling in an annulment action, it would have no *erga omnes* effect. In practice, however, it appears to have much the same effect, since the European Court has held that when an act has been declared invalid on a reference from a national court, though that ruling is binding only on the court which made the reference, 'it is sufficient reason for any other national court to regard that act as void'[34] (though such court may, if it wishes, refer the matter to the European Court again).[35] The strong implication of this judgment is that a ruling of invalidity is binding on other national courts, unless the European Court rescinds it on a subsequent reference – an unlikely occurrence. Moreover, the European Court has also ruled, on a reference from a national court, that an act may be invalid for

[31] *Ibid.* at 19–20.

[32] Cases 21–4/72, [1972] ECR 1219 at para. 5 of the judgment. See also *Racke*, Case C-162/96, [1998] ECR I-3655 at paras 25–28 of the judgment.

[33] At one time it was thought that there might be an exception where the Union act is contrary to an international agreement which is not directly effective. In the third *International Fruit Company* case (see n. 32) the European Court held that this could not be a ground of review under Art. 267 TFEU (then Art. 177 EEC) (see also *Schlüter*, Case 9/73, [1973] ECR 1135 at paras 24–31 of the judgment and *Bresciani*, Case 87/75, [1976] ECR 129 at paras 15–26 of the judgment). Some commentators took the view that this would be a ground of review under Art. 263. However, this has been rejected by the European Court in *Germany v. Council* (*Bananas* case), Case C-280/93, [1994] ECR I-4973, where it was confirmed that the position is the same under Art. 263 TFEU (then Art. 173 EEC) as under Art. 267 TFEU (then Art. 177 EEC): see paras 103–112 of the judgment.

[34] *International Chemical Corporation*, Case 66/80, [1981] ECR 1191 (first para. of the ruling).

[35] This could be to ask the European Court to reconsider its previous ruling; a more likely reason would be to request clarification on the temporal effect of the ruling (whether it applies only to the future or also to the past).

the future but valid for the past.[36] Such a ruling would be pointless if it was not applicable in later cases.[37]

§8 NON-EXISTENT ACTS

In the preceding discussion it has been assumed that the act subject to challenge, though invalid, is not non-existent (not void *ab initio*). If the act is non-existent, on the other hand, it is treated for all purposes as if it had never been adopted. As we saw in Chapter 11, § 4, it is not necessary for such an act to be annulled under Article 263 TFEU; indeed, it *cannot* be annulled because such proceedings would be inadmissible: the Court would lack jurisdiction *ratione materiae*, as there would be no reviewable act. As a result, it can be challenged indirectly – it might be more proper to say that its non-existence can be asserted – in *any* proceedings. Even the 'addressee' of a non-existent act can assert its non-existence, and it does not matter if the time limit under Article 263 has expired.[38]

FURTHER READING

Items are listed in date order, the most recent being at the end.

BEBR, 'Judicial Remedy of Private Parties against Normative Acts of the European Communities: The Role of the Exception of Illegality' (1966) 4 CMLRev. 7.

BARAV, 'The Exception of Illegality in Community Law: A Critical Analysis' (1974) 11 CMLRev. 366.

TRABUCCHI, 'L'effet "erga omnes" des décisions préjudicielles rendues par la Cour de Justice des Communautés européennes' [1974] RTDE 56.

BEBR, 'Examen en validité au titre de l'article 177 du traité CEE et cohésion juridique de la Communauté' [1975] CDE 379.

BEBR, 'Preliminary Rulings of the Court of Justice: Their Authority and Temporal Effect' (1981) 18 CMLRev. 475 (especially 475–83).

HARDING, 'The Impact of Article 177 of the EEC Treaty on the Review of Community Action' (1981) 1 YEL 93.

CAPDEVILA, 'The Action for Annulment, the Preliminary Reference on Validity and the Plea of Illegality: Complementary or Alternative Means?'(2006) 25 YEL 451.

VOGT, 'Indirect Judicial Protection in EC Law – The Case of the Plea of Illegality' (2006) 31 ELRev. 364.

ANGELA WARD, *Judicial Review and the Rights of Private Parties in EU Law*, 2nd edn (2007).

SCHWENSFEIER, 'The TWD Principle Post-Lisbon' (2012) 37 ELRev. 156.

[36] *Providence Agricole de la Champagne*, Case 4/79, [1980] ECR 2823; *Maïseries de Beauce*, Case 109/79, [1980] ECR 2883; *Roquette*, Case 145/79, [1980] ECR 2917. See also *Roquette*, Case C-228/92, [1994] ECR I-1445.

[37] See, further, Chap. 9, § 8.

[38] *Commission v. Greece*, Case 226/87, [1988] ECR 3611 at para. 16 of the judgment.

15

REVIEW AND ANNULMENT

§1 GROUNDS OF REVIEW

When the applicant has overcome all jurisdictional hurdles and problems of admissibility, he must convince the Court that the measure ought to be annulled. To do this, he must establish one or other of the grounds of review set out in Article 263 TFEU. These grounds apply not only in direct actions for annulment, but also in the case of an indirect challenge.[1] The grounds of review are four in number:

1. lack of competence;
2. infringement of an essential procedural requirement;
3. infringement of the Treaty or any rule of law relating to its application;
4. misuse of powers.

These grounds are derived from French administrative law; this does not, however, mean that they will necessarily be applied in the same way in EU law as in French law: the legal traditions of all the Member States, as well as the special circumstances of the European Union, will be taken into account by the European Court.

It will be noticed that these grounds are broad and cover almost every possible illegality. They also overlap to a considerable extent. In fact, if the third ground were given a sufficiently extensive interpretation, it could cover all the other three. Special considerations apply where a measure is attacked on procedural grounds or where a misuse of powers is claimed;[2] beyond this, it does not matter very much which formal ground is applicable. For this reason, the European Court does not normally state which of the four formal grounds is involved when it annuls a measure. Nevertheless, a word should be said about each of them.

§1.1 LACK OF COMPETENCE

Here 'competence' means legal power to adopt an act. The principle of the Treaties is that institutions have no power to adopt an act unless they are authorized to do so by a Treaty provision: the Union has no inherent legislative or executive power (principle of conferral, explained in Chapter 4, § 2). For every act, therefore, it must be possible to

[1] See Chap. 14, § 6. [2] This ground stands apart from the others because it involves subjective factors.

point to a Treaty provision (or to another legal act in turn based on a Treaty provision) which provides its legal basis. If there is no such basis, the act will be annulled for lack of competence.[3] The equivalent concept in English law is *ultra vires*.

Although it raises fundamental issues, this ground is rarely invoked because it is difficult – except, perhaps, in cases of delegation – to establish that the enacting authority lacked competence. It will be remembered from the discussion in Chapter 4, that the European Court gives a wide interpretation to empowering provisions in the Treaties; the theory of implied powers also extends the competence of the Council and Commission. On top of this, Article 352 TFEU is of such wide scope that, except in the case of matters wholly outside the ambit of the Treaty, it is almost always possible to find a legal basis for a Council act.[4]

A more common complaint is that the act was adopted under the wrong empowering provision, that is to say that the Council or Commission had the power to adopt it under one provision, but acted under another.[5] This was discussed in Chapter 4, and it will be remembered that the Court will annul the measure if resort to the wrong empowering provision had significant consequences – for example, if the provision under which the measure was adopted required unanimity while the correct provision provided for qualified majority voting. If there are no such consequences, the measure will not be annulled. In cases of this kind, the formal ground of review would appear not to be lack of competence – since the institution in question admittedly has the power to adopt the measure – but rather an infringement of an essential procedural requirement. It is, however, curious that the adoption of a measure by unanimity, instead of by a qualified majority, should constitute such an infringement, since a unanimous vote necessarily constitutes a majority.[6]

§1.2 INFRINGEMENT OF AN ESSENTIAL PROCEDURAL REQUIREMENT

This ground of invalidity includes requirements which may be regarded as procedural in the strict sense, such as a requirement to consult another authority, and also requirements concerning the form of the measure – for example, the requirement to give reasons.

The requirement may be laid down either in the Treaty or in secondary legislation (for example, in the case of delegation, a requirement to consult); it may also be

[3] See the first para. of Art. 5 [3b] EC.

[4] But for cases in which a Commission measure was annulled for lack of competence, see *France v. Commission*, Case C-327/91, [1994] ECR I-3641; *Germany v. European Parliament and Council* (*Tobacco Advertising* case), Case C-376/98, [2000] ECR I-8419.

[5] Such arguments are facilitated by the fact that regulations, directives, and decisions adopted by the Council or Commission must specify the empowering provision under which they were adopted: see § 1.2.

[6] For a bizarre incident in which the Council changed the legal basis of a measure *ex post facto* by means of another measure, see Regulation 2746/72, OJ 1972, L 291/148, amending Regulation 947/71, OJ 1971, L 106/1.

prescribed by a general principle of law. An example of the latter is the principle of *audi alteram partem*, which was held in the *Transocean Marine Paint* case[7] to be binding on the Commission even in the absence of an express legislative provision.[8]

It will be noticed that only an 'essential' procedural requirement is a ground of annulment. The distinction between essential and non-essential requirements, which was adopted from French administrative law,[9] is similar to the English distinction between procedural provisions that are mandatory and those that are merely directory. The philosophy behind this distinction is the same in all three systems: to invalidate an act for an insignificant procedural defect would unduly hamper administrative activity and would encourage excessive formalism and 'red tape', which in turn would stifle initiative and slow down the administrative process; on the other hand, not to annul for any formal defect at all would be detrimental to good administration and would prejudice the rights of individuals. The law therefore tries to achieve a compromise by restricting the sanction of invalidity to those cases where an important provision has been violated.

This compromise has many advantages; but it has the disadvantage of uncertainty: how does one tell whether a requirement is to be regarded as essential or not? Union provisions laying down procedural requirements do not normally state whether their infringement will lead to invalidity. Therefore, one must look to the function of the provision and to the likely consequences if it is not observed. Thus, if failure to observe it could affect the final content of the act, one would be justified in concluding that it was an essential requirement. For example, a requirement to consult another body, or to grant the person concerned a hearing, is classifiable as essential on the basis of this test: the facts and arguments that would be brought to the notice of the enacting authority through this procedure could induce it to alter the content of the measure.

It would be a mistake, however, to conclude that this is the sole test: procedural requirements which have no possible effects on the content of the act can also be classified as essential. For example, the most important objectives of the requirement to give reasons are, according to the European Court, to help the persons concerned defend their rights, to help the Court exercise its supervisory functions, and to enable third parties to appreciate the way in which the enacting authorities use their powers.[10] None of these considerations relates to the content of the measure;[11] yet the requirement to give reasons can certainly constitute an essential procedural requirement.

[7] Case 17/74, [1974] ECR 1063.

[8] See Chap. 5, § 6.

[9] The term used in French law for an essential procedural requirement is '*une forme substantielle*'; this is also the term used in the French version of the Treaties.

[10] See Chap. 4, § 7.2.

[11] It is, of course, true that another function of the requirement to give reasons is to clarify the enacting authority's objectives in adopting the measure; thus the discipline of formulating the reasons could induce it to reconsider the content of the measure. To this extent, the classification of this requirement as essential could be justified on the basis of the first test. This function has not, however, been mentioned by the European Court and it must be regarded as secondary.

Article 296, second paragraph, TFEU provides that legal acts must state the reasons on which they are based. This includes a requirement to specify the legal provision under which they were adopted (legal basis). In the *Tariff Preferences* case,[12] however, the Court held that failure to refer to a precise provision of the Treaty is not necessarily an infringement of an essential procedural requirement if it is possible to determine from other parts of the measure what its legal basis is. Where, however, the parties and the Court would otherwise be uncertain as to its precise legal basis, an explicit reference is, it held, 'indispensable'.[13] It would appear that in the former case there would be an infringement of a non-essential procedural requirement and in the latter of an essential one.[14] This shows that the terminology of the Treaty is misleading: what is important is not the nature of the procedural requirement infringed, but the consequences, in the particular circumstances of the case, of the infringement.

Requirements so far held to be essential include the requirement to give reasons, the requirement to grant a hearing (*audi alteram partem*),[15] the requirement to attain assent,[16] the requirement to consult,[17] and the requirement that a Council measure be based on a proposal from the Commission.[18]

The case of *United Kingdom v. Council*[19] establishes that the Council's Rules of Procedure can contain essential procedural requirements. Article 6(1) of the Rules of Procedure permitted measures to be adopted by the written procedure (without an actual meeting) provided no Member State objected. At a meeting of the Council held on 19 December 1985 it was decided, despite the contrary votes of the United Kingdom and Denmark, to adopt a particular directive by means of the written procedure before 31 December 1985. On 23 December, the Secretary General of the Council telexed the British Minister for Agriculture asking for his vote, which he was required to give by 30 December. In a letter dated 31 December, the Minister replied that the United Kingdom objected to the use of the written procedure and also to the directive itself. On the same day the Council notified the United Kingdom that the directive had been adopted.

The United Kingdom brought proceedings to annul the directive on the ground that resort to the written procedure violated Article 6(1) of the Council's Rules of Procedure. This raised the question whether the requirement of unanimity in that

[12] *Commission v. Council*, Case 45/86, [1987] ECR 1493.

[13] *Ibid.* at para. 9 of the judgment.

[14] It is not entirely clear whether, even here, the measure would be invalid if it had in fact been adopted under the correct empowering provision, or if resort to an incorrect empowering provision had not affected the procedure followed: see *per* Advocate General Lenz [1987] ECR at 1514–15 (paras 91–95).

[15] *Transocean Marine Paint v. Commission*, Case 17/74, [1974] ECR 1063.

[16] *Klöckner-Werke v. Commission*, Case 119/81, [1982] ECR 2627 at para. 6 of the judgment.

[17] *Italy v. High Authority*, Case 2/54, [1954] ECR 37 at 51–2; *Netherlands v. High Authority*, Case 6/54, [1955] ECR 103 at 112; *Roquette v. Council*, Case 138/79, [1980] ECR 3333; and *Maizena v. Council*, Case 139/79, [1980] ECR 3393 (duty to consult the European Parliament).

[18] In *United Kingdom v. Council*, Case 68/86, [1988] ECR 855 at para. 32 of the judgment, it was held that failure to identify the Commission proposal on which a measure is based is not an infringement of an essential procedural requirement, provided the measure is in fact based on a Commission proposal.

[19] Case 68/86, [1988] ECR 855.

provision constituted an essential procedural requirement.[20] The Court held it did, and therefore annulled the directive.

§1.3 INFRINGEMENT OF THE TREATY OR OF ANY RULE OF LAW RELATING TO ITS APPLICATION

If narrowly interpreted, this ground applies only to those cases where the act subject to challenge violates an express prohibition (in this respect, it contrasts with lack of competence, which applies in the absence of any relevant provision), but if given a wide interpretation it overlaps with virtually every other ground of annulment, since each could be said to involve an infringement of some rule of Union law. For this reason, it is almost always pleaded by litigants in addition to any other ground they might think appropriate.

What does it cover? First, it covers all provisions in the EU Treaties and all other Treaties amending or supplementing them; consequently it covers all the constitutive Treaties.[21] Secondly, it covers 'any rule of law' relating to the application of any of those Treaties. At first sight, the meaning of this phrase may give rise to doubt. The Dutch version of the Treaty uses the phrase *enige uitvoeringsregeling daarvan*, which means 'any rule executing it'. This suggests that the phrase applies only to implementing provisions, but this is too narrow an interpretation: the European Court has made clear that it applies to all rules of Union law other than those found in the constitutive Treaties.

Each of the following is a possible source of rules of law relating to the application of the Treaty:[22]

1. Union acts (including acts *sui generis*);
2. subsidiary conventions (provided they are part of the Union legal system);
3. acts of the representatives of the Member States (in so far as they are legally binding);
4. treaties with third countries binding on the Union (whether entered into by the Union or by the Member States);
5. the general principles of Union law;
6. international law.

Each of these will be considered in turn.

Violation of another Union act will be a ground of annulment if that other act was binding on the author of the act subject to challenge. This will occur where the latter is delegated legislation and also in those cases where the principle of legal certainty (protection of legitimate expectations) requires that the author of the act subject to

[20] The requirement of unanimity for the adoption of the written procedure is separate from the question whether unanimity is required for the adoption of the directive itself: see para. 47 of the judgment.

[21] See Chap. 3.

[22] See G Vandersanden and A Barav, *Contentieux Communautaire* (1977), pp. 188–201.

challenge abide by some previous act adopted by it. The *Staff Salaries* case[23] (discussed earlier)[24] furnishes an example of this: the Court there annulled a measure of the Council providing salary increases for EU staff because it violated a previous Council decision laying down the formula on the basis of which future salary increases were to be calculated. The Court held that the principle of legitimate expectations required the Council to adhere to its previous decision.

The question whether a subsidiary convention[25] prevails over a Union act is not free from doubt but it probably does not. If this is correct, violation of such a convention will not be a ground of annulment; but if the European Court takes the opposite view, there is no doubt that it would annul the act in question for violation of a rule of law relating to the application of the Treaty.[26] It will also be remembered that acts of the representatives of the Member States are in some cases a species of international agreement between the Member States. In such cases they will be of a similar status to the subsidiary conventions.

International agreements with non-member States concluded by the Union, or otherwise binding on it, are also covered; so any Union act contrary to such an agreement would be annulled by the Court, provided that the agreement was directly effective.[27]

The general principles of Union law play an important part in annulment actions.[28] An infringement of such a principle is a ground of invalidity except in those cases where the principle is merely interpretative or intended only to fill gaps in Union legislation.

In the *Racke* case,[29] the European Court held that the principles of customary international law may be applied to determine the validity of a Union regulation. The regulation in question had suspended a trade agreement between the Union and Yugoslavia, and it was argued by someone who claimed directly-effective rights under the agreement that the suspension was contrary to international law. The European Court held that customary international law is applicable as part of the Union legal system, but that a measure should be declared invalid for infringement of international law only when the Union institution adopting it made 'manifest errors of assessment' concerning the conditions for applying the relevant rules.[30]

§1.4 MISUSE OF POWERS

Though of great theoretical interest, this ground is only rarely established in practice. It is derived from French administrative law – where it is known as *détournement*

[23] *Commission v. Council*, Case 81/72, [1973] ECR 575. [24] See Chap. 5, § 3.2.

[25] On the meaning of this term, see Chap. 3, § 2.

[26] Though of importance in the past, most subsidiary conventions have now been replaced by Union acts.

[27] *International Fruit Company*, Cases 21–4/72, [1972] ECR 1219 at para. 5 of the judgment; *Schlüter*, Case 9/73, [1973] ECR 1135 at paras 24–31 of the judgment; *Bresciani*, Case 87/75, [1976] ECR 129 at paras 15–26 of the judgment; *Germany v. Council* (*Bananas* case), Case C-280/93, [1994] ECR I-4973 at paras 103–112 of the judgment.

[28] See Chap. 5.

[29] Case C-162/96, [1998] ECR I-3655. [30] *Ibid.* at para. 52 of the judgment.

de pouvoir – but is also found, in one form or another, in the legal systems of most Western countries. A misuse of powers has been defined by the Court as the adoption by a Union institution of a measure with the exclusive or main purpose of achieving an end other than that stated, or evading a procedure specifically prescribed by the Treaty for dealing with the circumstances of the case.[31] Put more simply, it is the exercise of a power for a purpose other than that for which it was granted.[32] It is a well-established ground of invalidity in English administrative law, where it is usually referred to, more informatively, as 'improper purpose'.

Unlike the other grounds of invalidity, which are objective in character, misuse of powers is subjective: in order to establish it, one has to discover the subjective purpose – the motive or intention – of the authority exercising the power.[33] For this reason, misuse of powers is more difficult to prove than other grounds: in the absence of a document emanating from the authority which indicates its purpose in adopting the measure, the applicant may have to rely on inference from the content of the measure and the general circumstances prevailing when it was enacted.[34] It is not, however, necessary to prove bad faith: an authority may quite innocently misuse its powers if it fails to appreciate the purpose for which they were given.

It will be apparent that misuse of powers is closely related to the doctrine of proportionality. This is one of the general principles of Union law (discussed in Chapter 5, § 4); it requires that burdens imposed on the citizen be proportionate to the objective pursued: the means chosen must be reasonably likely to attain the objective and the detriment inflicted on those concerned must not be disproportionate to the general benefit. The difference between proportionality and misuse of powers is that proportionality is purely objective: the terms of the measure are balanced against the objective of the provision under which it was adopted; in the case of misuse of powers, on the

[31] See, for example, *European Parliament v. Commission*, Case C-156/93, [1995] ECR I-2019 at para. 31 of the judgment.

[32] See *Netherlands v. High Authority*, Case 6/54, [1955] ECR 103 at 116; *Compagnie des Hauts Fourneaux de Chasse v. High Authority*, Case 15/57, [1958] ECR 211 at 230.

[33] In some of its earlier judgments, however, the European Court seems to have veered away from the pure doctrine of misuse of powers and allowed an objective element to enter its reasoning. Thus in *Hauts Fourneaux et Aciéries Belges v. High Authority*, Case 8/57, [1958] ECR 245 at 256, the Court said that violation of the principle of equality could constitute misuse of power; while in other cases there is a suggestion that lack of foresight could lead to misuse of power: see *Fédéchar v. High Authority*, Case 8/55, [1956] ECR 292 at 303, and *Chambre Syndicale de la Sidérurgie Française v. High Authority*, Cases 3–4/64, [1965] ECR 441 at 454–5; see further, G Vandersanden and A Barav, *Contentieux Communautaire* (1977), pp. 207–8. This extended concept of misuse of powers (which appears to have been derived from German law: see Dickschat, 'Problèmes d'interprétation des traités européens résultant de leur plurilinguisme' [1968] *Revue Belge de Droit International* 40 at 47) was probably adopted by the Court because of the special role played by misuse of powers in the ECSC Treaty, particularly with regard to the right of non-privileged applicants to challenge normative measures. By applying the wider concept, the Court could extend the right of non-privileged applicants to obtain judicial review under Art. 33 ECSC.

[34] The Court has said that the misuse of powers must be established 'on the basis of objective, relevant and consistent facts': see *Gutmann v. Commission*, Cases 18, 35/65, [1966] ECR 103 at 117 and *Lux v. Court of Auditors*, Case 69/83, [1984] ECR 2447 at para. 30 of the judgment.

other hand, the subjective intention of the author of the act is the relevant factor. If the authority is genuinely pursuing the proper objective, but uses inappropriate means, the measure will be annulled for lack of proportionality; if the objective is improper, misuse of powers will be the correct ground of review. However, though the two doctrines are quite distinct in theory, they can easily merge in practice, since the fact that the measure is inappropriate for the attainment of its ostensible objective will suggest that this was not the objective which its author was trying to attain.

In what circumstance will misuse of powers apply? French writers sometimes divide it into two categories, primary *détournement de pouvoir* and secondary *détournement de pouvoir*. The former comprises those cases where the power is not used in the public interest at all, but is used for some private objective of its author, perhaps to advance his own interests or to spite someone he dislikes. For example, if an official were refused a particular post because the decision-maker wished to appoint a family member, one would have a case of primary misuse of powers.[35]

Secondary misuse of powers occurs where the objective pursued is in the public interest but it is not one which the author of the act is entitled to pursue. The case of *Gutmann v. Commission*[36] furnishes a good example. The applicant in this case was an EAEC official who was transferred from the Research Centre at Ispra to Brussels on the basis of a provision authorizing the transfer of an official 'in the interests of the service'. The Court held, however, that this was not the real reason for the decision to transfer him: it was actually taken for disciplinary purposes. The decision was, therefore, annulled for misuse of powers.

Another case in which the plea was successfully invoked was *Giuffrida v. Council*.[37] This concerned an official called Signor Martino, who held an appointment at a particular grade, even though for many years he had performed duties appropriate to an official of a higher grade. In an attempt to remedy this anomalous situation, the Council organized a competition for a post at the higher grade. The sole object of this was, by the Council's own admission, to allow Signor Martino to be appointed to a post corresponding to his duties. Two officials applied, Signor Martino and the applicant in the case, Signor Giuffrida; Signor Martino was appointed and Signor Giuffrida brought proceedings to annul the appointment. The Court held that the objective of any recruitment procedure, including an internal competition, should be to appoint the best person for the job; by deciding in advance whom it would appoint, the Council was guilty of a misuse of powers. The appointment was therefore quashed.

A misuse of powers may also occur if an authority, for an improper reason, adopts a measure under one provision when another provision would have been more

[35] Compare *Mirossevich v. High Authority*, Case 10/55, [1956] ECR 333. Here similar allegations were made but were not proved.

[36] Cases 18, 35/65, [1966] ECR 103.

[37] Case 105/75, [1976] ECR 1395. See also *Fabrique de Fer de Charleroi v. Commission*, Cases 351, 360/85, [1987] ECR 3639, a case involving steel quotas in which the Commission adopted criteria designed to help a particular Member State rather than to spread the burden fairly among all steel enterprises.

appropriate. This was recognized by the Court in *Compagnie des Hauts Fourneaux de Chasse v. High Authority* where it said:[38]

> In this connexion it must be recognized that there might have been a misuse of powers if the High Authority had been faced with a situation covered by the procedure in Article 59 and, in order to evade the safeguards provided for in Article 59, had nevertheless deliberately decided to make use of Article 53(b) and of the financial arrangements provided for therein.

This rule would not, of course, apply if both provisions were appropriate and the authority's choice was not made on improper grounds.

It is important to note that a measure will not be annulled for misuse of powers if the improper purpose had no effect on its substance. After all, why should a measure be quashed if it would have been enacted in exactly the same terms even if its author had not been pursuing an illegitimate objective? Consequently, it will be valid if pursuit of the proper purpose would inevitably have led to the same result.[39]

It follows from this rule that if the authority has two objectives, one proper and one improper, the measure will not be annulled if the proper objective was the decisive one. In such a case, the improper objective will have no influence on the outcome. In *Fédéchar v. High Authority*[40] the Court said:

> Even if one unjustified reason were included among those which justify the action of the High Authority, the decision would not for that reason involve a misuse of powers, in so far as it does not adversely affect the basic aim of [the provision under which it was taken].

This statement suggests that, so long as the legitimate aim is attained, the presence of an improper purpose will be of no consequence. It seems to extend the rule slightly, since the improper purpose may have had some effect on the terms of the measure, even if it did not prevent the fulfilment of the legitimate objective. In other cases, there are suggestions that, where several motives are present, the applicant must prove that the improper motive was the sole, or at least the dominant, one.[41]

§2 THE TIME FACTOR

In all annulment actions, the validity of the act must be determined on the basis of the situation existing at the time when it was adopted. A measure cannot, therefore, be annulled because of a subsequent event. This is logical in view of the fact that

[38] Case 15/57, [1958] ECR 211 at 231. The Court actually found that misuse of powers had not been proved.

[39] *Fédéchar v. High Authority*, Case 8/55, [1956] ECR 292 at 300–1.

[40] Case 8/55, [1956] ECR 245 at 301. See also *France v. High Authority*, Case 1/54, [1954] ECR 1 at 16.

[41] See the *Fédéchar* case, Case 8/55, [1956] ECR 292 at 303; and *Hauts Fourneaux de Chasse v. High Authority*, Case 2/57, [1958] ECR 199 at 232. Compare the English decision of *R v. Brixton Prison Governor, ex parte Soblen* [1963] 2 QB 243 (Lord Denning's judgment).

annulment is normally retroactive: the Court declares the act to have been invalid *ab initio*.[42] It follows from this that an act cannot be annulled on the ground that it is in conflict with a superior rule of law contained in a measure enacted at a subsequent date. The superior measure will, of course, prevail and the first act will be inapplicable to the extent of the conflict; but the Court will not annul it.

These principles can be illustrated from the case-law of the European Court. *Schroeder v. Germany*,[43] for example, concerned a Union measure passed in order to limit imports of tomato concentrate from Greece. It was argued that the measure was not appropriate to achieve its objective – it was enacted under a power to pass 'appropriate' measures – because it could easily be circumvented. In dealing with this point, the Court said that the matter had to be approached on the basis of what was known when the measure was introduced: 'retrospective considerations of its efficacy' could not be taken into account.[44]

In the *Compagnie d'Approvisionnement* case,[45] the measure in issue was intended to counteract the effects of the devaluation of the French franc and it did this, in part, by granting subsidies to French exporters of agricultural produce. The applicant, which was a French exporter, maintained, however, that the subsidies were not high enough. One of its objections to the measure was that it infringed the principle of equality, since it was less generous than another regulation passed at a later date granting subsidies to German and Dutch importers consequent on a revaluation of the German and Dutch currencies. It alleged that this constituted discrimination against French exporters. The Court, however, ruled that the validity of the first regulation could not be called into question on the basis of subsequent events; consequently a comparison with the later measure could not be used to establish discrimination.[46]

This latter case raises some interesting issues: if two measures are passed dealing with situations which are sufficiently similar to bring the principle of equality into play, the possibilities of annulment might depend on which is passed first. If the less favourable measure is passed after the more favourable, it could be annulled for violation of the principle of equality. If, on the other hand, the less favourable measure is passed first, it is doubtful whether either could be annulled on this ground: the less favourable measure could not be annulled because of the time factor; the more favourable would not be quashed because the persons benefiting from it would not wish to challenge it and those covered by the less favourable measure would normally lack *locus standi*.

Is there no remedy in the latter case? One possibility is that those covered by the less favourable measure might request the enacting institution to amend it to bring it into line with the other measure; if this request were not met, proceedings could be brought for a remedy for failure to act. It will be remembered that in *Eridania v. Commission*[47] the Court ruled that an action for failure to act cannot be used for the purpose of

[42] See § 6.1. [43] Case 40/72, [1973] ECR 125. [44] *Ibid.* at para. 14 of the judgment.
[45] Cases 9, 11/71, [1972] ECR 391. [46] *Ibid.* at para. 39 of the judgment.
[47] Cases 10, 18/68, [1969] ECR 459, discussed in Chap. 3, §5.2.

obliging a Union institution to repeal an invalid act. It was, however, suggested in an earlier chapter[48] that there should be an exception to this rule where the act was initially valid but subsequently became incompatible with Union law as a result of a later development. If such an exception exists, the case where the less favourable measure is passed first would be precisely the situation in which it should be applied.

§3 INTEREST

The (rather strict) rules of *locus standi* applicable in Union law were discussed in Chapter 12: is it sufficient if these are satisfied and it is thus established that the applicant has a legally recognized interest in the annulment of the act; or must he also prove an interest in each ground of annulment pleaded? In the national systems of the Union countries there is a sharp divergence on this point:[49] in French, Belgian, and Italian law the view is taken that it is enough that the applicant has an interest in the annulment of the measure itself. If this is the case, he is entitled to put forward any ground recognized by law. In England, Scotland, Denmark, the Netherlands, and Germany, on the other hand, the applicant must, in at least some cases, show that he has an interest in the ground pleaded. This latter view has prevailed in Union law, at least with regard to staff cases.

In *Marcato v. Commission*,[50] a Commission official, who had been unsuccessful in his application for a more senior post, brought proceedings to annul the competition for the appointment. One of his objections was that the notice of competition did not lay down an age limit for candidates, as was required by the Staff Regulations. The applicant was, in fact, the second oldest of the candidates and, as the Commission pointed out, an age limit of fifty or sixty would not have eliminated any of the candidates, while a limit of forty would have eliminated the applicant himself. The Commission therefore argued that he could not object to the absence of an age limit, since his interests were not affected. This argument was fiercely rejected by Advocate General Mayras (a Frenchman) on the basis of the standard French doctrine. The Court, however, accepted it. The relevant passage of the judgment reads:[51]

> The setting of an age limit could only have resulted either in eliminating the applicant himself from the competition, which would have been directly contrary to his interest, or else in eliminating other, possibly qualified, candidates, which in the circumstances cannot be regarded as a legitimate interest of his.

The interesting point to note is that it is not enough for the applicant to have an actual interest in the ground pleaded; his interest must also be regarded as *legitimate*.

[48] See Chap. 13, § 5.2.

[49] See the Opinion of Advocate General Warner in *Deboeck v. Commission*, Case 90/74, [1975] ECR 1123 at 1140–1.

[50] Case 37/72, [1973] ECR 361.

[51] *Ibid.* at para. 6 of the judgment.

Presumably the Court considered that the rule regarding age limits had been enacted solely in the interests of the service and not in order to benefit rival candidates.[52]

Two other examples may briefly be mentioned.[53] In *De Dapper v. Parliament*,[54] another unsuccessful candidate complained that the persons who were appointed to the post had remained in the same grade: the Court held that only *they* could complain about this. In *Deboeck v. Commission*,[55] an unsuccessful candidate objected to the fact that the notice of competition had not been preceded by a notice of vacancy. The function of a notice of vacancy is to allow the appointing authority to consider whether the post might not be filled by transfer or promotion instead of by competition. The applicant, however, was not eligible for transfer or promotion to the post: her only chance of appointment lay in a competition; therefore, she was not entitled to object.[56]

It is not entirely clear exactly when an applicant will be regarded as not having an interest in a particular ground, but it is probably legitimate to formulate the rule as follows: where the complaint is that the author of the act failed to do something, the applicant will not be entitled to object if he would have been no better off if the omission had not occurred; where, on the other hand, something was done which ought not to have been done, the applicant will be able to rely on the irregularity only if his interests were prejudiced. An applicant will not, moreover, be regarded as affected unless he has a *legitimate* interest: an interest would probably be regarded as legitimate only if it was one which the rule of law violated might reasonably be supposed to have been intended to protect.

The cases do not indicate the scope of the rule. It will apply most often to procedural irregularities, but it appears also applicable to defects of substance: the allegations in *Marcato*, and even more so in *De Dapper*, go beyond what could be regarded as procedure. The rule will not of course apply to serious violations of the law: the Court usually investigates these of its own motion; so it will be irrelevant whether or not the applicant has an interest.

§4 MISTAKE OF FACT

A decision of fact is a determination whether or not a particular state of fact exists. It is quite different from a decision to act, though the two kinds of decision are frequently linked: the power to adopt a measure may be dependent on the prior existence of a situation of fact. The enacting authority must then determine the question of fact before

[52] A similar argument has been adopted in a number of English decisions: see, for example, *R v. Commissioners of Customs and Excise, ex parte Cooke and Stevenson* [1970] 1 All ER 1068.

[53] See also *Alfieri v. Parliament*, Case 35/64, [1965] ECR 261 at 267; *Serio v. Commission*, Case 115/73, [1974] ECR 341 at 349; and *De Vleeschauwer v. Commission*, Case 144/73, [1974] ECR 957 at 986.

[54] Case 29/74, [1975] ECR 35 at 40.

[55] Case 90/74, [1975] ECR 1123.

[56] Another possible objection to the omission was that it might have meant that certain potential candidates would not have known of the competition; but this did not affect the applicant: she *did* know of it.

it can exercise the discretionary power. If, however, it makes a wrong decision of fact, it may enact a measure when it has no power to do so: such a measure will be invalid and will be quashed by the European Court if appropriate proceedings are brought. The formal ground of annulment will usually be infringement of the Treaty or of a rule of law relating to its application.

A good example is provided by *Barge v. High Authority*.[57] This was another of the many cases under the ECSC Treaty concerning the scrap-iron equalization scheme. Under this scheme imported scrap was subsidized and the subsidy paid for by a levy on all users of scrap, both imported and home-produced. Since the levy was based on the quantity of scrap used, the Commission had to determine this before it could decide how much was owed by any given firm. Where the firm failed to provide the relevant figures, the Commission was obliged to make an estimate of scrap used. This was what occurred in the *Barge* case, where the estimate was based on the amount of electricity used by the steel foundry in question. The Commission then passed two decisions; one set out the estimated quantities of scrap used and the other fixed the amount due by way of the levy. These decisions were challenged by Barge, which succeeded in proving that the assessment of scrap consumed was inaccurate. The Court thereupon quashed both decisions.

Where a Union institution makes a mistake concerning a purely factual question of this kind, the Court will always quash the measure if its validity is dependent on the decision of fact. However, in many cases the relevant question is not one of 'pure' fact, but is rather an evaluation or judgment based on facts. For example, there are a number of provisions giving the Commission power to adopt measures if a given situation has produced 'economic difficulties' in a particular Member State or if there is a threat of 'serious disturbances' to the market in a given product. Clearly, a determination by the Commission that economic difficulties exist or that serious disturbances are threatened is a decision of a somewhat different nature from a determination that a particular firm has consumed X tons of ferrous scrap.

A decision of this kind is a complex determination containing, first, a number of purely factual decisions – for example, on the level of imports, exports, prices, profits, etc. – and, secondly, an evaluation of the situation thus revealed, in which it is decided that these 'primary' facts either establish, or do not establish, the existence of economic difficulties or a threat of serious disturbances, as the case may be. Though factual in one sense, this evaluation depends on the Commission's judgment, exercised on the basis of its experience. Though it does not, strictly speaking, involve a discretion,[58] it does contain a subjective element. Since the European Court lacks the political and economic expertise of the Commission and Council, it would be inappropriate if it were too ready to review it.

[57] Case 18/62, [1963] ECR 259. See also *Milac*, Case 131/77, [1978] ECR 1041 (where the question of fact on which the validity of the measure depended was whether the price of one product was dependent on that of another) and *per* Advocate General Mayras in *Westzucker*, Case 57/72, [1973] ECR 321 at 351.

[58] See *per* Advocate General Gand in *Germany v. Commission*, Case 50/69R, [1969] ECR 449 at 458.

In view of these considerations, it is not surprising that the ECSC Treaty contained a provision in Article 33 imposing restraints on the Court. This precluded the Court from examining the evaluation of the situation in the light of which the Commission adopted the act, unless it was alleged to have misused its powers or to have manifestly failed to observe the provisions of the Treaty or any rule of law relating to its application.[59]

The EU Treaties contain no equivalent provision, and at first the Court was prepared to consider the relevant economic data in some detail. One case in which this occurred was *Italy v. Commission*,[60] which concerned the problems caused by the increasing numbers of Italian refrigerators imported into France after 1961. The French invoked Article 226 EEC, as it then stood, and asked the Commission for permission to take protective measures. The Commission then took a decision allowing France to impose a special duty on Italian imports. Under Article 226 EEC, the Commission was entitled to authorize protective measures only where 'difficulties arise which are serious and liable to persist in any sector of the economy'. The Italian Government brought proceedings for the annulment of the Commission's decision, and in the course of these proceedings challenged the Commission's finding that this requirement had been satisfied. In dealing with this question, the Court gave quite detailed consideration to the relevant economic factors; however, it did so only in order to discover whether the Commission had misinterpreted the concept of serious difficulties.

In *Toepfer v. Commission*[61] the Court appeared to go further. The facts of this case have already been discussed;[62] here it will be sufficient to recall that the Commission had been slow to increase the levy on maize imports into Germany when the new French harvest came on to the market. Certain German grain importers were quick to take advantage of this and put in applications for import permits for fairly large quantities of maize (in all, approximately 125,000 metric tons, about 8–10 per cent of annual imports). The German intervention agency tried to block this by immediately asking the Commission for authorization to suspend all maize imports. This was granted.

Toepfer was one of the German importers who challenged the Commission decision granting the authorization. Under the relevant provision, the Commission could give authorization only if the imports in question threatened to cause 'serious

[59] On the application of this provision, see *Kergall v. Common Assembly*, Case 1/55, [1955] ECR 151 at 157 (the assessment of professional competence is normally a matter for the administration); *Mirossevich v. High Authority*, Case 10/55, [1956] ECR 333 at 342 (it is within the discretion of the competent authority to assess the aptitude of candidates for their duties, but the Court may review the methods by which such assessment is made); *Bourgaux v. Common Assembly*, Case 1/56, [1956] ECR 361 at 368 (the question as to which of five officials whose posts had been abolished were to be given three new posts was within the discretion of the Assembly, but it could be challenged on the ground of misuse of powers); *Leroy v. High Authority*, Cases 35/62, 16/63, [1963] ECR 197 (complex value judgments contained in a report assessing the professional competence of an official cannot be reviewed by the Court).

[60] Case 13/63, [1963] ECR 165.

[61] Cases 106–7/63, [1965] ECR 405.

[62] See Chap. 12, § 3.2.

disturbances' to the market. Toepfer claimed that this was not the case, and that the decision was consequently invalid for an infringement of the Treaty or a rule of law relating to its application. In ruling on this, the Court analysed the economic data and concluded that the quantity of maize in question was not sufficient to cause serious disturbances even if it were sold at low prices. The decision was therefore annulled.

In this case the Court seems to have come close to reviewing the Commission's evaluation of the situation, though it could be argued that the evidence showed that the Commission had misconceived the idea of 'serious disturbances'. In fact, though the Court did not decide the case on this basis, it could be maintained that there had really been a misuse of powers by the Commission: it had not actually been concerned with preventing a collapse of the market but rather with depriving the importers of the financial 'killing' they had expected. However, the evidence was probably insufficient to establish this.

The first express reference in an EU case to the doctrine of restraint is probably a statement by Advocate General Dutheillet de Lamothe in 1971 in *Rewe-Zentrale*.[63] This case concerned what was then Article 226 EEC, and it is desirable to say a little more about this provision in order to appreciate the remarks of the Advocate General. Article 226 was applicable only during the transitional period before the internal market (then the common market) was fully established, and was intended as a safeguard provision to deal with emergencies. Where it was established to the satisfaction of the Commission that such a situation had arisen, it was for the Commission to decide what measures were necessary. In deciding this, the Commission was obliged by Article 226(3) to give priority to 'such measures as will least disturb the functioning of the common market'. Advocate General de Lamothe began his discussion by commenting that, though Article 226 did not confer a discretion on the Commission, it granted it a wide power of appraisal, which was, however, subject to review by the Court.[64] He then continued:[65]

> I consider that it follows from this that, apart from a major infringement of a procedural requirement or a misuse of powers, decisions taken by the Commission in implementation of Article 226 are unlawful only in the following cases: first, where the Commission's appraisal is based on substantially incorrect facts. The illegality is thus established. Secondly: where, although the Commission's appraisal is based on substantially correct facts, it is nevertheless *clearly* wrong. Thirdly: where a measure derogating less substantially from the rules of the common market would *clearly* have sufficed to remedy the situation which called for the employment of Article 226.

The Court itself made no direct reference to the doctrine in *Rewe-Zentrale*. Two years later, however, such a reference was made in *Westzucker*.[66] This case concerned a

[63] Case 37/70, [1971] ECR 23.

[64] See also *per* Advocate General Gand in *Germany v. Commission*, Case 50/69R, [1969] ECR 449 at 458.

[65] [1971] ECR at 42.

[66] Case 57/72, [1973] ECR 321.

Commission decision suspending payment of a grant. In reviewing the validity of this decision, the Court said that the Commission enjoyed a 'significant freedom of evaluation' in fixing the level of the grant. It then continued:[67]

> When examining the lawfulness of the exercise of such freedom, the courts cannot substitute their own evaluation of the matter for that of the competent authority but must restrict themselves to examining whether the evaluation of the competent authority contains a patent error or constitutes a misuse of power.

This formula was repeated in later cases.[68] In *Racke*,[69] the Court expanded on it by adding to the two grounds of review already established – patent error and misuse of power – a third ground: that the competent authority had clearly exceeded the limits of its power of evaluation.[70] More recently, it has expressed the matter in the following words:[71]

> According to the case-law of the Court of Justice, not only must the Community judicature [the European Court and the General Court] establish whether the evidence relied on is factually accurate, reliable and consistent but also whether that evidence contains all the information which must be taken into account in order to assess a complex situation and whether it is capable of substantiating the conclusions drawn from it... However, when conducting such a review, the Community judicature must not substitute its own economic assessment for that of the Commission...

One can conclude from this that the position under the EU Treaties is now the same as it was under the ECSC Treaty: the absence of an express provision in Article 263 TFEU is irrelevant.

§5 FAILURE TO ACT

Special considerations apply where the action is for a remedy for failure to act. First, it is necessary to draw a distinction between a negative decision (a decision refusing to act) and failure even to reply to a request for action. Since the former is technically an act, and the proceedings technically an action for annulment, the grounds of review will in theory be those set out in Article 263 TFEU. However, since the proceedings are in reality designed to require the defendant to act, certain grounds will be inappropriate. For example, an applicant would hardly plead lack of competence: if the defendant has no competence in the matter, it would not be able to perform the act in question even if it wanted to; so any proceedings would be in vain. A negative decision may, on the

[67] *Ibid.* at para. 14 of the judgment.

[68] See *Deuka*, Case 78/74, [1975] ECR 421 at para. 9 of the judgment.

[69] Case 136/77, [1978] ECR 1245 at para. 4 of the judgment.

[70] The English text of the judgment mistranslates the French word *appréciation* as 'discretion'; it should, of course, be 'evaluation': compare the French and English texts of Art. 33 ECSC.

[71] *Spain v. Lenzing*, Case C-525/04 P, [2007] ECR I-9947 at para. 57 of the judgment.

other hand, be attacked on procedural grounds (including natural justice) or for defects of form (including lack of reasoning); however, if it is annulled on one of these grounds the applicant may find that he has won a hollow victory: the defendant may simply take the same decision over again after complying with the relevant requirements.

Where the defendant fails even to reply to the request for action, there can obviously be no question of pleading lack of form or failure to comply with the appropriate procedure: non-action, by its very nature, has no form, and no procedure applies to it. As in the case of a negative act, lack of competence is also inappropriate. This leaves only two possible grounds: infringement of the Treaty or any rule of law relating to its application, and misuse of powers.

When will these grounds apply? Article 265 TFEU states:

> Should the European Parliament, the European Council, the Council, the Commission or the European Central Bank, in infringement of the Treaties, fail to act, the Member States and the other institutions of the Union may bring an action before the Court of Justice of the European Union to have the infringement established. This Article shall apply, under the same conditions, to bodies, offices and agencies of the Union which fail to act.

This suggests that infringement of the Treaty is the only ground that may be pleaded. However, the matter is more complicated than this. In order to analyse it, we must make a distinction between a requirement to act and a power to act.

§5.1 REQUIREMENT TO ACT

Here there must be an obligation on the defendant to adopt a legal act. The main problem concerns the source of the obligation. Obviously an obligation contained in one of the constitutive Treaties will be sufficient: the phrase 'the Treaties' in Article 265 TFEU covers the EU Treaties, together with any amending or supplementing Treaties. Obligations contained in secondary legislation (Union acts) are not expressly mentioned; there can be little doubt, however, that the phrase 'in infringement of the Treaties' covers them as well, since an infringement of a measure passed under a Treaty is also an infringement of the Treaty itself: if a Treaty empowers a Union institution to enact legislation, it impliedly provides that it must be obeyed by other institutions – the essence of legislation is, after all, that it is legally binding. The same is probably true of an obligation contained in an international agreement binding on the Union.

Will an obligation derived from a general principle of law be sufficient? Though the position is not free from doubt, the European Court might hold that the obligation to respect the general principles of law is inherent in the Treaties. Article 19(1), second sentence, TEU could perhaps be invoked for this purpose.

§5.2 POWER TO ACT

It might be thought that no remedy for failure to act could be obtained where there is merely a discretionary power to act. For various reasons, however, this is not the case.

First of all, a power is almost always coupled with a duty, even if this duty is no more than to consider, with an open mind, whether the power should be exercised. Public authorities are not given powers to be exercised according to whim: a public authority must exercise its powers for the public good; and it must ascertain the public good according to the criteria laid down by law. Consequently, whenever granted a power, it must be willing to consider – in appropriate cases – whether to exercise it or not. This obligation applies to Union institutions as much as to any other public authorities. Therefore, if the power is granted by the Treaties or a provision of Union legislation, the institution will be guilty of an infringement of the Treaties if it fails to give the matter proper consideration.

Secondly, if the authority does apply its mind to the matter, but decides not to act, it will violate the law if it reaches its decision improperly. If it acts for the wrong motive, or takes improper considerations into account, or fails to take proper considerations into account, it will be guilty of a misuse of powers. This will be impliedly covered by the phrase 'infringement of the Treaties'. If the Treaties (or Union legislation passed under the Treaties) give a discretionary power, there is an implied obligation to exercise that power according to the proper criteria. A misuse of that power is therefore an infringement of the empowering provision in the same way that a failure to consider whether it should be exercised is an infringement of it.[72]

§6 ANNULMENT

If the applicant establishes that one of the grounds of review exists, the Court will annul the measure. Annulment is not, however, a simple matter. We shall now consider some of the problems.

§6.1 RETROACTIVITY

The basic principle of Union law is that invalid acts are voidable, but annulment is retroactive. This means, first, that invalid acts which are not annulled are valid to the extent that they cannot be challenged indirectly; and secondly, that if they *are* annulled, they are deemed never to have existed. Moreover, since an annulment operates *erga omnes*, its effects apply equally to persons who were not parties to the annulment proceedings.[73] These principles are, however, subject to exceptions. The first is that in certain

[72] See G Vandersanden and A Barav, *Contentieux Communautaire* (1977), pp. 242–3.

[73] It follows logically from these principles that once an act has been annulled, any subsequent action to annul it, even if brought by another party, should be declared inadmissible for lack of jurisdiction *ratione materiae*: there is no longer anything left to annul. However, the Court has not been consistent on this point: compare *Italy v. High Authority*, Case 2/54, [1954] ECR 37; *Assider v. High Authority*, Case 3/54, [1955] ECR 63; *ISA v. High Authority*, Case 4/54, [1955] ECR 91; *Italy v. High Authority*, Case 20/59, [1960] ECR 325; *Netherlands v. High Authority*, Case 25/59, [1960] ECR 355. See, further, Plouvier, *Les décisions de la Cour de Justice des Communautés Européennes et leurs Effets Juridiques* (1975), pp. 96–100.

rare cases an act will be absolutely void – in Union terminology, 'non-existent' – in which case annulment is neither necessary nor, indeed, possible, since the act is treated for all purposes as if it had never been adopted.[74]

Secondly, the principle that annulments are retroactive does not apply in certain cases. This is because retroactivity could have unfortunate consequences, especially in the case of an act of general application (regulation), since persons might have relied on it in good faith; moreover, other measures may have been taken under it, and, if the validity of these other measures depends on that of the annulled measure, they will be invalid too.

Since this could conflict with the principle of legal certainty, one aspect of which is non-retroactivity, there is a provision in the Treaties which enables the Court to avoid such a consequence. This is the second paragraph of Article 264 TFEU [231/174 EC] which, after providing that an act against which a successful challenge has been made will be declared void, states:

> However, the Court shall, if it considers this necessary, state which of the effects of the act which it has declared void shall be considered as definitive.

This provision allows the Court to limit the retroactive effect of the annulment in appropriate cases.[75] It could apply where the Commission took action under the act, for example by conferring benefits on particular individuals: the Court could then declare that benefits already conferred would not be affected by the annulment of the act.

In the *Staff Salaries* case,[76] the Court made a much more striking use of Article 264 TFEU (then Article 174 EEC). This was a case brought by the Commission against the Council to establish whether the annual salary increase granted to Union officials was large enough. The case was discussed in an earlier chapter,[77] and it will be remembered that the Council had decided, after discussions with the Commission and the staff associations, that future salary increases would be based on an agreed formula. However, when the next increase was made, it was – in the opinion of the Commission – below the minimum permissible under the formula. Now, the only way in which the Commission could bring the issue before the Court was to institute an action for the annulment of the Council regulation setting out the new salary scales. The action was successful: the Court ruled that the formula was binding on the Council and the new scales were indeed too low. However, the Court was then faced with a problem: if it annulled the regulation, the staff would not be entitled to *any* increases until such time as a new regulation was adopted. To avoid this, the Court resorted to Article 264 [174 EC] and ruled that the annulment would be projected into the future

[74] See Chap. 11, § 4.

[75] See *per* Advocate General Dutheillet de Lamothe in *Compagnie d'Approvisionnement v. Commission*, Cases 9, 11/71, [1972] ECR 391 at 411.

[76] *Commission v. Council*, Case 81/72, [1973] ECR 575. For another example, see *European Parliament v. Council*, Case C-360/93, [1996] ECR 1195.

[77] See Chap. 5, § 3.2.

so that the regulation would continue in force until such time as a new measure was adopted; only then would it take effect.

Article 264 TFEU has usually been applied with regard to regulations – prior to the Treaty of Lisbon it was expressly limited to regulations – but in the *Student Right of Residence* case[78] it was applied to a directive.[79] In this case, the European Parliament brought proceedings to annul a directive on the ground that it had been adopted on the wrong legal basis.[80] The Court annulled the directive; but, since it had already been implemented by the Member States, the Court ruled that the annulment would not take effect until a new directive had been adopted on the correct legal basis.

In *Portugal v. Commission*,[81] the Commission tried to pre-empt the Court's power to apply Article 264 (then Article 174 EC). It had adopted a regulation, parts of which admittedly went beyond its powers. When Portugal brought proceedings to annul the relevant parts, the Commission withdrew them with retroactive effect. However, the regulation withdrawing them stated that the withdrawal would not affect rights already acquired. It then asked the Court to declare that there was no need to adjudicate on the application brought by Portugal because it would serve no purpose. The Court rejected this. It annulled the relevant parts of the original regulation, and refused to apply Article 264 [174 EC].

§6.2 COMPLIANCE WITH THE JUDGMENT

Article 266 TFEU [233/176 EC] states:

> The institution, body, office or agency[82] whose act has been declared void or whose failure to act has been declared contrary to the Treaties shall be required to take the necessary measures to comply with the judgment of the Court of Justice of the European Union.

What are these measures likely to be? Besides the obvious fact that the author of the act will no longer operate or enforce it, positive action may have to be taken to undo the effects of past enforcement. In addition to the payment of damages (discussed in Chapter 16), it may be necessary to withdraw or amend other acts, perhaps because the reasoning in the judgment applies just as much to them.[83]

This provision was invoked in *AssiDomän Kraft Products v. Commission*,[84] a case in which the Commission had taken a decision imposing fines on a number of companies

[78] *European Parliament v. Council*, Case C-295/90, [1992] ECR I-4193.

[79] This was at a time when, according to the Treaty, it was still limited to regulations.

[80] It had been adopted under Art. 308 [235] EC; the Parliament thought it should have been adopted under the second paragraph of what was then Art. 7 EC and became, first Art. 6 and then Art 12. It concerned the right of students from one Member State to reside in another Member State while attending a course of study there.

[81] Case C-89/96, [1999] ECR I-8377.

[82] The words 'body, office or agency' were inadvertently omitted from the Consolidated Official Journal version of the Treaties.

[83] *SNUPAT v. High Authority*, Cases 42, 49/59, [1961] ECR 53 at 86–8 of the judgment; *Asteris v. Commission*, Cases 97, 99, 193, 215/86, [1988] ECR 2181.

[84] Case C-310/97 P, [1999] ECR I-5363 (appeal against Case T-227/95, [1997] ECR II-1185).

for breach of Union competition law. Some companies appealed to the European Court. The appeal was partly successful. The Court annulled parts of the Commission decision, in which it was held that certain offences had taken place. As a consequence, it annulled the fines imposed on some of the companies that had brought the appeal, and reduced those imposed on the others. The companies that had not appealed then asked the Commission to reduce the fines imposed on them in accordance with the same principles. When the Commission took a decision refusing to do so, they brought proceedings before the General Court (then the Court of First Instance) to annul that decision.

Two arguments were put forward. The first was that the Commission had infringed the principle that the annulment of a decision is retroactive and applies *erga omnes*. The General Court rejected this on the ground that the Commission's decision holding that the offences had occurred and imposing fines was not in reality one single decision, but rather a bundle of separate decisions, each addressed to a different defendant. So when the European Court annulled parts of it as a consequence of the appeal, what it really did was to annul parts of each of the decisions addressed to the appellants. The decisions addressed to the companies that had not appealed were not affected.

The second argument was based on Article 266 TFEU (then Article 176 EC). This argument was accepted by the General Court. It held that Article 266 required the Commission to reconsider the decisions addressed to the companies that had not taken part in the appeal and to reduce the fines imposed on them to the extent that the findings of the European Court were also applicable to them.

The Commission appealed against this judgment to the European Court, which allowed the appeal. It held that Article 266 applies only to the decisions annulled by the Court, not to other decisions addressed to other parties, even if they are similar.[85] It, therefore, held that the Commission had acted lawfully in refusing to reconsider the fines imposed on the companies that had not appealed, a ruling that could be regarded as putting formalism before justice.

It should finally be said that if the act was annulled on purely *formal* grounds – for example, for lack of natural justice or failure to give reasons – the enacting authority will not normally be precluded from re-enacting it according to the correct procedure. Subject to the principle of legal certainty, it could even be retroactive.[86] If, on the other hand, it was annulled for some reason of substance, such as lack of competence, infringement of the Treaties, or misuse of powers, re-enactment will not normally be permissible. It may, however, be necessary to replace it with a new measure containing different provisions.

[85] The Court distinguished the *SNUPAT* and *Asteris* cases, both cited in n. 83.

[86] *Amylum v. Council*, Case 108/81, [1982] ECR 3107; *Roquette v. Council*, Case 110/81, [1982] ECR 3159; *Tunnel Refineries v. Council*, Case 114/81, [1982] ECR 3189.

§6.3 PARTIAL ANNULMENT

The Court is not bound always to annul the whole measure: where the invalidity affects only certain provisions, and these provisions are severable from the rest of the instrument, it may annul them only. A provision will not be severable if the rest of the instrument will not make sense without it; nor will it be severable if the purpose of the instrument will be prejudiced to such an extent that the enacting institution would probably not have adopted it at all if it had known that the provision in question was illegal.

Transocean Marine Paint Association v. Commission[87] is a good example of the problems which can arise where the application is for the annulment of only part of a decision. The applicant in this case had applied to the Commission for an exemption under EU competition law, and had been granted it subject to certain conditions, one of which was that the Commission had to be informed of any financial links between the members of the association and other firms. The association maintained that this condition was unjustifiable and brought proceedings to have it annulled. The Court decided that it should be annulled because the Commission had not given the association advance warning that it had the condition in mind. The association was thus precluded from putting its case to the Commission before the decision was made. The Court held that this infringed the rules of natural justice.

The difficulty then confronting the Court was that, if it merely annulled the condition, the association might be in too favourable a position: even the latter was prepared to concede that the Commission was entitled to be given *some* information. The solution put forward by Advocate General Warner was to interpret Article 266 TFEU (then Article 176 EEC) as allowing the Court to refer the matter back to the enacting authority. He, therefore, proposed that the condition should be annulled and referred back to the Commission, which could then reconsider the matter and possibly replace it with a less onerous requirement. This suggestion was followed by the Court.

§6.4 REJECTION OF APPLICATION

Finally, it should be mentioned that the *rejection* of an application to annul does not definitively establish the validity of the measure; in particular, it does not preclude a new application by another party based on different grounds of invalidity.[88]

[87] Case 17/74, [1974] ECR 1063; discussed in Chap. 5, § 6.

[88] In *Assider v. High Authority*, Case 3/54, [1955] ECR 63, the application was directed against various measures, all of which had been the subject of a previous application in which some had been annulled and others not. As regards the measures that had not been annulled, the Court merely referred to the previous judgment and stated that, as no new grounds of invalidity had been put forward, the application would be dismissed. It is not entirely clear whether the previous judgment operated as *res judicata*, in the sense that it precluded a reconsideration of the arguments previously advanced, or whether it would be open to the applicant in the new proceedings to attempt to make the Court change its mind, perhaps by bringing new evidence. The fact that the application was held *admissible* suggests that the latter alternative may be correct. There is, however, no doubt that a fresh application may be made on *different* grounds.

§7 INDIRECT CHALLENGE

In theory, a declaration of invalidity resulting from an indirect challenge is applicable only to the case in question; in practice, however, its effects are much wider than this.[89]

To this extent, it has been assimilated to an annulment. In addition, the Court has applied Articles 264 and 266 TFEU by analogy to declarations of invalidity under Article 267 TFEU, thus narrowing the differences between the two remedies even more.

In the *Quellmehl* and *Gritz* cases,[90] the Council had given a subsidy both to starch producers and to the producers of two competing products, quellmehl and gritz. It subsequently passed a regulation withdrawing the subsidy from quellmehl and gritz, but not from starch. The quellmehl and gritz producers brought proceedings in the national courts and a reference was made to the European Court, which held that it was contrary to the principle of equality to subsidize the one and not the other. It did not, however, hold the regulation invalid (which would have allowed the quellmehl and gritz producers to succeed in their claim for payment of the subsidies). Instead, the Court ruled that the Council had to pass a new regulation either restoring the subsidy to the quellmehl and gritz producers or withdrawing it from the starch producers. It subsequently justified this ruling on the basis of Article 266 TFEU (then Article 176 EEC).[91]

In the *Maize* cases,[92] the Commission had passed a regulation applying a system for calculating monetary compensatory amounts for maize products. In proceedings resulting from a reference under Article 267 TFEU (then 177 EEC), the European Court held the regulation invalid. However, it applied the second paragraph of Article 264 TFEU (then Article 274 EEC) by analogy to enable it to hold that its ruling would not affect the payment of monetary compensatory amounts on transactions prior to its judgment. In effect, this meant that the regulation was annulled prospectively but not retrospectively.

FURTHER READING

Items are listed in date order, the most recent being at the end.

Auby, 'The Abuse of Power in French Administrative Law' (1970) 18 Am. Jo. Comp. L. 549.

Bebr, 'Preliminary Rulings of the Court of Justice: Their Authority and Temporal Effect' (1981) 18 CMLRev. 475.

[89] See Chap. 14, § 7.

[90] *Ruckdeschel*, Cases 117/76, 16/77, [1977] ECR 1753; *Moulins de Pont-à-Mousson*, Cases 124/76, 20/77, [1977] ECR 1795.

[91] See the *Maize* cases (n. 92).

[92] *Providence Agricole v. ONIC*, Case 4/79, [1980] ECR 2823 at paras 42–46 of the judgment; *Maïseries de Beauce v. ONIC*, Case 109/79, [1980] ECR 2883 at paras 42–46 of the judgment; *Roquette v. French Customs*, Case 145/79, [1980] ECR 2917 at paras 50–55 of the judgment.

Brown, 'Agrimonetary Byzantinism and Prospective Overruling' (1981) 18 CMLRev. 509.

Harding, 'The Impact of Article 177 of the EEC Treaty on the Review of Community Action' (1981) 1 YEL 93.

Waelbroeck, 'May the Court Limit the Retrospective Operation of its Judgments?' (1981) 1 YEL 115.

Toth, 'The Authority of Judgments of the European Court of Justice: Binding Force and Legal Effects' (1984) 4 YEL 1.

Takis Tridimas, *The General Principles of EC Law*, 2nd edn (2006).

Paul Craig, *EU Administrative Law*, 2nd edn (2012).

16

UNION OBLIGATIONS

This chapter is concerned with the liability of the European Union in contract, for restitution, and in tort.

§1 CONTRACT

The two main questions regarding contracts entered into by the European Union are the jurisdiction of the European Court and the law to be applied.

§1.1 JURISDICTION OF THE EUROPEAN COURT

The jurisdiction of the European Court (cases are heard by the General Court, with a right of appeal on points of law to the European Court) with regard to Union contracts is laid down by Article 272 TFEU [238/181 EC]:

> The Court of Justice of the European Union shall have jurisdiction to give judgment pursuant to any arbitration clause contained in a contract concluded by or on behalf of the Union, whether that contract be governed by public or private law.

It will be seen that this provision uses the phrase 'arbitration clause', thus suggesting that the European Court has jurisdiction only as an arbitrator. The significance of this is that in many countries the activities of arbitrators are subject to the supervision of the courts. There cannot, of course, be any question of this with regard to the European Court; so it would have been better if the Treaty had not used the terminology of arbitration. A preferable phrase would have been 'jurisdiction clause', which is used in private international law to describe a provision in a contract conferring jurisdiction on the courts of a particular country.[1]

It should also be noted that the provision does not state that the 'arbitration clause' must refer only to disputes arising out of the contract in which it is contained. A common clause would be of this type (for example, 'all disputes arising out of this contract shall be heard by the Court of Justice of the European Union') but it may also be possible for the parties to enter into a contract conferring jurisdiction on the European Court to hear disputes arising out of *another* contract.

[1] Alternative terms are 'choice-of-court' clause and 'forum-selection' clause.

If the European Court does not have jurisdiction by virtue of such a clause, the national courts will be entitled to hear the case.[2] This follows from Article 274 TFEU [240/183 EC].[3]

In determining whether it has jurisdiction under such a clause, the Court applies Union law alone: rules of national law on the validity of jurisdiction clauses cannot be taken into account.[4]

There is no indication in the Treaty as to the form which the clause should take, though the requirement in Article 44(5a) of the Rules of Procedure of the General Court that an application submitted under Article 272 TFEU must be accompanied by a copy of the contract which contains that clause implies that it should be in writing.[5] One solution would be for the Court to apply the rules laid down by Union law for the jurisdiction of Member State courts. At present, these are contained in Regulation 44/2001 on jurisdiction and the recognition and enforcement of judgments in civil and commercial matters, generally known as the 'Brussels I' Regulation.[6] However, Regulation 44/2001 will soon be replaced by Regulation 1215/2012, generally known as 'Brussels I (recast)'.[7] The relevant provision of the latter is Article 25(1) (Article 23(1) of the earlier version).[8] This provides that an agreement conferring jurisdiction on the courts of a Member State must be either:

(a) in writing or evidenced in writing;

(b) in a form which accords with practices which the parties have established between themselves; or

(c) in international trade or commerce, in a form which accords with a usage of which the parties are or ought to have been aware and which in such trade or commerce is widely known to, and regularly observed by, parties to contracts of the type involved in the particular trade or commerce concerned.

These rules are binding only on national courts but the European Court might look to them as a source of inspiration. This is especially appropriate since the European Court has jurisdiction to interpret them on a reference from a national court for a preliminary ruling.

In *Commission v. Zoubek*,[9] the Court referred to the Brussels Convention, the forerunner of Regulation 44/2001, though for a different purpose. In that case, the Commission brought proceedings against a journalist under a contract it had concluded with him. The Court had jurisdiction to hear this claim since the contract

[2] *Flemmer*, Cases C-80–82/99, [2001] ECR I-7211.

[3] This states that, save where jurisdiction is conferred on the Court of Justice of the European Union by the Treaties, disputes to which the Union is a party shall not on that ground be excluded from the jurisdiction of the courts of the Member States. In other words, the mere fact that the Union is a party is not a reason why the Member State courts should not hear a case.

[4] *Commission v. Feilhauer*, Case C-209/90, [1992] ECR I-2613.

[5] For an updated version of the Rules, see the Court's website, http://curia.europa.eu/.

[6] OJ 2000 L 12/1.

[7] OJ 2012 L 351/1. This was adopted on 12 December 2012 and will apply from 10 January 2015.

[8] The earlier version is the same in all material particulars.

[9] Case 426/85, [1986] ECR 4057.

contained an 'arbitration clause'. The Commission claimed that Zoubek had not performed his side of the contract: it asked for a declaration that the contract had been terminated and for an order that Zoubek should return an advance payment that had been made to him under the contract. Zoubek replied by bringing a counterclaim: he said that, under a separate contract with the Commission, it had been agreed that he could discharge his obligation to repay the money by supplying the Commission with certain publications.

Could the Court hear this counterclaim, in view of the fact that Zoubek did not claim that the separate contract contained an 'arbitration clause' conferring jurisdiction on the Court?[10] In answering this question, the Court referred to Article 6(3) of the Brussels Convention, which provides that a national court with jurisdiction over one claim may also hear a counterclaim arising 'from the same contract or facts on which the original claim was based'.[11] Although the Court did not purport to apply this provision directly, it reached the same conclusion: it held that it could consider a counterclaim only if it was 'directly connected' with the contract containing the 'arbitration clause'. On the facts of the case, it held that this requirement was met; it therefore had jurisdiction to hear the counterclaim.[12]

§1.2 CHOICE OF LAW

What law will be applied to a Union contract? The first paragraph of Article 340 TFEU [288/215 EC] purports to deal with this problem but does so in an unsatisfactory way. It reads: 'The contractual liability of the Union shall be governed by the law applicable to the contract in question.' In so far as it is more than a tautology, this means only that the liability of the Union is governed by the same law as governs the contract as a whole. This is, of course, what one would have assumed to be the case anyway. The provision does, however, have some value – though of a purely negative kind – in that it makes clear that the Union claims no special privileges or immunities.[13]

An inference may, perhaps, be drawn from what the first paragraph of Article 340 does *not* say: it does not expressly empower the European Court to build up a Union law of contract. This omission is noteworthy in that the second paragraph of Article 340, which deals with non-contractual liability, envisages the creation of a Union law of tort. It states that the non-contractual liability of the Union is to be governed by 'the general principles common to the laws of the Member States'. The contrast between

[10] The Court held that this question had to be decided by Union law, even though the original contract was governed by Belgian law (para. 10 of the judgment). This was obviously correct, since questions of jurisdiction always depend on Union law.

[11] There is an identical provision in Art. 8(3) of the Brussels I Regulation 2012 (Art. 6(3) of the 2000 version).

[12] In the end, it held that the counterclaim had not been established. It therefore dismissed the counterclaim and gave judgment for the Commission on the original claim.

[13] See PJ Verdam, 'De privaatrechtelijke contractuele aansprakelijkheid der EEG' in *Volkenrechtelijke opstellen aan Prof. Dr Gesina H. J. van der Molen* (International Law Essays in Honour of Gesina HJ van der Molen), p. 169 at pp. 174–5.

these two paragraphs of Article 340 indicates, therefore, that contractual liability is not in principle governed by Union law.

In the *Flemmer* case,[14] the European Court had to decide the law applicable to a contract concluded between a farmer, on the one hand, and the Council and Commission, on the other hand. The contract, which had been made through the agency of the relevant national authority, was to settle claims in tort arising out of the second *Mulder* case.[15] It contained no forum-selection clause or choice-of-law clause. Proceedings were brought before the German courts, which made a reference to the European Court. The European Court held that national law applied (it did not specify which national law, but it was presumably German law) provided it did not prejudice the 'scope and effectiveness' of Union law.[16] One can conclude from this that national law will normally apply to Union contracts, but it will be subject to any overriding rule of Union law and to what may perhaps be called Union public policy.

The choice of the appropriate system of national law must be determined by the rules of private international law. There is now an EU set of choice-of-law rules on contracts, contained in Regulation 593/2008, generally known as the 'Rome I' Regulation.[17] Although it is not expressly stated that it applies to proceedings before the European Court, it could nevertheless be applied by analogy.

The Commission normally insists on the insertion of a choice-of-law clause in its contracts, specifying the law of a Member State. The validity and effect of such a clause was disputed in one case – on the ground that the contract was more closely connected with the law of another country and contained express references to the law of that country – but the Court upheld it, saying that an express choice of law prevails over all other considerations.[18]

When the European Court applies the law of a Member State, it decides questions of law on the basis of its own knowledge, after hearing argument, even if no judge from the country in question is sitting on the case.[19] It does not require expert evidence, as would an English court if it had to apply foreign law.[20]

Different principles apply in the case of contracts of employment of Union officials.[21] In two early cases the European Court classified these as public law contracts. In the first of these cases, *Kergall v. Common Assembly*,[22] the applicant was a senior administrative official working for the Common Assembly (European Parliament). The Court

[14] Cases C-80–82/99, [2001] ECR I-7211.

[15] *Mulder v. Commission and Council*, Cases C-104/89, 37/90, [1992] ECR I-3061 (discussed later, in § 4.4).

[16] Para. 2 of the Ruling.

[17] OJ 2008, L 177/6.

[18] *Commission v. CO.DE.MI*, Case 318/81, [1985] ECR 3693 (see para. 21 of the judgment). This is largely in accord with the Rome I Regulation (then the Rome Convention), though there are some exceptions. The Court made no reference to the Convention.

[19] See, for example, *Commission v. CO.DE.MI* (n. 18) and *Pellegrini v. Commission*, Case 23/76, [1976] ECR 1807 (decided under Art. 188(1) EAEC).

[20] On possible limits to the application of national law, see *Commission v. Tordeur*, Case 232/84, [1985] ECR 3223.

[21] Such cases are rare because Union officials do not normally hold office on a contractual basis.

[22] Case 1/55, [1955] ECR 151.

held that his contract of employment was a public law contract since he was required to perform 'public law functions' and his contract referred to the internal regulations of the Common Assembly. In *Von Lachmüller v. Commission*,[23] the applicants worked in the translation service of the Commission. After the Court had established that the Commission was a public authority (public law corporation), it continued:[24]

> Moreover, those contracts were concluded to enable the Language Service of the Commission to function properly. The work of that service, which is responsible for ensuring that the contents of the acts of the Commission shall be identical in the four official languages of the Community [Union], constitutes an important element in the procedure which has as its purpose the formulation in each language of those acts; thus that service is of the same public nature as the Commission itself.
>
> Therefore the contracts at issue come under public law and are subject to the general rules of administrative law.

It appears from these extracts that it does not necessarily follow that all contracts of employment with Union institutions will automatically be classified as public law contracts. In both these judgments, the Court went to some pains to establish that the work performed by the applicants was of a governmental nature. It might be legitimate to conclude that where this is not the case the contract will be governed by private law.[25] The consequence in these cases of the Court's characterization of the contract as public was that it was governed by administrative law. There was no suggestion that national administrative law was to be applied; so one must conclude that where public law is applicable, it will be *Union* public law. This was not expressly stated but, since the Court decided the cases on the basis of legal rules that were not stated to be those of any national system, one can reach no other conclusion. If this is correct, it means that the classification of a contract as public not only affects the kind of law applicable (public rather than private) but also the legal system – Union, rather than national, law.

§2 RESTITUTION

Most Western legal systems recognize forms of liability that are based on neither contract (which requires agreement between the parties) nor tort (in which liability is based on the loss suffered by the claimant, rather than the enrichment of the defendant). Unjust enrichment is the best known. According to this principle, if the claimant can show that the defendant was unjustly enriched at his expense, the defendant is liable to make restitution to the extent that he has been enriched. *Negotiorum gestio* is another such concept. This applies where one person intervenes in the affairs of another, without the consent of the latter and without any desire to

[23] Cases 43, 45, 48/59, [1960] ECR 463. [24] At 473.
[25] Compare *Porta v. Commission*, Case 109/81, [1982] ECR 2469.

profit thereby, in order to protect the interests of the latter. An example is where someone puts out a fire on his neighbour's property. In certain circumstances, the person intervening can obtain restitution of his expenses up to the limit of the other person's enrichment.[26]

Although they are not expressly mentioned in the Treaties, the European Court has accepted that these forms of liability are part of Union law. The leading case is *Masdar (UK) Ltd v. Commission*,[27] in which a company made claims of unjust enrichment and *negotiorum gestio* against the Commission. The European Court said:[28]

> According to the principles common to the laws of the Member States, a person who has suffered a loss which increases the wealth of another person without there being any legal basis for that enrichment has the right, as a general rule, to restitution from the person enriched, up to the amount of the loss.

We will now consider the questions of substantive law and jurisdiction with regard to these forms of liability.

§2.1 SUBSTANTIVE LAW

Even prior to the *Masdar* case, there were a number of decisions in which the European Court applied these forms of liability. Most were staff cases and a typical example is *Wollast v. EEC*,[29] in which a Union employee was illegally dismissed from her job. The Court annulled her dismissal with the result that she was entitled to receive pay for the period since the dismissal. She had not, however, done any work during this period and she had thus been able to avoid certain expenses that she would otherwise have incurred; for example, she had not had to employ domestic help for her three young children. The Court held that she had been unjustly enriched at the expense of the Union and ordered that a deduction of 15 per cent be made from her salary for the period in question.

A different situation arose in *Mannesmann v. High Authority*,[30] where a scrap-iron subsidy had been wrongly paid and the Commission tried to recover it by taking a decision requiring Mannesmann, the user of the scrap, to refund it. Mannesmann brought proceedings under Article 33 ECSC to quash the decision. The European Court accepted that the Commission had the power to recover the money on the basis of restitution; nevertheless, it quashed the decision because the subsidy had been paid not to Mannesmann, but to his supplier.

[26] For a comparative discussion of this concept, see Sheehan, '*Negotiorum Gestio:* A Civilian Concept in the Common Law?' (2006) 55 ICLQ 253.

[27] Case C-47/07 P, [2008] ECR I-9761. For a comment, see Williams, (2010) 47 CMLRev. 555.

[28] *Masdar* (n. 27) para. 44 of the judgment.

[29] Case 18/63, [1964] ECR 85. See also *Degreef v. Commission*, Case 80/63, [1964] ECR 391 and *Willame v. Commission*, Case 110/63, [1965] ECR 649. In *Danvin v. Commission*, Case 26/67, [1968] ECR 315, a Union servant claimed that the Union had been unjustly enriched at his expense but was unable to establish that he had suffered any loss.

[30] Cases 4–13/59, [1960] ECR 113.

In *Masdar* (see earlier) the Commission had wanted to undertake a number of aid projects in CIS countries. It contracted with a Greek company, Helmico, to carry out the work. Helmico sub-contracted with a British company, Masdar. Masdar did the work and the Commission paid Helmico, but the latter did not (fully) pay Masdar. When Masdar wanted to sue Helmico, Helmico went bankrupt. It seems that Helmico had been guilty of deceitful conduct towards both Masdar and the Commission.

Masdar then sued the Commission, claiming that the latter was liable for its loss on the basis of unjust enrichment or *negotiorum gestio*. The European Court accepted that a claim could be brought on the basis of these principles, but ruled that the requirements of the claim had not been established. Although the Commission had obtained the benefit of Masdar's work, and had been enriched to that extent, its enrichment had not been unjust because the Commission had contracted with Helmico for the work to be done. There was thus a legitimate legal basis for its enrichment. It was not to blame for the fact that Helmico did not pay Masdar.

§2.2 JURISDICTION

The early cases in which the doctrine was applied were ones in which the Court had jurisdiction on some ground not specifically related to restitution: in the staff cases, it was Article 270 TFEU [236/179 EC] which gave the Court jurisdiction in disputes between the European Union and its servants; in *Mannesmann*, the issue arose incidentally in the course of review proceedings. The *Masdar* case appears to be the first in which a private citizen brought a claim for restitution which was not covered by some other jurisdictional provision of the Treaties.

This raised the question whether Article 268 TFEU [235/178 EC] can apply in such cases. This provision gives jurisdiction in disputes relating to 'compensation for damage' under Article 340, second paragraph. The latter provision talks of non-contractual liability, rather than tortious liability, and might therefore be thought to cover restitution as well as tort. However, Article 268 itself is concerned only with compensation for damage, and Article 340, second paragraph, requires the Union to 'make good any damage caused' by its institutions. This suggests that the basis of the liability covered by the provisions is the loss suffered by the applicant, rather than the enrichment of the defendant.

Despite these problems, the European Court has accepted that restitutionary claims are covered by Article 268 TFEU (then Article 235 EC) and Article 340, second paragraph, TFEU (then Article 288, second paragraph, EC). In *Masdar*, it said:

> 47 Given that unjust enrichment…is a source of non-contractual obligation common to the legal systems of the Member States, the Community cannot be dispensed from the application to itself of the same principles where a natural or legal person alleges that the Community has been unjustly enriched to the detriment of that person.
>
> 48 Moreover, since any obligation arising out of unjust enrichment is by definition non-contractual in nature, it is necessary to allow it to be invoked pursuant to Article 235 EC and the second paragraph of Article 288 EC…

49 Actions for unjust enrichment do not fall under the rules governing non-contractual liability in the strict sense, which, to be invoked, require a number of conditions to be satisfied, relating to the unlawfulness of the conduct imputed to the Community, the fact of the damage alleged and the existence of a causal link between that conduct and the damage complained of... They differ from actions brought under those rules in that they do not require proof of unlawful conduct - indeed, of any form of conduct at all - on the part of the defendant, but merely proof of enrichment on the part of the defendant for which there is no valid legal basis and of impoverishment on the part of the applicant which is linked to that enrichment.

50 However, despite those characteristics, the possibility of bringing an action for unjust enrichment against the Community cannot be denied to a person solely on the ground that the EC Treaty does not make express provision for a means of pursuing that type of action. If Article 235 EC and the second paragraph of Article 288 EC were to be construed as excluding that possibility, the result would be contrary to the principle of effective judicial protection, laid down in the case-law of the Court and confirmed in Article 47 of the Charter of fundamental rights of the European Union...

Though this is a rather strained interpretation of the Treaties, it ensures that claimants can obtain a legal remedy.

§3 TORT

Union tort liability is dealt with in Article 268 TFEU [235/178 EC] and Article 340, second paragraph, TFEU [288/215, second paragraph, EC]. Article 268 TFEU merely states that the European Court will have jurisdiction to decide disputes relating to compensation for damage as provided for in the second paragraph of Article 340. The latter reads as follows:

In the case of non-contractual liability, the Union shall, in accordance with the general principles common to the laws of the Member States, make good any damage caused by its institutions or by its servants in the performance of their duties.

The third paragraph of Article 340 creates an exception regarding the European Central Bank. This states:

Notwithstanding the second paragraph, the European Central Bank shall, in accordance with the general principles common to the laws of the Member States, make good any damage caused by it or by its servants in the performance of their duties.

Since the European Central Bank is itself an institution of the Union (see Article 13 TEU), this provision might seem pointless. However, it has the effect of imposing liability on the Bank itself, rather than the Union. Apart from this, it simply repeats the second paragraph. For this reason, the discussion that follows will focus on the second paragraph.

This contains the following elements. First, there must be an act or omission on the part of the Union; secondly, the applicant must have suffered damage; and thirdly, the act or omission must have caused the damage. The ECSC Treaty contained, in addition, the requirement of fault. The EU Treaties make no mention of this. They do, however, provide that Union liability will arise in accordance with the general principles common to the laws of the Member States. These principles do, of course, depend to a large extent on fault; but liability without fault is not unknown.

Before discussing these elements in detail, it is worth considering some preliminary matters. First of all, it should be noted that there is no limitation on the persons who may sue. The restrictive provisions of judicial review are absent. Nor does the short time limit within which review proceedings must be brought apply here. The period of limitation in tort actions is five years. This follows from Article 46 of the Statute of the Court of Justice of the European Union (Protocol No. 3), which provides:

> Proceedings against the Union in matters arising from non-contractual liability shall be barred after a period of five years from the occurrence of the event giving rise thereto. The period of limitation shall be interrupted if proceedings are instituted before the Court of Justice or if prior to such proceedings an application is made by the aggrieved party to the relevant institution of the Union. In the latter event the proceedings must be instituted within the period of two months provided for in Article 263 of the Treaty on the Functioning of the European Union; the provisions of the second paragraph of Article 265 of the Treaty on the Functioning of the European Union shall apply where appropriate.[31]

The second sentence of this provision might suggest that the period may be reduced if an application is made to the relevant institution of the Union, but this is not the case: the European Court held in *Kampffmeyer v. Commission*[32] that the period can never be less than five years. But an application to the institution can interrupt the running of time provided it is followed by the bringing of proceedings under Article 263 TFEU (or under Article 265); the period is also interrupted by the institution of proceedings before the Court.[33]

The expiry of the limitation period is not a bar to proceedings where the applicant only belatedly became aware of the event giving rise to the damage he suffered and he did not have a reasonable time to commence proceedings before the limitation period expired.[34] If the defendant does not plead that the claim is time-barred, the Court cannot raise the issue of its own motion.[35]

[31] This also applies to proceedings against the European Central Bank regarding non-contractual liability.

[32] Cases 5, 7, 13–24/66, [1967] ECR 245 at 259–60.

[33] See also *Giordano v. Commission*, Case 11/72, [1973] ECR 417.

[34] *Adams v. Commission*, Case 145/83, [1985] ECR 3539 at paras 48–51 of the judgment. See also *Birra Wührer v. Council and Commission*, Cases 256, 257, 265, 267/80, 5/81, [1982] ECR 85, which held that time cannot start to run before the damage has occurred, even if the defendant's action took place some time previously.

[35] *Roquette v. Commission*, Case 20/88, [1989] ECR 1553 at paras 11–13 of the judgment.

The second question concerns the person against whom the action should be brought. Article 340, second paragraph, says that 'the Union' must make good the damage.[36] However, the Union can act only through its institutions. Which institution should represent the Union before the Court? In the case of *Werhahn v. Council and Commission*[37] it was argued (by the Commission) that the Commission should always fulfil this role. This contention was based on Article 335 TFEU [282/211 EC] which provides that, in legal proceedings in *national* courts, the Union will be represented by the Commission. The Commission argued that this provision should be applied by analogy to proceedings in the European Court; but this was rejected by the Court, which held:[38]

> It is in the interests of a good administration of justice that where Union liability is involved by reason of the act of one of its institutions, it should be represented before the Court by the institution or institutions against which the matter giving rise to liability is alleged.

The case itself concerned a regulation enacted by the Council on the proposal of the Commission. Since both these institutions were responsible for the regulation which was the alleged wrongful act, the applicant had brought the action against both of them. The Court held that this was quite correct.

One can conclude from this that the action must be brought against the Union as represented by the institution which is responsible for the act or omission which forms the basis of the proceedings. Where there is joint responsibility, both institutions concerned must be named as defendants. Where the European Central Bank is responsible, the action must be brought against it: Article 340, third paragraph.

In proceedings under Article 340, second (or third) paragraph, the Court must give judgment in accordance with the 'general principles common to the laws of the Member States'. Since the Union is a public authority, it is to the law of *public* tort liability in the Member States that we must look.[39] In most Member States (including Britain) the liability of public authorities in tort is governed, in principle, by the same law as that of private individuals. But there are always a number of special rules which apply to public authorities so that even in these countries there are significant differences between the law applied in the public and the private spheres. In France, on the other hand, there is a completely separate system of public (administrative) tort law.

It is important to note that the Treaty refers to 'general principles', not 'rules', of law. It is, in fact, widely recognized that the Court is not obliged to look for the lowest common denominator and find the Union liable only where liability would exist under the legal system of each of the Member States.[40] Such a solution would stunt

[36] This is subject to the exception (set out earlier) concerning the European Central Bank.

[37] Cases 63–9/72, [1973] ECR 1229.

[38] *Ibid.* at para. 7 of the judgment.

[39] See *per* Advocate General Roemer in *Plaumann v. Commission*, Case 25/62, [1963] ECR 95 at 116–17, and *per* Advocate General Gand in *Kampffmeyer v. Commission*, Cases 5, 7, 13–24/66, [1967] ECR 245 at 352.

[40] See *per* Advocate General Roemer in *Zuckerfabrik Schöppenstedt v. Council*, Case 5/71, [1971] ECR 975 at 989, and *per* Advocate General Gand in *Sayag v. Leduc*, Case 9/69, [1969] ECR 329 at 340.

the growth of Union law. What is required is that the Court should look to the very general principles which apply in all the Member States – such as causation, damage, fault, and risk – and build up from these principles a system of law suited to the needs of the Union. The particular rules applied at the Union level need not necessarily be found in a majority of national systems and, where the special character of the Union so requires, it may even be permissible to apply rules not found in any national system. This means that the national systems are no more than a starting point for the judges of the European Court. They must, of course, respect the general legal tradition common to the Member States, but they are not bound to adopt specific solutions. This gives the Court considerable scope for a creative approach.[41]

§3.1 ACTS IMPUTABLE TO THE UNION

The first basic requisite of Union liability in tort is that there should be an act imputable to the European Union. The concept of an act in this context is very wide. It includes a physical act (for example, driving a motor car), an act intended to have legal effects (for example, a regulation), a verbal statement, and anything else that is capable of causing harm to others. It also includes a failure to act (omission), provided there was a duty to act. The special problems which arise in connection with acts intended to have legal effects are considered later, in § 4.

Under the second paragraph of Article 340 TFEU, an act is imputable to the Union either if it is an act of an institution of the Union ('damage caused by its institutions') or if it is an act of a servant of the Union and is performed in the course of his duties ('damage caused…by its servants in the performance of their duties').

The Treaties therefore recognize two categories of act for which the Union is responsible: acts performed by the Union itself (through its institutions) and acts performed by Union servants. Since Union institutions act through their servants (officials), it will be seen that there is a considerable overlap between these two categories. To an English lawyer, indeed, it might seem that the first category is entirely covered by the second and is therefore otiose. This is not entirely true, however, since there are certain acts which are more properly described as acts of the institution itself rather than of its officials. The best example consists of formal (official) acts, i.e., those performed by the official organs of the institution, such as decisions of the Commission or Council, or resolutions of the Parliament. The category would also include acts performed jointly by a number of officials over a period of time, for example monitoring of market conditions or supervision of subordinate authorities. The importance of the recognition by the Treaties of acts of the institutions themselves as a separate category is that an applicant in an action for damages does not have to name the official responsible; nor does it matter if no official was responsible. This is particularly important in the case

[41] For a general discussion, see Usher, 'The Influence of National Concepts on Decisions of the European Court' (1976) 1 ELRev. 359.

of a failure to act: it is enough to show that there was a duty on the institution to act; it need not be shown that any individual official was responsible.

The term 'institutions' in the second paragraph of Article 340 has a special meaning. It will be remembered that Article 13 TEU states that the Union has seven institutions:

- the European Parliament;
- the European Council;
- the Council;
- the European Commission;
- the Court of Justice of the European Union;
- the European Central Bank;
- the Court of Auditors.

These all constitute 'institutions' for the purpose of Article 340. In addition, the European Court held in *SGEEM v. European Investment Bank*,[42] that the term 'institutions' in Article 340 TFEU (then Article 215 EEC) also covers Union organs such as the European Investment Bank.[43] It is not clear what other bodies would constitute Union organs for this purpose, but it seems that any body established by the Treaty and authorized to act in the name of the Union would be covered.[44] It is likely that bodies, offices, and agencies of the Union – entities established under Union law – would be covered as well.[45]

In order to prove that an act of an official is imputable to the Union, it must be shown that the act was performed in the course of his duties. This concept will be familiar enough to English lawyers. In *Sayag v. Leduc*[46] the European Court had to consider what is meant by an act performed in the course of an official's duties. Mr Sayag was an engineer employed by the EAEC (Euratom), who was instructed to take Mr Leduc and another person, who were both representatives of private undertakings, on a visit to the installations at Mol in Belgium. He decided to drive them there in his private car and was given a travel order for this purpose. (The significance of the travel order was that it meant that his expenses would be paid by the Union.) While he was driving them, he was involved in a traffic accident in which he and his passengers were injured.

The passengers brought an action for damages in the Belgian courts against Sayag, but it was argued that he was acting in the performance of his duties when driving the car and that this meant that the action should have been brought against the Union instead.[47] The Belgian *Cour de Cassation* ordered that a preliminary reference be

[42] Case C-370/89, [1992] ECR I-6211.

[43] *Ibid.* at para. 16 of the judgment.

[44] See *ibid.* at para. 15 of the judgment.

[45] On these, see Chap. 1, § 8. If they are not covered on this basis, they would come under the doctrine laid down in *Worms v. High Authority*, discussed later (see n. 53).

[46] Case 9/69, [1969] ECR 329.

[47] This argument assumes that Union liability excludes individual liability, though this is not entirely certain: see later.

made to the European Court to determine what is meant by the phrase 'in the performance of their duties' in the second paragraph of Article 188 EAEC (equivalent to Article 340 TFEU).

The Court, following Advocate General Gand, gave a restrictive interpretation to the phrase. It ruled:[48]

> By referring at one and the same time to damage caused by the institutions and to that caused by the servants of the Community, Article 188 indicates that the Community is only liable for those acts of its servants which, by virtue of an internal and direct relationship, are the necessary extension of the tasks entrusted to the institutions.
>
> In the light of the special nature of this legal system, it would not therefore be lawful to extend it to categories of acts other than those referred to above.
>
> A servant's use of his private car for transport during the performance of his duties does not satisfy the conditions set out above.
>
> A reference to a servant's private car in a travel order does not bring the driving of such car within the performance of his duties, but is basically intended to enable any necessary reimbursement of the travel expenses involved in the use of this means of transport to be made in accordance with the standards laid down for this purpose.
>
> Only in the case of *force majeure* or in exceptional circumstances of such overriding importance that without the servant's using private means of transport the Community would have been unable to carry out the tasks entrusted to it, could such use be considered to form part of the servant's performance of his duties, within the meaning of the second paragraph of Article 188 of the Treaty.
>
> It follows from the above that the driving of a private car by a servant cannot in principle constitute the performance of his duties within the meaning of the second paragraph of Article 188 of the EAEC Treaty.

The result of this is that the liability of the Union for the acts of its servants is narrower than that of most Member States for the acts of their servants.[49] It is hard to see any justification for this.

Where the Union is not liable, it is of course possible to sue the servant in his personal capacity. Such proceedings must be brought in the national courts and are governed by national law. Union officials enjoy immunity from suit in national courts in respect of 'acts performed by them in their official capacity',[50] but it is hard to see how this can apply where the Union is not itself liable.[51]

[48] See *Sayag* (n. 46) at 335–6.

[49] See the comparative survey made by Advocate General Gand, *ibid.* at 340–1, where it is shown that in most of the original six Member States, liability for the acts of public servants is wide. The only exception appears to be Germany. In France there is authority relevant to the actual point at issue: it has been held that the State can be liable as a result of an accident caused by an official driving his private car on official business: *Bourrée, Conseil d'Etat*, 26 July 1944, Rec. Lebon, 217.

[50] Protocol (No. 7) on the Privileges and Immunities of the European Union, Art. 11(a). It is provided in Art. 17 that the immunity must be waived by the relevant institution whenever such waiver is not contrary to the interests of the Union.

[51] See *per* Advocate General Gand in an earlier case between the same parties, *Sayag v. Leduc*, Case 5/68, [1968] ECR 395 at 408. In this case the Court held that Sayag was not entitled to immunity, but it made clear (in

Another problem concerns the extent to which the Union will be liable for the torts of other bodies to which it delegates powers. The Treaties say nothing about the liability of the Union for the acts of its agents. It will be remembered, however, that in the field of judicial review, the Court held, in *SNUPAT v. High Authority*,[52] that, where the Union set up a subordinate body and delegated powers to it, the acts of that body could be regarded as acts of the delegating institution for the purpose of review. Might not a similar rule apply in the case of tort liability?

In *SNUPAT v. High Authority*, the Commission had set up two subordinate bodies, the *Office commun des consommateurs de ferrailles* (OCCF) and the *Caisse de péréquation de ferrailles importés* (CPFI), which were both incorporated under Belgian law, to administer an equalization scheme for ferrous scrap. Under this scheme, imported scrap was subsidized and the cost was met by a levy on all scrap users. The CPFI had demanded that SNUPAT pay a certain sum of money under the levy and SNUPAT brought an action in the European Court under Article 33 ECSC to annul the demand. The Court ruled that decisions of the CPFI should be imputed to the Commission for the purpose of the admissibility of the action.

A later case, *Worms v. High Authority*,[53] raised the question of liability in tort. Mr Worms was a Dutch scrap dealer who claimed that he had suffered damage because the OCCF had refused to do business with him. He sued the Commission under Article 40 ECSC, and the Court had to decide whether the Union could be liable for the acts of the OCCF. In its judgment the Court pointed out that the CPFI and the OCCF had different functions: the former had executive functions concerning the equalization scheme while the latter's functions were normally of a commercial nature and were concerned with the purchase of scrap on the open market. The Court then stated:[54]

> When carrying on its strictly commercial activities, the OCCF, a Belgian company under private law, is governed by national law. It is only in cases where the OCCF's acts concern the functioning of the equalization scheme, and on that account have the character of a public duty, that they can be considered as directly giving rise to the liability of the High Authority.

The Court went on to hold that the buying of scrap was an activity of a purely commercial nature and any damage caused by the OCCF's refusal to do business with a particular dealer was not the responsibility of the Commission. Worms would have to sue the OCCF directly in the national courts.

From this it may be concluded that, where a Union institution delegates governmental powers to some other body, the acts of that body in the exercise of those powers may be imputed to the Union; but where such a body carries out functions which are not of a governmental nature, its acts will not be imputable to the Union. This distinction between governmental and non-governmental functions appears to be akin to

the last paragraph of its judgment) that the immunity of the servant and the liability of the Union are separate questions. It is therefore possible, though unlikely, that in some cases they may both be liable. This would be the case only if it is possible for a Union official to be acting in the performance of his duties (the test for Union liability) without at the same time acting in his official capacity (the test for immunity).

[52] Cases 32–3/58, [1959] ECR 127. [53] Case 18/60, [1962] ECR 195. [54] *Ibid.* at 204.

that between public-law and private-law activities. Buying goods in the open market is a commercial (private-law) activity; but collecting levies is a public-law function and acts performed in this field would be imputable to the Union.

Worms v. High Authority appears to establish, therefore, that there are in fact *three* categories of acts which may be imputed to the Union: acts of Union institutions; acts of Union servants in the performance of their duties; and acts of other bodies performed in carrying out governmental (public) functions delegated to them by a Union institution.[55]

§3.2 DAMAGE AND CAUSATION

Once the existence of an act (or omission) imputable to the European Union has been established, the next requisite is that it should have caused damage to the applicant. The European Court has never laid down any general principles as to the kinds of loss for which compensation may be claimed or the way in which damages will be calculated. Instead, it has proceeded on an *ad hoc* basis and tried to reach a result that was just in the circumstances. For this reason, and because there have not in fact been many awards of damages, it is impossible to do more than make a few brief comments.

The Court has shown itself willing to award compensation for financial losses. In *Kampffmeyer v. Commission*,[56] for example, it was held that where, as a result of unlawful Union action, a firm was forced to break a contract, the cancellation fees incurred might be recovered from the Union; and in *CNTA v. Commission*[57] it was held that a firm was entitled to compensation for losses caused by currency fluctuations where the Union was responsible for its having been exposed to this risk.[58] It also seems probable, though it has not been finally decided, that compensation may be obtained for losses resulting from unlawful assistance given by Union institutions to competitors.[59]

In the *Kampffmeyer* case (see previously) the question also arose of whether an applicant could claim for loss of profit. A number of German grain dealers had applied for permits to import maize from France into Germany at a time when, because of the zero rate of levy, it was possible to make substantial profits. The German authorities wrongfully refused to grant the permits and the Commission upheld this action. The Court ruled that the Union was liable in principle to compensate the dealers for their

[55] The problems that arise when the Member States act on behalf of the Union are discussed later, in § 5.

[56] Cases 5, 7, 13–24/66, [1967] ECR 245. This decision is discussed further later.

[57] Case 74/74, decision of 14 May 1975, [1975] ECR 533; decision of 15 June 1976, [1976] ECR 797.

[58] See also *Commission v. Schneider Electric*, Case C-440/07 P, [2009] ECR I-6413 (Grand Chamber), in which the European Court appeared willing in principle to award damages for financial losses suffered by a company because, as a result of wrongful conduct by the Commission, it was unable to go through with a take-over bid. The claim failed on grounds of causation.

[59] There have been several cases in which damages have been claimed on this basis but they have been dismissed on other grounds. See, for example, *Bertrand v. Commission*, Case 40/75, [1976] ECR 1; and *Roquette v. Commission*, Case 26/74, [1976] ECR 677. These cases show that proof of causation in this situation will be difficult.

losses. The dealers who claimed for loss of profit fell into two categories: some had concluded contracts to buy grain in France and had cancelled them when import permits were refused; others had not concluded contracts before applying for permits. As regards the first category, the Court was prepared to award damages for loss of profit but it stated that, in view of the speculative nature of the transactions, it would award them only a sum equal to 10 per cent of what they would have had to pay by way of the levy if they had imported the maize after the levy rate had been raised to the normal level. Since their profits would probably have been at least equal to the normal levy rate, they were being awarded, in effect, only 10 per cent of the profits they could have made. Though it was reasonable to take into account the element of risk involved in transactions of this nature, this seems an excessively large reduction. The second category of applicants fared even worse: they were awarded no damages at all. The reason given by the Court was that their transactions lacked 'any substantial character'; but this does not seem entirely justifiable since they had taken a concrete step by applying for an import permit. Their decision not to conclude contracts until the permits had been obtained might be viewed as nothing more than normal business prudence. This case, therefore, shows a rather miserly attitude on the part of the Court; in later cases, however, it has been more generous.[60]

In staff cases, the Court has been prepared to award damages for anxiety and hurt feelings in the case of Union employees who have been wrongfully dismissed or otherwise unfairly treated.[61] The sums granted under this head have usually been small. In cases of personal injury, damages for physical and mental suffering have been awarded.[62]

The duty to mitigate loss is, the Court has held, a general principle common to the legal systems of the Member States, which applies also in Union law.[63] Failure to mitigate leads to a reduction of damages. Damages will also be reduced if the applicant is partly to blame for his loss.[64]

It is possible to bring proceedings before the damage has actually occurred: in such a case the applicant can obtain a declaration that he is entitled in principle to compensation.[65] This is possible, however, only if the damage is imminent and there is a high degree of certainty that it will take place. This would normally mean that the cause of

[60] *Mulder v. Council and Commission* (second *Mulder* case), Cases C-104/89, 37/90, [1992] ECR I-3061; *Stahlwerke Peine-Salzgitter v. Commission*, Case T-120/89, [1991] ECR II-279 (General Court); affirmed Case C-220/91 P, [1993] ECR I-2393 (ECJ).

[61] See, for example, *Algera v. Assembly*, Cases 7/56, 3–7/57, [1957] ECR 39 and *Willame v. Commission*, Case 110/63, [1965] ECR 649.

[62] *Grifoni v. Euratom*, Case C-308/87, [1994] ECR I-341 at paras 36–38 of the judgment.

[63] *Mulder v. Council and Commission* (second *Mulder* case), Cases C-104/89, 37/90, [1992] ECR I-3061 at para. 33 of the judgment.

[64] *Adams v. Commission*, Case 145/83, [1985] ECR 3539; *Grifoni v. Commission*, Case C-308/87, [1990] ECR I-1203.

[65] *Kampffmeyer v. Council and Commission*, Cases 56–60/74, [1976] ECR 711. However, time begins to run for limitation purposes only when the damage actually occurs: *Birra Wührer v. Council and Commission*, Cases 256, 257, 265, 267/80, 5/81, [1982] ECR 85.

the damage (the Union action) must already have occurred even if its consequences have not yet been fully realized.[66] The importance of this ruling is that it enables persons affected by Union measures to challenge them as soon as they have taken place and thus obtain a ruling as to their legality. In other words, an action for a declaration under the second paragraph of Article 340 TFEU could be used as a substitute for a review action under Article 263 TFEU; this could be valuable in view of the limitations placed on the right of private individuals to bring review proceedings.[67]

Where damages are calculated in one currency (for example, euros) and awarded in another (for example, the national currency of the applicant, if that is different), the appropriate date for conversion is that of the judgment.[68] If, as is often the case, the Court first gives an interlocutory judgment on the question of liability and, if the parties are unable to reach agreement, fixes the amount of damages in a later judgment, the relevant date is that of the interlocutory judgment.[69] Interest is usually awarded from the date of the interlocutory judgment. [70]

The European Court has had little to say about the problem of causation. One situation which raises the question of remoteness is where a Member State acts in violation of the Treaty and thereby causes loss to the applicant. If the Commission was aware of the facts but failed to take enforcement proceedings against the Member State, can the applicant bring an action in tort against the Commission on the ground that its failure to act was the cause of its loss? There have been several cases in which such proceedings have been brought, but they have all been dismissed on other grounds.[71] In some of the earlier cases, the European Court appeared to accept that liability could arise in this way;[72] subsequently, however, it has adopted a more hostile attitude.[73]

[66] See *per* Advocate General Reischl, *ibid.* at 753. [67] See Chap. 12.

[68] *Dumortier v. Council*, Cases 64, 113/76, 167, 239/78, 27, 28, 45/79, [1982] ECR 1733. [69] *Ibid.*

[70] *Ibid.* See also *Mulder v. Council and Commission* (second *Mulder* case), Cases C-104/89, 37/90, [1992] ECR I-3061 at para. 35 of the judgment. The European Court has never explained how it fixes the rate of interest, though it is normally between 6 and 8 per cent: Heukels (1993) 30 CMLRev. 368 at 385, note 56. It will not be greater than the rate requested by the applicant; thus in the second *Mulder* case, only 7 per cent was awarded in one joined case (because this was all that was asked for) and 8 per cent in the other. The highest rate awarded seems to be 12 per cent: *Berti v. Commission*, Case 131/81, [1985] ECR 645. In this case, the applicant was resident in Belgium and the Court applied the rate set out in the relevant Belgian legislation. However, the Commission did not formally dispute the applicant's claim in this respect.

[71] See *Vloeberghs v. High Authority*, Cases 9, 12/60, [1961] ECR 197; *Lütticke v. Commission*, Case 4/69, [1971] ECR 325; *Bertrand v. Commission*, Case 40/75, [1976] ECR 1; *Denkavit v. Commission*, Case 14/78, [1978] ECR 2497; *Société d'Initiatives et de Coopération Agricoles v. Commission*, Case 114/83, [1984] ECR 2589; and *GAARM v. Commission*, Case 289/83, [1984] ECR 4295.

[72] See the *Vloeberghs* case, [1961] ECR at 216 (also *per* Advocate General Roemer at 240) and the *Denkavit* case, [1978] ECR 2497 at para. 8 of the judgment.

[73] In *Asia Motor France v. Commission*, Case C-72/90, [1990] ECR I-2181, the Court declared such an action inadmissible on the ground that the Commission is under no duty to take action under Art. 258 TFEU (then Art. 169 EEC) (see para. 13 of the judgment). However, the possibility of an action might still arise if the Commission's decision not to act was taken on improper grounds.

§3.3 FAULT

Under the ECSC Treaty fault was an essential element of liability. There is no such requirement under the EU Treaties, but the European Court has always required the proof of fault in actions under Article 340, second paragraph, TFEU (though a violation of Union law, even if unintentional, can be sufficient).

There have been a number of cases in which the possibility of no-fault liability has been considered. One such case was *Compagnie d'Approvisionnement v. Commission*,[74] which concerned the measures taken after the devaluation of the French franc in 1969. In order to minimize disruption to the Common Agricultural Policy, the Council decided (among other things) that the French Government would grant subsidies on imports of cereal products. The amount of the subsidies was to be fixed by the Commission, and this was done by two Commission regulations. The applicants were cereal dealers who claimed to have suffered loss because the subsidies were fixed at too low a level to compensate for the devaluation of the franc. They put forward various arguments in order to establish the liability of the Union, including an argument based on the French doctrine of equal apportionment of public burdens (*l'égale répartition des charges publiques*) under which the State may be liable in certain circumstances in the absence of fault. To establish liability under this head in French law, it is necessary to show that measures taken by the State have placed an abnormal and unjustifiably severe burden on certain individuals who have thus suffered unusual and special damage and been required to make a disproportionate sacrifice in the general interest.

Advocate General Mayras considered this argument but decided that the applicants had not met the conditions imposed by French law.[75] The Court also rejected it without ruling on whether or not no-fault liability was part of Union law:[76]

> Any liability for a valid legislative measure is inconceivable in a situation like that in the present case since the measures adopted by the Commission were only intended to alleviate, in the general economic interest, the consequences which resulted in particular for all French importers from the national decision to devalue the franc.

In other words, the disputed measures did not impose a burden on the applicants; they gave them a benefit. Therefore, no question of liability under this head could arise.

For many years, the question remained uncertain. The possibility of no-fault liability was never ruled out, but it was not applied either.[77] The issue finally came to a head in *FIAMM v. Council and Commission*.[78] These cases were the product of the

[74] Cases 9, 11/71, [1972] ECR 391; see also *Biovilac v. EEC*, Case 59/83, [1984] ECR 4057 at paras 27–30 of the judgment, where reference was also made to the German concept of '*Sonderopfer*'; *Dorsch Consult v. Council and Commission*, Case T-184/95, [1998] ECR II-667; affirmed Case C-237/98 P [2000] ECR I-4549.

[75] [1972] ECR 391 at 422–3.

[76] At para. 46 of the judgment.

[77] See *Dorsch Consult v. Council and Commission*, Case T-184/95, [1998] ECR II-667 at paras 59 and 80 of the judgment; *Dorsch Consult v. Council and Commission*, Case C-237/98 P, [2000] ECR I-4549 at para. 6 of the Opinion of Advocate General La Pergola.

[78] Cases C-120–121/06 P, [2008] ECR I-6513.

Union's long-running dispute with the WTO over bananas. In proceedings before the Dispute Settlement Body of the WTO, it had been decided that Union measures on the importation and marketing of bananas were contrary to the WTO Agreement. When the Union failed to bring its legislation into line with the requirements of WTO law, the United States was given permission to apply countervailing duties on EU products.

The claimants in the case were European companies exporting goods to the United States. They had suffered financial loss when their products were selected for penal rates of duty. They argued that their loss had been caused by the unlawful failure of the European Union to comply with the WTO Agreement; so they brought proceedings against the Union under Article 340, second paragraph, TFEU (then Article 288, second paragraph, EC).

The case came initially before the General Court (then the Court of First Instance). It held that since the relevant provisions of the WTO Agreement were not directly effective, their violation was not a wrongful act for the purpose of establishing fault in a claim under Article 340. This was in line with earlier cases,[79] which held that the relevant provisions of the WTO Agreement could not be invoked for the purpose of annulling a Union act in proceedings under Article 263 TFEU [230/173 EC].[80]

Having failed to prove fault on the part of the Union, the claimants next argued that they were entitled to compensation on the basis of no-fault liability. The General Court held that no-fault liability was part of Union law, but rejected the claim on the ground that the damage they had suffered was not unusual in nature (a requirement under the French doctrine of equal apportionment of public burdens, discussed earlier). The claim was therefore dismissed.

The claimants appealed to the European Court, but the latter dismissed the appeals. It held that the General Court had been wrong to admit even the possibility of applying no-fault liability in the situation before it. The European Court said:

> 176 In the light of all the foregoing considerations, it must be concluded that, as Community law currently stands, no liability regime exists under which the Community can incur liability for conduct falling within the sphere of its legislative competence in a situation where any failure of such conduct to comply with the WTO agreements cannot be relied upon before the Community courts.
>
> ...
>
> 179 It follows from all of the foregoing that, in affirming in the judgments under appeal the existence of a regime providing for non-contractual liability of the Community on account of the lawful pursuit by it of its activities falling within the legislative sphere, the Court of First Instance erred in law.

[79] *Germany v. Council*, Case C-280/93, [1994] ECR I-4973; *Portugal v. Council*, Case C-149/96, [1999] ECR I-8395.

[80] See Chap. 6, § 9.3. There are some exceptions to this – see *Nakajima v. Council*, Case C-69/89, [1991] ECR I-2069; *FEDIOL v. Commission*, Case 70/87, [1989] ECR 1781 – but these did not apply on the facts of the *FIAMM* case.

Although this does not entirely rule out no-fault liability in all cases, it is difficult to envisage a situation in which it would apply. Paragraph 176 applies only where the Union acts within its sphere of legislative competence, but if it acted outside that sphere, that fact alone would probably constitute a fault. It seems, therefore, that fault will remain an essential feature of EU tort law for a long time to come.

What is meant by fault? In broad terms, it means that the act or omission which forms the basis of the action must be wrongful. In the case of an omission this means that there must have been a duty (as distinct from a mere power) to act; in the case of a positive act it means either that the action was wrongful in itself or that it was carried out in a wrongful way.

In general, any malfunctioning of the administrative system can constitute fault. One could perhaps say that there is a legal duty on Union institutions (and on other institutions to which Union functions are delegated and for whose acts the Union is responsible) to carry out their functions in a sensible and efficient manner – in other words, a duty of good administration. Consequently, any breach of this duty could constitute fault. Examples are: failure to adopt procedures necessary for the efficient functioning of the service, failure to supervise subordinate officials or outside bodies to whom functions have been delegated, failure to obtain all the facts before making a decision, taking a decision on the basis of erroneous or irrelevant facts, giving misleading information to the public, failure to give necessary information to the public, delay, or lack of foresight – in short, everything which English lawyers sum up under the heading of 'maladministration'.[81] In addition, of course, a violation of any written or unwritten rule of law may also constitute fault, provided the rule in question is intended for the protection of individuals.[82]

It should not, however, be thought that *any* deviation from the standard of an ideal service constitutes fault. The concept, after all, carries a connotation of blameworthiness and it is therefore necessary to consider whether the shortcoming in question is excusable. For example, in the case of a decision of fact (i.e., a judgment whether a certain state of facts exists) the institution concerned may be excused if it makes a mistake, provided it adopted the correct procedures and reached the conclusion which seemed to be indicated in the light of the information to hand.[83]

A good example is to be found in the case of *Richez-Parise v. Commission*.[84] The applicants in this case were a number of EU officials who had been given incorrect information concerning their pensions and had thereafter resigned from the service and taken certain decisions regarding their financial rights. The information in question was based on an interpretation of the relevant legal provisions, and, at the time at which it was given, the Commission had no reason to believe that it was wrong. Subsequently, the Commission discovered that its interpretation was of doubtful validity, but it took

[81] For an example, see *Fresh Marine Company v. Commission*, Case T-178/98, [2000] ECR II-3331; upheld on appeal, Case C-472/00 P, [2003] ECR I-7541.

[82] See § 4.3.

[83] See *per* Advocate General Gand in *Kampffmeyer v. Commission*, Cases 5, 7, 13–24/66, [1967] ECR 245 at 275–7.

[84] Cases 19, 20, 25, 30/69, [1970] ECR 325. For another case on misleading information, see *Compagnie Continentale France v. Council*, Case 169/73, [1975] ECR 117.

no immediate steps to inform the applicants of this. It was only some time later, after the applicants had committed themselves as regards the form in which they would take their accrued pension entitlements, that the position was rectified. The European Court held that the initial interpretation was not itself a wrongful act since the mistake was excusable, but the failure to correct it as soon as the Commission became aware of the true position did constitute fault.

In addition to administrative fault, there is also personal fault. This occurs where the individual officer acts wrongfully: where he fails to carry out instructions, or acts negligently, or illegally, or in bad faith – in other words, where the shortcoming is one of the individual rather than of the service.

Adams v. Commission[85] is one of the few cases in which an individual not employed by the Union has been awarded substantial damages. While working for a Swiss pharmaceutical company (Hoffmann-La Roche), Adams had, after requesting confidentiality, given documents to the Commission which showed that the company was violating Union competition law. The Commission then brought proceedings against the company and as a result it was fined. Subsequently the company discovered, partly as a result of documents supplied by the Commission, that Adams was the informant.

Under Swiss law Adams had committed a criminal offence by revealing the company's secrets to the Commission. By this time, Adams had ceased to work for Hoffmann-La Roche and gone to live in Italy. However, he came to Switzerland on a visit and the company had him arrested. The Swiss police kept him in solitary confinement and did not allow him to communicate with his family. As a result, his wife, who had also been interrogated, committed suicide. After his release (he was convicted but given a suspended sentence) he sued the Commission for damages.

The Court held that the Commission was bound by a duty of confidentiality and that it had violated this, in particular by not warning Adams when it discovered that Hoffmann-La Roche was planning to have him prosecuted. However, it held that Adams was partly to blame for his own misfortune (for example, by returning to Switzerland) and it decided that liability should be apportioned equally between him and the Commission. The Commission was, therefore, ordered to compensate him to the extent of one-half of the damage suffered.[86]

§4 LIABILITY FOR ACTS INTENDED TO HAVE LEGAL EFFECTS

Special considerations apply where the alleged wrongful act on the part of the Union is an act intended to have legal effects, i.e., a reviewable act as defined in Chapter 11.

[85] Case 145/83, [1985] ECR 3539.

[86] The amount of damages was settled in negotiations between the parties. According to *The Times*, 18 October 1986, Adams eventually accepted £200,000 (£100,000 for mental anguish and £100,000 for economic loss), plus £176,000 for costs.

Under the ECSC Treaty, there was a provision directly covering this situation, Article 34. This provided that where a Commission measure was annulled,[87] producers of coal or steel[88] which had suffered 'direct and special harm' could obtain redress if the Commission was guilty of a sufficient degree of fault. This provision applied only if the measure was first annulled;[89] however, this did not in itself establish that the requisite degree of fault existed.[90]

In addition to fault, the applicant had to establish that it had suffered direct and special harm. According to the General Court, the concept of special harm involved, on the one hand, 'harm of a particular intensity' and, on the other, 'an impact on a limited and identifiable number of economic agents'.[91] Direct harm referred to causation.

Since Article 34 applied only to producers of coal and steel, other applicants could not rely on it. Could they bring an action under Article 40, the ECSC equivalent of Article 340 TFEU? This question arose in *Vloeberghs v. High Authority*,[92] where a coal distributor (not producer) sued the Commission for damages under Article 40, because the latter had failed to take a decision requiring the French Government to allow its coal to enter France. The Commission claimed that the action was inadmissible, arguing that Article 34 provided the sole means of obtaining damages for loss caused by an act intended to have legal effects. It urged the Court not to allow Article 40 ECSC to be used as a means of circumventing the restrictions on judicial review imposed by Articles 33 and 35.

The Court rejected the Commission's argument. It pointed out that review actions and tort actions were quite separate remedies and that there was no reason why the restrictive conditions of the former should apply to the latter; it therefore concluded that it was not necessary for an applicant first to bring proceedings under Article 35. In the *Vloeberghs* case the Court left open whether the same applied where the basis of the action was a positive act rather than an omission, but the European Court subsequently held that it did.[93]

[87] It also applied where a failure to act was established: *Stahlwerke Peine-Salzgitter v. Commission*, Case T-120/89, [1991] ECR II-279; affirmed Case C-220/91 P, [1993] ECR I-2393 (ECJ).

[88] See the definition of 'undertaking' in Art. 80 ECSC.

[89] *Usinor v. Commission*, Cases 81, 119/85, [1986] ECR 1777.

[90] *Finsider v. Commission*, Cases C-363–4/88, [1992] ECR I-359. The European Court refused to accept the view of the General Court in *Stahlwerke Peine-Salzgitter v. Commission* (see n. 87) (para. 78 of the judgment) that the test applicable under Art. 340 TFEU for liability for a reviewable act (discussed later) should be applied under Art. 34 ECSC (*Stahlwerke Peine-Salzgitter v. Commission* (ECJ) (above), paras 27–30 of the judgment) though it is doubtful whether there was any marked difference in the requirements.

[91] *Stahlwerke Peine-Salzgitter v. Commission* (General Court) (see n. 87), at para. 131 of the judgment. On appeal, this was noted without comment by the European Court: Case C-220/91 P (ECJ), at paras 53–58 of the judgment. As interpreted by the General Court, this concept bears a striking resemblance to the concept of a manifest and grave violation, which, as will be explained later, has been held by the European Court to apply under Art. 340 TFEU.

[92] Cases 9, 12/60, [1961] ECR 197.

[93] *Finsider v. Commission* (n. 90), at para. 16 of the judgment; *Stahlwerke Peine-Salzgitter v. Commission* (ECJ) (n. 87), at para. 21 of the judgment.

The ECSC Treaty is no longer in force (though, as we have seen, cases decided under it are still relevant for present-day law). In the EU Treaties, the nearest equivalent to Article 34 ECSC is Article 266 TFEU [233/176 EC]. It reads:

> The institution whose act has been declared void or whose failure to act has been declared contrary to the Treaties shall be required to take the necessary measures to comply with the judgment of the Court of Justice of the European Union.
>
> This obligation shall not affect any obligation which may result from the application of the second paragraph of Article 340.

This gives no right to damages – unless the payment of damages were regarded as a 'necessary measure'[94] – but in view of its second paragraph it cannot hinder an action in tort.

§4.1 THE '*PLAUMANN* DOCTRINE'

The first case concerned with liability for a reviewable act under the EU Treaties was *Plaumann v. Commission*.[95] This case was discussed in Chapter 12, § 3. It will be remembered that the German Government had applied to the Commission for permission to lower the duty on clementines from 13 per cent to 10 per cent. The Commission took a decision addressed to Germany refusing this request. Plaumann was a German importer of clementines who claimed that the Commission's refusal was illegal. He brought proceedings under Article 263 TFEU (then Article 173 EEC) for the annulment of the decision and also under Article 340, second paragraph, TFEU (then Article 215, second paragraph, EEC) for damages. The amount claimed in damages was a sum equal to the additional duty he had had to pay.

It will be remembered from the discussion in Chapter 12 that the review proceedings were declared inadmissible on the ground that Plaumann lacked *locus standi*. The Court declared the tort action admissible but dismissed it on the merits. It gave its reasons as follows:[96]

> The conclusions of the applicant ask for payment of compensation equivalent to the customs duties and turnover tax which the applicant had to pay in consequence of the Decision against which it has at the same time instituted proceedings for annulment. In these circumstances it must be declared that the damage allegedly suffered by the applicant issues from this Decision and that the action for compensation in fact seeks to set aside the legal effects on the applicant of the contested Decision.
>
> In the present case the contested Decision has not been annulled. An administrative measure which has not been annulled cannot of itself constitute a wrongful act on the part of the administration inflicting damage upon those whom it affects. The latter cannot therefore claim damages by reason of that measure. The Court cannot by way of an action for

[94] According to Advocate General Roemer in *Nordgetreide v. Commission*, Case 42/71, [1972] ECR 105 at 115, the Court does not have the power to specify what measures must be taken to comply with its judgments.

[95] Case 25/62, [1963] ECR 95.

[96] *Ibid.* at 108.

compensation take steps which would nullify the legal effects of a decision which, as stated, has not been annulled.

The action brought by the applicant must therefore be dismissed as unfounded.

This reasoning will be familiar: exactly the same argument was put forward by the Commission in *Vloeberghs v. High Authority*. The argument rejected by the Court in that case was accepted in *Plaumann*. It is unclear why the Court changed its ground within so short a time (two years).[97] What should, however, be emphasized is that this restrictive approach was in no way required by the Treaties: there is nothing in them suggesting that a reviewable act which has not been quashed cannot form the basis of an action in tort; nor is this principle derived from the legal systems of the Member States.[98] As the Court said in the *Vloeberghs* case, actions for damages and applications for review are quite separate proceedings with different objectives.

This decision was subject to heavy criticism,[99] but it was almost eight years before the Court had an opportunity to reconsider it. This first occurred in *Lütticke v. Commission*,[100] in which a German company sued the Commission for damages because it had failed to address a directive or decision to Germany requiring it to modify certain taxes which the company had been obliged to pay. The Commission contended that the action was inadmissible because it was intended to establish a failure to act on its part, and its effect would be to circumvent the limitations imposed by Article 265 TFEU (then Article 175 EEC) on the application for a remedy for failure to act. This, of course, was precisely the argument unsuccessfully put forward in *Vloeberghs* and adopted by the Court in *Plaumann*. This time the Court rejected it. Its words were:[101]

The action for damages provided for by Article 178 [now 268 TFEU] and the second paragraph of Article 215 [now 340] was established by the Treaty as an independent form of action with a particular purpose to fulfil within the system of actions and subject to conditions for its use, conceived with a view to its specific purpose. It would be contrary to the independent nature of this action as well as to the efficacy of the general system of forms of action created by the Treaty to regard as a ground of inadmissibility the fact that, in certain circumstances, an action for damages might lead to a result similar to that of an action for failure to act under Article 175 [now 265 TFEU].

So the action was declared admissible (though it was dismissed on the merits on the ground that the Commission's failure to act was not wrongful).

[97] Plaumann could not have obtained a remedy in the national courts, since his complaint was that the Commission had failed to take a decision. There is no way in which a failure to act on the part of a Union institution can be challenged in the national courts. Consequently, the refusal by the Court to allow him to bring proceedings under Art. 340 TFEU (then Art. 215) meant that he was left without any remedy at all.

[98] See *per* Advocate General Roemer in *Zuckerfabrik Schöppenstedt v. Council*, Case 5/71, [1971] ECR 975 at 990, and the authors there cited.

[99] *Ibid.* at 991.

[100] Case 4/69, [1971] ECR 325.

[101] *Ibid.* at para. 6 of the judgment.

The position was confirmed in *Zuckerfabrik Schöppenstedt v. Council*,[102] where the act in question was a Council regulation which provided for compensation for stockholders of sugar who had suffered loss as a result of the price changes that came about when a Union regime for sugar was introduced. The terms of this regulation did not, however, entitle the applicant, a German company, to any compensation. The applicant claimed that this was wrong and sued the Council for damages. The Council contested the admissibility of the action on the ground that, in practical terms, its result would be the nullification of the legal effects of the regulation. This, it argued, would undermine the system of judicial review set up by Article 263 TFEU (then Article 173 EEC) under which private persons are not entitled to challenge the validity of regulations. The Court rejected this argument on the basis of the same reasoning as in the *Lütticke* case.[103]

The significance of this should be emphasized. The rule in *Plaumann* was more than a procedural one. It has already been shown that the rules of admissibility for applications to annul and applications for a remedy for failure to act are extremely strict: the narrow concept of *locus standi* and the short time limit impose stringent limitations on the right to bring these proceedings.[104] Therefore, if it had been accepted that such proceedings were a necessary precondition for an action for damages, the latter action would have been likewise restricted and Union liability would have been severely limited.

§4.2 THE '*SCHÖPPENSTEDT* FORMULA'

The *Schöppenstedt* case is important not only because it marked the final removal of the shackles imposed by *Plaumann*; it was also the first case in which the European

[102] Case 5/71, [1971] ECR 975.

[103] The argument was put again in a few subsequent cases but was always rejected by the Court. See, for example, *Compagnie d'Approvisionnement v. Commission*, Cases 9, 11/71, [1972] ECR 391 at paras 3–7 of the judgment and *Merkur v. Commission*, Case 43/72, [1973] ECR 1055 at paras 3 and 4 of the judgment. It appears, however, that the *Plaumann* doctrine still applies where the applicant claims not compensation for loss actually suffered, but the sum that would have been payable if the measure had not been adopted: see *Krohn v. Commission*, Case 175/84, [1986] ECR 753 at paras 30–34 of the judgment; *Birke v. Commission and Council*, Case 543/79, [1981] ECR 2669 at paras 23–28 of the judgment; *Bruckner v. Commission and Council*, Case 799/79, [1981] ECR 2697 at paras 14–20 of the judgment; *Cobrecaf v. Commission*, Case T-514/93, [1995] ECR II-621 at paras 58–61 of the judgment; *AssiDomän Kraft Products v. Commission*, Case C-310/97 P, [1999] ECR I-5363 (appeal against Case T-227/95, [1997] ECR II-1185) at para. 59 of the judgment; *Fresh Marine Company v. Commission*, Case T-178/98, [2000] ECR II-3331 at paras 41–53; upheld on appeal, Case C-472/00 P, [2003] ECR I-7541. In *Cobrecaf v. Commission*, the applicants brought proceedings to annul a Commission decision refusing to grant them increased aid. These proceedings were held inadmissible because they were brought outside the time limit. In addition, they asked for damages under Art. 340, second para., TFEU (then Art. 215 EC), the sum claimed being the amount of the additional aid which the contested decision had refused to give. The General Court held that, as an exception to the principle in the *Lütticke* case, 'the fact that a claim for annulment is held to be inadmissible renders the claim for damages inadmissible where the action for damages is actually aimed at securing withdrawal of an individual decision which has become definitive and would, if upheld, have the effect of nullifying the legal effects of that decision...' (para. 59 of the judgment). It is not clear exactly what the scope of this exception is, in particular whether it applies only when the applicant could have obtained another remedy if he had acted in good time.

[104] See Chap. 12.

Court made a general statement of the principles governing Union liability for an act intended to have legal effects. This statement, which will henceforth be referred to as the '*Schöppenstedt* formula', has been repeated, with small verbal differences, in most subsequent cases. In a later version it reads as follows: [105]

> The Court of Justice has consistently stated that the Community [Union] does not incur liability on account of a legislative measure which involves choices of economic policy unless a sufficiently serious breach of a superior rule of law for the protection of the individual has occurred.

We can analyse this as laying down three requirements for liability:

1. there must be a breach of a superior rule of law;
2. the breach must be sufficiently serious;
3. the superior rule of law must be one for the protection of the individual.

These requirements are intended to apply in addition to the general rules concerning damage and causation.

In *Bergaderm v. Commission*[106] (decided in 2000), the European Court held that the principles which it had previously laid down for the purpose of determining the liability of Member States under the *Francovich* doctrine (discussed in Chapter 7, § 11) should also apply to Union liability under Article 340. It said:[107]

> As regards Member State liability for damage caused to individuals, the Court has held that Community [Union] law confers a right to reparation where three conditions are met: the rule of law infringed must be intended to confer rights on individuals; the breach must be sufficiently serious; and there must be a direct causal link between the breach of the obligation resting on the State and the damage sustained by the injured parties...

Although differently formulated, this seems substantially the same as the *Schöppenstedt* formula. Rule 1 and Rule 3 of *Schöppenstedt* have been conflated into a single rule (the first), and the requirement of causation has been taken from the general rules. The requirement of a sufficiently serious breach remains the same. Later, we shall consider whether the verbal differences are of any significance.

According to its terms, the *Schöppenstedt* formula applies where the source of liability is a legislative measure (normally a regulation) involving choices of economic policy. However, in *Bergaderm*, the Court held that what is important is not the nature of the measure but the degree of discretion enjoyed by its author. If it has little or no discretion, any infringement of Union law may be sufficient to incur liability.[108] In determining this, the general (legislative) or individual (executive) nature of the measure is not the decisive criterion.[109]

[105] *HNL v. Council and Commission*, Cases 83, 94/76, 4, 15, 40/77, [1978] ECR 1209 at para. 4 of the judgment.

[106] Case C-352/98 P, [2000] ECR I-5291 (appeal from Case T-199/96, [1998] ECR II-2805).

[107] *Bergaderm* (n. 106) para. 42 of the judgment.

[108] *Ibid.* at para. 44 of the judgment.

[109] *Ibid.* at para. 46 of the judgment.

The *Bergaderm* case arose when a directive adopted by the Commission prohibited a particular substance in suntan lotions.[110] Only one company used the substance, and it was driven into liquidation. The company sued the Commission for damages, but lost in the General Court (then the Court of First Instance). On appeal to the European Court, one of its arguments was that the General Court had been wrong to regard the directive as a legislative measure in terms of the *Schöppenstedt* formula, since it affected the position of only one producer (itself). The European Court rejected this argument on the ground that it did not matter whether the measure was legislative or executive.

One can conclude from this that the nature of the measure is important only as a pointer to the degree of discretion enjoyed. A legislative act will almost always involve a high degree of discretion. In some cases, this will also be true of an executive act – but not always. The test for determining whether there is discretion is whether the adoption of the act involves policy choices. It can hardly matter, however, whether these are economic, social, or political. The statement in the *Schöppenstedt* case that the formula applies only to liability on account of legislative measures that involve choices of economic policy must, therefore, be regarded as misconceived. The formula should rather be regarded as applying to any measure involving policy choices.

We shall now consider the three requisites laid down in the *Schöppenstedt* formula, as modified by *Bergaderm*.

§4.3 FIRST REQUISITE

The first requisite is that there must be a breach of a superior rule of law. *Bergaderm* requires merely that a rule of law must be infringed. This change makes no difference. Any rule of Union law can constitute a 'superior rule of law', provided it is binding on the author of the allegedly tortious act.

A general principle of law can constitute such a rule of law.[111] *CNTA v. Commission*[112] is an example. This case arose out of the system of monetary compensatory amounts (MCAs), which were intended to compensate for fluctuations in exchange rates. These payments had originally been granted on exports of colza seed from France, but on 26 January 1972 the Commission passed a regulation which abolished the system as from 1 February. The applicant was a French firm which had entered into a number of export contracts before the regulation was passed, and these were to be performed after the ending of the scheme. It claimed that it had entered into the contracts on the assumption that MCAs would be payable and had calculated its price on that basis. It argued that it had suffered loss by reason of the sudden ending of the scheme without warning and without any provision being made for transactions which were in the

[110] It was thought by some scientists to cause cancer.

[111] *FIAMM v. Council and Commission*, Cases C-120–121/06 P, [2008] ECR I-6513 at paras 182–184 (fundamental rights, including the right to property and the freedom to pursue a trade or profession).

[112] Case 74/74, [1975] ECR 533.

process of completion when it came into force. It therefore sued the Commission for damages.

In order to establish liability it had to prove that the Commission had been guilty of a wrongful act. It claimed that the regulation was such an act because it infringed the principle of legal certainty and in particular the principle of the protection of legitimate expectations.

The Court stated that, though the system of MCAs could not be regarded as furnishing a guarantee to exporters that they would not suffer loss as a result of fluctuations in the exchange rate, it nevertheless had the effect in practice of shielding them from such a risk. Consequently, even a prudent exporter might decide not to cover himself against it. The Court then continued:[113]

> In these circumstances, a trader may legitimately expect that for transactions irrevocably undertaken by him because he has obtained, subject to a deposit, export licences fixing the amount of the refund in advance, no unforeseeable alteration will occur which could have the effect of causing him inevitable loss, by re-exposing him to the exchange risk.
>
> The Community [Union] is therefore liable if, in the absence of an overriding matter of public interest, the Commission abolished with immediate effect and without warning the application of compensatory amounts in a specific sector without adopting transitional measures which would at least permit traders either to avoid the loss which would have been suffered in the performance of export contracts, the existence and irrevocability of which are established by the advance fixing of the refunds, or to be compensated for such loss.
>
> In the absence of an overriding matter of public interest, the Commission has violated a superior rule of law, thus rendering the Community liable, by failing to include in Regulation No. 189/72 transitional measures for the protection of the confidence which a trader might legitimately have had in the Community rules.

The Court went on to hold, however, that the European Union was not liable to pay the full amount of the MCAs applicable to the transactions in question. The Union's obligation was solely to ensure that the exporter did not make an actual loss on the transaction as a result of a change in the exchange rate. In later proceedings,[114] it was established that payment for the shipments had been made in French francs. Therefore, CNTA had suffered no loss and it consequently obtained no damages. It is important to note that the Court did not hold the regulation invalid. If it had done so, CNTA would have been entitled to the MCAs at the normal rate. The wrongful act was not the passing of the regulation but the failure either to give reasonable notice to interested parties that the system would soon be ended or, alternatively, to include transitional provisions to protect exporters who had already committed themselves. It was this omission which violated the principle of the protection of legitimate expectations, which, according to the Court, was a superior rule of law in the terms of the *Schöppenstedt* formula.

[113] *Ibid.* at paras 42–44 of the judgment.
[114] [1976] ECR 797.

§4.4 SECOND REQUISITE

The second requisite is that the breach must be sufficiently serious. This is the same under the *Bergaderm* restatement. It is the most important aspect of the *Schöppenstedt* formula and it constitutes the most difficult hurdle for the applicant to surmount. The first decision to consider is *HNL v. Council and Commission*,[115] more commonly known as the second *Skimmed-Milk Powder* case. This arose out of the over-production of milk in the European Union and the creation of a skimmed-milk-powder 'mountain'. In an attempt to get rid of this, the Council passed a regulation obliging animal-feed producers to purchase skimmed-milk powder from the intervention agencies. The idea was that skimmed-milk powder would replace soya as a source of protein in the animal feed. The drawback to this, however, was that skimmed-milk powder was much more expensive than soya and the consequence of the scheme was that farmers had to pay more for their animal feed.

The farmers objected and various actions were brought to contest the legality of the regulation. Some were brought in the national courts and referred to the European Court; others were actions for damages brought in the European Court. Judgment was given first in the cases in which preliminary references were made: the Court ruled that the regulation was invalid because it obliged the producers to purchase skimmed-milk powder 'at such a disproportionate price that it was equivalent to a discriminatory distribution of the burden of costs between the various agricultural sectors' without being justifiable for the purpose of disposing of the stocks of skimmed-milk powder.[116] In other words, the regulation offended against the principles of equality and proportionality.[117]

The following year the Court gave judgment in the tort actions. Since the regulation had already been ruled invalid, there could be no dispute regarding the first requirement of the *Schöppenstedt* formula; nor did the Court have any difficulty in holding that the third requirement was satisfied. The difficulties centred on the second requirement: was the violation sufficiently serious?

It might have been thought that if the violation were serious enough to result in a ruling that the regulation was invalid, it would be serious enough to justify the award of damages; but the Court held that this was not the case. A ruling of invalidity merely satisfies the first requirement in the *Schöppenstedt* formula; it does not necessarily satisfy the second. The Court tried to justify this strict approach by pointing out that in national law it is only in exceptional cases that public authorities incur liability for legislative measures. It may be doubted, however, whether analogies with national law are very apposite in this regard, since the legislative process in the Union is so different from that in the Member States.

[115] Cases 83, 94/76, 4, 15, 40/77, [1978] ECR 1209.

[116] See *ibid.* at para. 3 of the judgment. See further *Bela-Mühle*, Case 114/76; *Granaria*, Case 116/76; and *Ölmühle Hamburg*, Cases 119–20/76, [1977] ECR 1211 *et seq.*

[117] These principles are discussed in Chap. 5, §§ 4 and 5.

The Court then stated that, in a legislative field involving wide discretion, the Union will not be liable unless the institution concerned has 'manifestly and gravely disregarded the limits on the exercise of its powers', a requirement that was affirmed in *Bergaderm*, where the Court said that the decisive test for finding that a breach of Union law is sufficiently serious is whether the Union institution manifestly and gravely disregarded the limits on its discretion.[118]

The requirement of a serious violation has thus been enlarged: where the Union enjoys a wide measure of discretion, applicants must now establish a *manifest* and *grave* violation. The Court held that these requirements were not satisfied in the case. It gave four reasons: first, the regulation affected a wide category of persons, namely all buyers of protein animal feed; secondly, the price increase had only a limited effect on production costs; thirdly, the increase was slight in comparison with increases caused by fluctuations in world prices; and lastly, the effect of the regulation on profits did not exceed the normal level of risk inherent in activities in the agricultural sectors concerned.

One can conclude from this that liability will not result from measures of this kind unless the violation of the law has a serious impact on the interests of the applicants. The last three factors mentioned are all concerned with the degree of harm suffered by the victims. The first factor indicates that liability will be less likely to result where the loss is spread over a wide class of persons than where it is concentrated on a small number of victims.

The *HNL* case was followed a year later by a group of cases concerning two rather unusual products, quellmehl and gritz.[119] The former is made from maize or wheat and is used in bread production to keep the dough damp; the latter is also derived from maize and is used in brewing. The history of these cases began some years prior to the judgment when the Union decided to subsidize starch so it could compete with synthetic products. Starch is, however, to some extent interchangeable with quellmehl and gritz and the subsidy enabled it to undercut quellmehl in baking and gritz in brewing. To prevent this, the subsidies were granted to the latter products as well.

The trouble started when the Council passed a regulation withdrawing the subsidies for quellmehl and gritz but not for starch. The quellmehl and gritz producers objected and brought actions in the national courts. In proceedings for preliminary references, the European Court ruled that the Council had been guilty of discrimination in treating quellmehl and gritz differently from starch.[120] The Council then restored the subsidies, but only from the date of the Court's judgment. The quellmehl and gritz producers claimed that they should have been backdated to when they were

[118] *Bergaderm v. Commission* (n. 106), at para. 43 of the judgment.

[119] *Dumortier v. Council*, Cases 64, 113/76, 167, 239/78, 27, 28, 45/79, [1979] ECR 3091; *Ireks-Arkady v. Council and Commission*, Case 238/78, [1979] ECR 2955; *DGV v. Council and Commission*, Cases 241, 242, 245–50/78, [1979] ECR 3017; *Interquell v. Council and Commission*, Cases 261–2/78, [1979] ECR 3045.

[120] *Ruckdeschel*, Cases 117/76, 16/77, [1977] ECR 1753 and *Moulins de Pont-à-Mousson*, Cases 124/76, 20/77, [1977] ECR 1795.

originally withdrawn and brought proceedings under Article 340, second paragraph, TFEU (then Article 215, second paragraph, EEC), for compensation for the loss they had suffered during the period when they were without subsidies.

There was again no difficulty in proving that the regulations which withdrew the subsidies violated a superior rule of law for the protection of the individual. Was the violation manifest and grave? The Court held that it was. Its reasons were not very clear, but it emphasized that the quellmehl and gritz producers were a small, clearly defined group, and stated that the loss they had suffered went beyond the risks normally inherent in their business. The Court therefore ruled that they were entitled to damages based on the amount of the subsidy they would have received if they had been treated on the same basis as the starch producers. However, this was to be reduced to the extent to which they had been able to pass on any part of the loss to their customers.[121]

This decision may be contrasted with the judgment given by the Court only two months later in the *Isoglucose* cases.[122] Isoglucose is a sweetener which competes with sugar in a certain sector of the market (soft drinks, jams, and similar products). It was first put on the market in 1976 and the Union authorities immediately took steps to meet the threat it posed to sugar, a product which was in surplus. The result was a regulation imposing on isoglucose a levy of such large proportions that, according to the producers, it would have made all production uneconomical. Two of the main factories were in England, and proceedings were brought in the English courts to challenge the validity of the regulation. The European Court held, on a preliminary reference, that the regulation infringed the principle of equality because it discriminated against isoglucose in comparison with sugar.[123] The levy was then withdrawn with retroactive effect.

This did not, however, end the troubles of the isoglucose manufacturers. They had been obliged to suspend production while the levy dispute was pending: if the levy had been upheld, their plants would have had to switch to other products or close entirely. They had therefore incurred heavy expenses from lost production and financial overheads. Hardest hit was the Dutch firm Koninklijke Scholten-Honig (KSH), which had been forced into liquidation. It had constructed a large plant at Tilbury which had been sold at a loss. It claimed that its total loss resulting from the imposition of the levy was over 147 million guilders (over £30 million). The other two producers, Amylum and Tunnel Refineries, had suffered less but their losses were quite considerable: Amylum claimed over 100 million Belgian francs and Tunnel Refineries over £1 million. No one could contend that these losses were within the normal risk of manufacturing even a new product.

[121] The Court did not actually fix the amount of damages: this was left over for determination in later proceedings. See, further, [1982] ECR 3271 and 3293.

[122] *Amylum and Tunnel Refineries v. Council and Commission*, Cases 116, 124/77, [1979] ECR 3497; *KSH v. Council and Commission*, Case 143/77, [1979] ECR 3583 (second *Isoglucose* cases).

[123] *Royal Scholten-Honig*, Cases 103, 145/77, [1978] ECR 2037 (first *Isoglucose* cases).

The producers therefore brought actions for damages. There was again no problem with the first and third requisites under the *Schöppenstedt* formula, but was the violation manifest and grave? On the basis of the tests in the previous cases, one would have thought that it was. Isoglucose manufacturers were an even more restricted group than quellmehl and gritz producers: their numbers were limited by the heavy investment required and the fact that some of the technology involved was still under patent. Moreover, the impact of the regulation on their business was little short of catastrophic.

In spite of this, the Court held that they were entitled to no compensation. Its reasoning was sparse – suggesting that the judges were divided among themselves – and no consideration was given to the degree of harm suffered; instead, the Court concentrated on the extent to which the law had been violated. One would have thought that this was at least as great as in the previous case – the Court itself said that the charges borne by the isoglucose manufacturers were 'manifestly unequal' as compared to those imposed on sugar producers – but the Court ruled that the defendants' errors were not of such gravity that their conduct could be regarded as 'verging on the arbitrary' (a point on which opinions might differ).

It appears from these cases, which were all decided in the late 1970s, that the requirement that the violation be manifest and grave has two aspects to it: one is the degree of harm suffered and the extent to which it is concentrated on a small group of victims; the other is the extent to which the law has been violated. Moreover, the *Isoglucose* cases suggest that the Union will be liable only if the defendant's conduct verges on the arbitrary, a more stringent criterion than was applied in the earlier cases.

Evidence of a more liberal attitude became discernible in the 1990s. In *Stahlwerke Peine-Salzgitter v. Commission*[124] the European Court went out of its way to state that conduct verging on the arbitrary is *not* a requirement,[125] and in *Sofrimport v. Commission*[126] it awarded damages to an apple importer whose goods had been wrongfully excluded from the Union. Its most startling decision, however, was *Mulder v. Council and Commission*,[127] usually known as the second *Mulder* case. This concerned measures taken by the European Union to curb over-production of milk. Initially, the Union introduced a scheme under which dairy farmers were paid a premium for agreeing not to market milk during a five-year period. Over 100,000 farmers took advantage of this scheme. Some time later, the Union introduced a system of milk quotas, under which a special levy – a 'superlevy' – was payable by farmers who produced more than their quota of milk. The quotas were based on the quantity marketed during a year specified in the regulation. The problem was that the regulation did not take account of farmers who had produced no milk during the year in question because they had given an undertaking under the previous scheme. When this scheme

[124] Case C-220/91 P, [1993] ECR I-2393 (ECJ), at para. 51 of the judgment.

[125] The case was actually an action under Arts 34 and 40 ECSC, but the statement concerning arbitrariness was made with reference to Art. 340, second para., TFEU (then Art. 215, second para., EEC).

[126] Case C-152/88, [1990] ECR I-2477.

[127] Cases C-104/89, C-37/90, [1992] ECR I-3061.

ended, they had the worst of both worlds: they no longer received a premium, nor did they have a quota.

In proceedings for a preliminary reference, the European Court held that the regulation introducing the quota system breached their legitimate expectations and was *pro tanto* invalid.[128] As a result, the Council adopted another regulation allowing the farmers in question a special quota of 60 per cent of the quantity marketed in the year immediately preceding that in which they had given their undertaking. In later proceedings, however, the Court held that a quota of only 60 per cent was too low.[129] So the Council introduced another regulation giving them a higher quota.

This put matters right for the future, but the question of compensation for past losses still remained. In the second *Mulder* case, some of the farmers brought an action for damages under Article 340 TFEU (then Article 215 EEC). It had already been established in the earlier cases that the Union had violated the principle of legitimate expectations, a principle which the Court characterized as a superior rule of law for the protection of the individual; the case therefore hinged on the question whether the violation was sufficiently manifest and grave to entail the liability of the Union.

The Court held that, in the case of the regulation totally denying the farmers a milk quota, this requirement was met: the farmers in question were a clearly defined category and the risk of being permanently denied a milk quota was unforeseeable and went beyond the risks normally inherent in milk production. In the case of the regulation granting them a quota of 60 per cent, on the other hand, the violation was not sufficiently serious: the Council had made a choice of economic policy, which had involved balancing the need to avoid over-production of milk against the interests of the farmers who had previously entered into undertakings.[130] Though flawed, that choice did not constitute a sufficiently manifest and grave violation of the limits to the Council's discretionary power. Consequently, the applicants were entitled to damages to compensate them only until the entry into force of this latter regulation.

These damages were to compensate them for loss of profit based on the difference between what they might reasonably have been expected to earn if they had not been denied their rightful quotas and what they actually earned by selling milk outside the quota system, together with what they actually earned, or could have earned,[131] by carrying on alternative activities.

The judgment in this case is remarkable because the number of producers affected was so large that it was impossible for the Council and the Commission to negotiate separately with each one; so the Council had to adopt a regulation setting out the

[128] *Mulder* (first *Mulder* case), Case 120/86, [1988] ECR 2321; *Von Deetzen*, Case 170/86, [1988] ECR 2355.

[129] *Spagl*, Case C-189/89, [1990] ECR I-4539; *Pastätter*, Case C-217/89, [1990] ECR I-4585; *Von Deetzen*, Case C-44/89, [1991] ECR I-5119.

[130] The Council evidently considered that if the farmers who had given undertakings were allowed a greater quota, over-production would result unless the quotas given to the other farmers were reduced.

[131] An application of the principle that there is a duty to mitigate loss.

compensation offered.[132] It seems, therefore, that the Court has abandoned the policy of restricting damage awards to cases where there are few potential claimants.

One can conclude that the 'manifest and grave' requirement is now settled law, as is the requirement that the harm suffered must be outside the normal risks inherent in the activity in question.[133] It is not, however, necessary to prove that the conduct of the Union was verging on the arbitrary, nor is it any longer impossible to obtain damages where there are a large number of potential claimants.

§4.5 THIRD REQUISITE

The third requisite is that the rule of law infringed must be for the protection of the individual, or, in the words of *Bergaderm*, it must be intended to confer rights on individuals.[134] What this appears to mean is that the purpose of the violated rule must be to confer rights on individuals of the category to which the applicant belongs. If this is correct, the requirement is no more than a restatement of a principle which had been applied in cases decided before *Schöppenstedt*.

The principle was first laid down in *Vloeberghs v. High Authority*.[135] This case was discussed at the beginning of § 4, and it will be remembered that it concerned a failure to take a decision under Article 88 ECSC. Vloeberghs was a Belgian coal dealer which had a number of customers in France to whom it wanted to sell coal which it had imported from the United States and which was in stock in Belgium. The French authorities refused to allow the coal to enter France. Vloeberghs regarded this as a violation of the Union principle of free circulation of goods which, it claimed, applied to coal originating outside the Union provided that it had been lawfully imported into a Member State. It therefore asked the Commission to institute enforcement proceedings against France under Article 88 ECSC. When the Commission failed to do so, Vloeberghs brought proceedings against it for damages on the ground that the Commission's failure to act was a violation of the Treaty, especially Article 8 ECSC which imposed a duty on the Commission to ensure that the objectives of the Treaty were attained.

The Court accepted that the principle of free circulation of goods applied to coal originating outside the Union provided it had been lawfully imported into a Member State. However, it stated that this principle had been established in the interests of Union production and, though it had been extended to coal produced outside the

[132] Regulation 2187/93, OJ 1993, L 196/6. For further developments, see *Quiller v. Council and Commission*, Cases T-195 and 202/94, [1997] ECR II-2247; *Dethlefs v. Council and Commission*, Case T-112/95, [1998] ECR II-3819; *Flemmer*, Cases C-80–82/99, [2001] ECR I-7211.

[133] It seems that these risks must be assessed on the basis of the position as it existed when the applicant embarked on the venture which ultimately resulted in the loss incurred: see *Grands Moulins de Paris v. Council and Commission*, Case 50/86, [1987] ECR 4833, where the Court apparently considered that the risks are inherently greater in the case of a new product, and that loss is more easily foreseeable if there is a legislative trend in the direction of the measure which ultimately caused it.

[134] *Bergaderm v. Commission* (n. 106) para. 42 of the judgment.

[135] Cases 9, 12/60, [1961] ECR 197.

Union, it was not intended to benefit such coal and those dealing in it: the purpose of extending the principle to imported coal was merely to ensure that measures taken to restrict the movement of imported coal did not indirectly impede the circulation of Union coal. Consequently, though the Commission owed a duty to Union producers to enforce the principle of free circulation, it owed no such duty to dealers in non-Union coal. The action was therefore dismissed.

Another case in which the applicant failed to establish that the measure in question was intended to confer rights on persons in his position was *Vreugdenhil v. Commission*.[136] This concerned a Council regulation allowing goods which had been exported from the Union to be re-imported free of duty. The Commission, acting under a power delegated to it by the Council under another regulation, had provided that the right would not apply in certain cases. In earlier proceedings for a preliminary reference,[137] the Court had held that in doing this the Commission had gone outside the power delegated to it and had trespassed on the territory of the Council. The Commission measure was therefore declared invalid. In *Vreugdenhil v. Commission* the persons concerned claimed damages, but the Court held that the division of powers between the different Union institutions is intended to uphold institutional balance: it was not for the protection of individuals. The claim therefore failed.

Kampffmeyer v. Commission[138] contains the most illuminating discussion on this point. The case was discussed earlier in this chapter (at the beginning of § 3) and will be considered again later; here it is sufficient to say that the applicants were German grain importers who had applied to the relevant German authority for licences to import maize from France. Under Article 22 of Regulation 19, the German authority could refuse such applications only if a serious disturbance of the market was threatened. Any such decision had to be confirmed by the Commission, which was under an obligation not to confirm it unless it considered that this condition was fulfilled. In the *Kampffmeyer* case, the German authority suspended imports and this decision was confirmed by the Commission. The applicants then sued the Union for damages.

The Court held that the condition laid down in Article 22 of Regulation 19 had not, in fact, been fulfilled and that the Commission decision confirming the German measures was consequently invalid. Was the rule of law violated (Article 22 of Regulation 19) intended to benefit the applicants? The Court held that it was. Its reasoning was as follows:[139]

> With regard to the argument that the rule of law which is infringed is not intended to protect the interests of the applicants, the said Article 22, together with the other provisions of Regulation No. 19, is directed, according to the wording of the fourth recital in the preamble to the Regulation, to ensuring appropriate support for agricultural markets during the transitional period on the one hand, and to allowing the progressive establishment of a single market by

[136] Case C-282/90, [1992] ECR-1937.

[137] *Vreugdenhil v. Minister van Landbouw en Visserij*, Case 22/88, [1989] ECR 2049.

[138] Cases 5, 7, 13–24/66, [1967] ECR 245.

[139] *Ibid.* at 262–3.

> making possible the development of the free movement of goods on the other. Furthermore, the interests of the producers in the Member States and of free trade between these States are expressly mentioned in the preamble to the said Regulation. It appears in particular from Article 18 that the exercise of freedom of trade between States is subject only to the general requirements laid down by its own provisions and those of subsequent Regulations. Article 22 constitutes an exception to these general rules and consequently an infringement of that article must be regarded as an infringement of those rules and of the interests which they are intended to protect. The fact that these interests are of a general nature does not prevent their including the interests of individual undertakings such as the applicants which as cereal importers are parties engaged in intra-Community trade. Although the application of the rules of law in question is not in general capable of being of direct and individual concern to the said undertakings, that does not prevent the possibility that the protection of their interests may be – as in the present case it is in fact – intended by those rules of law. The defendant's argument that the rule of law contained in Article 22 of Regulation No. 19 is not directed towards the protection of the interests of the applicants cannot therefore be accepted.

The task of determining the purpose of a legal rule often involves more than pure legal analysis, and for this reason it is impossible to lay down general rules. It is, however, interesting that the Court in the passage just quoted expressly rejected two arguments. First, the fact that a provision has been enacted in the general interest does not mean that it cannot *also* have been intended to protect the interests of particular individuals. It is sufficient, therefore, if it is intended in part to protect their interests. Secondly, the fact that an individual would not have *locus standi* to challenge it in review proceedings, because it is not of direct and individual concern to him,[140] does not necessarily mean that the provision is not intended to protect his interests.

§4.6 CONCLUSIONS

It was said earlier that the advantage of a tort action is that it is not subject to the restrictive conditions applicable to actions for judicial review, especially the short time limits and the strict rules for *locus standi*. This, however, is balanced by the fact that a more serious degree of misconduct has to be established on the part of the Union.

§5 CONCURRENT LIABILITY: THE UNION AND THE MEMBER STATES

The question to be considered here is the extent to which the liability of the European Union is affected by the fact that there is concurrent liability on the part of a national authority. This often occurs, since it is normal practice for Union policies to be carried out by national authorities. Policy decisions are taken by Union institutions and

[140] See Chap. 12.

the requisite legal acts are adopted; but the implementation of these policies is usually entrusted to agencies of the national Governments acting on behalf of the Union. The citizen usually deals with the latter and if he suffers damage it is usually through the instrumentality of these authorities. If, therefore, he is forced to pay a sum of money that is not due, or refused a grant to which he is entitled, it is the national authority which acts or fails to act. The root cause of the trouble may be some act or failure to act on the part of the Union but, since the matter is implemented by the national authority, the possibility arises of a right of action against the national authority as well as against the Union. The action against the national authority may be in tort, for restitution, or on the basis of a statutory obligation, and will have to be brought in the national courts, as there is no provision for a private person to sue a national government in the European Court.[141]

Will the existence of such a remedy affect any right of action the applicant may have against the Union in the European Court? Obviously applicants cannot be allowed to obtain compensation twice over, so any compensation already obtained in the national courts will have to be deducted from what is awarded in the European Court. But what will happen if no compensation at the national level has yet been obtained either because no proceedings have been instituted or because they are still pending?

The first occasion on which the Court had to consider this problem was in *Kampffmeyer v. Commission*.[142] This case, which has already been discussed, concerned German grain dealers who had been refused permits to import maize from France into Germany. By the time the ban was lifted, the import levy had been increased; so those dealers who went through with their transactions were forced to pay a sum which would not otherwise have been payable. The decision to ban imports was taken by the German Government but it was approved, as required under Union law, by the Commission. In earlier proceedings[143] the Court annulled the Commission decision; now the importers brought proceedings against the Commission for damages. The Court held that by approving the German measures in circumstances in which they were not justified, the Commission had committed a wrongful act which could result in liability. The Court was prepared to consider compensation only for those importers who had concluded contracts to buy maize in France before the applications for import permits had been refused. The loss suffered fell into two categories: in some cases the grain bought had subsequently been imported and the levy paid; in others the contracts had been cancelled. In the former cases the loss suffered was equal to the levy paid; in the latter it was equal to the payments involved in cancellation plus loss of profit.[144]

As far as concurrent liability was concerned, there were two possible grounds on which a claim could be made against the German authorities. One was restitution. This

[141] Actions against a Member State in the European Court may be brought only by the Commission or another Member State: Arts 258 and 259 TFEU.

[142] Cases 5, 7, 13–24/66, [1967] ECR 245. See also *Becher v. Commission*, Case 30/66, [1967] ECR 285.

[143] *Toepfer v. Commission*, Cases 106–7/63, [1965] ECR 405 (discussed in Chap. 12, § 3.2).

[144] The question of damages was dealt with when the case was discussed earlier in this chapter.

applied only where the maize had been imported into Germany and the levy paid. The Court pointed out that the levy was paid into the German treasury and that it might be possible to recover it through proceedings in the German courts. It therefore ruled that this possibility must first be exhausted before it would consider awarding damages under this head against the Union.

The second possible cause of action against the German authority was in tort. The German decision to ban imports was illegal and the German authority was consequently just as much at fault as the Commission: the Germans had imposed the ban; the Commission had confirmed it. Proceedings against the German Government had, in fact, already been instituted but the German court had stayed them to await the outcome of the Union proceedings. The European Court held that, before it could decide the extent of the Union's liability, the German courts should be given the opportunity to decide whether the German authority was liable. It therefore stayed the proceedings.

Was this decision justifiable? It seems clear that the basic premise of the judgment was that primary liability rested on the German authority and that Union liability was only subsidiary.[145] There was considerable justification for this view as regards the levy, since, under the provisions applicable at that time, such levies were not handed over to the Union. If there was a right under German law to recover the levy, it was not unreasonable to regard this aspect of the claim as one where Union liability was subsidiary.

The ruling on the tort issue, however, is hard to justify. This was a case of joint liability, and there was no obvious reason why the liability of the Union should be subsidiary to that of the German authorities. The German proceedings had already been stayed to await the outcome of the Union action; now the European Court was staying the Union action to wait for the German court to give judgment. What if neither was prepared to act first? The European Court was sacrificing the interests of the applicants, who should have been permitted to sue whichever joint tortfeasor they chose, in order to shift the liability on to the German authority. The Court's justification for this was that it was necessary in order to 'avoid the applicants' being insufficiently or excessively compensated for the same damage by the different assessment of two different courts applying different rules of law'.[146] The German court could, of course, have given exactly the same reason for its ruling.

It is hard to know why the Court adopted this approach.[147] Perhaps it thought that if it were more liberal it would be swamped by actions for damages; perhaps it was afraid that the Commission would be outmanœuvred by the German authorities and the Union would end up having to meet the whole of the claim itself. Whatever the

[145] See *per* Advocate General Gand in *Becher v. Commission*, Case 30/66, [1967] ECR 285 at 305.

[146] *Ibid.* at 300.

[147] It should be noted that the solution adopted by the Court had been rejected by Advocate General Gand: see [1967] ECR at 278–9.

reasons, the decision produced totally unsatisfactory results for the applicants, who struggled for years to obtain a remedy.[148]

It was not until five years later that the problem again came before the European Court. This was in *Haegeman v. Commission*,[149] decided in 1972. Haegeman was a Belgian firm which imported wine from Greece (which was not then a Member State). A countervailing duty had been imposed on these imports by a Union regulation and Haegeman claimed that this was illegal as it was contrary to the association agreement between the Union and Greece. It therefore wrote to the Commission and requested the return of the money it had paid. When this was refused it brought an annulment action in the European Court to quash the decision refusing to refund the money.

It should be noted that the countervailing duty, though imposed by Union regulations, was collected by the Belgian authorities. In this respect it was similar to the levy in *Kampffmeyer*. There had, however, been an important development since that decision. The Council Decision of 21 April 1970 on the Replacement of Financial Contributions from Member States by the Communities' Own Resources[150] provided that as from 1 January 1971 the revenue from certain levies and duties would go to the Union. According to the Court, the countervailing duty in question came within the scope of this provision. In other words, while in *Kampffmeyer* the levies were paid into national funds, in *Haegeman* the money went into the Union treasury.[151]

One would have thought that this new factor would have greatly strengthened the case for holding that the Union was under an obligation to refund the money. The Court, however, ruled that because the collection of these funds was a matter for the national authorities, claims for refunds had to be made to them. Any ensuing litigation would then be brought in the national courts. The Commission was, therefore, not obliged to consider Haegeman's application and the annulment action was inadmissible.

This reasoning is hard to accept. The fact that the mechanics of collection are a matter for national provisions and the collection is carried out by national officials does not affect the question of who is liable to make repayment. The duties were imposed by Union provisions and collected on behalf of the Union. The national authorities were agents of the Union and the money was handed over to the Union. If the duties were illegal, it was the Union, not the national authorities, which was unjustly enriched. It was, therefore, unjustified to hold that the national authorities alone were liable to make restitution.[152]

[148] See Schermers, 'The Law as It Stands on the Appeal for Damages' (1975) 1 LIEI 113 at 135 and J Boulouis and RM Chevallier, *Grands arrêts de la cour de justice des communautés européennes*, Tome 1, (1974) p. 417, note A1. After nine years the majority of the applicants did, in fact, obtain compensation in the German courts; but some had still not exhausted the remedies under national law: see Durand, 'Restitution or Damages: National or European Court?' (1976) 1 ELRev. 431 at 433.

[149] Case 96/71, [1972] ECR 1005. [150] Decision 70/243, OJ 1970, L 94.

[151] It is not clear from the case whether all the payments were made after 1 January 1971 but the Court assumed in its judgment that all the payments went into Union funds.

[152] But see René Joliet, *Le droit institutionnel des Communautés européennes: Le contentieux* (1981), p. 228.

Haegeman also claimed damages in tort for various losses it had suffered as a result of the imposition of the duty, but the Court held that, as the question of Union liability depended on the legality of the duty, this claim would be dismissed 'at the present stage'. It is not entirely clear what was meant by this, but it seems that the Court intended that Haegeman should first establish the illegality of the levy through proceedings in the Belgian courts with a reference to the European Court for a preliminary ruling. Then, if it were successful in this, it could return to the European Court with its tort action.

It is interesting that in a case decided only a few months before, *Compagnie d'Approvisionnement v. Commission (No. 2)*,[153] Advocate General Dutheillet de Lamothe had given careful consideration to just this possibility. In this case the applicants, which were French dealers in cereals, complained that a subsidy, granted under a Council regulation, had been fixed by the Commission at too low a level. They therefore brought proceedings against the Commission under Article 340, second paragraph, TFEU (then Article 215, second paragraph, EEC). One argument put forward by the Commission was that the action was inadmissible because the applicants should first have brought proceedings in the French courts to establish that the Commission regulation fixing the level of the subsidy was illegal. This would have been referred to the European Court and a ruling on the point would have been made. Only if this was successful, argued the Commission, could the applicants bring their action against the Union.

Advocate General Dutheillet de Lamothe rejected this argument. First, he pointed out that in view of the various levels of the national court system through which the case would have to pass, it might well be over five years before the matter was finally concluded. By this time the period of limitation for the action against the Union would have expired. (In his view there was no ground on which the running of time could be interrupted in these circumstances.) He also pointed out the extreme difficulties which similar doctrines had caused in France and other countries and suggested that the end result could be a denial of justice. Finally, he stated that there was nothing in the Treaties to justify such a procedure.

The Court declared the action admissible. Thus, though it did not explicitly deal with this particular point, it implicitly rejected the Commission's argument. One wonders why, so soon afterwards, it should have required Haegeman to make what Advocate General Dutheillet de Lamothe had referred to as the 'long march' through the national courts.

However, in a similar case decided a year after *Haegeman*, the European Court held that the action was admissible. This was in *Merkur v. Commission*,[154] in which it said that, as it already had the case before it, it 'would not be in keeping with the proper administration of justice and the requirements of procedural efficiency to compel the applicant to have recourse to national remedies and thus to wait for a considerable

[153] Cases 9, 11/71, [1972] ECR 391.

[154] Case 43/72, [1973] ECR 1055.

length of time before a final decision on his claim is made'.[155] It is hard to regard this ruling as anything other than a rejection of the decision in *Haegeman*.[156]

For the next few years little was heard of the *Haegeman* ruling and one might possibly have thought that it had been quietly forgotten. In one case, *Holtz and Willemsen v. Council and Commission*,[157] it was argued by the Commission that the applicant's claim (for a subsidy) should have been brought in the national courts. This was rejected by Advocate General Reischl,[158] and the Court, though it did not deal with the point, found the proceedings admissible. In *CNTA v. Commission*[159] the point was not even really argued. In 1975, however, the Court again changed tack[160] and since then there have been many cases in which applicants have been sent to the national courts.

In order to give an explanation of what the present position appears to be, it is necessary to distinguish between three separate situations: first, where the applicant's loss lies in the fact that he was unlawfully obliged to pay a sum of money to the national authority; secondly, where his loss lies in the fact that the national authorities unlawfully refused to make a payment to him; and thirdly, where his loss is of some other kind. In the first situation, his right of action against the national authority will be for restitution; in the second, it will be on the basis of a statutory obligation; in the third, it will be in tort. Each situation will be considered separately.

§5.1 RESTITUTION

Where the applicant's loss consists in the fact that he was unlawfully obliged to make a payment to the national authority, he will normally have a remedy for restitution against the national authority. In such a situation, he will not be entitled to bring proceedings against the Union even if the national authority acted as agent for the Union and handed the money over to it. In *Kampffmeyer*,[161] the proceedings in the European Court were held admissible and the Union was held liable in principle; in the later cases, the proceedings were held inadmissible. The latter is the rule today.[162]

§5.2 STATUTORY OBLIGATION

The second situation is where the national authority has wrongfully refused to make a payment to the applicant. In spite of the earlier cases discussed previously, the general

[155] At para. 6 of the judgment.

[156] See Van Gerven, 'De niet-contractuele aansprakelijkheid van de Gemeenschap wegens normatieve handelingen' [1976] SEW 2, at 7–8.

[157] Case 153/73, [1974] ECR 675.

[158] *Ibid.* at 700–1.

[159] Case 74/74, [1975] ECR 533 (discussed earlier).

[160] The doctrine was resurrected (somewhat ambiguously) in *Grands Moulins des Antilles v. Commission*, Case 99/74, [1975] ECR 1531 and (more emphatically) in *IBC v. Commission*, Case 46/75, [1976] ECR 65. For a discussion of these, and later cases, see Hartley, 'Concurrent Liability in EEC Law: A Critical Review of the Cases' (1977) 2 ELRev. 249.

[161] See n. 56.

[162] *Vreugdenhil v. Commission*, Case C-282/90, [1992] ECR I-1937 at para. 12 of the judgment.

rule now is that such an action will be inadmissible, even if the basis of the obligation was a Union measure, and the national authority obtained its funds from the European Union.[163]

§5.3 NO NATIONAL REMEDY

In both the situations discussed so far, the position is different where it is not possible for the applicant to obtain a remedy in the national courts. Since the alternative would be a denial of justice, the European Court has, after some hesitation,[164] held that proceedings can be brought directly before it against the appropriate Union institution.[165]

Roquette v. Commission[166] provides a good illustration. This was a sequel to an earlier case[167] in which a number of French grain exporters had been obliged to pay MCAs under Union regulations they claimed to be invalid. They brought proceedings in the French courts for the return of the sums paid (which had been collected by the French authorities on behalf of the European Union). On a reference for a preliminary ruling, the European Court held that the regulations were indeed invalid, but nevertheless the applicants could not recover money already paid. Roquette then brought proceedings in the European Court under Article 340 TFEU for damages to compensate it for the loss it had suffered. In these circumstances, as the European Court pointed out, Roquette could not obtain a remedy in the French courts because such a remedy had been barred by the European Court itself in the earlier case.[168] Despite the protestations of the Commission,[169] therefore, the proceedings were admissible.[170]

The circumstances in *Roquette* were unusual. A more common situation is where the sole cause of the problem is the failure of the Commission or Council to adopt a legal act. In such a case, the applicant cannot bring proceedings in the national court and ask it to decide the case on the basis that the measure has been enacted.[171] Not even the European Court can do this: in actions for a remedy for a failure to act, all it can do

[163] *Asteris v. Greece*, Cases 106–20/87, [1988] ECR 5515 at para. 25 of the judgment and the cases there cited.

[164] *Roquette v. Commission*, Case 26/74, [1976] ECR 677. This case concerned an exporter who had been obliged to pay a levy under a provision of Union law. The levy was collected by the national authority and handed over to the Commission. The exporter considered that he had not been liable to make the payment and brought proceedings for its recovery, with interest, in both the national courts (against the national authority) and the European Court (against the Commission). The national court made a reference for a preliminary ruling, and the European Court held in favour of the exporter (*Roquette v. France*, Case 34/74, [1974] ECR 1217). The national court then ordered the repayment of the sum in question, but refused to award interest, partly on the ground that the Union had had the use of the money during the period in question. The exporter then continued his action against the Commission in the European Court in order to obtain the interest. The European Court, however, held this claim inadmissible on the ground that it was ancillary to the claim for the repayment of the levy, a claim which was within the exclusive jurisdiction of the national courts. This seems unfair.

[165] *Unifrex v. Commission and Council*, Case 281/82, [1984] ECR 1969 at paras 1–13 of the judgment; *Krohn v. Commission*, Case 175/84, [1986] ECR 753 at paras 24–29 of the judgment; see also *De Boer Buizen v. Council and Commission*, Case 81/86, [1987] ECR 3677 at paras 9–10 of the judgment (claim in tort).

[166] Case 20/88, [1989] ECR 1553.

[167] *Roquette v. French Customs*, Case 145/79, [1980] ECR 2917.

[168] See *ibid.* paras 14–17 of the judgment

[169] See *ibid.* para. 9 of the judgment.

[170] The Court nevertheless held that the ruling in the earlier case required it to dismiss the claim on the merits.

[171] *Port*, Case C-68/95, [1996] ECR I-6065 at para. 53 of the judgment.

is to declare that the defendant's failure to act is contrary to the Treaties; it cannot itself adopt the measure.[172] In these circumstances there is, therefore, no procedure under which the applicant can bring his complaint before the national courts; consequently, he can bring proceedings before the European Court under Article 340.[173]

This situation must be contrasted with another situation, superficially similar but in fact very different, in which the right in question already exists by virtue of a previous measure, but is wrongfully withdrawn by a later measure. Here a remedy would normally exist in the national courts since the applicant could argue that the later measure was invalid and of no effect. A reference could be made to the European Court and, if it held this was the case, the earlier measure could be applied as being still in force.[174]

§5.4 TORT

In an action in tort, the applicant is claiming not a specific sum of money, but compensation for loss suffered. It now appears to be settled that if this is the true nature of his claim, he can proceed directly against the Union in the European Court.[175]

This is shown by *Dietz v. Commission*.[176] Dietz was a German firm which entered into a contract to export sugar to Italy. After the contract was made but before it was performed, a levy was introduced on imports into Italy. The result was that Dietz made a loss on the transaction, and it brought an action against the Union in the European Court on the ground that the sudden imposition of the charge was a violation of the principle of the protection of legitimate expectations.

It will be remembered that in the *CNTA* case, which had been decided a couple of years previously, the Court had ruled that a claim of this nature is possible.[177] As that case made clear, however, an applicant in Dietz's position cannot claim a full refund of the levy; all it can claim is the amount of any actual loss – not loss of profit – that it suffered. For this reason, Dietz's claim was not for a fixed sum but was a true tort action; consequently it was admissible.

The *Quellmehl* and *Gritz* cases establish this even more firmly. It will be remembered[178] that the essence of the claim was that subsidies had been withdrawn from quellmehl and gritz but not from starch. Since starch was in competition with quellmehl and gritz, this constituted discrimination. The Court, however, held that

[172] See Chap. 13. [173] *Unifrex v. Commission and Council*, Case 281/82, [1984] ECR 1969 (see n. 165).

[174] *IBC v. Commission*, Case 46/75, [1976] ECR 65.

[175] In addition to the cases discussed in the text, see *Zuckerfabrik Bedburg v. Council and Commission*, Case 281/84, [1987] ECR 49 at paras 10–12 of the judgment; *Vreugdenhil v. Commission*, Case C-282/90, [1992] ECR I-1937 at paras 9–15 of the judgment. In *Assurances du Crédit v. Council and Commission*, Case C-63/89, [1991] ECR I-1799, Advocate General Tesauro argued that, even in the case of a tort action, proceedings cannot be brought in the European Court if the applicant could have obtained an adequate remedy in the national courts. This contention, which was not considered by the Court, is, however, contrary to the judgment in *Zuckerfabrik Bedburg*, which drew a clear distinction between tort actions and actions for sums due; it is also contrary to the judgment in *Vreugdenhil*, which drew a similar distinction.

[176] Case 126/76, [1977] ECR 2431. [177] See § 4.3. [178] See § 4.4.

the quellmehl and gritz producers did not have a claim to the subsidy as such; all they were entitled to was compensation for the loss they had suffered (though on the facts of the case it came to the same thing). This, too, was a true tort action and was therefore admissible.

It should finally be emphasized that no question of Union liability can arise unless the harm suffered was caused by an act of the European Union; if it was caused by the national authorities acting independently, the Union cannot be held responsible: concurrent liability arises only where the national authorities are acting as agents of the Union or on the instructions of a Union institution.

§5.5 CONCLUSIONS

The cases that have been discussed in this section illustrate the severe problems often faced by private litigants trying to obtain a remedy in situations involving both the national authorities and the European Union. The inconsistent decisions given by the Court can make it difficult to decide on the best course of action. In some cases, moreover, it is hard to avoid the suspicion that the Court has been prepared to sacrifice the interests of the citizen in order to protect those of the Union.

FURTHER READING

Items are listed in date order, the most recent being at the end.

Durand, 'Restitution or Damages: National Court or European Court?' (1976) 1 ELRev. 431.

Harding, 'The Choice of Court Problem in Cases of Non-Contractual Liability under EEC Law' (1979) 16 CMLRev. 389.

Lewis, 'Joint and Several Liability of the European Communities and National Authorities' [1980] CLP 99.

Barav, 'La répétition de l'indu' [1981] CDE 507.

René Joliet, *Le droit institutionnel des Communautés européennes: Le contentieux* (1981), pp. 243–71.

Bridge, 'Procedural Aspects of the Enforcement of European Community Law through the Legal Systems of the Member States' (1984) 9 ELRev. 28.

Henry G Schermers, Ton Heukels, and Philip Mead (eds), *Non-Contractual Liability of the European Communities* (1988).

Wils, 'Concurrent Liability of the Community and a Member State' (1992) 17 ELRev. 191.

Ton Heukels and Alison McDonnell (eds), *The Action for Damages in Community Law* (1997).

Tridimas, 'Liability for Breach of Community Law: Growing Up and Mellowing Down?' (2001) 38 CMLRev. 301 (pp. 321–32).

Andrea Biondi and Martin Farley, *The Right to Damages in European Law* (2009).

Gutman, 'The Evolution of the Action for Damages against the European Union and its Place in the System of Judicial Protection' (2011) 48 CMLRev. 695.

BIBLIOGRAPHY

Only general works are listed here; specialized materials are found in the 'Further Reading' after each chapter.

PAUL CRAIG, *EU Administrative Law*, 2nd edn, (2012).

SIONAIDH DOUGLAS-SCOTT, *Constitutional Law of the European Union* (2002).

WALTER VAN GERVEN, *The European Union, A Polity of States and Peoples* (2005).

TREVOR C HARTLEY, *Constitutional Problems of the European Union* (1999).

RENÉ JOLIET, *Le droit institutionnel des Communautés européennes: Le contentieux* (1981).

RENÉ JOLIET, *Le droit institutionnel des Communautés européennes: Les institutions; Les sources; Les rapports entre ordres juridiques* (1983).

RH LAUWAARS, *Lawfulness and Legal Force of Community Decisions* (1973).

HENRY G SCHERMERS AND DENIS F WAELBROECK, *Judicial Protection in the European Communities*, 6th edn (2001).

AG TOTH, *Legal Protection of Individuals in the European Communities* (1978).

TAKIS TRIDIMAS, *The General Principles of EC Law*, 2nd edn (2006).

G VANDERSANDEN AND A BARAV, *Contentieux Communautaire* (1977).

ANGELA WARD, *Judicial Review and the Rights of Private Parties in EU Law*, 2nd edn (2007).

INDEX

Abortion 150–1
Abstract theory 295–7
***Acte Clair* doctrine** 305–6
Acts
  legal *see* **Legal acts**
  Member States, of *see* **Acts of Member States**
  non-existent acts *see* **Void *ab initio* acts**
  non-member States *see* **non-member States**
  representatives of Member States, of *see* **Acts of representatives**
  reviewable *see* **Reviewable acts**
Acts of institutions established by agreements with third countries
  direct effect, and 243
  generally 191
  preliminary references 287–8
Acts of Member States
  acts of representatives 94–5
  conflicting treaties 98–104
    conflicts between EU treaties 99
    conflicts with non-Union treaties 100–1
    European Convention on Human Rights 101–4
    United Nations law 104–6
  constitutive treaties 87–89
    amending the treaties 89–92
    principal treaties, list of 87–8
    supplementary instruments 88–9
  subsidiary conventions 94
  treaties among a sub-group of Member States 95–8
Acts of representatives of Member States 94–5
  preliminary references 284
Administrative law
  annulment
    compliance with judgment 438–9
    failure to act 434–6
    generally 427–8, 436–8
    indirect challenge, effects of 441
    mistake of fact 430–4
    misuse of powers 424–7
    partial annulment 440
    procedural infringements 420–3
    rejection of application 440
    retroactivity, and 436–7
    time factor 427–9
    treaty infringements 423–4
  failure to act
    examples of 395–6
    introduction to 392–3
    judgment, form of 408–9
    locus standi 394, 401, 405–8
    negative decisions 393–4
    parties to proceedings 396
    position, definition of 395–6
    request for action 394, 395, 402–5
    reviewable omissions 396–402
    treaty provisions 392–3
    unity principle 393, 397, 405–6
  indirect challenge
    definition of 410
    description of 411
    effect of successful 417–18, 441
    general application acts, challenging 412
    grounds for challenge 416–17
    individual acts, problems of challenging 413–15
    introduction to 410–11
    invalidity ruling binding 417
    locus standi of privileged applicants 415
    non-existent acts 418
    normative/individual acts distinguished 412–15
    proceedings, limitations in which to challenge 416
    treaty provisions 411–12
  introduction to
    citizens' challenges 345–6
    jurisdiction 346
  locus standi
    direct concern 386–90
    failure to act 405–8
    individual concern 369–71
    justification for unlimited *locus standi* 368
    non-privileged applicants 368–9, 383–4
    quasi-judicial determinations 379–83
    privileged applicants 367–8
    semi-privileged applicants 368
    small groups 371–2
  review, grounds of
    acts *see* reviewable acts *below*
    application infringement 423–4
    competence, lack of 419–20
    essential procedural infringement 420–23
    failure to act 434–6
    grounds of 419
    locus standi 429–30
    mistake of fact 430–4
    misuse of powers 424–7
    patent error 434
    time factor 428–9
  reviewable acts
    acts of Council, Commission and European Central Bank 350
    acts producing legal effects *vis-à-vis* third parties 349
    author of the act 364–6
    features of 350

Administrative law (*cont.*)
'having legal effects' requirement 350–1
invalid acts 360–4
jurisdiction *ratione materiae* 346, 349, 360
legislative acts 350
letters signed by Commission 361–2
negative decisions, as 393–4
Noordwijks Cement Accoord case 351–3
problem cases 353–9
treaty provisions 349–51
void acts 360–4
voidable acts 360–4
Union obligations, contract
choice of law 445–7
jurisdiction of the European Court 443–5
Union obligations, tort
acts imputable to EU 453–7
anxiety and hurt feelings, damages for 458
applicant's conduct 458
causation 459–60
concurrent liability 479–83, 485–6
currency conversion 459
damage 457–9
declaration of entitlement to damages 458–9
defendants 58, 452
direct actions 58
duty to mitigate loss 458
elements 451
employment, claims arising out of 458
European Central Bank, and 450, 452
fault 460–3
financial loss, compensation for 457
general 450–3
general principles of law common to Member States 452–3
interest 459
limitation 451
locus standi 451
profit, claims for loss of 457–8
remoteness 459
treaty provisions 450–2
Admissibility 60–1
Advocates General
Documentation Service 53
First Advocate General 51, 52
function of 51–2
horizontal direct effect 224–5
impartiality 52
importance of role 52
independence 52
judges acting as 55
judges compared 50, 51
numbers of 51
opinions of 52–3
role of 51–2
status of 51
Agreement Establishing the World Trade Organization (WTO) 183
Agreement on Trade-Related Aspects of Intellectual Property Rights (TRIPS) 183
Agreements with third countries
acts of institutions established by
Association councils 191
direct effect, and 243
generally 191
competence, exclusive and shared 174–5
complementarity, principle of 181
conferral, principle of 175–6
direct effect, and 240–3
effect to, courts giving
European court, proceedings in 198
general principles 196–7
national courts, proceedings in 197
kinds of agreement
Member States/non-member States 175
'mixed' agreements 175
Union/non-member States 175
legal personality of Union 174
legal proceedings 189–91
Member States, binding on 196
parallelism, doctrine of 176–7, 178, 179, 184–5
preliminary references 285–7
primary powers of treaty-making 176, 177
secondary powers of treaty-making 176–85
source of EU Law, as 174
treaty-making procedure 187–9
Treaty of Lisbon 185–6
Union, binding on
Member States concluded agreement 193–4
mixed agreements 194–6
Union concluded agreements 84, 192
Union legal system, and 84, 191–2
Animals
maltreatment of 252–3
Annulment
compliance with judgment 438–9
failure to act 434–6
generally 427–8, 436–8
indirect challenge, effects of 441
mistake of fact 430–4
misuse of powers 424–7
partial annulment 440
procedural infringements 420–3
rejection of application 440
retroactivity, and
erga omnes 436
general rule 436
non-application of rule 437–8
non-existent acts 436
regulations, and 437–8
time factor 427–9
treaty infringements 423–4
Anti-dumping
General Court, and 59
reviewable act 380–2
Appeals
Civil Service Tribunal, from 55, 60
European Court, none from 52
General Court, from 54, 59
preliminary references, and 281, 309–10
Association councils 191

***Audi alteram partem* rule** 53, 171, 320, 421–2
Austria
Constitution 160
seats in European Parliament 14
tort, government liability in 254–5

Belgium
direct effect, response to 259–60
monist doctrine, acceptance of 260
seats in European Parliament 14
Bodies, offices and agencies
Committee of the Regions 36
Economic and Social Committee 35–6
European agencies 36
generally 34–5
preliminary references, and 282
Budgetary procedure 42–3
Bulgaria
seats in European Parliament 14

Cabinet
Chefs de Cabinet 29
Commissioner assistance 29
Certainty *see* **Legal certainty**
Charter of Fundamental Rights 156–7, 158
Choice of law 445–7
choice-of-law clauses 446
EU employment cases 446–7
Rome I Regulation 446
Civil Service Tribunal
appeals to General Court 55
function of 55
judges 55
legal aid 65
procedure
admissibility 60–61
costs 64
English Courts distinguished 60
execution of judgment 62
judgments 60, 62
language choice 67–8
lawyers 64–5
oral procedure 60, 61
preliminary rulings 63–4
preparatory inquiry 61
rules of 60
special procedure after judgment 62–3
written proceedings 60
treaty provisions 56
'Closed category'
decisions 370–1, 372–3
individual concern 369–71
meaning 370
regulations 370–1, 374–9
test 369–70
Closer co-operation *see* **Enhanced co-operation**
Commission, EU *see* **European Commission**
Committee of the Permanent Representatives of the Member States (COREPER) 24
Committee of the Regions 36
Committees 17
Common Foreign and Security Policy (CFSP)
Common Security and Defence Policy 34
development of 33–4
features of 33
High Representative of the Union for Foreign Affairs and Security Policy 34
terrorism, and 160
voting 33
Common Security and Defence Policy 34
Competence
exclusive areas of 119
subsidiarity, and 123–4
treaty provisions 119
exclusive and shared 119
treaty-making competence 174–5
generally 119
shared, areas of 119
supplementary 119
Competition
Noordwijks Cement Accoord case 351–3
restrictive agreements 351
reviewable acts 379–80
Complementarity, principle of 181
Conciliation
Conciliation Committee 39, 40–1
generally 40
Conciliation Committee 40–1
Concurrent liability
generally 478–83
no national remedy 484–5
restitution 483
statutory obligation 483–4
tort 479–83, 485–6
Conferral, principle of
competence 119
implied powers, theory of 113–14
'Kompetenz- Kompetenz' 112–13, 207
meaning of 112–13
open-ended powers
treaty-making powers of EU 174–5
treaty provisions 114–19
ultra vires acts 113
Consistent interpretation, doctrine of
directives, and 235–8
origins 236
uncertainty, and 238
Constitutional Courts
Czech 9
Danish 207
German 7, 77, 147, 152, 207, 261–2, 263–6
Italian 244
Polish 271–2
Constitutions
Belgium 260
Danish 207, 266–7
European, draft 8–9
French 267
German 7, 147, 159, 167, 258, 261–2
Ireland 258
Italy 258
Netherlands 206
United States 205–6
Constitutive treaties 83, 87–9
amending the treaties 89–92
ECSC Treaty, as 87
principal treaties, list of 87–8
supplementary instruments 88–9
Contractual obligations
choice of law 445–7
choice-of-law clauses 446

Contractual obligations (*cont.*)
EU employment cases 446–7
Rome I Regulation 446
jurisdiction of the European Court 443–5
agreements conferring jurisdiction, form of 444
arbitration/jurisdiction clauses 443–4, 445
Conventions, subsidiary
acts of Member States, as 94
preliminary references, and 284
Co-operation procedure 121–2
COREPER 24
Council
budgetary procedure 42–3
configuration of meetings 23
constituent members of 23–4
Council of Europe, distinguished 21
COREPER 24
European Council, distinguished 21
General Secretariat 24
institution of Union, as 13
locus standi
privileged applicant, as 367–8
Presidency of the Council 23–4
reviewable acts 350
role of 22
treaty-making procedure 187–9
voting
additional rules 26
allocation of votes 25
'Luxembourg Accords' 26–7
negative tactics of 26
qualified majority 25–6
simple majority 24–5
unanimity 25
Council of Europe 11
Council, distinguished 21
European Council, distinguished 21
Court of Auditors
constituent members 32
fraud, and 33
function of 32
institution of Union, as 13, 32, 33
President 32
reviewable acts 364
Court of First Instance *see* **General Court**
Court of Justice of the European Union *see* **European Court**
Court procedure
admissibility 60–1
costs 64
English Courts distinguished 6
execution of judgment 62
judgments 60, 62
language choice 67–8
lawyers 64–5
oral procedure 60, 61
preliminary rulings 63–4
preparatory inquiry 61
rules of 60
special procedure after judgment 62–3
written proceedings 60
Courts
Court of First Instance *see* **General Court**
Court of Justice *see* **European Court**
General Court *see* **General Court**
preliminary references *see* **Preliminary references**
procedure *see* **Court procedure**
specialized courts *see* **Civil Service Tribunal**
Croatia
seats in European Parliament 15
Currency
attitudes towards membership of Euro Area 11
European Central Bank, and 31
establishment of euro 8
financial crisis
impact of 10–11
response to 96–8
tort actions, conversion in 459
Cyprus
financial crisis, impact of 10
seats in European Parliament 15
Czech Republic
Constitutional Court 9
seats in European Parliament 14
Damages
anxiety and hurt feelings, damages for 458
applicant's conduct 458
causation 459–60
concurrent liability 479–83, 485–6
currency conversion 459
damage 457–9
declaration of entitlement to 458–9
employment, claims arising out of 458
enforcement actions 327–8, 332–4
financial loss, compensation for 457
government liability 252
causation 252
damages 252
interest 459
loss, proving 58
profit, claims for loss of 457–8
remoteness 459
Decisions
binding nature of 109
direct effect, and 239–40
disguised 109
individual acts, as 412
legal act, as 108–9
locus standi
non-privileged applicants 368–9
open and closed categories 369–70
publication of 141–2
reviewable act, as 350
supremacy of EU law 244
Declaration of Fundamental Rights and Freedoms 153
Declaration of invalidity
enforcement actions 325
indirect challenges, and 441
Delegated acts 111
imputable to EU 456–7
Delegation
Commission, to 129–31
implementing powers 134–5
advisory procedure 135
examination procedure 135

liability for delegated acts 456–7
meaning of 128–9
Member States, to 133–4
outside bodies, to 131–3
Union institutions, to 131

Denmark
conferral, principle of 113
Constitution 207, 258, 266–7
direct effect, response to 266–7
seats in European Parliament 14
Treaty on European Union, ratification of 266

Direct actions
'accelerated procedure' 311
annulment 419
categories of 56
costs 64
defendants 58
'expedited procedure' 311
judgments 57
judicial review 58
jurisdiction
conferred by agreement between the parties 57
conferred by direct operation of law 57–8
head of jurisdiction, as a 56
language choice 67–8
lawyers, right to appear 64
tort actions 58
written proceedings, and 60

Direct concern
administrative law, and 368, 386–90

Direct effect
acts of institutions established by agreements with third countries 243
agreements with third countries 240–3
consistent interpretation, doctrine of 235–8
criminal proceedings, and 239
decisions, and 239–40
directives, and
cases on 218–22
deadline, importance of 221–2
exclusionary effect 227–8
horizontal effect, and 224–31
new principle 219–21
regulations distinguished 222–4
'state', meaning of 231–5
steps towards 218
treaty provisions 218
vertical effect 224–31
dualist doctrine
generally 204–6
exclusionary effect 227–8
horizontal effect
cases 224–31
generally 224–31
indirect effect 235–9
introduction to 203–7
law, general principles of 240
meaning of 203–4
monist doctrine
generally 83–4, 204–6, 258
national powers, restriction of 243–5
non-implementation, governmental liability 239
principle of
basic ideas 209–10
clarity 210–11
further action, no dependency on 213–14
unambiguity 210–11
unconditional 211–13
procedure in national courts 245–8
regulations, and
directives, differences between 222–4
horizontal effect 224–31
national implementing rules 216–18
treaty provisions, and 215–18
vertical effect 224–31
remedies in national courts
damages, *a priori* limit 248
equal availability of national, principle of 245–6, 251
generally 245–8
interim relief 247
states
capacity in which acting 232
cases 231–5
meaning of 'state' 231–5
nationalized industries 232–4
organizations as emanation of the state 232–4
public authority, and 232
public sector employment 234
public services 234
substitution effect 227, 228
supremacy of EU law, and 243–5
tort, government liability in
animals, maltreatment of 252–3
cases 248–55
causation 252
damages 252
directives, transposition of 254
effectiveness, principle of 251
judges, incorrect decisions of 254–5
treaty provisions 214
triangular situations, theory of 227
United Kingdom, and 274
vertical effect
cases 224–31
generally 224–31

Directives
consistent interpretation, doctrine of 235–8
definition of 108, 109
direct effect, and
cases on 218–22
deadline, importance of 221–2
exclusionary effect 227–8
new principle 219–21
regulations, differences between 222–4
'state', meaning of 231–5
steps towards 218
supremacy of EU law 244
treaty provisions 218
vertical effect 224
legal act as, 108
publication of 141–2
reviewable act, as 350
transposition of 254

Directorates General 29

Discrimination
equality, principle of 168–9
nationality 168, 169, 234
producer/consumers in agriculture 168–9
religion 169–70

Discrimination (*cont.*)
remedies, availability of 245–6, 251
sex 169, 236
Documentation Division 54
Dualist doctrine
generally 204–6
United Kingdom, and 206, 260

Economic and Social Committee 35–6
ECSC Treaty
constitutive treaty, as 87
expiry of 87, 465
failure to act 328
fault, as element of liability 460
French text of 65
generally 3–4
human rights 145
rule-making powers 30
validity rulings 299–300
EEC Treaty 3–4
Enforcement actions
actions by Member States
reasoned opinions, request for 329
treaty provisions 329–30
administrative stage
audi alteram partem rule 320
Commission discretion 321–3
formal stage 320–21
general 319–21
informal stage 320
observations 320
procedural defects, consequences of 324–5
time limit for Commission action 323–4
treaty provisions 319–20
violation, recording the 323
compliance
defying the court 335–6
fines 336–8
damages 327–8, 332–4
fines
calculation of 337–8
criteria for 337
environmental pollution 338
fixing penalties in advance 338–9
general infringements 339
lump-sum 336, 337
periodic penalty payment 336, 337
persistent infringements 339
problems of imposing 339–40
procedure for 336
standard flat-rate amount 337
interim measures
cases illustrating 331–2, 333, 336
interlocutory injunctions 331
main considerations 331
treaty provisions 331
introduction to 315
judicial stage
binding nature of judgment 326–7
de novo consideration 325
declaration of invalidity 325, 326
plenary jurisdiction 325
scope of proceedings 325–6
north/south gradient willingness to observe EU law 335
problems of 339–40
remedies on failure of Commission
actions for failure to act 327–8
damages 327–8
private individuals 327
reasoned opinions/ decisions distinguished 327
restitution 332–4
reviewable acts 327
tort actions 328
violations of EU law
judiciary of Member State, by 317–19
legislature of Member State, by 317–19
popular action, by 319
provisions covered 316–17
Enhanced co-operation
generally 8, 43–4
treaty provisions 43–4
Environmental pollution
fines for 338
Equality
doctrine of 145, 168–9
equal pay 169
nationality 168, 169, 234
non-discrimination as general principle 145, 169
producer/consumers in agriculture 168–9
religious discrimination 169–70
sex equality 169, 236
Treaty provisions 168–9
Erga omnes
annulment, and 436
indirect challenges, and 417
Essential procedural requirement
review, and 420–3
Estonia
seats in European Parliament 15
EU Treaties
conflicts between 99
general principles of law, origin of 145
United Nations law, conflicts with 104–6
Euratom 3–4, 5, 10, 99, 324, 455
Euro *see* **Currency**
European agencies
executive 36
generally 36
regulatory 36
European Arrest Warrant 265, 271–2
European Central Bank
Executive Board 31, 32
Governing Council 31
institution of Union, as 13, 31
President 31
term of office 31–2
tort liability 450, 452
role 31
European Commission
approval by Parliament 20
assessment of 31
censure by Parliament 20–1
Commissioners *see* **European Commissioners**
composition of 27–30
decision-making procedure 30–1
delegation, and 129–31
Directorates General 29
importance of role 31
institution of Union, as 13

President *see* **President of the Commission**
privileged applicant, *locus standi* as 367–8
reasoned opinions/decisions distinguished 327
rule-making powers 30
Santer Commission 31
treaty-making procedure 187–9
written procedure 30–1

European Commissioners
appointment 27–8
Cabinet assistance 29
compulsory retirement 28
dismissal of 28
income tax 30
legal proceedings 30
lobbying of 29
national loyalties 28
privileges 30
resignation of 28
tenure 28

European Communities Act 1972
direct effect 259, 274
enforcement of judgments 275–6
general 272–3
implementation 274–5
preliminary rulings 313
supremacy of EU law 206, 259, 276–8
Union Treaties 273

European Convention on Human Rights and Fundamental Freedoms
conflicts with EU Treaties 101–4
EU, and 153–6
'inspiration' for EU 153
United Kingdom, and 206

European Council 11–12
constituent members of 23–4
Council, distinguished 21
Council of Europe, distinguished 21
decision-making body 21
High Representative of the Union for Foreign Affairs and Security Policy 22–3
history of 21–2
institution of Union, as 13
President
election of 22
role of 22

European Court
Advocates General 51–3
agreements with third countries 198
appeals, none from 52
chambers, division into 50
future of 77–8
General Court, appeals from 54
general principles of law/non-enacted law 84, 144–6
Grand Chamber 50
Information Office 54
institution of Union, as 13
interpretative role 72–3
judges
appointment of 49–50
background of 51
chambers, sitting in 50
election 50
full court 50–1
incorrect decisions of 254–5
independence of 49–50, 51
judgments 51, 53
judicial psychology 144
majority decisions 50
numbers of 49
President of the Court 50
reappointment 50
removal of 50
retirement age 50
term 50, 51
judgments 51, 53, 56, 60, 62
form of judgment 70–1
multilingualism, 68–9
jurisdiction 55–8
direct actions *see* **Direct actions**
judicial review *see* **Judicial review**
preliminary rulings *see* **Preliminary references**
principal heads of jurisdiction 56
tort liability *see* **Tort liability**
legal aid 65
legal secretaries 53–4
multilingualism *see* **Multilingualism**
opinions 56–7
plenary (full) formation 50–1
policies of 73–7
precedent 71–2
preliminary references 310–11
procedure
admissibility 60–1
costs 64
English Courts distinguished 60
execution of judgment 62
language choice 67–8
lawyers 64–5
oral procedure 60, 61
preliminary rulings 63–4
preparatory inquiry 61
rules of 60
special procedure after judgment 62–3
written proceedings 60
registrars 53
rule of law, and 345–6
Research and Documentation Division 54
specialized services 54
Translation Directorate 54
treaty provisions 56

European Investment Bank 35
EU tort liability, and 454

European Parliament 11–12
Commission, approval of 20
Commission, censure 20–1
committees 17
composition 13–16
consultation 18–20
democracy, and 1, 45–6
digressively proportional representation 15
enhanced co-operation, consent to 44
immunities 16
inquiries, right to set up 17
MEPs *see* **Members of the European Parliament (MEPS)**
Ombudsman 18
parliamentary questions 17
petition, citizens' right to 18
political parties 17
powers, increase in 21
proposals, right to request 17
privileged applicant, *locus standi* as 367–8
privileges 16
proposals, right to request 17
representing citizens 13
treaty-making 187–9
veto rights 20

European Road Transport Agreement 109–10
European Stability Mechanism 37–8, 96–8
European Union
attitudes to EU in North and South 11
creation of 7–8
financial crisis 10–11, 37–8, 96–8
history 3–11
hybrid nature of 11–12
legal system *see* **Union legal system**
widening membership 4–6

Failure to act
examples of 395–6
introduction to 392–3
judgment, form of 408–9
locus standi 394, 401, 405–8
negative decisions 393–4
annul, action to 394
generally 393
locus standi 394
meaning 393
'necessary measures' 394
parties to proceedings 396
position, definition of 395–6
requests for action 394, 395, 402–5
general 394, 395, 402–3
time limit for request 404–5
reviewable acts 394
parties to proceedings 396
position, definition of 395–6
reviewable omissions
failure to repeal an act 399–402
generally 396–8
'narrow interpretation' 397–8, 400, 406
preliminary acts 398–9
'wide interpretation' 397, 398, 400
treaty provisions 392–3
unity principle 393, 397, 405–6
Financial crisis 10–11, 37–8
European Stability Mechanism 37–8, 96–8
Fiscal Compact 96–7
impact 10
role of EU institutions 10–11, 37–8, 97–8
Fines
calculation of 337–8
criteria for 337
environmental pollution 338
fixing penalties in advance 338–9
general infringements 339
lump-sum 336, 337
periodic penalty payment 336, 337
persistent infringements 339
problems of imposing 339–40
procedure for 336
standard flat-rate amount 337
Finland
seats in European Parliament 14
Fiscal Compact 96–8
Form for legal acts
preliminary acts 136
reasons 136–41
essential procedural requirement, as 421, 422
incorporating reasons by reference 139
obligation to give 136, 420, 421, 422
purpose 136–7, 140–1
sufficiency of 137–40
requirements 136
signature 141
France
application of EU law
cases 268–71
Constitution, amendments to 258, 270
courts differing attitudes towards 267–71
directives 269–70
generally 267–71
fined in conservation of fish case 338
seats in European Parliament 14
separate system of public tort law 452
Fundamental rights *see* **Human rights**

General Agreement on Trade in Services (GATS) 183
General Court
appeals
European Court, to 54, 59
grounds of 59
interveners 59
appeals from Civil Service Tribunal 55, 60
chambers of 55
composition 54–5
establishment/purpose 54
function 49
judges 54–5
Advocate General, judge acting as 55
appointment 54
Chambers, sitting in 55
plenary sessions, sitting in 55
President 55
qualifications 54–5
jurisdiction of 55–7, 58–9
types of cases 58–9
legal aid 65
multilingualism *see* **Multilingualism**
preliminary references, and 282
procedure
admissibility 60–1
costs 64
English Courts distinguished 60
execution of judgment 62
judgments 60, 62
language choice 67–8
lawyers 64–5
oral procedure 60, 61
preliminary rulings 63–4
preparatory inquiry 61
rules of 60
special procedure after judgment 62–3
written proceedings 60
treaty provisions 56
workload 54
Germany
abortion, and 150
application of EU law 261–6
conferral, principle of 112–13
Constitution (*Grundgesetz*)
amendment 258
directives, and 263
fundamental rights 147–50, 159, 261–2
Kompetenz-Kompetenz 112–13, 207
limitations on federal Europe participation 7
proportionality, and 167–8
transfer of powers 258

Treaty of Lisbon compatibility 265
Constitutional Court
democracy, principle of 265–6
direct effect, and 262
European Arrest Warrant 265
federal Europe 7
fundamental rights 147, 148, 159, 261–2
human rights 17, 147, 152
legitimate expectations 165–6
seats in European Parliament 14

Greece
financial crisis, impact of 10
fine for environmental pollution 338
seats in European Parliament 14

Hearing, right to a
English law, influence of 170
general principle of law, as 171
legal professional privilege 171
legal representation, rights of 171
non-self-incrimination, right to 171
'rights of the defence' 171

High Representative of the Union for Foreign Affairs and Security Policy
European Council, and 22–3
generally 34
political post, as 13

Horizontal direct effect
cases 224–31
generally 224–31

Human rights
abortion 150–1
Charter of Fundamental Rights 8, 153, 156–7, 158
equality
doctrine of 145, 168–9
nationality 168, 169
non-discrimination as general principle 145, 169
producer/consumer in agriculture 168–9
religious discrimination 169–70
sex equality 169
Treaty provisions 168–9
EU binding Member States 157–8
EU concept, development of
controversial rights 150–1
enhancement 152–3
generally 146–53
Germany, and 147–50
European Convention on Human Rights and Fundamental Freedoms 152, 153–6
hearing, right to a
English law, influence of 170
general principle of law, as 171
legal professional privilege 171
legal representation, rights of 171
non-self-incrimination, right to 171
'rights of the defence' 171
'inspired rights', sources of
international treaties 151–2
national constitutional traditions 147–8
international law, and 159–62
justification for infringement, as 158–9
legal certainty
concept of 162
legitimate expectations 165–7
retroactivity 162–4
revocation of decisions 167
vested rights 162–4
legal professional privilege 171
proportionality 167–8

Hungary
seats in European Parliament 14

Iceland
non-member State, as 96

Immunities and privileges
European Commissioners 30
MEPs 16

Implementing acts
definition of 111

Implied powers, theory of 113–14

Indirect challenge
description of 411
definition of 410
effect of successful 417–18, 441
general application acts, challenging 412
grounds for challenge 416–17
individual acts, problems of challenging 413–15
introduction to 410–11
invalidity ruling binding 417
locus standi of privileged applicants 415–16
non-existent acts 418
normative/individual acts distinguished 412–15
proceedings, limitations in which to challenge 416
treaty provisions 411–12

Indirect effect *see* **Consistent interpretation, doctrine of**

Information Office 54

Interim measures
cases illustrating 331–2, 333, 336
interlocutory injunctions 331
main considerations 331
treaty provisions 331

Institutions
assessment of 31
auditors *see* **Court of Auditors**
bank *see* **European Central Bank**
Commission *see* **European Commission**
Council *see* **Council**
Council of Europe *see* **Council of Europe**
courts *see* **Civil Service Tribunal; European Court; General Court**
established by agreements with non-member States 243
European Council *see* **European Council**
Parliament *see* **European Parliament**

Institutions (*cont.*)
political posts
High Representative of the Union for Foreign Affairs and Security Policy 13, 22, 34
President of the Commission 13, 20, 27, 29
President of the European Council 13, 22–3
tort actions, as defendants to 452
Interlocutory injunctions
enforcement actions, and 331
International agreements
administrative law, and 424
categories of 175
concluded by EU 174–5, 185–9, 192–6
conflicts between treaties 100–1
direct effect, and 258
institutional structures set up by 191
national courts, and 197
source of EU law, as 84, 174, 191–2
subsidiary conventions 94
Union legal system, and 84, 191–2
International Labour Organization 190
International law
human rights, and 159–62
treaties conflicting with 101–4
Interveners 59
Ireland
abortion, and 150–1
Constitution, amendment of EU membership provision 258
financial crisis, impact of 10
illegal dumping of waste 339
seats in European Parliament 15
Italy
financial crisis, impact of 10
seats in European Parliament 14

Joint Declaration against Racism and Xenophobia 153
Judge-Rapporteur 61, 70
Judges
Civil Service Tribunal 55
European Court
appointment of 49–50
background of 51
chambers, sitting in 50
election 50
full court 50–1
incorrect decisions of 254–5
independence of 49–50, 51
judgments 51
judicial psychology 144
majority decisions 50
numbers of 49
President of the Court 50
reappointment 50
removal of 50
retirement age 50
term 50, 51
General Court
Advocate General, judge acting as 55
appointment 54
Chambers, sitting in 55
plenary sessions, sitting in 55
President 55
qualifications 54–5
Judgments *see under* **European Court**
Judicial review
direct actions 58
legal acts, and 112
remedies 58
reviewable acts *see* **Reviewable acts**
subsidiarity, infringement of 126–8
Jurisdiction
Civil Service Tribunal 55–7
contractual obligations, and 443–5
criteria classifying jurisdiction 56–7
European Court 55–7
General Court, and 55–7
principal heads of 56
ratione materiae 346, 349, 418
ratione personae 346
ratione temporis 346
restitution, and 449–50

Latvia
seats in European Parliament 15
Law, principles of general
direct effect, and 240
equality *see* **Equality, doctrine of**
hearing, right to 170–1
human rights *see* **Human rights**
independent source, as 146
judicial reasoning
deductive 145
inductive 145
legal certainty *see* **Legal certainty**
legal professional privilege 172
origin of 145
preliminary references, and 284
proportionality *see* **Proportionality**
role of 144
treaty provisions 145–6
Lawyers
European Court procedures, and 64–5
'Laying-Up Fund for Inland Waterway Vessels' 181–2
Legal acts
acts *sui generis* 109–10, 178
classification of
functional 111
limitations of 109–10
nominal 108–10
procedural 111
competence
exclusive 119
exclusive and shared 119
generally 119
shared 119
supplementary 119
treaty-making competence 174–5
treaty provisions 119
decisions 108
delegated acts 111
liability for 456–7
delegation of powers
Commission, to 129–31
delegation, what it means 128–9
implementing powers 134–5
Member States, to 133–4
outside bodies, to 131–3
Union institutions, to 131
directives 108, 109
disguised decisions 109

entry into force 141
form for *see* **Form for legal acts**
implementing acts 111
intended effects, liability for
generally 463–5
Plaumann *doctrine* 465–7
Schöppenstedt formula 467–78
judicial review, and 112
legal basis for 120–2
legislative acts 111–12
non-legislative acts 111
normative act 111
notification 141–2
opinions 108
ordinary legislative procedure 111
proportionality 124
publication 141–2
recommendations 108
regulations 108, 109
reviewable act, as 349, 351–3
see also **Reviewable acts**
special legislative procedure 111
subsidiarity 122–4
treaty provisions 108–12
Legal certainty
legitimate expectations
German law derivation 165–6
meaning of 165
protection principle 166–7
protection of 360
retroactivity
generally 162–4
interpretation rule 164
legislation 164
non-application of rule 427–8
prohibition of 164
quasi-retroactivity 162–3
true 162, 163, 164
vested rights 162–4
revocation of decisions 167
Legal personality 174
Legal professional privilege
generally 172
procedure for 172
right to a hearing, and 171
Legal secretaries 53–4
functions 54
Legislative procedure
conciliation 39, 40–41
Conciliation Committee 40–41
first reading 39
general rule 39
ordinary 38–41
second reading 39
third stage 40
treaty provisions 39–41
Legitimate expectations
German law derivation 165–6
meaning of 165
protection principle 166–7
Lithuania
seats in European Parliament 15
Locus standi
direct concern 386–90
failure to act 405–8
individual concern
case law 369–71
closed categories: decisions 372–3
closed categories: regulations 374–9
closed category test 369–70, 376, 378, 380, 385
meaning of 369–70
Plaumann test 369–70, 376, 378, 380, 385
small groups 371–2
justification for 368
non-privileged applicants
basic requirements 368–9
decisions, and 109, 369
direct concern 386–90
individual concern 369–71, 384
regulatory acts 383–4
three ways to bring proceedings 368–9
treaty provisions 368
quasi-judicial determinations
anti-dumping proceedings 380–2
competition proceedings 379–80
liberal approach 383
state aid 382–3
privileged applicants
Commission 367–8
Council 367–8
European Parliament 367–8
semi-privileged applicants
Committee of the Regions 368
Court of Auditors 368
European Central Bank 368
tort actions 451
Treaty of Lisbon
changes introduced by 384–6
individual concern 384–6
regulatory acts 384–6
treaty provisions 367–8
Luxembourg
seats in European Parliament 15
'Luxembourg Accords' 26–7

Malta
seats in European Parliament 15
Member States
acts of
conflicting treaties 98–104
constitutive treaties 87–9, 174
representatives 94–5
sub-groups of Member States, treaties among 95–8
subsidiary conventions 94
acts of representatives of 94–5
agreements with third countries
binding Member States 175, 196
concluded by Member States 193–4
concurrent liability 478–86
delegation to 131–3
direct effect *see* **Direct effect, principle of**
enforcement actions by 329–30
general principles of law, origin of 145
human rights binding 157–8
national responses to EU law
Belgium 259–60
Denmark 266–7
France 267–71
Germany 261–6
Poland 271–2
United Kingdom 272–8
non-member *see* **non-member States**
preliminary references *see* **Preliminary references**
supremacy of EU law, and 206

Members of the European Parliament (MEPS)
abstentions by 39
Conciliation Committee, and 39, 40–1
election of 13–16
immunities 16
legislative procedure, and 39–40
national Parliaments, and 16
numbers of 14–15
offices unable to be held 16
political parties, and 17
privileges 16
proportional representation 16
Monist doctrine
Belgium, acceptance by 260
generally 204–6
Netherlands, and 258
Multilateral Agreements in Trade in Goods 183
Multilingualism
court procedure 67–8
judgment drafting 68–9
linguistic equality, principle of 65
official languages 65
multilingual texts, interpretation of 66–7

National parliaments
MEPs, and 16
Protocol 44
role of 44–5
National responses to EU law
Belgium 259–60
Denmark 266–7
France 267–71
Germany 261–6
Poland 271–2
United Kingdom 272–8
direct effect, and 274
enforcement of judgments 275–6
European Communities Act 272–3
implementation 274–5
supremacy of EU Law 206, 259, 276–82
Union Treaties 273
Negotiorum gestio
restitution, and 447–8
Netherlands
monist doctrine, and 258
seats in European Parliament 14
non-member States
acts of institutions established by agreement with 287–8
agreements with 285–7
international agreements with 84, 174, 191–2, 423
preliminary references 285–7
Non-privileged applicants
basic requirements 368–9
direct concern 386–90
individual concern
case law 369–71
closed categories: decisions 370–1, 372–3
closed categories: regulations 370–1, 374–9
closed-category test 369–70
meaning of 369–70
post-Lisbon 384–90
small groups 371–2
privileged applicants *see* **Privileged applicants**
regulatory acts 384–6
three ways to bring proceedings 368–9
treaty provisions 368
Non-union treaties
conflicts between 100–1
Noordwijks Cement Accoord case 351–3
Norway
non-member State as 96

Official Journal of the European Union 141
Ombudsman 18, 35
Opinions
Advocates General 52
judgments, and 56–7
legal act, as 108
reasoned 327, 329, 334, 336
Ordinary legislative procedure 111, 385
Ordinary revision procedure
treaties, and 89

Parallelism, doctrine of 176–7, 178, 179, 184–5
Parliaments *see* **European Parliament; National parliaments**
Parliamentary questions 17
Partial annulment 440
Plaumann doctrine
reviewable act, liability for 465–7
'Plea of illegality' *see* **Indirect challenge**
Poland
conferral, principle of 113
national response to EU Law 271–2
seats in European Parliament 14
Police
judiciary, co-operation with 33
simplified revision procedure 89, 90–1
'state', and 232
Political parties 17
Portugal
financial crisis, impact of 10
seats in European Parliament 14
Precedent 71–2
Preliminary references
appeal and, differences between 281
application of 311–12
contrived proceedings 300–2
'court', meaning of 282
courts covered
obligation to refer 295–9
power to refer 290–5
effects of 57, 313
English courts procedure 308
entities covered 282–3
European Court procedure 310–11
hypothetical questions 300–2
importance of 57
interpretation of 311–12
issues covered
effect of Union provision 83–4, 283
interpretation 283
validity 283
procedure
appeals 309–10
content of reference 309
English courts 308

European Court 310–11
form of reference 309
provisions referred
acts of institutions established by agreement with third countries 286–8
acts of representatives 284
agreements with non-member States 285–7
conventions, subsidiary 284
law, general principles of 284–5
national 284
treaty provisions 288–9
Union acts, and 284
timing of
discretion, exercise of 307–8
law relating to 303–7
treaties 283
validity, and 299–300
Presidency of the Council 23–4
President of the Commission
election of 20, 27
political post, as 13
portfolio, allocation and reshuffle 29
President of the European Council
election of 22
political post, as 13
role of 22
Privileged applicants
indirect challenge, and 415–16
locus standi, and 367–8
non-privileged applicants *see* **Non-privileged applicants**
Privileges
European Commissioners 30
legal professional privilege 171
MEPs 16
Proportionality, principle of
application of, Protocol on 124–5
courts, and 168
definition of 124, 168
economic law, and 168
general principle of law, as 167
generally 167–8
Germany, and 148, 167–8
misuse of powers, and 425–6
procedure 124–6
Protocol on the Application of the Principles of Subsidiarity and Proportionality 124–5

Reasoned opinions
decisions distinguished 327
request for 329
Recommendations
legal act, as 108
Registrars
functions of 53
role of 53
term of 53
Regulations
definition of 108, 109
direct effect, and
directives, differences between 222–4
national implementing rules 216–18
supremacy of EU law 244
treaty provisions, and 215–18
legal act, as 108
locus standi
open and closed categories 374–9
normative act, as 412
publication of 141–2
reviewable act, as 350
Remedies
damages
a priori limit 248
enforcement actions 332–4
enforcement actions *see* **Enforcement actions**
equal availability of national remedies 245–6, 251
generally 245–8
interim relief 247
restitution 332–4
tort, national governments liability in 248–52
Research and Documentation Division 54
Resolutions 109–10
Restitution
concurrent liability 479–80, 483
enforcement actions, and 332–4
jurisdiction, and 449–50
negotiorum gestio 447–8
substantive law 448–9
unjust enrichment 447–8
examples 448–9
Retroactivity
annulment 436–8
legal certainty
generally 162–4
interpretation rule 164
legislation 164
prohibition of 164
quasi-retroactivity 162–3
true 162, 163, 164
vested rights 162–4
Review
acts *see* **Reviewable acts**
application infringement
generally 423–4
rules of law, possible sources of 423
what it covers 423–4
competence, lack of
competence, definition in context 419–20
delegation, and 420
ultra vires, equivalent concept 420
wrong empowering provision 420
essential procedural infringement
essential/non-essential distinction 421
essential requirements, examples of 422–3
generally 420–23
uncertainty disadvantage 421
failure to act
negative decisions/failure to reply distinction 434–5
power to act 435–6
requirement to act 435
grounds of 419
locus standi
staff cases 429–30
mistake of fact
decisions of fact 430–1
'economic difficulties' 431
examples of 431–4
generally 430–4
'primary' facts 431
'pure' fact mistake 431

Review (*cont.*)
misuse of powers
definition of 425
derivation of 424–5
difficulties in proving 425
generally 424–7
primary 426
proportionality, and 425–6
secondary 426
subjective character of 425–6
patent error 434
time factor
case law 428–9
Reviewable acts
acts intended to have legal effects, liability for
general 463–5
Plaumann doctrine 465–7
Schöppenstedt formula 467–78
acts of Council, Commission and European Central Bank
decisions 350
directives 350
regulations 350
sui generis acts 350
author of the act 364–6
treaty provisions 364–5
features of 350
'having legal effects' requirement
definition of 351–3
invalid acts 360–64
jurisdiction *ratione materiae* 346, 349, 360
legislative acts, definition of 350
letters signed by Commission 361–2
negative decisions, as 393–4
Noordwijks Cement Accoord case 351–3
problem cases 353–9
third parties, acts producing legal effects *vis-à-vis* 349
treaty provisions 349–51
void acts 360–4
consequences of 360–1
defects 361
general rule 360
secret legislation 363–4
ultra vires 361
voidable acts 360–64
general rule 360
Romania
seats in European Parliament 14
Rule of law
principle of EU, as 345–6

Santer Commission 31
Schengen Agreement 95, 96
Schöppenstedt formula
first requisite 469–70
generally 467–9
second requisite 471–6
third requisite 476–8
Simplified revision procedure
treaties, and 89, 90–1
Slovakia
seats in European Parliament 14
Slovenia
seats in European Parliament 15
Social chapter 95–6
Sources of EU law
decisions *see* **Decisions**
directives *see* **Directives**
international agreements *see* **International agreements**
law, general principles *see* **Law, general principles of**
regulations *see* **Regulations**
Treaties *see* **Treaties**
Spain
Civil Code 236
environmental pollution 338
financial crisis, impact of 10
seats in European Parliament 14
Special legislative procedure 111
Standing *see* ***Locus standi***
State aid 382–3
Subsidiarity, principle of
definition of 123
exclusive competence, and 123–4
generally 122–4
judicial review for infringement 126–8
procedure 124–6
Protocol on the application of 124–5
requirements 123
Subsidiary conventions
act of Member State, as 94
preliminary references 284
rule of law, as 423–4
United Kingdom, and 273
violations, and 317
***Sui generis* acts** 109–10, 178
reviewable act, as 350
Supremacy, doctrine of 147
direct effect, and 243–5
monist country, and 204–6
United Kingdom, and 205, 260, 276–8
Sweden
seats in European Parliament 14

Third countries
acts of institutions established by agreements with
direct effect, and 243
generally 191
preliminary references 287–8
direct effect 240–3
Time limits
enforcement actions 323–4
failure to act 404–5
tort actions 451
Tort liability
acts imputable to EU 453–7
delegated powers, acts through 456–7
institutions, acts performed through 453–4
officials, acts performed through 453, 454–5
wide concept of 'acts' 453
anxiety and hurt feelings, damages for 458
applicant's conduct 458
causation 459–60
concurrent liability 479–83, 485–6
currency conversion 459
damage 457–9
declaration of entitlement to damages 458–9
defendants 58, 452
direct actions 58
duty to mitigate loss 458
elements 451
employment, claims arising out of 458
European Central Bank, and 450, 452
fault 460–3
blameworthiness 462

loss, proving 58
meaning of 462
mistakes, correcting 462–3
no-fault liability 451, 460–2
personal fault 463
financial loss, compensation for 457
general 450–3
general principles of law common to Member States 452–3
government liability
animals, maltreatment of 252–3
cases 248–55
causation 252
damages 252
directives, transposition of 254
effectiveness, principle of 251
judges, incorrect decisions of 254–5
interest 459
limitation 451
locus standi 451
profit, claims for loss of 457–8
remoteness 459
treaty provisions 450–2
Translation Directorate 54
Travaux préparatoires 73, 263
Treaties
amendments to 89–92
challenges 90
consent of Member States 91
inter-governmental conference 89
international law 91–2
Member States' constitutional requirements 89–90
ordinary revision procedure 89
ratification 90
simplified revision procedure 89, 90–1
Annexes 88
conflicting treaties 98–104
amendments 92
EU treaties, conflicts between 99
European Convention on Human Rights conflicts 101–4
non-Union treaties, conflicts with 100–1
United Nations law 104–6
constitutive treaties 83, 87–9
amending the treaties 89–92
principal treaties, list of 87–8
supplementary instruments 88–9
new members 93
preliminary references, and 283
principal treaties, list of 87–8
Protocols 88
sub-group of Member States, treaties among 95–8
subsidiary conventions 94
supplementary instruments 88–9
suspending membership rights 93–4
treaty-making *see* **Treaty-making**
Treaty-making *see* **Agreements with third countries**
Treaty of Lisbon
generally 185–6
German Constitution, compatibility with 265
Triangular situations, theory of 227

Ultra vires
appeals from General Court 59
EU acting beyond its powers 113, 128
lack of competence 420
void acts 361
Union acts *see* **Legal acts**
Union legal system 83–5
competence *see* **Competence**
enacted and non-enacted law 84
instruments 84–5
international agreements 84
sources 84
treaties *see* **Treaties**
Union obligations
acts intended to have legal effects, liability for
general 463–5
Plaumann doctrine 465–7
Schöppenstedt formula 467–78
contract *see* **Contractual obligations**
restitution *see* **Restitution**
tort *see* **Tort liability**
United Kingdom
application of EU law 272–8
direct effect 274
dualist doctrine, and 206, 260, 272
European Convention on Human Rights, and 206
European Communities Act 1972
direct effect 274
enforcement of judgments 275–6
implementation 274–5
preliminary rulings 313
supremacy of EU law 206, 260, 276–8
Union Treaties 273
Euroscepticism 11
preliminary references 313
seats in European Parliament 14
supremacy of EU law, and 206, 260, 276–8
United Nations law
EU law, conflicts between 104–6
human rights 104–6
Unjust enrichment
restitution, and 447–8
substantive law 448–9

Vertical direct effect
cases 224–31
generally 224–31
Veto rights 20
Void *ab initio* acts
annulment 436–7
indirect challenge, and 418
reviewable acts, and 360–4
Voidable acts 360–4
annulment 436
Voting
additional rules 26
allocation of votes 25
'Luxembourg Accords' 26–7
negative tactics of 26
qualified majority 25–6
simple majority 24–5
unanimity 25

Written proceedings 60